The Handbook of Narrative and Psychotherapy

The Handbook of Narrative and Psychotherapy

Practice, Theory, and Research

Edited by

LYNNE E. ANGUS
York University

JOHN McLEOD
University of Abertay Dundee

SAGE Publications
International Educational and Professional Publisher
Thousand Oaks ▪ London ▪ New Delhi

Copyright © 2004 by Sage Publications, Inc.

All rights reserved. No part of this book may be reproduced or utilized in any form or by any means, electronic or mechanical, including photocopying, recording, or by any information storage and retrieval system, without permission in writing from the publisher.

For information:

Sage Publications, Inc.
2455 Teller Road
Thousand Oaks, California 91320
E-mail: order@sagepub.com

Sage Publications Ltd.
6 Bonhill Street
London EC2A 4PU
United Kingdom

Sage Publications India Pvt. Ltd.
B-42, Panchsheel Enclave
Post Box 4109
New Delhi 110 017 India

Library of Congress Cataloging-in-Publication Data

The handbook of narrative and psychotherapy: Practice, theory, and research/editors, Lynne E. Angus and John McLeod
   p. cm.
Includes bibliographical references and index.
ISBN 978-0-7619-2684-9 (Cloth)
   1. Narrative therapy—Handbooks, manuals, etc. 2. Psychotherapy—Handbooks, manuals, etc. 3. Psychiatry—Handbooks, manuals, etc. I. Title: Narrative and psychotherapy. II. Angus, Lynne E. III. McLeod, John.
RC489.S74H36 2004
616.89′165—dc22

2003016014

03 04 10 9 8 7 6 5 4 3 2 1

Acquiring Editor:	Jim Brace-Thompson
Editorial Assistant:	Karen Ehrmann
Production Editor:	Diana E. Axelsen
Copy Editor:	Jacqueline A. Tasch
Typesetter/Designer:	C&M Digitals (P) Ltd.
Indexer:	Teri Greenberg
Cover Designer:	Michelle Lee Kenny

Contents

Preface ix

PART I. THE "NARRATIVE TURN": WHY STORIES MATTER IN PSYCHOTHERAPY — 1

1. The Narrative Creation of Self — 3
   Jerome Bruner

2. Folk Psychology and Narrative Practices — 15
   Michael White

3. Narrative Therapy and Postmodernism — 53
   Donald E. Polkinghorne

PART II. WORKING WITH NARRATIVE IN PSYCHOTHERAPY — 69

4. The CCRT Approach to Working With Patient Narratives in Psychodynamic Psychotherapy — 71
   Howard Book

5. "What's the Story?" Working With Narrative in Experiential Psychotherapy — 87
   Lynne E. Angus, Jennifer Lewin, Beverley Bouffard, and Debra Rotondi-Trevisan

6. Nurturing Nature: Cognitive Narrative Strategies — 103
   Óscar F. Gonçalves, Margarida R. Henriques, and Paulo P. P. Machado

7. Working With Narrative in Psychotherapy: A Relational Constructivist Approach — 119
   Luis Botella, Olga Herrero, Meritxell Pacheco, and Sergi Corbella

8. A Poststructuralist Approach to Narrative Work   137
   GENE COMBS AND JILL FREEDMAN

PART III. NARRATIVE IDENTITY AND SELF-MULTIPLICITY: IMPLICATIONS FOR PSYCHOTHERAPY   157

9. Narrative Identity and Narrative Therapy   159
   DAN P. MCADAMS AND LISA JANIS

10. The Innovation of Self-Narratives: A Dialogical Approach   175
    HUBERT J. M. HERMANS

11. Assimilation and Narrative: Stories as Meaning Bridges   193
    KATERINE OTASUKE, MEREDITH J. GLICK, MICHAEL A. GRAY, D'ARCY J. REYNOLDS JR., CAROL L. HUMPHREYS, LISA M. SALVI, AND WILLIAM B. STILES

12. Minding Our Therapeutic Tales: Treatments in Perspectivism   211
    ROBERT L. RUSSELL AND FRED B. BRYANT

PART IV. NARRATIVE ASSESSMENT STRATEGIES IN PSYCHOTHERAPY   227

13. Self-Defining Memories, Narrative Identity, and Psychotherapy: A Conceptual Model, Empirical Investigation, and Case Report   229
    JEFFERSON A. SINGER AND PAVEL S. BLAGOV

14. The Narrative Assessment Interview: Assessing Self-Change in Psychotherapy   247
    KAREN K. HARDTKE AND LYNNE E. ANGUS

15. Disorganized Narratives: The Psychological Condition and Its Treatment   263
    GIANCARLO DIMAGGIO AND ANTONIO SEMERARI

16. Story Dramaturgy and Personal Conflict: JAKOB—A Tool for Narrative Understanding and Psychotherapeutic Practice   283
    BRIGITTE BOOTHE AND AGNES VON WYL

PART V. EMERGING TRENDS AND FUTURE DIRECTIONS — 297

17. Narrative Activity: Clients' and Therapists' Intentions in the Process of Narration — 299
    HEIDI M. LEVITT & DAVID L. RENNIE

18. "To Tell My Story": Configuring Interpersonal Relations Within Narrative Process — 315
    TIMOTHY ANDERSON

19. The Contributions of Emotion Processes to Narrative Change in Psychotherapy: A Dialectical Constructivist Approach — 331
    LESLIE S. GREENBERG AND LYNNE E. ANGUS

20. Social Construction, Narrative, and Psychotherapy — 351
    JOHN MCLEOD

21. Toward an Integrative Framework for Understanding the Role of Narrative in the Psychotherapy Process — 367
    LYNNE E. ANGUS AND JOHN MCLEOD

Name Index — 375
Subject Index — 383
About the Editors — 397
About the Contributors — 399

Preface

Over the last 10 years, the "narrative turn" in philosophy, psychology, and social science has had an important impact on the field of psychotherapy. An increasing number of practitioners regard their work as based in an appreciation of the significance of client storytelling, and they define change in therapy as entailing the re-authoring of life stories. In an important way, these new narrative perspectives, emerging in the context of individual, couples, and family therapy models, are beginning to be supported by advances in psychotherapy research and training. The domain of "narrative-informed" therapy draws on a rich vein of existing theory and research in disciplines such as philosophy, social anthropology, and sociology, and linguistics and literary criticism, as well as psychology.

We are at an exciting stage in the development of a narrative-informed understanding of therapy. Many aspects of the role of narrative and storytelling in therapy have been explored by different theorists and researchers. To a large extent, these ideas and practices have existed in isolation from each other—each set of ideas has been articulated and discussed within its own specific research and practice community. The present book brings together for the first time the many strands of thinking about narrative and psychotherapy, with the intention of promoting dialogue, stimulating further innovation, and providing a resource for practitioners seeking to integrate narrative strategies into their work with clients.

Many psychotherapists who find meaning and utility in narrative approaches have found it necessary to learn a different way of hearing and understanding the therapeutic process. Paying attention to stories, and the process of storytelling, can involve learning to think about therapy in new ways. Historically, the development of narrative approaches to psychotherapy can be traced back to the writings of philosophers such as Paul Ricoeur, Michel Foucault, and Alasdair MacIntyre, who established the primacy of narrative as a basic structure for human knowing and action. These philosophers argued that the structure of narrative reflected fundamental dimensions of human existence, such as personal agency and intention, living in and through time, and the experience of belonging within a culture and tradition. The implications of these philosophical insights for psychology and psychotherapy began to be articulated in the 1980s through the work of Jerome Bruner, Miller Mair, Donald Polkinghorne, and Theodore Sarbin. Part I of the *Handbook* includes chapters by Jerome Bruner, Michael White, and Donald Polkinghorne, which capture the practical relevance of these underlying conceptual issues and debates.

Bruner shows how an understanding of narrative can be enhanced by adopting a philosophically informed interdisciplinary framework. White builds on some of Bruner's early work by suggesting that the ways of making sense of people that have emerged within mainstream academic psychology are in conflict with an older "folk psychology," which gives priority to narrative ways of knowing. Polkinghorne questions whether the postmodern themes in the narrative therapy developed by Michael White and his colleague, David Epston, may have gone too far in downplaying the importance of the individual subject. Many of the contributors to later chapters in the *Handbook* locate their thinking within these philosophical debates.

Within the psychotherapy community, the influence of narrative perspectives has been expressed largely through the assimilation of narrative ideas into existing approaches to therapy. Part II of the *Handbook* includes a range of examples of this process in action. A substantial number of psychoanalytic and psychodynamic practitioners and theorists have found that narrative provides an effective means of engaging with unconscious processes. The chapter by Howard Book describes an approach to psychodynamic therapy that is based on the analysis of psychodynamic core conflictual relationship themes that can be identified by attending to the structure and content of relationship narratives told by the client in therapy. The chapter by Lynne Angus and her colleagues explores some of the ways in which narrative perspectives can be integrated into experiential approaches to therapy, approaches that emphasize emotional processing, client agency, and empathic engagement. The chapters by Oscar Gonçalves and by Luis Botella and their colleagues represent the integration of narrative concepts into cognitive and constructivist approaches to therapy, which seek to enable clients to change the cognitive schemas or constructs through which they create personal realities. The final chapter in this section, by Gene Combs and Jill Freedman, describes their work within the narrative therapy tradition, which takes a socially oriented approach in working with clients to deconstruct dominant cultural narratives and to establish more satisfactory relationships with other members of their families and communities. In all of these chapters, contributors provide case material to illustrate their ways of working.

One of the significant implications of adopting a narrative perspective on therapy is that it reveals the extent to which the stories that people tell tend to highlight the multiple, fragmented nature of personal identity. Within psychotherapy, concepts such as ego or self assume a high degree of unity within a person's sense of who he or she is. Listening closely to stories, on the other hand, invites an appreciation of the situated, fluid, dialogical nature of personal being. The chapters in Part III examine the implications for psychotherapy of narrative identity and self-multiplicity. Dan McAdams provides an outline of some of the findings from his substantial program of research into personality and life narrative and discusses how his ideas, which combine ideas of both unity and multiplicity in self-narration, can be applied within psychotherapy. The chapters by Hubert Hermans and by Katerine Otasuke, Bill Stiles, and their colleagues offer two contrasting yet similar ways of conceptualizing narrative multiplicity: voice and I-positions. The work of Robert L. Russell and Fred B. Bryant explores these issues from a developmental perspective, in the context of research and practice in child psychotherapy.

The stories that people tell are complex, multifaceted phenomena and carry meaning at a variety of levels. An important theme that runs through the *Handbook* is concerned with the issue of how to define and observe narratives. This issue is of relevance in research and in the assessment of clients entering psychotherapy, and it also informs therapist training and selection in a number of ways. The chapters in Part IV consider this set of issues from a number of contrasting perspectives. Jefferson Singer and Pavel Blagov suggest that their research into the role of self-defining or autobiographical memories in the construction of personal identity may provide a useful assessment resource for psychotherapy researchers and practitioners. Karen Hardtke and Lynne Angus introduce a method of eliciting client narratives before and after therapy for the purposes of both assessment and research. Giancarlo Dimaggio and Antonio Semerari offer a set of criteria for deciding on the level of disorganization in therapy clients, who may be highly emotionally damaged, and describe how their framework can be used to inform therapeutic practice. Brigitte Boothe and Agnes von Wyl give an account of a psychoanalytically oriented method for analyzing stories told by clients in therapy for the purpose of bringing to light unconscious drives and relationship patterns.

The final section of the *Handbook* looks to the future, offering a series of proposals for further integrative work in the area of narrative and psychotherapy. The chapter by Heidi Levitt and David Rennie addresses the issue of client intentionality and personal storytelling in psychotherapy sessions. Timothy Anderson looks at the impressive body of research in interpersonal theory and makes a number of suggestions for ways in which it might be used to improve the sensitivity of narrative-informed psychotherapists to interactional factors within therapy. Leslie Greenberg and Lynne Angus present a powerful argument for the central role that emotional processing plays in all psychotherapy and for greater attention to the interplay between emotional experiencing and the construction of narrative. John McLeod suggests that the primary value of a focus on narrative may be to refocus therapeutic work on the relationship between the person and the culture or community within which he or she has constructed a personal niche. In the closing chapter, the editors take a look at the field of narrative and psychotherapy as a whole and offer a framework that may begin to make it possible to integrate the wide range of ideas and practices that exist within this area.

The aim or intention of the *Handbook* has been to create a meeting ground where some of the best of recent thinking and innovative practice in psychotherapy can come together. All of the authors were invited to address issues of theory, research, and practice. In their writing, there is a strong sense of interconnectedness, which is grounded, we believe, in the fundamental importance of narrative in human relationships. There are also major areas of divergence, however, where groups have staked out territories that are rarely if ever visited by others. As editors, we have operated from a stance of having a genuine interest in, and respect for, all of the theoretical positions and practices that are represented in this *Handbook*.

We would to take like this opportunity to thank Jim Brace-Thompson, our editor at Sage, who has consistently been a source of support and guidance, and Barbara Thurston for her editing expertise and care in the preparation of the manuscripts for publication. We would also like to express our deep appreciation to our "other halves," Ken Ainsworth and Julia McLeod, who have acted with remarkable patience and forbearance throughout what has been a long journey. Finally, we would like to thank all the contributors to the *Handbook*, who have been a pleasure to work with. We hope that their writing will inspire, inform, and intrigue you as readers as much as it has us as editors.

Part I

The "Narrative Turn": Why Stories Matter in Psychotherapy

CHAPTER 1

The Narrative Creation of Self

JEROME BRUNER

I

"Self" is a surprisingly quirky idea—intuitively obvious to common sense yet notoriously evasive to definition by the fastidious philosopher. The best we seem to be able to do when asked what it is, is to point a finger at our forehead or our chest. Yet "self" is the common coin of our speech: no conversation goes long without its being unapologetically used. And the legal code simply takes it for granted when it speaks of such legal concepts as responsibility and privacy. We would do well, then, to have a brief look at what the self is, the subject that narrative creation of self is supposed to be about.

Is there some essential self inside that, somehow, is just there? If so, why would we ever need to tell ourselves about ourselves, and why would there be such injunctions as "Know thyself" or "To thine own self be true"? Surely, if our selves were just there, we'd have no need to *tell* ourselves about them. Yet we spend a good deal of time doing just that, either alone, or with friends, or vicariously at the psychiatrist's, or at confession if we are Catholics. What function does such self-telling serve?

The standard twentieth-century answer to this question was that much of our selves was unconscious, created *sub rosa,* and adroitly defended from our conscious probings by various mechanisms that concealed or distorted it. We needed to find ways around these defenses—with the help of a psychoanalyst, in interaction with whom we would reenact the past and overcome our resistance to discovering ourselves. Where there was id, now there shall be ego, to paraphrase Freud. Little question that Freud's solution to our puzzle was a brilliant metaphor and that it had profound effects on our image of self (Bruner, 1958).

AUTHOR'S NOTE: Copyright © 2002 by Jerome Bruner. Reprinted from *Making Stories: Law, Literature, Life* (2002), with permission from the author and from the publisher, Farrar, Straus and Giroux, LLC.

Yet we would do well to continue our inquiry. Freud's implied drama of id, ego, and superego, for all its metaphoric brilliance, is unfinished business, and it is to the pursuit of this unfinished business that this chapter is dedicated. The question why we need to tell stories in order to elucidate what we mean by "self" has even come to preoccupy mainstream psychoanalysis (Spence, 1982, 1987).

I want to begin by proposing boldly that, in effect, there is no such thing as an intuitively obvious and essential self to know, one that just sits there ready to be portrayed in words. Rather, we constantly construct and reconstruct our selves to meet the needs of the situations we encounter, and we do so with the guidance of our memories of the past and our hopes and fears for the future. Telling oneself about oneself is like making up a story about who and what we are, what's happened, and why we're doing what we're doing.

It is not that we have to make up these stories from scratch each time. Our self-making stories accumulate over time, even pattern themselves on conventional genres. They get out-of-date, and not just because we grow older or wiser but also because our self-making stories need to fit new circumstances, new friends, new enterprises. Our very memories fall victim to our self-making stories. It is not that I can no longer tell you (or myself) the "original, true story" about my desolation in the bleak summer after my father died. Rather, I would be telling you (or myself) a new story about a twelve-year-old "once upon a time." And I could tell it several ways, all of them shaped as much by my life since then as by the circumstances of that long-ago summer.

Self-making is a narrative art, and though it is more constrained by memory than fiction is, it is uneasily constrained, a matter to which we shall come presently. Self-making, anomalously, is from both the inside and the outside. The inside of it, we like to say in our Cartesian way, is memory, feelings, ideas, beliefs, subjectivity. Part of this insideness is almost certainly innate and species-specific, like our irresistible sense of continuity over time and place and our postural sense of ourselves. But much of self-making is from outside in—based on the apparent esteem of others and on the myriad expectations that we early, even mindlessly, pick up from the culture in which we are immersed.

Besides, narrative acts of self-making are usually guided by unspoken, implicit cultural models of what selfhood should be, might be—and, of course, shouldn't be. Not that we are slaves of culture, as even the most dedicated cultural anthropologists now appreciate. Rather, there are many possible, ambiguous models of selfhood even in simple or ritualized cultures. Yet all cultures provide presuppositions and perspectives about selfhood, rather like plot summaries or homilies for telling oneself or others about oneself.

But these self-making precepts are not rigid commands. They leave ample room for maneuver. Self-making is, after all, our principal means for establishing our uniqueness, and a moment's thought makes plain that we distinguish ourselves from others by comparing our accounts of ourselves with the accounts that others give us of themselves.

Telling others about oneself is, then, no simple matter. It depends on what *we* think *they* think we ought to be like—or what selves in general ought to be like. Nor do our calculations end when we come to telling ourselves about ourselves. Our self-directed self-making narratives early come to express what we think others expect us to be like. Without much awareness of it, we develop a decorum for telling ourselves about ourselves: how to be frank with ourselves, how not to offend others. A thoughtful student of autobiography has proposed that self-narratives (at least written autobiographies) conform to a tacit *pacte autobiographique* governing what constitutes appropriate public self-telling. We follow some variant of it even when we are only telling ourselves about ourselves. In the process, selfhood becomes *res publica,* even when talking to ourselves (Lejeune, 1975, 1989).

It hardly requires a postmodern leap to conclude, accordingly, that self is also other. Classicists, interestingly, see this phenomenon even in the ancient world. Did not the Roman art of rhetoric, originally designed to aid in arguing convincingly to others, eventually turn inward to self-telling? And might it have produced the resoluteness so characteristic of Roman masculinity? And so the sharp-minded Roman, clear about who and what he was and what was expected of him. Did that self-certainty even shape the emperor Justinian, pushing him at the peak of his career to cleanse all local ambiguity from the administration of Roman law? Is empire affected by the long reach of self-narratives?

Take another example from antiquity, offered by the distinguished Cambridge classicist Sir Geoffrey Lloyd. Lloyd notes, with impressive evidence, that the ancient Greeks were much more confrontational and autonomy-seeking than the then contemporary Chinese. The Greeks, not the Chinese, invented the "winner-takes-all" syllogism for resolving their arguments, while the Chinese, surely as gifted mathematically, avoided such showdown procedures like the plague. Showdowns fit Chinese decorum poorly. Did their method of proof make the Greeks even more confrontational until, as with the rhetoric of the later Romans, it sharpened their sense of their selfhood? Do we invent tools to further our cultural bent and then become their servants, even developing ourselves to fit them?

Americans, it has been said, no longer show as much overt affection as they used to: men worry that it might be taken as sexual harassment if affection is directed toward women, adults worry that it might appear like child abuse if directed toward kids. All of this is the side effect of well-intended prohibitive statutes. A posted notice in one California school district (Oxenhandler, 2001), for example, expressly forbids "showing your affections" (on a list of prohibitions that includes "Don't spit"). Will our new guardedness end up obscuring the tender side of our selfhood? Will it become taboo to take account of that tenderness in telling ourselves about ourselves?

I I

Selfhood seems to have become an astonishingly public issue in our times. Endless books tell us how to improve it, how to keep from becoming "divided," narcissistic, isolated, or un-situated. Research psychologists, ordinarily proud of their neutrality, warn us of our "errors" in judging self, that we usually see others as guided by enduring beliefs and dispositions while seeing ourselves as more subtly steered by our circumstances. They call this the primary attribution error.

But hasn't self always been a matter of public, moral concern, even a topic of debate? Self and soul have forever been yin and yang in the Judeo-Christian tradition. Confession of sins and appropriate penance purged the soul—and raised the spirits of one's secular self. Doctrinally, the soul was cursed with original sin, and we know from magisterial works on the history of childhood how important it was considered to purge that sin from selfhood. Calvin's version of original sin was so compelling that it took Rousseau's irony and courage to bid it a bitter farewell in *Émile.*

But the good self has also been an issue in that perpetual cockpit of secular moral debate called pedagogy. Does education make the spirit more generous by broadening the mind? Does selfhood become the richer by exposure to "the best which has been thought and said in the world," in Matthew Arnold's classic phrase? Education was *Bildung*—character building, not just subject matter. Hegel thought he had diagnosed the difficulty: The young (or anybody) had to be inspired to rise above immediate demands by being instructed in the culture's noble history. He went so far as to suggest that pedagogy should "alienate one from the present." Even the allegedly pragmatic John Dewey debated the issue of how to create a self fit for a good society. No generation, it seems, has ever been able to heed the advice of the title of James Thurber's little classic *Let Your Mind Alone!*

One cannot resist the conclusion that the nature and shape of selfhood are indeed as much matters of cultural concern, *res publica*, as of individual concern. Or, to put it another way, selfhood involves a commitment to others as well as being "true to oneself." Selfhood without such commitment constitutes a form of sociopathy—the absence of a sense of responsibility to the requirements of social being. Even so basic a concept in the law as *mens rea*, a guilty mind, and the legal determination of criminal intent would be impossible without this element of social commitment in selfhood.

Small wonder, then, that the self is a public topic and that its "betterment" is regarded not just as a personal matter but as meriting the care of those charged with maintaining a proper moral order—the church, the school, the family, and, of course, the state itself.

We must return to the puzzling question of what selfhood is and how it is fashioned. Let's leave the matter by noting only that self-making and self-telling are about as public activities as any private acts can be. And so are critiques of them.

III

Why do we naturally portray ourselves through story, so naturally indeed that selfhood itself seems a product of our own story making? Does the research literature of psychology have any answers? One gifted psychologist, Ulric Neisser (Neisser, 1988, 1993; Neisser & Fivush, 1994; Neisser & Jopling, 1997; Neisser & Winograd, 1998), has gathered much of that literature together in several learned volumes containing articles by leading scholars in the field. I've gone back over those volumes with our question in mind—Why narrative?—and have condensed what I found into a dozen "one-liners" about the self:

1. It is teleological and agentive, replete with desires, intentions, and aspirations and endlessly in pursuit of goals.

2. In consequence, it is sensitive to obstacles, real or imagined: responsive to success or failure, unsteady in handling uncertain outcomes.

3. It responds to its judged successes and failures by altering its aspirations and ambitions and changing its reference groups (Bruner, 1991).

4. It relies on selective remembering to adjust the past to the demands of the present and the anticipated future.

5. It is oriented toward "reference groups" and "significant others" who set the cultural standards by which it judges itself (Shweder, 2000; Wang, 2001).

6. It is possessive and extensible, adopting beliefs, values, loyalties, even objects as aspects of its own identity.

7. Yet it seems able to shed these values and possessions as required by circumstances without losing its continuity.

8. It is experientially continuous over time and circumstances, despite striking transformations in its contents and activities.

9. It is sensitive to where and with whom it finds itself in the world.

10. It is accountable and sometimes responsible for formulating itself in words, becoming troubled when words cannot be found.

11. It is moody, affective, labile, and situation-sensitive.
12. It seeks and guards coherence, eschewing dissonance and contradiction through highly developed psychic procedures.

Not very surprising, hardly counterintuitive in even the smallest detail. It becomes more interesting, though, if you translate it into a set of reminders about how to tell or write a good story. Something like:

1. A story needs a plot.
2. Plots need obstacles to goals.
3. Obstacles make people reconsider.
4. Tell only about the story-relevant past.
5. Give your characters allies and connections.
6. Let your characters grow.
7. But keep their identities intact.
8. And also keep their continuities evident.
9. Locate your characters in the world of people.
10. Let your characters explain themselves as needed.
11. Let your characters have moods.
12. Worry when your characters are not making sense—and have them worry, too.

Should we say, then, that all the psychological research on selfhood was simply a rediscovery of the wheel, that all we've learned from it is that most people learn how to tell passable stories with themselves as the chief protagonists? That would surely be unjust and also plainly untrue. But we could certainly fault the psychologists with a failure to tell the dancer from the dance, the medium from the message, or however one puts it. For their "self" comes out to be little more than a standard protagonist in a standard story of a standard genre. She sets out on a quest, runs into obstacles and has second thoughts about her aims in life, remembers what's needed as needed, has allies and people she cares about, yet grows without losing herself in the process. She lives in a recognizable world, speaks her mind when she needs to but is thrown when words fail her, and wonders whether her life makes sense. It can be tragic, comic, a *bildungsroman*, whatever. Does selfhood require more than a reasonably well-wrought story, a story whose continuing episodes tie together (like stories generally, or like lines of precedent in the law)?

Maybe we're faced with another chicken-and-egg puzzle. Is our sense of selfhood the *fons et origo* of storytelling, or does the human gift of narrative endow selfhood with the shape it takes? But perhaps that oversimplifies. There is an old adage in linguistics that "thinking is for speaking"—that we come to think in a certain way in order to say what we want to say in the language we've learned to use, which hardly means that *all* thinking is shaped just for the sake of talking. Dan Slobin (2000), a gifted scholar and a seasoned student of how language and thought influence each other, puts it well: "One cannot verbalize experience without taking a *perspective,* and . . . the language being used often favors particular perspectives. The world does not present 'events' to be encoded in language. Rather, in the process of speaking or writing, experiences are filtered through language into *verbalized events.*" Selfhood can surely be thought of as one of those "verbalized events," a kind of meta-event that gives coherence and continuity to the scramble of experience. However, it is not just language per se but narrative that shapes its use—particularly its use in self-making. Is it so surprising? Physicists come to think in those equations they scrawl on blackboards. Musicians are so adept at thinking musically that they need to look at the score as well as listen to the music to see where something went wrong. Don't we, too, have to tell the event in order to find out whether, after all, "this is the kind of person I really mean to be"?

IV

Most people never get around to composing a book-length autobiography. Self-telling is usually provoked by episodes related to some longer-term concern. Though linked to or provoked by particular happenings, it ordinarily presupposes those longer-term, larger-scale concerns—much like history writing, where the *annales*, the records, of particular events are already determined or shaped by a more encompassing *chronique*, which itself bears the stamp of an over-arching *histoire*. An account of a battle takes for granted the existence of a war, which takes for granted the larger notions of competitive nation-states and some kind of world order.

No autobiography is completed, only ended. No autobiographer is free from questions about which self his autobiography is about, composed from what perspective, for whom. The one we write is only one *version*, one way of achieving coherence. Autobiography turns even a seasoned writer into a doppelgänger—and turns its readers into sleuths. How can any version of an autobiography strike a balance between what one actually was and what one might have been? We play games with ourselves about this would-be balance. A writer friend and neighbor of mine, a gifted journalist engaged in writing an autobiography, as was I, responded to my doubts with: "No problem for me; I am faithful to memory." Yet she was renowned locally as a delicious fabulist who, in the words of a witty fellow townsman, "could make a shopping trip to Skibbereen sound like a visit to ancient Rome itself." Like her, we are forever balancing what was with what might have been—and, in the main, mercifully unaware of how we do it.

Literary autobiography, for all its pitfalls, has much to teach us about what we leave implicit in more spontaneous, episode-linked, briefer self-accounts. It can even give us hints about the writer's crypto-philosophical notion of what a self is. And that is no idle matter.

A recent book highlights this point vividly—James Olney's (1998) thoughtful *Memory and Narrative: The Weave of Life-Writing*. Olney is particularly concerned with the rise and fall of the narrative form in self-accounting and with the question why, in recent times, it has begun losing its allure for literary autobiographers, even if they can't escape it in their more spontaneous and episodic self-telling.

Four famous life writers come under his scrutiny, their work extending over more than a millennium, starting with Saint Augustine, whose *Confessions* virtually pioneered the autobiographical genre in the fourth century, and ending with Samuel Beckett. Augustine sees his search as one for his true life, his true self, and conceives autobiography as a quest for true memory, for reality. For him, one's true life is that which has been given one by God and Providence, and narrative's inherent, unique orderliness reflects the natural form of memory, the form truest to Providence—given being. True memory mirrors the real world, and Augustine accepts that narrative is its medium. His is a narrative realism, and the self that emerges is the gift of revelation, leavened by reason.

Contrast Giambattista Vico in the eighteenth century, next on Olney's historical trajectory. Vico's reflections on the powers of mind led him to cock his eye at Augustine's narrative realism. For him, a life is crafted by the mental acts of those who live it, not by an act of God. Its storylikeness is of our doing, not God's. Vico was perhaps the first radical constructivist, though he was protected by a rationalism that guarded him from the skepticism usually associated with that stance.

Enter Jean-Jacques Rousseau about a half century later, who, alerted by Vico's reflections and emboldened by the new skepticism of his own revolutionary times, raised new doubts about Augustine's stable and innocent narrative realism. Rousseau's *Confessions* are laced with high-spirited skepticism. Yes, acts of mind, not Providence, shape an autobiography, but Rousseau also pokes fun at these acts of mind—their passionate follies and vanity-serving uses. Life stories for Rousseau are more like social games than quests for some higher truth, and that may be one reason he has little patience with notions like original sin. He turns Vico's respect for reason into a rueful and impious skepticism.

Jump ahead two centuries to Samuel Beckett and our own times. Beckett is at one with Vico's reasoned rejection of Augustine's narrative realism and even more in sympathy with Rousseau's wry skepticism. But he explicitly rejects narrative as reflecting the inherent order of life. Indeed, he denies the very notion that there is any inherent order. His is a thoroughgoing fictionalism, his mission to free life writing (as well as literature) from its narrative straitjacket. Life is problematic, not to be shackled in conventional genres. So even his somewhat autobiographical dramas, like *Waiting for Godot,* pose problems rather than answer them. For him, the road is better than the inn: let one be not lulled by the illusion of narrative.

Each—Augustine, Vico, Rousseau, and Beckett—is a child of his historical time, cultivating a fresh image of selfhood and rejecting what was stale. For Augustine, self is the product of revelation-guided narrative, revealing what God had wrought; by the time we reach Beckett, self-told narrative has become a mere *façon d'écrire,* a man-made noose strangling the imagination. But for each of them, the nature and origin of selfhood were issues of deep and debatable concern, and the concern seems not to have diminished, though the issues may have changed drastically. Why did Thomas à Kempis call his account of true monastic selfhood *Imitatio Christi?* Was he pushing Augustinian narrative realism, proposing Christ's depiction of the serving self as the true model? Were the monks and nuns of his times convinced that their selves were trying to be true imitations of Christ's? Reading Thomas with modern eyes, one senses he is like a recruiter glorifying the kind of selfhood that might lure novices into the monastic life or justify staying in it. The contrast implied throughout his stirring little book is with the selfish, secular self. And so it seems with all disquisitions about selfhood. In some indirect way, they are all advertisements for a *right* selfhood, each with its own version of the tempting competition.

And so it is with Virginia Woolf's metaphoric "room of one's own," her feminist appeal for a change in women's conceptions of their selfhood. Was Jack Kerouac's *On the Road* tuned to reducing the teleological intensity in his generation's style of self-telling and self-making?

One regrets that in Olney's brilliant account of the great innovations in conceptions of selfhood, he did not explore more fully the struggles his heroic authors underwent in their times—Augustine's against blind faith, Vico's against the spirit of the Enlightenment, Rousseau's against an oppressive *ancien régime,* and Beckett's against literary realism. The four of them obviously shaped new images of selfhood. But like their images, no image of selfhood ever gains a monopoly. We would do well to inquire why this is so. And our inquiry will bring us back to the issues of autonomy and commitment touched on briefly before.

V

A self-making narrative is something of a balancing act. It must, on the one hand, create a conviction of autonomy, that one has a will of one's own, a certain freedom of choice, a degree of possibility. But it must also relate the self to a world of others—to friends and family, to institutions, to the past, to reference groups. But the commitment to others that is implicit in relating oneself to others of course limits our autonomy. We seem virtually unable to live without both, autonomy and commitment, and our lives strive to balance the two. So do the self-narratives we tell ourselves.

Not everyone succeeds. Take one Christopher McCandless, a twenty-three-year-old whose dead body was found several years ago in a deserted bus in the Alaska wilderness. Some autobiographical fragments showed up among his meager possessions, and they tell the story of a "radically autonomous identity gone wrong" (Eakin, 1999). "Dealing with things on his own" was his ideal, and he understood Thoreau's injunction "simplify, simplify" to mean that he should depend on nobody, strive for unfettered autonomy. His self-narrative fit this formula: at the end of his days, he was living in remote Alaska, eating only edible plants, and after three months he died of starvation. Shortly before his death, he went to the trouble of taking a self-portrait, the film of which was found in his camera. In it the young man is seated, with one hand raised and holding in the other a block-letter note on which he has written, "I have had a happy life and Thank the Lord. Goodbye and may God Bless All." On a plywood-covered window of the deserted bus that became his last refuge, he scratched this message: "Two Years He walks the Earth ... Ultimate Freedom. An Extremist. An Aesthetic Voyager Whose Home is *The Road* ... No Longer To Be Poisoned By Civilization He Flees, And Walks Alone Upon the Land To Become *Lost* in the *Wild*." In the end, even poor Christopher McCandless felt some commitment to others—his commitment offered, mind you, as an act of free will. As he lay alone, starving to death, he still felt impelled to offer God's blessings to those he had spurned, which was an act of grace, a balancing act. Then, perhaps nostalgically, perhaps bitterly, he died. Was he victim or victor in his own story? More than seventy years ago, the great folklorist Vladimir Propp demonstrated how characters and events in folk stories serve as functions in narrative plots: they do not exist on their own. What function did Christopher McCandless's final act play in his story, and how did he tell it to himself?

I once knew a young doctor, disillusioned with the humdrum of private practice, who upon hearing about the organization *Médecins sans Frontiéres* began reading its literature and raising money for it at his county medical association meetings. Finally he spent two years doctoring in Africa. On his return, I asked him if he had changed. "Yes," he said, "my life's more all of a piece now." All of a piece? Scattered over two continents? Yes, for now he is not only practicing medicine back where he'd started but researching the roiling history of the town he'd left to go off to Africa, the better to find the sources of his discontent, to reconcile his autonomy with his commitment to a town which he is making part of the wider world he had longed for. In doing so, he has created a viable self. He's even enlisted the town fathers as his allies in the effort!

How indeed does one balance autonomy and commitment in one's sense of self, let alone make it all of a piece? I had studied that question as a psychologist in the usual indirect way we psychologists do and dutifully contributed my chapter to one of those Neisser volumes I mentioned earlier. But somehow the balance comes out more plainly in ordinary conversation. So I've been asking people about it casually when the topic seems right—friends, people with whom I work, acquaintances. I simply ask them outright about themselves whenever the topic of balancing seems natural. One was a law student, a young woman who was deeply committed to child advocacy in support of parents during child-related litigation. I asked her how she got into that work, which seemed to suit her to a T. She said she'd send me an e-mail, and here is what it said:

> It was in some ways inadvertent. I had graduated with a B.A. in English and creative writing, and didn't want to go into education or publishing, etc., but did want to do something . . . to better the lives of poor children. By a peculiar turn of circumstances I fell into an internship with the Community Legal Aid Society in a middle-sized city in the East, where I worked closely with an attorney who was representing parents (often with mental disabilities) in abuse and neglect cases. I was immediately drawn to the work. Most of all, I was astounded by the strength of these parents in the face of tremendous environmental adversity, but also by the way their voices were heard by no one. When they encountered someone (the attorney I worked with, myself) who was truly interested in listening to them, they often weren't able to trust the relationship, and this in turn interfered with effective legal representation. Having done a lot of my own work to "find my voice" and to learn firsthand the healing, even transformative power of being in a relationship with someone who really listened, I felt very connected to these parents, despite our differences in background, etc. So, in the end, it is a continuation of my very deep, very personal interest.

Both the doctor and the child advocate had reached impasses: bored and discontented, going on and on with foreseeable duties to fulfill established commitments. Medical school, then internship, then small-town private practice. The well-brought-up daughter of literary bent, on to college and on to teaching high-school English. Both were following trajectories shaped early in life by conventional commitment. Neither was in material need; they did not have to continue. Both foresaw the next step too clearly, as if possibility had been closed off by the sheer predictability of what lay ahead.

Commitment under these conditions is a narrative that is dominated by precedent—obligations in one's own life. Medical graduates go on to internships and then into practice—with small-town practice perhaps being an off-the-track wit fillip. Circumstances change. The balancing act between commitment and autonomy no longer satisfies as the range of possibilities narrows. One's self-narrative seems lacking in those possible worlds that imagination generates and that novelists and dramatists cultivate.

We can think of these times in life in several ways. We can think of them as akin to the times at which circumstances are ripe for a landmark decision by a court of law. And like landmark decisions, where an earlier doctrinal principle is expanded to take account of new conditions, turning points in life honor old aspirations in new ways. Medical care is not just for the safe and the hometown familiars but also for the deprived and beleaguered beyond a horizon one had not realized existed. Or one gives one's more developed voice to those who need it in their defense, not just to those who would routinely find it on their own. Or poor Christopher McCandless: if self-sufficiency is good, then let it be total. Or one can conceive turning points in one's self-telling as like a self-generated *peripeteia*, one's previously coping with trouble having now generated trouble of its own.

The bald fact of the matter is that one rarely encounters autobiographies, whether written or spontaneously told in interview, that are without turning points. And they are almost always accompanied by remarks such as "I became a new woman," or "I found a new voice," or "It was a new me after I walked out." Are these an integral part of growing up—like the *Sturm und Drang* of adolescence? Perhaps, though they certainly are not a feature only of youth, for turning points often occur later in life, particularly as retirement approaches. It may well be that Erik Erikson's renowned "life stages," marked by a shift in concern from autonomy to competence to intimacy to continuity, set the stage for autobiographical turning points.

Some cultures provide for them ritually, as *rites de passage,* and they are often sufficiently painful or taxing to get the idea across. A !Kung Bushman boy is put through a painful ceremonial (which includes having ashes rubbed into fresh cuts in his cheeks, tomorrow's proud scars of manhood) designed to mark his passage out of childhood. Now he is fit to be a hunter, ready to reject a child's ways. He's taken on a hunt soon after, and much hoopla is made about his role in killing a giraffe or whatever gets snagged. The rite of passage not only encourages but legitimates change.

It is not only in *rites de passage* (or in Erikson's life stages) that turning points are conventionalized. Self-narrating, if I may state it again, is from the outside in as well as from the inside out. When circumstances ready us for change, we turn to others who have lived through one, become open to new trends and new ways of looking at ourselves in the world. We read novels with new interest, go to political demonstrations, listen with a more open ear. Lawyers bored with the routines of mergers and copyright-infringement suits pay new attention to what the American Civil Liberties Union is up to. A rising and discontented Jane Fonda, on her own testimony, begins reading the "new" feminist literature to help her understand a divorce through which she has just gone. And, indeed, feminism offers changing versions of a woman's selfhood: from feminine consciousness in a Willa Cather or a Katherine Mansfield, to the protest feminism of a Simone de Beauvoir or a Germaine Greer, to today's activist "equality" feminists.

Self-making through self-narrating is restless and endless, probably more so now than ever before. It is a dialectical process, a balancing act. And despite self-assuring homilies about people never changing, they do. They rebalance their autonomy and their commitments, usually in a way that honors what they were before. Decorum keeps most of us from the sorts of wild adventure in self-making that brought Christopher McCandless down.

V I

What is there to say in conclusion about the narrative art of self-making?

Sigmund Freud (1956), in an interesting book too seldom read, remarked that each of us is like an entire cast of characters in a novel or play. Novelists and playwrights, he wrote, construct their works of art by splitting up their interior cast of characters, putting them on the page or onstage to work out their relations with each other. Those characters can be heard in the pages of any autobiography. Perhaps it is a literary exaggeration to call our multiple inner voices characters. But they are there to be heard, trying to come to terms with each other, sometimes at loggerheads. An extensive self-making narrative will try to speak for them all, but we know already that no single story can do that. To whom are you telling it, and to what end? Besides, we are too Hamlet-like to make it all of a piece—too torn between the familiar and the possible.

None of this seems to discourage us. We go on, constructing ourselves through narrative.

Why is narrative so essential, why do we need it for self-definition? The narrative gift seems to be our natural way of using language for characterizing those deviations from the expected state of things that characterize living in a human culture. None of us knows the just-so evolutionary story of its rise and survival. But what we do know is that it is irresistible as a way of making sense of human interaction.

I have argued that it is through narrative that we create and recreate selfhood, that self is a product of our telling and not some essence to be delved for in the recesses of subjectivity. There is now evidence that if we lacked the capacity to make stories about ourselves, there would be no such thing as selfhood. Let me offer this evidence.

A neurological disorder called *dysnarrativia*, a severe impairment in the ability to tell or understand stories, is associated with neuropathies like Korsakov's syndrome and Alzheimer's disease. It is more than an impairment of memory about the past, which is itself highly disruptive of one's sense of self, as Oliver Sacks's (1973) work has made plain. In Korsakov's syndrome particularly, where affect as well as memory is severely impaired, selfhood virtually vanishes. Sacks (1986) describes one of his severe Korsakov patients as "scooped out, de-souled."

One characteristic symptom in such cases is an almost complete loss of the ability to read other minds, to tell what others might have been thinking, feeling, even seeing. Sufferers seem to have lost not only a sense of self but also a sense of other. An astute critic of autobiography, Paul John Eakin (1999), commenting on this literature, takes this evidence as further proof that selfhood is profoundly relational, that self, as noted earlier, is also other.

The emerging view is that dysnarrativia is deadly for selfhood. Eakin (1999) cites the conclusion of an unpublished paper by Kay Young and Jeffrey Saver (1995): "Individuals who have lost the ability to construct narratives have lost their selves." The construction of selfhood, it seems, cannot proceed without a capacity to narrate.

Once we are equipped with that capacity, we can produce a selfhood that joins us with others, that permits us to hark back selectively to our past while shaping ourselves for the possibilities of an imagined future. We gain the self-told narratives that make and remake our selves from the culture in which we live. However much we may rely on a functioning brain to achieve our selfhood, we are virtually from the start expressions of the culture that nurtures us. And culture itself is a dialectic, replete with alternative narratives about what self is or might be. The stories we tell to create ourselves reflect that dialectic.

REFERENCES

Bruner, J. (1958). The Freudian Conception of Man. *Daedalus, 8(1),* 77-84.

Bruner, J. (1991). *Acts of Meaning,* Cambridge, Mass.: Harvard University Press.

Eakin, P. J. (1999). *How Our Lives Become Stories: Making Selves.* Ithaca, NY: Cornell University Press.

Freud, S. (1956). *Delusion and Dream: An Interpretation in the Light of Psychoanalysis of "Gradiva," a Novel by Wilhelm Jensen,* ed. P. Rieff. Boston: Beacon Press.

Lejeune, P. (1975). *Le Pacte autobiographique* Paris: Seuil.

Lejeune, P. (1989). *On Autobiography.* Minneapolis: University of Minnesota Press.

Lloyd, G. (1979). *Magic, Reason, and Experience.* Cambridge, UK: Cambridge University Press.

Lloyd, G. (1999). *Science, Folklore, and Ideology.* Indianapolis: Hackett.

Neisser, U. (1958). The Freudian Conception of Man. *Daedalus, 8(1),* 77-84.

Neisser, U. (1988). Five Kinds of Self-Knowledge. *Philosophical Psychology, 1,* 35-59.

Neisser, U. (1993). *The Perceived Self.* Cambridge: Cambridge University Press.

Neisser, U. & Fivush, R. (1994). *The Remembering Self*. Cambridge: Cambridge University Press.

Neisser, U. & Jopling, D. (1997). *The Conceptual Self in Context*. Cambridge: Cambridge University Press.

Neisser, U. & Winograd, E. (1988). *Remembering Reconsidered*. Cambridge: Cambridge University Press.

Olney, J. (1998). *Memory and Narrative: The Weave of Life-Writing*. Chicago: University of Chicago Press.

Oxenhandler, N. (2001). *The Eros of Parenthood*. New York: St. Martin's Press.

Sacks, O. (1973). *Awakenings*. London: Duckworth.

Sacks, O. (1986). *The Man Who Mistook His Wife for a Hat and Other Clinical Tales*. New York: Alfred A. Knopf.

Shweder, R. (2000). The Psychology of Practice and the Practice of the Three Psychologies. *Asian Journal of Social Psychology*, 3, 207-22.

Slobin, D. (2000). Verbalized Events: A Dynamic Approach to Linguistic Relativity and Determinism. *Current Issues in Linguistic Theory*, 198, 107.

Spence, D. (1982). *Narrative Truth and Historical Truth: Meaning and Interpretation in Psychoanalysis*. New York: W. W. Norton.

Spence, D. (1987). *The Freudian Metaphor: Toward Paradigm Change in Psychoanalysis*. New York: W. W. Norton.

Wang, Q. (2001). Culture Effects on Adults' Earliest Childhood Recollection and Self-Description. *Journal of Personality and Social Psychology*, 81(2).

Young, K. & Saver, J. (1995). The Neurology of Narrative. Paper presented at a session titled *Autobiography and the Neurosciences*, Modern Language Association Convention, New York.

CHAPTER 2

Folk Psychology and Narrative Practice

MICHAEL WHITE

In the first part of this chapter, I link many of the practices of narrative therapy to a historical tradition of understanding life and identity that is at times referred to as "folk psychology." This tradition, which was largely displaced by the modern psychologies, began to be reinstated when the social sciences went through an "interpretive turn" in the late 1960s and early 1970s. I discuss the extent to which many of the practices of narrative inquiry can be located within the context of this interpretive turn, and within the tradition of folk psychology. In the second part of this chapter, I clarify some of the proposals for therapeutic practice that are shaped by this tradition of folk psychology. Finally, in the third part, I focus on considerations of history and culture, and on the implications of these considerations for therapeutic practice. To begin these explorations, I describe a therapeutic conversation that I had with Paul, who consulted me about his work as a counselor.

1. FOLK PSYCHOLOGY

Paul*

Paul consulted me about some concerns that he had about his work. He was a counselor in a local agency, working mostly with heterosexual couples. Although there was much that he enjoyed about his work, in recent times he had become increasingly uncomfortable about some of his responses to the expressions of the male partners of these couple relationships. These were responses of

---

AUTHOR'S NOTE: I would like to thank David Epston for his helpful comments on an earlier draft of this chapter. This chapter was presented at the "Narrative Therapy and Community Work Conference" in Adelaide, South Australia, February, 2001, and published in the *Dulwich Centre Newsletter*, 2001, 2, pp. 4-37. Reprinted with permission from Dulwich Centre Publications, Adelaide, South Australia.
*The names of people appearing throughout this paper are pseudonyms.

anxiety and uncertainty, and Paul had reached the conclusion that this had to do with deep-seated fears and insecurities that were the outcome of his "unresolved issues." This specter of unresolved issues weighed heavily on him, spinning him into uncertainty, and provoking dread. As well, the fact of the presence of these unresolved issues had Paul questioning his fitness to be working with people.

Paul So that is where I am at with this fear thing. Sometimes it's more than fear. I'm shaking inside, virtually terrified. And I have been having a lot of questions about what I am doing in this work. I have even thought that maybe it is a sick thing. You know, that I am in this for the wrong reasons, that I have some weird motive. You know, for the motive of trying to work through the things that are unresolved, to do this for myself through my work. This has got to be pretty bad, you know.

M Would you say a little more about this motive that . . .

Paul Well, it's probably because I haven't sorted things out with my father, that I am, and this is without realizing it too, that I am doing this through my work. Which I reckon is pretty screwed up.

M You have had this idea for a while?

Paul Yeah.

M Has it helped a lot?

Paul Nope. Not so far. In fact, not one little bit *[laughs]*. But then, I don't know what the answer is.

M Could we go back a step or two? Do you have a sense of what it is that you are responding to in these men when you feel this apprehension most? What it is that you are experiencing at the time in your conversations with these men? Do you have any thoughts about what it is that you witness, that contributes to this fear and anxiety?

Paul Just little things really. Nothing much. It's pretty silly really. Sometimes I think it is just my imagination.

M Like?

Paul Like a look, hmm . . . or a way of sitting or, let me see . . . certain words or a tone of voice, and . . . maybe a gesture. Like I said, just little things really. Lots of really silly little things can get me going, that can trigger it. You know, it's like . . . it's like as if I am always on the alert.

M On the alert? Tell me this. You said unresolved issues, and you mentioned your father, so I am making a guess. What would expressions like these have alerted you to at earlier times in your life?

Paul Well . . . yeah, that's it. Of something brewing in my father, of a mood coming on . . . Probably trouble, lots of trouble. Of manipulation too . . . yeah, he was really into that. Yeah, there would be things that would have alerted me to danger.

M Your mother too?

Paul You mean, alerted me to danger from her?

M No. I mean did she also have a sensitivity to these early-warning signs?

Paul Yeah. I think we got together on this and helped each other out. We could see things coming.

M And what sort of actions did you take in response to these early-warning signs, in response to these cues?

Paul   Well, we couldn't do much really. My mum could distract him sometimes. And so could I. You know, I always worried so much about my mum. When I think about it, I guess that knowing how to read these cues did help us to get out of harm's way at times. But, it wasn't enough . . . *[trails off]*

M   I take it that you and your mother validated this sense for each other. This sense that you had of the potential for harm. You joined with each other in developing this sensitivity to these cues. And you also supported each other in the limited actions that were available to you both.

Paul   We would work together on it. Yeah. But . . . *[tears welling and chest heaving]* . . . there I go again *[brushing away the tears]*.

M   Would you mind saying a little about those tears?

Paul   It's OK. Just thinking about my mum you know, and about, well, what she went through and how hard she tried. And, and, about how unfair it was and about what she achieved despite all of this. And about our connection. Other things too.

M   What would she think about the work experiences that you are consulting me over? What is your guess about how she would be responding if she was present and hearing what I am hearing?

Paul   I think that she would feel for me a lot, and that she would be worried for me *[now openly crying]*.

M   If I could ask her for her thoughts about why you had chosen to work in this area, what do you think she would say?

Paul   Well, she was mostly respectful of my decisions, not always though *[now grinning through tears]*. Sometimes she would get really mad at me. Maybe she'd say: "Are you stark raving mad? What in the hell are you doing this to yourself for, after all that we went through?"

M   If she did see your choice of work as a significant decision, one not taken lightly, then what do you reckon she would say?

Paul   Yeah. Actually, I really think she would, you know. She would probably say that it was because I wanted everyone to have a fair go. She would probably say that I knew what it was all about in lots of ways. She would probably understand that I just couldn't leave it.

M   So she might connect the fact of your working in this area with a purpose?

Paul   I reckon she would. She would probably say something about what I stood for, back then you know, although I wished that I'd been able to do more, I just . . . I do want everyone to have a fair go, that's true, and no one should have to live under a cloud like this.

M   Could it be that these are the sort of purposes that you and your mother's life were joined in?

Paul   For sure. For sure. But she never had a chance.

M   What do you reckon it would have been like for your mum to know that these purposes live on in your work in the way that they do?

Paul   *[crying again]* I reckon it would have meant heaps to her. Just heaps. And hey, the surprising thing is that I hadn't really thought much about this.

M   What is your guess about how she would feel about her own life, just knowing this?

Paul   *[still crying]* She wouldn't feel empty. She wouldn't feel that all the hard work had been for nothing.

As this conversation evolved further there was an opportunity to evoke the presence of Paul's mother (who was deceased). Later, the theme of sensitivity to cues returned to the center of the conversation.

M   Picking up on this sensitivity to cues that you and your mother helped one another develop. Would you say that there was a skill in this?

Paul   Well, I have never really thought about that. Till now I have just seen it as a liability.

M   What would you say now?

Paul   Yeah. Now I would definitely say that.

M   Say what? That it is a skill?

Paul   Yeah. Although I haven't thought of it in this way before. Hey!

M   What?

Paul   I really like thinking about this.

M   Could I check something with you? I understand, from all that you have said, that the insecurities, fears and unresolved issues that you have talked of are, well, that they are part of a bundle of things. That these things speak of a sensitivity to certain cues about danger and potential for harm—of skills in reading these cues. That they speak of insider knowledges about the effects of intimidation and disrespect and abuse. That they speak about a valuing of and belief in other ways of being in life, of the sort that were reflected in your connection with your mother. And that they speak of a purpose that has been present through the history of your life, about contributing to everyone having a fair go, that you are joined with your mother in. I wanted to check this understanding out with you.

Paul   That's great! I can relate to all of that, and it feels so good *[grinning again]*.

M   What is the good feeling? Could you say something about this?

Paul   Relief . . . relief . . . because this isn't all so bad is it, after all. I mean, I had been feeling like I was a fake counselor with the insecurities and all of those unresolved issues. But this isn't so bad, is it? *[now laughing]*

M   I was thinking something similar. In fact I was thinking about what your work would look like if everything that has been bundled up in this anxiety and fear was more explicitly present in your work with the couples that are consulting you.

Paul   I can't imagine. But I would put myself up for a conversation about that.

The ensuing conversation centered on this exploration. In it, Paul determined that he could more explicitly take up, into his work, the sensitivity that he had to these cues, as well as these insider knowledges about the practices and consequences of intimidation and disrespect. He developed some specific ideas about how he might give expression to this sensitivity and to these knowledges, and about how this could open space for conversations about that which usually cannot be spoken of. In this conversation Paul also settled on some ideas about alternative avenues for the expression of what he had previously referred to as his insecurities. He practiced some of these ideas in the context of our meetings with me playing the part of the male partners of some of the couples that had been consulting him. For example, he would try out preludes to inquiries addressing practices of intimidation such as: "Right now I would like to share with you the sort of questions that I would be asking you if it wasn't for my apprehension about how you might respond to them. I would appreciate it if you would reflect on these questions, and then tell me about whether or not this apprehension would be valid if I was to ask you these questions."

Paul also thought of options for addressing the sort of circumstances that would make it difficult to proceed with these therapeutic conversations, and other options for openly negotiating the sort of circumstances that would make progress possible. I had two subsequent meetings with Paul, in which he caught me up with some really exciting developments in his work in addressing the power relations of gender with heterosexual couples. In one of these meetings he also informed me that he had found himself more able to provide an account of his work to friends in terms of his purposes without feeling embarrassed. He then joked that he longed for some more unresolved issues that we might turn upside down in our conversations with each other, and hoped that I would be able to detect a few of these. I suggested that he go down the street to get some of these, and bring them back with him next time. We both laughed.

Folk Psychology

Many aspects of this account of my conversation with Paul are shaped by questions and reflections that are informed by what I refer to as narrative practices. Invariably I find that the people who consult me relate to these practices quite instantaneously, and this provides the basis for many wonderful adventures in the context of therapeutic conversations. I believe that the familiarity that people have with this sort of therapeutic inquiry has to do with the fact that many of the practices of narrative therapy are closely linked to a particular tradition of understanding life and identity that is deeply historical. At times this centuries-old tradition is referred to as "folk psychology" (Bruner, 1990).

> All cultures have as one of their most powerful constitutive instruments a folk psychology, a set of more or less connected, more or less normative descriptions about how human beings "tick," what our own and other minds are like, what one can expect situated action to be like, what are possible modes of life, how one commits oneself to them, and so on. . . . Coined in derision by the new cognitive scientists for its hospitality toward such intentional states as beliefs, desires, and meanings, the expression of "folk psychology" could not be more appropriate. (pp. 35 and 36)

According to this definition, we routinely employ folk psychology as we make our way through everyday life. We put this folk psychology into service in our efforts to understand our own lives and in making sense of the actions of others. Folk psychology equips us with a range of notions about what makes people "tick," and provides a foundation for our responses to the actions of others—our responses to the actions of others are premised on these understandings about what makes them tick, and by our conclusions about the nature of these actions. Folk psychology also comes to the fore in our efforts to make out just what it is that is going on in the world. Among other achievements, Bruner (1990) illustrates the way that folk psychology shapes our endeavor to come to terms with the unexpected in life, provides a basis for our efforts to address obstacles and crises, and makes it possible for us to come to terms with a range of predicaments and dilemmas that confront us in everyday life.

What are the features of this folk psychology? Perhaps first and foremost, it is distinguished by the notion of "personal agency." It casts people as active mediators, negotiators, and as representatives of their own lives, doing so separately and in unison with others. It is a psychology that is about people living their lives out according to certain intentions and purposes, in the pursuit of what matters to them. It is a psychology that is about people going about the business of satisfying certain wants and achieving sought-after goals. It is a psychology that foregrounds matters of values and beliefs, and one that associates these values and beliefs with commitments to ways of life that characterize people. This emphasis on personal agency, on the significance that is assigned to notions of purpose, and on the weight that is given to notions of beliefs, values, and commitments, is a reflection of this folk psychology's theory of mind. In its appreciation of what it is that informs people's expressions of life, this tradition of folk psychology invokes "mind."[1]

In regard to traditions of understanding human life, folk psychology is one of many psychologies that are now available to people for these purposes. The last century or two has seen burgeoning developments in these traditions of human understanding, and many of these developments have had the effect of displacing, in some arenas, the tradition of folk psychology that I have been drawing out here. Others have changed the shape of some strains of folk psychology—folk psychology has not remained invariant, and has taken in many of the modern psychological notions that have been manufactured in this era of extraordinary expansion in the psychologies. However, in the face of these developments, the emphasis on the significance of personal agency and on intentional states is still strongly featured in the great majority of folk psychological accounts of human action.

The New Psychologies

Although folk psychology has continued to enjoy a degree of popular success, it hasn't fared all that well in the arena of the professional psychologies. It is lowly ranked and marginalized by these psychologies. It is considered to be naïve in its conceptions of life and identity, mired in the biases of local culture, and nonscientific in the priority that it gives to the notions of human agency and intentional states. In the domain of the professional psychologies, folk psychology is considered not up to the sophistication and rigor required of a modern psychology for the development of adequate or, for that matter, even reasonable, understandings of human expression.

There have been many developments that have significantly impinged on the status of folk psychology in this way. The nineteenth century saw the bringing together, into a system of professional psychology, a number of "modern" and interlinked developments of the preceding century or two. These included the following:

1. The development of humanist notions of the presence of a human "nature" that is considered to be the foundation of personal existence, and that is understood to provide the source of human expression.

2. The evolution of the conception of a "self" as an essence that is understood to occupy the center of personal identity. Although this idea of a self is a relatively novel idea in the history of the world's cultures, it has been a hugely successful idea, and is today quite taken for granted in the West.

3. The progressive development, from the seventeenth century on, of a new system of social control in which the normalizing judgment of people's lives has steadily displaced moral judgment.[2]

This new professional psychology was dismissive of the capacity of folk psychology to provide an adequately reasoned and rational explanation of human action. It de-emphasized the relevance of personal agency and intentional states. In the stead of these intentional state notions it substituted a notion of "internal states" that were considered to be universal to the human condition.[3] Human expression was now interpreted as a surface manifestation of these internal states—a manifestation of unconscious motives, instincts, drives, traits, dispositions and so on. Various intrapsychic mechanisms (who hasn't heard of defense mechanisms?) were constructed to provide an account of how these internal states were transformed into human expression. The development of these intrapsychic mechanisms provided the foundation of a new category of mind, the "unconscious mind," and this quickly displaced the "mind" of folk psychology.

Not all psychologies that construct intrapsychic mechanisms are founded on these internal state notions. For example, some fascinating developments in the exploration of mind were initiated during this era by psychologists of the ilk of William James (1890, 1892, 1902). Although these developments featured various premises about what might be called intrapsychic processes, they did not construct internal state notions. This Jamesian tradition of understanding human life has been significantly renewed over the last decade or two. For example, see Russell Meares' *Intimacy and Alienation* (2000).[4]

In contrast to the "intentional state" notions of folk psychology, and the psychologies influenced by James, notions of the internal state psychologies were increasingly taken up and applied to the identification of and treatment of a whole range of human maladies, the real causes of which were now considered inaccessible to ordinary human consciousness. These causes could only be discovered and known through archaeological processes guided by those equipped with the knowledge and skills in establishing the conditions under which true insight might be revealed. In many circles, these claims to the identification of an underlying and universal structure to human expression were heralded as a breakthrough in the scientific understanding of life and identity. Apart from anything else, these understandings of the new psychologies were considered to be beyond the culturally tainted understandings that are a characteristic of folk psychology. It was widely accepted that these developments would lay the foundations of a truly cross-cultural psychology.

Despite the early success of these internal state psychologies, they were soon faced with a significant challenge. During the period of World War I a new psychology emerged, one that consolidated itself in the 1920s and that became the dominant paradigm in professional psychology over the next two or three decades. This new psychology was a radical behaviorism that was inspired by the era of positivist science and by the extraordinary success of machine mechanics during the period encompassing the world wars. Radical behaviorism was dismissive of the traditions of psychology that preceded it, considering them irrational. This new psychology made concerted efforts to erase any notions of mind—folk conceptions of mind and the unconscious mind of internal state psychologies—in understandings of human action. In the domain of the professional disciplines it was largely successful in this objective (if not in popular imagination), for a time establishing virtual hegemony. The laboratory had become the context for human inquiry and for advancement in the psychology of what was now human "behavior," not human action.

In acknowledging the general success of radical behaviorism in its ambitions for professional psychology, I am not suggesting that it went unchallenged. There were many other developments in the psychologies that were questioning of the claims of radical behaviorism, but these were assigned little legitimacy and few avenues of expression.

Then came the so-called "cognitive revolution" of the 1950s, which initially endeavored to erect meaning as a central tenant in psychology. It was in the context of this development that "meaning" was accorded a priority in the understanding of human action. According to this, it was people's constructions of meaning that shaped their actions. An appreciation of how people went about making meaning out of their experiences of the world was considered the proper focus of a human psychology. Although this cognitive revolution successfully challenged the hegemony of the positivist behavioral traditions, as well as the personality theories of the intentional state psychologies, unfortunately many of [its] early initiatives to install meaning as a central concept in psychology were subsequently derailed.[5]

Very soon, in what was no longer the era of machine mechanics in technology but the information era, this cognitive focus turned away from the production of meaning and onto "information." This shaped inquiry not into processes that people engage with in the construction of meaning but into the processing of information, not into the shape that these social constructions give to human expression but into the computation of information, and not into studies of the significance of constructions of meaning in regard to identity formation but into studies regarding precision in control inputs. As an outcome of these developments, notions of human agency and of intentional states were again rendered irrelevant to an adequate understanding of life and identity.

This brief account that I have given of the history of the development of traditions for understanding human action over the past century is partial. In the professional disciplines there have been many other developments, some of them relatively peripheral, and others that have, for a time, rivaled some of the more mainstream ideas. For example, most people who work in the family therapy field would be aware of the very significant influence of the "new functionalism" of the 1950s, the legacy of which is so visible in many of the assumptions of "systems theory" and in the practices of family therapy of recent decades. And I am sure that most people who work in this field would be aware of the spectacular success of cognitive behavior therapy over the last decade or two. Since it is not possible for me in the space of this [chapter] to draw an overview of developments such as these, I have had to be content to provide an account of a few of the specific, major, and historical mainstream developments that have played a significant role in displacing the relevance attributed to the mind of folk psychology in explanations of human action and expression.

Revival of the Internal State Psychologies

I came to my social work training in the wake of these developments. At this time, nothing much was settled. As a student studying psychology in 1967, I remember well being introduced to the claims of behaviorism and of information theory, to the debate surrounding these different representations of human action, and to some of the controversy associated with this debate. I was introduced to several versions of the internal state psychologies, including those that located these internal states in the "family," not just the individual, and that provided the foundation for the manufacture of a new range of family pathologies and relationship dysfunctions. I was also introduced to the new functionalism in systems theory which also had the family as its primary focus. The only thing that did seem settled in the context of all of these claims and counterclaims was this: In any consideration of human action and identity, notions of human agency and intentional states were irrelevant and inconsequential.

In the context of this climate, I am sure that readers could imagine, or perhaps even recall, the sort of reception provoked by the raising of unpopular lines of inquiry through questions like: "And what about student participation in the anti-Vietnam War movement? Could this really be adequately explained away in the terms of unresolved family-of-origin issues? What if this was understood to be action that was principled, and therefore value and belief driven?"

In any case, whatever debate was taking place in the professional disciplines at this time, this was soon to be overshadowed by the phenomenal rise of the internal-state "popular psychologies" in the late 1960s and early 1970s. These popular psychologies were not so much a resurgence of folk psychology, but an amalgam of

- specific developments of the professional psychologies,
- aspects of the personal liberation philosophies that were the vogue of the 1960s,
- elements of the new consumer culture of the 1970s,
- bits of the structuralist developmental psychologies of Piaget and Erickson,
- pieces of Eastern spiritual and mystical traditions,
- facets of the new functionalism, and more.

What unified most of these popular psychologies was the status given to the self—the notion of "essential self" was assigned an unquestioned status, even in the face of some extraordinary contradictions that this notion at times aroused in the realm of ideas and practice. It was a taken-for-granted fact that this was a self to be found at the center of identity and that it existed independently of efforts to describe it.

This was the era of the great self revival. These popular psychologies were almost entirely "self psychologies." There was a self to be discovered at the core of personhood, one that was composed of certain essences that are of human nature. Life was considered to be either a direct expression of these essences, or, more often, a manifestation of the repression of, or distortion of, these essences. Strongly associated with this emphasis on the self was the catharsis injunction. At this time this injunction was the foremost of all psychological injunctions. Cathartic happenings were everywhere to behold, virtually pandemic. In fact, in some circles in the early 1970s, so all encompassing were the outbreaks of catharsis that it became virtually impossible to find social spaces untouched by this phenomenon in some way. These self psychologies were linked to this catharsis injunction through a powerful ethical obligation to discover the "truth" of who one was and to seek to live a life that was an accurate and authentic expression of this truth.

Meaning, Narrative, and the Reinstatement of Folk Psychology

In here describing the emergence of popular psychology, I am not suggesting that this idea about self as an essence was new—in fact it is a centuries-old idea that significantly informed the internal state psychologies of the nineteenth century. And the quest for "the truth of who we are" wasn't new either–it had been a major preoccupation of philosophical inquiry for several centuries. These developments of the 1960s and 1970s in popular psychology represented a resurgence and reinvigoration of some longstanding traditions of thought and practice. In recent times, these traditions have been enormously successful in capturing the popular imagination, and have undoubtedly influenced contemporary folk psychological understandings of life in many ways. However, many of these influences do not sit at all comfortably with those strains of folk psychology that emphasize human agency and intentional states, strains that remain ever present. These strains have remained highly visible in many domains of cultural life, including in the drama of much contemporary theater and literature, especially the novel. As well, there have been a number of initiatives in recent decades to reinstate this tradition of folk psychology as a tradition relevant to inquiry in the human sciences and social sciences.

In fact, at the very time of the resurgence of internal state notions in the popular psychologies, some of the social sciences were going through what has been referred to as an "interpretive turn" (Geertz, 1973, 1983). It was in the context of this interpretive turn that meaning was placed firmly at the center of social inquiry. This development was perhaps most visible in the emergence of the "new" cultural anthropology. This was a form of inquiry based on the idea that people respond to each other in terms of their understandings of each others' actions, in terms of their own theories about what they and others are up to—that people respond to each other in terms of their own psychology. This premise placed the focus of inquiry firmly on meaning—on the constructions and categories of meaning that characterized communities of people. It brought the focus of inquiry to the significance of the meanings that people attributed to experiences of life. It sponsored studies into the life-shaping effects of these meanings, and their role in the construction of people's identities.

With meaning at the center, this new cultural anthropology took the focus of inquiry to the social construction of people's realities. These were realities that were not radically derived through one's independent construction of the events of one's life. These realities were not the outcome of some privileged access to the world as it is. They were not arrived at through some objective grasp of the nature of things. Rather, people's realities were understood to be historical and social products, negotiated in and between communities of people and distributed throughout these communities. This was the case for identity as much as for any other construction; identity was understood to be a phenomenon that was dispersed in communities of people, its traces to be found everywhere, including in

- socially negotiated self narratives,
- the impressions and the imagination of others,
- the performance of drama,
- dance, in play, in song and in poetics,
- ritual, ceremony and symbol,
- attire and in habits of life, and
- personal and public documentation, dispersed through the inscriptions entered into community stories, into personal diaries, into correspondences in the form of letters and cards, into public files in the form of profiles, assessments, and reports, and in the longstanding tradition of autobiography.

With meaning making now at the heart of social inquiry, the very processes by which people rendered their experiences of their lives sensible to themselves and to each other began to receive significant attention. This focus was the outcome of understandings that meaning does not pre-exist the interpretation of experience, and that all meanings are linguistic and social achievements. This was also the outcome of the understanding that people give meaning to their experiences of life by taking these into frames that render them sensible or intelligible. The question that was raised in this inquiry was: "What sort of frames of intelligibility are employed by people and by communities of people in their interpretive acts?"

The outcome of this exploration was a deepening appreciation of the extent to which people routinely construct meaning by trafficking in stories about their own and others' lives, an appreciation that in turn

[led] to an understanding of the profoundly significant part that narrative structures play in providing a principal frame of intelligibility for everyday-life experience. People make sense of the world by taking their experiences of life into narrative frames, by locating these experiences in the familiar stories of their lives. In taking these experiences of life into narrative frames they become situated in sequences of events that are unfolding through time according to particular themes.

This development also reinstated the mind of folk psychology in understandings of people's acts of living. There is a homologous relationship between folk psychology notions of mind and the traditional structure of narrative. In the tradition of story making and storytelling, agents are implicated in actions that are shaped by their intentional states and these actions have the objective of achieving certain goals. In the terms of this tradition of storytelling, it is understood that the means employed in these strivings are influenced by and are revealing of what people believe, value, hope for, and dream of. Taken together, these beliefs, values, hopes, and dreams come to represent what people's lives are about in general terms, and, in more specific terms, what they are committed to in terms how they wish to live their lives. The practices of life embraced by people in the pursuit of these sought-after ends are seen to reflect their preferred ways of being in the world. In considerations of acts of life, the mind was back. And it was the mind of folk psychology, not a version of mind that invoked notions of internal states, of rational conception, of objective perception, of formal logic, or of the computation of information.

Before long this interpretive turn was gathering momentum in the social sciences, radically altering the shape of practices of inquiry into a whole range of social phenomena (for example, see Clifford, 1988; Geertz, 1973, 1983; M. Rosaldo, 1984; R. Rosaldo, 1993; Turner & Bruner, 1986). It also began to touch the human sciences (for example see Gergen & Gergen, 1984; Spence, 1982), and by the 1980s it had set off, in the social psychologies, numerous explorations into identity formation and human action. However, these developments in some of the human sciences did not much touch mainstream psychological and counseling practices over this time.

I believe that many of my own explorations of narrative therapy can be located within the context of this interpretive turn, and within this tradition of folk psychology. Many of the practices of this therapy routinely evoke notions of personal agency and contribute to the rich description of a range of intentional states. These practices have the potential to bring forth the mindedness of folk psychology even in circumstances in which people's actions are routinely perceived to be discontinuous with what is known about them, and, on account of this, constructed as mindless or pathological or crazy. Practices that reinstate "mindedness" also can have the effect of restoring people's cherished understandings and preferred identity claims, and can contribute to a range of options for people to respond to untoward events in ways that are in keeping with these preferred claims. I believe that the story of Jill and her family is illustrative of some of these practices.

Jill's Family*

I am meeting with Anne and David, and their son and daughter, Sam and Belinda, for the first time. They have come to talk about a tragic event in their family—the death of their eldest daughter, Jill, through a fatal overdose that was not an accident, some three years ago. Things had gone OK in Jill's life for much of her childhood, but had then unraveled somewhat in her later years. Being from a relatively remote country region, she had gone away to school at twelve years of age, and things didn't work out all that well for her there. She struggled with peer abuse and with feelings of acute loneliness, but did not confide much of this to her parents. According to them, she eventually fell in with the wrong crowd, and seemed to embrace values that were totally at variance with those that she had grown up with, and which they could not understand.

The fact that she had been such a "strong and adventurous and funny little kid" before things went so totally off the track had given Anne and David the sense that they had never really known Jill in her later years. Or was it that they hadn't really known her in her earlier years? It was all so confusing for them. Whichever the case, Anne and David felt [bad] about this. And Jill's distancing from them in the period leading up to her suicide had been very painful, particularly for Anne, who had such a strong sense of having failed Jill in her time of greatest need. Sam had also taken it very hard, as he felt that, over this time, there had been some opportunities to talk with Jill that he hadn't taken up.

Had it all been for nothing? It had become all just too sad and painful to think about, let alone to talk to each other about, and, as an outcome of this, the memory of Jill's existence was a rapidly diminishing sense for the members of this family. And no one in this family wanted to be on these terms with their memories of Jill.

Anne   So, I guess that this brings you up to the present, and why we decided to make this appointment. So where do we go? *[throws arms into the air in an expression of despair]*

M   Is it OK for me to ask some questions about the circumstances surrounding Jill's suicide?

Anne   Yeah. That's OK. We expected that you would want some of the details, didn't we. *[turning to David]*

David   Yeah. We have been preparing ourselves for this.

M   *[glancing at Sam and Belinda]*

Sam   Yeah. It's OK. *[turning to Belinda]* Isn't it sis.

Belinda   *[nods]*

M   I have the sense from what you have been telling me that Jill was strongly resolved to do this. To take her own life. I was thinking about all the thought that she must have put into it, and about the preparations that were . . .

Anne   That's true. Yes.

David   *[nods]*

M   Were these sort of actions in character for Jill?

Anne   Well, I don't know. I don't think that she really prepared for much at all really. I'm just thinking about how everything went off the rails, you know.

M   What about occasions upon which she was strongly resolved to do something big or difficult or daunting, that she followed through on? Can you think of any?

Anne   Well . . . I . . . *[looks to David]* Can you?

David   This has me thinking of other times. Yeah. When she was younger, she was really plucky. She really was a plucky little kid. Wasn't she?

Anne   That's true.

David   Do you remember that time we were at the beach. She must have been four years old, and it was time to go, and she was carrying all of those toys and her hat and her

	clothes and trying to eat a sandwich at the same time as she was trying to get up those sand hills. And you knew she wouldn't let anyone help. And along came a woman who scowled at us. One of those telling off looks. She tried to pick things up for Jill. You remember.
Anne	Yeah. Yeah. *[smiling]* Jill shouted: "It's my life!" And she was only four years old! Can you believe that? She was only four years old! And what did she do? She just chucked everything back down the hill again, the sandwich and all, and then went tumbling after them, trying to grab them all up again as she went, much to this woman's horror. *[Anne is now laughing, along with David]*
David	There she was standing at the bottom, all covered in sandwich and sand, and grinning from ear to ear.
Belinda	*[laughing]* Yeah, I've heard that story before.
Sam	I can think of lots of others just like that one. *[also laughing]*
M	So when thinking about the strength of her resolve, it doesn't totally surprise you? The way that she took her life, I mean.
Anne	Well, actually no. I guess not. Not really. But I reckon she had lost this for a while.
David	Yeah, for sure.
M	So, it sort of fits with the plucky person she was. And anything else?
Anne	Well I don't know what this has got to do with it. But she always kept trying at things when others would give up. When she was younger that is.
Belinda	Yeah. But also when she was older. I remember how hard it was for her with all of the teasing she went through. It would have been better if she'd let us do something about it, but she wouldn't have it. But she sure didn't give up trying to tackle it. She went against it, didn't she? She didn't just accept this. She had these ideas about what was right and fair, about what was OK and what wasn't.
Sam	Yeah, that's sure true in one way, but . . .
David	But then she got into some bad things and did some things that really were really scary and not OK, that caused other people a lot of pain and heartache. So, I don't know . . . It just doesn't make sense, does it?
M	I wonder how this fits in. If it does fit in, that is.
David	What do you mean?
M	Belinda said something about where Jill stood on what was right and what wasn't, on what was OK and what wasn't OK. If Jill had witnessed herself doing things that went against these values, how would this be for her?
David	Actually, I reckon this would have been difficult for her. She wouldn't have been at all happy with herself.
M	Do you have any thoughts about whether or not this could relate to the decisions that Jill was making about her life prior to her death?
Anne	I didn't think about this, but maybe there is something in it. I reckon that she went against so many of her principles, and in lots

	of ways she did this. So, maybe there is some connection, that this was in a funny way about her principles. It could have been, it really could have.
M	I want to check to see if I am getting your meaning. Are you saying that there may have been something about taking her life that was principled? Not in the way that anyone would have wished, but...
David	Yeah. I guess... like Anne said, in funny sort of way. I guess that is what we are saying. *[sighs]*
M	*[turning to Anne, who had echoed David's sigh]* Anne, is that where are you with this?
Anne	Yeah. This is something I can see. But I am really surprised to hear myself admitting this. Shocked even.
M	You both sighed. Could I ask what these sighs are about?
Anne	It's a strange sense of relief really. I mean there would have been a lot of other ways for her to do something. But this is something to hold onto, and... well, I am desperate for that, totally desperate for that.
M	David?
David	For me too. Some relief I guess.
M	Going back to the circumstances of her death, I understand that she distanced from you in the period leading up to this. And that this was very hard for all of you.
Anne	*[starts crying]*
M	Would you say something about those tears? Would you help me understand what they are about?
Anne	*[pause]* I was thinking about my connection with Jill. I thought that we had always been so close. But I must have been wrong. *[pause]* I can't help but feel that I not only failed to understand, but that I failed her.
M	Tell me. How did you reach this conclusion?
Anne	Because she didn't come to me in what must have been her time of greatest need. I'm sure that I failed her *[sobbing] [pause]*. Even though the special relationship that we once had was gone, well... anyway, clearly she didn't think that she could rely on me or that I had anything to offer.
M	Did anyone else here also think that there was a special connection between Anne and Jill?
Belinda	Yeah. Sure. Sure there was. She was always sending mum cards and things, *[turning to Sam]* wasn't she?
Sam	Yeah. If she was going to tell anyone anything, it was mum she would tell.
M	So what's your sense of how she regarded her connection with your mum?
David	She just treasured it, I know it. That's so clear to me as well. To all of us. *[Belinda and Sam nod in agreement]*
M	OK. So, in the light of this, what sense do you make out of this distancing from Anne in the period leading up to her death? Would this distance have made it more or less possible for Jill to take her life?

David	I don't know if this is right but I think that I've got an answer for that. I don't reckon that there is anyway that Jill could have followed through on this decision to end her life if she had been close to Anne at the time, and I reckon that Jill knew this. I'm not saying things were perfect. I know that there were some hard times and some differences, you know the usual sort of thing . . . But she just treasured her relationship with her mother.		having now, are these the same tears? Or are they different tears?
M	So, there could have been a purpose to this distancing from Anne, and from the rest of you? That . . .	Anne	For me they are different.
		M	OK, so they are different tears for you. Are they taking you to the same place though, or to a different place. To where you have been before, or are they journeying you to somewhere else?
David	Yeah. Now that I think about it, I'm sure of it.	Anne	It is to a different place.
Sam	I can see it too.	M	Would you be prepared to tell me about this, or would you prefer not to?
Anne	[now sobbing]		
David	[holding her in his arms, also crying]	Anne	It is to a place where . . . let's see . . . I still feel very sad. But it is different somehow. How is it different? [pause] Well . . . these tears are not taking me down that well and into the void, into the nothingness that I feel that I have been drowning in. It is easier . . . these tears that is, and it is with some new thoughts, taking me into a . . . yes . . . a lighter place. [pause] I am sure that I will never lose this sadness, but if I can hold on to what I am feeling now, I know that I am not going to be so overwhelmed. And yes [pause]. Of course, there are lots of good memories.
M	In some way—and I know this might sound like a strange way of putting it from what you are saying it is my understanding that this distancing may have been a testimony to Jill's connection with Anne? Can I check this understanding with you?		
Sam	[also crying] Yeah, I can see this too.		
Belinda	[also crying] Me too.		
M	[also tearful] You have given me a strong sense of what your tears are about. But I would like to ask a couple of questions about what's happening for you? Is that OK?	M	I was just . . .
		Anne	There is something else . . . yeah . . . I've got something back that I thought I had lost. And I didn't expect this, I really didn't.
Anne	It is OK.	M	What's your guess about how Jill would be responding to this, responding to this development?
M	I know that you have had lots of tears. These tears that you are		
		Anne	Well . . .

Folk Psychology and Narrative Practice | 29

Belinda She would want this for mum. *[turning to Anne]* Mum, she would want this for you so much, I just know she would *[turning to Sam]*. Wouldn't she Sam?

Sam Yeah, and for us too.

M Do you mean that she wouldn't want the fact of her death to take away from . . .

Belinda Her connection with all of us.

Sam Yeah.

M Would it be OK if I asked some questions that could have the effect of evoking Jill's presence here? Because I would like to get a sense of the words that she might use to say all of this, and a sense of the way that she would say it. I had some other ideas for our conversation as well. I am curious to know more about how your lives are different for having had Jill as a daughter and as a sister. Because it is my guess that this has changed you all in some way, that there are some ways that you think and that you are in this world that are a testimony to her life. Would these directions fit for you, or do you have some other ideas about where it might be best for us to go now?

The family members wanted to follow up both of these lines of inquiry, and this provided a basis for some extraordinary conversations over the course of three or four meetings. Following this, Anne and David called a gathering of extended family and friends for the purposes of honoring Jill's life and the legacy of her life. In the context of this ceremony, Anne, David, Sam and Belinda talked openly of Jill's suicide, rendering this and the events surrounding it sensible to all present in terms of what they understood she had lived for, in terms of what they understood she had stood for in her life, and in terms of the significance of her relationships with the members of her family. In this ceremony, the conclusions it appeared Jill had reached that called for her suicide were acknowledged. Even though her death would always be powerfully lamented, there was now some acknowledgment of the fact that Jill's suicide did fit with many of the things that they knew of her, and that it wasn't mindless or crazy. Anne, David, Sam, and Belinda successfully renegotiated the terms of their memories of Jill. The facts of her existence, and the significance of this to their lives, were experiences that could now be readily called upon by them all.

I believe that this account of my conversations with Jill's family illustrates the sort of options that become available to people when space is created for the generation of the "mindedness" of folk psychology. It was in the context of these conversations, through explorations that were deriving of notions of personal agency and intentional states, that Jill's actions were rendered mindful. These were explorations that were consistent with a reinstatement of the "mind" of the folk psychology traditions that I have been describing in this chapter.

2. PERSONAL AGENCY AND INTENTIONAL STATES

In several places in this chapter, I have made reference to the significance that is attributed to notions of personal agency and intentional states in the context of narrative explorations of human action and identity formation. At this juncture I will make a number of clarifications about what is being proposed in this. I believe that this is appropriate because this emphasis on the significance of these notions of personal agency and intentional states is often construed as a proposal for traditions of understanding that do not fit at all well with the folk psychology tradition that I have been describing. In attending to these clarifications I will draw attention to the part that therapeutic practices shaped by this folk psychology tradition can play in the production of "multi-intentioned" lives, of "joined" lives, of "multiple authenticities," and of "inhabited" lives.

The Production of Multi-Intentioned Lives

At times the emphasis given to notions of personal agency and intentional states in narrative practices is read as a proposal for

1. strictly rational understandings of life,
2. the privileging of contemporary ideas about individual and autonomous thought and action,
3. a renewal of the internal state psychologies in which these intentional states are cast as phenomena that are intrinsic to people's lives, or for
4. the revival of highly deterministic cause/effect accounts of human action.

However, this is not what is being proposed. Rather, this "take" on personal agency and intentional states is to propose that, in response to a person's expressions of life, there is a range of opportunities for people to engage with each other in the negotiation and renegotiation of the sort of identity conclusions that are informed by a tradition of folk psychology. It is in this tradition that notions of personal agency and intentional states are attributed to and implicated in people's acts of living. These notions of personal agency and intentional states are present in those conclusions about people's actions that are shaped by categories of identity that feature purposes, values, beliefs, hopes, dreams, visions, and commitments to ways of living. These categories of identity can be likened to "filing cabinets" of the mind, into which people routinely file and cross-reference a range of identity conclusions about their own and each other's lives.

These identity conclusions are not independently and autonomously manufactured, but are socially negotiated and renegotiated in communities of people. And they are not singular. These identity conclusions exist within the context of a multiplicity—as an outcome of the ongoing social negotiation of these identity conclusions, people's lives become multi-intentioned. This emphasis on the significance of the social negotiation of people's identity conclusions is not reproducing of internal state notions. These identity conclusions are not taken to be a reflection of phenomena that are intrinsic to people's lives that are manifested in their actions. Rather, what is being proposed is that it is these conclusions themselves that have consequences for people's lives and relationships. People's acts of living, including their responses to each other, are shaped by the identity conclusions that are filed into the identity categories of the mind, which are circumscribed by contemporary culture's favored notions of identity. These identity conclusions significantly constitute people's existence.

For the purposes of further clarification, I will here contrast the opportunities that I believe folk psychology offers for the renegotiation of identity conclusions with those associated with the internal state psychologies. The categories of identity associated with notions of personal agency and intentional states are distinct in relation to those of the internal state psychologies categories of "motives," "drives," "needs," "attributes," "traits," and so on. In the context of the internal state psychologies, human expression is understood to be a surface manifestation of some essence or force or element that resides at the center of identity, or to be a manifestation of a distortion or disturbance or imbalance in these forces. In the context of people's difficulties in life, these expressions are invariably considered to be expressions of pathology, deficit, or dysfunction. It is upon the basis of such conclusions that many of the knowledges of the professional disciplines, and the systems of analyses that are constructed through these knowledges, are called forth. It is proposed that through recourse to these systems of analyses the pathologies, disorders and dysfunctions of people's lives can be identified and definitively known, and that these then can be subject to "treatments of choice."

In contrast, I believe that the intentional states of folk psychology are radically open to the sort of renegotiations that have the potential to throw people's expressions of life into a multiplicity of different lights. When it comes to people's difficulties in life, in the context of these intentional state understandings, human action is not indicative of disturbances of the internal states. Rather, these difficulties raise options for people to traffic in conceptions of personal agency and intentional states notions, and in this there are options for the attribution of alternative purposes not previously appreciated, for the restoration of cherished understandings and preferred identity claims (as in the story of my work with Jill's family), and for the elaboration of moral commitments that diverge from those that have been previously acknowledged. In the context of these understandings nothing is settled—considerations of life are taken into the subjunctive, a great deal is open to renegotiation, diversity is emphasized, and people's lives become multi-purposed and multi-layered.

The Production of Joined Lives

Externalizing conversations are often, but not always, featured in the practices of narrative therapy. In response to the problems of their lives, it is not uncommon for people to form highly negative conclusions about their own and each other's identity, and about the identity of their relationships. It is in these circumstances that externalizing conversations open options for people to redefine or revise their relationships with the problems of their lives, and to so break their lives from these highly negative identity conclusions. In this redefinition of one's relationship with problems, the negative identity conclusions that invariably invoke some internal state of some sort—usually associated with some account of deficit, pathology, or dysfunction—no longer speak to people of the totality of who they are. It is in the context of these conversations that people derive a sense that their identity is not at one with the problems of their lives. Among other things, this opens space for yet other conversations that contribute to the generation of alternative stories of people's lives, and to the renegotiation of identity conclusions. People invariably respond to these conversations by engaging in the performance of some of the preferred claims about their lives that are associated with these alternative identity conclusions.

I have always regarded these alternative identity conclusions that are derived in these conversations to be socially negotiated in communities of people, and to be products of history and culture. I raise this point here because, despite the care that I have taken in my writing and teaching to consistently emphasize the social basis of these alternative identity conclusions, it is sometimes assumed that these externalizing conversations are associated with the proposal of an autonomous self that is being freed from the oppression of the problem. I believe that the vigor of this assumption is a reflection of the pervasiveness of western culture's taken-for-granted understandings that construct a self at the center of personhood.

I believe that the proposal of an autonomous self has been strongly supported in the development of the internal state psychologies. If it is so that the proposal of the autonomous self is associated with modern developments in the cellularization of life (and this is argued quite convincingly by many historians of thought), the internal state categories of identity contribute to developments in the sub-cellularization of life. According to Foucault (1973, 1979), the proposal of the autonomous self seems closely associated with the development of modern systems of social control in which people are separated from each other by being allocated precise locations in a range of continuums of health and tables of performance—locations that specify one's distance from the socially constructed and desirable norms regarding the healthy and fully functioning individual. It would appear that the proposal of internal state categories of identity take the cellularization a step further—the autonomous individual is separated into relatively autonomous internal states that life becomes an expression of. As an outcome of this development, people are alone in their "motives," isolated in their "deficits," and vulnerable in their "psychological needs."

In contrast, I believe externalizing conversations that contribute to options for people to separate from the sort of negative identity conclusions that invoke accounts of deficit, pathology, and dysfunction, and re-authoring conversations that provide opportunities for people to generate new identity conclusions that feature folk psychological notions of personal agency and intentional states, have the potential to overturn this cellularization of life. Rather than contributing to the sort of internal state conclusions that are potentially isolating of people from each other, these conversations contribute to the development of identity conclusions that provide people with a sense of their lives being joined with the lives of others around shared themes that are characterized by a range of purposes, values, beliefs, hopes, dreams, visions, commitments, and so on (in this respect, consider how transporting the therapeutic conversation was for Paul—from being isolated in his deficits to becoming joined with his mother's life around shared purposes and skills).

In summary, therapeutic conversations that provide options for people to traffic in intentional state notions raise new possibilities for the joining of identities, provide an antidote to the normalizing judgment that is so intimately associated with the development of the autonomous self, and contribute to the de-cellularization of life.

The Production of Multiple Authenticities

In discussing the processes of therapy, I have from time to time made reference to dominant and alternative stories, and frequently contrasted these (for example, see White, 1989, 1992). There have been many occasions in which others have taken this distinction into humanist renderings. These are renderings that substitute "dominant story" with "oppressive" or "false story," and that substitute "alternative story" with "true" or "real" or "authentic" story. In these renderings the alternative stories of people's lives are accorded a naturalistic status in much the same vein that this status is attributed to the identity categories of the internal state psychologies. By this account it is understood that the conversations of narrative therapy are libratory conversations—it is considered that these conversations make it possible for people to overthrow the oppressive stories of their lives, and provide a context for the discovery and unveiling of their true or authentic stories. At times these renderings of the dominant story/alternative story distinction endure, despite the fact that this is contrary to what I have proposed, and the fact that many of the ideas associated with narrative therapy raise very specific questions about such renderings.

Rather than contrast stories as oppressive and authentic or as false and true, I have been interested in the constitutive or shaping effects of all stories. Stories about life and identity are not equal to each other in their constitutive effects. It is clearly apparent that some stories sponsor a broader range of options for action in life than do others. For example, I am sure that everyone would appreciate the fact that the deficit-centered stories of people's lives sponsor a particularly narrow range of options for action. In addition to my interest in the constitutive or shaping effects of all stories, I have been interested in conversational processes that are richly describing of those stories of people's lives that open more options for action in the world rather than fewer. It is in the context of these conversations that people not only experience their lives as multi-storied, but clearly become more narratively resourced. It is in the context of becoming more narratively resourced that people are able to attribute significance to a range of experiences of life that would otherwise be neglected.

In calling into question the rendering of the dominant story/alternative story distinction that establishes the juxtaposition of oppressive and real or authentic stories, and that casts therapeutic conversations as libratory, what becomes of the notion of authenticity? Rather than understanding authenticity to be a phenomenon that is discovered as an outcome of some private and individual achievement in which the "truth" of a person's identity is revealed, or as an outcome of the identification of their "true" story, within the context of the tradition of thought associated with narrative therapy, authenticity is regarded as a public and social achievement in which a person's preferred identity claims are acknowledged. It is understood that people are dependent upon social processes of acknowledgment for the "authentication" of their preferred identity claims; that, as an outcome of this social acknowledgment, people experience being "at one" with these preferred claims.

Preferred claims about people's identities are embedded in the alternative stories of their lives, and therapeutic conversations that are structured by the "definitional ceremony" metaphor (Myerhoff, 1982, 1986) present a range of options for the rich description of these stories.[6] These are conversations that engage people as outsider witnesses in the telling and retelling of the stories of others' lives. It is in the context of these tellings and retellings that people experience themselves being at one with the preferred claims about their identities. Therapeutic practices that are shaped by this understanding contribute to the development of circumstances under which a range of preferred identity claims can be acknowledged, under which there are options for people to experience "multiple authenticities."

The outsider witnesses that contribute to retellings of the stories of people's lives that are powerfully authenticating of their preferred identity claims can be drawn from these people's families and wider kinship networks, from their friendship networks, from the professional disciplines, from the local community, from lists or registers of people who have previously sought therapeutic consultation and who have volunteered to contribute to the therapist's work with those who follow in their footsteps, and from elsewhere.[7] Jill's family called together friends and extended family members to a ceremony that was honoring of Jill's life and actions. This ceremony was structured around a series of tellings and retellings of the stories of Jill's life. These tellings and retellings were powerfully authenticating of the preferred identity claims about the lives and relationships of the members of this family, and of their sense of Jill's ongoing presence in their lives.

The Production of Inhabited Lives

There appears to be intimate link between narrative structures and the fantastic capacity that people have for reflexive engagements with life. This reflexivity is a capacity to achieve distance in relation to the immediacy of life. It is witnessed in our ability to stand out of the flow of lived experience, sometimes only momentarily, and to review the events of our lives from other vantage points. It is largely in the reading of our lives as lived through the structure of narrative that we are afforded the purchase to stand back from our lives. This reading of our lives through narrative structures provides the opportunity for us to render meaningful that which previously wasn't, and to re-conceive of that which has already been rendered meaningful. This generation and regeneration of meaning allows for a sense of narrative authority, and for an experience of living that people describe as akin to stepping in and out of the flow of life.

This generation and regeneration of meaning also occurs across time. Our reflexive capacity provides us with new alternatives for what to make out of

1. the past in response to any new meanings that are assigned to our experiences of the present,
2. the present in response to any new meanings that are assigned to our experiences of the past,
3. the future in response to any new meanings that are assigned to our experiences of the past and/or the present, and
4. the past and/or the present in response to any new meanings assigned to proposed or hypothetical futures.

An example: Those therapeutic conversations which are tracing of the history of a unique outcome or exception through the trajectory of a person's life often introduce options for a creative re-engagement with one's past. This is a re-engagement that provides possibilities for the identification of purposes that were not previously fully grasped, of commitments not previously felt, and of moral considerations that were previously unconsidered. In turn, it is through these recountings that people arrive at new understandings of current predicaments and dilemmas, of why events took the turn that they did, and of what these might mean for the future of their lives. All this occurs in the backwards and forwards movement of therapeutic conversations.

When in the past I have described various options that therapeutic conversations can provide for these reflexive re-engagements with life, at times it has been assumed by others that narrative practices deal with abstractions of life, rather than life itself—that this contributes to a certain therapist detachment in therapeutic practice, and requires the people who consult therapists to participate in therapeutic conversations in a detached fashion that takes them away from more direct expressions of their experiences of life. However, detachment is not synonymous with the sort of distance that provides opportunities for the reflexive engagements with life that I have described in the above paragraphs. The distance that is achieved in the reading of life through narrative structures is one that provides people with wonderful opportunities for a more significant and dramatic engagement with their own lives. It is a distance that opens possibilities for people to explore new options in self-regulation, and in the habitation of their own bodies. It is a distance that presents options for people to more fully inhabit their lives, as the following account of my conversations with Ricky illustrates.

Ricky*

Ricky consulted me over a personal crisis following a recent relationship break-up.

This break-up had occurred eleven months before our first consultation. At the time, Peter, Ricky's partner of seven years, suddenly announced his intention to depart from the relationship, declaring that he had never really loved Ricky. He then listed his complaints and dissatisfactions with Ricky, about which he had never previously spoken, or even hinted. Peter's parting comment was that Ricky and relationships don't go together. Ricky was shattered: "Is there anywhere that one can go from here when so racked with self doubt, with one's sense of ability to judge the intentions of others in tatters, and with one's trust in ruins? Is there anywhere that one can go from here with all of this baggage, quite apart from the loss that one is experiencing?" Ricky concluded that his ability to trust had been damaged beyond repair, and he began to stand back from his social network. A friend had responded to this by talking Ricky into seeing me.

Ricky   So, there you are. All of this was shattering. Apart from everything else, it has taken away my trust. It is a fear of trusting. I have this inability to trust, and . . . well, you know . . . I think it has damaged me. And I don't know if I could ever learn to trust again.

M   Would you say a little more about this. About this sense of a loss of trust, or an inability to trust?

Ricky   It is like, well . . . like I just feel that I can't fully trust anymore, and what's life going to be like for me, because I am not getting over this. I feel like I am stuck with this deficit.

M   Is this something that has become evident to you in your connections with others? Has it been noticed by any of your friends?

Ricky   Yeah. That's how I got to here, seeing you. Only the other day I was talking to a friend who felt that I was being a bit guarded. And they said, this friend, that is, said: "You have a problem with trust. You should see someone about this."

M   And so here you are. I understand that Peter's announcement and his subsequent actions were quite unexpected at the time. Looking back, are you aware of anything that might have prepared you for what was to come?

Ricky   I suppose, but you know what they say about hindsight.

M   It is always easy to be wise . . .

Ricky   Yeah. It is always easy to be wise after the event, isn't it.

M   Tell me about some of that wisdom of hindsight.

Ricky   Well, of course, I should have seen it coming, shouldn't I. And I have been giving myself a hard time over this, haven't I.

M   Are you telling me that there are some things that you are conscious of now, or aware of now, that you were not before?

Ricky   You could say that. Yeah, I guess that would be right. At least I hope that is right. Well, a wish, maybe. Perhaps even that's a bit strong.

M   If faced with similar circumstances today, and being aware of what you are now aware of, perhaps even to the extent of being able to predict such a turn of events, do you think that you would be investing so much trust in a relationship? Would this be appropriate?

Ricky   No. No, it wouldn't. I would withhold it. But then, I didn't see [it]

	coming then, so how could I do this? Well, I really don't know, do I?
M	Let's just speculate. If you did see something like this coming, what would you be doing with this trust? What sort of attitude would you be having towards this trust?
Ricky	I am not sure what you mean.
M	Would withholding trust in such a circumstance suggest that you were putting a high value on your trust or a low value on it, respecting it more or less, preserving it or being reckless with it, or holding it back or . . . Or perhaps none of these, but something else maybe?
Ricky	Well, thinking about it like that, I would say the other ones. The first ones. I would say that I would be being respectful of my trust, that I would be valuing it more.
M	You said that you had become guarded in your present day-to-day connections with people, so I have the sense that you haven't just continued to live your life as you had previously lived it, and that you haven't cast your trust about freely in an attempt to recreate the life that you had. In the light of what we have just been talking about, what are your thoughts about what this says about your position on trust?
Ricky	Let's see. Well, I can only think that I am, well, let's see, maybe cherishing this trust now. Do you think that I am cherishing this trust more? [pause] Yeah, I guess that is it.
M	OK. Does this mean that you now wouldn't make this trust so available to others in certain circumstances, or that . . .
Ricky	Yeah. Look, I didn't think that I would hear myself saying this, but I guess that is what I am saying.
M	Why didn't you think that you would hear yourself saying this?
Ricky	Because it is nothing that I would have put to words before. There really is a shift here, but I really hadn't stood back from it and given much thought to this until now. I mean until right this minute.
M	Do you have any thoughts about why you have been cherishing this trust more? And about what it might say about other developments in your life?
Ricky	I suppose it is about a . . . [pause] Yeah, more of a determination to be respected. Yeah, that's probably it. And perhaps I'm not going to let it be taken for granted. My trust, that is. I've had enough of that, I have.
M	Anything else that this might reflect? Like . . .
Ricky	Well, like what?
M	What's your guess about what this says about your purposes, or about what you value?
Ricky	Maybe it is that I don't intend to give up on how I want to live my life.
M	On how you want to [live] your life? Tell me, of all the people who have known you, can you think of anyone who might have appreciated these things about you? Who might have appreciated this determination, or who might have acknowledged the choices that you made about how you wanted to live your life?
Ricky	Well . . .

Ricky identified two figures of his history whom he believed had appreciated him in these terms—an ex-lover and an aunt. I encouraged him to provide accounts of what it was that these figures might have witnessed that could have contributed to this appreciation of him. The accounts given by Ricky established a basis for yet further explorations about what it was he had intended for his life. Following this meeting, Ricky contacted this ex-lover and his aunt, told them about our conversation, and shared with them his conclusions about how their acknowledgment of him had contributed to his life. For our third meeting, at Ricky's invitation, we were joined by these two people.

Apart from other things, these conversations provided a foundation for establishing a clear account of the circumstances under which Ricky would be prepared to offer trust in his connections with others, and the circumstances under which this trust would not be available. He subsequently met again with the friend that he had mentioned early in our first conversation. In this meeting, Ricky described the circumstances that he understood were favorable and unfavorable to his trusting of others, and informed this friend that in any act in which he extended this trust he was presenting a gift that was offered provisionally. This led to some significantly new and positive developments in this connection. Ricky no longer had a sense of having "a problem with trust."

This brief description of my conversations with Ricky provides an account of the way that narrative structures can provide a foundation for reflexive engagements with life. Upon being encouraged to speculate about his likely responses should he have been conscious of what he hadn't been conscious of in his relationship with Peter, Ricky concluded that he would have withheld trust. This conclusion provided the basis for a flurry of meaning-making activity in which Ricky's responses to the day-to-day events of his life were redefined, in which specific developments in his relationship to trust were named, and in which what this reflected about his intentions for his life were determined and richly described.

In these therapeutic conversations, the structure of narrative provided Ricky with purchase to stand back from life and to reconceive of that which had already been rendered meaningful. This provided a frame for a regeneration of meaning in which constructions of integrity displaced constructions of deficit. It was from the distance achieved in this reflexive engagement that Ricky was able to discern the circumstances under which this trust would be available to others. And the subsequent performance of this discernment in his conversation with his friend is an example of the way that the distance achieved through reflexive engagements provide[s] possibilities for people to more fully inhabit some of the domains of their own lives. Among other things, these are possibilities in the regulation of their own actions in response to the actions of others.

In the next and final section of this chapter, I turn to considerations of history and culture.

3. HISTORY AND CULTURE

To argue that culture is socially and historically constructed, that narrative is a primary, in humans perhaps *the* primary mode of knowing, that we assemble the selves we live in out of materials lying about in the society around us and develop a theory of mind to comprehend the selves of others, that we do not act directly on the world but on beliefs we hold about the world, that from birth on we are all active, impassioned meaning makers in search of plausible stories, and that mind cannot in any sense be regarded as natural or naked, with culture thought of as an add-on—such a view amounts to rather more than a midcourse correction (Geertz, 2000, p. 196).

In various places in this chapter, I have addressed the notion that life is a social phenomenon. For example, I have reviewed how constructions of life and identity are socially negotiated in communities of people, and I have drawn attention to the central role that processes of social acknowledgment play in the authentication of people's identity claims. But life is also a social phenomenon in that it is the outcome of people's engagements with specific modes of thought and life that are cultural and historical. These modes of thought and life compose life.

Our understandings of life and identity are not arrived at in an historical and cultural vacuum. Whether these understandings pertain to our sense of personal identity, to our accounts of other people's actions, to what one might do to change the way things are, or whatever, they are all informed by specific ways of thinking that are based on a stock of cultural knowledges. Not only are these knowledges historical and cultural products, but so too are the skills that are evident in our ways of living, in our acts of life. I am using the word "skills" in an unconventional sense—these are those skills that are represented in all of those little everyday acts of life that have to do with the making of a "living," with getting through the day, with the forging of an identity, and with the fabricating of relationships. It is only through such a definition of skills that we can conceive of what might be referred to as practical "insider know-how," that we can come to fully appreciate this know-how in the lives of the people who consult us, and that we can join with people in the co-researching of what might be described as "local knowledge."

These skills are shaped by cultural modes of living that include specific practices of relationship–for example, those practices that constitute relations of power–and specific practices of self-formation, at times referred to as "technologies of the self" or "disciplines of the self" (Foucault, 1979). These practices of relationship and practices of self formation are linked to cultural knowledges of life and identity in relationships of mutual dependency.

Over many years of writing and teaching, following Foucault I have drawn attention to the relationship between these knowledges and cultural practices, and to their constitutive role in expressions of life (for example, see White & Epston, 1989). And I have also described and illustrated the relevance of these considerations to the practice of therapy. However, at times these considerations pertaining to the relationship between knowledge and practice or knowledge and power ("power" on account of the fact that many of these practices constitute relations of power) have, in my view, been misinterpreted. For example:

1. When I am describing the relations of mutual dependency of these knowledges and practices, it is at times assumed that what is being proposed is a new version of that familiar refrain: power is knowledge and knowledge is power.

2. When drawing attention to the constitutive role of cultural knowledges and cultural practices in the formation of life and identity, it is at times assumed that I am proposing a direct causal relationship between these knowledges and practices and people's expressions of living—that people's expressions of living are directly determined by these knowledges and practices.

3. When describing and illustrating the relevance of these considerations to a therapeutic practice that brings into focus the stories of people's lives, it is at times assumed that I am conflating the idea of narrative with these cultural knowledges and practices, serving to obscure many things, including the power relations of local culture.

In order to further emphasize the significance of this understanding that life is a social phenomenon that is constituted through specific modes of life and thought that are historical and cultural, and to further clarify these considerations pertaining to knowledge and practice, I will address these three relatively common misinterpretations in turn.

Power/Knowledge

Contrary to interpretations that substitute knowledge with power and power with knowledge, attempts to describe the relations of mutual dependency between these culturally informed knowledges on the one hand, and these practices of relationship and techniques of the self on the other, do not lend themselves at all well to the familiar refrain "knowledge is power and power is knowledge." In explorations of these practices of relationship and techniques of self, our attention is drawn to relational practices, and to a "know-how," that is manifest in skillful practice of life. Although these practices and skills are linked to and supported by certain cultural constructs, they are not in themselves constructs. When I meet with men who are referred to me for engaging in abusive actions, these actions are shaped by a technology of power, which is a practical know-how that is shaped by specific skills. These skills make possible the overpowering of whomever happens to be the subject of these actions (usually women and children), the isolation of this subject from others, the destruction of this subject's trust in his or her own perception of events, the assignment of culpability for the abuse to the subject, and so on. Although these actual relational practices are linked to and supported by knowledges that construct, among other things, male supremacy and entitlement, they are not one and the same.

Another example: When I am engaged in therapeutic conversations with people who are struggling with anorexia nervosa and bulimia (usually, but not always, women) I am introduced to concepts of identity and to constructions of the body that are informed by knowledges of life that are of contemporary culture. I am also introduced to a history of relational practices, which, among other things, include various operations of power that these people have been subject to. As well, I am introduced to a range of techniques of the self that include self evaluation, the precise documentation of inputs and outputs (of all manner of things from calories to one's thoughts), the rigorous policing of one's life that makes possible the achievement of "life as ritual," and so on. Again, although these relational practices and techniques of self formation are linked to and find their support in cultural knowledges that construct life and identity, they cannot be reduced to these knowledges. Rather these practices are linked to cultural knowledges through relations of mutual dependency. This consideration is highly relevant to therapeutic conversations, for it calls attention [not only] to the importance of addressing people's constructions of their own and each others' identities, but also to the importance of addressing the very practices of relationship and techniques of self that accompany these constructions.

Indeterminacy Within Determinacy

In regard to these observations about the constitutive role of cultural knowledges and practices in the formation of life, what about those conclusions that assume that what is being proposed is a direct causal relationship between these knowledges and practices on the one hand, and people's expressions of life on the other? Attention to the constitutive role of cultural knowledges and cultural practices in the formation of life and identity is not necessarily associated with an assumption that life and identity are strictly determined by cultural modes of life and thought–attention to these considerations is not necessarily associated with the proposal that there is a one-to-one relationship between these cultural knowledges and practices on the one hand, and life as it is lived on the other. In fact, I have always assumed that this is not the case–that in constructing their lives and identities, people do not passively reproduce these cultural knowledges and practices. I have never considered these knowledges of life and practices of living to be "inputs" that are directly reproduced as "outputs" in people's acts of life. Rather, considerations of the constitutive role of cultural knowledges and practices have provoked my interest in questions such as these:

- How do people engage with these cultural modes of life and thought?
- How do these cultural forces that are composed of knowledges of life and practices of living find their way into people's minds and into their expressions of life?
- How is it that people pull the materials of culture together to form an identity, to make a life?
- If expressions of life are versions of these knowledges and practices, how are these versions achieved?

It is questions like these that have led me to further explorations of meaning making. For it is so clearly apparent that in engaging with these cultural modes of life and thought, in pulling together the materials of culture into a life, people are performing acts of meaning–the recomposition of these modes of life and thought requires acts in the discernment of meaning. And I believe that it is also apparent that this discernment of meaning is an achievement, one that is often hard-won. So, it is my fascination with these questions that has powerfully reinforced my interest in the activity of meaning making, and in the structures, frames, and circumstances that facilitate this.

Some twenty years ago this interest in the discernment of meaning took me to the work of Gregory Bateson (1972, 1979), who described two principal mechanisms at work in this achievement. He proposed that all responses in the "world of the living" are founded on the drawing of distinctions around contrasting descriptions of the experiences of life–according to Bateson, it is this "double description" that provides a basis for the drawing of distinctions in the world, that establishes conditions for the discernment of meaning. Bateson also described the conditions that were required to establish, in people's minds, a receiving context for "news of difference." This receiving context was a network of presuppositions that provided a frame for the receipt of news of difference, one that would render this news sensible or comprehensible. Bateson often referred to these receiving frames as "restraints of redundancy," and, according to him, it was these restraints that made it possible for people to respond selectively to their experiences of the world–for people to "pluck the new from the random." I have always understood the network of presuppositions that form the basis of these restraints of redundancy to be culturally informed, and the meanings that these restraints give to the events of the world to be carriers of culture.

More recently, considerations that are aroused by these questions have taken me to the work of Jacques Derrida (1978) who, like Bateson, proposes a relational understanding of all meanings. In focusing on texts, Derrida strongly challenged the idea of "presence"—that is, the idea that meanings inhere in whatever it is that is being described and are "present" within people's consciousness—and asserted that all descriptions are arrived at through a process of discernment. In his textual analyses, Derrida sought to demonstrate that all description is achieved in response to other contrasting descriptions that are absent from but implicit in the text.

Although I have not considered people's lives to be texts, I do believe people's expressions of living to be based on a foundation of discernment, which is a meaning-making achievement. And I have explored ways in which these absent but implicit descriptions might be excavated through the deconstruction or unpacking of the stories of people's lives (White, 2000).

While the ideas of Bateson and Derrida provide some account of how people assemble their lives out of "materials lying about in the society" through the activity of meaning making, it is those propositions about the centrality of the structure of narrative in this achievement that have more significantly shaped my explorations. According to these propositions, it is narrative structures that provide people with the receiving frames that make it possible for them to attribute meaning to the events of the world—the structure of narrative provides a principal frame of intelligibility through which people engage in the activity of making sense of their experiences of life. In structures of narrative, events are linked together in unfolding sequences through time according to a theme or a plot. These structures also provide the basis for people to derive a range of conclusions about what these events might say about their own intentional states, and the intentional states of others–including purposes, values, beliefs, hopes, dreams, and commitments in life. The mind of folk psychology is invoked by these means. These structures of narrative, and the specific narratives that are formed in the context of these, are not strictly determining of the meanings that people give to their experiences of life. Rather, they contribute to conditions of indeterminacy[8] within determinacy (White, 1991). This indeterminacy within determinacy provides a vexing and challenging conundrum.

> The extent to which persons are self-interpretive—they are not passive in their response to lived experience, but active in ascribing meaning to this—leads us to a second consideration of the significance of agency and the subject in the constitutionalist account of identity.... As the interpretation of experience according to narrative is an achievement, then so is identity. There are always contingencies thrown up in life for which a person's dominant self narrative is not tailor-made. These must be managed. As well, there are many gaps in personal narratives. Such gaps are the outcome of the degree to which ambiguity and uncertainty feature in all stories. In the living of, or in the performance of, self-narrative, these gaps must be filled. And there are always dilemmas to be resolved in the performance of self-narrative: dilemmas that arise from the extent to which inconsistencies and contradictions are a feature of all stories. (White, 1992, p. 41)

To summarize, to propose life to be a direct reproduction of the knowledges and practices of culture excludes considerations of how these knowledges and practices find their ways into people's minds and into their expressions of life, of how it is that people pull the materials of culture together to form an identity and a life, and of the processes by which these cultural knowledges and practices are reworked in people's expressions of living. To propose life to be a direct reproduction of culture renders invisible the specific achievement of meaning making, along with a range of experiences associated with this. This includes the complexities of the social negotiations that provide the basis of this achievement, as well as all of the personal exertions, compromises, struggles, and dilemmas associated with the production of meaning.

Narrative as a Vehicle of Culture

I have briefly reviewed some considerations relating to the activity of meaning making, to the structure of narrative, and to the constituting role of cultural knowledges and practices. I have proposed that in this constituting role, these knowledges and practices are not strictly determining of life. It is my understanding that the narratives of people's lives are not radically constructed—not derived in a social, cultural and political vacuum—but are shaped by these knowledges and practices that are cultural and historical. It is also my understanding that these narratives are carriers of culture—they are a vehicle for these knowledges and practices. Embedded in these narratives are knowledges of life that sponsor particular ways of living, and that are associated with specific practices of relationship and techniques of self formation.

This understanding of narrative as a cultural vehicle is featured in therapeutic conversations that are unpacking of the stories of people's lives and identities. Not only does this unpacking contribute to the deconstruction of the negative identity conclusions associated with these stories, but it also renders more visible the modes of life and thought that are carried in them—that is, through the unpacking of the stories of people's lives, the extent to which these are the bearers of historical and cultural ways of being in the world and thinking about the world becomes more explicitly known. These therapeutic practices bring the world into therapy in the sense that many routine and unquestioned understandings about life and ways of living become visible as cultural and historical products, and these are no longer accepted as certainties about life or truths about human nature and identity. In this way, what might be termed "the politics of people's experiences" are made visible and contestable.

The understanding of narrative as a cultural vehicle is also featured in the re-authoring conversations of narrative therapy. In these conversations people do not radically construct alternative stories of their lives and claims about their identities. The alternative identity claims and stories of life that are derived in these conversations are the bearers of other ways of being in the world, and other ways of thinking about the world, that are also cultural and historical. On account of this consideration, these re-authoring conversations are not just about drawing out the alternative stories of people's lives. In addition they also provide a context for the identification of and the rich description of the knowledges of life and practices of living that are associated with these stories. Thus, it is not just those therapeutic conversations that are unpacking of the stories of people's lives and identities that bring the world into therapy. Re-authoring conversations achieve this as well.

This appreciation of the cultural and historical character of these other knowledges and practices has the effect of expanding therapeutic inquiry into the broader realms of living, providing people with new possibilities for drawing on and seeing through culture and history in their efforts to address their predicaments and their concerns. This gives people a basis for the development of some familiarity with ways of thinking and with practices of relationship that were previously little known, for options in self-formation previously unseen, and for the recognition of problem-solving skills not previously acknowledged or available.

The following account of my meetings with Larry and his family provides an example of the sort of possibilities that can become available when the cultural and historical aspects of the alternative stories of people's lives are considered.

*Larry and His Family**

I am meeting with Larry and his parents, Imelda and Eric. I am hearing that Larry, now thirteen years of age, has been a long-standing source of concern to his parents. He has also been a source of concern to the police, to his schoolteachers and to the parents of other children. Imelda and Eric are particularly worried about Larry's frequent tantrums, his general aggression, and his risky actions. He has already come to the attention of several social service agencies, and has at times been considered "uncontrollable." From all accounts Larry has been unmoved by the many efforts so far initiated to encourage him to reform his ways.

Imelda and Eric decided to seek further consultation following a recent crisis. In a "fit of anger" Larry had held a knife to his mother's throat. This was the "last straw" for Imelda. In response, she packed her bags and left the family home, vowing never to go back. She stayed with a cousin for a couple of days, and then returned, stating that she would give things one last try. Consulting me was part of the terms of this one last try.

In the early part of my consultation with this family I heard about how angry Larry gets toward his mother, and I learn that it is not at all unusual for him to threaten her at these times. In response to this I seek information about the specificity of his actions when angry:

M   OK, so I am hearing about how angry you get toward your mother. I'm curious. Do you ever get this angry toward your father?

Larry   Yeah.

M   Would you say more angry, less angry, or about the same?

Larry   Same.

M   So, have you ever held a knife to your father's throat?

Eric   [shakes his head]

Larry   No.

M   Would you ever consider it?

Larry   No.

Eric   [shakes his head]

The fact that Larry would raise a knife to his mother's throat when angry with her but not follow suit with his father when angry with him had me speculating about the gender politics expressed in his actions. It is not unusual for sons to advocate for the power relations of gender in their interactions with their mothers. On account of this speculation, I was curious to know about Eric's position on Larry's actions:

M   Larry, do you know what your father thought about this?

Larry   What?

M   What he thought about you holding a knife to your mother. Was he for it or against it?

Eric   [takes a quick breath, registering surprise at my question]

Larry   Against it I s'pose.

M   How did you know that?

Larry   [shrugs his shoulders] Just do.

M   [to Eric] Is that right?

Eric   I am surprised you would ask this question. Of course I was against it!

M   [to Imelda] Is this something that you would have known? That Eric was against this?

Imelda   Of course I did. I wouldn't have stayed if I hadn't known this.

M   Have you always known this about Eric, that he would be opposed to Larry threatening you?

Imelda   Eric isn't always that tuned in to what is happening, and we have had words about this. But in the end I

	do get his attention, and he's always been respectful.
M	*[to Eric]* Is this something that you would relate to?
Eric	Yeah. Imelda's right about this. It is true that I have let her down at times, but I feel I have done my best to respect her as woman. It's a principle with me.
M	Is your respect here specific, or is it a general principle in your interactions with women?
Eric	I would like to believe that it is general. What do you think Imelda?
Imelda	Yeah. I reckon it is a general thing. He doesn't treat women bad.
M	*[to Eric]* I guess that you have witnessed men's disrespect of women.
Eric	Sure have. Why, even at work there has been some harassment. I never want any part of it. I won't join in.
M	Does anyone in your workplace know how you feel about this? Would anyone there know what your position is on this?
Eric	*[shrugs]* I guess so.
M	Right now I am curious about what has provided you with a foundation for this principle of respect, about how you have managed to hang on to this, and about whether you have found this difficult at times. I was also curious to know about what hanging onto this says about the sort of values and beliefs that might be important to you. What are your thoughts about this?

It was with this question that I initiated a line of inquiry that I hoped would provide a framework for Eric to more richly describe these other ways of being for men in relation to women. However, despite the fact that Eric was clearly interested in these questions, his responses were quite sparse. In the context of our conversation, the knowledges and practices associated with these ways of being remained thinly known. But I did learn that Eric's father, Kevin, would have also disapproved of Larry's threatening of his mother, and that he would support what Eric had been saying about respect.

Larry's abusive actions toward Imelda had been the focal point of our initial conversation, and I had a strong appreciation of the importance of Larry assuming full responsibility for these actions. However, while such considerations about a person's responsibility for perpetrating abusive actions are paramount, so too are considerations about who might best assume responsibility for addressing such actions—about whom it might be appropriate to engage in acts of redress. And this is a different consideration. It was my understanding that Larry's abusive actions were shaped by knowledges that contribute to particular constructions of men's and women's identities, and by practices of power that are associated with these knowledges. I did not believe that Larry was a primary author of these knowledges and practices–they are out there, at large, in our communities. On account of this, I believed that it would not be appropriate for me to establish a context in which it was required of Larry that he take sole responsibility for initiating acts of redress. Rather, as these knowledges and practices have been developed and finely honed in men's culture, I believed that in these circumstances it would be more appropriate for a community of men to join with Larry in this initiative.

It was with these considerations in mind that I began to ask questions about Larry's evident surprise at much that he was now hearing from Eric. The responses to these questions determined that Larry was open to further explorations of men's ways of being in relation to women, and the option of a separate meeting with Larry, Eric, and Kevin was suggested. The purpose of this meeting would be to put Larry more in touch with his father and grandfather's position on matters of men's relationships with women, to generate some proposals for steps that Larry might take to mend what might be mended, and to assist Larry in explorations of other ways of being in the world as a young man. As part of the plan, if Larry wished he could invite another young man to the meeting to be a support person for him (he eventually chose his cousin, Peter), and it was agreed that all proposals arising from the meeting would be taken back to Imelda to give feedback on. Eric liked the idea, and thought that Kevin would be more than happy to play this part. Larry said that this was OK by him because "it takes the heat off." Imelda was very relieved to hear this plan, as, for so long, she "had born the brunt of responsibility for stopping Larry's abuse." This meeting took place two weeks later, and the following transcript is taken from a point midway through:

M   So, Kevin, that is how your name came up. Eric implicated you in his ability to resist these disrespectful ways of relating to women. Does this strike a chord for you? Do you have a sense that you might have contributed to such a foundation? Or are you surprised to hear this?

Kevin   Well, I can't recall it ever being discussed, but I do strongly believe that women are to be respected, and I haven't liked what Larry says and does at times. *[turning to Larry]* You know that, don't you son? *[turning back to me]* But I don't know how much it is OK for me to interfere.

M   Eric, you talked with me about your father's respect of women. From what you have seen, how does that translate into action? What does your father do that is a demonstration of this respect?

Eric   Well, he does listen to women. He doesn't put down their ideas, and he doesn't raise his voice when he disagrees with my mother, or when he is feeling frustrated. And I have seen him frustrated.

M   What has this meant to you?

Eric   Well, I guess he has been a good example for me in lots of ways.

M   *[turning to Kevin]* What is it like for you to hear this?

Kevin   A bit of a surprise really!

M   What is it like for you to be implicated in Eric's actions in this way?

Kevin   Well, let me see. I've also got lots of shortcomings. But I would have to say that it is pleasing, because we all want a good life for everybody. It isn't anything that I really knew, because it is nothing that we have talked about. To be honest, I would also have to say that this is something that I probably don't think about enough.

M   *[addressing Kevin and Eric]* Would you now have a go at talking to Larry about two things. First, would you have a go at catching him up on what this says about what you both value and what you believe, and on your understandings about what responsibilities are to be honored in men's relationships with women. And second, would you have a go at catching him up on your ideas about how this can be put into practice in men's relationships with women. This second point is important. It is one thing to know something, it is another thing to have the skills to act on this knowledge.

Kevin That's a lot. But we will give it a try.

Eric Yeah, we could do that.

M And maybe I could help to break it up a bit by asking you some more questions as we go along?

Eric Yeah. That would definitely help a lot.

Over the course of the ensuing conversation, other ways of being for men in relation to women were drawn out. This included knowledges that differently shape gender constructions, and, as well, a range of practical examples about how to put these knowledges to work. At points during this conversation I encouraged Larry and his cousin, Peter, to engage in a retelling of what they were hearing. It was apparent that both Larry and Peter were genuinely surprised over much of this, and by what it was that Eric and Kevin were respecting in each other. At this juncture, I introduced some questions about the broader contexts of these ways of being as men:

M Kevin, I would like to know about how you got introduced to these ways of being a man in relation to women. Would it be OK with you if I asked some questions about this?

Kevin Fine, fine. Go ahead. Maybe I'll learn a few things. [chuckles]

M Earlier in our conversation Eric was telling me that you can make yourself available to things that are hard for you to hear. When you think of this ability, who else do you think of?

Kevin Let me see now. The first thing that comes to mind is an uncle of mine who was a youth leader in a boys' club when I was young. He had a position of authority, and I remember some of the blokes that were in this position were pretty strong about the correct line, like little dictators. But my uncle wasn't like this. You could still have an opinion around him. And he could cope with hearing things that were hard to hear. Everyone just knew this about him. And I can remember him taking advice from my aunt. Which, I know now, at the time, I know wasn't that usual. *[meaning that it was unusual to witness men in these positions taking advice from their women partners]*

M Do you know how he achieved this?

Kevin Never asked him. But it might have had to do with the fact that he came from a family with a "background."

M A background?

Kevin Well, his family was different. I remember something about Quakers, but don't have a lot of details.

M Did your father have this background too?

Kevin No, when it comes to patience and understanding, he wasn't too flash. This uncle was his brother-in-law.

M *[turning to Eric and Larry]* Did you know this about Kevin's uncle?

Eric No way.

M What about you Larry?

Larry Nope.

M Peter?

Peter Me neither.

M Kevin, could you tell us some stories about your uncle. I would like to know what you saw in his actions. This way we might get some clearer ideas about what he thought about things, and about how he went about things. For example, about what he knew to do in responding to what was difficult. About what he knew about respecting women. And about the ways that he held himself open to other people's opinions when these other people weren't male friends, or men with authority.

Kevin Sure, let's do it.

In the ensuing conversation, many particularities of the knowledges and practices of living that characterized this uncle's ways of being were described.

I met with Kevin, Eric, Larry, and Peter on two further occasions, and then on three more occasions with Eric, Larry, and Imelda, pursuing further this inquiry into alternative ways of being for men in relation to women. In these meetings, these ways of being became more richly known to all of the members of this family, and it became evident that these were becoming more influential in guiding Larry's actions. It was also evident that Eric was becoming more proactive in addressing some of the gender politics expressed in his workplace. Imelda happily provided feedback on a range of proposals for how Larry might respond to her in a variety of circumstances, including those in which he experienced frustration, and on proposals for the steps that he might take to mend what might be mended in his relationship with her.

It was established that any future concerns about Larry's relationship with Imelda could be referred back to this committee of men who would take the responsibility of joining with him in the development of further proposals for addressing these concerns, and of supporting him in initiating actions based on these proposals. I would be available to join this committee of men if this was found to be necessary. It wasn't. Subsequently, on two occasions when Larry was having difficulty in figuring out how to respond to Imelda's concerns, the committee was reconvened, and a range of options caucused on. Larry experienced no difficulties in taking up some of those options deemed most appropriate.

In this work with Larry and his family, I understood the claims about Eric's preferred ways of being in the world as a man to be associated with knowledges of life and practices of relationship that were cultural and historical. This consideration shaped an inquiry that provided a basis for the development of a familiarity with ways of thinking and with practices of relationship that were previously little known, of options in self-formation previously unseen, and for the recognition of problem-solving skills not previously acknowledged or relatively available.

SUMMARY

At the outset of this chapter, I proposed that the familiarity that people have with narrative inquiry, and their responsiveness to this inquiry, has to do with the fact that many of the practices of this inquiry are closely linked to a particular tradition of understanding life and identity that is deeply historical. Following Bruner (1990), I referred to this tradition as "folk psychology." This is a tradition of understanding that is distinguished by the notions of personal agency and intentional states, and is one that was displaced over the period of the development of the modern psychologies.

This folk psychological tradition of understanding life and identity was reinstated in the social sciences in the 1960s and 1970s, particularly through the "interpretive turn" in cultural anthropology. This reinstatement of folk psychology was accompanied by renewed interest in the activity of making meaning, and in the structures of narrative. This activity and these structures are the primary focus of many of the practices of narrative therapy that bring forth the mind of folk psychology.

In clarifying some of the proposals for therapeutic practice that are shaped by this tradition of folk psychology, I discussed the production of "multi-intentioned" lives, of "joined" lives, of "multiple authenticities," and of "inhabited" lives. I then discussed some of the implications of the acknowledgment that personal and community narratives are historical and cultural products, and the carriers of specific knowledges of life and practices of living that shape people's ways of being in the world.

At different points in this chapter, I included transcripts of therapeutic conversations along with brief summaries of my conversations with Paul in regard to the unpacking of "unresolved issues"; with Jill's family in relation to rendering her suicide sensible; with Ricky about his relationship with trust; and with Larry and his family over addressing the power relations of gender. Through the inclusion of these stories it was my intention to illustrate some of the ways in which the practices of narrative therapy are shaped by notions of personal agency and intentional states, and, on account of this, strongly linked to a particular historical tradition of human understanding referred to as "folk psychology."

NOTES

1. For a fuller account of the constituents of folk psychology, see Jerome Bruner's *Acts of Meaning* (1990).

2. I have a longstanding interest in Foucault's (1973, 1979) analysis of the significance of this development in the shaping of modern psychological understandings and practices. According to this analysis, in the context of this normalizing judgment, people are assigned a precise location in relation to norms about life that are chiefly constructed in the modern disciplines. This normalizing judgment also provides certain incitements for people to operate on their own lives in specific ways in order to close the gap between these assigned locations and these norms. In as much as this assignment of a precise location in relation to these norms is cellularizing or individualizing of life, the introduction of the idea of internal states that shape human expression contributes to the sub-cellularization of life. According to this analysis of modern power, the sub-cellularization of life that is achieved through the construction of internal states contributes yet further to mechanisms of social control. This sub-cellularization provides further opportunities for people to engage in the normalizing judgment of their own and others' lives. And it has the effect of inciting people to operate on their own and others' lives in efforts to reproduce the psychological norms that have been constructed through the history of the professional disciplines.

3. In contrasting internal and intentional states I am following Jerome Bruner (1990). Other contrasts work equally well. For example there are the essentialist/non-essentialist, structuralist/non-structuralist, and the naturalistic/constitutionalist distinctions.

4. The Jamesian tradition was displaced following Freud's Clark University lectures in 1908. It is interesting to speculate as Beels (2001) does on what would have happened to the early twentieth century's psychologies if this had not occurred and had not captured the professional and public imagination.

5. Jerome Bruner (1990), a figure who contributed significantly to this cognitive revolution, provides an interesting account of this history and the outcome of this development.

6. For discussion of this definitional ceremony metaphor and of its relevance to therapeutic practice, see White (1995, 1997, 1999).

7. Over the past two decades David Epston and I have explored many possibilities for recruiting audiences to the preferred developments of people's lives. We have never considered

these explorations to be peripheral to our consultations. Rather we have viewed them as highly significant to the authentication of the identity claims associated with these preferred developments, and to the endurance of these developments. Engaging with the work of the cultural anthropologist Barbara Myerhoff (1982, 1986) in the latter part of the 1980s contributed further to our understanding of the processes associated with the audience's contribution to the authentication of the preferred developments and identity claims of people's lives (for example, see White & Epston, 1989). Our acquaintance with Barbara Myerhoff's notion of the definitional ceremony also contributed to further developments and refinements in what we came to call (following Myerhoff) "outsider-witness" practices. These retellings are invariably quite transformative in their effects.

8. I have borrowed this term and its sense from Wolfgang Iser (1978) and Jerome Bruner (1986).

REFERENCES

Bateson, G. (1972). *Steps to an Ecology of Mind*. New York: Ballantine.

Bateson, G. (1979). *Mind and Nature: A necessary unity*. New York: Dutton.

Beels, C. (2001) *A Different Story: The rise of narrative in psychotherapy*. Phoenix, Arizona: Zeig, Tucker & Theissen.

Bruner, J. (1986). *Actual Minds, Possible Worlds*. Cambridge, MA: Harvard University Press.

Bruner, J. (1990). *Acts of Meaning*. Cambridge, Mass: Harvard University Press.

Clifford, J. (1988). *The Predicament of Culture: Twentieth century ethnography, literature and art*. Cambridge, Mass: Harvard University Press.

Derrida, J. (1978). *Writing and Difference*. Chicago: University of Chicago Press.

Foucault. M. (1973). *The Birth of the Clinic: An archaeology of medical perception*. London: Tavistock.

Foucault, M. (1979). *Discipline and Punish: The birth of the prison*. Middlesex: Peregrine Books.

Foucault, M. (1980). *Power/Knowledge: Selected interviews and other writings*. New York: Pantheon Books.

Geertz, C. (1973). *The Interpretation of Cultures*. New York: Basic Books.

Geertz, C. (1983). *Local Knowledge: Further essays on interpretive anthropology*. New York: Basic Books.

Geertz, C. (2000). *Available Light: Anthropological reflections on philosophical topics*. New Jersey: Princeton University Press.

Gergen, M. M. & Gergen, K. J. (1984). "The social construction of narrative accounts." In Gergen, K. J. & Gergen, M. M. (Eds.), *Historical Social Psychology*. Hillsdale: Lawrence Erlbaum Associates.

Iser, W. (1978). *The Act of Reading*. Baltimore, MD: John Hopkins University Press.

James, W. (1890). *Principles of Psychology*, Vol. I and II. New York: Holt.

James, W. (1892). *Psychology: Brief course*. London: Macmillan.

James, W. (1902). *Varieties of Religious Experience*. New York: Longmans.

Meares, R. (2000). *Intimacy and Alienation: Memory, trauma and personal being*. London: Routledge.

Myerhoff, B. (1982). "Life history among the elderly: Performance, visibility and remembering." In Ruby, J. (Ed.), *A Crack in The Mirror: Reflexive perspectives in anthropology*. Philadelphia: University of Pennsylvania Press.

Myerhoff, B. (1986). "Life not death in Venice: Its second life." In Turner, V. & Bruner, E. (Eds.), *The Anthropology of Experience*. Chicago: University of Illinois Press.

Rosaldo, M. (1984). "Toward an anthropology of self and feeling." In Shweder, R. A. & Le Vine, R. A. (Eds.), *Culture Theory: Essays on mind, self, and emotion*. Cambridge: Cambridge University Press.

Rosaldo, R. (1993). *Culture and Truth: The remaking of social analysis*. Boston: Beacon Press.

Spence, D. (1982). *Narrative Truth and Historical Truth: Meaning and interpretation in psychoanalysis*. New York: Norton.

Turner, V. & Bruner, E. (Eds.) (1986). *The Anthropology of Experience*. Chicago: University of Illinois Press.

White, M. (1991). "Deconstruction and therapy." *Dulwich Centre Newsletter*, No. 3. Reprinted in Epston, D. & White, M. (1992), *Experience, Contradiction, Narrative and Imagination: Selected papers of*

David Epston and Michael White, 1989-1991. Adelaide, Australia: Dulwich Centre Publications. Reprinted in Gilligan, S. (Ed.) 1993: *Therapeutic Conversations*. New York: W.W. Norton.

White, M. (1992). "Men's culture, the men's movement, and the constitution of men's lives." *Dulwich Centre Newsletter*, Nos. 3 & 4. Reprinted in McLean, C., Carey, M. & White, C. (Eds.) (1993), *Men's Ways of Being*. Boulder, Colo.: Westview Press.

White, M. (1995). "Reflecting teamwork as definitional ceremony." In White, M.: *Re-Authoring Lives*. Adelaide, Australia: Dulwich Centre Publications.

White, M. (1997). 'Definitional ceremony.' In White, M.: *Narratives of Therapists' Lives*. Adelaide, Australia: Dulwich Centre Publications.

White, M. (1999). "Reflecting-team work as definitional ceremony revisited." *Gecko*, Vol. 2. Reprinted in White, M. (2000), *Reflections on Narrative Practice*. Adelaide, Australia: Dulwich Centre Publications.

White, M. (2000). "Re-engaging with history: The absent but implicit." In White, M., *Reflections on Narrative Practice: Essays and interviews*. Adelaide, Australia: Dulwich Centre Publications.

White, M. & Epston, D. (1989). *Literate Means to Therapeutic Ends*. Adelaide, Australia: Dulwich Centre Publications. Republished as White, M. & Epston, D. (1990), *Narrative Means to Therapeutic Ends*. New York: W.W. Norton.

CHAPTER 3

Narrative Therapy and Postmodernism

DONALD E. POLKINGHORNE

Narrative therapy is based on the understanding that the language form in which people understand their lives is the storied or narrative form. Narrative is the form that displays life as a temporal unfolding. Rather than viewing people as a something, such as a male or a depressive or an anorexic, narrative therapy views people as unique histories. As histories, people give meaning to the events that happen to them and to the actions they undertake through the stories they construct about their lives. A repertoire of life stories is provided by the culture in which a person lives. These stories are often internalized and employed by people to make sense of their lives; however, these culturally provided stories are regularly constrictive and blaming. Narrative therapy works to assist clients to revise these internalized culture stories into ones that are more inclusive and appreciative of clients' personal power and responsibility.

The development of what came to be termed *narrative therapy* was primarily the work of practicing marriage and family therapists. It took place outside of the mainstream elaboration of psychotherapy by university-based research and training programs and outside the commentary of clinical and counseling psychologists. (Schafer, 1992, and Spence, 1984, however, who are practicing psychoanalysts, not practicing family therapists, have also contributed to the development of a broader use of narrative ideas in therapy through their narrative interpretation of psychoanalytic practice.) Narrative therapy theory has come to have

---

AUTHOR'S NOTE: Correspondence regarding this chapter should be sent to Donald E. Polkinghorne, University of Southern California, Rossier School of Education, Waite Phillips Hall, Los Angeles, CA 90089-0031 or to polkingh@usc.edu.

such a close relationship with postmodern philosophy that some narrative therapists have called it *postmodern therapy*. It is a purpose of this chapter to call into question the identification of narrative therapy as a postmodern therapy.

The name *postmodern therapy* is of recent origin, first appearing in the narrative therapy literature in the late 1980s. It was adopted by several therapists (de Shazer, 1991; White & Epston, 1990) as a characterization of the narrative approach to the therapy they had already been developing. The development of a new narrative approach to therapy preceded the appeal to the ideas of some postmodernist writers as theoretical support for and explanation of the newly developing therapeutic practice. These narrative therapists were selective in what they drew from postmodern writers. Some of the postmodern ideas, such as the centrality of language and discourse, were adopted, whereas other themes, such as the rejection of the creative subject, were not adopted. Narrative therapy, then, was developed as a practice before it conscripted supportive postmodern ideas to provide philosophic support. It is my position that narrative therapy primarily makes use of existential themes, such as self-agency, empowerment, and responsibility, in its therapeutic work while using postmodern themes for diagnostic purposes.

This chapter begins by locating narrative therapy within the late developments of family therapy, with its existential emphasis on client strengths, client-therapist partnership, and constructive meaning. The next section discusses the addition of narrative ideas to the already developed themes of family therapy. This is followed by a section dealing with the use of postmodern themes by narrative therapy. The concluding section calls for a reassessment of the existential dimensions of narrative therapy.

HISTORICAL DEVELOPMENTS IN FAMILY THERAPY

Marriage and family counseling traces its roots to the 1880s and the application of pedagogy to parenting. It was professionalized in the 1940s and entered into an "era of research" in the 1950s (Thomas, 1992). During this era of research, significant changes in understanding families were introduced. Until this time family therapy had been informed by the sociological traditions in family research (using verbal reports of the mother) and the psychoanalytic tradition of family dynamics (Levant, 1984). The most influential of the new ideas was introduced by Bateson and his research group (which included Erickson, Satir, Rosen, Laing, and Jackson). Bateson refocused family therapy theory away from the intrapsychic personality characteristics of individual family members to a view of the family as a communication system. The behavior of individual members of a family was seen as the effect of the communication patterns that existed in the family system. The introjection of a focus on the family as a system set family therapy in a direction that, over the next three decades, would evolve into a practice consistent with the narrative emphasis on discourse and context.

Family therapy theory moved through several phases before the current narrative theories flowered in the 1990s. The first phase was the structural approach, in which symptoms of individual family members were understood as efforts to maintain the homeostatic equilibrium of the family system. The family system could become stuck in recurring loops of disruptive behavior or in improperly balanced hierarchical interactions. It was the role of the therapist to fix the family system by rearranging the interactions so that the family would become stable and functional.

In the second phase, the view that the goal of therapy was to stabilize the family system changed to the view that functioning families were systems that were able to change and evolve. The metaphors from the first phase—mechanic cybernetics concepts of governors, thermostats, and feedback loops—were changed to biological and ecological images. The metaphor of the therapist was also changed; instead of being a detached repair person who stands outside the system, the therapist became a part of the very system that he or she was serving. Becoming a part of the system meant that the therapist was no longer in a position to make objective assessments and prescriptions. Thus, changes in family systems that have incorporated the therapist into themselves occurred as a co-evolutionary or co-creative process.

During both of these phases, the primary focus was on the behavior or actions of the members of the family system. Therapeutic intervention involved figuring out what the family members were doing that maintained problems and producing changes in these behaviors so that the system would function more smoothly (Eron & Lund, 1996). However, under the influence of Watzlawick (e.g., Watzlawick, Weakland, & Fisch, 1974), the idea of reframing was introduced to family therapy. Reframing is based on the notion that people's behaviors are based on their interpretation of situations or others' behavior. That is, rather than the other's behavior per se, it is the meaning that one attaches to the other's behavior that is the source of one's own behavior. As a technique for change within the family system, the therapist assists family members in reinterpreting or changing the meaning they attach to a situation. Reframing, and its notion that action is informed by meaning, can be seen as providing the opening for the development of a more meaning-focused narrative theory of therapy.

THEMES IN NARRATIVE THERAPY

The primary focus of narrative therapy is on the interpretations or meanings people attribute to the happenings and events in their lives. The interpretative understanding that people have of events can limit or expand their possible actions. Narrative therapists assist clients to come to more expansive and inclusive interpretations of themselves and situations. Aspects of their selves that were covered over by limiting interpretations are allowed to come into view when looked at through a more open narrative understanding.

Four overlapping developments in family therapy in the late 1980s contributed to the move to a meaning-based approach within family therapy. Not only have these developments strengthened and enlarged the practice of family therapy, but also their themes have provided the basic elements of the current practice of narrative therapy (Eron & Lund, 1996). The four developments were: (a) emphasis on client strengths, (b) view of clients and therapists as partners, (c) adaptation of a constructionist approach to meaning, and (d) emphasis on the narrative or story form of meaning.

Emphasis on Client Strengths

The first of the developments toward a narrative-based family therapy was a shift of strategy from identifying client weaknesses and inadequacies as the source of their problems to attending to client strengths as the source of solving their problems. This shift was part of what was termed *solution-focused therapy* (de Shazer, 1985; O'Hanlon & Weiner-Davis, 1989). Solution-focused therapy is "a shift in focus from pathology and deficits to strengths, capabilities, and resources in therapy" (O'Hanlon & Weiner-Davis, 1989, p. 7). The therapist engages clients in conversation about the competencies they can employ to make changes in their lives. The talk is about what clients are engaged in when the problem does not occur rather than when it does occur.

View of Clients and Therapists as Partners

The idea that clients are objects to be observed and classified by a detached therapist-observer was called into question by narrative therapists. With the introduction of the use of reflecting teams (Andersen, 1991) as part of the therapeutic process, the concept of the therapist him- or herself as partner in the therapeutic dialogue was reinforced as a theme of narrative therapy. The development of the use of a reflecting team was to overcome clients' impression that they were objects to be observed and analyzed, an impression symbolized by the one-way mirror behind which sat unknown observers. The one-way mirror was a demonstration of the position that clients were objects under view by experts who were detached from the clients' problems. Through observation the experts could determine the type of problem a client had and then prescribe what needed to be done to solve that type of problem.

In the reflecting-team approach, therapy is conducted by a team rather than a single therapist. Some members of the team serve as observers of the therapeutic work, while another member serves as the primary therapist. The observers come out from behind the one-way mirror into the room in which the therapy is taking place. At various intervals, the observers engage the clients in conversation about their experience of the therapy and the therapist. The team and the clients reflect on whether or not the therapeutic process is being helpful and what the clients themselves can do and the therapist can do to achieve the goals of the therapy. The implied message of the location and content of the reflection process is that the control and responsibility of the therapeutic work is shared among the members of the therapist-client group. The point of the client and therapist as partners theme is that therapy is a specialized discursive interpersonal activity rather than a subject knower seeking to comprehend a client as an at-a-distance object.

Adaptation of a Constructionist Approach to Meaning

The third development in family therapy was the shift in focus from family members' behavior or intrapsychic tensions such as drives or defense mechanisms to the meaning that events have for family members. A simple illustration of meaning is "a red light *means* stop." The central idea of meaning is that something is conveyed by something else, such as a word, an action, a gesture, or a situation. Narrative therapy holds that humans are meaning seekers; that is, their interaction with their environment, others, and themselves is such that their attention is focused on what these denote, signify, or mean. How one acts depends on the meaning one understands is signified by an event or feeling. For example, because a red light is understood to mean stop, one stops. Human activity is a response to meaning rather than to uninterpreted sense data.

At issue in attention to meaning is what the source of people's understanding is, such that certain events or objects have particular meanings. The view that humans innately know what things mean, or that events or objects have meaning in themselves, is not adequate to understand human actions and feelings. Rather, humans themselves are the authors of the meanings they attach to events or objects. The general notion that humans author their meaning was first termed *constructivism*. Mascolo and Pollack (1997), in a recent article in the *Journal of Constructivist Psychology*, offered this definition of constructivism: "Constructivism consists of the proposition that meaning is a constructed product of human activity rather than an innate characteristic of the mind or an inherent property of objects or events in the world" (p. 1).

The general idea that humans are constructors of the meaning that events and happenings have for them has been the source of significant psychotherapy literature within and beyond the family therapy field. The constructivist approach to psychotherapy was founded on the personal construct theory of Kelly (1955). Neimeyer and Mahoney (1995) have produced the edited volume, *Constructivism in Psychotherapy*, and Hoyt (1994, 1996) has edited two volumes titled *Constructive Therapies*. In addition, Neimeyer and Neimeyer (1997) edit the *Journal of Constructivist Psychology* (titled *Journal of Personal Construct Psychology* in its earlier volumes). Constructivist psychotherapy does not describe itself as a postmodern therapy. However, Neimeyer (1995) acknowledges that "constructivist thinking ... like any stream of thought ... has been responsive to the broader contours of the intellectual landscape that surrounds it. In this instance, the landscape has been shaped by the influence of postmodernism" (p. 12).

The broad stream of constructivist thought in psychotherapy carries within it several conflicting notions. One of these conflicts concerns the source and locus of meaning in human experience. One position is that meaning is derived only from the social/linguistic system of the culture in which one is immersed. The other position is that meaning is derived from multiple sources, such as personal experiences, the social environment, physical maturation (Piaget, 1971), and schemas that occur through people's developmental processes. The first position proposes that the social system is the locus of meaning; the second retains the idea that the self is central to the construction of one's meaning system.

The first position has been termed *social constructionism* and the second position, *constructivism*. Further confusion resulting from the *ion* and *iv* distinction results from the fact that some authors who identify themselves as social construct*ion*ists, retain the notion of the individual as source of meaning and action (see Danziger's 1997 review, *The Varieties of Social Construction*). Narrative therapy theory as developed at the Houston Galveston Institute (Goolishian & Anderson, 1987) has made use of the view of social construct*ion*ism, particularly as it is spelled out in the writings of Gergen (e.g., 1985). An edited collection of applications of these social constructionist ideas to psychotherapy, *Therapy as Social Construction*, has been published (McNamee & Gergen, 1992b).

As I understand social constructionism, it holds that language serves as the model for meaning generation. A group of letters, such as *c-a-t*, does not inherently mean anything. The letters come to have meaning only as I participate in public conversation and observe how these letters are used. Different public discourses organize and relate meanings in different ways. A red light does not inherently mean *stop*; rather its meaning is determined by social convention. In addition, different language systems provide different sets of meaning. For example, in the medieval discourse, the appearance of a comet meant that a catastrophic natural event would occur. In the contemporary discourse, the appearance of a comet does not mean catastrophe and, thus, does not evoke fear. The origin of meaning is social and not individual, and "our formulations of what is the case are guided by and limited to the systems of language in which we live" (McNamee & Gergen, 1992a, p. 4).

Some social constructionists hold that the meaning is not something words stand for but rather that meaning is essentially language; that is, they understand "language as the very fabric of meaning rather than its incidental clothing" (Dews, 1987, p. 17). "All human systems are linguistic systems" (Anderson & Goolishian, 1992, p. 27), and without a socially generated language, meaning would not exist, in this view. Although this does not indicate that there is nothing outside language, it does mean that people's understandings of themselves, others, and the environment are constructed out of the limited set of meanings that are provided by the conventions of their particular discourse setting. Thus, the meanings of one's own actions are reflections and instances contained within one's social discourse.

Emphasis on the Narrative or Story Form of Meaning

In addition to the three themes described above—emphasis on patient strengths, view of therapist and client as partners, and adaptation of a constructionist approach to meaning—narrative therapy added a fourth theme from which it derives its name; that is, the use of self-narratives or stories. Self-narratives are the stories people tell about themselves, and these stories are the central focus of narrative therapists' work with clients. Life stories are seen as the linguistic expression or presentation of clients' understanding of the meaning of their life events.

Narrative is a form of discourse that links events together across time, and, thus, it can display the temporal dimension of human existence. Narrative form captures the notion that human lives are "becomings" or journeys in which actions and happenings occur before, after, and at the same time as other actions and happenings. The previous analogy used in family therapy to refer to people's understanding of the meaning of events was Bateson's notion that meanings are like maps of a territory. The map analogy shows meaning as static, unable to capture movement and change. The new narrative analogy is that of a text. A text is a group of sentences joined together to produce a level of meaning that ties together the sentences into a unified story with a beginning, middle, and end. White (in White & Epston, 1990) describes his adoption of the text analogy of meaning as a replacement of the map metaphor:

> In considering the text analogy, I perceived a family resemblance of ideas between the notion of map and the notion of narrative. However, the notion of narrative, in that it requires the location of events in cross-time patterns, clearly has some advantages over the notion of map. (p. 3)

A person's self-narrative provides the context in which the happenings and events of his or her life take on meaning. The meaning of life events is given through their placement in and importance for the plot of one's self-narrative. The plot is what one's life story is about; the plot selects from the possible meanings of events those meanings that relate to the outcome. The plot not only governs which meanings are attributed to events, but it also selects which events are included and which are left out of the story. Events that do not contribute to the denouement of the plot or are irrelevant to it are dismissed as unimportant. For example, the plot of a daughter's story about how her stepfather is trying to bring about her ruin will describe the meaning of the event of her stepfather's imposition of a curfew as an attempt to remove her from her friends; while events such as the times he has driven her to activities at his inconvenience will be left out of her story.

Narratives draw on the constructivist idea that the meaning of events and happenings of one's life is underdetermined by those events and happenings themselves. The events receive meaning from one's life stories. If one's life story is revised, the meanings assigned to life events change, and the feelings toward and actions from these events change. The essential theoretical foundation of narrative therapy is based on the idea that as people change their life stories, through which they have interpreted their life events, the meanings assigned to those events will change. The purpose of narrative therapy is to assist clients in changing the narrative meaning they have given to their lives from one that is restrictive and victimizing to one that opens possibilities and is empowering.

An issue within narrative therapy is how indeterminate the relationship between life occurrences and the meaning assigned to them is. Some (e.g., Freedman & Combs, 1996) seem to emphasize an almost indiscriminant relation between meaning and event. This position is based on the notion that words, and therefore meaning, have no inherent relation to the things they signify. For example, the use of the sound *dog* to signify the canine animal is completely arbitrary. By extending this analogy to meaning, meaning is held to be arbitrarily related to events. Thus, clients can somewhat arbitrarily revise their life stories.

The more mainstream narrative therapy position (White & Epston, 1990) holds that life events constrict the meaning attached to them but do not determine it. The social system or discourse in which one participates provides a set of meanings that govern how community members will generally interpret events. Using the red light example again, in our society, the meaning of a red light typically means stop. However, within the social system, many events are allowed multiple interpretations. Again, using language for the analogy, some words are polysemous, for example, bat, which can mean either the animal, a stick (baseball), or a wink (to bat an eye). Most often, the particular meaning assigned is constrained by a context. In a like manner, events and actions often allow for multiple interpretations. For example, a pinch from another person can denote a playful move or an intended hurt expressing anger. Thus, while clients can re-author their life stories, they cannot simply choose any story for their lives; clients are constrained to those revisions that can be applied to the actual happenings in their lives. Revisions in one's life plot need to attend to actual significant life events, such as an accident or a father's absence.

Cultural Plots as Constricting

The plots that people employ as templates for interpreting the events in their lives often are provided by their cultural discourse. The repertoire of cultural plots is thought to reflect plots in which the person's performance matches the functional needs of the society. Best and Kellner (1991) describe this process as "one in which the ultimate goal and effect of discipline is normalization, the elimination of all social and psychological irregularities and the production of useful and docile subjects through a refashioning of minds and bodies" (p. 47). White and Epston (1990), drawing on postmodern philosopher Foucault's analysis of contemporary society, hold that socially authored plots are the products of those whose standing in the social order gives them the power to construct the meaning that people give to their lives. These plots, in general, serve to construct people's lives as meaningful when they perform the consumptive and accepting roles required by a bureaucratically organized and information-based social order.

The socially acceptable plots are adapted by people to make sense of their particular lives. The plots provide meaning and value to their past actions; that is, they have served to forward the plot (good actions) or have impeded the plot development (bad actions).

Plots also serve in the planning of future actions, in that people choose those actions which are consistent with the needs of the plot's completion (to live a good life). The socially authored plots adapted to the local circumstances of individuals are termed *dominant stories*. For some, the socially dominant story they have internalized produces problems in interpersonal relations or causes psychological pain. In their attempt to fulfill the requirements of their dominant plot, they are led to believe that they themselves are the source of their problems.

Overcoming the Dominant Story

When people seek therapy, the narrative therapist works with the person to deconstruct his or her dominant plot (White, 1991). The first step in overcoming an internalized, culturally imposed self-story is to bring the story to awareness. By the articulation of the dominant story, clients become alert to how it has operated to produce distorted and limited interpretations of their life events. Once the dominant story has been extracted, it can be held out for examination and deconstruction. In deconstruction, what has been taken for granted in the dominant story is questioned, to the point that the dominant life story begins to appear as simply one possible view of one's self, not necessarily the correct view. The cultural story begins to loosen its dominance or hold over the client's life. The deconstructive move makes possible the replacement of a client's socially supplied life story with a story that incorporates the client's full life events and that positions the client as the agent and responsible protagonist of his or her story. A number of techniques have been devised in narrative therapy to assist in the deconstruction. The most notable of these are termed *unique outcomes* and *externalizing the problem*. In the unique outcomes technique, clients are asked to recall events that have been dismissed and left out by the dominant plot. The recognition of events that cannot be integrated into the dominant plot serves to undo the dominant plot and open space for the development of a new and more complex plot that includes these now recalled but previously dismissed events and actions.

In externalizing the problem, clients are asked to view the problem as external to them, not as a part of what or who they are. For example, clients who are suffering from anorexic symptoms are asked to view the anorexia as something other than themselves, which is trying to defeat them and take control of their lives. They are asked to recall the times when they successfully fought against the anorexia. Remembrance of these times allows clients to incorporate their strengths and past victories over their problems into the stories they have been constructing about their lives.

The work of deconstruction of the operating dominant plot and the reconstruction of a new plot takes place through a conversational partnership between client and therapist. The new plot emerges out of the deconstruction of the dominant plot without concerted effort by the client to consciously design it. The new plot does not come about by simply accepting another alternate, already available, socially authored plot. The new plot needs to integrate the contents of the old story with the newly available contents. The new contents require a plot that recognizes the agency of one's self (through externalization of the problem). The new plot also opens up a further review of the previously assigned meanings to past life events. Assignments of self-responsibility for previous actions and reinterpretations of the meaning of others' actions are also altered as they are reconfigured into the new story.

The re-visioning of one's life plot (Parry & Doan, 1994) thus changes the meaning assigned to past events and happenings and serves to re-vision one's future. The denouement of the new plot requires a different set of future actions. The altered meaning of the self generated by the new story calls into question future behaviors and plans that had been derived from the old dominant story.

The therapeutic work of narrative therapy is also aimed at bringing about a unified view of oneself. Gergen (1991) has noted that in contemporary Western society, people are often flooded with various dominant plots. Clients' problems can result from the difficulty of finding a personally integrating story. Yet, the development of a meaningful existence seems to require a plot inclusive enough to include the variety of activities and purposes people undertake. Kerby (1997), in *Memory, Identity, Community: The Idea of Narrative in the Human Sciences,* writes: "There is still, I believe, the legitimate though often unconscious desire for unification; it is basic to the human project for generating a meaningful presence with others" (p. 136). The experience of narrative therapists is that when the dominant story is deconstructed, the new story that emerges for the client's identity is both more complex and more integrating than the old culturally dominant story.

POSTMODERN INFLUENCES IN NARRATIVE THERAPY

The philosophers called postmodernist do not have a set of common attributes but rather seem to have what Wittgenstein's analogy referred to as a family resemblance. The analogy points out that although one can see a certain resemblance among the family members, when they are studied up close one may find that there is no feature common to all the members. Narrative therapists have been quite selective in their appeal to postmodern philosophers. Their featured postmodern philosopher is Foucault; he is the only postmodern philosopher White and Epston (1990) cite, although White does make use of Derrida's term *deconstruction.* Derrida's work is important in the writings of de Shazer (1991), but besides a few references to Lyotard, I have not found references to other postmodern philosophers such as Deleuze and Guattari or Baudrillard.

The specific writings of the postmodern philosophers have also been used selectively by narrative therapists. Fish (1993) points out that White's discussion of Foucault's ideas on power is severely skewed:

> While subscribing to Foucault's concept of discourse, he does not examine the archaeological implication inherent in this concept that the subject is irrelevant. Meanwhile, White and Epston ignore Foucault's genealogical admission that, on the local level, differences in power relations are used volitionally and with effect. (p. 224)

In the judgment of Fish (1993), narrative therapists have chosen only those aspects of postmodern philosophy that permit a view that tends "to conceptually isolate the therapist-family system from any social, historical, economic, or institutional context, and to deny the existence or relevance of differences in power at an interpersonal level" (p. 228).

The influence of postmodern ideas on narrative therapy came more directly from what has become postmodern anthropology than from postmodern philosophy. Epston, White's partner, had been an anthropologist before becoming a family therapist. Geertz's interpretive approach to anthropology was called on to support family therapy's turn to meaning. In the introduction to *Local Knowledge,* Geertz (1983) wrote about his earlier book, *The Interpretation of Cultures* (1973):

> Ten years ago, the proposal that cultural phenomena should be treated as significative systems . . . was a much more alarming one for social scientists—allergic, as they tend

to be to anything literary or inexact—than it is now. In part, it is a result of the growing recognition that the established approach to treating such phenomena, [with] laws-and-causes social physics, was not producing the triumphs of prediction, control, and testability . . . that had been promised. (p. 3)

Geertz's work bolstered the idea that people's actions are based on the interpretative meaning they assign to the experiences of self, others, and environment rather than on direct knowledge of these phenomena.

In support of the importance of narrative as a meaning-producing form of text, White cites Bruner (the anthropologist) for support. Bruner, in a passage quoted by White (in White & Epston, 1990), proposed that it is storytelling that determines the meaning ascribed to experience. In Bruner's (1986) view,

> We begin with a narrative that already contains a beginning and an ending, which frame and hence enable us to interpret the present. It is not that we initially have a body of data, the facts, and we then must construct a story or theory to account for them. Instead . . . the narrative structures we construct are not secondary narratives about data but primary narratives that establish what is to count as data. New narratives yield new vocabulary, syntax, and meaning in our ethnographic accounts; they define what constitute the data of those accounts. (p. 143)

White also notes the influence of sociologist Goffman (1974) on his idea of narratives as interpretative frameworks; White also adopted Goffman's (1961) term *unique outcomes* as the name for actions and experiences that have been left out and neglected by a client's socially dominant story.

Narrative therapy is primarily an internal development within family therapy. Its approach evolved from the traditions of the field, the creative development of new ideas and techniques, and the experiences with clients that derived from the use of these new techniques. Theoretical support and stimulation for these new ideas have been drawn from the other social sciences and from postmodern philosophy. Narrative therapy, however, cannot be understood as simply the application of the ideas of postmodern philosophy to psychotherapy.

EXISTENTIAL THEMES IN NARRATIVE THERAPY

Human beings can be understood as the confluence of three realms: the biological, the personal, and the social. Social constructionist and postmodern philosophical theory (in contrast to narrative therapy) assert that the social realm is predominant and the other two realms are under its auspices. The creation of meaning is a function of the social realm. In this view, the personal realm is a construct of the social realm, having no inherent structure of its own. This idea is reflected in the prominence of the notions of the "death of the subject" and "decentering of the self" in postmodern literature. Postmodern philosophical and social constructionist theory contend that people are not centers or agents of meaning and actions but that they can be understood as performers playing roles written for them in the social discourse. The bodily realm, too, is under direction of the social realm in that the social realm controls the body's actions by its imposed rhythms of work, rest, and holidays; by its instructions regarding eating habits; and by its moral approval of only a limited set of possible bodily activities. The social realm, which is a languaged system, has an existence independent of its individual speakers. Like language, social systems are in place before and remain after the life of any individual person.

Within the threefold confluence of biological, personal, and social realms, most therapists who identify themselves as narrative therapists practice on the existential assumption that the personal realm is itself a possible creator of meaning. However, narrative therapists do not retreat to the position that the personal realm is the realm that creates and maintains the social realm. Nor do they maintain that there is an essential essence or structure to the personal realm; that is, they hold that there is no "real" self that one is and that can be discovered. Instead, narrative therapists understand that people can operate within the social discourse to produce creative and original meanings for themselves. They are not limited to adopting for their own lives the meanings prearranged for them in the storied characters supplied by their social discourse. Clients are not merely playing out the roles written for them but, instead, have the capacity to rewrite their own, more inclusive life stories. Language, once again, can be used as an analogy. Although the structures of a language (the social discourse) provide the tools for expression, they do not determine what can be expressed with them. Using a language's syntax and words, one can create new meanings and speak sentences never spoken before. Thus, the meanings that can be expressed by a language are relatively open ended. New meaning can arise in a language system through the metaphoric extension of old meanings, the creation of new words, and fresh combinations of words into new phrases. Thus, the social realm does not simply impose its meaning on its subjects; it provides the discursive tools that enable persons to originate new meanings other than the ones that are dominant in the social order.

Narrative therapy differs from postmodern philosophy and social constructionism in its recognition that a person is not simply a creation of social discourse but also a center that has power to overcome the meaning-generated plots imposed on him or her by the social system. The person has the capacity to revise received plots and, thereby, to come to a new self-understanding. This belief that people have the capacity to use the meaning-generating tools provided by the social discourse to revise and alter prior understandings of themselves is, however, an adaptation, rather than an uncritical adoption, of the traditional existential view of the person as unfettered by the social world. White and Epston (1990, p. 67) favorably quote Geertz (1976):

> The Western conception of the person as a bounded, unique cognitive universe, a dynamic center of awareness, emotion, judgment and action organized into a distinctive whole, is however incorrigible it may seem to us, a rather peculiar idea with the concept of the world's cultures. (p. 225)

This view of people is a long way from the dual substance theory of Descartes and its notion of a knower separated from the world it knows. The idea of the person held by narrative therapists has a combined postmodern-existential hue in that people are understood as co-constructors of meaning, in partnership with the social discourse in which they are located.

CONCLUSIONS

The primary thrust of narrative therapy is the importance of focusing on meanings or interpretations clients have of life events or actions rather than simply on the events in themselves. Narrative therapists understand that meanings are generated by self-plots. Plots select from the possible meanings of particular events and actions those that contribute to the unfolding of a person's operating self-story. Postmodern thought emphasizes that people's self-stories are imposed on them by the cultural discourse in which they are immersed. The skeptical postmodern portrait of our contemporary social world is one in which people are structured into self-identities that serve to promote the desires of those in power by normalizing people into roles that make them more easily managed by a computerized bureaucracy and make them more facilely lured into incessant consumption of commodities. The postmodern philosophers warn that our social system has become totalized and that all of our society's discursive meanings have integrated into a single discourse. The more skeptical postmodern philosophers doubt if there is a way out of the control of the system because they find no position outside the system from which it can be critiqued. The meaning of people, objects, and activities has become related to their fiscal value and cost-effectiveness.

Narrative therapy can be understood as a response to the degradation and management of individual lives within the situation described by postmodern thinkers. Narrative therapy draws on the existential themes of personal agency and responsibility as it works to assist clients in gaining some power of self-creation by deconstructing the plots imposed on them by the social system. Narrative therapy works to bring some play into the society's totalizing discourse by assisting clients to revise and construct personal plots that incorporate the full breadth of their lives. This assistance takes the form of helping clients recall previous actions that do not fit into their adopted dominant self-stories. These now-remembered actions and events no longer fit the internalized social plot; the awareness of these events requires re-vision of the self-story into one that is more realistic, though more complex. The new self-story is more realistic in that it incorporates the fullness of one's life instead of only those parts that fit the social plot.

However, the skepticism of many postmodern writers recently has been tempered by their use of existential themes in their call for liberation and for freedom from the restraints imposed by social discourse. Foucault, the most quoted postmodern philosopher in the postmodern therapy literature, had in his late writings (1980s) turned to the notion of the self-constituting subject, which he had previously rejected as an existentialist fiction. Although these late writings of Foucault are not cited in the postmodern therapy literature, they support the notion of a subject capable of creating new self-meaning. Foucault with Sennet (1982), reflecting on his earlier work, wrote, "When I was studying asylums, prisons, and so on, I perhaps insisted too much on techniques of domination.... I would like, in the years to come, to study power relations starting from techniques of the self" (p. 10). Techniques of the self refer to practices "which permit individuals to effect by their own means or with the help of others a certain number of operations on their own bodies and souls, thoughts, conduct, and way of being, so as to transform themselves in order to attain a certain state of happiness, purity, wisdom, perfection, or immortality" (Foucault, 1988, p. 18). Foucault's previous deterministic view of the subject is rejected, and he turns to a concern of how individuals can transform their own subjectivities. Foucault suggests that the Greek and Roman cultures "offer contemporary individuals elements of a model for overcoming modern forms of subjectivity and creating new forms of life that break with coercive normalizing institutions of modernity" (Best & Kellner, 1991, p. 63). Foucault (1982) says, "We have to promote new forms of subjectivity through the refusal of this kind of [normalized] individuality which has been imposed on us for centuries" (p. 216). Foucault is not returning to a concept of a subject endowed with an inner essence or original will that precedes and stands out from the social realm. However, he now proposes that individuals have the power to define their own identity. These ideas in the late writings of Foucault seem more suitable support for postmodern or narrative therapy than his earlier emphasis on the domination of the social world.

In Danziger's (1997) review of 11 social constructionist volumes, mentioned previously, he concludes that "many of the contributors are far from being signed-up members of the social constructionist or postmodernist clubs" (p. 409). I believe, because of their retention of a creative and authorial subject, the same comment applies to narrative therapists.

It is this revised postmodern theme of the self-constructing subject, which is closest to the narrative therapy notion of the re-authoring subject. The process of narrative therapy is built on the existential view that people have a capacity to revise and re-author the narratives in which they have been acculturated. The task of narrative therapists is to assist people in the exercise of this capacity. That people have this capacity is demonstrated in the many case studies reported in the narrative therapy literature. Even books (e.g., Freedman & Combs, 1996) whose theoretical sections lean toward describing the self as socially controlled picture narrative therapeutic work as opening space for new stories. The very idea of psychotherapy, in general, is based on the premise that people have the capacity to change the meaning they have given to their life events and thereby open up new avenues of action and self-understanding. Psychoanalysis and the cognitive therapies, as well as narrative therapy, operate on this premise. Even current behavioral therapies include the notion of changes in attributed meaning through changes in behavior.

In an issue of *The Family Therapy Networker,* mainly devoted to articles about narrative therapy, Wylie (1994) provides a description of White's narrative therapy work: "White liberates little pockets of noncooperation, moments of personal courage and autonomy, self-respect and emotional vitality beneath the iron grid of lived misery and assigned pathology" (p. 45). Narrative therapists believe in personal transformation through the generation of revised life stories. This belief separates these therapists from what has been the view of postmodern philosophers that the subject is a passive creation of the social discourse. I think narrative therapists should be more assertive in their rejection of the empty and powerless subject. Their therapeutic experience has given them a more complex and complete understanding of human existence than that proposed by the postmodern social philosophers. Indeed, the view of the passive subject seems to have played itself out within some of the postmodern philosophical writers. More recent developments in postmodern philosophy, which are not cited in the narrative therapy literature, may be helpful to narrative therapists in their defense of people's creative powers. Examples of helpful postmodern developments include Foucault's turn to a recognition of the creative subject and Derrida's ideas about the slippage of meaning within a language system and his warnings about the apartheid dangers inherent in language's tendency to divide people into bifurcated categories—male and female, black and white, and so on—and to elevate one category over the other.

Postmodern therapists have their own tale to tell about human transformation and the creative capacity of the subject. I think they need to be less impressed by the version of postmodernism developed in the work of the early skepticism of the French postmodern philosophers and more aggressive in the presentation of their own version of an existentially informed postmodernism of human self-creation.

REFERENCES

Andersen, T. (Ed.). (1991). *The reflecting team*. New York: Norton.

Anderson, H., & Goolishian, H. (1992). The client is the expert: A not-knowing approach to therapy. In S. McNamee & K. J. Gergen (Eds.), *Therapy as social construction* (pp. 25-39). Newbury Park, CA: Sage.

Best, S., & Kellner, D. (1991). *Postmodern theory: Critical interrogations*. New York: Guilford.

Bruner, E. M. (1986). Ethnography as narrative. In V. W. Turner & E. M. Bruner (Eds.), *The anthropology of experience* (pp. 139-155). Urbana: University of Illinois Press.

Danziger, K. (1997). The varieties of social constructionism. *Theory and Psychology, 7*(3), 399-416.

de Shazer, S. (1985). *Keys to solutions in brief therapy*. New York: Norton.

de Shazer, S. (1991). *Putting difference to work*. New York: Norton.

Dews, P. (1987). *Logics of disintegration: Poststructural thought and the claims of critical theory*. New York: Verso.

Eron, J. B., & Lund, T. W. (1996). *Narrative solutions in brief therapy*. New York: Guilford.

Fish, V. (1993). Poststructuralism in family therapy: Interrogating the narrative/conversational mode. *Journal of Marital and Family Therapy, 19*(3), 221-232.

Foucault, M. (1982). The subject and power. In H. L. Dreyfus & P. Rabinow (Eds.), *Michel Foucault: Beyond structuralism and hermeneutics* (pp. 208-226). Chicago: University of Chicago Press.

Foucault, M. (1988). Technologies of the self. In L. M. Martin, H. Gutman, & P. H. Hutton (Eds.), *Technologies of the self* (pp. 16-49). Amherst: University of Massachusetts Press.

Foucault, M., & Sennet, R. (1982). Sexuality and solitude. In D. Rieff (Ed.), *Humanities in review* (Vol. 1.). London: Cambridge University Press.

Freedman, J., & Combs, G. (1996). *Narrative therapy: The social construction of preferred realities*. New York: Norton.

Geertz, C. (1973). *Interpretation of cultures*. New York: Basic Books.

Geertz, C. (1976). From nature's point of view: On the nature of anthropological understanding. In K. Basso & H. Selby (Eds.), *Meaning in anthropology*. Albuquerque: University of New Mexico Press.

Geertz, C. (1983). *Local knowledge: Further essays in interpretative anthropology*. New York: Basic Books.

Gergen, K. J. (1985). The social constructionist movement in modern psychology. *American Psychologist, 40*, 266-275.

Gergen, K. J. (1991). *The saturated self: Dilemmas of identity in contemporary life*. New York: Basic Books.

Goffman, E. (1961). *Asylums: Essays in the social situation of mental patients and other inmates*. New York: Doubleday.

Goffman, E. (1974). *Frame analysis*. New York: Harper.

Goolishian, H., & Anderson, H. (1987). Language systems and therapy: An evolving idea. *Psychotherapy, 24*, 529-538.

Hoyt, M. F. (Ed.). (1994). *Constructive therapies*. (Vol. 1). New York: Guilford.

Hoyt, M. F. (Ed.). (1996). *Constructive therapies*. (Vol. 2). New York: Guilford.

Kelly, G. A. (1955). *The psychology of personal constructs*. (Vol. 1). New York: Norton.

Kerby, A. P. (1997). The language of the self. In L. P. Hinchman & S. K. Hinchman (Eds.), *Memory, identity, community: The idea of narrative in the human sciences* (pp. 125-142). Albany: State University of New York Press.

Levant, R. F. (1984). *Family therapy: A comprehensive overview*. Englewood Cliffs, NJ: Prentice Hall.

Mascolo, M. F., & Pollack, R. D. (1997). Frontiers of constructivism: Problems and prospects. *Journal of Constructivist Psychology, 10*(1), 1-5.

McNamee, S., & Gergen, K. J. (1992a). Introduction. In S. McNamee & K. J. Gergen (Eds.), *Therapy as social construction* (pp. 1-6). Newbury Park, CA: Sage.

McNamee, S., & Gergen, K. J. (Eds.). (1992b). *Therapy as social construction*. Newbury Park, CA: Sage.

Neimeyer, R. A. (1995). Constructivist psychotherapies: Features, foundations, and future directions. In R. A. Neimeyer & M. J. Mahoney (Eds.), *Constructivism in psychotherapy* (pp. 11-38). Washington, DC: American Psychological Association.

Neimeyer, R. A., & Mahoney, M. J. (1995). *Constructivism in psychotherapy*. Washington, DC: American Psychological Association.

Neimeyer, R. A., & Neimeyer, G. J. (Eds.). (1997). *Journal of constructivist psychology*. London: Taylor & Francis.

Neisser, U. (1993). The self perceived. In U. Neisser (Ed.), *The perceived self: Ecological and interpersonal sources of self knowledge* (pp. 3-21). Cambridge, UK: Cambridge University Press.

O'Hanlon, W. H., & Weiner-Davis, M. (1989). *In search of solutions: A new direction in psychotherapy*. New York: Norton.

Parry, A., & Doan, R. E. (1994). *Story re-visions: Narrative therapy in the postmodern world*. New York: Guilford.

Piaget, J. (1971). *Psychology and epistemology: Toward a theory of knowledge*. New York: Viking.

Schafer, R. (1992). *Retelling a life: Narration and dialogue in psychoanalysis*. New York: Basic Books.

Spence, D. P. (1984). *Narrative truth and historical truth*. New York: Norton.

Thomas, M. B. (1992). *An introduction to marital and family therapy: Counseling toward healthier family systems across the lifespan*. New York: Macmillan.

Watzlawick, P., Weakland, J., & Fisch, R. (Eds.). (1974). *Change: Principles of problem formation and problem resolution*. New York: Norton.

White, M. (1991). *Deconstruction and therapy*. Adelaide, Australia: Dulwich Centre Newsletter.

White, M., & Epston, D. (1990). *Narrative means to therapeutic ends*. New York: Norton.

Wylie, M. S. (1994). Panning for gold. *The Family Therapy Networker, 18*(6), 40-48.

Part II

Working With Narrative in Psychotherapy

CHAPTER 4

The CCRT Approach to Working With Patient Narratives in Psychodynamic Psychotherapy

HOWARD BOOK

The Core Conflictual Relationship Theme (CCRT) approach to patient narratives in psychodynamic psychotherapy is a focused (Luborsky, 1984), reliable (Luborsky & Diguer, 1998a), valid (Luborsky, 1998a), and easily constructed (Book, 1998; Luborsky, 1984) conceptualization of the patient's primary psychodynamic conflicts (Luborsky, 1984). The CCRT is a highly researched paradigm explored at more than 75 research centers worldwide (Luborsky, personal communication, 1996). As such, it links psychotherapy to psychopathology, transposes theory into practice, embodies scientific principles and findings, aids in crisply formulating the patient's pivotal conflicts, serves as a blueprint that guides therapy, acts as a marker for change, leads to more accurate interventions, encourages patient acceptability of interpretations, and respects the uniqueness and humanity of the person in question (Eells, 1997; Luborsky, 1997).

In his historical overview of the development of the CCRT, Luborsky (1984) describes the gestation of the CCRT as occurring from 1974 to 1977. During this period, Luborsky began reviewing and scoring psychotherapy sessions with the goal of tracking cues that illuminated repetitive relationship patterns that were central to the patient's difficulties (Luborsky, 1997). The birth of the CCRT occurred on Saturday, January 17, 1976, at 2 p.m., at a scientific and clinical meeting hosted by the Department of Psychiatry at the Downstate Medical Center, when Luborsky presented his paper, "The Early Life of the Idea for the

AUTHOR'S NOTE: Correspondence regarding this chapter should be sent to Howard Book, MD, Suite 101, 2900 Yonge Street, Toronto, Ontario, Canada M4N 3N8 or to hbwork@netsurf.net.

Core Conflictual Relationship Theme Method in Understanding Transference" (Luborsky, 1998b). In carrying out this self-imposed exercise, Luborsky noted that most of the inferences he made occurred when he was paying attention to the patient's narratives about interactions that he or she had with other people.

Luborsky realized that within these narratives, three items seemed to demand his attention. The first was what the patient wished for, wanted, or desired in this relationship with the person about whom he or she was speaking. Luborsky went on to describe this item as the Wish, shorthanded as W. The second item was how the patient believed this other person would respond if the patient were to articulate or act on his or her Wish. This item was referred to as the Response of the Other, shorthanded to RO. Given this belief about the other person's response (the RO), the third item was how the patient then did actually react. This was referred to as the Response from the Self, shorthanded to RS. The RS described how the speaker behaved and what he or she felt.

WHAT THE CCRT LOOKS LIKE

As this chapter will later illustrate, the CCRT is put together by the therapist during the assessment (evaluation) phase and then presented to the patient during the feedback session following evaluation and prior to beginning formal therapy. It is expressed in two or three sentences that contain the patient's Wish (W), Response from Other (RO), and Response from Self (RS) (Book, 1998; Luborsky, 1984). In terms of the reliable identification of the core components of the CCRT formulation, Luborsky and Diguer (1998) have reported encouraging findings. They studied the interrater reliability of the CCRT by comparing the CCRT scoring of 35 cases. Using two psychodynamically oriented clinicians as judges, the weighted kappa for the W was 0.61 (fair to good, toward the good ranking), the negative RS was also 0.61, and the negative RO was 0.70 (almost reaching the minimum 0.75 ranking of excellent).

In another series, on a small sample (eight patients) using standard reliability methods to evaluate whether CCRT formulations by three trained judges were basically similar or dissimilar, all three judges agreed 75% of the time (six out of eight cases), and two of the three judges made similar formulations 100% of the time (Luborsky & Diguer, 1998). Finally (Luborsky, 1997), a number of studies support the validity of the CCRT by showing impressively similar results between the CCRT and other researched formulations (Horowitz, Luborsky, & Popp, 1991; Luborsky et al., 1993).

Studying the pervasiveness of the CCRT in different levels of consciousness (in two separate studies), Popp, Luborsky, and Crits-Christoph (1998) and later Popp, Diguer, et al. (1998) compared the CCRTs derived from dreams of patients with the CCRTs derived through narratives about interactions with others in their waking lives. The researchers found "significant similarities between the recurrent relationship themes in dreams and those in waking narratives, with the highest similarity being for the RO." They concluded,

> A finding of similar CCRTs in the waking narratives and dreams implies similarity of CCRTs across different states of consciousness, [and that] these results support the concept of a central relationship pattern that shows itself in two different states or modes of thinking: in dreams and in waking narratives. (Popp, Luborsky, et al., 1998).

The following paragraph illustrates the CCRT that the therapist generated during the assessment phase and presented to her patient, Steven Wright, a 42-year-old architect, in a session after the assessment was completed but before formal therapy began. This therapist stated:

> Over the past three sessions [here the therapist is referring to the evaluation interviews] you and I have discussed a lot about what's been going on in your life, currently and in the past. We have talked about a number of issues, but there is one issue that is quite prominent, seems to run like a red thread through most of what you describe in your relationships with others, and appears to be closely connected to the tension that brought you to seek treatment. And this is how I see it [this is the stem introducing the CCRT that is about to follow].
>
> It seems to me that you want to be in a relationship where you can respond assertively and actively voice your concerns when you feel you have been unfairly treated [this is the patient's Wish or W] but you figure that if you do so, the other person is going to blast you out of the water [the RO-expected]. So, instead of voicing these concerns you bite your tongue, say nothing [the RS-behavior] and end up feeling tense, angry, humiliated, and small [RS-affect].
>
> And it seems to me that these feelings [RS-affect] relate to the ongoing sense of tension and irritability that brought you to see me in the first place [here the therapist is connecting the patient's CCRT to the patient's entrance complaints].

The therapist then asks: "What do you think of what I've said? Is this an important area we might explore?" It is essential that the patient experience the therapist's conceptualization—that is, the CCRT—as highly meaningful. The degree of meaningfulness that the patient experiences on hearing the CCRT motivates the patient to understand more about the roots of the CCRT in therapy and also offers a directional map that helps orient the patient to the work that needs to be done. The CCRT is sandwiched between the stem ("We've talked about many things . . . but one issue seems to run like a red thread . . .") and the exploratory sentence ("What do you think of what I've said?").

The CCRT contains the three components previously described: a Wish that occurs in the context of a relationship, a Response of the Other that may be either expected (RO-expected) or actual (RO-actual), and a Response from the Self that has behavioral and affective arms (RS-behavior and RS-affect). These three components do not exist in isolation but are linked to each other in a cascading manner. The RO is what the patient expects would happen *if* he or she acted on the W. Less frequently, the RO is what actually happens when the patient does act on the W.

In the illustration above, the anticipated Response of the Other—that of being blasted out of the water—is what the patient expects should he speak up when he's feeling unjustly treated. Similarly, the Response from the Self is linked to the RO. That is, the RS is what the patient does and feels in the context of the expected (or actual) RO. In the above example, *because* the patient expects to be blasted out of the water by the other person (RO) *should* he speak up (W), he actually responds (RS) by not speaking up, biting his tongue (behavior) and feeling tense, frustrated, and small (affect). It is an if-then-so instead connection between these three components. *If* you were to speak up (W), *then* you expect others would respond by blasting you out of the water (RO-expected), *so instead* you remain silent but feel tense and insignificant (RS-behavior and affect).

A second guiding principle is that the Response of the Other is always from the patient's perspective. This patient expects others to blast him out of the water should he speak up, and it is irrelevant whether an objective third party might state. "Oh, the woman Steven was talking to is a meek, mild soft-spoken individual who not only doesn't blast people out of the water, she has trouble raising her own voice!" In developing the RO, it is irrelevant what an objective observer might state; the only relevancy is what the patient's expectation might be.

How the CCRT Is Developed

When is the CCRT developed? CCRT is developed by the therapist during the usual assessment format he or she carries out on all patients. Psychologists, social workers, and psychiatrists will use whatever assessment format, evaluation protocol, or other assessment is typical in their practice. However, in addition to carrying out the usual discipline-specific evaluation, to develop a CCRT the therapist listens for and immediately transcribes Relationship Episodes (REs).

A Relationship Episode is simply a narrative the patient tells about an *interaction* with another person. It is not merely a comment about that other person, such as: "This new boss of ours is an absolute jerk. A self-centered pompous know-it-all." This is not an RE. It is simply a description of another person. An RE must be a narrative about an *interaction* between the patient and a person. It is fairly easy, though, to turn a description into an RE by asking the patient—in this case, Steven, the architect whose CCRT was used as an example previously—what has transpired between him and his boss that left him with that impression. This was the interchange that followed:

Therapist Can you give me an example of what went on between the two of you that left you viewing your boss as a jerk?

Steven Sure, he comes barging into my office—without knocking—and says "Stevie, I need that Adams report you're working on completed by tomorrow morning!" And I think to myself: "You've got to be out of your mind. The Adams report is one of four that I'm working on and you're acting like it's the only one I've got. Why didn't you ask instead of ordering? And what about Stevie? My name is Steven. Last time I was Stevie was in grade six." Man, I really felt like telling him to screw himself.

By asking the question, "It sounds like something happened between the two of you. Can you give me an example?" the therapist redirects the patient to describe a Relationship Episode. As soon as Steven begins with "He comes barging into my office," the RE begins.

Usually, therapists do not have to encourage or redirect patients to bring up Relationship Episodes. If anything, it is more of a task to get them to stop. Patients are forever describing unsatisfying encounters with spouses, significant others, coworkers, rude strangers, drivers, service personnel, and previous therapists. In fact, Luborsky, Barber, and Diguer (1992) found that on average, there were 4.1 relationship narratives told in the psychodynamic therapy sessions drawn from the Penn Psychotherapy Project and sample of patients experiencing major depression. In addition, they found that most of the narratives identified in this study were about recent events that had occurred within the two weeks before the therapy session. All therapists have to do is become adroit at identifying and writing down these REs as they occur.

The therapist collects approximately four to six Relationship Episodes to ensure consistency in choosing the most accurate Wish, Response of the Other, and Response of Self to create the CCRT that will be presented to the patient. After the evaluation session, the therapist looks at each RE that he or she has written down and attempts to find a W that the patient desired in that interaction; an RO either that the patient expected to occur or that did occur in the context of the W; and the RS, how the patient actually and behaviorally felt given the RO.

What was Steven's Wish? He tells us in the narrative: "I wanted to tell him to go screw himself." The closer the therapist can get to the data, the actual words the patient uses about what he or she wanted or wished to do, the more accurate and powerful will be the ultimate CCRT.

What about the Response of the Other? Is it there? No. However, at the time that Steven was describing this Relationship Episode, the therapist could inquire in such a way that encourages him to describe how he thought the other might have responded (the RO—in this case the RO-expected) had he acted on his wish.

Therapist So, you were quite offended by his intrusiveness, rudeness, and demandingness?

Steven You betcha.

Therapist And you wanted to tell him to go screw himself. *[the Wish]*

Steven Yeah.

Therapist Did you?

Steven No way!

Therapist I'm not saying you should have, but did you say anything to him about your displeasure?

Steven No, actually I didn't.

Therapist Why not?

Steven Well, he's new and the boss. And I don't want to ruffle his feathers.

Therapist What might have happened had you spoken up and ruffled his feathers?

Steven Well, you know the old saying, "A new broom sweeps clean." He's new here and probably has associates that he wants to bring in from his previous job. You know what happens, these guys get rid of the old and bring in people they've worked with and know.

Therapist You're saying had you spoken up you might have become a prime candidate for being fired?

Steven Yeah.

Therapist So what did you do?

Steven Nothing. I just bit my tongue.

Therapist And how did you feel doing that?

Steven Well, I still felt angry, but I also felt humiliated and small.

By asking the question, "What did you want to do?" the therapist encouraged Steven to flesh out and articulate his Wish. When he goes on to inquire, "If you had spoken up what might have happened?" he is gently directing this patient to put into words how he expected his boss to respond—the Response of Other. By asking what Steven ultimately did do and what he did feel—as compared to what he wanted to do (W)—the therapist is gently orienting the patient to describe the behavioral and affective components of his Response of Self. Now the therapist can transcribe these components, as the following chart illustrates.

RE #1: Boss

Wish	Response of the Other	Response of Self
tell him to screw himself	fire him	says nothing (behavior) feels small (affect)

By posing appropriate questions, a very brief Relationship Episode containing none of the three components that make up a CCRT can be expanded to contain all components. For example, during the assessment, this same patient mentioned, "On the drive to work, this idiot cut me off, but I didn't let it spoil my day." This is an RE, albeit brief. It describes an interaction between the patient and a stranger in which the patient felt cut off by the stranger. There is no obvious Wish, Response of Other, or Response of Self. Since this RE is impoverished of Ws, ROs, and RSs, the therapist can simply disregard it and wait for the patient to describe another, more fleshed-out RE. Or the therapist might ask exploratory questions that uncover the unspoken W, RO, and RS, as the following interchange illustrates:

Therapist So, he cut you off?

Steven Yeah, that s.o.b. in his yuppie Porsche.

Therapist What did you want to do when he cut you off?

Steven Give him a piece of my mind.

Therapist Did you?

Steven No.

Therapist Why not?

Steven I don't know.

Therapist Well, what do you figure would have happened if you did tell him off?

Steven You can never tell. Road rage.

Therapist Yeah, there seems to be more and more of that these days.

Steven Yeah, people get shot over parking spots.

Therapist So, you did nothing.

Steven No. I said nothing, I did nothing. Didn't even give him a dirty look.

Therapist And how'd you end up feeling?

Steven Angry, frustrated, and kind of disappointed in myself for not even looking at him.

These exploratory questions yield a fuller Relationship Episode, replete with Wish, Response of Other, and Response of Self. The therapist then writes down #2: Porsche driver, and fills in the columns with the information he has from this.

RE #2: Porsche

Wish	Response of the Other	Response of Self
give him a piece of my mind, give him a dirty look	get shot	does nothing (behavior), feels irritated, frustrated, disappointed in self (affect)

One Relationship Episode does not a CCRT make. During the assessment phase, the therapist should collect four to six REs in order to ensure consistency, relevance, and accuracy of the components. After the four to six REs and their components (Wish, Response of Other, and Response of Self) have been collected, the therapist scans down the columns of Ws, ROs, and RSs looking for overarching themes, bundling together those Ws that seem to be related. He or she does the same for those ROs and those RSs.

With Steven, the four Wishes (only two of which appear here) seem to be to let his boss know not to call him Stevie; certainly to let him know that he has other reports to work on and cannot get the Adams report out on short notice; to give the rude driver a piece of his mind; to give the driver at least a dirty look. These four Ws seem thematically related, can be bundled together, represented by an overarching W: to speak up assertively when feeling mistreated. The same process is repeated by bundling and developing an overarching Response of Other and an overarching Response of Self. With this patient, the overarching W, RO, and RS are:

W: to speak up assertively when wronged

RO: to retaliate

RS: to say nothing; to feel angry, humiliated, and small

The therapist would present these overarching components to the patient as his or her CCRT *after* the assessment phase but before beginning formal therapy. A sample of how this might sound is provided on page 73, above.

The therapist then asks the patient: "What do you think of what I've said. Is this an important area we might explore?" Usually, patients embrace the CCRT and find it quite illuminating. Steven responded, "Absolutely. It's important. That's exactly what I've been saying. I never thought about it so clearly before, but that's what's really been happening to me." Why do patients find the CCRT so engaging? They connect with it so well because all the therapist is doing is offering the patient a highly distilled, concentrated, and integrated narrative of what the patient has already told him! It is all in the patient's words and, most important, from the patient's perspective.

In the occasional situation where the patient does not take to the CCRT, the therapist might ask, "What seems to be wrong or inaccurate with it?" Or the therapist might say, "Well, let's look at it a piece at a time." The therapist then explores each of the three components to discover which one doesn't seem to jibe with the patient's experience. For example, the therapist might say,

> I mentioned you have a wish to speak up when you feel wronged, and I got this idea from, for example, your telling me how much you wanted to give that Porsche driver a piece of your mind when he cut you off; or how you wanted to let your boss know that calling you "Stevie" was insulting. Does that make sense to you?

Evaluating each of the three components with the patient usually allows some fine-tuning—using a different word or two—which then allows the patient to feel comfortable with the CCRT. The following section of this chapter will focus on the descriptive and psychodynamic goals of the CCRT approach in the context of psychodynamic psychotherapy.

GOALS OF PSYCHODYNAMIC PSYCHOTHERAPY USING THE CCRT APPROACH

Descriptively, the goals of CCRT psychotherapy are a reduction in the patient's symptoms and a promotion of personality maturation. Psychodynamically, these twin goals are achieved by the patient's being able to actualize his or her Wish rather than respond by a defensive Response of Self. The actualization of the W and subsequent elemination of the need to respond in the self limiting, regressive RS manner are accomplished in therapy by the patient's identifying, working through, and resolving the transference-based perspective of the Response of the Other.

With Steven Wright, one of the goals is facilitating his actualizing the Wish, that is, facilitating his capacity to speak up and voice his concerns when unfairly or unjustifiably treated instead of regressively saying nothing, but feeling angry, frustrated, and small (Response of Self). The work that catalyzed this process resulted in his increasing awareness of how his present expectation of "being blown out of the water" (Response of the Other) was a transference to others in the present as if they were the overbearing, enraged father of his childhood. Previously unconscious memories and affects surfaced during treatment and were worked through by being repetitively recalled, reconstructed, and re-experienced. As this working through occurred, the influence of his past relationship with his father on his present view of others loosened. As a result, Steven was less at risk for viewing individuals in the present the way he experienced his father in the past, and the distorted view that they were poised to "blow him out of the water" should he speak up diminished.

The "Regressive Wish" Caveat

Although the dynamic goal is to facilitate the patient's actualizing his or her Wish, there are certain situations where it is countertherapeutic to aid the patient in actualizing his or her W. This situation occurs when the W is regressive: having to do with desires to destroy, mutilate, or be sadistic, or representing desires to be overly dependent, to retreat, or to isolate oneself from others. For example, a patient might say,

> I really can't stand my mother-in-law. She treats me in an intolerable, demeaning way. There actually were times when I think about punching her in the face. If there were not a law against it, who knows? I might. I really don't want to go to jail though.

Here, the Wish seems to be "I'd like to punch her in the face." This is a regressive wish, and the therapist does not help the patient actualize regressive wishes.

Once identified, a regressive wish is viewed as a Response of Self and not as a Wish. The therapist then searches for and identifies the unarticulated real W. For example, with the above patient, the therapist might inquire:

Therapist What makes you so mad at her?

Patient She's rude and very demeaning to me. I can't stand it.

Therapist So, you wish that she would treat you with respect?

Patient Absolutely. I mean it doesn't even have to be with respect. If she would just treat me in a friendly way, it would really help our relationship.

With a bit of exploration, the Wish becomes "I wish my mother-in-law would treat me in a friendly, likeable manner"; the Response of Other is "She treats me with disdain"; and the Response of Self is "I've kept this bottled up for a long time, feel hurt and angry, and have fantasies of punching her in the face." The real W, "I wish she would treat me in a friendly and civil manner," is something that we can help him attain in treatment.

THE CCRT METHOD OF PSYCHODYNAMIC PSYCHOTHERAPY

Once the therapist has presented the CCRT to the patient and the patient embraces its relevance, formal psychodynamic psychotherapy can begin. During psychotherapy, the therapist listens almost exclusively for Relationship Episodes, for narratives about interactions the patient has with others, and pays little attention to anything else. Therapy falls into three phases, and the therapeutic focus and goals differ in each phase.

Beginning Phase: Demonstrating the Ubiquity of the CCRT

The goal during the beginning phase of psychotherapy is focused on helping the patient become more aware of how frequently the CCRT is activated and rules his or her life (Book, 1998). With Steven, this meant listening to narratives that he spontaneously related and pointing out to him how frequently he automatically shuts down and says nothing (Response of Self) rather than appropriately speaking up (Wish), out of a fear that to do so would invite retaliation (Response of the Other)—that is, how frequently his CCRT controls his behavior. The goal is to make a repetitive, unconscious behavior conscious, so that Steven would have more of an opportunity to see the price he pays for such automatic, maladaptive behavior. Simultaneously, the therapist encourages him to attempt new and more successful ways of behaving. The major technique the therapist uses is one of confrontation: bringing the patient's awareness to an external or internal reality to which he or she is oblivious. The following scenario, which occurred in the fourth session, is one such example:

Steven: Sorry I'm late. It took me a little longer than I thought to get some shopping done.

Therapist: What happened exactly?

Steven: Well, I could have been on time, but as I was waiting in line, this woman inadvertently got in front of me and then, when she was at the cashier, she couldn't find her credit card right away.

Noting that with his words, "this woman inadvertently got in front of me," Steven is beginning an RE narrative, the therapist is poised to further explore the influence of Steven's CCRT on this interaction, as this vignette goes on to show:

Therapist: What do you mean, "she inadvertently cut in front of you?"

Steven: Well, I was standing there and she just walked in front of me while she was digging around in her purse for a credit card.

Therapist: So, how did you feel...what happened when she did this?

Steven: Nothing happened.

Therapist: How did you feel?

Steven: I felt a bit irritated, but it was no big thing.

Therapist: You felt irritated. What went on in your mind?

Steven: Well, I wanted to tell her to get to the back of the line.

Therapist: And?

Steven: And I didn't.

Therapist: It sounds familiar, doesn't it?

Steven: What do you mean?

Therapist: Well, she unfairly cut in front of you and you had a wish to tell her to move, but you didn't. Instead, you kept quiet but ended up feeling irritated, frustrated, and small. And this is what we've been talking about, isn't it? How frequently you find yourself in positions when you've been treated unfairly, you have a wish to speak up, but instead of doing so you remain quiet and feel small. And this is why I've suggested you feel tense.

Steven: Oh, my goodness! I hadn't thought of it. It's exactly that same pattern. It's like you pointed out in the last session when I didn't say anything about my steak being well done instead of rare at that restaurant. It ruined my dinner, but I never said a thing! This seems to happen all the time.

In this interchange, the therapist confronts Steven with the hitherto unseen power of his CCRT. The more aware the patient is of the ubiquity of how he or she inhibits the Wish, the more motivated and poised he or she is to explore more about the reasons why this behavior continues.

Second Phase: Working Through the Response of the Other (RO)

This phase is crucial to the promotion of personality growth that liberates the patient from those unconscious forces that constituted his or her Response of the Other, so that he or she is free to actualize his or her Wish. In particular, the focus in this phase is helping the patient understand that the RO—the expectation, in Steven's case, of being "blown out of the water"—is related to early childhood experiences with his or her caretakers more than it is the reality of the current situation.

With Steven, it is helping him understand how being raised by a sharp-tempered, highly critical father who frequently yelled at and fought with Steven's mother, along with his sense of frightened helplessness, was an ongoing childhood experience that unconsciously colored his expectations of others in his adult life. Put somewhat differently, because of his experiences in a household with an angry, critical father, Steven approached everyone in his adult world with the unconscious expectation that, like his father, they too would treat him in a frighteningly angry manner if he were to actualize his wishes to speak up. This information about Steven's family was elicited during the assessment phase.

By using confrontational and interpretive techniques, the goal in this phase is to help Steven link his early childhood experiences to his current adult expectations of others. A second crucial goal is to facilitate Steven's increasing awareness of how his unconscious feelings about his parents for exposing him to these battles, and never having had the safety to experience and discuss these forbidden, frightening feelings, maintains this transference response to others in his adult life, as the next vignette illustrates:

Therapist Steven, we've seen over and over again in the last number of sessions how you tend to remain silent instead of speaking up when wronged. And it seems—from what you and I have discussed—that you remain quiet out of a fear that if you speak up you're going to be blasted out of the water. So, I'm wondering where in the world you got this idea that speaking up will end in your being blasted out of the water?

Steven I'm not sure. I don't know.

Therapist Well, I'm more interested in what comes to mind than what you know for sure. So, what comes to mind when you think about this?

Steven Well, maybe it has something to do with my childhood, growing up in a home where there was a lot of yelling and screaming.

Therapist Tell me more about that. What do you remember?

Steven It was terrible; he would rant and rave. It made me very frightened. I couldn't stand it.

Therapist And so what did you do?

Steven Nothing. What could I do? I was just a little kid. I was scared stiff. I wanted them to stop. I wanted him to stop all that yelling at mom. I couldn't do anything. I was just a little kid.

Therapist It is understandable that as a little tyke you would be so frightened and fearful of speaking up. And I tend to think that that experience and those feelings have become carried over to everyone in your life.

This interpretive focus is repeated over and over. At one point, as Steven becomes more aware of how angry he is at being inconvenienced with people in his present, the therapist also interprets how he might have also felt angry at his father in the past.

Therapist Yes. You certainly sounded angry at that salesperson for his disdainful rudeness. Makes me wonder whether you recall ever feeling angry as a child, at your father, for example.

Steven No. As a child I was a goody-two-shoes like I told you. No angry thoughts at all . . . except, when I couldn't fall asleep . . . now that I think of it . . . I used to count as high as I could. To give myself a focus I used to pretend I was in an airplane dropping bombs, and I'd count the bombs as they made these wonderful floral patterns when they exploded. This counting lulled me to sleep.

Therapist Well that's something. You know, maybe the floral patterns helped disguise how angry and destructive these images were—after all, they were fantasies of bombs falling and exploding. And maybe these images had something to do with how angry you felt. Like a ticking time-bomb waiting to go off.

More interpretive work like this helped Steven become aware of how angry he felt as a child toward his father. With more exploration, it became apparent that his repression and denial of any angry feelings as a child was a reflection of what is called his "denied identification with the aggressor." That is, because Steven so despised his father's behavior, he could not tolerate any angry feelings within himself, because he interpreted any anger, or even assertiveness, as meaning that he was as furious and potentially as destructive as the father he hated. The last thing he wanted was to be like his father. Steven also recognized how he feared that any suggestion of assertion—any behavior more than passivity—might result in his father's becoming enraged with him. Further interpretive work helped him to identify and become more comfortable with the angry feelings he had as a child toward his father and angry feelings he had toward others in his adult life, and his ongoing belief that to be angry was to be like his father and to invite retaliation.

As Steven began to tolerate angry feelings and recognize his denied anger at his father (based on his fears that being angry would mean being a terrible person as he viewed his father to be and that being angry would simply invite massive retaliation from his father), he became freer to experience, tolerate, and contain his angry feelings in the present. Tolerating his anger allowed him to speak up appropriately when wronged without fear of retaliation. That is, he was able to actualize his Wish. As he became more able to do so, he no longer had to rely on his previously inhibiting traits of remaining quiet and passive, feeling angry, small, and tense. That is, he no longer had to respond in a Response of Self manner.

Third Phase: Termination

In the final phase of treatment, termination is brought up, and common issues relating to loss, abandonment, sadness, and anger are all scanned for, identified, and worked through. When using the CCRT approach, however, the therapist particularly scans for enactments. Enactments are the phenomena by which the patient silently pantomimes his Response of Self, because at an unconscious level he or she experiences the therapist as behaving in a Response of the Other manner. In researching the consistency of the CCRT as it emerges to the therapist and as it is experienced with others, Fried, Crits-Christoph, and Luborsky (1998) concluded that "patients demonstrate pervasive relationship patterns that can be discerned when they interact with the therapist as well as with other people." They found that correctly matched pairs of therapists' Relationship Episodes and other-person CCRTs were more similar than were mismatched pairs. This was found for all CCRT components and reached statistical significance for the W and RS components. Their study concluded that "the patient's relationship with the therapist has parallels with the patient's relationships with other people" concerning the CCRT.

These researchers also draw attention to how this study reinforces Freud's concept of transference: that the patient's experience with the therapist partially parallels the pattern of experience with other people in the present as well as in the past. This latter conclusion supports findings from an earlier study by Luborsky, Mellon, et al. (1985), which demonstrated a correspondence between nine of Freud's observations about transference with the Response of the Other in the CCRT.

For example, after 18 months of therapy, Steven brought up the idea of termination, stating that many of his goals had been met: He was feeling far better most of the time, was no longer tense and anxious, and was able to easily speak up when appropriate (Wish) without fearing that doing so would provoke retaliation (Response of the Other). After discussing this for two sessions, both therapist and Steven agreed that they would terminate after four more weekly sessions.

In the next session, the therapist was aware that Steven was no longer speaking up as actively and forcibly as he had. He wondered if this was a mini-regression associated with termination and whether this resurgence of passivity represented a return of Steven's old Response of Self—biting his tongue, remaining silent, and looking tense. He also conceptualized that this shift in Steven's behavior might represent the reemergence of his old Response of the Other—retaliation—that may have been stimulated by the decision to terminate. In other words, from a CCRT perspective, the therapist's hypothesis was that Steven unconsciously equated the mutual decision to terminate as reflecting the therapist's anger at him (the reemergence of his RO).

As he pointed this out, Steven was able to say,

> You know it's funny. Both of us agreed to stop, but I began to think that you agreed too quickly. Now that you mention it, somehow I had these ideas that you were pissed off at me. That maybe I was rude to you, or that you found it offensive that I would even bring up this idea of stopping after you had been so helpful to me. I think I kind of saw you as retaliating because I had offended you by bringing up the idea of stopping.

With these words, Steven describes his awareness of the reemergence and resurgence of his old Response of the Other—expecting retaliation—and the reemergence of his old Response of Self—remaining silent and passive in order to ward off the expected retaliation.

Enactment during termination is not an unwelcome phenomenon because it allows the therapist and patient a "second chance" to revisit, understand, and further resolve the patient's CCRT in a here-and-now, affect-laden way. This second chance further consolidates the gains the patient has made during treatment. As Steven and his therapist used this enactment to further consolidate the gains he made during treatment, Steven began working actively and assertively on his ambivalent feelings around stopping therapy. Although he wondered if he would maintain these gains after termination, his therapist said,

> Although you will be stopping treatment soon, it doesn't mean that therapy ends. You have learned a great deal about yourself, your concerns about speaking up, and your fears about retaliation that are based on your early childhood experiences. The skills you have developed you will be able to use on your own.

At the completion of therapy, Steven had become more spontaneous in speaking up in situations where he felt unfairly treated and was far less concerned that doing so would irritate or anger others. When contacted 3 months later for a brief follow-up interview, Steven said that there had been situations when he spoke up where others did become irritated with him, but he found that although distressed, he was still able to stand his ground. He also found that such experiences did not interfere with his newly found capacity to speak up in subsequent situations where he felt wronged.

Most probably, his Relationship Episodes at this time would illustrate his actually speaking up in situations where he felt wronged, rather than merely *wishing* to speak up but instead remaining silent while feeling belittled.

CONCLUSIONS

The CCRT approach in psychodynamic psychotherapy enables clinicians to identify, conceptualize, address, and resolve transference distortions, repetition compulsions, and compromise solutions, as they are contained in everyday narratives that the patients tell about interactions between them and others in their environment. This process results in a decrease in symptoms and, in many cases, a promotion of positive personality growth. From an outcome perspective, Crits-Christoph and Luborsky (1998) measured the pervasiveness of the CCRT in sessions drawn from the early parts of treatment with the pervasiveness of the CCRT in sessions from the latter parts of treatment. The pervasiveness was measured by the frequency with which relationship conflicts appeared in Relationship Episodes. They compared the frequency of each of the three components from early sessions to later sessions in treatment. Finally, they measured the presence of symptom occurrences in sessions from early as compared to later parts of treatment. These researchers found that CCRT pervasiveness decreased from early to late treatment, that the frequency of the Wish remained rather constant but that frequency of the Response of the Other and Response of Self decreased significantly, and that the decrease in the CCRT pervasiveness was associated with a decrease in symptom occurrence.

These findings support the dynamic goal of psychotherapy: that the Wish should not decrease but rather should be actualized. This occurs dynamically by working through the Response of the Other and its transference implications, so that the RO diminishes as does the defensive Response of Self. These findings also support the concept that changes in the CCRT are associated with a decrease in symptoms.

Benefits of the CCRT approach lie in the ease and validity with which these underlying dynamics can be clearly uncovered, the guidance it offers the clinician in responding empathically and therapeutically, and the rigorous research that has supported its conceptual and therapeutic utility.

Future developments of the CCRT may include research into how therapeutic benefits may accrue as a result of modifying the CCRT approach to particular diagnostic categories, specific age groupings, and particular therapeutic modalities (couple therapy, family therapy, group therapy). How combined therapies—such as brief CCRT psychotherapy and medication—amplify benefits to the patient is another promising area. Recent advances in neuroimaging may allow researchers to link brain activity and CCRT accuracy.

Finally, in nonclinical settings, psychodynamic organizational consultants have an opportunity to use the CCRT as a method of understanding role problems in organizations and illuminating how specific maladaptive organizational cultures interfere with the corporation's tasks, goals, and ultimately its profitability (Kets de Vries, 2002).

REFERENCES

Book, H. (1998). *How to practice brief psychodynamic psychotherapy: The Core Conflictual Relationship Theme method.* Washington, DC: American Psychological Association.

Crits-Christoph, P., & Luborsky, L. (1998). Changes in CCRT pervasiveness during psychotherapy. In L. Luborsky & P. Crits-Christoph (Eds.), *Understanding transference: The Core Conflictual Relationship Theme method* (pp. 151-164). Washington, DC: American Psychological Association.

Eells, T. D. (1997). Psychotherapy case formulation: History and current status. In T. D. Eells (Ed.), *Handbook of psychotherapy case formulation* (pp. 1-2). New York: Guilford.

Fried, D., Crits-Christoph, P., & Luborsky, L. (1998). The parallel of the CCRT for the therapist with the CCRT for other people. In L. Luborsky & P. Crits-Christoph (Eds.), *Understanding transference: The Core Conflictual Relationship Theme method* (pp. 165-174). Washington, DC: American Psychological Association.

Horowitz, M., Luborsky, L., & Popp, C. (1991). A comparison of the role relationship models configuration and the Core Conflictual Relationship Theme. In M. Horowitz (Ed.), *Person schemas and maladaptive interpersonal behavior* (pp. 213-109). Chicago: University of Chicago Press.

Kets de Vries, M. F. R. (2002). *The leadership mystique: A user's manual for the human enterprise.* New York: Prentice Hall.

Luborsky, L. (1984). *Principles of psychoanalytic psychotherapy: A manual for supportive-expressive treatment.* New York: Basic Books.

Luborsky, L. (1997). The Core Conflictual Relationship Theme (CCRT): A basic case formulation method. In T. D. Eells (Ed.), *Handbook of psychotherapy case formulation* (pp. 58-83). New York: Guilford.

Luborsky, L. (1998a). The convergence of Freud's observations about transference with the CCRT evidence. In L. Luborsky & P. Crits-Christoph (Eds.), *Understanding transference: The Core Conflictual Relationship Theme method* (pp. 307-325). Washington, DC: American Psychological Association.

Luborsky, L. (1998b). The early life of the idea for the Core Conflictual Relationship Theme method. In L. Luborsky & P. Crits-Christoph (Eds.), *Understanding transference: The Core Conflictual Relationship Theme method* (pp. 3-14). Washington, DC: American Psychological Association.

Luborsky, L., Barber, J. P., Binder, J., Curtis, J., Dahl, H., Horowitz, L. M., Horowitz, M., Perry, J. C., Schacht, T., Silberschatz, G., & Teller, V. (1993). Transference-related measures: A new therapy-based class. In N. Miller, L. Luborsky, J. P. Barber, & J. Docherty (Eds.), *Psychodynamic treatment research: A handbook for clinical practice* (pp. 326-421). New York: Basic Books.

Luborsky, L., Barber, J. P., & Diguer, L. (1992). The meanings of narratives told during psychotherapy: The fruits of a new observational unit. *Psychotherapy Research*, 2(4), 227-290.

Luborsky, L., & Diguer, L. (1998). The reliability of the CCRT measure: Results from eight samples. In L. Luborsky & P. Crits-Christoph (Eds.), *Understanding transference: The Core Conflictual Relationship Theme method* (pp. 97-108). Washington, DC: American Psychological Association.

Luborsky, L., Mellon, J., Cohen, K., van Ravenswaay, P., Hole, A., Childress, A., Ming, S., Crits-Christoph, P., Levine, F., & Alexander, K. (1985). A verification of Freud's grandest clinical hypothesis: The transference. *Clinical Psychology Review, 5,* 231-246.

Popp, C., Diguer, L., Luborsky, L., Faude, J., Johnson, S., Morris, M., Schaffer, N., Schaffler, P., & Schmidt, K. (1998). Study 2: The parallel of the CCRT from waking narratives with the CCRT from dreams: A further validation. In L. Luborsky & P. Crits-Christoph (Eds.), *Understanding transference: The Core Conflictual Relationship Theme method* (pp. 187-196). Washington, DC: American Psychological Association.

Popp, C., Luborsky, L., & Crits-Christoph, P. (1998). Study 1: The parallel of the CCRT from waking narratives with the CCRT from dreams. In L. Luborsky & P. Crits-Christoph (Eds.), *Understanding transference: The Core Conflictual Relationship Theme method* (pp. 175-187). Washington, DC: American Psychological Association.

CHAPTER 5

"What's the Story?"
Working With Narrative in Experiential Psychotherapy

LYNNE E. ANGUS

JENNIFER LEWIN

BEVERLEY BOUFFARD

DEBRA ROTONDI-TREVISAN

OVERVIEW

The contribution of emotional processes (Greenberg, 2002), empathy (Bohart & Greenberg, 1997), and client reflexivity (Rennie, 1998) to productive experiential psychotherapeutic outcomes has been well documented in the psychotherapy practice and research literature. In contrast, the importance of client narrative expression—in particular the narrative disclosure of emotionally salient, autobiographical memories—for the facilitation of experiential engagement, emotional arousal, and personal meaning-making has rarely been addressed. In this chapter, we hope to fill this gap in the experiential practice and research literature.

Specifically, it is our view that clients' disclosure of emotionally charged personal narratives is foundational to the emergence of emotional responses in therapy sessions and contributes to the concretization of new meanings in brief experiential psychotherapy. Moreover, the sharing of emotionally significant personal memories is central to the construction of shared contexts of meaning and understanding between clients and therapists and the development of a strong therapeutic bond and alliance. In this chapter, we will first present a comprehensive Narrative Process model of therapeutic

AUTHORS' NOTE: Correspondence regarding this chapter should be sent to the authors at York University, 4700 Keele Street, Toronto, Ontario, Canada M3J 1P3 or to langus@yorku.ca.

change that is coherent with the fundamental assumptions of experiential approaches generally and process experiential psychotherapy (Greenberg, 2002; Greenberg, Rice, & Elliott, 1993) in particular. Next we will provide evidence for the importance of narrative expression in process experiential therapy practice. Finally, we will identify key narrative strategies undertaken by experienced process experiential therapists and their clients when they achieved successful outcomes.

THE NARRATIVE PROCESS MODEL

The Narrative Process Model (Angus, Levitt, & Hardtke, 1999) views narrative expression as arising out of a dialectical interplay of autobiographical memory, emotion, and reflexive meaning-making processes. While personally significant narratives are marked by the expression and evocation of emotions, the significance of emotions can only be understood when organized within a narrative framework that identifies what is felt, about whom, and in relation to what need or issue. The Narrative Process Model is in agreement with a dialectical constructivist view of experiential therapeutic change. Core assumptions underlying this model include (a) client agency, (b) human reflexivity and meaning-making, (c) the importance of emotion schemes and emotion processing for the facilitation of second order or identity change, and (d) the co-constructive nature of the client-therapist dialogue. While we are in full agreement with the basic tenets of a dialectical-constructivist model (Greenberg & Pascual-Leone, 1995, 1997, 2001), which views emotional processing and emergent meaning-making processes as central to the inception of change in psychotherapy, we also believe that narrative expression and the disclosure of salient personal memories are foundational to the inception of change experiences in experiential therapy.

According to the Narrative Process Model of self-change, all forms of successful psychotherapy involve the articulation, elaboration, and transformation of the client's life story (Angus & Hardtke, 1994; Angus, Hardtke, & Levitt, 1996; Angus et al., 1999). Personal identity is construed as the coherent integration of emotionally salient personal narratives, which either explicitly or implicitly represent core beliefs about self and others. The emotional tone of the narrative—anger, sadness, joy, or fear—appears to be one of the primary ways in which personal memories and narratives are linked to one another. Accordingly, implicit emotion themes and the personal memories they contain become the lens through which we classify, tell a story about, and make meaning of our new interpersonal experiences with others in the world.

In the Narrative Process Model, therapeutic change is viewed as entailing a process of dialectical shifts between narrative storytelling (external narrative mode), emotional differentiation (internal narrative mode), and reflexive meaning-making modes of inquiry.

External Narrative Sequences

In psychotherapy, it is crucial that clients remember and articulate real or imagined, past or recent events to fill in the gaps in the narrative that may have been forgotten or never fully acknowledged and therefore not understood (Angus et al., 1999). This therapeutic process is represented by the external narrative mode of the Narrative Processes Model, which addresses the question of "what happened?" (Angus & Hardtke, 1994). An external narrative sequence can be a personal story that is either autobiographical or nonautobiographical in content. Recent research findings have established that 75% of all external sequences, extracted from 180 experiential therapy sessions, contained an autobiographical memory.

In addition, external sequences may entail either a description of a specific event, a general description of many repeated similar events, or a composite of many specific events (Angus et al., 1996). The autobiographical external provides the client with the chance to engage in storytelling, to create a visually rich picture for the therapist by means of verbally descriptive and specific details of life experiences and events (Angus et al., 1999). In fact, the description of "what happened" might also entail nonautobiographical information or chronicles of factual information or events.

Internal Narrative Sequences

Clients also need to be fully engaged in the lived experience of an event in order to bring to awareness and fully articulate tacit feelings and emotions. This is achieved when both the therapist and client engage in the detailed unfolding and exploration of associated sensations and emotions, which can emerge in the retelling of an autobiographical memory. The internal narrative process mode is associated with this process and entails the description and elaboration of subjective feelings, reactions, and emotions connected with an event and addresses the question of "what was felt?" during the event. In addition, the internal narrative mode addresses what was felt during the therapy session in relation to the event.

The function of the internal mode of inquiry for clients is to share with the therapist their reexperienced feelings and emotions that are associated with the retelling of a particular event (external mode) or to articulate newly emerging feelings and emotions occurring during the therapy hour (Angus et al., 1999). Research supports the notion that emotional disclosure regarding traumatic events can result in positive immunological and psychological effects for survivors (Harber & Pennebaker, 1992; Pennebaker & Seagal, 1999).

Reflexive Narrative Sequences

The final goal of productive therapy involves the reflexive analysis of articulated experiences, which often leads to the construction of new meanings and perspectives on situations and can result in a reconstructed narrative. This reconstructed narrative may either support or challenge the implicit beliefs about self and others that contribute to the client's life story or *macronarrative* (Hardtke, 1996). The reflexive narrative mode represents this therapeutic process and is characterized as the reflexive analyses of events and subjective feelings. Therefore, this narrative process mode addresses the question of "what does it mean?" in relation to what happened or what was felt during an event.

Each of the narrative process modes of inquiry has a corresponding therapeutic goal: (a) to help clients to fill in the gaps of what has been forgotten or never fully acknowledged and, hence, understood; (b) to help clients to "re-live" the event and to better articulate and understand it, perhaps for the first time; and (c) to aid the client in forming new understandings about the self and others. Together, the three narrative modes of inquiry and their accompanying therapeutic goals are vital and contribute to the development of more coherent, emotionally differentiated personal narratives, which provide individuals with a greater understanding of themselves and their interactions with others. In essence, the narrative process modes are viewed as essential components of a distinctive mode of human meaning-making, which constructs, maintains, and, when needed, revises our sense of self in the world.

The developmental psychologist Jerome Bruner (1986, 1990) points out that narrative organizes and integrates actions, emotions, and meanings within the context of an unfolding sequential timeline. He suggests that coherent personal narratives entail the articulation and integration of the dual landscapes of narrative action (e.g., describing the scene, setting, and actions of the actors) and consciousness (e.g., articulating the emotions, beliefs, intentions, goals, and purposes of self and others) from the situated perspective of the narrator. From a Narrative Process Model (Angus et al., 1999) perspective, accessing and articulating the client's world of emotions, beliefs, expectations, intentions, and goals—what Bruner (1990) has termed the landscape of consciousness—is critical for the emergence of new ways of seeing and experiencing longstanding relationship problems and coming to terms with significant personal loss. The reflexive decentering from and then reengagement with distressing life experiences, from different relational vantage points, facilitates the articulation of new understandings about the self in relation to others. It is the reflexive processing of emotions, beliefs, hopes, needs, motives, intentions, and goals (landscape of consciousness)—and their inclusion in the events of the problem stories or narratives (landscape of action)—which enables the experience to be fully understood and accepted as part of the life story. In essence, it is the integration of the landscape of action (a description of the sequential, linear unfolding of an event which answers the question of what happened) with the landscape of consciousness (the internal responses of self and others which address the questions of what was felt and what it means) that enables the construction of a coherent and meaning-filled narrative account of our interpersonal experiences with others in the world.

To conduct an empirical investigation of narrative processes in psychotherapy, a systematic method for the identification of therapy discourse parameters associated with narrative-processing modes was developed (Angus & Hardtke, 1994; Angus et al., 1999). The Narrative Processes Coding System (NPCS) and revised manual (Angus et al., 1996) has evolved from the Narrative Process Model and was designed for application to psychotherapy transcripts. The NPCS provides researchers with a rational, systematic method of segmenting therapy transcripts, regardless of therapeutic modality. The NPCS has demonstrated both construct validity and good levels of interrater agreement in a series of recent psychotherapy process studies (Angus & Hardtke, 1994; Angus et al., 1999; Gonçalves, Korman, & Angus, 2000; Gonçalves, Machado, Korman, & Angus, 2002; Hardtke, Levitt, & Angus, in press; Levitt & Angus, 2000; Levitt, Korman, & Angus, 2000; Levitt, Korman, Angus, & Hardtke, 1997).

The NPCS entails a two-step process that enables the researcher to (a) reliably subdivide and characterize therapy session transcripts into topic segments according to content shifts in verbal dialogue and (b) further subdivide and characterize these topic segments in terms of one of three narrative-process mode types. The narrative types are (a) External Narrative Process Sequences, which include descriptions of events (past, present, and/or future; actual or imagined); (b) Internal Narrative Process Sequences, which include a subjective/experiential description of experience; and (c) Reflexive Narrative Process Sequences, which entail recursive questioning and meaning-making processes in relation to beliefs, actions, and emotions represented in current, past, and/or future events. The NPCS provides an empirical method for identifying the occurrence of the three narrative process modes as well as the dialectical shifts between modes, as they occur over time and across sessions. Accordingly, the Narrative Process Model and NPCS can be used as a heuristic to explore the interplay of the dual landscapes of action and consciousness in the context of psychotherapy sessions.

Over the past 5 years, we have had the opportunity to intensively investigate narrative process modes and shifts in the context of 12 full case analyses of clients undergoing brief process experiential therapy treatment for depression (Angus et al., 1999) and unfinished business (Angus & Bouffard, 2002). The findings emerging from this extended inquiry into narrative, emotion, and meaning-making processes will now be presented, with clinical examples for key findings.

NARRATIVE PROCESSES AND PROCESS EXPERIENTIAL PSYCHOTHERAPY

Process experiential psychotherapy is a distinctive, emotion-focused, constructivist therapy rooted in an integration of both gestalt (Perls, 1973) and client-centered (Rogers, 1951) psychotherapy approaches. As such, it shares a common faith in humanity's innate capacity for self-reflective awareness and for movement toward positive growth and self-development (Greenberg et al., 1993). While the gestalt approach provides therapists with a set of interventions designed to evoke problematic thoughts, feelings, and behaviors, the client-centered approach encourages therapists to adopt an empathic, prizing (positive, accepting), and genuine attunement to the client's emotionally salient experiences.

To build a strong therapeutic alliance, process experiential therapists first establish a secure, empathic relationship with their clients. Once established, gestalt techniques are introduced to facilitate the resolution of longstanding problems in living. The objective of the therapy is to access and restructure habitual maladaptive emotional states—worthlessness, anxious dependence, powerlessness, abandonment, and invalidation—that are viewed as the source of psychological distress such as depression (Greenberg, Watson, & Goldman, 1998). Through the therapeutic process, adaptive emotions are accessed to transform maladaptive emotions and to organize the person for adaptive responses. This process of changing emotion is thought to work by the use of specific therapeutic techniques that help stimulate arousal of emotion and its processing.

In two-chair work, clients articulate their experience or perception of an event from two different viewpoints: the critical self and the experiencing self. The critical self is instructed to express harsh criticisms or negative self-statements to the experiencing self to evoke a strong emotional response or reaction. Reactions such as hopelessness, fear, or shame are then transformed by accessing primary emotions, such as sadness in response to loss or anger in response to violation. When more primary emotions are activated, clients are encouraged to combat the negative cognitions with these and their associated needs. This leads to a softening of the harsh criticism and a negotiation and integration of the two previously disparate aspects of self (Greenberg et al., 1993).

Unfinished business is a gestalt therapy term that signifies the presence of longstanding, unresolved relationship concerns, which are often accompanied by feelings of burden and resentment. Empty chair work for unfinished business involves emotional expression of previously suppressed primary emotion, such as hurt and anger toward the imaginary significant other in the chair. This intervention leads to an expression of unmet needs. Clients take the perspective of the other at this point, which leads to the accessing of a new, often more positive view of the other. The resolution involves accepting and forgiving the other or, in cases of abuse, holding the other accountable for his or her actions.

Greenberg (2002) states that a central task for experiential psychotherapists is the facilitation of client emotional processes such that primary adaptive emotional responses can be accessed, articulated, and meaningfully understood. From a Narrative Process Model perspective, it is the client's narrative description of emotionally salient, autobiographical memory narratives—external narrative sequences—that provides the essential experiential starting point for reflexive processing of evoked emotions and the subsequent articulation of related personal meanings. It is our view that emergent personal meanings, arising from the processing of adaptive emotions, exist within a tacit narrative schema in which a new story emerges to account for what was felt, in relation to whom, and about what need or concern. Moreover, when emotions shift, clients are impelled to articulate and story the new emotional landscape they find themselves inhabiting. New views of self and other in terms of probable intentions, beliefs, and goals also shift and change in the quest to create an emotionally coherent story that integrates the dual narrative landscapes of action and consciousness.

An intensive analysis of more than 18 therapy dyads and 200 therapy sessions, drawn from process experiential therapy clients undergoing treatment for depression and unfinished business make it clear that clients specialize in the narration and disclosure of salient personal memories in their therapy sessions. In the context of sessions drawn from six brief process experiential therapy dyads undergoing treatment for depression (Greenberg & Angus, 1995), Rotondi-Trevisan (2002) found that 74% of the external narrative sequences, or 668 external sequences, met criteria for personal autobiographical memory narrative (Singer & Moffitt, 1992). Stated another way, clients disclosed six autobiographical memories, on average, to their therapists in the context of process experiential treatment sessions.

These findings support the notion that it is through the telling of personal stories that we show ourselves to others and construct shared understandings with engaged listeners. Moreover, our intensive narrative-process analyses indicate that therapists' attunement to clients' autobiographical memory narratives serves two key functions in a successful experiential therapy relationship: (a) the development of a strong therapeutic alliance and (b) the evocation and differentiation of emotion processes for the articulation of new meanings and perspectives on self. We will now provide a fuller description of each of these key contributions in the context of clinical examples drawn from process experiential therapy sessions.

Narrative Expression and the Therapeutic Alliance

Clients use the description of vivid autobiographical memories to tell their stories to therapists and to be more fully understood. Autobiographical memory storytelling facilitates the development of a strong, trusting therapeutic bond in which both client and therapist co-create a sense of shared experiencing, knowing, and interpersonal understanding. The therapist's capacity to attend empathically to a client's key concerns, as conveyed in personal stories, contributes to an early development of a strong, secure therapeutic alliance by instilling a sense of basic trust in the client toward the therapist. Experiential therapists, in turn, invite their clients to affectively and reflexively explore and expand on these vivid memories in the therapy sessions. New meanings that emerge from the exploration of emotion and meaning schemes are then concretized by clients in the context of telling new stories about life experiences, stories that represent new ways of seeing or interacting with others.

In the following sequences, the process experiential therapist empathically supports the client (a) to describe a detailed unfolding of the sequence of events that frame a traumatic episode (landscape of action; External Narrative Sequences) and (b) to differentiate emotions, intentions, and appraisals experienced in the context of the trauma event (landscape of consciousness; Internal and reflexive narrative sequence shifts). It is the integration of the landscape of action and consciousness that facilitates the co-construction of a coherent trauma narrative in the therapy session. The following sequence was drawn from one process experiential therapy dyad with good outcome who participated in a clinical trial for unfinished business at the York Psychotherapy Center.

Client I just can't you know, because the images of certain things like that are so clear in my mind and it was so long ago *[shift to external narrative mode and the description of a single event memory]* And I said that to my sister yesterday, that night is so clear to me

Therapist the night she died

Client the night she killed herself. It's so clear, I can remember everything

Therapist just like it happened yesterday

Client and I remember *[shift to a narrative of childhood]* and it sort of came into clear focus of me as a kid, and I hate it, I mean I hate it. *[shift to internal/emotional differentiation]* I remember the night that my mother died, that's what it was like *[emergence of single-event narrative of suicide scene and external shift/landscape of action]* I was walking and my brother and sister, my sister was supposed to be babysitting my brother in the house, and um, it was quiet and I thought they were waiting to jump out and go "boo!" you know? kid's stuff

Therapist mm-hm.

Client so I tiptoe, tiptoe up the sidewalk and open the front door very carefully and listen, still nothing, just the sound in my eardrums *[shift to internal/landscape of consciousness]*

Therapist this deafening silence *[therapist's evocative reflection of internal experience]*

Client so quiet, and I'm thinking *[shift to reflexive/landscape of consciousness]* this is really berserk, really crazy, because usually by now they've jumped out and scared the living daylights out of me and we've all laughed

Therapist mm

Client and punched each other or whatever kids do. And I remember walking in *[shift to external]* and still nothing, and thinking this is really funny, *[shift to reflexive/ landscape of consciousness]* and I took my boots off and I went creeping down into the kitchen and I saw my mother's foot first and—*[shift to internal]* I was in absolute shock and not knowing what to do.

Therapist and your heart almost stopped *[therapist's evocative elaboration of client internal experiencing]*

Client *[shift to external narrative mode]* and I started shouting because I thought my sister was supposed to be there and I started screaming for my sister and then I

Client   noticed that on the table there was a note saying that she was over at my aunt's and uncle's at a New Year's party and they had put my little brother to bed there and *[reflexive shift/landscape of consciousness]* that was really, because of all the turmoil as a child too I was frightened to call anybody because you know your own business stays within the four walls of your house so

Therapist   sure, sure

Client   it felt like 10 hours, I'm sure it was a minute but it seemed like 10 hours.

Therapist   so then you walked in and saw what had actually happened *[therapist invites a return to the differentiation of the suicide scene and shift to external/landscape of action]*

Client   I tried waking her up, I thought she might just have, you know

Therapist   who knows as a child

Client   and I'm just shaking her and shaking her and trying to wake her up, and thinking *[shift to reflexive/landscape of consciousness]* you know, oh god, what do I do, who do I call, what do I do

Therapist   mm

Client   so the first thing I did, *[shift back to external/landscape of action]* I called my aunt she came over with my sister because of course I said,—I don't know what I said, I have no idea and of course when she came in *[shift to reflexive/landscape of consciousness]* my heart also goes out to her because I can't imagine an adult, myself now walking in on a situation like that—with your family.

Therapist   yeah.

In this sequence, both the client and therapist collaborate in a detailed unfolding of a trauma scene, in the context of a narrative description that provides a clear beginning, middle, and end to the event. In addition, a clear scene and setting is provided, along with the internal experiences of both the protagonist and significant others (the aunt) involved in the event. For the first time, a coherent narrative of the trauma memory begins to take shape for the client. A continual interplay between external and internal/reflexive narrative shifts seamlessly interweaves the unfolding narrative scene with the emotions, intentions, and expectations that the client experienced at the time of his mother's suicide.

The following example is also drawn from a good-outcome therapy dyad and illustrates how the process experiential therapist helps the client to access and disclose salient personal memories:

Client   and *[external narrative shift]* especially in the spring—in around May of this year I was really um thinking, the memories were flooding back from 20 years ago in the spring when I left home, and I first discovered I was pregnant.

Therapist   I see.

Client   Really, the weather—the weather in the springtime of this year brought back memories of what happened in May and April of '87.

Therapist   Oh I see, uh-huh, is there anything about it that you can sort of recapture and tell me

Client	uh
Therapist	what specifically kinds of memories came back?
Client	I just remember pulling together—hastily pulling together that wedding, and all the running around we did to pull it together in 2 weeks.

In another example drawn from the same therapy dyad, the therapist probes for the disclosure of a specific autobiographical memory narrative,

Therapist	Uh-huh. So see if any specific memory comes up of any, of a time when you really felt
Client	uh,—oh yes
Therapist	uh-huh
Client	I took, I remember the time when I called home. I called . . . I called my mother's home just to hear whoever's voice answered. I did it four or five times and then I would just hang up
Therapist	hm
Client	just to hear [her family name], just to get in touch with that house that seemed so far away and gone and lost.

The client responds to the therapist's request for a memory with a narrative that conveys the sense of the client's poignant longing for the family that she had to leave behind—"lost"—when she chose to leave home, as a teenager, to live with the father of her newborn baby. It is clear that in all of these examples, the therapist is actively encouraging the client to shift to the recollection of emotionally significant personal memories and to describe these experiences to the therapist.

Narrative Processes and Emotional Meaning Making

Process experiential therapists focus on their clients' retelling of emotionally salient autobiographical memory narratives, or external narrative sequences, to enable clients to further differentiate emotions that are experienced during the retelling of the personal memory. Based on the process experiential model, it is clear that a key therapist task is the active facilitation of client processing shifts toward the differentiation and elaboration of emotional experiences, internal narrative mode.

One of the unique insights generated by the NPCS to date has been the discovery that the transition from storytelling to emotional differentiation was most successful when it was first preceded by the client's active exploration of his or her own experiential responses to the narrative, in the context of a reflexive inquiry mode. Specifically, process experiential therapists invite clients to shift from external narrative modes to reflexive and internal narrative modes to elaborate the landscape of consciousness and facilitate emotional meaning-making and new perspectives on self and others in the world. In turn, the differentiation and narrative organization of painful emotion enables the client to reflexively explore and symbolize emergent meanings of distress, trauma, and loss.

In her intensive case analysis of three good-outcome and three poor-outcome process experiential therapy dyads, Lewin (2001) found that reflexive to internal mode shifts made up almost a third (30%) of all narrative process mode shifts undertaken by therapists involved in the good-outcome therapy relationships. In contrast, poor-outcome therapists initiated significantly fewer reflexive to internal mode shifts (16.75%). In essence, it appeared that the therapist's specific focus on emotional meanings, in the context of the client's self-reflections, helped the client to enter more fully into a sustained elaboration of his or her own internal world of felt emotions, as experienced in the therapy session. The client's exploration of intense feelings of vulnerability and emotional pain were also sustained by a sense of safety and trust in the person of the therapist.

The following excerpt from one good-outcome process experiential therapy dyad illustrates this process of empathic attunement, reflexive meaning making, and emotional differentiation in the context of salient personal memories.

Client   [*external narrative sequence*] Rob's brother Peter was my friend initially and we used to spend a lot of time together at the newspaper.... most of the reason that I'm unable—that I am terrified of running into Rob in front of other people is because I cannot sit there and be quiet but I cannot say things in front of Peter that would incur his wrath at all... [*shift to reflexive narrative sequence*] like just the idea of him not liking me for some reason—and I have yet to figure this out—is extremely upsetting to me and has been for a long time.... [*shift to new relational context associated with similar feelings*] and it is becoming that way with Mark too... my biggest problem with Mark is everything I can see he's a person that I could love and respect but I have this nagging doubt about me

Therapist   this is an inner doubt within you.... [*empathic reflection/reflexive mode*]

Client   yeah.... that it's all put on, that I'm being lied to all over again because ultimately the way I feel, what happens with Mark is I feel emotion toward him... [*shift to internal mode*] just like different emotions but up until about a week ago, like friendship.

Therapist   Is that kind of like... a feeling of warmth? [*empathic conjecture, differentiating emotional experience/internal mode*]

Client   Exactly! I was about to say a trust, a warmth... just this complete contentment

Therapist   that feels really good inside

Client   exactly and um it's followed by this gut-wrenching, sick feeling of dread [*shift to reflexive mode*] because the only other person in the last 4 years that has made me feel that way was Raoul and it turned out to be exactly opposite to everything that was really going on.... like when I thought he most liked me, and most accepted me for who I was, it was a huge act.

In this excerpt, both client and therapist participate in a collaborative differentiation of implicit emotions and meanings (Bruner's notion of the narrative landscape of consciousness) that suffuse problematic events (the landscape of action) unfolding in intimate relationships. Process experiential therapists enable clients to access and symbolize implicit emotion schemes and bring new understandings to the actions of self and others through or by means of the facilitation of reflexive and internal narrative process shifts. It should be noted, however, that this facilitation process was most successful when preceded by the client's active self-exploration of his or her own heightened experiential arousal, evoked by either the retelling of significant relationship events or participation in empty-chair or two-chair gestalt interventions during the therapy hour.

Process experiential therapists also focus on client descriptions of emotionally salient autobiographical memory narratives, or external narrative sequences, for the assessment of emotion process markers such as heightened emotional arousal and the introduction of chairing interventions. In the case of emotional harm, empty chair interventions are designed to help clients undertake an experiential entry into the internal world or perspective of the significant other with whom they have experienced relationship problems.

In the quest for emotional understanding, a key question that will need to be addressed is the intentions of the person whose actions caused the client such emotional pain: "Why did they hurt me?" The issue of intention goes directly to fundamental issues of trust and attachment and the belief that others are trustworthy and loving. When the actions of loved ones cause us emotional pain, we are often left confused and unable to meaningfully integrate feelings of anger, betrayal, fearfulness, and sadness. Central to the quest for understanding is the construction of a new, emotionally coherent account that integrates the narrative landscape of action—what happened—with a more differentiated and rich account of the narrative landscape of consciousness, in which the questions of "what do I feel?" and "what does it mean?" are more fully addressed.

The following example of an empty-chair intervention, drawn from the same therapy dyad as the first excerpt, demonstrates the important role that the process experiential therapist's empathic reflections, selective questions, and suggestions play in helping the client to further articulate the landscape of consciousness (emotions and meanings) in relation to experiences of trauma and loss. The therapist's responses help scaffold the client's reflexive processing of implicit meanings attendant to the personal memory as well as to differentiate new emotional responses emerging from his active engagement in his inner experiential world. In this sequence, the therapist first has the client imaginatively place his mother, who committed suicide when he was an adolescent, in an empty chair and then asks the client to describe the trauma scene (an external narrative shift) followed by an encouragement to elaborate felt emotions (an internal narrative mode). The client, in turn, shifts back and forth between describing the remembered suicidal scene and articulating felt emotions evoked by the terrifying images. In this therapeutic dance, the therapist empathically follows the client's lead and facilitates the expression of painful emotions and deep fears. Finally, the client shifts to a reflexive questioning mode at the end of the sequence in an attempt to bring understanding to this trauma experience.

Therapist   Tell her what you remember about the things, about the memories *[therapist invites shift to external narrative mode]*

Client   the horror and the terror *[in tears] [client focuses on felt emotions, internal narrative mode, experienced in response to internalized image of mother at the suicide scene]*

Therapist   let it go *[therapist stays with the client focus on felt emotions in the internal mode and differentiates fear, horror, and terror]* tell her about your fear *[client takes a Kleenex]* the horror and the terror stay with it, you're doing well—what do you remember? Tell her what it's like for you. It's important . . .

Client   *[crying]* I feel these memories are absolutely horrific and things I never should have seen.

Therapist Tell her.

Client It's etched so deeply in my mind I can't erase it. When I think of you I can't even think of you because I just remember you. . . .

Therapist Tell her what you see. *[therapist invites a shift to external narrative mode to elaborate image of the trauma scene]*

Client All I see is just you laying there. . . . I can't believe it and you're not waking up *[shift to reflexive and elaboration of appraisals unfolding in the suicide scene]*

Therapist not waking up. What's it like for you? *[therapist invites a shift to internal narrative mode]*

Client I'm just so afraid *[client shift to internal/emotional differentiation]*

Therapist I feel terrified *[therapist's empathic reflection and emotional differentiation]*—that's good, keep breathing. I feel terrified. What's going on? *[therapist's question invites the client to elaborate internal experiencing]*

Client and absolute disbelief—*[client shifts to reflexive mode]* how could you, how could you . . .

Therapist So how could you do this? *[therapist invites client to confront his mother directly with his reflexive questions in a search for understanding and meaning]* Tell her this.

Client I don't really understand why you did it.

Therapist Stay with those memories—and what do you want to say? . . . what are you feeling now? *[therapist invites client to elaborate felt emotions and a shift to internal narrative mode]*

Client *[client continues in reflexive narrative mode]* I'm thinking that um, how can I, how can something that happened so long ago control me so much now.

A primary goal of process experiential task interventions—such as two-chair and empty chair tasks—is the heightening of client emotional arousal to facilitate shifts in client emotional processes. Emotion shifts can be in the form of movement from maladaptive secondary emotions to more primary adaptive emotional responses or the accessing of new adaptive emotional responses in the context of personal memory narratives. Experiencing new and sometimes contradictory emotional responses in the context of past life events can lead to significant shifts in the intentions, hopes, beliefs, wishes, and feelings we attribute to the actions of self and others. At these moments, we see ourselves and others in a new light and are impelled to construct a new, emotionally coherent narrative that accounts for what happened and why it occurred, what was felt, in relation to whom, about what need or issue. It is our contention that emotions are "understood," and have personal meaning, when they are organized within a narrative framework that identifies what is felt, about whom, and in relation to what need or issue.

In contrast to the therapists engaged in good-outcome process experiential therapy, Lewin (2001) found that poor-outcome therapists were twice as likely to try to initiate shifts to internal emotion-focused modes directly from external narrative sequences. Similarly, poor-outcome clients initiated more internal to external narrative shifts than good-outcome clients. Lewin suggests that the two findings may be related. Poor-outcome clients may have initiated more shifts from internal narrative modes back to external storytelling modes when resisting their therapist's attempts to have them focus on and differentiate distressing and painful emotions.

In the context of intensively analyzing the following poor-outcome process experiential therapy dyad, Lewin found that most of the client's emotional experiences involved the therapist either (a) doing the majority of the emotional processing or (b) focusing more on the client's bodily sensations rather than her inner psychological state. The client also appeared to play a more passive role than good-outcome clients when exploring her feelings and preferred to focus on bodily sensations rather than discussing her emotions. The following excerpt, taken from Session 4, highlights the client's focus on her bodily sensations as she describes how she feels out of breath a lot of the time.

Client   Yeah yeah. I find that I'm, I'm ah I feel short of breath a lot. *[shift to internal narrative sequence]*

Therapist   Short of breath a lot?

Client   mm-hm. And just panting and huffing and puffing you know I *[lets out breath]* breathing and yawning and like I can't get enough air.

Therapist   So it's almost as if you're suffocating *[therapist empathic conjecture/metaphor]*

Client   Yeah.

Therapist   So, what's that sense of suffocating . . . ? *[therapist invites client to differentiate experiential felt sense]*

Client   Well, I'll pick up the phone, I can be sitting. . . . *[client shift away from internal narrative sequence to an external/storytelling narrative sequence]*

It is of interest to note the client's movement away from focusing on her internal experiencing and back to storytelling rather than reflection, despite the therapist's evocative metaphoric representation of the client's felt distress. The preceding excerpt also suggests that it is not only the activation of emotional schemes but the client's reflexive engagement with and movement into the elaboration of personal meanings connected with emotionally charged events that is crucial for therapeutic change.

CONCLUSIONS

In conclusion, it appears that clients' disclosures of personal stories, and the subsequent elaboration of the dual landscapes of narrative action and consciousness, are fundamental to the facilitation of significant client shifts and personal change in process experiential psychotherapy. Findings emerging from the intensive empirical analyses of productive process experiential sessions indicate that therapists explicitly focus on strategies that enable clients to dwell in and articulate more fully key components of the narrative landscape of consciousness. These components included the differentiation of adaptive emotions, implicit beliefs, hopes, intentions, and expectations of self and others caught up in the unfolding events of the narrative landscape of action.

Less evident in the process experiential model, but clearly present in good-outcome therapy sessions, was therapists' active facilitation of clients' disclosures of emotionally salient personal memories for the purpose of meaning-making and emotional differentiation. In addition, the disclosure of personal stories seems to be the fundamental means by which clients disclose to therapists "who they are" and is key to the establishment of a sense of shared understanding, and trust, in the therapy relationship. Process experiential therapists, in turn, invite their clients to reflexively explore and affectively engage these vivid memories in the therapy sessions. New meanings that emerge from the experiential exploration of emotion schemes is then concretized by clients in the context of telling new stories, which represent new ways of seeing, experiencing, and interacting with others in the world.

In conclusion, in the context of intensively exploring the interplay of narrative, emotion, and meaning-making modes in productive therapy sessions, a more differentiated understanding of the essential contributions of both emotion and narrative processes for self-change has emerged. These findings would appear to have important implications for both the theory and practice of experiential psychotherapy, and we are looking forward to participating in the ongoing evolution of experiential therapy practice and research.

REFERENCES

Angus, L., & Bouffard, B. (2002). "No lo entiendo": La busqueda de sentido emocional y coherencia personalante una perdida traumatica durante la infancia. *Revista Psicoterapia, 12*(49), 25-46.

Angus, L., & Hardtke, H. (1994). Narrative processes in psychotherapy. *Canadian Psychology, 35*, 190-203.

Angus, L., Hardtke, K., & Levitt, H. (1996). *Narrative processes coding system training manual.* Unpublished manuscript, York University, North York, Ontario, Canada.

Angus, L., Levitt, H., & Hardtke, K. (1999). The narrative processing coding system: Research applications and implications for psychotherapy practice. *Journal of Clinical Psychology, 55*, 1255-1270.

Bohart, A., & Greenberg, L. S. (1997). *Empathy reconsidered: New directions in psychotherapy.* Washington, DC: American Psychological Association.

Bruner, J. S. (1986). *Actual minds, possible worlds.* Cambridge, MA: Harvard Press University.

Bruner, J. (1990). *Acts of meaning.* Cambridge, MA: Harvard University Press.

Gonçalves, O. F., Korman, Y., & Angus, L. (2000). Constructing psychopathology from a cognitive narrative perspective. In R. A. Neimeyer & J. D. Raskin (Eds.), *Constructions of disorder: Meaning-making frameworks for psychotherapy* (pp. 265-284), Washington, DC: American Psychological Association.

Gonçalves, O. F., Machado, P. P., Korman, Y., & Angus, L. (2002). Assessing psychopathology: A narrative approach. In L. E. Beutler & M. L. Malik (Eds.), *Rethinking the DSM: A psychological perspective* (pp. 149-176). Washington, DC: American Psychological Association.

Greenberg, L. S. (2002). *Emotion-focused therapy: Coaching clients to work through their feelings.* Washington, DC: American Psychological Association.

Greenberg L. S., & Angus, L. (1995). How does therapy work? *Social Sciences and Humanities Research Council Standard Research Grant (1995-1998).*

Greenberg, L. S., & Pascual-Leone, J. (1995). A dialectical constructivist approach to experiential change. In R. A. Neimeyer & M. J. Mahoney (Eds.), *Constructivism in psychotherapy* (pp. 169-194). Washington, DC: American Psychological Association.

Greenberg, L. S., & Pascual-Leone, J. (1997). Emotion in the creation of personal meaning. In M. J. Power & C. R. Brewin (Eds.), *Transformation of meaning in psychological therapies: Integrating theory and practice* (pp. 157-173). New York: John Wiley.

Greenberg, L. S., & Pascual-Leone, J. (2001). A dialectical constructivist view of the creation of personal meaning. *Journal of Constructivist Psychology, 14*, 165-186.

Greenberg, L. S., Rice, L. N., & Elliott, R. (1993). *Facilitating emotional change: The moment-by-moment process.* New York: Guilford.

Greenberg, L. S., Watson, J. C, & Goldman, R. (1998). Process-experiential therapy of depression. In L. S. Greenberg & J. C. Watson (Eds.), *Handbook of experiential psychotherapy* (pp. 227-248). New York: Guilford.

Harber, K. D., & Pennebaker, J.W. (1992). Overcoming traumatic memories. In S. Christianson (Ed.), *The handbook of emotion and memory: Research and theory* (pp. 359-387). Hillsdale, NJ: Lawrence Erlbaum.

Hardtke, K. (1996). *Characterizing therapy focus and exploring client process: Investigating therapeutic modalities from a narrative approach.* Unpublished master's thesis, York University, Toronto, Ontario, Canada.

Hardtke, K., Levitt, H., & Angus, L. (in press). Investigating narrative processes in psychotherapy discourse: The Narrative Processes Coding System. *Zeitschrift fuer qualitative Bildungs-, Beratungs- und Sozialforschung.*

Levitt, H., & Angus, L. (2000). Psychotherapy process measure research and the evaluation of psychotherapy orientation: A narrative analysis. *Psychotherapy Integration, 9*(3), 279-300.

Levitt, H., Korman, Y., & Angus, L. (2000). A metaphor analysis in treatments of depression: Metaphor as a marker of change. *Counselling Psychology Quarterly, 13,* 23-35.

Levitt, H., Korman, Y., Angus, L., & Hardtke, K. (1997). Metaphor analyses in good and poor outcome psychotherapy: Unloading a burden vs. being burdened. *Psicologia: Teoria, Investigao e Practica, 2,* 329-346.

Lewin, J. K. (2001). *Both sides of the coin: Comparative analyses of narrative process patterns in poor and good outcome dyads engaged in brief experiential psychotherapy for depression.* Unpublished master's thesis, York University, Toronto, Ontario, Canada.

Pennebaker, J., & Seagal, J. (1999). Forming a story: The health benefits of narrative. *Journal of Clinical Psychology, 55,* 1243-1254.

Perls, F. S. (1973). *The Gestalt approach and eye witness to therapy.* New York: Dell.

Rennie, D. (1998). *Person-centered counseling: An experiential approach.* Thousand Oaks, CA: Sage.

Rogers, C. (1951). *Client-centred therapy.* London: Constable.

Rotondi-Trevisan, D. (2002). *Memory narrative analysis and micro-narrative coherence in brief experiential psychotherapy for depression: An exploratory analysis.* Unpublished master's thesis, York University, Toronto, Ontario, Canada.

Singer, J. A., & Moffitt, K. H. (1992). *A scoring manual for narrative memories.* Unpublished manuscript, Department of Psychology, Connecticut College, New London, CT.

CHAPTER 6

Nurturing Nature
Cognitive Narrative Strategies

ÓSCAR F. GONÇALVES
MARGARIDA R. HENRIQUES
PAULO P. P. MACHADO

PSYCHOPATHOLOGY AND PSYCHOTHERAPY AS A NARRATIVE PROCESS

One of the characteristics marking our distinctiveness as human beings is our capacity to use our language abilities to construct personal experiences as narratives. Narratives are central to our capacity to symbolize experience, both to ourselves and other human beings. In this sense, we may state that, at the psychosocial level, we can be essentially defined as *narrative beings*. Likewise, at the biological level, narrative seems to be the essential process that facilitates the integration of our personal experiences by means of coordinated action from a diverse array of brain structures and processes (Cozolino, 2002). Almost every brain structure is involved in the process of narrative construction, and thus, we may say that the human mind is, indeed, a *narrative brain*.

One of the most striking proposals of narrative psychology is the idea that the world is not a function of what exists but of what happens. The notion of "what happens" is a crucial element of the narrative process—narrative is what happens. We defend the idea that psychopathology is not the result of an underlying internal mechanism (biological or psychological) but a product of the patient's narrative construction (Angus, Levitt, & Hardtke, 1999; Botella & Herrero, 2000; Dimaggio & Semerari, 2001; Gonçalves, 1995b; Hermans & Hermans-Jansen, 1995; McLeod, 1997; Neimeyer, 2000; Omer &

AUTHORS' NOTE: Correspondence regarding this chapter should be sent to the authors at University of Minho, Gualtar Campus, Department of Psychology, 4710 Braga, Portugal, or to pmachado@iep.uminho.pt.

Alon, 1997; White & Epston, 1990). More specifically, what we call psychopathology is a result of a narrative construction that, for some reason, became less viable in the experiential reality of the patient (Gonçalves, 2001).

We can also see psychopathology as social production; this view allows narrative approaches to conceptualize patients' suffering without using stigmatizing diagnostic labels. Alternatively, psychopathology becomes a signifying process, inseparable from narrative production, and a result of co-construction of both patient and therapist language systems embedded in a given social and historical context. Narrative analysis requires that we focus on the narrative plot, exploring the potential and limits of each patient's narrative and the process of its construction and the social discourse that helps to maintain it.

There is currently a large body of research that supports the applicability of the narrative model to clinical practice, namely, studies showing the relationship between degree of narrative coherence and structure and patients' well-being (Baerger & McAdams, 1999; Pennebaker, 1993; Russell & Wandrei, 1996). Other studies have shown that patient outcome seems to be associated with a progressive narrative differentiation in the direction of more complexity, internality, and meaning creation (Angus et al., 1999; Pennebaker, 1993). In contrast, studies on spontaneous narratives of agoraphobic patients (Gonçalves, Henriques, Alves, & Soares, 2002) have shown very low levels of narrative differentiation in terms of process.

In addition, there is some evidence that different psychopathological organizations might be associated with different prototype narratives in terms of particular meaning systems (Capps & Ochs, 1995; Gonçalves et al., 1996). Our research on this topic will be presented at the end of the chapter, and although it is not yet conclusive, it tends to support the hypothesis that psychopathology can be conceptualized as some form of social construction. In essence, the findings suggest that there is an essential mismatch between the fictional psychopathology created by the patient and the fictional reality created by the therapist (Gonçalves, 2001). We suggest that the experience of well-being has limited overlap with the experience of psychopathological suffering, and not surprisingly, there are different ways of narrating such experiences. In a creative, functional, and adaptive narrative existence, we find a tendency to discursive multiplicity that inhibits any kind of prototypical narrative. When this discursive multiplicity is challenged, psychological disturbance tends to emerge. Instead of conceptualizing reality as a negotiation process between multiple possibilities of the world itself, the individual tends to see an absolute, unchangeable reality for which he or she must take sole responsibility.

We suggest that rigidity in the process of narrative construction of experience creates a psychomorbid nucleus that affects dimensions of narrative construction and inhibits an existential multipotentiality that constitutes the basis for well-being. Psychotherapy, in turn, emerges from a need to repair human beings' narrative constructions and justifies the essential relevance of patient narrative productions for both clinicians and psychotherapy researchers. Not surprisingly, narrative models of psychotherapy aim at re-owning and expanding the experiential idiosyncratic meaning of self-experiences and promoting a more coherent, complex, multiple, and flexible narrative. With this approach, psychotherapy is not conceptualized within a cure or problem-solving paradigm but within a creating paradigm. The purpose of therapy becomes the promotion of self-change without defining limits.

To promote this movement toward reconceptualizing narrative and change in psychotherapy, we will present the cognitive narrative model of psychotherapy, which evolves from a cognitive behavioral tradition within a constructivist paradigm (Gonçalves, 1995b, 1995c, 1998). This model sees psychotherapy as an experiential context for the co-construction (i.e., conversations) of multiple voices (i.e., deconstruction) of narratives lived in the past, experienced in the present, and projected into the future.

THE PROCESS OF COGNITIVE NARRATIVE PSYCHOTHERAPY

We have seen so far how psychopathology can be conceptualized as narrative fiction and psychotherapy as a process of narrative creation. The main objective of cognitive narrative psychotherapy is to promote a narrative exercise that makes the patient open him- or herself to the proactive and multivoiced construction of his or her own experience. The therapeutic process develops in three stages: (a) recollection, (b) adjectivation, and (c) projection. All these stages have a common framework; they begin with an introduction and modeling phase, and then several exercises are proposed in the therapeutic session and prescribed for homework activities as applied to daily and life narratives. Future narratives are addressed in the final phase of therapy. Each exercise, both in session and homework, is followed by an evaluation of the provoked experience. Homework activities are always discussed in the following session.

At each stage, two distinct but complementary foci are addressed in terms of specific patient tasks. At the synchronic level (i.e., focused on the patient's current experience), the therapeutic work is focused on patients' micronarratives, or the narrative construction of their daily life episodes. At the diachronic level (i.e., across the patient's life span), the focus is on the patients' macronarrative, or the narrative construction applied to the central themes of their life experience. Tasks addressing the diachronic exploration of patients' macronarratives are preceded by relaxation exercises in order to promote the free association of remembered experiences.

Although the three phases of the therapeutic process are presented as if they occur sequentially, it is expected that at times, patients will spontaneously provide narrative productions early in therapy that are more representative of later stages of the cognitive narrative model. We suggest however that the therapeutic work is focused on the particular aspect of narrative construction that is being explored in any given phase.

Phase I: Recollection

The goal of the recollection stage is to help patients become aware of their experiences and self narratives, which is crucial for completion of the meaning exploration process. The recalling process is an active task that by itself promotes the construction of alternative realities, a process that is central to therapeutic change. In this stage, patients engage in a circular creative process that entails shifts between episodic memory narratives and semantic memory (Tulving, 1985a, 1985b). In contrast with a semantic memory, a narrative episode implies the presence of contextualized elements connected by temporal relationships. For example, if the patient states, "It was a nice day," the therapist tries to promote the elaboration of a narrative event using statements like "Tell me something specific that happened that day." By exploring episodes and their related memories, it is possible to create new meanings.

It is precisely this episodic element of experience that creates a narrative context that will allow a new semantic differentiation because by exploring the different dimensions of the experience, we allow the emergence of new meanings while at the same time the multipotentiality of the experience is stressed. Thus, the therapeutic goal at this stage is the intentional recollection of a detailed, episodic memory narrative.

With this approach, recollection includes all the elements of the creative process, contrasting with a positivist view of memory as a photographic static process. We use recall, not to evoke historical truth, but to create potentially alternate narrative constructions. The goal is to elaborate and differentiate the narrative structure of the episodic memory in terms of *orientation, structural sequence,* and *narrative integration*.

In the clinical context, therapists facilitate the development of a more sophisticated level of structural narrative coherence by engaging patients in four therapeutic tasks: introduction to episodic recall—the guided imagery exercise, daily narratives episodic recall, life span narratives episodic recall, and prototype narrative construction. We will now present the most important activities of this phase.

Introduction to episodic recall: The guided imagining exercise. The patient is encouraged to remember and narrate episodic memories occurring across the life span and to elaborate each memory in terms of the canonic elements of narrative structure. The first phase consists of the *construction of an associative availability* through a relaxation induction exercise. The second phase consists of a *temporal regression* exercise in which the therapist guides the patient, inviting him or her to identify narrative episodes in different moments of the life span and to talk about them in the present tense.

Daily episodic narratives recall. This task promotes the synchronic, creative construction of everyday narrative episodes, through the prescribed assignment of recalling and recording one narrative per day. Patients are asked to narrate, in the present, the sequence of events, its context, and impact of its recall on themselves and how it relates to the narrative.

Life span episodic narratives recall. In a diachronic perspective, the patient begins generalizing the exploration and structuring of life events. One particular aspect of this exercise is that patients are asked to recall one episode for each year of their life (from age zero to the present) and write it down on a numbered (year) piece of paper.

Prototype narrative construction. In the final stage of the recalling process, the thematic invariants of the patients' narratives are identified. We try to select a narrative that is a good example (i.e., a prototype) of the themes of the patient. From all of the recalled life episodes, the patient is asked to select the one episode that best typifies the thematic nature of his or her functioning. It is this narrative prototype that will be used as a diachronic organizer of the patient's life themes in the therapy sessions.

The Process of Recollection: Amanda

Amanda is a 30-year-old university lecturer. A lively, attractive, and intellectually sophisticated woman, she is experiencing communication problems with her family. While she feels overwhelmed by the almost daily conflicts in her family and at work, she is especially affected by conflictual interactions with her stepson. She has intense verbal exchanges with him. The selection of daily and life events highlights recurrent self-narratives dominated by anger. The predominant emotional tone of these narratives is both anger and desperation. Her jaws look tense, and her teeth and fist clench when she tells her stories. As the recalling work progresses, new contrasting narratives emerge, such as when the patient spent a couple of hours at the hairdresser. At the beginning, this story was only a proto-narrative, and so we promoted its structural development in the therapy session. She tells us that when she arrived at the hair salon, she was hoping to have her hair done quickly to be ready for a social event. Initially, she was tense at the hair salon, anticipating that she would not have enough time to be ready for her social event, and she was not looking forward to that outcome. As the hairdresser was taking care of her, massaging and washing her head, she began to feel more relaxed and willing to "chit chat" about trivial events, such as her vacation plans for the holiday season. Her attitude and nonverbal body language became more relaxed. At the end of the recalling phase, when asked to select a prototype narrative, she describes a traumatic event that she repeatedly recalls: the sexual assault and rape she experienced at age 17. She says that after 13 years whenever she feels that she's losing control of a given situation, the context, the sensation, and the emotions of the episode are automatically activated.

Phase II: Adjectifying

The main goal of the adjectifying phase is to allow the patient to elaborate on the remembered event by giving it color, shape, scent, taste, texture, emotion, thoughts, and meaning. Adjectifying enlivens an experience through a process of narrative symbolization. This phase focuses on the elements of the narrative process with the goal of increasing complexity. This goal is attained through the differentiation of the sensorial, emotional, cognitive, and metaphoric aspects of the narrative. This will develop in the subphases: objectifying, emotional and cognitive subjectifying, and metaphorizing.

Objectifying: Adjectifying Sensations

We use the term *objectifying* to refer to the process of separating different sensorial components of the remembered experience: visual, auditory, olfactory, gustatory, and kinesthetic. In this phase, the therapist alerts patients to the fact that the basis of our experience is either internal or external sensorial experiences, a fact that patients usually overlook. Patients are encouraged to explore the multiplicity of their sensorial experience and to realize that there is no need to become a prisoner of a singular sensory experience. This exercise proposes an alternative to the limited, pathologically saturated sensorial representation of lived experiences and encourages patients to become aware of and articulate a diverse range of sensorial experiences. While the goals of the recalling phase include the creation of narrative coherence, the goals of the adjectifying phase entail the elaboration of sensorial differentiation and greater narrative complexity.

Daily narratives objectification. The goal is to both promote patients' ability to narrate past experiences in their total sensorial complexity and to use this enhanced skill in the daily management of situations. We begin by asking patients to select one daily narrative that will be fully explored in terms of its sensorial multiplicity and plurality. We ask patients to, in the here-and-now, explore the visual, auditory, gustatory, olfactory, and kinesthetic aspects of their experience. We then review the other daily narratives using the same procedure. When a patient has progressed through these exercises, we will begin to objectify the prototype narrative.

The Process of Adjectifying: Antonio

Antonio is a 40-year-old self-employed professional that seeks therapy due to complaints of sadness, failure, low self-esteem, and recent alcohol abuse. During the recalling exercise, Antonio selected an early episode, when he was 6 years old, which he called "my original sin." In one of his first days of elementary school, he had decided to bring a pocketknife to sharpen his pencils. Unfortunately, on that same day, one of his schoolmates found that his coat had been cut by a knife. As Antonio was the only student in the class with a pocketknife, the teacher asked him in a confronting way, "Why did you cut the coat, Antonio?" He almost fainted in response to his teacher's question. He had never expected that he would be accused of something that he had not done. He repeatedly denied that he had been responsible for the damage to the coat. However, the teacher was not satisfied with his response and decided to call his mother and request that she attend a meeting at the school. Facing his mother at the school, sobbing and distressed, he confessed to the "crime" he had not committed.

At the start of the objectification exercise, Antonio had a self-devaluating tone in his voice and stated that he was finding it difficult to complete the exercise. His sensations were limited to physical sensations connected to an oppressive feeling of sadness, which alcohol seems to soothe. Over time, he became more open to a broader range of sensorial experiences and described a state of "sensorial amazement." The following episode demonstrates this change in sensorial awareness. Recently, Antonio was supposed to meet a friend at a local café, a situation in which he usually felt uncomfortable and self-conscious. He was particularly uncomfortable walking into the café alone, as he imagined a critical audience watching and evaluating his every move. As Antonio was walking towards the café, he used his experience as a therapeutic prescription, and the objectification procedure had its first proactive effect. He sat down, ordered coffee, and spent the rest of the time writing down the multiplicity of sensations that he was experiencing in the café. He was surprised to realize that half an hour had gone by, and he had written a couple of pages in his diary before realizing that his friend had not arrived to meet him as planned.

The next week, Antonio began objectifying his prototype narrative. It was hard for him to reexperience the sensorial dimension of his story, but in doing so, Antonio realized—for the first time—that he was able to analyze the narrative as an observer, as if he was a movie director, in a curious process of decentering. It was also in the context of decentering moments that he recalled the tenderness in his mother's face, the scent of her hair, the familiar faces of many peers, which had been lost in time, and all of the dimensions that the creative construction of memories allows us.

Subjectifying: Cognitive and Emotion Adjectivation Process

Subjectifying aims at achieving a heightened differentiation—or complexity—of what is usually described as the internal world of patients (cf. Lakoff & Johnson, 1980). From an internal perspective, we live in a chaotic and a fascinating world of emotions and thoughts of which we are only partially aware most of the time. Rather than viewing psychological dysfunction as the result of the pathogenic presence of some negative emotion or automatic thought, it can be construed as the inability to articulate the full diversity of our subjective experiences as reflected in our emotional experiences and train of thought. Dysfunction can be understood as the outcome of being exclusively dedicated to one kind of emotional experience or one thought content. Subjectifying aims at promoting this awareness of the complexity and diversity of our internal experience.

The subjectifying stage, as a means of narrative construction, is the process of the creation of internal experience. From a narrative standpoint, the distinction between emotion and thought is not crucial because they are both forms of internal symbolic experience. However, from a methodological standpoint, this distinction can help patients to center on the most undifferentiated aspects of their experience (i.e., basic emotions) and expand its narrative symbolization (i.e., cognitions).

The therapeutic tasks that facilitate the development of the subjectification phase entail three strategies analogous to those identified in the previous phase: subjectifying introduction and modeling, subjectifying daily narratives, and subjectifying prototype narrative.

Subjectifying daily and prototype narrative. The therapist facilitates the process of broadening the diversity of emotions and thoughts associated with each narrative throughout five distinct stages: (a) emotional activation, wherein the therapist asks questions regarding objectivation; (b) focalization, wherein the therapist facilitates the intensification of sensations by repetition or exaggeration, while the patient describes the experience; (c) symbolization, wherein the therapist asks patients to select a word or symbol that best describes what is being experienced, followed by a return to the physical sensation, as a way of validating the symbolization (a process similar to the task of fine-tuning an old analogue radio receiver); (d) thoughts listing, where the first thoughts associated with each emotion are explored; and (e) in a process of progressive association, encouraging the patient to keep a train of thought from the first mentioned to those eventually associated with it, until several thoughts are explored, and we're back to the first thought or emotion.

Subjectifying Processes : Alvaro

Álvaro is a 27-year-old engineer who came to therapy complaining about cyclical episodes of euphoric and depressive humor. In the past, his mother and grandfather had been diagnosed with bipolar disorder, and Álvaro was afraid that he might be at risk for the disorder. Álvaro admitted that the moments of euphoria were beginning to cause him social embarrassment. Although married, he was frequently involved in extramarital affairs. These relationships had a curious pattern. His extramarital partners were usually married, and the relationship always began in a very emotionally intense fashion, accompanied by strong feelings and promises of eternal love. But, after a few weeks, the relationship would end painfully, and a great sadness would overcome Álvaro. This depressive period would last a couple of weeks and was interrupted only by the start of a new affair. Álvaro reported feeling very dependent on these affective cycles and considered them organizers of his own life.

When the subjectifying work began, something new emerged for Álvaro. He selected a narrative about an autumn night spent at a friend's farmhouse. The objectivation exercise brought out a panoply of farm sensations for Álvaro, dominated by the scent of firewood and the heat of the fire on his face. As he deepened his physical sensations, Álvaro reported a sense of peace and thoughts of relaxation that stimulated the recollection of calm and tranquil events from his past. Associated with this tranquility, the thought of being in "slow motion" arises, and he becomes more contemplative. When questioned about the exercise, Álvaro makes a curious comment: "interesting these hybrid feelings." The strangeness of new emotional discriminations brought the sensation of a complex feeling state. However, a new path to the complexity of his subjective experience appeared, and emotional polarity created the possibility of constructing new emotional experiences. Automatic thoughts gave way to a kind of slow-motion reflection and contemplation. In his daily narratives, Álvaro now tries to find examples of such tranquility from which to explore new experiences. The sadness and the euphoria are still present but no longer the exclusive organizers of his subjective experience.

Metaphorizing:
The Adjectivation of Meaning

Lakoff and Johnson (1980) argue that our conceptual system construes reality through metaphors. Even if this is so, our view is that metaphors are narrative condensations of meaning. Our flexibility as human beings rests in the ability to reflect on the thinking process and create multiple meanings.

We believe that there is no unifying or final meaning, and that reality is, in fact, the product of a constant search for narrative meaning. The metaphorizing stage invites the patient to experience the relativity of meaning, accept its indetermination, and become willing to explore multiple meanings (Gergen & Kaye, 1992). It is hoped that patients will find multiple meanings for all of their experiences, and despite the prevalence of some meaning modes, active questioning will open up more complex paths to more complex constructions of reality.

For the metaphorizing phase, we use three strategies analogous to those of the previous phases: metaphorizing introduction and modeling, daily narratives metaphorizing, and prototype narrative metaphorizing.

Metaphorizing daily and prototype narratives. Once patients have been introduced to the sensorial, emotional, and cognitive reexperiencing of their narrative, the exploration of meanings is the next step to complete. This step is obtained by asking patients to select a metaphor (e.g., name, object, concept, image, plant, and animal) that constitutes a title symbolizing an experience. Once this is completed, patients are asked to elaborate other metaphors that can be construed from the original metaphoric image and, finally, to identify one final metaphor that synthesizes the meaning of the other figurative expressions.

Metaphorizing Processes: Ana

Ana is a 46-year-old medical doctor who came to therapy following a major depressive episode. Ana lived most of her life without experiencing psychological distress, always thinking of herself as self-sufficient and strong. She is the eldest of five siblings and was the most obedient and responsible of all the children. Her parents, particularly her father, had controlled her life in the most subtle way. As the eldest, she was expected to take care of her younger brothers and sisters, achieve academically in medical school, marry an engineer after graduation, and have children of her own. All of these expectations were met, but two episodes would tragically affect this perfect narrative. The birth of her third child became her final opportunity to have children, due to medical complications. Almost simultaneously, her father died. Ana felt severely depressed and confused; the idea that she had never lived her own life emerged for the first time.

In the process of metaphorizing weekly narratives, it was clear that most of Ana's metaphoric expressions were freedom metaphors: water, ocean, sailing, rivers. Ana assumed that the current week had been unusual, with moments of happiness and calm that she had not experienced for quite a while. During the week, she had only one "difficult" day, and the associated metaphor had been "feeling imprisoned." The moment of returning to the prototype narrative had arrived. The patient had described her feelings of inadequacy as a trained doctor when she was not able to save her father from the stroke that finally killed him. The metaphor that emerged was "mortgaged." She realized that her life had been lived as if it had been mortgaged for the prior 46 years, and therapy would help her to determine how to live the next 46 years. It was time to pay the mortgage.

Phase III: Projection

The final phase of the therapeutic process intentionally deals with the content of patient narratives and promotes the introduction of a multiplicity of themes, characters, actions, and contexts. In this way, the subject construes different possibilities of existence. Markus and Nurius (1986) called this process the exploration of "possible I's," a process that leads to the proactive construction of a diversity of experiential responses.

While the patient plans, tests, and evaluates narratives with alternate contents, a new sense of authorship emerges. In this phase, the patient engages in an intentional search for new narratives. It is a moment of creativity and existential lightness. At the end, the patient will discover a surprising diversity of contents, emotions, and sensations in the narratives disclosed to the therapist in the therapy sessions. In other words, the narratives have lost their dysfunctional sense of singularity and saturation. At this point, psychotherapy is no longer needed.

The activities of this stage of therapy include (a) projection introduction and modeling, (b) construction of an alternate narrative, (c) historical grounding of the alternate narrative, (d) identification of daily alternate narratives, and (e) projection of alternate narratives.

Construction of the alternate narrative. First, the therapist begins with a first projection exercise based on either the exploration of alternatives to the root metaphor that patients have elaborated or their prototype narrative. Given that the metaphor symbolizes an invariant of meaning for a patient, the therapist will begin this process from contrasting points of view to promote diversity of meanings. This procedure is followed by the selection of alternate narrative episodes, encouraging patients to identify a variety of self-narratives from their lives in which they operated in a way different from the root metaphor. Then we explore the metaphorizing of these alternative episodes, through the construction of multiple metaphors. Finally, we ask patients to select an alternative metaphor, one that synthesizes the previous ones or best symbolizes what patients would like to implement as an alternative to their regular functioning.

Historical grounding of the alternative metaphor. The objective of this phase is the reconstruction of the patient's past life story from the standpoint of a new perspective or vantage points. Patients are invited to select episodes from their lives to illustrate these contrasting forms of meaning, being careful to find them in a variety of contexts, themes, actions, and characters.

Identification of daily alternative narratives. After rooting the alternative metaphor in a historical timeframe, patients are asked to find evidence of daily narratives that can be symbolized by the alternative metaphor, as well as other contrasting with the root metaphor.

Projection of alternative narratives. This is active planning of life experiences through the projection of alternative metaphors. The procedure involves the following steps: (a) selection of an episode that is going to happen during the week in which the patient would like to represent the alternative metaphor; (b) projection of the experience, in which the therapist suggests that the patient construes in imagery the objectifying emotional and cognitive subjectifying of the experience; (c) implementation of the alternative narrative and recording of the adjectivation of the experience; and (d) projection of new narratives in the therapy session, promoting diversity of themes, characters, actions, and contexts. The process continues until it is clear for both the patient and the therapist that there is sufficient diversity in the content of the patient's narratives and the permanent nature of the patient's change process.

Projecting processes: Armando

Armando was a 23-year-old college student who had remained a freshman in mathematics for a number of years. The patient was sent to therapy because of his persistent academic problem. This academic problem appeared to be associated with symptoms of intense test anxiety and feelings of personal devaluation. From the beginning of the therapeutic process, it was clear that Armando's difficulties were also generalized to the majority of social situations where, besides anxiety, he showed lack of adequate social skills.

Armando selected as prototype narrative an episode that occurred in his first day of classes, when the professor asked students their SAT scores. This questioning was accompanied with comments about low scores and how a strong background in mathematics was crucial to academic success in that course. When Armando's turn arrived, he panicked and had persistent thoughts of being ridiculous, childish, and cowardly. His root metaphor was a *crawling bug*, meaning both his insignificance (insect) and his inability to leave the ground (crawling).

It took some time for Armando to get familiar with the challenges and possibilities of a projection attitude. Slowly, he became enthusiastic about the idea of construing new possibilities for his narratives, with diverse contexts and characters. As the work of construing alternative metaphors continued, he changed his "look," with a new haircut and clothes, and began a physical exercise program. A new metaphor emerged: private eye. In fact his hypersensitiveness to social circumstances allowed the development of considerable observation skills; that is, he was a good listener and evaluator of others' reactions (but he had used those skills against himself until now). Sherlock Homes was one of his favorite characters, and he was invited to go back to read some of his favorite books and to try and look for contact points between the character and the metaphor he was trying to develop. He began to realize that throughout his life, and in the present, there were moments when he could identify the skills of distancing from himself and observing others, as well as possessing the problem-solving creativity that characterizes a private eye. Strategies for narrative implementation of this metaphor were generated for a variety of situations and contexts.

Close to the end of the therapeutic process, Armando told us that he had decided to quit his major and switch to psychology. His decision came as a surprise to us, and the idea of some kind of identification with the therapist crossed our minds. We then questioned him about the reasons behind that decision. He answered with an arrogant and somewhat superior expression: "Obviously, my Dear Watson, it doesn't take much to move from a private eye to the eye of the private."

This model has been used for clinical work with patients of different ages and psychological problems. There are adaptations of this model for specific health-related problems such as myocardial infraction and dyspepsia. Other developments are associated with specific populations, namely, heroin dependents and children, although future developments are planned.

RESEARCHING COGNITIVE NARRATIVE PSYCHOTHERAPY

Thus far, we have presented the different phases of the therapeutic process of the model. We will now describe some of the research currently in progress at the University of Minho (Portugal) that supports this therapeutic approach. A more extensive description of this research is presented elsewhere (Gonçalves & Machado, 1999).

In a first set of studies, we interviewed 24 agoraphobic, 18 opiate-dependent, 20 alcoholic-dependent, 11 anorexic, and 20 depressed patients. During the interview process, significant life narratives were collected from each subject and analyzed.

In general, the prototype narrative for the opiate-dependent sample can be described as an episode taking place in a public setting and activated by some uncontrolled situation. Individuals were guided in this situation by the objective of pain avoidance and pleasure seeking. Their actions were typically nonconfrontational and externally controlled, with a mixture of internal states that oscillated between the dialectic of pain/suffering and pleasure/relief. The outcome of the narrative was typically the maintenance of the status quo, with the subjects ending up with a sense of social loss and loss of personal power.

For the alcoholic sample, the prototype narrative can be summarized as an episode taking place in a personal context and activated by an experience of loss. Individuals were guided in this situation by the goal of overcoming and escaping the situation. Their actions were of crying and escaping with accompanying feelings of sadness and tension. The outcome of the narrative was typically feelings of isolation, with the subjects ending up with a sense of the beginning of a personal collapse.

The prototype narrative of the anorexic patients was an episode where the central scenario was of the school or the house. In the situation, they were confronted and disappointed by the attitude of significant others. Subjects tried to assert themselves in this confrontation by opposing and crying while experiencing sadness, anxiety, disappointment, and anger. The typical outcome was the failure of subjects to assert their own wishes, ending up disappointed with themselves and others.

The prototype narrative of the depressed patients was an episode where the central scenario was at home. In the situation, they were confronted with an unexpected or sudden death. the person was assaulted by feelings of disbelief, refusing to accept the news and becoming paralyzed. This was followed by feelings of deep sadness and anger. As a result, the subject felt fragile, wanted to withdraw, and decided to isolate him- ot herself. The subject felt that his or her world was falling apart.

Finally, for the agoraphobic subjects, the prototype narrative took place somewhere between hospital and home and was activated by a situation that was seen as a both a separation and a risky challenge. The subjects tried to maintain security and overcome this challenge by a mixture of avoidance, crying, and searching for help while at the same time challenging themselves. They experienced in this process a composite of different feelings such as fear, insecurity, loss of control, abandonment, sadness, despair, offense, revenge, and personal affirmation. Individuals tried to restore a sense of calm and tranquility by avoidance, crying, challenging themselves, and searching for help. The situation typically ended with a dichotomous experience: on one hand, an increased awareness of the dangers and, on the other, a sense of self-competence and efficacy.

We then computed convergent validity of the prototype narratives, following the proposal of Howard, Maerlender, Myers, and Curtin (1992). We tested the verisimilitude of each prototype narrative for a sample of the dysfunctional subjects and the comparison groups. All subjects were confronted with the prototype narrative and asked to rate on a 5-point Likert scale the degree to which that narrative could be understood as something plausible as a personal life event. The results showed that the sample experiencing psychopathology evaluated the prototype narrative as being significantly more related to their personal lives than the control sample.

As stated before, an assumption underlying the present research was that some nuclear narratives acquire a central role in knowledge development, assuming the role of core prototypes from which further experiences are categorized, reordered, and intentionalized. The convergent validity found for the prototype narratives for these three types of dysfunction supports the specific nature of cognitive organization in these dysfunctions as well as the possibility of identifying this specificity in prototype narratives.

Following this study, we tested the divergent validity of the prototype narratives. Each subject rank-ordered the five prototype narratives (i.e., agoraphobic, opiate dependent, depressed, anorexic, and alcoholic) in terms of the degree of similarity of the narrative to a personally significant life event; then, they evaluated each of the five narratives in terms of verisimilitude (i.e., how close to a personal significant life event was each narrative). Subjects were the patients themselves, their family, friends or significant others, and clinicians.

Results showed that clinicians were able to identify the prototype narrative for each psychopathological subgroup. Depressed patients identified themselves more with the depressed prototype narrative than with any other one, but this did not happen at a significant level for other clinical groups and their corresponding narratives. However, agoraphobic patients identified themselves more with the corresponding narrative than with the drug-dependent and anorexic ones. Friends and family and significant others of agoraphobic patients showed results similar to those of the patients themselves. Other groups didn't show significant results.

In an ongoing study, we are currently analyzing the structure, process, and content of spontaneous narratives (i.e., patients were asked to describe a significant life episode) provided by agoraphobics and heroin addicts. The three manuals developed to evaluate structure, process, and content have aided in achieving good interrater agreement (Gonçalves et al., 2002). Preliminary data analyses indicate that for both the agoraphobic and opiate-dependent subgroups, the spontaneous narratives evidenced higher levels of narrative structure with less evidence of narrative process and content elaboration. These results tend to support the idea that patients tend to structure their narratives coherently but lack diversity and flexibility.

In another study, (Gonçalves, Machado, & Rosas, 1997), 60 myocardial infarction patients leaving an intensive care unit were randomly distributed between a treatment (cognitive narrative therapy) and control group condition. The therapy group had a total of three 1-hour daily sessions of cognitive narrative psychotherapy (objectifying, subjectifying, metaphorizing, and projecting the narrative). The control group was exposed to an equivalent amount of nonstructured discussion on trivial aspects of life. Participants were evaluated on measures of emotional well-being at pretest, posttest, and follow-up, and of physical well-being at follow-up. Preliminary results reported elsewhere (Gonçalves, Machado, & Rosas, 1998) have shown that the narrative group improved along several measures of psychological adjustment in comparison to the control group.

In summary, the current research at the University of Minho and the Center for Cognitive Psychotherapy aims at increasing our understanding of the role of the narrative in the amelioration of physical and psychological conditions of patients with both physical and psychological problems. We expect that this research will shed some light on some of the important variables in the therapeutic process and the effect of narrative strategies in psychotherapy.

Another study carried out at the University of California, Santa Barbara, used an adaptation of cognitive narrative psychotherapy as one of the active treatments for comorbid depressed and chemically dependent patients together with cognitive therapy and prescriptive therapy (Beutler et al., in press). Overall, mean treatment effects were clinically significant, but probably because of the small statistical power of the reported preliminary results, no significant differences among treatments were revealed. However, mean effect sizes of .30 on outcome variables increased to a range from .39 to .63 when matching variables were considered. These results tend to suggest that narrative therapy can be effective for the treatment of these conditions.

Finally, sessions from these three treatments were compared to evaluate the clinical change of patients in terms of the complexity of process, multiplicity of content, and coherence of structure of their narratives. The first, middle, and last therapy session for each patient in the sample was transcribed and coded using the narrative process, context, and structure manuals. Changes in the narratives of patients who improved the most and the ones who improved the least in each treatment group revealed an interesting pattern. The narratives of those clients who demonstrated the most treatment gave evidence of changes in complexity of process, multiplicity of content, and coherence of structure, when the three sessions were compared. Those patients who improved the least did not show this pattern. Another interesting result was that among the patients who improved the most and those who improved the least, it was the narrative therapy group that demonstrated a positive development of narrative complexity of process, multiplicity of content, and coherence of structure in the spontaneous narratives analyzed for this study (Moreira, Gonçalves, Beutler, & Harwood, 2003).

CONCLUSIONS

Human beings are symbolic species (Deacon, 1997) with a pervasive language instinct (Pinker, 1994). It is this language instinct that allows room for the narrative construction of experience. We use stories not only to communicate with others but also, and above all, to communicate with ourselves. More than a tool devised to communicate, narrative is a way of organizing experience. Amazingly enough, narrative production seems to be a central executive function by which neural integration is achieved. For example, research by Michael Gazzaniga and his colleagues has consistently shown that parts of our brain act as "interpreters," contributing to a continuous and integrated narration as a way of providing structure and coherence in our daily experience (Gazzaniga, 2000). As Siegel (1999) has pointed out, "vertical, dorsal-ventral, lateral, interhemispheric, and spatiotemporal forms of integration are all present within the narrative process" (p. 331). Narrative can be seen as a way by which we nurture our brain in achieving increased neural plasticity.

We believe that this decade will witness a better understanding of how different aspects of the brain cooperate in narrative construction and the specific role of narrative in brain development. We will be in a better position then to understand the role of narrative in psychological disorders and how narrative can be clinically used to increase neural plasticity. Maybe that will finally help us to stop seeing psychotherapy within the straitjacket of nature versus nurture. In a not too distant future, psychotherapy will finally be regarded as an ideal way for nurturing nature.

REFERENCES

Angus, L. E., Levitt, H., & Hardtke, K. (1999). The narrative processes coding system: Research applications and implications for psychotherapy practice. *Journal of Clinical Psychology, 55*, 1255-1270.

Baerger, D. R., & McAdams, D. P. (1999). Life story coherence and its relation to psychological well-being. *Narrative Inquiry, 9*, 69-96.

Beutler, L. E., Moleiro, C., Malik, M., Harwood, T. M., Romanelli, R., Gallagher-Thompson,

D., & Thompson, L. (in press). A comparison of the Dodo, EST, and ATI factors among co-morbid stimulant-dependent, depressed patients. *Clinical Psychology & Psychotherapy.*

Botella, L., & Herrero, O. (2000). A relational constructivist approach to narrative therapy. *The European Journal of Psychotherapy, Counselling & Health, 3,* 407-418.

Capps, L., & Ochs, E. (1995). *Constructing panic: The discourse of agoraphobia.* Cambridge, MA: Harvard University Press.

Cozolino, L. (2002). *The neuroscience of psychotherapy.* New York: Norton.

Deacon, T. (1997). *The symbolic species.* London: Penguin.

Dimaggio, G., & Semerari, A. (2001). Psychopathological narrative forms. *Journal of Constructivist Psychology, 14,* 1-24.

Gazzaniga, M. (2000). Right hemisphere language following brain bisection: A 20-year perspective. In M. S. Gazzaniga (Ed.), *Cognitive neuroscience* (pp. 411-430). Malden, MA: Blackwell.

Gergen, K. J., & Kaye, J. (1992). Beyond narrative in the negotiation of human meaning. In S. McNamee & K. J. Gergen (Eds.), *Therapy as social construction* (pp. 166-185). London: Sage.

Gonçalves, O. F. (1995a). Cognicion, constructivismo y narrativa: En busca de un sentido para las silabas. *Revista de Psicoterapia, 6,* 45-52.

Gonçalves, O. F. (1995b). Cognitive narrative psychotherapy: The hermeneutic construction of alternative meanings. In M. J. Mahoney (Ed.), *Cognitive and constructive psychotherapies: Theory, research, and practice* (pp. 139-162). New York: Springer.

Gonçalves, O. F. (1995c). Hermeneutics, constructivism, and cognitive-behavioral therapies: From the object to the project. In R. A. Neimeyer & M. J. Mahoney (Eds.), *Constructivism in psychotherapy* (pp. 195-230). Washington, DC: American Psychological Association.

Gonçalves, O. F. (1998). *Psicoterapia cognitiva narrativa: Um manual de psicoterapia breve.* Sao Paulo, Brazil: Edipsy.

Gonçalves, O. F. (2000). *Viver narrativamente: A psicoterapia como adjectivação da experiência.* Coimbra, Portugal: Quarteto Editora.

Gonçalves, O. F. (2001). Da psicoterapia como ficção à psicoterapia como criação: As más notícias. In M. M. Gonçalves & O. F. Gonçalves (Coords.), *Psicoterapia, discurso e narrativa: A construção conversacional da mudança* (pp. 7-25). Coimbra, Portugal: Quarteto.

Gonçalves, O. F., Alves, A., Soares, I., Duarte, Z., Henriques, M., & Maia, A. (1996). Narrativa e psicopatologia. *Psicologia: Teoria, Investigação e Prática, 1,* 307-318.

Gonçalves, O. F., Henriques, M. R., Alves, A., & Soares, L. (2002). Analyzing structure, process, and content in narratives of patients diagnosed with agoraphobia. *Revista Internacional de Psicología y de la Salud/International Journal of Clinical and Health Psychology, 2,* 389-406.

Gonçalves, O. F., & Machado, P. P (1999). Cognitive narrative psychotherapy: Research foundations. *Journal of Clinical Psychology, 55,* 1179-1191.

Gonçalves, O. F., Machado, P. P., & Rosas, M. (1997). A elaboração narrativa dos aspectos psicotraumáticos do enfarte do miocárdio: Um manual terapêutico. *Psicologia: Teoria, investigação e prática, 1,* 381-392.

Gonçalves, O. F., Machado, P. P., & Rosas, M. (1998, June). *Outcome and follow-up data on the impact of narrative elaboration of the psychotraumatic aspects of the myocardial infraction on patient's physical and emotional recovering.* Paper presented at the Annual Meeting of the Society for Psychotherapy Research, Snowbird, Utah, United States.

Hermans, H. J. M., & Hermans-Jansen, E. (1995). *Self-narratives: The construction of meaning in psychotherapy.* New York: Guilford.

Howard, G. S., Maerlender, A. C., Myers, P. R., & Curtin, T. D. (1992). In stories we trust: Studies on the validity of autobiographies. *Journal of Counseling Psychology, 39,* 398-405.

Lakoff, G., & Johnson, M. (1980). *Metaphors we live by.* Chicago: University of Chicago Press.

Markus, H., & Nurius, P. (1986). Possible selves. *American Psychologist, 41,* 954–969.

McLeod, J. (1997). *Narrative and psychotherapy.* London: Sage.

Moreira, P., Gonçalves, O., Beutler, L. E., & Harwood. M. (2003). *Besides tests results, what changes in psychotherapy?* Braga, Portugal: Universidade do Minho. Manuscript in preparation.

Neimeyer, R. (2000). Narrative disruptions and the construction of the self. In R. Neimeyer & J. Raskin (Eds.), *Constructions of disorder* (pp. 207-242). Washington, DC: American Psychological Association.

Omer, H., & Alon, N. (1997). *Constructing therapeutic narratives*. Northvale, NJ: Jason Aronson.

Pennebaker, J. (1993). Putting stress in words: Health, linguistic, and therapeutic implication. *Behaviour, Research & Therapy, 31*, 539-548.

Pinker, S. (1994). *The language instinct*. New York: Harper.

Russell, R. L., & Wandrei, M. L. (1996). Narrative and the process of psychotherapy: Theoretical foundations and empirical support. In H. Rosen & K. Kuehlwein (Eds.), *Constructing realities: Meaning making perspectives for psychotherapists* (pp. 307-336). San Francisco: Jossey-Bass.

Siegel, D. J. (1999). *The developing mind*. New York: Guilford.

Tulving, E. (1985a). How many memory systems are there? *American Psychologist, 40*, 385-398.

Tulving, E. (1985b). Memory and consciousness. *Canadian Psychology, 26*, 1-12.

White, M., & Epston, D. (1990). *Narrative means to therapeutic ends*. New York: Norton.

CHAPTER 7

Working With Narrative in Psychotherapy
A Relational Constructivist Approach

LUIS BOTELLA
OLGA HERRERO
MERITXELL PACHECO
SERGI CORBELLA

OVERVIEW

Stories are everywhere. Human meaning-making processes are so embedded in narrative forms that it is quite difficult to locate instances of human life that are alien to narratives. The very history of humankind is a story full of stories. Religious traditions are rich in stories, from biblical parables to Zen Buddhist or Sufi tales. We live in (and through) stories; family myths, traditions, and anecdotes. We fall in love through (and sometimes with) stories, from Shakespearean dramas to pop love songs. We grow up, work, rest, dream, suffer, and even die according to narrative patterns. Stories are the fabric of our private lives, our relational networks, our social traditions, and our cultural and historical institutions. However, psychology has been somehow blind to the pervasiveness of narrative, probably because, in its attempt to constitute a "respectable science," it traditionally adopted forms of "paradigmatic (versus narrative) thought" (Bruner, 1986), which appeared more scientific in the past. Paradoxically, and with

AUTHORS' NOTE: Correspondence regarding this article should be sent to the authors at Ramon Llull University, Department of Psychology, Cister 22-24, 08022 Barcelona, Spain, or to Lluisbg@blanquerna.url.es.

some remarkable exceptions, for instance, Sir Frederic Bartlett's classical studies on remembering in the early 20th century, it was not until postmodernism began to problematize grand metanarratives (Lyotard, 1993) that psychology began to pay attention to narratives in a host of domains. Throughout these years, narrative approaches to a variety of human psychological processes have gained popularity, and some of them are nowadays part of mainstream psychology as well as a growing body of research and practice. The appeal of narrative as a root metaphor for human psychological functioning seems to be particularly noticeable among constructivists and social constructionists.

Our aim in this work is to make a contribution to this ongoing development, one that rests on our own understanding of narrative and psychotherapy from a *relational constructivist* approach (Botella, 2001; Botella & Herrero, 2000). Thus, the chapter is divided in three main sections: (a) a brief outline of our understanding of relational constructivism and its main guiding assumptions; (b) a series of guidelines for the practice of working with narrative in therapy, informed by a relational constructivist approach to both clinical practice and research; and (c) some closing thoughts about what we consider the main challenges of narrative therapy in the near future.

RELATIONAL CONSTRUCTIVISM: A HISTORICAL AND CONCEPTUAL CONTEXT

The first section of this chapter will deal with how our approach has developed, including a brief discussion of the location of our practices within historical, social, and cultural traditions.

What we call relational constructivism (Botella, 2001; Botella & Herrero, 2000) constitutes our attempt to press the dialogue between constructivism and social constructionism further (see Botella, 1995) and to enrich it with the voice of narrative and postmodern approaches. We have been developing the ideas presented here during the last 10 years of our academic and therapeutic work, and nowadays, these ideas inform and inspire our own practice as psychotherapists at the *Servei d'Assessorament i Atenció Psicològic Blanquerna* (Blanquerna Psychotherapy Unit) in Barcelona as well as our research programs at the Constructivism and Discourse Processes Research Group at Ramon Llull University. If the theoretical assumptions that we present in this chapter were originally proposed by its senior author (LB), they have been developed, applied, tested and refined in the context of our joint work, both in clinical practice and research. Thus, coherently with our own approach, we present them as discursive productions belonging to an ongoing conversation, not to any single individual participating in this conversation. Of course, we also acknowledge the significant role of the rest of our research group members, especially Antonia María Gomez and Paola Velázquez. What follows, then, is a brief outline of the 10 main assumptions of relational constructivism in our present conceptualization of it.

1. *Being human entails construing meaning.* From a constructivist standpoint, human psychological processes can be equated to "efforts after meaning" (Bartlett, 1932). Human beings are proactively oriented toward a meaningful understanding of the world in which they live and their own place in it. Being human entails active efforts to interpret experience, seeking purpose and significance in the events that surround us (Neimeyer & Neimeyer, 1993).

2. *Meaning is an interpretative and linguistic achievement.* Experiences in themselves do not carry meaning. To render the otherwise

"purposeless drift" (Efran, Lukens, & Lukens, 1990) of life events meaningful and more or less predictable, we need to pattern them, to find similarities and contrasts between them, and to place them in unfolding frames of intelligibility, that is, to *interpret* them. As we shall see, intelligibility and transformation (i.e., agency) are two crucial goals of narrative therapy from a relational constructivist approach.

3. *Language and interpretations are relational achievements.* As discussed by, among others, Ludwig Wittgenstein (1953), language is not the private property of any particular individual's cognitive processes but a form of game we play together, that is, the relational product of shared discursive practices and joint actions. Our interpretations of experience are patterned by and located in the context of shared forms of intelligibility. The process of becoming a member of our social network entails learning how to make sense of life events in forms that do not push us into a corner of relational isolation. Even when we do not want to be accepted, the forms of action we undertake to become outcasts are also socially and relationally sustained patterns of meaning-making.

4. *Relationships are conversational.* Since relationships and interactions are mediated by language, they adopt the form of conversations. In the context of a conversation, meaning is not an exclusively individual responsibility (or property). The meaning of our words or actions is always open to a process of supplementation (Gergen, 1994); that is, our words or actions need to be supplemented by the others' to mean anything at all. Thus, the meaning attributed to our words or actions is never a final one and, potentially, they may be interpreted in many ways: Meaning can always be reconstrued, reframed, transvaluated. Every new interpretation clears the space for a new version of events while it also reduces competing ones to the not-yet-said.

5. *Conversations are constitutive of subject positions.* Conversations are constitutive of selves; such a constitutive force derives from their provision of subject positions. Since the meaning of our words or actions does not depend exclusively on ourselves but on a process of unfolding supplementation, conversations create subject positions that are contingent to the very conversation taking place. In this sense, we can position ourselves differently depending on the conversation in which we are taking part. Such an amalgam of subject positions becomes constitutive of our self-concept—conceived of not as a totally private process but as the result of internalizing significant conversations.

6. *Subject positions are expressed as voices.* When a subject position is discursively expressed, it becomes a voice. Voices are thus the discursive expressions of different subject positions constituted in internalized conversations. As Mikhail Bakhtin (1986) aptly noted, authorial voices are likely not to be totally coherent but to maintain a dialogical relationship among them, some being more dominant than others. Both inner dialogue and externalized conversations assume the form of a dialectical interchange, in the sense that our words are not only addressed to the object of our discourse but also to every other competing discourse of which we can think.

7. *Voices expressed along a time dimension constitute narratives.* Since the essence of narrative is time, the expression of a voice along a time dimension assumes a narrative form. Given the dialogical nature of subject positions and discursively expressed narrative voices, there is always more than one way to tell our life story, more than one voice

to be heard, and more than one plot to be voiced. In this reconstructive potential lies the essence of human change in general and psychotherapy in particular; were it not for the indeterminacy of meaning-making processes, the only way left in some cases would be to abandon the scene altogether.

8. *Identity is both the product and the process of self-narrative construction.* Certainly, the answer to the question, "Who am I?" shapes and defines our identity in a given moment. However, the way we select the events to be included in (or excluded from) our narrative, the main themes we organize it around, the characters we regard as significant or nonsignificant, the voices we privilege or silence when telling it . . . all of it is as constitutive of our own identity as the content of our life story. When seen in this light, identity becomes synonymous with authorship. From what has been said so far, it is obvious that there is never a single fixed, final, or true life story to tell, nor a single way to tell it, but a plethora of possibilities.

9. *Psychological problems are embedded in the process of construing narratives of identity.* What we call "psychological problems" or "disorders" constitute a "fuzzy set" of human ways to belong and relate to the world. What seems to be common to practically all of them, however, is the subjective experience of *unintelligibility* and *loss of personal agency* that they introduce in people's narratives of identity. Under a myriad of different discursive expressions, people who complain about psychological suffering refer naturally to one or both of the aforementioned narrative blocks. It is as if, somehow, our position relative to our narrative of identity had been pushed to a state of authorial powerlessness. Life (as in the Simon and Garfunkel song) seems "a scene badly written in which one must play."

10. *Psychotherapy can be equated to a collaborative dialogue addressed to transform the client's narratives of identity.* Psychotherapy takes place in language. Despite the pervasiveness of the medico/biological model and the drug metaphor, psychotherapy derives its transformative potential not from being a treatment or a cure, but from being a specialized form of human conversation in which new subject positions are voiced, new narratives are told, new forms of intelligibility emerge, and the not-yet-said finds room to be consciously and mindfully heard. The skill of the therapist is the skill of clearing the space for such a transformative dialogue to take place.

We will discuss this last point further in the next section of this work. Before closing the present one, however, we want to briefly elaborate on the position of relational constructivism in the context of other approaches to narrative psychology and psychotherapy, particularly regarding the constitutive (versus representative) nature of self-narratives.

As Singer (1996) noted after carefully reviewing the main assumptions underlying earlier narrative approaches, some of them shared the common notion that the study of individual or collective narratives should clear the way for the study of an "actual world" transcending narrative itself. This is typical of earlier narrative traditions inspired by traditional sociology or anthropology, and Singer refers to this assumption as an *objectivist* one. In contrast, other approaches (particularly the ones inspired by symbolic interactionism, personology, and, more recently, cognitive psychology) addressed narratives as a way to access the "inner reality" of narrating individuals. Singer refers to this assumption as a *subjectivist* one.

Our position in this context is neither objectivist nor subjectivist. We consider narratives not as a *representation* of a different domain of experience but as a form of relationally situated and *constitutive* action in their own right. That is, we assume that we *are* the stories that we *live* and *tell,* and we *live* and *tell* the stories that we *are.* To put it in more technical terms, relational constructivism is based on the assumption of a constitutive relationship between narrative and lived experience, in the sense that each one mutually defines and shapes the other. Thus, the more life is lived, for example, as a series of irreparable failures at critical points, the more it is told (to ourselves and to others) as such; and the more it is told in this painful and depressive way, the more it is lived as such.

Having briefly outlined the main theoretical assumptions that inform our practice, it is now time to discuss our practice itself.

GUIDELINES FOR PSYCHOTHERAPEUTIC PRACTICE

It is in an integrative spirit that our proposal is best understood. As we tried to highlight in the first section of this chapter, we envision our main theoretical assumptions as common principles, that is, general dimensions of narrative and human meaning-making processes that are implicitly or explicitly involved in any form of psychotherapeutic practice. However, we do not conceive of these common principles as unspecific or atheoretical; all of the 10 main assumptions we sketched in the preceding section entail quite specific professional skills in order to be implemented in psychotherapy, and all of them are theoretically coherent with our own attempt to bridge the gap between constructivism and constructionism. In this sense, our own approach to therapeutic practice is embedded in the constructivist tradition of theoretical coherence and technical eclecticism. Our own experience as (a) practitioners, (b) trainers and supervisors of psychotherapy trainees at a master's level, and (c) psychotherapy researchers validate the usefulness of this general framework.

What follows is a synthesis of what we regard as the main implications of the conceptual assumptions discussed in the preceding section for working with narrative in psychotherapy. We have clustered some of these assumptions in terms of their main underlying themes, and the implications we mentioned before will be presented, emphasizing their connection to these clusters. Also, we have identified in each instance one or more basic guiding questions, so that they can be used as roadmaps to orient and pattern the therapist's focus of attention and action when working with client narrative expression, as well as the selected procedures and techniques he or she decides to use in therapy. Table 7.1 presents a synthesis of the main conceptual assumptions of relational constructivism as well as the guiding questions they entail—already clustered so as to facilitate their interpretation.

This is obviously only one of all the possible sets of guiding questions that could be derived from our main assumptions, and in fact, we keep the table "under construction" as we continue to develop and test our ideas in practice and research. Notice, however, that the emphasis is not on specific techniques but on the conceptual principles that guide the thoughtful selection of them.

We have also included clinical vignettes to illustrate our main points, as well as selected results from our applied research programs that lend empirical support to our discussion (for a comprehensive description of our research programs, see our Web site at http://fpce.blanquerna.edu/constructivisme).

Experience, Meaning, Interpretation, and Language

Guiding Question: How do our clients construe meanings from their experience,

Table 7.1 Conceptual Assumptions of Relational Constructivism and Guiding Questions for Clinical Practice

Conceptual Assumption	Guiding Question
1. Being human entails construing meaning.	How do our clients construe meanings from their experience and what are the main difficulties and/or blocks that they experience in this process?
2. Meaning is an interpretative and linguistic achievement.	
3. Language and interpretations are relational achievements.	What are the relational contexts in which the ways our clients construe meanings have been generated? What forms of relationship are invited by these constructions? Which ones are discouraged?
4. Relationships are conversational.	How can we use language so as to generate therapeutic conversations that clear the space for changes in our clients' subject positions?
5. Conversations are constitutive of subject positions.	
6. Subject positions are expressed as voices.	How can we foster a transformative dialogue between our clients' different voices?
7. Voices expressed along a time dimension constitute narratives.	How can we foster meaningful transformations in our clients' narratives of identity?
8. Identity is both the product and the process of one's self-narratives construction.	What is the constitutive relationship between our clients' processes of identity construction and their presenting complaint?
9. Psychological problems are embedded in the process of construing one's narratives of identity.	How can we create a therapeutic relationship that helps to bring forth meaningful changes, in terms of both increased intelligibility and agency?
10. Psychotherapy can be equated to a collaborative dialogue addressed to transform the client's narratives of identity.	

and what are the main difficulties and/or blocks that they experience in this process? As is the case with the rest of the guiding questions we are proposing, every therapist is likely to answer this one in terms of his or her preferred theoretical framework and/or personal style. In our case, one of the conceptual models that we find more useful and theoretically coherent with our own approach in addressing this first guiding question is the cycle of experience, which was originally proposed by Kelly (1970) and formalized by Neimeyer (1987) within the realm of personal construct psychology.

Basically, the cycle of experience describes the process of meaning construction as a five-stage ongoing process according to which we human beings face an experience by first subjectively anticipating its outcome. To the extent that such an anticipation is perceived as self-relevant, our investment in its outcome is likely to be greater or lower. Through our encounter with the event, anticipations will either be confirmed or disconfirmed (i.e., validated or invalidated). In narrative terms, the greater the relevance of the narrative being validated or invalidated to one's core themes, the higher the intensity of emotions aroused by such validation or invalidation. Particularly if anticipations are invalidated, we will face the need to constructively revise our construct system. A constructive revision of core themes and narratization processes is needed. Thus the "last" stage of the cycle is recursively connected to the "first" one, because the result of our constructive revision influences the way we meet new experiences.

Careful attention to what our clients tell us (and how they tell it) in therapy can help us therapists "draw a map" of their construing processes and how they can be better mobilized. In this section, we will use as an example one of the case studies of our in-depth qualitative research project on the narrative emplotment (ascribing of a narrative plot to a series of otherwise unrelated events) of loss (see Botella et al., 2002). In this particular study, we did a qualitative analysis of an autobiographical narrative written by a middle-aged father (Luis Alberto) whose son committed suicide. Luis Alberto was a successful South American businessman who sought overseas training in psychology, for the first time, in the wake of this tragic event. It was in the course of this study that he encountered constructivist ideas through contact with one of the authors (LB), finding in them a helpful reformulation of the perturbing questions generated by his son's fateful decision. In particular, Kelly's (1955/1991) discussion of suicide as an "elaborative choice" whose goal was to preserve a person's system of meaning by warding off further invalidation struck him deeply and instigated the written reflections that became his diary. (Space restrictions do not allow us to go into a full discussion of the study, or even to include lengthy fragments of the narrative we analyzed. Thus, interested readers can refer to Botella et al., 2002.)

Data from this study, as well as from others related to the same project (see Botella & Herrero, 2001), demonstrated that even if this reconstructive and reincorporating process is possible, it may be particularly difficult in some instances. This difficulty arises from the inevitable loss of coherence in one's self-narrative and interpersonal positions after such a core invalidation. Loss of narrative coherence stems from the fact that the traumatic event violates almost by definition the core themes in one's self-narrative. Thus, one may be confronted with the difficult task of reconstruing an invalidated narrative that *must* make sense of an event incompatible with the core themes that sustained the previous narrative. Some instances of traumatic loss may be extremely difficult to cope with (i.e., to effect a narrative reconstrual) because they involve the violation of what seem to be fundamental cornerstones of human existence. For example, the death of a child violates the almost commonsensical idea that "children outlive their parents," and it is hard to reconcile such an event with belief in a forgiving God or a just Fate. Also, loss brought forth by a suicidal action faces the bereaved with the need to deal with issues of agency in the deceased's actions, questioning not only spiritual issues but the very essence of human freedom. In this sense, Luis Alberto's experience is probably one of the most difficult ones to reconstruct, since it involves the suicide of his son.

Dialogue, Relationships and Subject Positions

Guiding Questions: What are the relational contexts in which the ways our clients construe meanings have been generated? What forms of relationship are invited by these constructions; which ones are discouraged? To the extent that we assume that language and interpretations are relational achievements, and not exclusively individual ones, then it makes sense to ask what are the relational contexts (the "language games," in Wittgenstein's 1953 term) that contributed to our clients' construing experience the way they do.

The joint exploration of such relational contexts in therapy can take place in many ways.

In general, we find questions addressed to the elaboration of similarities and contrasts between the subject positions of our clients and their significant others very useful. For instance, if clients define themselves as powerless (as opposed to powerful), we ask them who is the more powerless person in their family and who is the more powerful one. We may even invite them to locate all other significant people in their relational network along the powerful-powerless continuum and to assign a rating to each one as if it were an informal repertory grid (see Kelly, 1955/1991). We can also introduce more subtle nuances in our dialogue, asking clients in what relational narrative or context each of these persons is more or less powerful or powerless, or during which moment of their lives they have been closer to one or the other end of the continuum (the procedure is parallel to what solution-focused therapists refer to as "scaling questions"; e.g., Kim Berg & de Shazer, 1993).

We also find it useful to ask our clients about the personal history of the terms they use. For example, in the case we mentioned above, we could ask the client when he or she heard the word *powerless* (or *powerful*) for the first time, who used it, to whom it was addressed, where it came from, and so on.

Results from our own research projects also shed some light on how some therapists use language so as to foster change in their clients. One research project is dedicated to the conversational analysis of the unfolding of clients' narrative reflexivity through therapeutic dialogue (see Botella, Pacheco, Herrero, & Corbella, 2000). Our point of departure in one of these studies was the notion that the development of clients' narrative reflexivity is related to a good therapeutic outcome. The study examined the process of unfolding reflexive narrative processing modes (instead of an external or internal mode; see Angus, Levitt, & Hardtke, 1999) as a result of the joint construction of meaning via the therapeutic dialogue. We attempted to shed some light on the conditions of the therapeutic conversation and relationship that facilitate client change, in terms of their narratives and how these conditions function. We adopted a qualitative and discovery-oriented approach to this particular study. Transcripts of one complete good-outcome brief process-experiential therapy (15 sessions) for depression, drawn from the York I Depression Study, were coded and analyzed. The types of narrative processes used by the client were identified by means of the Narrative Process Coding System (Angus, Hardtke, & Levitt, 1996; Angus et al., 1999). The dialogical dimensions of the therapeutic conversation were coded and analyzed using a hierarchical tree that we developed by using a research strategy inspired by grounded theory methodology (Glaser & Strauss, 1967).

Our results indicated that throughout all the therapy sessions the therapist positioned herself as a collaborative and reflexive voice that facilitated and commented aloud on the client's reflections. This allowed the client to give voice to a position quite opposite to the one that was dominant in her other relationships. Instead of being focused on the other (in this case, the therapist), as was the case with her position relative to her father and her husband, the client found herself participating in a dialogue whose main focus was herself.

Also, our study demonstrated that as a result of the dialogical positioning previously discussed, the therapeutic conversation unfolded as a joint language game that allowed the client to assume a reflexive position. Conversational processes previously initiated by the therapist were now almost impossible to causally attribute to only one speaker. Even if our results come from a particular from of therapy (process-experiential), they can probably be extrapolated to other ones—at least to all therapies that consider increasing the client's level of reflexivity as a therapeutic goal.

Narrative and Identity

Guiding Question: How can we foster meaningful transformations in our clients' narratives of identity? In regaining a feeling of intelligibility and transformation over one's narrative of identity, the dialectic tension between continuity and discontinuity plays a crucial role. Very often the narratives we hear our clients tell us have been critically fragmented by some life event that has introduced an unexpected discontinuity in them—be it frustration, abuse, trauma, loss, illness, or a given symptom. This is likely to be the reason why most of our clients express their main goal in therapy as "I want to be the one I used to be." Unfortunately, such a "narrative rewinding" is impossible by definition, since we cannot turn back time. Nevertheless, quoting Kierkegaard, life is lived forward, but it is understood backward. Thus, as M. C. Bateson (1993) discusses, "Much of coping with discontinuity has to do with discovering threads of continuity. You cannot adjust to changes unless you can recognize some analogy between your old situation and your new situation" (p. 45).

Most of what we have discussed so far can also be seen as an answer to this guiding question. However, for the sake of clarity and structure, we will focus this section on a brief discussion of the narrative dimensions we use so as to address our therapeutic action to the introduction of meaningful changes in one or more of them (see Table 7.2).

Results from a host of our studies dealing with in-depth conversation analysis of successful therapies (see Pacheco & Botella, 1999; Pacheco, Botella, & Corbella, 1999) demonstrate that all of these narrative dimensions are sensitive to therapeutic change, that is, they change when the client changes as a result of successful therapy. What follows is a series of fragments from Nicole's pre-therapy self-narrative, written as a therapeutic assignment after her intake session. Nicole was a 32-year-old woman, diagnosed as agoraphobic, whose therapeutic narratives were analyzed in one of our studies. The dramatic shifts in her narrative before and after successful therapy are a good representation of the dimensions of self-narratives presented in Table 7.2 as well as a demonstration of how they change as a result of psychotherapy.*

(. . .) My mother has always been a fearful and quite conservative woman. She would see dangers in almost anything and anyone. I remember how she used to warn me against boys when I was a teenager, against all kind of terrible things that could happen to me if I tried to do things on my own. My father had just given up trying to change her, and he would isolate himself from her warnings and look at me in a sort of hopeless way when she became almost paranoid. (. . .) I don't know where my panic comes from. I guess I must suffer from some nervous disease . . . maybe it's something in my genes, since I seem to resemble my mother more and more. (. . .) Most of the time I think there's nothing I can do to stop my fears. My mother once told me that I was so weak that even my weaknesses were stronger than me, and I think she was right in her own cruel way (. . .) When my fear takes over me, everything seems to be extremely dangerous and threatening,

---

* In the following dialogue, the author uses (. . .) to designate areas where he deleted material that was irrelevant to his point, whereas . . . indicates a pause in the speaker's presentation.

Table 7.2   Selected Dimensions of Self-Narratives

Narrative endpoint   Narrative goal, event to be explained, state to be reached or avoided, outcome of significance, or "point." The point of a narrative is the answer to the question "so what"?

Plot   Construction and interconnection of events such that meaningful structures are developed.

Theme   A general thought or idea of which a set of propositions is taken to be an illustration.

Characters' construction   Attributes assigned to the narrative's characters by its author.

Origin   Cause attributed to the narrated events by its author. It can be internal, when such an origin is attributed to the author's self, or external, when it is attributed to sources other than the author's self.

Agency   Possibility of modifying the course of the narrative events as perceived by its author. According to its degree of modifiability, any narrated event can position its author as active when such a modification is seen as possible or passive when such a modification is seen as impossible.

Relevance   Extent to which an event is thematically connected to the narrative endpoint. It can be high or low.

Coherence   Extent to which an event is in accordance with the narrative endpoint. According to its degree of coherence, any narrated event can be noncontradictory or contradictory.

Narrative form   Narrative movement relative to its evaluative shifts over time. A narrative is progressive to the extent that it links together events so that the movement along the evaluative dimension over time is incremental. A narrative is regressive to the extent that it links together events so that the movement along the evaluative dimension over time is decremental. A narrative is stable to the extent that it links together events so that the movement along the evaluative dimension over time remains unchanged. (Gergen, 1994)

Narrative consciousness level   Level of reflection of the author as manifested in the narrative. It can be external when the narrative consists of a mere descriptive representation of events; internal when it includes references to mental processes or states than can only be known by the author; or reflexive when it includes references to a metalevel, that is, to mental processes or states referring to the moment when the narrative is told and not only to the moment when the events took place. (see also Angus, Hardtke, & Levitt, 1996)

Openness to alternatives   Extent to which the narrated events could be interpreted alternatively. According to its degree of openness, an event can be tight when it imposes a large amount of textual constraint, that is, when it allows only one correct answer to the questions asked by the reader. It can be loose when it imposes a small amount of textual constraint, that is, when it allows many alternative answers to the questions asked by the reader.

---

particularly the way other people look at me in the streets, or in the subway ... I can't barely stand it ... they seem to be able to see inside me and see how weak I am. (...) Sometimes I can overcome my fear ... but it happens so rarely that it feels like a drop of water in an ocean of anxiety and insecurity. (...) I feel trapped in my fear, and I can only foresee a future even worse and more and more isolated.

The endpoint of Nicole's self-narrative was, "how did I become who I am," since in fact that was the assignment that the therapist asked her to write about. The origin that Nicole attributed to her suffering was almost completely external, as can be seen in her mentioning "nervous disease" or even "something in her genes." Probably as a result of that, Nicole's feelings of agency were almost inexistent ("there's nothing I can do"). Her own feelings of weakness and vulnerability turned almost everything (and particularly social interaction) into a relevant threat. Nicole's self-narrative form was extremely regressive, leading only to the anticipation of an even worse future. Also, Nicole's construction of the other characters in her self-narrative (in this case, her parents) were far from flattering and contributed to her feelings of fatality. The level of coherence in her self-narrative was quite high, except for the fact that she mentioned some isolated episodes of "overcoming fear." The level of openness to alternatives in Nicole's self-narrative was very low, since her way of emplotting her life events left almost no space for interpretations other than her own. Interestingly, however, her level of self-narrative consciousness was predominantly internal, even if the tone of the emotions and thoughts that she was aware of were almost entirely negative, threatening and fearful.

After 6 months of weekly psychotherapy sessions that combined behavioral exposure techniques, open discussion of her self-defeating and negative construction of herself, family therapy, and attendance at a supportive therapy group as well as a self-help group, Nicole wrote a narrative on how therapy was helping her. These are fragments from that narrative:

> (. . .) I've learnt to see other people as just this: other people. The person looking at me is obviously a human being with her own fears, weaknesses, strengths, dreams . . . with her own story just as I have mine. In fact, I caught myself sometimes laughing secretly at the thought that maybe the one who's looking at me is also in therapy for some other reason! (. . .) Episodes of "success" are now more frequent and, believe me, this is the best reinforcement one can have! (. . .) Exposure helped me control my fear, as well as relaxation, breathing, and meditation exercises. However, now I realize that was only the beginning . . . the surface. Fear will always be an uncontrollable enemy until I can be reasonably sure that the world is not a dangerous place, that people are not out there to harm me, and that even if that was the case, I could protect me and survive. Some of the group sessions helped me a lot to see that point; I could resonate deeply with some of the group members' craving for shelter and protection. Also, family therapy sessions helped me see myself in context. (. . .) Sharing some of my family experiences with other members of the self-help group has made me realize that there are striking similarities among us. It's obvious to me now that our (and particularly my own!) parents were fallible human beings, and even if their way to relate to me has left scars in my self-esteem, learning to live with such scars and help them make me stronger is a challenge I must face . . . and I'm not the only one! (. . .) Well . . . maybe I have a future after all. However, this idea has led me to a newly found sense of responsibility that I didn't know existed. And it is a bit frightening somehow. But I would not call this fear . . . it's more like unexpected excitement.

Nicole's narrative had shifted in most of the dimensions we analyzed. The origin that Nicole attributed to her suffering was now more internal, in the sense that she attributed part of her feelings of fear and weakness to her own construction of the social world. Thus, her feelings of agency increased—which were probably connected to the success of behavioral exposure in this case. People were seen not so much as a relevant threat but as fellow human beings (who can even be in therapy themselves). Nicole's self-narrative form shifted from regressive to progressive, even if she admitted that the feelings of responsibility this entailed were not always totally pleasant. Her construction of the other characters (her parents) seemed to be more compassionate. A new sense of coherence emerged in Nicole's self-narrative, one that revolved around success instead of weakness, fear, or failure exclusively. Also, her level of self-narrative consciousness was still internal but also reflexive, and the tone of the emotions and thoughts that she was aware of were now not only negative but positive in many instances.

In the case of Luis Alberto's narrative, which deals extensively and in detail with his reconstructive process, a pattern of meaning reconstruction was observed. First, his narrative focused on a particular guiding theme (professional and social success) and included emplotted life events that were coherent with the identified theme. Then the occurrence of traumatic loss in his life shattered his sense of self-coherence by introducing a threatening and unpredictable event (his son's suicide), one that was incompatible with the original narrative's guiding theme: How can Louis Alberto keep considering his life a success after his son has committed suicide? Despite Luis Alberto's attempts to recover coherence by "never until now accepting the suicide thesis, devoting myself again fully to my professional and academic functions (that I never left in front of the others) and looking at life skeptically, with the same success as before" the impact of the traumatic event was too strong to be easily marginalized from his narrative.

As in other cases we have analyzed, the reconstructive process he exemplified in his narrative consisted precisely in finding a new guiding theme for his life and his identity, one that did not marginalize his loss but included it and even used it as a cornerstone. Thus, the emerging narrative was no longer focused exclusively on professional and social success but on a newly found sense of "spirituality, emotionality, love, intellectuality, physical strength and a proactive view of one's future and life, creative strength, and sociability." Luis Alberto equated this process to the creation of "a new system of constructs" that "give a different meaning to a life that undoubtedly has a before and an after." Such constructs allowed him to "live again, probably more intensely than before, enjoying life in all that it means: at home, at the workplace, with one's friends and acquaintances" to "laugh again, simply put, to live."

We have also analyzed successful therapies in terms of conversation analysis of episodes of dialogical self-narrative transformation, that is, episodes in which the therapeutic dialogue revolves around client-initiated stories (see Pacheco & Botella, 1999; Pacheco et al., 1999). Our results indicate that during such episodes, the narrative consciousness level of both client and therapist was predominantly reflexive. Also, a significant number of these episodes followed a pattern of loosening-tightening (temporal narrative disorganization-reorganization) during the reconstructive process.

This twofold process of increased reflexivity and disorganization-reorganization can be seen in the following example. The client had just explained to the therapist an episode during which he initiated an open dialogue with his parents about a series of painful memories from his childhood that included his parents. The client developed his narrative in a chiefly internal narrative mode, mentioning his own feelings and emotions as the conversation with his parents took place, as well as how he thinks his parents were feeling. Then the following interchange took place:

Therapist I am aware that you were feeling a lot of mixed emotions at that moment, as you were talking to your parents, and I'd like to go back to these in a moment. But I am also wondering how are you feeling here and now as you talk to me about your experience of

	the conversation with your parents...
Client	You know... it's sort of funny, because I feel part of the same ambivalence that I felt then... you see; that sort of dilemma between "this is going to clarify things" on the one hand, and "this is going to make things even worse" on the other.
Therapist	It feels as if there are two voices activated at the same time. I wonder if they are in a dialogue or one is opposing the other, or...
Client	Yeah... I can feel this duplicity too... I don't know if *dialogue* would describe what's going on inside me... However, I can also notice a difference between now and then...
Therapist	And that would be...?
Client	...that now I don't need to be defensive, I'm not risking being defeated if I make a mistake or show some weakness... I don't know, I'm not sure if I can express myself more clearly...
Therapist	Maybe this feeling is somehow related to our relationship here being different from the one with your parents, or your occupying a different position in both...
Client	Yeah, I think so. I don't need to be defensive here because I don't feel under attack. *[5 seconds silence; the client begins to weep]* It's painful to myself to hear me say that I feel under attack when talking to my parents...

The shift to a reflexive narrative mode is initiated by the therapist's focusing the conversation in the "here and now," thus encouraging the client to literally reflect on his recent past experience from the viewpoint of the present. Nevertheless, as the therapeutic conversation unfolds as a joint language game that allows the client to assume a reflexive position, conversational processes previously initiated by the therapist are almost impossible to attribute causally to only one speaker. Also, the loosening-tightening cycle can be seen as the client's initial difficulties in finding precise words to describe his experience give way to the more definite and insightful awareness revealed in his last speech turn in the example.

Results from the studies mentioned before (see Pacheco & Botella, 1999; Pacheco et al., 1999) also demonstrated a strong relationship between the narrative categories *origin* and *agency* (see Table 7.2). Clients presented events as impossible to modify by themselves when the cause attributed to these events was external to themselves (lack of agency-external origin). Conversely, they presented events as modifiable by themselves when the cause attributed to these events was internal to themselves (active agency-internal origin).

Our first result confirmed the significance of the process also described by Adams (1997): the role of reflexive questions as a way of promoting psychotherapeutic change. As for the recurrent pattern of strong relationship between the categories *origin* and *agency*, our results confirm the generally agreed upon observation that the initial experience of clients in psychotherapy is one of lack of control over their difficulties. This experience leads to a feeling of self-fragmentation between a "controlling self" and another self that escapes from such control. As in the episodes analyzed, trying to achieve some level of integration between these two selves could be a good strategy to help clients approach the events in their self-narratives in a way that allows their feelings of agency to increase.

Psychotherapy and the (Re)Construction of Narrative Identity

Guiding Question: What's the constitutive relationship between our clients' processes of identity construction and their presenting complaint? From our present position, our clients' complaints make sense in the context of a life story and a tradition of relational positionings that constitute their identity. This does not mean that we always find it necessary to conduct a long-term therapy oriented to modify core aspects of our clients. In fact, our outcome research evidence points to the conclusion that, on average, our therapeutic style results in what could be considered brief therapy. We routinely ask our clients to respond to the outcome measure inventory of the Clinical Outcomes in Routine Evaluation (CORE) system (see Mellor-Clark, Barkham, Connell, & Evans, 1999), as well as the Symptom Check List (SCL-90R; Derogatis, 1992), before therapy begins and after every four therapy sessions, as well as at the end of therapy and in follow-up interviews at 3, 6, 9, and 12 months. Results from the analysis of 200 cases indicate that the average number of sessions in our good-outcome therapies is between 12 and 13. The analysis of outcome measures yields clinically significant differences from pretherapy to end of therapy. These differences (on average) are already statistically significant between pretherapy and Session 4, and their statistical significance increases between Session 4 and Session 8. However, we do consider it essential to take into account the experiential logic that connects our clients' presenting complaints with their identity-construing processes. Our experience indicates that acting otherwise leads only to a state of systemic and biographic shortsightedness.

For example, Maria was a client who consulted us because, in her own words, she could not "live without suffering," which was giving way to a feeling of permanent dissatisfaction with almost every context of her life. As her biographical narrative unfolded, a pattern emerged showing that Maria felt ignored by her parents throughout her childhood because they devoted almost all of their resources, love, and attention to Maria's elder brother (who had been diagnosed as schizophrenic). At a given point in therapy, we told Maria that her statement, "I cannot live without suffering," could perhaps be deconstructed as:

1. I have never received the love and care I deserve.

2. I cannot live without being loved and cared for.

3. The only way I conceive of being loved and cared for is to adopt the subject position of someone who is suffering.

We told Maria that Point 1 seemed to us a very sad situation that would have affected anyone profoundly; Point 2 something absolutely natural; and Point 3 an unfortunate consequence of the lack of viable alternatives. We suggested that all of this could be changed by means of reflexive and mindful awareness and proactive efforts to transform it. We asked Maria to write the three points on a card and to take the card with her so she could read it reflexively every time she found herself thinking "I cannot live without suffering" during the next weeks (this is one of the procedures proposed by Ecker & Hulley, 2000, in their depth-oriented brief therapy). The result was that Maria was able to make a liberating turn in her life and, even if not all of the changes she experienced in therapy are attributable to this procedure, it really worked as a trigger to foster a very meaningful series of them.

Reflexivity, Agency, and Narrative Change in Psychotherapy

Guiding Question: How can we create a therapeutic relationship that helps bring forth meaningful changes, both in terms of increased intelligibility and agency? We have already discussed the fundamentals of our view of therapy as transformative dialogue. However, in this section, we would like to briefly discuss what we consider crucial attitudes in an optimal therapeutic relationship. From our present perspective, therapy must give the client all possible power and initiative. This notion is based not only on ample research results that demonstrate the importance of clients' factors in successful therapy (see Duncan & Miller, 2000) but also on our ethical commitment to the notion of psychotherapy as liberation, not as correction or medical cure.

We try to foster our clients' active implication in the co-construction of the therapeutic agenda by means of some questions typical of systemic and solution-focused therapies, such as: How would you like to use our time today? What would be useful for us to know? What would be a change that indicates that things are getting better? In the long run, by positioning ourselves this way as therapists, we try to address therapy to validate our clients as active agents in their own change processes by honoring, encouraging, and supporting their creativity in developing solutions.

To test our theoretical assumptions about the therapeutic relationship from a relational constructivist approach, we conducted a series of studies dealing with therapeutic alliance and helpful/unhelpful events in therapy (see Herrero, Jiménez, Poch, & Botella, 2000; Pacheco, Corbella, Gómez, Velázquez, & Botella, 2001). In one of them (Pacheco et al., 2001), we performed a qualitative analysis of helpful events in psychotherapy with clients whose presenting complaint was depression. At the end of Sessions 1 to 8 and every four sessions after that, 17 clients were asked to answer an open-ended questionnaire concerning what they found helpful in that particular session. Their answers were analyzed by means of grounded theory methodology (Glaser & Strauss, 1967) and arranged as a hierarchical concept tree. Three superordinate categories emerged from our analysis: reflexivity, narrative transformation, and working alliance. We found a close relation between reflexivity and narrative transformation, with reflexivity being a prerequisite to achieve narrative transformation. All the categories included in narrative transformation involved client discovery of new elements in their story.

For example, one of the clients who participated in these studies mentioned the following as a "helpful event" in one of her psychotherapy sessions:

> One of the things that helped me in today's session was realizing how I was unconsciously contributing to my feeling that the others do not take my needs into account by not expressing them because I feel I do not have the right to do it. I think that now that I'm aware of it I'll be more capable to speak up for myself and let others know that I have needs too. In fact, I've done that (even if very rarely) in the past, so I guess it's not that impossible!

Notice how this particular client relates her reflexive awareness of her own subject position in such situations to the tentative emergence of a new narrative in which what previously were "rare exceptions" begin assuming a higher narrative relevance.

In another study within the same research project (Herrero et al., 2000), we performed the same kind of analysis with a sample of 40 women suffering from breast cancer. They were participants in three different therapy groups, in which 10 weekly sessions were conducted following relational constructivist principles. We found both similarities and differences between what clients identified as helpful events in this study and in the previous one, probably due to the differences in the therapy format (individual versus group) and clients' problem (depression versus breast cancer).

In this case, our results demonstrated that participants identified the therapeutic ingredient as the group itself (i.e., as a whole), and not its individual members. There was also a sense of coordinated action (Gergen, 1994). That is, the group felt members were moving in harmony to generate meaning together by means of, for instance, sharing and talking, group cohesion, commonality, or empathy. Both aspects (the group format as therapeutic in itself and coordinated action as a helpful event) were absent from our clients' responses in the previous study, since they were in individual therapy. Also, participants in the group therapy for breast cancer format viewed the multiple perspectives generated in their dialogue with the therapists and with each other as a helpful event, since they fostered alternative views, interchanging opinions, or giving advice. Interestingly, only five people considered reflexivity a helpful event in this case.

CONCLUSIONS

We would like to bring our reflections to a (momentary) end by means of a story.

> Some time ago a Congress on Jokes took place. Attendees were reputed joke tellers, so knowledgeable about popular jokes that, in fact, they had numbered the jokes as a handy referencing system. Thus, for instance, during the social gatherings and coffee breaks one of the presenters would say, "Number 102," and everyone would roll with laughter. At a given point, a newcomer to the congress said, "Number 560," but unexpectedly nobody laughed. He insisted: "Hey, I said Number 560!" only to find himself confronted with cold looks again. Shocked by such coldness, he asked his colleagues: "Now, what's wrong with Joke #560?" They said to him, "You know . . . it's not the joke, it's the way you tell it. . . ."

Contemporary psychotherapy finds itself in the middle of a series of contrasting trends with respect to which it is called to position itself. One is the trend toward the establishment of a list of so-called empirically supported treatments (see, e.g., Barlow, 1996; Shapiro, 1996). Another one is the traditional fascination of many therapists with what is in vogue at the moment. Both of these trends can, in the long run, bring the development of narrative-informed therapy to an end. In the first case, this would occur by turning therapy into a series of treatment manuals that leave little or no room for creativity. In the second, it would occur by blurring what is unique in working with narrative in therapy and giving the false impression that "everything is a form of narrative-informed therapy" or that "everybody works with narrative in therapy." A more detailed discussion of how to face such challenges is beyond the scope of this work, and some tentative answers from a constructivist position can be found in Botella (2000). However, in both cases we would like to keep in mind that "it's not the joke, it's the way you tell it."

REFERENCES

Adams, J. F. (1997). Questions as interventions in therapeutic conversation. *Journal of Family Psychotherapy, 8,* 17-35.

Angus, L. E., Hardtke, K., & Levitt, H. (1996). *The narrative process coding system manual: Revised edition.* Unpublished manuscript, York University, North York, Ontario, Canada.

Angus, L., Levitt, H., & Hardtke, K. (1999). The narrative processes coding system: Research applications and implications for psychotherapy practice. *The Journal of Clinical Psychology, 55*(10), 1255-1270.

Bakhtin, M. (1986). *Speech genres and other late essays*. Austin: University of Texas Press.

Barlow, D. H. (1996). The effectiveness of psychotherapy: Science and policy. *Clinical Psychology: Science & Practice, 3*, 236-240.

Bartlett, F. C. (1932). *Remembering*. Cambridge, UK: Cambridge University Press.

Bateson, M. C. (1993). Composing a life. In C. Simpkinson & A. Simpkinson (Eds.), *Sacred stories* (pp. 39-51). New York: Harper Collins.

Botella, L. (1995). Personal construct psychology, constructivism, and postmodern thought. In R. A. Neimeyer & G. J. Neimeyer (Eds.), *Advances in personal construct psychology* (Vol. 3, pp. 3-36). Greenwich, CT: JAI Press.

Botella, L. (2000). Personal construct psychology, constructivism, and psychotherapy research. In J. W. Scheer (Ed.), *The person in society: Challenges to a constructivist theory* (pp. 115-125). Giessen, Germany: Psychosozial-Verlag.

Botella, L. (2001). Diálogo, relações e mudança: uma aproximação discursiva à psicoterapia construtivista [Dialogue, relationships, and change: A discursive approach to constructivist psychotherapy]. In Ó. Gonçalves & M. Gonçalves (Eds.), *Abordagens construcionistas à psicoterapia* (pp. 50-61). Coimbra, Portugal: Quarteto.

Botella, L., & Herrero, O. (2000). A relational constructivist approach to narrative therapy. *European Journal of Psychotherapy, Counselling, and Health, 3*, 1 12.

Botella, L., & Herrero, O. (2001). El entramado narrativo de la pérdida y el duelo: Un estudio de caso desde la terapia familiar constructivista [The narrative emplotment of loss and grieving: A case study from the standpoint of constructivist family therapy]. In C. Pérez (Ed.), *La familia: Nuevas aportaciones* (pp. 258-274). Barcelona, Spain: Edebé.

Botella, L., Neimeyer, R. A., Herrero, O., Pacheco, M., Figueras, S., & Werner-Wildner, L. A. (2002). The meaning of your absence: Traumatic loss and narrative reconstruction. In J. Kauffman (Ed.), *Loss of the assumptive world* (pp. 31-47). New York: Bruner-Mazel.

Botella, L., Pacheco, M., Herrero, O., & Corbella, S. (2000, June). *The unfolding of client's narrative reflexivity through therapeutic dialogue in process-experiential therapy: A qualitative case study*. Paper presented at the 31st Annual Meeting of the Society for Psychotherapy Research, Chicago.

Bruner, J. S. (1986). *Actual minds, possible worlds*. Cambridge, MA: Harvard University Press.

Derogatis, L. R. (1992). *SCL-90-R, administration, scoring & procedures manual-II for the R(evised) version and other instruments of the Psychopathology Rating Scale Series*. Townson, MD: Clinical Psychometric Research, Inc.

Duncan, B., & Miller, S. (2000). *The heroic client: Doing client-centered, outcome-informed therapy*. New York: Jossey-Bass.

Ecker, B., & Hulley, L. (2000). The order in clinical "disorder": Symptom coherence in depth-oriented brief therapy. In R. A. Neimeyer & J. D. Raskin (Eds.), *Constructions of disorder* (pp. 63-89). Washington, DC: American Psychological Association.

Efran, J. S., Lukens, M. D., & Lukens, R. J. (1990). *Language, structure, and change: Frameworks of meaning in psychotherapy*. New York: Norton.

Gergen, K. J. (1994). *Realities and relationships*. Cambridge, MA: Harvard University Press.

Glaser, B. G., & Strauss, A. (1967). *The discovery of grounded theory: Strategies for qualitative research*. Chicago: Aldine.

Herrero, O., Jiménez, B., Poch, G., & Botella, L. (2000, September). *Helpful and unhelpful events in constructivist/narrative psychotherapy groups with breast cancer patients*. Poster presented at the 7th International Congress on Constructivism in Psychotherapy, Geneva, Switzerland.

Kelly, G. A. (1970). Behavior is an experiment. In D. Bannister (Ed.), *Perspectives in personal construct theory* (pp. 10-26). London: Academic.

Kelly, G. A. (1991). *The psychology of personal constructs*. London: Routledge. (Original work published 1955)

Kim Berg, I., & de Shazer, S. (1993). Making numbers talk: Language in therapy. In S. Friedman (Ed.), *The new language of change* (pp. 5-25). New York: Guilford.

Lyotard, J.-F. (1993). *The postmodern condition: A report on knowledge* (G. Bennington & B. Massumi, Trans.). Minneapolis: University of Minnesota Press.

Mellor-Clark, J., Barkham, M., Connell, J., & Evans, C. (1999). Practice-based evidence and standardized evaluation: Informing the design of the CORE system. *European Journal of Counselling, Psychotherapy and Health, 2,* 357-374.

Neimeyer, G. J., & Neimeyer, R. A. (1993). Defining the boundaries of constructivist assessment. In G. J. Neimeyer (Ed.), *Constructivist assessment: A casebook* (pp. 1-30). London: Sage.

Neimeyer, R. A. (1987). An orientation to personal construct therapy. In R. A. Neimeyer & G. J. Neimeyer (Eds.), *Personal construct therapy casebook* (pp. 20-35). New York: Springer.

Pacheco, M., & Botella, L. (1999). La transformació narrativa-dialògica durant el procés psicoterapèutic: Una proposta d'anàlisi qualitativa de narratives amb suport computat [Dialogical narrative transformation in constructivist psychotherapy: A process research using a computer-assisted method for qualitative analysis]. *Aloma: Revista de Psicologia i Ciències de l'Educació, 5,* 195-208.

Pacheco, M., Botella, L., & Corbella, S. (1999, July). *Dialogical narrative transformation in constructivist psychotherapy: A process research using a computer-assisted method for qualitative analysis.* Paper presented at the XIIIth International Congress on Personal Construct Psychology, Berlin, Germany.

Pacheco, M., Corbella, S., Gómez, A. M., Velázquez, P., & Botella, L. (2001, June). *Helpful events in psychotherapy with depressed people.* Poster presented at the 32nd Annual Meeting of the Society for Psychotherapy Research, Montevideo, Uruguay.

Shapiro, D. A. (1996). "Validated" treatments and evidence-based psychological services. *Clinical Psychology: Science & Practice, 3,* 256-259.

Singer, J. A. (1996). The story of your life: A process perspective on narrative and emotion in adult development. In C. Magai & S. H. McFadden (Eds.), *Handbook of emotion, adult development, and aging* (pp. 443-463). New York: Academic Press.

Wittgenstein, L. (1953). *Philosophical investigations.* New York: Macmillan.

CHAPTER 8

A Poststructuralist Approach to Narrative Work

GENE COMBS

JILL FREEDMAN

Narrative therapy, as we use the term, refers to an ever-shifting stream of ideas, attitudes, and practices that flow from the work of Michael White and David Epston (Epston & White, 1992b; White & Epston, 1990). Narrative therapists draw on the ideas of poststructuralist scholars such as Michel Foucault (1980), Jerome Bruner (1990), and Barbara Meyerhoff (1986) to articulate and embody their approach to therapy in diverse ways according to their particular contexts. Because this approach is more a philosophy or a way of life than it is a set of techniques, we will discuss several aspects of the narrative worldview before we write in any detail about practices that flow from it.

THE NARRATIVE METAPHOR

Narrative therapy takes its name from the poststructuralist notion that meaning is carried in the retelling and reenacting of stories (Bruner, 1990; Meyerhoff, 1986; Turner, 1986). The sun rises every morning, but not all sunrises are meaningful. The sunrises (and all other events) that are meaningful to any particular person are those that get incorporated into that person's life narrative. A story, perhaps one told only to oneself in pictures and sensations, will be part and parcel of the meaningfulness of any sunrise that is memorable. For a sunrise to be socially, interpersonally meaningful, its story must be circulated—retold or reenacted—among the members of a social grouping.

When we look through the lens of the narrative metaphor, we see that stories shape our experience. We live out our biographies as we compose them. In this process, we do not attend to or remember each and every event of our moment-to-moment, day-to-day lives. Only a few of our myriad experiences get incorporated into the stories we enact with each other. Yet, these stories that we act out with each other are not *about* our lives; in the domain of meaning, they *are* our lives.

Therapists who have begun to use the narrative metaphor to guide their practice have experienced quite a large shift in their worldview. Instead of trying to solve problems, we have become interested in collaborating with people to change their lives through enriching the narratives they and others experience concerning their lives. We work to bring forth and develop "thick descriptions" (Geertz, 1973; Ryle, 1971/1990)—rich, meaningful, multi-stranded stories of those aspects of people's life experience that would not be predicted by the problem-saturated story line. It seems that through these more complex and robust stories, people can live out new identities, new possibilities for relationship, and new futures.

Because there are always many events in any life that have not yet been "storied," it is always possible to develop a thicker description of anyone's life and relationships. In the tapestry formed by the multiple threads of a thick description, the problematic thread is less significant; it can be seen as a small flaw or an interesting texture.

POWER

People do not make up their life narratives from scratch. We are all born into stories, and those stories shape our perceptions of what is possible; but we rarely think of the stories we are born into as stories. We think of them as "reality." For example, the U.S. Declaration of Independence states that "all men are created equal." When that phrase was written, the stories of their day led people to perceive a reality in which *men* (when applied to the right to vote, for instance) meant "land-owning white males." It took, among other things, a civil war to change societal stories so that the taken-for-granted meaning of *men* in relation to the right to vote was "males of any color, as long as they are U.S. citizens and not in jail." It took lots more sweat and strife to change the stories so that *men* applied to females as well. Stories have the power to shape our social reality. Conversely, societies have the power to shape the stories that circulate in them. Michel Foucault is perhaps best remembered for his studies of the interrelatedness of knowledge and power (Foucault, 1980). He carefully and thoroughly described ways in which knowledge (what is considered to be known and to be worth knowing) in particular domains such as madness, illness, criminality, and sexuality shifted from one historical period to the next or from one culture to the next. He described how the workings of power shifted with the shifts in knowledge and vice versa.

Foucault described two types of power: traditional power and modern power. Traditional power is the sort that we associate with kings and other patriarchs. It emanates from a center and is enforced in public through harsh external means. It establishes social control through a system of moral judgments that invite people to look to representatives of a god, king, or other central authority for approval based on their moral worth. Modern power is more insidious and invisible. It develops and circulates in widely dispersed and shifting communities. It is based on norms and scales and is enforced largely through self-policing and the normative judgments of peers. It invites people to look to test scores or self-comparisons with idealized norms (such as *Vogue* models) for approval based on their normative worth.

Narrative therapists are especially interested in the workings of modern power. We see modern power as carried in the stories we tell each other about what is worth pursuing and what is not worth pursuing, what constitutes success or failure, who is "in" and who is "out," and where we measure ourselves to be on this or that continuum of normality. We believe that the thin, unsatisfying stories that lead people to consult with therapists are supported by the workings of modern power, which tend to be invisible. They are easily taken for granted because of the way they hide in the norms, standards, and scales that we so willingly use to measure ourselves and each other.

We study the workings of modern power so that we can develop awareness of the discourses that support people's problems. This makes it possible for us to interact with people in ways that invite them to see each other in the light of different stories. In that light, they can imagine, experience, and live out more possibilities for satisfying life stories.

Foucault was especially interested in how the "truth claims" carried in the "grand abstractions" of reductionist science constituted a discourse that dehumanized and objectified many people. He was interested in finding and circulating marginalized discourses—stories that exist but are not widely circulated or powerfully endorsed—that might balance the excessive power of the reductionistic scientific discourse. He wrote of the "amazing efficacy of discontinuous, particular, and local criticism" in bringing about a "return of knowledge" or "an insurrection of subjugated knowledges" (Foucault, 1980, pp. 80-84).

Following Foucault, we believe that even in the most disempowered of lives, there is always lived experience that lies outside the dominant stories. Narrative therapists have developed ways of thinking and working that bring forth "discontinuous, particular, and local" stories so that people can inhabit and lay claim to the many possibilities for their lives that lie outside of the norms and standards set by dominant narratives.

THE INTERPRETIVE TURN

We value the meaning people make of their own experience over the meaning that we, as "experts," might make of that experience. This attitude has been referred to as "the interpretive turn" (Bruner, 1986; Geertz, 1983). Under its influence, we situate ourselves as interested people who are skilled at asking questions to bring forth the knowledge and experience of the people who come to consult with us. We work to help people notice the influence of taken-for-granted cultural stories in their lives, not by pointing them out, but by asking questions that invite people to consider the expectations, norms, cultural ideas and the like that in their experience might support problems with which they struggle. Instead of assessing people so as to fit them into general, normative categories and using techniques based on assumptions about what they should do in light of such assessment, we ask questions about previously neglected aspects of their experience. We invite them to remember, make meaning of, and evaluate those aspects of their experience and decide if these new stories might more meaningfully contribute to their identities, lives, and relationships than do the problematic stories. People find wisdom and direction in their own experience rather than in expert ideas. Because (thinking it might be useful to others facing similar dilemmas) people are often willing to circulate stories of their lived experience, we find ourselves acting as archivists of local knowledge so that it can be passed on to others (Epston, Morris, & Maisel, 1995; Epston & White, 1992a). We believe that circulating these stories of lived experience contributes to keeping our local cultures (and, on our more grandiose days, the whole world) lively and multitextured.

A NARRATIVE WORLDVIEW

The ideas we are describing constitute a worldview or a way of life. We do not draw a sharp distinction between our work lives and the rest of our lives. We seek out ways of living that support collaboration, social justice, and local, situated, context-specific knowledge rather than normative thinking, diagnostic labeling, and the general, noncontextualized, rules of expert knowledge. This worldview leads to improvisation and creativity. It supports us in a commitment continually to educate ourselves about discourses that limit or subjugate people so that they cannot fully pursue their preferred directions in life. We think that situating ourselves in this worldview is a continuing process. It requires ongoing reflection on the effects of our actions. We have found questions such as those that follow helpful in this process. This list has changed over the years, but it started out as a personal communication from David Epston, which was his response to a request from us for his thinking about ethics and the narrative approach.

- Whose language is being privileged here? Am I bringing forth the stories that these people want to tell in their own words, or am I pushing for the stories that I want to hear, told in my favorite jargon?
- Are there dominant stories that are limiting or creating problems in these people's lives?
- Am I inviting awareness of those stories without becoming dominant myself?
- Am I evaluating these people, or am I inviting them to evaluate things (how therapy is going, the effects of various practices, preferred directions in life, etc.)?
- Who am I viewing as the expert here, myself or the people I am working with?
- Am I working so as to require these people to enter my expert knowledge, or so as to require myself to enter their experiential worlds?
- Is what I am doing dividing and isolating these people or bringing forth a sense of community and collaboration?
- Am I situating my opinions in my personal experience? Am I being transparent about my context, my values, and my intentions so that these people can evaluate the effects of my biases?
- Do the questions I am asking conserve dominant societal practices or propose alternative practices?
- How am I embodying professionalism? Which am I concerned with: how I look to my professional colleagues or how I am being experienced by the people who seek my help?

NARRATIVE PRACTICES

In the day-to-day work of narrative therapy, we start by getting to know people as they would want to be known. In an initial interview, we want to hear at least a few things about people's lives outside of the problems (their interests, their living situation, etc.). Through such conversation, we hope to show that we consider people to be more than their problems. Also, we want to hear from the very first about a broader spectrum of stories than we could ever know through talking about problems.

We listen to stories. This is a very different mind-set from listening for symptoms, for surface clues to deep meaning, for self-defeating cognitions, or for "facts." As we listen, we try to understand what is problematic in people's stories, and we listen for problem names that are "experience near" (fitting with their vocabulary and worldview, not ours). We provide space and time for people to reflect on their own narratives as they emerge, thus becoming their own witnesses. When working with couples or families, we tend to work so that one person at a time is in a telling/performing mode while the others are in a witnessing mode. We promote a rhythmic alternation between telling and listening, between acting and reflecting, throughout the course of people's visits with us.

We do not try to lead people toward some predetermined outcome. At the same time—and this can be a tricky balancing act—we do not want to let the workings of modern power predetermine the outcome. That is, since modern power operates through recruiting people to live their lives according to culturally constructed norms, if we don't take the time to think with people about how modern power may be playing out in their lives and supporting the problems they face, they may describe their goals and preferences in terms of these same culturally constructed norms. Only when the effects of these norms are made visible can people really delineate what they want, separate from what the dominant culture indicates they should want. We are not neutral. We try to influence people toward exposing the role of modern power in their lives and toward honoring their own preferences for their lives.

Asking Questions About Problems

As we listen, we ask questions that invite people to consider the effects of problems on their lives and relationships. The combined focus on discourses of modern power and the effects of problems tends to bring forth stories of people's struggles with normative judgment, self-policing, and dominant discourses. This kind of inquiry tends to deconstruct problematic stories, opening space for the perception of "unique outcomes" (events that would not have been predicted by the problematic story). As unique outcomes appear, we ask questions that invite people to expand or thicken them into memorable, experientially vivid stories that can be interwoven with the problematic stories. In this way, people's lives come to be more thickly described and multistoried. Michael White (1991) defines deconstruction actively and politically, as

> procedures that subvert taken-for-granted realities and practices: those so-called "truths" that are split off from the conditions and the context of their production; those disembodied ways of speaking that hide their biases and prejudices; and those familiar practices of self and of relationship that are subjugating of person's lives. (p. 27)

In similar fashion, Foucault (1977) suggested that the workings of modern power can lead people to a sense of themselves as "docile bodies," subject to knowledge and procedures in which they have no active voice. There are subjugating stories of gender, race, class, age, sexual orientation, and religion (to name a few) that are so prevalent and entrenched in our culture that we can get caught up in them without realizing it. We believe it is our responsibility as therapists to cultivate a growing awareness of the dominant (and dominating) stories in our society and to develop ways of collaboratively examining the effects of those stories when we sense them at work in the lives and relationships of the people who consult with us.

Rachel Hare-Mustin (1994) has used the metaphor of a "mirrored room" to talk about how the only ideas that can come up in therapy are the ideas that the people involved bring into the therapy room:

> The therapy room is like a room lined with mirrors. It reflects back only what is voiced within it... If the therapist and family are unaware of marginalized discourses, such as those associated with members of subordinate gender, race, and class groups, those discourses remain outside the mirrored room. (p. 22)

This notion implies that therapists must continually reflect on the discourses that shape our perceptions of what is possible, both for ourselves and for the people with whom we work. Such reflection puts us in the position to ask deconstructive questions—questions whose aim is respectfully and patiently to examine problems in detail and expose discourses and normative judgments that support them.

Externalizing Conversations

White (1987, 1988/1989, 1989; see also Epston, 1993) has introduced the idea that the person is not the problem, the problem is the problem. Externalization is a practice supported by the belief that a problem is something operating on, impacting, or pervading a person's life, something separate and different from the person.

We believe that listening with the belief that problems are separate from people has a powerful deconstructive effect. It biases us to interact differently with people than we would if we saw them as intrinsically problematic. It creates a different receiving context for people's stories, one in which we can work to understand their problems without seeing the people themselves as problematic or pathological. In therapy with couples and families, externalization makes space for people to see each other beyond the problems. In this kind of context, people's stories almost always become less restrictive.

We can expose limiting discourses by asking externalizing questions about contextual influences on the problem. What "feeds" the problem? What "starves" it? Who benefits from it? In what settings might the problematic attitude be useful? Which people would proudly advocate for the problem? What groups of people would definitely be opposed to it and its intentions? Questions such as these invite people to consider how the entire context of their lives affects the problem and vice versa. As problems are externalized, it becomes established that, rather than being problematic in and of themselves, people have relationships with problems.

In externalizing conversations, we want to hear about the effects of problems. When we ask about the effects of a problem on people's lives and relationships, they can stop thinking about themselves or their relationships as inherently problematic and, instead, consider their relationships with problems and whether they want to revise them.

Mapping a Statement of Position

Michael White (Mann & Russell, 2002, White, 2002) has developed a set of practices that we find very helpful in conducting externalizing conversations. He describes four steps that can be followed in constructing a "Statement of Position Map."

The first step is to negotiate an experience-near and particular definition of a concern or problem. We strive to talk with people about their problems in the language and images that they use to describe them. If a label does not emerge from conversation, we ask questions like these:

- What would you call this thing that you have been struggling against?
- How would you describe what it is that is holding you back?
- You mention "sadness." Would that be the best label for what is coming between you two? If so, can you say a little more about just exactly what sadness means to you?

The second step is to map the effects of the problem through different domains of living. We do this by asking questions like these:

- How does sadness make itself known to you?
- What has the reputation got people thinking about you? What has it got you thinking about yourself?
- What is it like when those messy accidents make an unexpected appearance?
- How does the heaviness come between you and your mother? Does it affect each of you

differently as well as coming between you? What impact do these effects have on the rest of the family?

- What does the fear keep you from doing?
- Who else does raging and fussing and fuming and all that stuff affect? How?

Once we have collaboratively generated a list of effects, the third step is to invite people to evaluate each effect carefully. Questions like those that follow are helpful in this step.

- Is that a good thing or a bad thing?
- What do you feel about the messy accidents?
- Do you like for the heaviness to come between you and your mother?
- Does it make you happy, sad, or something else when the fear keeps you from going to the movies?

The fourth step is to ask people to justify their evaluations. By this, we mean the therapist should inquire about the reasons, motivations, values, and so on that shape people's evaluations. We do this with questions like:

- Why do you think this is something you don't want in your life?
- How come you don't like it?
- Why does it make you sad when fear keeps you from going to the movies?
- What makes it so awfully embarrassing for you when inertia keeps you from finishing something?

The third and fourth steps are done in concert. That is, we ask people to evaluate each effect and to justify their evaluations before moving on to evaluate the next effect.

As people answer all these questions about a specific problem, it is repeatedly presented in externalized language. Through this process, the problem usually comes to be perceived as solidly and clearly separate. People get a well-defined sense of where they stand in relation to the problem, and they often describe how they would prefer to act and feel toward it in the future. Instead of struggling with each other, family members often join together to struggle with the problem. At such a juncture, it is often useful to name a project.

Naming the Problem and the Project

Naming a problem often leads to a way of examining and thinking differently about that problem. As we focus on them and continue to inquire about them, the names for problems can become poetic and compelling.

We recently saw a young heterosexual couple. The man described the problem as waking him in the middle of the night with a gun to his head. When we asked him to name the problem (which he had been referring to as "anxiety attacks"), he called it "the thief" because it was trying to steal his sleep. His partner, who had been scornful of the fear and difficulty sleeping until this point, could easily relate to the terror of a burglary in the dark of night. She began to appreciate her partner's bravery in facing it alone. She suggested that he wake her so that she could help him face the thief. His poetic and compelling name for the problem helped her sign on for a project of helping him stand up to it.

Once problems are clearly named, we begin to listen for and ask about projects. We listen for words in people's descriptions that might serve as good names for projects. If we don't hear clear statements of projects or directions in life, we can ask questions that directly invite people to name them. Some problems and projects are shared by several people. Others are of concern to one family member but not to others, even if they are working together in family therapy. Witnessing each other's stories and hearing the problems and projects that shape them may be very important to family members, even though each person focuses on a different problem or project.

The explicit and direct discussion of projects and their contrast to problems can be a vital part of therapy. As people name problems and projects, we keep track of them so that, together, we can bring forth and thicken the counterplots. This contrasting heightens the meaning that is made of particular experiences. Without an identified counterplot, experiences that lie outside the problem story may go unnoticed or seem trivial. With a counterplot, people can perceive shape and meaning in their nonproblematic experiences. For example, once a person has declared a project of "listening more with my hopes and less with my fears," any conversation in which she participates can be plotted into the narrative of how hopes and fears influence her listening. Until such a project is explicitly discussed and agreed upon, conversations could be given many different meanings or no meaning at all.

The names of projects often shift as the therapy progresses, and it is the therapist's job to keep up with people's changes in language and conceptualization. Throughout this process, we seek personal, evocative, and poetic names for projects. We ask questions that invite people to shape their perceptions, thoughts, feelings, and actions into stories according to the ever-shifting plots and counterplots they identify as meaningful for their lives.

Unique Outcomes

Our entryway for inviting people to tell and live new stories is through "unique outcomes." A unique outcome is any event that would not have been predicted by the plot line of a problem-saturated story. A unique outcome may be a plan, action, feeling, statement, desire, dream, thought, belief, ability, or commitment (Morgan, 2000). Unique outcomes constitute openings that, through questions and reflective discussion, can be developed into new stories.

Sometimes, people offer unique outcomes quite directly. For example, in describing a problem, someone may say, "It's not always like that," and go on to describe a unique outcome. It is not unusual, as people become involved in the reauthoring process, for them to save up new unique outcomes to tell their therapist. At other times, unique outcomes are so buried in people's descriptions of their problematic stories that it is important to listen very carefully if we are not to miss them. For example, if a person says, "Once in a while I get through it OK, but usually. . ." and then proceeds to tell a problematic story, only if we are listening closely can we be curious about the "once in a while."

Most often, openings develop spontaneously in ways similar to those we have been describing, as we listen deconstructively, asking people about the effects of problems on their lives and relationships. If openings do not develop spontaneously, we can inquire more directly about them. When we are working with an externalized problem, a straightforward way of looking for openings is to ask about a person's influence on the life of the problem. That is, we ask questions such as, "Has there ever been a time when the problem tried to get the upper hand, but you were able to resist its influence?" or "Have you ever been able to escape the problem for even a few minutes?" or "Is the problem *always* with you?" When questions of this sort follow a detailed inquiry into the effects of the problem on the person, people can usually find instances in which they were able to elude the problem's influence. Each such instance is a potential opening onto an alternative life narrative.

Developing Stories From Unique Outcomes

Once we have agreed on a preferred opening that seems relevant, we ask questions that invite people to develop it into an alternative story. We do not have a formula to follow in this process, but we do keep in mind that stories involve events organized by plot through time in particular contexts and that they usually include more than one person.

In telling the story of a preferred event, people are performing meaning (Meyerhoff, 1986). We work to make the therapy context a ritual space in which the meaning is meaningfully performed. Ideally, we want people to relive the events surrounding a unique outcome as they tell them. We facilitate this kind of experiential involvement by asking questions to develop a story rich in detail and meaning (Freedman & Combs, 1993, 1996).

White (White & Epston, 1990), following Bruner (1986), speaks of the "dual landscapes" of action and consciousness (or, in his more recent work, identity). He suggests that the stories that constitute people's lives unfold in both those landscapes and that it can be helpful for therapists to inquire about both. Let us look first at the landscape of action.

The landscape of action includes detail in multiple modalities involving the viewpoints of multiple characters in a particular scene or setting. It also includes the action itself. What happened, in what sequence, involving which characters?

Taking the very simple example of Jeff at an initial therapy appointment saying that his happiness had been deteriorating for years and that this was the first time he had sought out therapy, we might wonder if simply deciding to come to therapy and actually showing up are unique outcomes. The following are some questions we might ask:

- When did you actually decide to seek out therapy?
- What difference did it make to decide? Did you notice a shift in what you were feeling or thinking?
- Were other people involved in making the decision? What did they say or do that influenced you at the time? Or was it remembering something from a past interaction with them?
- Do you remember what it felt like to make the appointment to come here tonight? What were you thinking as you hung up the phone?
- Who would be most pleased that you have taken this step? What would they say about it?

In the landscape of action, we are interested in constructing an "agentive self" with people. That is, we ask questions with an eye to enhancing those aspects of the emerging story that support personal agency (Adams-Westcott, Dafforn, & Sterne, 1993). The very act of reauthoring requires and demonstrates personal agency, and most people experience that in this work. We go a step further in making personal agency apparent by asking, in a variety of ways, how people have accomplished what they have.

In the example above, we might ask the following questions for this purpose:

- Given the hopelessness you described, I can see how deciding to do something in the face of it would be quite a struggle. Can you tell me more about how you stood up to the hopelessness?
- Were you preparing somehow to take this step? What went into that preparation?
- How did you keep the hopelessness sufficiently out of the picture that you could show up here tonight?

We think about the shape of a story as it comes forth: What happened before the unique outcome? How smoothly did things unfold? Were there false starts involved? What did this particular episode lead to? In this regard, we are especially interested to know if there is a turning point, a place where the story changes for the good. Although *turning point* is not a fitting metaphor for everyone in every situation, when it is, it distinguishes a significant event that we can plot in time. We believe it is useful to focus special attention on this sort of event, bringing forth even more shape and detail, perhaps even treating it as a story within a story.

No matter how vivid a story is in the landscape of action, if it is to have meaning, it must also be developed in the landscape of identity. By *the landscape of identity,* we refer to that imaginary territory in which people plot the meanings, desires, intentions, beliefs, commitments, motivations, values, and the like that relate to their experience in the landscape of action. In other words, in the landscape of identity, people reflect on the implications of experiences storied in the landscape of action.

To explore the landscape of identity, we ask what we (Freedman & Combs, 1993) call meaning questions. These are questions that invite people to step back from the landscape of action and reflect on the meaning of the actions they have recounted. For example, we may ask:

- What do you think it says about your hopes that you have decided to pursue therapy?
- Does it characterize the way you do things to have secret hope in the face of hopelessness?
- If your partner had witnessed your preparation for this step, what would it have meant to her?

In coauthoring stories, we move between the landscape of action and the landscape of identity, weaving the two back and forth again and again.

Time: Developing a "History of the Present" and Extending the Story Into the Future

In striving to make sense of life, people face the task of arranging their experiences of events in sequences across time in such a way as to arrive at a coherent account of themselves and the world around them (White & Epston, 1990, p. 9).

Once a preferred event has been identified, we want to link that event to other preferred events across time, so that their meanings survive and so that the events and their meanings can thicken people's narratives in preferred ways. Therefore, once a preferred event is identified and storied, we ask questions that might link it to other past events and develop the story of those events. Here are some examples of questions that might identify such events:

- When you think back, what events come to mind that you might be building on, that reflect other times when you could have given up hope, but you didn't?
- If we were to interview friends who have known you throughout your life, who might have predicted that you would have been able to accomplish this? What memories might they share with us that would have led them to predict this?

As people free more and more of their pasts from the grip of problem-dominated stories, they are able to envision, expect, and plan toward less problematic futures. To bring forth experience of such futures, we might ask:

- We have just been talking about an accomplishment and several events in the past that paved the way for this accomplishment. If you think of these events as creating a kind of direction in your life, what do you think the next step will be?
- You have learned some things that have changed your view of the possibilities for your life. If you keep this new view in your heart, how do you think the future might be different?

Reflecting

It is through reflecting on our experience that we make meaning of it. Although the practice of reflection may occur even when we do not structure or encourage it, such "natural" reflection does not necessarily focus on the preferred experiences or new narratives that are developing in therapeutic conversations.

Whenever possible, we use reflecting teams (Andersen, 1987) or outsider witness groups (White, 1995, 1997, 2000) to increase the audience for tellings and retellings. We structure such groups in a very particular way, which includes four parts (Cohen, Combs, DeLaurenti, DeLaurenti, Freedman, Larimer, & Shulman, 1998; Freedman, 2002; White, 1995).

In the first part, the therapist interviews the people who have come for help while the outsider witness group observes the interview from behind a one-way mirror (or at a bit of a distance). In the second part, the witness group switches places with the people who have been talking, who then listen as the witness group has a conversation, raising questions and reflecting on what they have watched. In the third part, the therapist and the people who have come for help switch back to their original places and the people respond to the reflections as the witness group observes. In the fourth part, everyone meets together for the purpose of deconstructing the interview or making it transparent. The therapist and outsider witness group members respond to questions anyone has about their questions, purposes, and the directions they pursued in the interview.

In the second part of the interview, if an outsider witness group or a reflecting team with little experience is reflecting, the therapist may ask questions drawing out team members, keeping the focus on what moved team members and on possible preferred directions that emerged during the interview. We ask team members to situate their reflections in their own experience, to acknowledge the trust people are showing in opening their lives to the presence of others, and to comment on the difference being part of the conversation makes to their own lives.

When no reflecting team is available, we look for other ways to invite reflection. By talking with one person at a time, other family members can serve in some of the ways that a team can. *Virtual* teams can be useful. We can set them up by asking people to briefly describe a few people who they wish could have been listening in on the therapy. We then ask them what they think each of these virtual members would have been struck by and what effect that would have had on the person. We can also ask people to be a team of one for themselves. We often invite this by saying something like, "If you had been sitting over there in that corner eavesdropping on this session, what would stand out for you at this point?" Then, we can interview the person in the same manner that we would interview an inexperienced reflecting team.

Documenting and Circulating New Stories

Because we believe that the new stories that emerge in therapy become transformative only when they are enacted outside of the therapy room, we are interested in documenting and circulating the new stories (White & Epston, 1990). We take notes in therapy, using people's own words specifically to document new stories as they develop. We often refer back to these notes and read them aloud. When people take a stand, or describe a new achievement, or reach a turning point, we might create a document or certificate together to formalize and commemorate it. We sometimes make videotapes for people's personal use in which they reflect on how far they have come. We may make tapes or documents about what people have learned so that they can be used by others facing similar problems (Epston & White, 1992b; White & Epston, 1990). Through this kind of exchange, people can band together in virtual leagues.

We sometimes write letters between therapy meetings. In these letters, we reflect on unique outcomes and ask questions that we did not ask in the therapy conversation. We hope that this will thicken and extend the knowledge that had begun to emerge there. We sometimes generate formal documents that list important elements of new narratives (Freedman & Combs, 1997). To encourage the circulation of this knowledge, we invite people to share these documents with other people in their lives.

Another way we facilitate circulation of alternative stories as they develop is by inviting members of people's social networks (friends, coworkers, supervisors, teachers, neighbors, ministers, etc.) to therapy sessions. They may act as an outsider witness group or be more directly interviewed as part of the therapy.

NARRATIVE THERAPY IN PRACTICE: AN ILLUSTRATIVE EXAMPLE

We offer the following transcript to illustrate some of the ideas we have described in practice. In the transcript I (Jill) am talking with Celestina, who came to see me because she experienced difficulties in intimate relationships. Earlier in our work together, she told me something she had never told anyone before: She had been physically abused by her father throughout her childhood. She had also witnessed her mother being abused.

In conversations prior to the one transcribed here, as part of developing a statement of position map, I had asked about the effects of abuse. Celestina had listed fears, self-blame, lack of self-confidence, difficulties in relationships, and a constant watching for danger. In our previous sessions, she had decided to do something about all of these effects, rather than just focussing on the difficulties in relationships. She had named the problem "the effects of the abuse" and the project "feeding my spirit."

We spent some time considering what larger cultural stories supported the problems. We talked about stories of patriarchy—women and children as the property of men—and stories that portrayed abused people as damaged goods. In Celestina's experience, these stories contributed to feelings of shame and fear. Celestina grew up in Puerto Rico, and only by moving to Chicago and achieving a physical distance from her father had she found it possible to separate enough from the problematic stories to believe it was possible and appropriate to get help.

This is a very abbreviated sketch of some of the subjects Celestina and I addressed in conversations about the problematic stories and the larger cultural stories supporting them. As I (Jill) listened to these stories, I was interested in understanding them and also in noticing unique outcomes. At the beginning of the interview that we have transcribed, Celestina mentions a new experience she is having: enjoying being with herself and appreciating time alone. This experience is something that would not be predicted by the fear and self-blame. After hearing some details about the new way of enjoying time alone, in order to develop a history of the present, I ask about roots of this experience. This leads Celestina to link the experience with a thoughtfulness that she recognizes she has had for a long, long time, even as a little girl. As she makes distinctions, I am interested in relating them to the problem (the effects of the abuse) or to the project (feeding her spirit).

We offer some commentary in italics to relate the transcript to the practices we have described.

Celestina I appreciate more the time that I'm with myself... when I'm writing my journal... when I'm

	just laying down in my house. And when I don't have the time I feel like it's bad. I need to isolate myself in a good sense. In a good sense... just to have time to relax and slow down and read and reflect. And, it was very interesting because it's like this has never really been a part of my life. And now I'm so conscious that if I don't do it, I feel like I need it.
Jill	So. Um. That's giving me the idea that part of "feeding your spirit" is "having a new relationship with yourself."

[*I am interested here in relating what Celestina is talking about to the name of her project. If this new development is not part of her project, it may not be relevant for our conversation. If it is relevant, tying it to the project name could help thicken Celestina's experience of alternative stories and her sense of putting the effects of the problem behind her.*]

Celestina	Yes.
Jill	Is that right?
Celestina	Yes.

[*This checking in is very important and relates to the interpretive turn. I want to make sure I am honoring Celestina's ideas, rather than mine.*]

Jill	Uh huh. What would have it been like, say three years ago, if you found yourself with time to be with yourself?
Celestina	Um... Wow! Ah...
Jill	Maybe if I ask you this way: What's the difference now, finding time to be with yourself, than if you'd been in that same position three years ago?

[*Asking questions to contrast experience over time can make changes more apparent and available.*]

Celestina	Ah, well. First of all, it's a different feeling. It's not like I'm isolating myself because I don't want to see anybody, or I don't want to face whatever is happening in my life at that moment. It's not escaping from anything. It's like taking time to be with myself and enjoy it.
Jill	Umm... So, you're saying that in the past it would have been about escaping something? But, now it's about...
Celestina	Yeah, because I remember that I always wanted to do something like that. But, it wasn't really clear in my mind, what, how, and, and what really I wanted to do. I remember saying to my friends, "I want to take a weekend to go where nobody knows me and where I can be just alone." But, I wasn't really thinking about taking time for myself. It was like, "I just want to go." And I never did it.
Jill	That's sort of interesting to me. It makes me wonder if even though you didn't have that relationship with yourself yet, somehow you knew it was possible. Do you think?
Celestina	Yeah.
Jill	What do you think... If we could sort of look back through time... What do you think we might see?... sort of the roots of

this relationship you're developing with yourself. *[Here I am interested in developing a history of the present.]*

Celestina   Ah. Wow... I don't know. I always liked to think about anything. About anything that was happening or affecting my life in some way. And, I used to have a lot of self-talking, which I still do. But, now it is not self-doubt. It's just, like... I don't know. Maybe it was a way for me to, to calm myself; to survive in some way the abuse that was happening at home, and all the stress.

Jill   So, OK.... Do you think, though, that the way that you've been able to create a relationship with yourself even though the abuse and stress was great, the way that you've been able to immerse yourself in your thoughts, was sort of a precursor to this? Is it something that sort of set the stage for being able to have this luxurious relationship with yourself?

Celestina   I can say so.

Jill   Mm hmm. Is that something you appreciated back then—your thoughtfulness and talking to yourself as a way of getting through what was going on in your own house?

Celestina   Yeah. Yeah.

Jill   If you had known back then, if you had been able back then to see ahead, to see how you're spending the time now, just wanting to be with yourself, slowing down, enjoying being with yourself... What would it have meant to you back then, if you had been able to see this in your future? *[Here I am asking a meaning question.]*

Celestina   Ah... Hope!... Hope. I think that's the only word. Hope.

Jill   Mm hmm.

Celestina   Like it's going to happen. And you're going to get there. And...

Jill   Uh huh. So, let me ask you a question then. Would you say that this, um, "appreciating time with yourself," would you say that that's an anti-abuse kind of thing? Or would you say it's a *beyond* abuse kind of thing?

Celestina   Both!

Jill   Both?

Celestina   Yeah. Both. Because it's to create this—and I like that—anti-abuse environment. I like this term. And, at the same time it's like going beyond. It's like just going further.

Jill   Mm hm.

Celestina   It's both. Both! Well, I think I told you once that I felt like I've been all my life running. Running, and doing everything so fast. Sometimes, like, running away from a lot of things. And I'm a very hyper person, and active, and I'm always there. But, now I don't feel like I'm running. I feel like I'm *doing*.

Jill   Yeah.

Celestina   You know, it makes a very different feeling.

Jill   How is it different?

Celestina	Because I have no hurry. I'm enjoying better what I'm doing and I can manage my stress in a better way.
Jill	Uh huh. So, can you just tell me about a time that would be an example of doing, instead of running? *[Celestina has mentioned a unique outcome. I am now hoping to develop its story.]*
Celestina	Let me see. One I don't really ... probably I had moments.
Jill	It doesn't have to be a fancy, big time. Just a moment. Any moment.
Celestina	Recently?
Jill	Yeah.
Celestina	OK. Maybe this is going to sound like it doesn't have to do with it, but it's the only example I can think of. And I think I told you that I was in a ... a lot of different stressors. You know, going to school. I was taking a training which was just taking all my time. And I really didn't have too much time to be in the office to do the work. And the first week, I was so, so stressed out. You know. I was almost in tears because I was like, I just can't do this. But, I remember everything that I've been doing. And I was talking to myself, like, "Take one day at a time." And, "You're going to do everything you have to do."
Jill	Hmm.
Celestina	And, it's true. I slow down. And I was thinking about, "Well, if I can do it, I can do it. That's it." "You need to rest." I was saying to myself, "You need to take rests. You need not to worry too much about whatever needs to be done." And, ah, "Summer is close and you will have more time to do other things." And ...
Jill	Can I just ask you a question?
Celestina	Uh huh.
Jill	Were you saying this to yourself in English or Spanish?
Celestina	*[laugh]* Actually, this is going to sound funny. Both!
Jill	Both? Could you do it that way? Just like, so I could hear what it was like? Would that be all right? To do it in English and Spanish, like how you were doing it?
	[I thought it would be useful in the retelling for Celestina to reexperience this alternative story. I didn't want translating for me to hamper her experience. I also wondered if there might be important experience that would be of use here that is part of Celestina's Puerto Rican language and culture.]
Celestina	Oh my gosh! Ah ... Oh.
Jill	I won't understand it, but I'd just sort of like to hear what it sounds like.
Celestina	Well, usually I start in Spanish like, um, "Cogelo con calma este ... estas muy estress." And then I start to talk in English like, "You're going to do it. Nobody is pushing you." And it's like a back and forth in English and in Spanish all the time. "No apurre ... No hay problema ...

	Nadie esta empujando, so take it easy."
Jill	Uh huh.
Celestina	Something like that.
Jill	Now, was the voice of running... What language was that?
Celestina	Oh. Spanish most of the time.
Jill	OK. So, do you think it's significant to have both [languages] in this feeding your spirit?
Celestina	Actually, now that you brought it up, when I think in English I have to speak slowly, because if I try to speak as fast as I can speak Spanish, I just can't do it. Actually, I'm learning how to speak it in Spanish not too loud. And it's a very good feeling, because it's like when I don't speak loud, I don't speak fast.
Jill	OK. So, that would be... Um, would you say that this feeding your spirit—doing instead of running—is... You thought it was slow? And now you're saying it's also not loud?
Celestina	Um hmm.
Jill	OK. So, I'm imagining this little girl, who found this way of being thoughtful and talking to herself, even in this environment of abuse and stress...
Celestina	Mm hm.
Jill	... and that little girl growing up and creating this whole antiabuse environment where she's really appreciating herself and appreciating time with herself. If I had to fit... Is there some... When you see that from here to here, [*holding my hands out widely*], what memory sort of is in the middle of those two that would support this direction? [*I am asking for another memory that could be storied to support the direction these preferred stories are establishing.*]
Celestina	Ah. Well. Now that I look back... I'm the only daughter. So, I had my own room, with everything, it seems. I was very young. I don't remember what age, but probably younger than 10 years old. And in some ways, my room was like my refuge. So, I used to spend a lot of time in my room. And I had my own stereo. And listening to music, I was able to spend the whole night in my room reading, or just listening to music—sitting on the floor, very relaxed. And sometimes, if it was very late, I used some headphones. So, I was able to do that. And it was always part of my life. And when I was doing some kind of work for school, I used to do it in my room—alone—because I had almost everything. I had my desk, I had my stereo, with my music, and I had almost everything that I needed. So... Maybe that was something that was always taking me to this direction.
Jill	So, even though you didn't think about that as appreciating time with yourself...
Celestina	No, no, not at that time.
Jill	... somehow, that might have been a beginning? Something that would begin this relationship that you have now that's feeding your spirit?

Celestina	Yeah.	Celestina	Yes. The lyrics, the words... And the music is a little different; it's not too loud. You don't have too many instruments. Probably a lot of guitars and soft music. But, the lyrics make you think about different things.
Jill	Do you like that idea?		
Celestina	To be alone? To be...?		
Jill	That you, even way back then, in that house, that you were sort of creating this path.		
Celestina	Yeah.	Jill	Like what?
Jill	Why do you like the idea?	Celestina	Like politics, social problems. Like, to think about yourself, your relationship with other people; your relationship with the world, with mother earth, with nature. And since I was very young I like that kind of music. And when I wanted to be relaxed, and reflect a little bit about who I am, and what I like, and what I do... I listen to that music.
Celestina	Ah. In some way it was my time to be calm. Even when I wasn't really thinking about it, this was time to be with myself.		
Jill	Mm hmm...		
Celestina	It was a time of not being running. Or not being involved in whatever was going on.		
Jill	Mm hmm...		
Celestina	That's why I said it was like my refuge. I was there.	Jill	Mm hmm...
		Celestina	It makes me think.
Jill	So, what music were you listening to? [*My intention with this question was to invite details that would make the story more experientially vivid.*]	Jill	And you still do that?
		Celestina	Yeah. I still do that. I still have those tapes.
Celestina	Oh, my God, everything. I love music! It depends on the mood. But, what I wanted... And I still do it when I want to be relaxed and calm... I listen to soft music. It can be in English or in Spanish. It really doesn't matter. And it's very interesting now that I'm thinking about it, I like some music that not everybody listens to. And I don't think it's too known here in the United States, but it could be defined like, a little bit of social conscience kind of music.	Jill	OK, so, if we are listening to that right now, together, and you are reflecting on who you are, and what you do, what thoughts do you think you might be telling me with that music playing in the background?
			[*I am thinking about time. We started with a recent unique outcome, then historicized it, and now I am wondering about the possibility of bringing this whole strand of story into the present in a different way.*]
Jill	Really? How so? Is it the words you're talking about?	Celestina	Well, I can think of a song in particular.

Jill	Mm.
Celestina	It is a man who is singing it. Actually, let me see if I can translate that title, the name of the song. It's like, "Everybody with Their Own World, Their Own Thing." You know, you like something. And this is who I am, and this is what I like. And he is singing about "I prefer . . ." um, "I prefer to be who I am, [rather] than to make up someone just to please other people. I prefer be in with a lot of trees around me and to see . . ." um, I don't know, ". . . the water" (or whatever) ". . . than to be in the city, with a lot of smog." And he is comparing.
Jill	Mm.
Celestina	And I love that song because it's like, "That's who I am too!" You know?
Jill	Um hum.
Celestina	I prefer to be free. To be whom I am. To be honest. And, I prefer not to have too much, but to live in peace.

Much of narrative work involves telling and retelling, and—through the retellings—experiencing stories that wouldn't be predicted by the problematic stories. It may also include making new meaning of problematic stories or telling them from different points of view or in the light of what people learn about themselves through alternative, preferred stories. For Celestina, making a tape of a therapy conversation served as a document that she can watch again and again.

At another point in our work together, Celestina created another document for herself called "My Journey," in which she recorded what she learned and how she changed through the process of separating from the abuse (what we call externalization). She read this document to me, to some of her closest friends, and to her mother. In this way, she circulated her preferred stories to an audience.

At the point when Celestina had separated from the effects of the abuse and was "feeding her spirit," we invited an outsider witness group to two of her therapy meetings. The support and reflections of the team were a monumental contribution to her new developments.

Celestina also served as an outsider witness for a young man I was seeing in therapy who was struggling with the effects of violence at the hands of his father. This was of great help to the young man and also offered a way of honoring Celestina's knowledge about such problems.

Giving us permission to publish this transcript of her work and trusting readers with the details of her life are yet other ways that Celestina has created an audience for her new, preferred stories. She has restoried the experiences with abuse and its effects so that they are no longer focused on pathology. She takes joy in the notion that her work can contribute to the way other people may work together in challenging abuse and its effects.

REFERENCES

Adams-Westcott, J., Dafforn, T., & Sterne, P. (1993). Escaping victim life stories and co-constructing personal agency. In S. Gilligan & R. Price (Eds.), *Therapeutic conversations*. New York: Norton.

Andersen, T. (1987). The reflecting team: Dialogue and meta-dialogue in clinical work. *Family Process, 26*, 415-428.

Bruner, J. (1986). *Actual minds/possible worlds*. Cambridge, MA: Harvard University Press.

Bruner, J. (1990). *Acts of meaning*. Cambridge, MA: Harvard University Press.

Cohen, S. M., Combs, G., DeLaurenti, B., DeLaurenti, P., Freedman, J., Larimer, D., & Shulman, D. (1998). Minimizing hierarchy in therapeutic relationships: A reflecting team approach. In M. Hoyt (Ed.), *Handbook of constructive therapies: Innovative approaches from leading practitioners* (pp. 276-293). San Francisco: Jossey-Bass.

Epston, D. (1993). Internalizing discourses versus externalizing discourses. In S. Gilligan & R. Price (Eds.), *Therapeutic conversations* (pp. 161-177). New York: Norton.

Epston, D., Morris, F., & Maisel, R., (1995). A narrative approach to so-called anorexia/bulimia. In K. Weingarten (Ed.), *Cultural resistance: Challenging beliefs about men, women, and therapy* (pp. 69-96). New York: Haworth.

Epston, D., & White, M. (1992a). Consulting your consultants: The documentation of alternative knowledges. In D. Epston & M. White (Eds.), *Experience, contradiction, narrative, and imagination: Selected papers of David Epston and Michael White*. Adelaide, Australia: Dulwich Centre Publications.

Epston, D., & White, M. (1992b). *Experience, contradiction, narrative, and imagination: Selected papers of David Epston & Michael White*. Adelaide, South Australia: Dulwich Centre Publications.

Foucault, M. (1977). *Discipline and punish: The birth of the prison* (A. Sheridan, Trans.). New York: Panatheon.

Foucault, M. (1980). *Power/knowledge: Selected interviews and other writings, 1972-1977* (C. Gordon, Ed.). New York: Pantheon.

Freedman, J. (2002). Using reflecting teams. In A. R. Roberts & G. J. Greene (Eds.), *Social workers' desk reference*. New York: Oxford University Press.

Freedman, J., & Combs, G. (1993). Invitations to new stories: Using questions to explore alternative possibilities. In S. Gilligan & R. Price (Eds.), *Therapeutic conversations* (pp. 291-303). New York: Norton.

Freedman, J., & Combs, G. (1996). *Narrative therapy: The social construction of preferred realities*. New York: Norton.

Freedman, J., & Combs, G. (1997). Lists. In C. Smith & D. Nylund (Eds.), *Narrative therapies with children and adolescents* (pp. 147-161). New York: Guilford.

Geertz, C. (1973). *The interpretation of cultures*. New York: Basic Books.

Geertz, C. (1983). *Local knowledge: Further essays in interpretive anthropology*. New York: Basic Books.

Hare-Mustin, R. (1994). Discourses in the mirrored room: A postmodern analysis of therapy. *Family Process, 33*(1), 19-35.

Mann, S., & Russell, S. (2002). Narrative ways of working with women survivors of childhood sexual abuse. *The International Journal of Narrative Therapy and Community Work, 3*, 3-21.

Meyerhoff, B. (1986). "Life not death in Venice": Its second life. In V. W. Turner & E. M. Bruner (Eds.), *The anthropology of experience* (pp. 261-286). Chicago: University of Illinois Press.

Morgan, A. (2000). *What is narrative therapy? An easy-to-read introduction*. Adelaide, Australia: Dulwich Centre Publications.

Ryle, G. (1990). *Collected papers: Critical essays and collected essays 1929-68*. Bristol, UK: Thoemmes Press. (Original work published 1971)

Turner, V. (1986). Dewey, Dilthey, and drama: An essay in the anthropology of experience. In V. Turner & E. Bruner (Eds.), *The anthropology of experience* (pp. 33-44). Chicago: University of Illinois Press.

White, M. (1987, Spring). Family therapy and schizophrenia: Addressing the "in-the-corner" lifestyle. *Dulwich Centre Newsletter*, pp. 14-21.

White, M. (1988/1989, Summer). The externalizing of the problem and the re-authoring of lives and relationships. *Dulwich Centre Newsletter*, pp. 3-20.

White, M. (1989). *Selected papers*. Adelaide, Australia: Dulwich Centre Publications.

White, M. (1991). Deconstruction and therapy. *Dulwich Centre Newsletter, 3*, pp. 21-40.

White, M. (1995). *Re-authoring lives: Interviews and essays*. Adelaide, Australia: Dulwich Centre Publications.

White, M. (1997). *Narratives of therapists' lives*. Adelaide, Australia: Dulwich Centre Publications.

White, M. (2000). *Reflections on narrative practice: Essays and interviews*. Adelaide, Australia: Dulwich Centre Publications.

White, M. (2002). Workshop notes. Retrieved from www.dulwichcentre.com.au/articles/mwworkshopnotes.

White, M., & Epston, D. (1990). *Narrative means to therapeutic ends*. New York: Norton.

Part III

Narrative Identity and Self-Multiplicity

Implications for Psychotherapy

CHAPTER 9

Narrative Identity and Narrative Therapy

DAN P. MCADAMS

LISA JANIS

Narrative approaches to counseling and psychotherapy have risen to prominence over the past decade and a half (e.g., McLeod, 1997; White & Epston, 1990). During that same time, research psychologists have likewise turned their attention toward narratives, scripts, plots, and other aspects of what Sarbin (1986) has called "the storied nature of human conduct" (p. 1). Cognitive scientists have conducted hundreds of studies on how people encode, store, and retrieve storied information pertaining to real-life events and personal experiences (e.g., Conway & Pleydell-Pearce, 2000). Social psychologists have employed narrative methods to test hypotheses regarding the dynamics of close relationships (Murray & Holmes, 1994).

Developmental psychologists have examined the origins of story comprehension and storytelling in preschoolers (Fivush & Kuebli, 1997). Narrative theories of personality, developed from the premise that human beings are storytellers by nature, have been developed by Gregg (1991), Hermans and Kempen (1993), McAdams (1985), Tomkins (1987), and Singer and Salovey (1993). Outside psychology, life-narrative research methods and theories have enjoyed a renaissance in sociology (Denzin & Lincoln, 1994) and education (Casey, 1996). Investigators from many different backgrounds today speak of the narrative study of lives as a broad-based, interdisciplinary effort to understand social life—at the level of the individual, the community, and even the

AUTHORS' NOTE: Correspondence regarding this chapter should be sent to the authors at Northwestern University, Department of Psychology, Annenberg Hall, Room 209, 2115 North Campus Drive, Evanston, IL 60208, or to Dmca@northwestern.edu.

state—in terms of the implicit stories that people live by (Josselson & Lieblich, 1993; Josselson, Lieblich, & McAdams, 2003).

The central idea animating narrative-based approaches to theory and research in the behavioral and social sciences is that human beings make sense of their lives and their worlds through stories. In his narrative model of identity, McAdams (1985, 1993, 1996) has argued that identity itself takes the form of an inner story, complete with setting, scenes, character, plot, and themes. In late adolescence and young adulthood, people living in modern societies begin to reconstruct the personal past, perceive the present, and anticipate the future in terms of an internalized and evolving self-story, an integrative narrative of self that provides modern life with some modicum of psychosocial unity and purpose. Internalized life stories are based on biographical facts, but they go considerably beyond the facts as people selectively appropriate aspects of their experience and imaginatively construe both past and future to construct stories that make sense to them and to their audiences, that vivify and integrate life and make it more or less meaningful.

Narrative identities are psychosocial constructions coauthored by people and the cultural context within which their lives are embedded and given meaning. As such, individual life stories reflect cultural values and norms, including assumptions about gender, race, and class. Life stories are intelligible within a particular cultural frame, and yet they also differentiate one person from the next. People differ from each other with respect to their narrative identities in ways that are not unlike the ways they differ from each other on more conventional psychological characteristics—such as traits, motives, intelligence, and so on. For example, life stories may be compared and contrasted with respect to the salience of such thematic lines as agency versus communion (Singer, 1997) and redemption versus contamination (Maruna, 2001; McAdams, Reynolds, Lewis, Patten, & Bowman, 2001). Life stories differ from each other with respect to their structural complexity (Woike, Gersekovich, Piorkowski, & Polo, 1999) and their coherence and intelligibility (Baerger & McAdams, 1999). A person's narrative identity is a key component of what constitutes the individuality of that particular person, situated in a particular family and among particular friends and acquaintances (Thorne, 2000) and living in a particular society at a particular historical moment (Gregg, 1991).

WHAT IS IDENTITY?

The point of departure for McAdams's (1985) narrative model is Erikson's (1963) developmental concept of *ego identity*. In late adolescence and young adulthood (the fifth of eight stages in his developmental scheme), Erikson maintained, people first confront the problem of identity versus role confusion. At this time in the human life course, people first explore ideological and occupational options available in society and experiment with a wide range of social roles, with the aim of eventually consolidating their beliefs and values into a personal ideology and making provisional commitments to life plans and projects that promise to situate them meaningfully into new societal niches (Marcia, 1980). During this developmental period, people first seek to integrate their disparate roles, talents, proclivities, and social involvements into a patterned configuration of thought and activity that provides life with some semblance of psychosocial unity and purpose (Breger, 1974).

Identity, then, is an integrative configuration of self-in-the-adult-world. This configuration integrates in two ways. First, in a synchronic sense, identity integrates the wide range of different, and likely conflicting, roles and relationships that characterize a given life in the here and now. "When I am with my father, I feel sullen and depressed; but when I talk with my friends I feel a great surge of optimism and love for humankind." Identity needs to integrate those two things so that while they appear very different, they can be viewed as integral parts of the same self-configuration. Second, identity must integrate diachronically, that is, in time. "I used to love to play baseball, but now I want to be a social psychologist." Or "I was a born-again Christian but now I feel that I am agnostic." Identity needs to integrate these kinds of contrasts so that while self-elements are separated in time (and in content quality), they can be brought meaningfully together into a temporally organized whole. Put starkly, identity becomes a problem when adolescents or young adults first realize that they are, have been, and/or could be many different (and conflicting) things, and they experience a strong desire, encouraged by society, to be but *one* (large, integrated, and dynamic) thing. Of course, perfect unity and purpose in life form an ideal and may not be fully desirable anyway (Gergen, 1992; McAdams, 1997). But Erikson's concept of identity underscores an integrative tendency in selfhood that becomes especially salient for the first time in that period of life (late teenage years through the mid-20s) which Arnett (2000) has recently labeled *emerging adulthood*. Before this developmental period, there is no identity.

This is not to say that there is no "self." Nor is it to say that people don't "know who they are" before late adolescence. Ask any 10-year-old or 3-year-old. They can tell you who they are. They will tell you their name. They may list traits, roles, relationships, favorite foods, things they don't like, and on and on. It would be absurd to suggest that children have no sense of self. But in Erikson's terms, children typically have no identity because the integration of selfhood is not yet a psychosocial problem for them. Erikson's (and McAdams's) use of the term *identity*, therefore, is rather more technical and delimited than its common usage in psychology, sociology, and everyday parlance. From this perspective, identity is not synonymous with the "self" or the "self-concept" or even with "who I am"; rather it refers to a particular quality or flavoring of people's self-understandings, a way in which the self can be arranged or configured. To the extent that a person's self-understanding is integrated synchronically and diachronically such that it situates him or her into a meaningful psychosocial niche and provides his or her life with some degree of unity and purpose, that person "has" identity. Identity, then, is something people do not begin to "work on" and do not have until the emerging adulthood years. At this time, people begin to put their lives together into self-defining stories. It is an internalized and evolving story of self that integrates the self synchronically and diachronically, explaining why it is that I am sullen with my father and euphoric with my friends and how it happened—step by step, scene by scene—that I went from being a born-again Christian who loved baseball to an agnostic social psychologist.

Why does identity wait so long? Why is it not until the emerging adulthood years that people first construct life stories to provide their lives with unity and purpose? Showing his Freudian roots, Erikson suggested that the timing is linked to sex. The eruption of genital sexuality in adolescence helps to launch the identity project, Erikson maintained, because it signals the coming of full-fledged adult status in love and work. Furthermore, as a qualitative change in how the body looks and feels, puberty may usher in a realization that I am no longer a child, and with that realization comes a new apprehension of one's personal history: "I don't know what I am now, but I am no longer what I was" (McAdams, 1985). Childhood becomes the remembered past and adulthood the anticipated future.

Just as important, Erikson (1959) asserted, are changing social relationships and societal expectations: "It is of great relevance to the young individual's identity formation that he be responded to, and be given function and status as a person whose gradual growth and transformation make sense to those who begin to make sense to him" (p. 111). Parents, high school teachers, siblings, friends, college admissions counselors, the business world, the media, and many other aspects of modern society explicitly and implicitly urge adolescents and young adults to "get a life" (Habermas & Bluck, 2000). It is time to make some decisions about the future, about school, the armed services, work, and (for some) marriage and family. In general, Western societies "expect" adolescents and young adults to begin to examine the occupational, interpersonal, and ideological offerings of society and, eventually, to make commitments, even if only temporary, to personalized niches in the adult world. This is to say that both society and the emerging adult are ready for the individual's identity experiments by the time he or she has in fact become an emerging adult. Accordingly, Erikson (1959) wrote:

> The period can be viewed as a psychosocial moratorium during which the individual through free role experimentation may find a niche in some section of his society, a niche which is firmly defined and yet seems to be uniquely made for him. In finding it the young adult gains an assured sense of inner continuity and social sameness which will bridge what he was as a child and what he is about to become, and will reconcile his conception of himself and his community's recognition of him. (p. 111)

Advances in cognitive development may be instrumental for the emergence of identity at this time in the life course. Following Breger (1974) and Elkind (1981), McAdams (1985) argued that formal operational thinking in adolescence helps to supply the cognitive wherewithal for identity exploration. With the advent of formal operations, young people are able to engage in hypothetico-deductive thinking and to entertain systematically an infinite range of hypothetical scenarios and ideals as they might apply to their lives. Identity becomes an especially engaging abstraction for the abstract thinker. Breger (1974) writes: "The idea of a unitary or whole self in which past memories of who one was, present experiences of who one is, and future expectations of who one will be, is the sort of abstraction that the child simply does not think about." But "with the emergence of formal operations in adolescence, wholeness, unity, and integration become introspectively real problems" (p. 330). The idea that one's life, as complex and dynamic as it increasingly appears to be, might be integrated into a meaningful and purposeful whole may represent, therefore, an especially appealing possibility to the self-reflective emerging adult.

In McAdams's view, emerging adults begin to work on such an integration by putting their lives together into culturally meaningful stories. Accordingly, Habermas and Bluck (2000) argue that the construction of integrative life stories requires cognitive tools to which people do not have full access until adolescence and young adulthood. According to Habermas and Bluck, the full articulation of an integrative life story requires the understanding and utilization of four types of coherence. By the time they enter elementary school, children have an implicit understanding of what constitutes a well-formed story, and they are able to narrate single experiences in their own lives as little stories embodying what Habermas and Bluck call *temporal coherence*. During their grade school years and up through puberty, they gather the cultural knowledge they need to imagine what constitutes a typical life in their society, developing what Habermas and Bluck call *biographical coherence*. They come to understand, for example, that people typically grow up in families and school but then leave home in their late teens, that people eventually get jobs as adults and often get married and have children, that people ideally move forward or upward in a career over time, that they retire before they are extremely old, and so on.

Still, it is not until adolescence, Habermas and Bluck (2000) contend, that individuals craft causal narratives to explain how different events are linked together in the context of a biography. *Causal coherence* is exhibited in the increasing effort across adolescence to provide narrative accounts of one's life that explain how one event caused, led to, transformed, or in some other way is meaningfully related to other events in one's life. Traits, attitudes, beliefs, and preferences may now be explained in terms of the life events that may have caused them. Adolescents may, for example, explain why they reject their parents' liberal political values, or why they feel shy around members of the opposite sex, or how it came to be that their junior year in high school represented a turning point in their understanding of themselves in terms of personal experiences from the past that have been selected and, in many cases, reconstructed to make a coherent explanation. In *thematic coherence*, furthermore, they may identify an overarching theme, value, or principle that integrates many different episodes in their lives and conveys the gist of who they are and what their biography is all about. Studies reported by Habermas and Bluck (2000) suggest that causal and thematic coherence are rare in autobiographical accounts in early adolescence but increase substantially through the teenage years and into young adulthood. By the time individuals have reached the emerging adulthood years, therefore, they are typically able and eager to construct stories about the past and about the self that exhibit temporal, biographical, causal, and thematic coherence. Autobiographical memory and narrative understanding have now developed to the level whereby they can be called into service in the making of identity.

THE LIFE STORY AND THE LIFE COURSE

Although the cognitive and psychosocial prerequisites for full life-story making may not be in place until late adolescence and early adulthood, it is not as if the individual suddenly begins working on the story at this time, with no preparation or background. Versions of the life story may emerge earlier, as documented by Elkind (1981) in work on the personal fable. As indicated in diaries and other personal sources, young adolescents may construct fantastical autobiographical stories about their own potential greatness or uniqueness, stories that embody a high degree of coherence but may have little relation to the reality of their lives. Elkind suggests that personal fables fade over the course of adolescence, but they may be viewed as initial rough drafts of life stories (McAdams, 1985). Long before adolescence, moreover, people relate personal memories in story form, as studies of parent-child conversations show (Fivush & Kuebli, 1997), and children are collecting and processing experiences of all kinds that will eventually make their way into or have some important influence on the integrative life stories they later construct to make sense of their lives. McAdams (1993) argues that even early attachment patterns with caregivers may ultimately be reflected in the overall narrative tone and quality that adult life stories show. Children are not explicitly making identity, in the sense of constructing integrative life stories that provide their lives with unity and purpose and position them meaningfully within psychosocial niches in the modern world, but they are still implicitly gathering material for the identities they will someday make. The dominant images and themes of adult life stories, therefore, may reflect influences from the earliest years of life.

Although full-fledged life stories may begin to reveal themselves as identity formats in the adolescent and young-adult years, identity construction does not end when this developmental epoch is over. Erikson's (1963) original stage model confined identity formation to a single psychosocial stage (emerging adulthood), but McAdams's narrative model emphasizes the continuation of identity work across the adult years. Life stories develop and change across the life course, reflecting various on-time and off-time happenings and transitions. McAdams (1993) argues that people may work on different facets or qualities of the story at different times in life. For example, individuals in late adolescence and young adulthood are likely to focus some of their identity work on crystallizing the basic values and beliefs that ground their stories within an ideological setting (Perry, 1970). Being able to identify a clear and compelling belief system that organizes a person's life proves to be a powerful mechanism for establishing thematic coherence in the life story. In early-to-middle adulthood, many American men and women appear to focus their identity work on articulating, expanding, and refining the story's main characters, or personal *imagoes*. An imago is an idealized personification of the self that functions as a protagonist in the narrative (McAdams, 1984). Akin to what Markus and Nurius (1986) call "possible selves," imagoes personify important motivational trends in the life story, such as strong needs for power, achievement, or intimacy (McAdams, 1985). The construction of imagoes helps to integrate a life by bringing into the same narrative format different personifications of the me—the self-as-loving-wife, the self-as-ardent-feminist, the self-as-devoted-mother, the self-as-the-young-girl-who-longed-to-escape-the-suburbs, the self-as-future-retiree-who-will-escape-to-that-country-home, and so on. By constructing a single life story that integrates a wide range of self-characterizations as imagoes, the adult can resolve what William James first identified as the "one-in-many-selves paradox" (Knowles & Sibicky, 1990, p. 676).

The midlife years may occasion considerable identity work for many modern adults. Life span theorists have written about how the realization that one's life is now more than half over can bring to the psychological fore concerns about loss and mortality and can stimulate the actualization of long-suppressed tendencies, such as traditionally masculine tendencies among women and feminine tendencies among men (Gutmann, 1987; Levinson, 1978). Life course theories emphasize changing social roles and relationships in the midlife years and shifting contingencies in the ecology of everyday life (Elder, 1995). Theorists of different stripes tend to agree that midlife can be the psychosocial prime of life for many people, for during this period, they assume their most influential roles in families, the workplace, and society. In Erikson's (1963) view, adults ideally realize their greatest powers of generativity during the midlife years, as they focus time, attention, and resources on caring for and contributing to the well-being of the next generation. A recent flurry of empirical research documents the psychological and social importance of generativity in midlife (e.g., McAdams, 2001a; McAdams & de St. Aubin, 1998; Peterson & Klohnen, 1995).

In two different but related senses, generativity becomes an increasingly important issue in narrative identity during the midlife years. First, as men and women move into and through midlife, themes of caring for the next generation, of leaving a positive legacy for the future, of giving something back to society for the benefits one has received, and other generative motifs become increasingly salient in life stories (McAdams, de St. Aubin, & Logan, 1993). Second, as adults move into and through midlife, they may become more and more concerned with the endings of their life stories. It is in the nature of stories that beginnings and middles lead inevitably to endings and that endings provide a sense of closure and resolution (Kermode, 1967). The imagery and rhetoric of generativity provides adults with an especially appealing way to conceive of "the end," even as people are deeply immersed in the middle of the life course. By suggesting that one's own efforts may generate products and outcomes that will outlive the self, by framing a life story in terms of those good things (and people) that become the self's enduring legacy, life narrations that emphasize generativity implicitly provide stories with what may be perceived as good and satisfying endings (Kotre, 1984; McAdams, 1985). These endings, in turn, feed back to influence beginnings and middles. Consequently, it should not be surprising to observe considerable revising and reworking of one's narrative identity, even the reimagining of the distant past, in light of changing psychosocial concerns in the adult years and changing understandings of what the near and distant future may bring.

While generativity may represent a developmental challenge for many adults in midlife, adults differ dramatically from each other with respect to how they address this challenge. Quantitative research using self-report scales and rating procedures has shown marked individual differences in the strength of adults' generativity inclinations (see McAdams, 2001a, for a review). Some adults are much more generative than others. Individual differences in generativity, furthermore, appear to be associated with differences in narrative identity.

For example, McAdams, Diamond, de St. Aubin, and Mansfield (1997) contrasted the life stories constructed by adults scoring high on objective (behavioral and self-report) indices of generativity to those constructed by a matched sample of adults scoring in the intermediate to low range on generativity. The investigators found that as a group the highly generative adults tended to formulate narrative identities that more closely approximated a commitment story compared to their less generative counterparts. In the prototypical commitment story, the protagonist (a) enjoys an early family blessing or advantage, (b) is sensitized to the suffering of others at an early age, (c) is guided by a clear and compelling personal ideology that remains relatively stable over time, (d) transforms or redeems bad scenes into good outcomes (redemption sequences), and (e) sets goals for the future to benefit society. As an internalized narrative of the self, the commitment story may help to sustain and reinforce the generative adult's efforts to contribute in positive ways to the next generation. While many different kinds of life stories might be constructed by highly generative people, adults who work hard to guide and foster the next generation may make sense of their strong commitment in terms of an internalized narrative that suggests that they were "called" or destined to do good things for others, that such a personal destiny is deeply rooted in childhood, reinforced by a precocious sensitivity to the suffering of others and bolstered by a clear and convincing belief system that remains steadfast over time. Perceiving one's life in terms of redemption sequences (bad scenes are transformed into good outcomes), furthermore, provides the hope that hard work today will yield positive dividends for the future, a hope that may sustain generative efforts as private as raising one's child and as public as committing oneself to the advancement of one's own society. Stories in literature, myth, and folklore that celebrate generativity often display the kinds of themes identified as part of the commitment story (McAdams, 1993).

A prominent theme in the commitment story is the transformation of bad events into good outcomes, which McAdams et al. (1997) call a *redemption sequence*. The theme of redemption is a powerful motif, as well, in life stories of reformed drug addicts (Singer, 1997) and ex-convicts who have renounced a life of crime (Maruna, 2001). McAdams, Reynolds, et al. (2001) coded narrative accounts of key life story scenes among students and adults, looking for redemption sequences and for the contrasting narrative form of *contamination sequences*. In a contamination sequence, an emotionally positive event goes suddenly bad. Their results show that redemption sequences in life stories are positively associated with self-report measures of life satisfaction, self-esteem, and sense of life coherence and negatively associated with depression. By contrast, contamination sequences are positively associated with depression and negatively associated the three indices of well-being. The results are consistent with the literature in health psychology showing that people who construe benefits as having followed from their injuries, illnesses, or misfortunes tend to show faster recovery from their setbacks and more positive well-being overall (Affleck & Tennen, 1996). Therefore, while life storytelling functions to provide the self with ego identity, it is also instrumental in mood repair (Josephson, Singer, & Salovey, 1996) and in the overall maintenance of mental health.

CULTURE AND THE NARRATIVE STUDY OF LIVES

People tell stories in all human cultures. They tell them to other people. The very concept of a story is inherently social in that stories exist to be told in a social context. "The narrative structure of autobiographical memory appears indistinguishable from the narrative structure of other social communications," writes Rubin (1998), "and the recall of autobiographical memories is usually a social act that can define a social group" (p. 54). Developmental psychologists emphasize how children and adults share personal memories in conversation, how autobiographical memory is socially constructed. Thorne (2000) argues that the term *personal memory* is a misnomer, for the majority of important memories are shared with other people. A better term might be *intimate memory*, she suggests. For Thorne (2000), the construction of self-defining memories and life stories is always a social enterprise, and "families and friends collude in self-making" (p. 45). Even when families and friends are absent, however, life stories may retain their social character. Hermans and Kempen (1993) view the self as akin to a *polyphonic novel*, containing within it a multitude of internalized voices that "speak" to each other in dialogue. McAdams (1998) contends that all life stories are formulated with both external and internalized audiences in mind. Someone is always listening, or watching—be it friends and acquaintances, parents and children, or Freud's superego, Mead's generalized other, internalized attachment objects, or God.

Life stories mirror the culture wherein the story is made and told. Stories live in culture. They are born, they grow, they proliferate, and they eventually die according to the norms, rules, and traditions that prevail in a given society, according to a society's implicit understandings of what counts as a tellable story, a tellable life. As Rosenwald (1992) puts it, "when people tell life stories, they do so in accordance with the models of intelligibility specific to the culture" (p. 265). As noted above, Habermas and Bluck (2000) contend that before people can formulate convincing life stories, they must become acquainted with the culture's concept of biography. In modern Western cultures, biographies are expected to begin in the family, to involve growth and expansion in the early years, to trace later problems back to earlier conflicts, to incorporate epiphanies and turning points that mark changes in the protagonist's quest, and to be couched in the discourse of progress versus decline (McAdams, 1996). Other societies tell lives in different ways and have different views of what constitutes a good story to tell (Gregg, 1991).

Furthermore, even in a given society, different stories compete for dominance and acceptance. Feminists such as Heilbrun (1988) argue that in Western societies, many women "have been deprived of the narratives, or the texts, plots, or examples, by which they might assume power over—take control over—their lives" (p. 17). It is painfully clear that life stories echo gender and class constructions in society and reflect, in one way or another, prevailing patterns of hegemony in the economic, political, and cultural contexts wherein human lives are situated. Power elites in society privilege certain life stories over others, and therefore, a number of narrative researchers and clinicians seek to give voice and expression to forms of life narrative that have traditionally been suppressed or marginalized (Franz & Stewart, 1994; Gergen & Gergen, 1993; White & Epston, 1990).

A wide-ranging and loosely coordinated movement in the social sciences, the narrative study of lives has emerged in recent years as an interdisciplinary effort to write, interpret, and disseminate people's life stories, with special attention paid to the accounts of women, people of color, and representatives of other groups whose lives and whose stories have historically been ignored or even suppressed (Josselson & Lieblich, 1993; Josselson et al., 2003; McAdams, Josselson, & Lieblich, 2001). Many of the studies undertaken by scholars in this arena use inductive and hermeneutical methods to examine in depth small samples of life stories collected from clearly defined sociodemographic and cultural groups. For instance, Modell (1992) identified common themes and narrative strategies in the stories that birth parents tell about why they gave up their children for adoption. Walkover (1992) found that married couples on the edge of parenthood crafted stories about their imagined future in which they romanticized and idealized the children they were about to have, suggesting an implicit (but irrational) belief in the perfectibility of childhood. Linn (1997) identified common life-narrative types among Israeli soldiers who refused to engage in what they believed to be immoral acts of aggression. Gregg (1996) identified a hybrid life-narrative form that mixes themes of modernity and traditional Islamic faith among contemporary young Moroccans. Cohler, Hostetler, and Boxer (1998) analyzed conflicts, frustrations, and potentialities in generativity in the life stories of gay couples. Crossley (2001) explored how HIV-positive people turned the sense of place and the meaning of home into themes in their life stories.

RELATIONS TO THERAPY

In modern life, counseling and psychotherapy provide prime opportunities for the telling and transformation of life stories. As modern adults work to improve their lives and make sense of the confusing world in which they live, therapists and counselors provide support and guidance in life narration. Narrative therapists offer a wide range of strategies for intervening in the psychosocial construction of everyday life (e.g., Hermans & Hermans-Jansen, 1995; McLeod, 1997; Singer, 1997). A key metaphor for many approaches, however, is *emancipation*. Therapists help to free clients from the culturally dominant narratives within which the clients may feel trapped (e.g., White & Epston, 1990). Through a variety of techniques (such as the process of externalizing the clients' presenting problem), therapists help to free up the "subjugated discourses" and "alternative stories that incorporate vital and neglected aspects of lived experience" (White & Epston, 1990, p. 31). The new stories that are generated in narrative therapy are ideally more closely attuned to the rich, lived experience of daily life and more likely, therefore, to feel "helpful, satisfying, and open-ended" (White & Epston, 1990, p. 15).

The narrative therapy movement and the upsurge of narrative research in the social sciences have developed on parallel tracks over the past two decades. Yet, in many areas, developments in one track might have implications for the other. In particular, McAdams's work on narrative identity, along with related research areas in the narrative study of lives, would appear to hold important implications for conceiving and practicing narrative therapy. We see four implications that are worth considering.

First, research and theory on narrative identity suggest that the kind of change that narrative therapy achieves has substantial effects on the very development of identity and personality. McAdams (1996) has argued that personality itself consists of three levels of individuality: dispositional traits (e.g., depressiveness, neuroticism, extraversion), characteristic adaptations (e.g., motives and goals, coping strategies, defenses), and integrative life narratives (e.g., identity). Because no form of psychotherapy is likely to have a big impact on basic temperament traits, some critics have claimed that therapy only works around the periphery of personality and produces changes that are likely to be ephemeral and domain specific. Recent research, however, suggests that people's specific strategies and adaptations and their internalized life narratives have as much impact on behavior as do dispositional traits (McAdams, 2001b). In changing people's goals and strategies and in providing new stories to use in making sense of their lives, narrative therapists are affecting the personalities of individuals as much as they are changing the dynamics in families and other social relationships.

Second, work on narrative identity shows that therapists need to consider carefully the developmental dimensions of life stories. It is not until late adolescence and young adulthood that individuals living in modern societies begin to put their lives together into integrative life narratives. Before this time, they do not have the cognitive wherewithal to do so; nor are their lives situated in a social ecology that encourages such identity construction. By the age of 5, children understand what stories are, but they are many years from seeing their own lives in full narrative terms (Habermas & Bluck, 2000). Therapeutic interventions need to be geared accordingly. For example, grade school children cannot be expected to derive thematic conclusions from different incidents and narratives in their lives, even if such conclusions seem patently obvious to adults (and the therapist). Teenagers may begin to derive such conclusions, but with this group, the danger may be that abstract conclusions are too readily drawn, as Elkind's (1981) research on personal fables shows. Quick to embrace totalistic solutions and abstract ideologies, some teenagers may lack the cognitive flexibility and tolerance for ambiguity that are required for making narrative sense of what a complex world has to offer. Midlife adults are likely to be concerned with generativity and the sense of an ending in life stories. Especially in family counseling, narrative therapists need to comprehend and coordinate the different developmental demands that shape the ways in which different family members apprehend their stories and their lives.

Third, a person's narrative identity says as much about the person's world as it does about the person. Narrative researchers and therapists have both shown a keen appreciation for the power of culture in the making of life stories. But some forms of narrative therapy seem to imply that the most authentic and emancipating life narratives are those that defy cultural constraints (e.g., White & Epston, 1990). From this perspective, dominant cultural narratives are hegemonic and repressive, whereas the subjugated discourses that ring truer to the individual's lived experience seem to exist outside culture, as if there were a culture-free core of personal experience. Narrative researchers appear to be somewhat less sanguine about the possibilities of transcending culture through life narrative (Rosenwald, 1992). From the most skeptical point of view, the emancipation of subjugated discourse may simply be the substitution of one culturally shaped narrative for another. Life stories are always psychosocial constructions, coauthored by the person and the person's world. The coauthorship is likely to prevail even in the therapeutic setting, as narrative therapists intentionally and unwittingly encourage certain identity constructions and discourage others. Even if the therapist were able to remain neutral, the change process itself would surely reflect cultural categories and expectations. The new and improved self that may arise from narrative therapy may be no less a cultural construct than its oppressive predecessor.

Fourth, both narrative therapists and researchers would do well to think more carefully about what kinds of stories they hold out as psychological ideals. White and Epston (1990) write that good stories transcend dominant cultural narratives to capture the rich phenomenology of lived experience. A good story solves problems and broadens a person's life. A good story is "helpful, satisfying, and open-ended" (White & Epston, 1990, p. 15). Rosenwald (1992) speaks of "satisfactory" life stories that "help to advance living action" (p. 284).

Among the psychological criteria that McAdams (1993) sets forth for mature and identity-promoting life narratives are coherence, openness, credibility, differentiation, reconciliation, and generative integration. From McAdams's standpoint, life stories are more than psychological discourses. They are also cultural texts that present particular moral perspectives (MacIntyre, 1981; Taylor, 1989). The psychological language of adaptation, fulfillment, coping, happiness, and the like is helpful but not sufficient for a full understanding and evaluation of an individual's life narrative. All stories promote certain goods and particularize certain images of what it means to be a good person and live a good life in a certain cultural context (Taylor, 1989). Narrative therapists must bring these extrapsychological categories to bear in their work with children, adults, and families. As narrative change agents, they must become fluent in the psychological, cultural, and moral discourses wherein their clients' lives have meaning.

The issue of what constitutes a good life story, in both therapy and research, leads naturally to the thorny issue of narrative truth. Narrative approaches tend to adopt variations on a constructivist epistemology. In other words, stories are seen as meaning-making constructions that bear an indeterminate relation to objective reality. McAdams's life story theory of identity adopts an intermediate position of psychosocial constructionism. Narrative identity has fictive elements to it, but it is not purely a fiction. Unlike a story in the *New Yorker*, a well-designed and psychosocially effective life story is grounded in the social and material reality of an individual's life. A narrative's credibility, therefore, is one important criterion for maturity in identity and integrity in social life. Life stories are jointly constructed by the person whose story it is and the culture within which the story has its constitutive meanings. Narrative identities are forms of discourse that, although culture bound and likely to change over time, have a substantive integrity that renders them more or less interpretable and a psychological reality that enables them to shape and direct human lives.

Theorists who find a purer social constructionism more to their liking, however, may find problematic the idea that identity should correspond, in some sense, to the social and material realities of life, arguing instead that these realities cannot be objectively known anyway (e.g., Gergen, 1992) and that therefore there exists no standard against which to consider the veracity of a life story. Focusing on therapy, White and Epston (1990) seem to come close to this view when they assert that because "we cannot know objective reality, all knowing requires an act of interpretation" (p. 2). In the extreme, this perspective suggests that revising a life story through therapy is less a process of discarding falsehoods in favor of truth and more a process of determining what dominant story a patient is stuck in and searching for pieces of experience that contradict or fall outside that dominant story. Using these newly discovered aspects of life, therapist and patient work together to fashion an alternative and, ideally, more helpful, satisfying, and open-ended story.

A thoroughgoing constructivist view, however, may be criticized for what Rosenwald (1992)—a prominent narrative theorist himself—describes as its "note of freewheeling arbitrariness" (p. 285). In other words, the extreme constructivist view seems to imply that, insofar as stories reflect only social convention and not objective reality, any story is as good as the next so long as it is deemed useful in ameliorating a patient's presenting problem. For Rosenwald (1992), however, this criterion for a "better" story is too liberal: "Does a story become better because its elements have been conveniently reshuffled to fit the occasion? If this were all, it would be rightly called fiction. But can a fiction reduce suffering?" (p. 285).

Rosenwald proposes that the truth of a narrative is neither representational nor pragmatic but dialectical. The therapist's task is not simply to generate a new authoritative story from a collection of newly unearthed experiences but also to help the patient become adept at the art of story revision and develop an appreciation for the process and an expectation that the process will continue throughout the course of life. Rosenwald suggests that life is lived in the shadow of the latest version of a narrator's story; in living, the narrator tries both to live up to what has been expressed in the story and to build in whatever is felt to be missing. In time, actions undertaken can reconfirm certain features of the story while complicating or even refuting other aspects. New living action prepares the ground for newer versions of the story, and new stories, in turn, determine future action. The more the patient becomes proficient in thoughtful revision of his or her narrative, the more this cycle continues, and the stories become increasingly more coherent and expressive. Life stories, then, do not conform fully to either objective reality or pragmatic concerns, but neither are they simply discontinuous fictions tailored to specific situations. Newer versions answer to past accounts. The later accounts are more satisfactory insofar as they overcome the self-damaging effects of past stories. Thus, stories relate to each other as do speakers engaged in dialogue; as Rosenwald points out, a dialogue may be quite productive and illuminating even if no single truth is attained and no particular problem fully solved. The ongoing dialectic is the narrative process, and what the narrative can reflect "truly" is this very labor.

In conclusion, narrative therapists are in the business of changing people's life stories. Narrative researchers are in the business of studying those stories from a scientific perspective. To date, therapists and researchers have not had too much to say to each other on the topic of life stories. We believe that the future holds many opportunities for fruitful dialogue between clinicians and researchers who work with life stories. The current chapter focuses on but one particular theoretical and research approach in the narrative study of lives. McAdams's model of narrative identity appears to resonate with and connect to the narrative therapy movement in many ways. Narrative therapy, research, and theory will all benefit to the extent clinicians and researchers share ideas and perspectives in the future.

REFERENCES

Affleck, G., & Tennen, H. (1996). Construing benefits from adversity: Adaptational significance and dispositional underpinnings. *Journal of Personality, 64,* 899-922.

Arnett, J. J. (2000). Emerging adulthood: A theory of development from the late teens through the twenties. *American Psychologist, 55,* 469-480.

Baerger, D., & McAdams, D. P. (1999). Life story coherence and its relation to psychological well-being. *Narrative Inquiry, 9,* 69-86.

Breger, L. (1974). *From instinct to identity: The development of personality.* Englewood Cliffs, NJ: Prentice Hall.

Casey, K. (1996). The new narrative research in education. In M. W. Apple (Ed.), *Review of research in education* (Vol. 21, pp. 211-253). Washington, DC: American Educational Research Association.

Cohler, B. J., Hostetler, A. J., & Boxer, A. (1998). Generativity, social context, and lived experience: Narratives of gay men in middle adulthood. In D. P. McAdams & E. de St. Aubin (Eds.), *Generativity and adult development* (pp. 265-309). Washington, DC: American Psychological Association.

Conway, M. A., & Pleydell-Pearce, C. W. (2000). The construction of autobiographical memories in the self-memory system. *Psychological Review, 107,* 261-288.

Crossley, M. (2001). Sense of place and its import for life transitions: The case of HIV positive individuals. In D. P. McAdams, R. Josselson, & A. Lieblich (Eds.), *Turns in the road: Narrative studies of lives in transition* (pp. 279-296). Washington, DC: American Psychological Association.

Denzin, N., & Lincoln, Y. (Eds.). (1994). *Handbook of qualitative research.* London: Sage.

Elder, G. H., Jr. (1995). The life course paradigm: Social change and individual development. In P. Moen, G. H. Elder, Jr., & K. Luscher (Eds.), *Examining lives in context* (pp. 101-139). Washington, DC: American Psychological Association.

Elkind, D. (1981). *Children and adolescents* (3rd ed.). New York: Oxford University Press.

Erikson, E. H. (1959). Identity and the life cycle: Selected papers. *Psychological Issues, 1*(1), 5-165.

Erikson, E. H. (1963). *Childhood and society* (2nd ed.). New York: Norton.

Fivush, R., & Kuebli, J. (1997). Making everyday events emotional: The construal of emotion in parent-child conversations about the past. In N. L. Stein, P. A. Ornstein, B. Tversky, & C. Brainerd (Eds.), *Memory for everyday and emotional events* (pp. 239-266). Mahwah, NJ: Lawrence Erlbaum.

Franz, C., & Stewart, A. J. (Eds.). (1994). *Women creating lives: Identities, resilience, and resistance.* Boulder, CO: Westview.

Gergen, K. J. (1992). *The saturated self: Dilemmas of identity in contemporary life.* New York: Basic Books.

Gergen, M. M., & Gergen, K. J. (1993). Narratives of the gendered body in popular autobiography. In R. Josselson & A. Lieblich (Eds.), *The narrative study of lives* (Vol. 1, pp. 191-218). Thousand Oaks, CA: Sage.

Gregg, G. (1991). *Self-representation: Life narrative studies in identity and ideology.* New York: Greenwood.

Gregg, G. (1996). Themes of authority in life-histories of young Moroccans. In S. Miller & R. Bourgia (Eds.), *Representations of power in Morocco.* Cambridge, MA: Harvard University Press.

Gutmann, D. (1987). *Reclaimed powers.* New York: Basic Books.

Habermas, T., & Bluck, S. (2000). Getting a life: The emergence of the life story in adolescence. *Psychological Bulletin, 126,* 748-769.

Heilbrun, C. G. (1988). *Writing a woman's life.* New York: Norton.

Hermans, H. J. M., & Hermans-Jansen, E. (1995). *Self-narratives: The construction of meaning in psychotherapy.* New York: Guilford.

Hermans, H. J. M., & Kempen, H. J. G. (1993). *The dialogical self: Meaning as movement.* New York: Academic Press.

Josephson, B. R., Singer, J. A., & Salovey, P. (1996). Mood regulation and memory: Repairing sad moods with happy memories. *Cognition and Emotion, 10,* 437-444.

Josselson, R., & Lieblich, A. (Eds.). (1993). *The narrative study of lives* (Vol. 1). Thousand Oaks, CA: Sage.

Josselson, R., Lieblich, A., & McAdams, D. P. (Eds.). (2003). *Up close and personal: The teaching and learning of narrative research.* Washington, DC: American Psychological Association.

Kermode, F. (1967). *The sense of an ending.* New York: Oxford University Press.

Knowles, E. S., & Sibicky, M. E. (1990). Continuity and diversity in the stream of selves: Metaphorical resolutions of William James's one-in-many-selves paradox. *Personality and Social Psychology Bulletin, 16,* 676-687.

Kotre, J. (1984). *Outliving the self: Generativity and the interpretation of lives.* Baltimore, MD: Johns Hopkins University Press.

Levinson, D. J. (1978). *The seasons of a man's life.* New York: Knopf.

Linn, R. (1997). Soldiers' narrative of selective moral resistance: A separate position of the connected self? In A. Lieblich & R. Josselson (Eds.), *The narrative study of lives* (Vol. 5, pp. 94-112). Thousand Oaks, CA: Sage.

MacIntyre, A. (1981). *After virtue.* Notre Dame, IN: University of Notre Dame Press.

Marcia, J. E. (1980). Identity in adolescence. In J. Adelson (Ed.), *Handbook of adolescent psychology* (pp. 159-187). New York: John Wiley.

Markus, H., & Nurius, P. (1986). Possible selves. *American Psychologist, 41,* 954-969.

Maruna, S. (2001). *Making good: How ex-convicts reform and rebuild their lives.* Washington, DC: American Psychological Association.

McAdams, D. P. (1984). Love, power, and images of the self. In C. Z. Malatesta & C. E. Izard (Eds.), *Emotion in adult development* (pp. 159-174). Beverly Hills, CA: Sage.

McAdams, D. P. (1985). *Power, intimacy, and the life story: Personological inquiries into identity.* New York: Guilford.

McAdams, D. P. (1993). *The stories we live by: Personal myths and the making of the self.* New York: William Morrow.

McAdams, D. P. (1996). Personality, modernity, and the storied self: A contemporary framework for studying persons. *Psychological Inquiry, 7,* 295-321.

McAdams, D. P. (1997). The case for unity in the (post)modern self: A modest proposal. In R. Ashmore & L. Jussim (Eds.), *Self and identity: Fundamental issues* (pp. 46-78). New York: Oxford University Press.

McAdams, D. P. (1998). The role of defense in the life story. *Journal of Personality, 66,* 1125-1146.

McAdams, D. P. (2001a). Generativity in midlife. In M. Lachman (Ed.), *Handbook of midlife development* (pp. 395-443). New York: John Wiley.

McAdams, D. P. (2001b). *The person: An integrated introduction to personality psychology* (3rd ed.). New York: John Wiley.

McAdams, D. P., & de St. Aubin, E. (Eds.). (1998). *Generativity and adult development: How and why we care for the next generation.* Washington, DC: American Psychological Association.

McAdams, D. P., de St. Aubin, E., & Logan, R. (1993). Generativity among young, midlife, and older adults. *Psychology and Aging, 8,* 221-230.

McAdams, D. P., Diamond, A., de St. Aubin, E., & Mansfield, E. (1997). Stories of commitment: The psychosocial construction of generative lives. *Journal of Personality and Social Psychology, 72,* 678-694.

McAdams, D. P., Josselson, R., & Lieblich, A. (Eds.). (2001). *Turns in the road: Narrative studies of lives in transition.* Washington, DC: American Psychological Association.

McAdams, D. P., Reynolds, J., Lewis, M. L., Patten, A., & Bowman, P. T. (2001). When bad things turn good and good things turn bad: Sequences of redemption and contamination in life narrative, and their relation to psychosocial adaptation in midlife adults and in students. *Personality and Social Psychology Bulletin, 27,* 472-483.

McLeod, J. (1997). *Narrative and psychotherapy.* London: Sage.

Modell, J. (1992). "How do you introduce yourself as a childless mother?" Birthparent interpretations of parenthood. In G. C. Rosenwald & R. L. Ochberg (Eds.), *Storied lives: The cultural politics of self-understanding* (pp. 76-94). New Haven, CT: Yale University Press.

Murray, S. L., & Holmes, J. G. (1994). Storytelling in close relationships: The construction of confidence. *Personality and Social Psychology Bulletin, 20,* 650-663.

Perry, W. C. (1970). *Forms of intellectual and ethical development in the college years.* New York: Holt, Rinehart & Winston.

Peterson, B. E., & Klohnen, E. C. (1995). Realization of generativity in two samples of women at midlife. *Psychology and Aging, 10,* 20-29.

Rosenwald, G. C. (1992). Conclusion: Reflections on narrative self-understanding. In G. C. Rosenwald & R. L. Ochberg (Eds.), *Storied lives: The cultural politics of self-understanding* (pp. 265-289). New Haven, CT: Yale University Press.

Rubin, D. C. (1998). Beginnings of a theory of autobiographical remembering. In C. P. Thompson, D. J. Hermann, D. Bruce, J. D. Read, D. G. Payne, & M. P. Toglia (Eds.), *Autobiographical memory: Theoretical and applied perspectives* (pp. 47-67). Mahwah, NJ: Lawrence Erlbaum.

Sarbin, T. (Ed.). (1986). *Narrative psychology: The storied nature of human conduct.* New York: Praeger.

Singer, J. A. (1997). *Message in a bottle: Stories of men and addiction.* New York: Free Press.

Singer, J. A., & Salovey, P. (1993). *The remembered self.* New York: Free Press.

Taylor, C. (1989). *Sources of the self: The making of the modern identity.* Cambridge, MA: Harvard University Press.

Thorne, A. (2000). Personal memory telling and personality development. *Personality and Social Psychology Review, 4,* 45-56.

Tomkins, S. S. (1987). Script theory. In J. Aronoff, A. I. Rabin, & R. A. Zucker (Eds.), *The emergence of personality* (pp. 147-216). New York: Springer.

Walkover, B. C. (1992). The family as an overwrought object of desire. In G. C. Rosenwald & R. L. Ochberg (Eds.), *Storied lives: The cultural politics of self-understanding* (pp. 178-191). New Haven, CT: Yale University Press.

White, M., & Epston, D. (1990). *Narrative means to therapeutic ends.* New York: Norton.

Woike, B. A., Gersekovich, I., Piorkowski, R., & Polo, M. (1999). The role of motives in the content and structure of autobiographical memory. *Journal of Personality and Social Psychology, 76,* 600-612.

CHAPTER 10

The Innovation of Self-Narratives
A Dialogical Approach

HUBERT J. M. HERMANS

OVERVIEW

The therapeutic assessment and intervention approach, which is presented in this chapter, has emerged from 30 years of listening to the self-narratives of clients in psychotherapy. Over the course of time, many of my thoughts about psychotherapy have changed as I try out various procedures, read different sources of literature and, last but not least, learn from discussions with clients. However, three strong impressions, even convictions, have remained over the years and continue to influence my present work in psychotherapy.

First, when clients tell the stories of their lives or significant parts of their lives, they not only tell the story but also listen to the same story. They tell it not only to the therapist but also, via the therapist, to themselves. It is precisely this listening which opens the gate to the retelling of the story. Certainly, the therapist significantly, and even necessarily, influences the quality of this *feedback listening,* but the basic idea is that clients retell their stories by listening to their own formulations and reformulations.

Second, by telling their stories to the therapist and to themselves, a *dialogical space* is created that instigates the retelling of the story in such a way that new relationships are established between existing story parts or new elements are introduced. This dialogical space functions as a field of tension in which a gradual transition is realized between the assessment of the story and its change or innovation.

Third, the construction of a dialogical space is facilitated when the two parties, client and psychotherapist, contribute to the process from their own specific expertise.

AUTHOR'S NOTE: I thank Els Hermans-Jansen for her contribution in the presented case study and Ingrid Josephs for her constructive comments on this chapter. Correspondence regarding this chapter should be sent to the author at University of Nijmegen, Department of Clinical Psychology and Personality, P.O. Box 9104, 6500 HE Nijmegen, The Netherlands, or to HHermans@psych.kun.nl.

Clients have an enormous database available on their own lives from which they select events for the organization of a story. Moreover, they are knowledgeable on the meanings of these events as part of their life story. The therapist, on the other hand, has experience with a variety of other clients and is, moreover, knowledgeable on theories, methods, and specific procedures for the assessment and change of the client's narrative. With these areas of expertise as a starting point, the two parties develop a cooperative relationship that aims at a reconstruction of the story. These three impressions (self-listening, gradual transition between assessment and change, and acknowledgment of the client's specific expertise) form the basis of a dialogical approach to the innovation of clients' self-narratives.

THE DIALOGICAL SELF: A POLYPHONY OF VOICES

The dialogical self (Hermans & Kempen, 1993) serves as the background theory of the narrative approach presented in this chapter. In its most succinct formulation, the dialogical self can be described as a dynamic multiplicity of (voiced) positions in the landscape of the mind, intertwined as this mind is with the minds of other people. This formulation aims at a far-reaching decentralization of the self, which is assumed to consist of a number of relatively autonomous spatial positions (actual, remembered, or imagined) in which the *I* is located, with the possibility of moving from one position to another. These movements can lead to dialogical relationships among positions in terms of question and answer or agreement and disagreement. The concept of the dialogical self can be further elaborated by examining its two components, dialogue and self, in somewhat more detail.

The notion of a decentralized dialogue is most explicitly expressed in the metaphor of the polyphonic novel proposed by the Russian literary scholar, Mikhail Bakhtin (1929/1973) after reading Dostoyevsky's impressive oeuvre. The principle feature of the polyphonic novel is that it is composed of a number of independent and mutually opposing viewpoints embodied by characters involved in dialogical relationships. Each character in such a novel is considered ideologically authoritative and independent, implying that each character is perceived as the author of his or her own view of the world, instead of being the object of Dostoyevsky's all-encompassing, artistic vision. The characters in Dostoyevsky's novels are not "obedient slaves" subjected to his centralized worldview. Rather, the characters are capable of standing next to their creator, disagreeing with the author, and even rebelling against him. Taking the shape of some of his characters gives Dostoyevsky the opportunity to present different and even opposing views of the world, representing a multiplicity of differently located voices of the "same" Dostoyevsky. The characters pose questions and give answers to each other, agree and disagree with each other, try to convince and ridicule each other. As a result of these dialogues, new meanings emerge, both between and within people. As in a polyphonic composition, the several voices or instruments have different spatial positions and accompany and oppose each other in dialogical relationships. The introduction of the polyphonic novel marked the beginning of what in literary circles is described as the "retreat of the omniscient narrator" (Spencer, 1971).

The *self* component of the theory can be understood by going back to the main originator of the concept in the history of psychology, William James (1890), who introduced the distinction between the *I* and the *Me*, according to Rosenberg (1979), a classic distinction in the psychology of the self. In James's view, the *I* is equated with the self-as-knower and the *Me* with self-as-known. The *I* has three features: continuity, distinctness, and volition (see also Damon & Hart, 1982). The continuity of the self-as-knower is characterized by a sense of personal identity, that is, a sense of sameness through time. Feeling distinct from others, or having a sense of individuality, also follows from the subjective nature of the self-as-knower. Finally, a sense of personal volition refers to the agency of the self, as represented by the continuous appropriation and rejection of thoughts by which the self-as-knower proves itself to be an active processor of experience.

James (1890) depicted the *Me* as being composed of a variety of empirical elements that seem to belong to oneself. Crucial for dialogical self theory is James's observation that there is a gradual transition between *Me* and *mine*. He considered the self-as-object as being composed of all that the person can call his or her own, "not only his body and his psychic powers, but his clothes and his house, his wife and children, his ancestors and friends, his reputation and works, his lands and horses, and yacht and bank-account" (p. 291). As this formulation suggests, people and things in the environment belong to the self insofar as they are perceived to be "mine." This definition has the important implication that not only "my mother" belongs to the self but even "my enemy," even though my enemy may be perceived as very different from or even opposed to myself. As Rosenberg (1979) has rightly argued, James's view of the self extended to the environment. With his conception of the self, James paved the way for later theoretical developments in which the self is considered to be a highly open construct that leaves room for contrasts, oppositions, and negotiations between voices that are part of the social environment.

In dialogical self theory the theoretical term, *I*-position, is not restricted to the internal domain of the self. The external positions, as parts of an extended self, are also conceived as *I*-positions, that is, the other is conceived as "another I." This point of view is consistent with Bakhtin (1929/1973), who said, "For the author the hero is not 'he,' and not 'I' but a full-valued 'thou,' that is another full-fledged 'I'" (p. 51). This point of view goes beyond James's notion of the self because his extension took place primarily on the level of the *Me* (the self-as-known). In line with Bakhtin, it can be claimed that the social other is part not only of the *Me* but also of the *I*. Thus, the other as part of the external domain of the self is seen not only as "mine" but also as "another I," which, rather than being an extension of the self on the object level, is a person like myself on the subject level or is an object with personlike qualities (e.g., a piece of art, a toy, a picture, nature, or a beautiful place which "speaks" to you). The other as *alter ego* has two implications: The other is like me (ego) and at the same time another one (alter). Self-knowledge is, then, not only knowledge of myself (internal domain of the position repertoire) but also knowledge of the relationship with the other as alter ego (external domain of the position repertoire). In this way, self-knowledge and knowledge of the other are intimately related.

The concept of the dialogical self emerges from a reformulation of the Jamesian *I-me* relationships in terms of Bakhtin's polyphonic novel. The spatial term *position* and the dynamic terms *positioning* and *repositioning* (see also Harré & Van Langenhove, 1991) are used to express the theoretical idea that the *I* is decentralized, that is, positioned in time and space and not, in any way, hovering above itself or the world. Like parts of a polyphonic novel, the different *I*-positions are embodied as voices who entertain dialogical relationships, both internal and external, with other voices.

On the basis of these considerations, the dialogical self can be described in terms of a dynamic multiplicity of relatively autonomous *I*-positions, contextualized in a spatial structure in which the *I* is able to move from one spatial position to another in accordance with changes in situation and time. The *I* fluctuates among different and even opposed positions and has the capacity to imaginatively endow each position with a voice so that dialogical relations between positions can be established. The voices function as interacting characters in a story. Each of them has a story to tell about its own experiences from its own stance. As different voices, these characters exchange information about their respective *Me*s, resulting in a complex, narratively structured self (Hermans, 2001b; Hermans, Kempen, & Van Loon, 1992).

As the preceding analysis suggests, internal and external voices are intimately intertwined and function even on a common base. Self and society have in common that they consist of a polyphony of consonant and dissonant voices. Self and society share two main features that are necessary for understanding dialogical relationships. First, both in a multivoiced society and in a multivoiced self, there is opportunity for intersubjective interchange. Second, both in society and in the self, the relationships between the several positions are shaped by dominance or social power. As some individuals or groups in a society have more social power and influence than other individuals and groups, the voices of some positions in the self are more easily heard and have, in a particular situation, more chance for expression and communication than others. In sum, dialogical interchange and dominance are intrinsic features of the dialogical self (Bhatia & Ram, 2002; Gregg, 1991; Hermans & Kempen, 1993, 1998; Linell, 1990; Taylor, 1991).

PSYCHOTHERAPY AS A RECONSTRUCTION OF THE POSITION REPERTOIRE

Narrative-informed psychotherapy, from a dialogical point of view, aims at a reconstruction of the client's position repertoire in such a way that the client is able to move flexibly from one position to another. This aim has an important implication for the power relationships between positions. If one or a few positions are so dominant in the system that the movement to other desirable positions is seriously inhibited, the self-system can be considered dysfunctional. The aim of psychotherapy, then, is to change dominance relations in such a way that the dialogue between the several positions can take place more fluently (see also Honos-Webb, Surko, Stiles, & Greenberg, 1999).

Insofar as psychotherapy aims to change dominant relationships and the dialogical interchange of positions, it aims at the innovation of the position repertoire as an organized system. There are three ways in which the repertoire can be innovated. First, a new position can be introduced into the system and included in the organization of the self. Potentially, each new situation can lead to a new position in the self, but the openness to new positions strongly depends on the existing organization of the repertoire. If a particular position or coalition of positions dominates the organization of the repertoire, any new position is suppressed, split off, or at least subordinated to the existing power regime before it has a chance to innovate the system in any productive way. For an effective introduction of a new position, it is therefore necessary first to have insight into the existing organization of the repertoire and into those positions in particular that block movement (e.g., *I* as a victim or *I* as always angry). If this requirement is fulfilled, therapeutic strategies can be applied for the introduction of new positions that form an effective answer to the dominant position. In the course of the psychotherapeutic process, a dominance reversal is intended so that the new positions can match or even surpass the influence of the "old" positions in the system

(Hermans, 1996a, 1996b; Honos-Webb et al., 1999; Leiman, 2002).

A second form of innovation exists when positions move from the background of the system to the foreground. In that case, the positions are already part of the system, but they become accessible as the result of psychotherapy. Lysaker and Lysaker (2001), for example, studied schizophrenia as a "collapse of the dialogical self" and followed a client through three phases: before, during, and after a schizophrenic period. One of their findings was that particular positions, active in the first phase (e.g., *I* as a lover of music), seemed to disappear in the second phase but could be activated again in the third phase. Such data suggest that particular positions may be pushed to the background for a shorter or longer period in a person's autobiographical history. They seem to have disappeared entirely, but the fact is that they are no longer accessible. The goal of psychotherapy is, then, to restore the accessibility of existing positions.

A third form of innovation can be realized when two or more positions come to support each other in new ways or to develop some form of cooperation to form a new subsystem in the self. Positions that have similar purposes can go together and form a coalition (e.g., *I* as enjoyer of life and *I* as playful). However, it is also possible that a coalition emerges between positions that were previously opposites or even enemies of each other.

An example may be a client who suffered from extreme doubts about his own capacities and finally felt burned out. Over the course of his psychotherapy, I had the opportunity to follow the development of his position repertoire over a period of 18 months. In the beginning, it became clear that three positions played main roles in his present life: the doubter, the perfectionist, and, somewhat in the background but very important to him, the enjoyer of life. Although the latter position was very important to the client, it was strongly suppressed by a coalition between the doubter and the perfectionist, the second one compensating for the anxiety aroused by the first one. Over time, the client and I discovered that the persistent dominance of the perfectionist position could be reduced by learning to delegate tasks to other people at the right moment and by learning a new style of working. When we examined his repertoire for a second time, it appeared that the perfectionist and the enjoyer had formed a coalition that was strong enough to push the doubter to the background of the self-system. The client was increasingly able to enjoy working hard and doing a good job without the persistent urge to complete the task in every small detail. The new coalition represented a reorganization of a significant part of the repertoire with the advantage that the energy of the perfectionist was not blocked but used in cooperation with the enjoyer of life. Such case studies show that it is possible to form a new coalition between positions that were previously opposed and seemed to exclude each other as cooperative partners (for more detail, see Hermans, 2001a).

In summary, the goal of psychotherapy is the reorganization of the position repertoire in such a way that a flexible movement between positions is realized and subjective well-being is increased. The repertoire can be changed by the introduction of new positions, the movement of background positions to the foreground of the system, and the formation of new coalitions between existing positions. As the preceding formulations and examples suggest, it is not realistic to qualify some positions as functional (the "good guy") and others as dysfunctional (the "bad guy"). Rather, their place in the organization of the repertoire makes positions functional or dysfunctional. Let's illustrate this with an actual case.

Table 10.1 Some of Leo's Positions

Internal Positions	External Positions
I as child of my parents	My father
I as colleague	My mother
I as vulnerable	My ex-partner Laura
I as revenger	My sport-mates
I as sacrificing	My brother Tim
I as demanding	My sister Sheila
I as accepting	My colleague Frank
I as sexual	Problematic person: Arthur
I as dreamer	Fantasy girlfriend
I as disillusioned	Card-playing group
I as thinker (C)	Therapist: Els
I as stalker (C)	Nature: Skiing
I as not accepting (C)	The ladies (C)

Note: C = Internal positions chosen by Leo.

Leo's Repertoire: Stalker, Revenger, and Dreamer

Leo, a 29-year-old man, contacted a psychotherapist (Els Hermans-Jansen) after he received a bad evaluation from his superiors about his functioning in his work situation. He was criticized as being arrogant and lacking empathy in contact with his colleagues. In the same period, his partner, who was strongly idealized by Leo, broke off the relationship with him. In an uncontrolled fit of temper, he wrote an extremely aggressive letter in which he accused her of being the cause of all of his problems. For his partner, this letter was reason to refuse any contact with him. Although she was unapproachable, Leo could not stop thinking of her, and she increasingly became an obsession for him. The way he expressed his feelings for her was by following her and her new friend around all day and terrorizing them with frequent nightly telephone calls. Leo was aware that he was increasingly behaving like a stalker, and this behavior, in combination with the bad job evaluation, was his reason for contacting the psychotherapist.

After listening to his story, the therapist (in cooperation with me as cotherapist) proposed that Leo examine his position repertoire as a starting point for psychotherapy. The therapist provided Leo with a list of internal and external positions that were collected by the psychotherapist and me as being relevant to most clients and as relevant in the psychological literature (e.g., Rowan & Cooper, 1999). The client was invited to check the list and mark those positions he experienced as playing some role in his life. Some of the positions that Leo considered relevant are presented in Table 10.1 (for a full list of provided positions, see Hermans, 2001a). After Leo had selected a variety of positions in the provided list, he was invited to add some positions that he proposed himself and formulated in his own language. He then added three internal positions (marked as C in Table 10.1). One of the added positions was "I as stalker," which Leo thought was one of the most significant positions to examine as playing an influential role in his present life. In the external domain, Leo added also an extra position: "the ladies," a word he used for the prostitutes whom he frequently visited, a habit that was increasingly detrimental to his financial reserves.

To make the list as personal as possible, Leo was permitted to add names to the provided external positions. He added, for example, the name Laura to his ex-partner, who had broken off the relationship. For his fantasy girlfriend, he added no name. She seemed to be a character on a suprapersonal level who was fantasized as gratifying all the longings and desires he had as a dreamer.

By inviting clients to introduce positions into the repertoire from their own perspective and by adding their names to the positions involved, it is possible to combine two kinds of language systems, ones related to the psychotherapist and to the client. An advantage of this procedure is that the client's terms can be investigated in the context of the terms introduced by the psychotherapist. On the other hand, the terms provided by the psychotherapist receive meaning in the context of the client's language system. In this way, the position repertoire functions as an interface between two parties taking each other's perspectives.

After the construction of the repertoire as described above, the nature of the relationship between internal and external positions is examined. In this part of the investigation, therapist and client focus on the relation between a particular internal position and a particular external position and explore this relationship in the context of the other positions of the repertoire. In Leo's case, the relationship between the stalker (internal) and his ex-partner, Laura (external), was strongly colored by the association between the stalker and the revenger. Leo admitted that his stalking behavior was an act of revenge and agreed that the latter word, provided by the therapist, correctly reflected his intention. In the external domain, his contact with Laura was meaningfully connected with his fantasy figure: As long as he experienced a good connection with Laura, Laura and the fantasy girlfriend were almost identical, almost two shapes of the same person.

However, after Laura ended the relationship with Leo, the fantasy figure functioned as a compensation for Laura as she continued to fulfill Leo's desires. His visits to the "ladies" had a similar compensating function as he felt that they met his need for attention and respect.

In discussing the relationships between the several parts of the repertoire, the therapist and Leo discovered that there was a highly influential background position: the dreamer. Leo explained that this position was very important to his relationship with Laura, who always had been an ideal person for him (see Table 10.2 for a visual representation of the several positions and their relationships).

Valuation of Significant Story Parts

To investigate the background positions of the stalker in more depth, the psychotherapist proposed that Leo tell about his life and about his relationship with Laura in particular from both the perspective of the revenger and the dreamer. In this part of the investigation, the therapist used some open-ended questions that invited Leo to tell about the meaning of significant events in his life.

These questions are part of the self-confrontation method (Hermans & Hermans-Jansen, 1995), which invites clients to tell their stories or parts of stories about their past, present, and future. One question about the past is this: "Has there been anything of major influence in your past life which still continues to exert a strong influence on you?" Client and therapist read these questions sitting side by side. This spatial position symbolizes a relationship of cooperation between client and therapist. The procedure requires clients to give their associations after which the therapist helps them to formulate a sentence. These sentences are written down on small cards so that they can easily be taken up in a later phase of the therapeutic

Table 10.2 Valuations and Affective Indices From the Revenger, the Dreamer, and the Accepting Self

	S^a	O^a	P^b	N^b
Valuations From the Revenger				
1. When I have nothing more to lose, I can enjoy destroying somebody; I derive some pride from that	12	1	18	16
2. When I have the feeling that somebody (my ex-partner) is not honest with me, and I discover this, I want to give a lesson to that person with verbal violence and with telephone calls. . . . I want to make somebody suffer	13	3	18	21
Valuations from the Dreamer				
3. I was fantasizing that I would later get a rich and easy life; I played that with Lego	10	7	28	0
4. I am the reformer of the world, a well-known figure who traces criminals, a kind of private-detective, a hero who gets much admiration and attention	2	7	22	2
Valuations from the Accepting Self				
5. When the accepting self is not there, there are emotions like attacking, being short-sighted, reproaching with communication . . . then I give room to the revenger	1	0	0	37
6. Whereas Johnson (previous employer) reacted with some amusement to my self-image (dreamer), I see now that I receive respect from Peters (present employer), for example, my suggestions are followed and I receive respect from the administration	19	4	41	4

Note: S = affect referring to self-affirmation; O = affect referring to contact and union with the other; P = positive affect; N = negative affect.

a. S and O indices range from 0 to 20
b. P and N indices range from 0 to 40.

process and compared with other sentences. Similar questions are also asked about the client's past and future (Hermans & Hermans-Jansen, 1995, p. 35).

In the framework proposed here, it is important that the client answer these questions not from an undefined position (as is usual in tests and interviews) but from several positions made explicit beforehand. For Leo, this meant that first he entered into his revenger's position and answered the questions from his thoughts and feelings as a revenger. Then, he told about one or more events that have a personal meaning for him in a positive (pleasant) or negative (unpleasant) sense. Such meanings are called *valuations*. A number of valuations from the revenger's position are given in Table 10.2. Next, Leo placed himself in the dreamer's position from which, by means of the same open-ended questions, he likewise gave his most important valuations. These are also listed in Table 10.2.

The basic idea behind the described procedure is that when people tell stories of their lives to another person and to themselves, they give positive or negative value to the events and circumstances that are part of their stories. People bring together a variety of events or circumstances into a valuation, which functions as a meaning unit in which these events and circumstances are organized. A valuation may refer to a dear memory, a difficult problem, an important contact with another person, a fantasy, an unreachable goal, and so on. One purpose in the process of psychotherapy is to examine which valuations are associated with a particular position. The advantage of exploring valuations is that they are more specific and concrete than positions and are closer to the client's experience in particular situations. Moreover, it is easier to investigate their affective significance. In this way, the valuations function as a bridge between positions and affective experience.

The Affective Components of Storytelling

The affective component not only is necessary for an understanding of a particular valuation but also provides an insight into the organization of several valuations as part of a system. Valuations that refer to different situations may nevertheless have a common affective base. This assumption is in agreement with recent developments in narrative therapy that emphasize the central role of affect in storytelling (e.g., Angus, Levitt, & Hardtke, 1999).

In valuation research, four kinds of affect are distinguished: affect referring to self-affirmation or S-affect (e.g., strength and self-esteem), affect referring to contact and union with somebody or something else or O-affect (e.g., tenderness and love), general positive (P) affect (e.g., enjoyment and internal calm), and general negative (N) affect (e.g., anxiety and powerlessness). After formulating valuations from the perspective of a particular position with the assistance of the therapist, the client then assesses each valuation in terms of a series of affect terms or words, which refer to different kinds of affect. For each valuation, the client rates, on a scale of 0 to 5, the extent to which a particular affect is experienced in relation to each valuation. This procedure is completed by the client, working alone, with a computer program. When the client is finished, the computer program combines the different types of affect into the affective indices S, O, P, and N, which are sum scores of the intensity levels of the corresponding affect terms. The therapist is then ready to discuss affective patterns of the valuations with the client (Hermans & Hermans-Jansen, 1995).

The rationale behind this procedure is that people, in developing and organizing their positions and associated valuations, are at a deeper level fulfilling basic motives, S and O motives, or in the terms of Bakan (1966), agency and communion (see also McAdams, Hoffman, Mansfield, & Day, 1996, for a discussion of these motives from a narrative point of view). When people succeed in gratifying these motives, positive feelings emerge; when they meet insuperable obstacles, negative feelings are predominant. It is assumed that these basic motives are expressed in the affective component of the valuation. By examining the combination of S, O, P, and N affect, insight can be gained into the affective organization of valuations and their corresponding positions.

The affective component of some of Leo's valuations is presented at the right side of Table 10.2, in the form of S, O, P, and N patterns. When the valuations from the revenger are compared, we see a predominance of S affect over O affect and a clear ambivalence in the levels of P and N affect. On a basic affective level, this means that the revenger affirms himself by destruction and aggression. However, his revenge is only partly "sweet" because the presence of negative affect suggests that he is not very happy about this attitude.

The valuations that Leo formulated from the perspective of the dreamer not only have an entirely different content but also different affective tone. There is no clear predominance of S or O affect. Rather, his fantasies seem to be positive without a strong involvement of self-affirmation or contact. It seems that his dream world is not clearly rooted in his basic motives.

The most crucial finding during the discussion of these valuations of significant story parts and their affective meanings was that the dreamer functioned as a most influential background position of the revenger. Leo experienced the dreamer as opposite to the revenger, but the dreamer played a significant role in his relationship with Laura. The discussion resulted in the insight that the stalker, the revenger, and the dreamer functioned as a coalition in which the revenger was aroused in an effort to restore the threatened ideals of the dreamer. In the service of the unrealistic dreamer and the self-affirming revenger, Leo became a stalker. The implication for the therapy was that Leo was challenged to respond to the position of the dreamer, who was seen as the central character directing Leo's behavior from behind the scenes.

THERAPEUTIC PROCESS: ATTENDING, CREATING, ANCHORING

So far, we have focused on the construction of a position repertoire, on the selection of one or more positions that are relevant in the client's present life and represented in self narratives, and on the construction of valuations and affect as emerging from the selected positions. Together, these investigations are designed to begin a gradual transition from self-narrative and valuation assessment to the inception of self-change. Constructing positions and valuations is not purely an assessment technique in which the client is studied or assessed by the therapist. Rather, the client contributes significantly to the process by adding positions or significant story parts, formulating valuations, and identifying affective responses. The client is continuously invited by the therapist to participate in the discussion and interpretation of the results. In other words, the client is involved as a coinvestigator during the entire process (Hermans & Bonarius, 1991).

This phase of investigation, however, is not the end of the approach we use. It is followed by a second phase called, in light of Kelly's (1955) model, the validation/invalidation process. In this phase, the client is encouraged to elaborate, in the form of concrete actions and personal stories, on the insights that emerged from the investigation phase. The client is invited to relate the emerging insights to specific situations or self narratives and to check them on the level of lived experience.

In the beginning of the validation process, Leo discovered that, almost hidden in the background of his repertoire, was a position that seemed highly significant to his future development. This position, "I as accepting," was already selected as relevant during the construction of his repertoire (see Table 10.1), but it did not play a central role in his present life. Instead, he introduced an opposite position, "not accepting" (see Table 10.1), as playing a more prominent role in his present life. Leo and his therapist realized that the accepting position was highly relevant as an effective counterweight to the more egocentric positions such as stalker, revenger, and dreamer. For Leo, *acceptance* meant accepting that he was only as ordinary or exceptional as most other people in his environment and that he was not the unique reformer of the world. At the same time, Leo was invited to give more attention than before to the people in his environment and to accept their wishes, successes, and failures as realities.

The validation/invalidation phase is articulated in three subphases: attending, creating, and anchoring. In the attending phase, the client learns to become sensitive to those experiences or self-narratives that are relevant to both the original position (dreamer) and to the counterposition (accepting), which functions as the main route or pathway to innovation in the client's position repertoire. An important narrative-structuring technique used in this phase is a diary based on: *where* did it happen, *when* did it happen, *who* was present, and *how* did it go. Leo was asked to focus on one or two specific situations in which he did not succeed in accepting and describe them in detail so that they could be discussed in one of the following sessions.

In the next subphase, entitled creating, the client is invited to try out new behavior as a first attempt to act in a different way than what is usual for him. In Leo's case, this meant experimenting with accepting himself and others in specific situations (e.g., accepting that his new girlfriend talks with another man without becoming angry). In the creating subphase, several techniques are introduced to the client. A typical one is the validation ladder. The client selects and describes together with the therapist a number of situations of increasing difficulty with regard to the selected position. Next, the client experiments with one or more situations at the lower end of the scale, with the advantage that the probability of success is increased.

In the third subphase, anchoring, the client applies the new behavior to a variety of situations with increasing difficulty. The purpose of this phase is to establish the desired behavior as a new habit by repeating it across situations and time. In this phase, Leo was confronted with an event that was quite dramatic: His new girlfriend broke off her relationship with him. This was, in fact, the ultimate test of his acceptance. Would he again become extremely aggressive, and would the revenger take precedence over all other positions? In the sessions following this event, Leo discussed the new situation with the therapist and succeeded in keeping himself under control. He and his girlfriend decided to continue their relationship as friends but not as lovers.

In summary, the therapeutic procedure aims at a gradual transition between assessment and change. This is realized in two cycles. The larger cycle has three phases: Investigation-Validation-Investigation (IVI). The middle phase, Validation, is in turn divided into three subphases: Attending-Creating-Anchoring (ACA). The latter cycle is basically in agreement with Stiles's Assimilation of Problematic Experience Scale (APES), which describes how voices that are initially dominated by other voices are increasingly integrated in the larger community of voices (Honos-Webb et al., 1999).

Evaluation of Therapy Success

Five months after the beginning of the validation process, a second investigation was performed. In the meantime, the accepting position was so far developed that Leo was able to formulate some valuations from the perspective of this position. Some examples of these valuations are presented in Table 10.2. As the formulation of Valuation 5 indicates, Leo critically discusses his own position as revenger and gives a meaningful and adequate response to this character. In Valuation 6, he establishes a coalition between the accepting self and the dreamer. As the formulation of this valuation suggests, the dreamer is no longer merely fantasizing and building castles in the air but has become integrated into the accepting self position with the result that Leo is now finding a more realistic way of receiving respect and attention.

More generally, the dialogical approach we present distinguishes several criteria for therapy improvement or success: (a) the inclusion of a new position, the establishment of a coalition, or the foregrounding of a background position that is strong enough to present an effective counterweight to the position that hitherto dominated the client's position repertoire and personal narratives; (b) the sensitivity to see a clear connection between the relevant positions and counterpositions, on the one hand, and the experiences of everyday life on the other hand; (c) the ability to experiment with new behavior in such a way that the desirable position is developed and strengthened; (d) the application of the counterposition in a variety of situations so that it becomes a new habit; (e) the development of positions and valuations that are associated with affect referring to positive self-affirmation; and (f) the development of a meta-position from which the client has an affectively rooted insight into the relationships between other positions in their dynamic relationships (Dimaggio, Salvatore, Azzara, & Catania, 2003; Georgaca, 2001; Hermans, 2003).

In the evaluation of successful therapy, the affective dimension is particularly important. For more than 25 years, we have studied the affective patterns of a great variety of valuations from clients of different socioeconomic backgrounds and educational levels (Hermans & Hermans-Jansen, 1995). On the basis of the combination of the affective indices referring to self-affirmation, contact and union with the other, and positive and negative affect, we have distinguished six main valuation types (see Figure 10.1). As Van Geel (2000) concluded in a psychometric study of several thousand valuations, more than 60 percent of all valuations can be represented by a circle with six segments, representing these six types. Moreover, Van Geel compared a group of clients at the start of psychotherapy with a group of university students and found that valuations referring to positive self-affirmation (type +S) clearly distinguished between the two groups: Students had more valuations of this type in their system than clients. On the other hand, clients had more valuations in their system referring to the absence of self-affirmation and contact and union (type LL).

These findings are compatible with my clinical experience, which suggests that, in the course of successful therapy, clients move in the direction of increasing self-affirmation, suggesting that they become increasingly able to cope with their problems in an autonomous way.

Research regarding stories, positions, and valuations in larger samples sharpens our insight into factors that determine successful therapy. It should be added, however, that results of such research should be applied to the individual case with much caution. A personal position repertoire and corresponding valuations are structures organized on an individual basis. Therefore, any general finding should be interpreted in light of the client's specific biography and the client's organization of positions and valuations.

The Therapeutic Relationship

Our method of assessment and change of a client's position repertoire depends on a cooperative relationship between client and psychotherapist. Given the notion of the extended self, the therapist functions as "another *I*" for the client and represents an

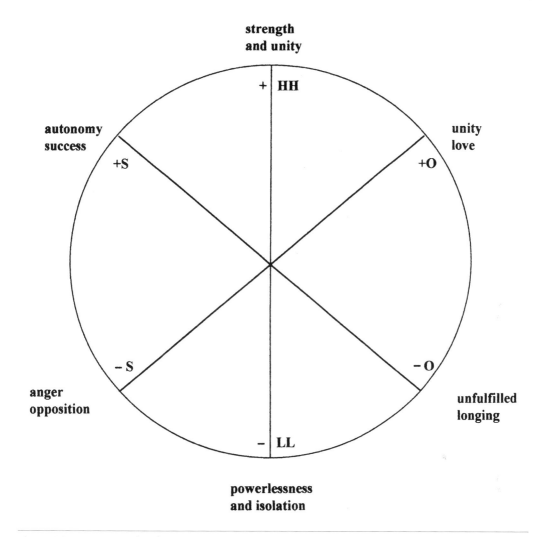

Figure 10.1   Types of Valuation

Note: +S = positive self-affirmation, −S = negative self-affirmation, +O = positive contact with other, −O = negative contact with other, +HH = high affirmation and high contact, −LL = low self-affirmation and low contact.

innovating position in the external domain of the client's self. Moreover, the therapeutic value of this position is in its dialogical relationship with a variety of other positions in the internal and external domain. Thus, the therapist represents a meta-position in the client's repertoire and contributes in significant ways to insights about the dynamic relationships among positions both between the internal and external domains of the self and within these domains. Moreover, the therapist facilitates the inclusion of a new position, the establishment a coalition of positions, or the foregrounding of a desirable position. The special position of the therapist can be illustrated with Leo's case.

Leo's main positions are depicted in Figure 10.2. The circles mark three domains:

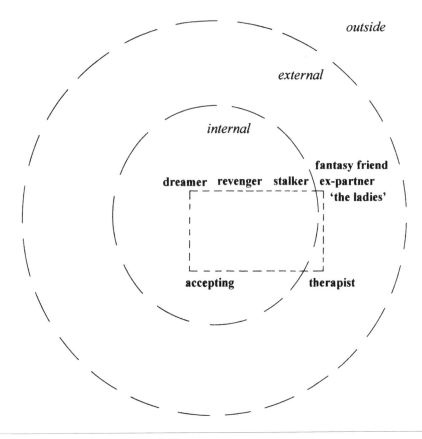

Figure 10.2   Leo's Position Repertoire

internal, external, and outside. As we have seen, the first two areas represent the extended self. The latter area, however, does not belong to the self but represents an unlimited area from which new positions may enter the self. The open circles suggest that positions may move from the outside to the inside of the self, from the external to the internal domain, and vice versa. In this way, positions may come and go depending on changes in situation and time. The rectangle in Figure 10.2 marks a dialogical space in which innovation of the self takes place (see also Goolishian & Anderson, 1992; Reichelt & Sveaass, 1994). This space is created as a field of tension between two groups of positions. One group is placed at the upper line of the rectangle and the other at the bottom line. The positions on the upper line represent the coalition of Leo's dysfunctional repertoire at the start of therapy. He compensated for the loss of his partner by dreaming about his always-available fantasy girlfriend and by making frequent visits to "the ladies." At the same time, the revenger was activated as an ineffectual attempt to compensate for the damage to his dream images.

The therapist's strategy was to activate a position that can replace the compensatory relationships between the positions with a complementary relationship (Benjamin, 1997).

The accepting position has the potential to give an adequate dialogical answer to the opposite groups in both the internal domain (dreamer, revenger, stalker) and the external domain (ex-partner, fantasy figure, ladies). Whereas compensatory relationships keep the original power structures intact, complementary relationships, acknowledging the existence of established positions, create a counterweight strong enough to change the power structure of the system as a whole. In Leo's case, the therapist locates herself as a facilitator of complementary relationships on the bottom line of the rectangle and does so in cooperation with the growing accepting character in the internal domain of the self. In fact, the therapist is far from neutral. She takes sides with the accepting character and strategically facilitates the growing dominance of this position in order to reorganize and innovate the system.

In summary, the therapist has two functions: (a) she instigates the creation of new structures in the self, which provide a complementary answer to the existing but less effective structures; and (b) she serves as a beginning meta-position for the client, who increasingly gets an affectively based insight into the nature of the relationships between those positions that are relevant to the client's problem.

Indicators and Contraindicators

On the basis of clinical experience up to this point, some indications and contraindications can be formulated in a preliminary way. The dialogical approach presented here can be applied in cases of (a) identity problems and confusion in self-image or self-story, (b) fragmentation of one's self-narrative, (c) traumatic experiences that are not of a serious nature, (d) the feeling of not being able to set personal goals, (e) problems in social systems (e.g., social problems between two or more people who are members of a family or another social system); (f) a lack of clarity in the personal meaning of psychosomatic problems, (g) monothematic restriction of one's self-narrative, and (h) the investigation of transference and countertransference.

The following contraindications should be taken into account: (a) heavy traumatic experiences with clients who are not able to talk about their problems; (b) apparent incapacity to organize events in a comprehensible self-narrative; (c) use of substances that change, temporarily or permanently, one's self-consciousness to a large degree; (d) serious neurocognitive impairment that restricts the client's self-awareness or self-insight; (e) deficient psychiatric care that is not acknowledged but is instead pushed off on the clients; and (f) therapists who object to being engaged in a cooperative project with clients. (For indications for and against a dialogical approach, see also Lysaker & Lysaker, 2001.)

SELF AND SOCIETY IN THE FUTURE

The dialogical approach, as presented in this chapter, aims at a reconstruction and innovation of the client's self-narrative. The underlying theory rejects the idea of a centralized and omniscient storyteller, who is located above his story and tells about events from a god's viewpoint. As in the metaphor of the polyphonic novel, the therapeutic method invites the client and the psychotherapist to construct a dialogical space in which counterpositions are developed that create a dominance reversal in existing power structures and lead to the innovation of the self.

Among the most significant challenges that I see in the future are cultural changes that have repercussions for the construction of the self. As many discussions in the social sciences over the past decades have suggested, our theories and therapeutic procedures are bounded by cultural limitations and biases. However, in what is increasingly developing into a globalized society, the psychology of the self and its psychotherapeutic implications are challenged in unprecedented ways. Like a society, the self is populated by voices, and as a consequence, cultural changes in the larger society have immediate repercussions for the organization of the self as a "society of mind." In terms of Figure 10.2, the circle between the self and the outside world is more open than ever, and a large number of heterogeneous voices enter and leave the realm of the contemporaneous self within relatively short periods of time. At the interface of different cultures, people are challenged to give an answer to the increasing multiplicity of cultural voices, including their power differences (Bhatia & Ram, 2002; Hermans & Kempen, 1998; Josephs, 2002).

In light of these developments, narrative psychotherapy is faced with an increasing heterogeneity of stories told by people of mixed cultural origin. As different cultures become members of a globalized society, most of us, or perhaps all of us, are becoming people of mixed cultural origin. If this is so, the dialogues with our clients are becoming more complex and of a multipositional nature.

REFERENCES

Angus, L., Levitt, H., & Hardtke, K. (1999). The narrative processes coding system: Research applications and implications for psychotherapeutic practice. *Journal of Clinical Psychology, 55*, 1255-1270.

Bakan, D. (1966). *The duality of human existence.* Chicago: Rand McNally.

Bakhtin, M. (1973). *Problems of Dostoevsky's poetics* (2nd ed.) (R. W. Rotsel, Trans.). Ann Arbor, MI: Ardis. (Original work published 1929 under the title, *Problemy tvorchestva Dostoevskogo* [Problems of Dostoevsky's Art])

Benjamin, L. S. (1997). Human imagination and psychopathology. *Journal of Psychotherapy Integration, 7*, 195-211.

Bhatia, S., & Ram, A. (2002). Acculturation, dialogical voices, and the construction of the diasporic self. *Theory & Psychology, 12*, 55-77.

Damon, W., & Hart, D. (1982). The development of self-understanding from infancy through adolescence. *Child Development, 4*, 841-864.

Dimaggio, G., Salvatore, G., Azzara, C., & Catania, D. (2003). Rewriting self-narratives: The therapeutic process. *Journal of Constructivist Psychology, 16*, 155-181.

Georgaca, E. (2001). Voices of the self in psychotherapy: A qualitative analysis. *British Journal of Medical Psychology, 74*, 223-236.

Goolishian, H. A., & Anderson, H. (1992). Strategy and intervention versus nonintervention: A matter of theory? *Journal of Marital and Family Therapy, 18*, 5-15.

Gregg, G. S. (1991). *Self-representation: Life narrative studies in identity and ideology.* New York: Greenwood.

Harré, R., & Van Langenhove, L. (1991). Varieties of positioning. *Journal for the Theory of Social Behaviour, 21*, 393-407.

Hermans, H. J. M. (1996a). Opposites in a dialogical self: Constructs as characters. *The Journal of Constructivist Psychology, 9*, 1-26.

Hermans, H. J. M. (1996b). Voicing the self: From information processing to dialogical interchange. *Psychological Bulletin, 119*, 31-50.

Hermans, H. J. M. (2001a). The construction of a personal position repertoire: Method and practice. *Culture & Psychology, 7*, 323-365.

Hermans, H. J. M. (2001b). The dialogical self: Toward a theory of personal and cultural positioning. *Culture & Psychology, 7*, 243-281.

Hermans, H. J. M. (2003). The construction and reconstruction of a dialogical self. *Journal of Constructivist Psychology, 16*, 89-130.

Hermans, H. J. M., & Bonarius, H. (1991). The person as co-investigator in personality research. *European Journal of Personality, 5*, 199-216.

Hermans, H. J. M., & Hermans-Jansen, E. (1995). *Self-narratives: The construction of meaning in psychotherapy.* New York: Guilford.

Hermans, H. J. M., & Kempen, H. J. G. (1993). *The dialogical self: Meaning as movement.* San Diego: Academic Press.

Hermans, H. J. M., & Kempen, H. J. G. (1998). Moving cultures: The perilous problems of cultural dichotomies in a globalizing society. *American Psychologist, 53,* 1111-1120.

Hermans, H. J. M., Kempen, H. J. G., & Van Loon, R. J. P. (1992). The dialogical self: Beyond individualism and rationalism. *American Psychologist, 47,* 23-33.

Honos-Webb, L., Surko, M., Stiles, W. B., & Greenberg, L. (1999). Assimilation of voices in psychotherapy: The case of Jan. *Journal of Counseling Psychology, 46,* 448-460.

James, W. (1890). *The principles of psychology* (Vol. 1). London: Macmillan.

Josephs, I. E. (2002). "The Hopi in me": The construction of a voice in the dialogical self from a cultural psychological perspective. *Theory & Psychology, 12,* 161-173.

Kelly, G. A. (1955). *The psychology of personal constructs.* New York: Norton.

Leiman, M. (2002). Toward semiotic dialogism: The role of sign mediation in the dialogical self. *Theory & Psychology, 12,* 221-235.

Linell, P. (1990). The power of dialogue dynamics. In I. Marková & K. Foppa (Eds.). *The dynamics of dialogue* (pp. 147-177). New York: Harvester Wheatsheaf.

Lysaker, P. H., & Lysaker, J. T. (2001). Psychosis and the disintegration of dialogical self-structure: Problems posed by schizophrenia for the maintenance of dialogue. *British Journal of Medical Psychology, 74,* 23-33.

McAdams, D. P., Hoffman, B. J., Mansfield, E. D., & Day, R. (1996). Themes of agency and communion in significant autobiographical scenes. *Journal of Personality, 64,* 339-378.

Reichelt, S., & Sveaass, N. (1994). Therapy with refugee families: What is a "good" conversation? *Family Process, 33,* 247-262.

Rosenberg, M. (1979). *Conceiving the self.* New York: Basic Books.

Rowan, J., & Cooper, M. (1999). *The plural self: Multiplicity in everyday life.* London: Sage.

Spencer, S. (1971). *Space, time, and structure in the modern novel.* New York: New York University Press.

Taylor, C. (1991). The dialogical self. In D. R. Hiley, J. F. Bohman, & R. Shusterman (Eds.), *The interpretative turn* (pp. 304-314). Ithaca, NY: Cornell University Press.

Van Geel, A. L. M. (2000). *Agency and communion: A psychometric study of the self-confrontation method.* Unpublished doctoral dissertation, University of Nijmegen, the Netherlands.

CHAPTER 11

Assimilation and Narrative
Stories as Meaning Bridges

KATERINE OSATUKE

MEREDITH J. GLICK

MICHAEL A. GRAY

D'ARCY J. REYNOLDS, JR.

CAROL L. HUMPHREYS

LISA M. SALVI

WILLIAM B. STILES

Clients come to therapy to tell their stories (Hermans, 1999; Neimeyer & Mahoney, 1995; Sarbin, 1986). Narratives can preserve the rich complexities of lived experience. A good life story is rich in characterization, plot, and theme; it draws listeners into the person's complexly textured world; and it is always becoming richer, deeper, and more differentiated (McAdams, 1996). Researchers have attempted to show how clients' narratives or stories change as a result of therapy (Angus, Levitt, & Hardtke, 1999; Gonçalves & Machado, 1999; Grafanaki & McLeod, 1999; Lowe, 1999; McLeod, 1997, 2000, 2002; McLeod & Balamoutsou, 1996; McNamee & Gergen, 1992; Neimeyer, 2000b). The assimilation model (Stiles, 1999, 2002; Stiles et al., 1990)

AUTHORS' NOTE: Correspondence regarding this chapter should be sent to the authors at Miami University, Department of Psychology, Benton Hall, 500 East High Street, Oxford, OH 45056, or to osatukk@muohio.edu.

can build on these approaches by providing a systematic method for tracking changes in clients' stories and a set of concepts for understanding the observed changes. The model describes how problematic experiences become assimilated into the client's self in psychotherapy. It offers a language to describe how experiences become problems, how they can stop being problems, and how they can become integrated and transformed into personal resources. Thus, it serves as a lens through which problematic experiences and stories can be examined.

Stories are a way that people put their therwise inchoate experiences in order and communicate about them—with other people and within themselves (Gonçalves & Machado, 1999). As we explain later, the assimilation model considers stories as *meaning bridges*— the semiotic glue that holds our experiences together (by *semiotic*, we mean constructed of words and other signs). The process of assimilation involves building meaning bridges between the many disparate parts of the self. Each successive story represents an assimilation of the diverse constituent experiences of people, places, and events that compose it. Some stories work better than others, however, and psychotherapy can be understood as mending or replacing stories to better assimilate people's problematic experiences. To explain this, we begin by acknowledging the storied context in which psychotherapy takes place.

We Live in a Storied World

We live in a storied world. Our reality can be seen as composed of stories in which we are embroiled (Bruner, 1986, 1990). When we are born, we emerge into a plot thick with anticipation of our arrival. We are raised in families that have their own intricate narratives, and we become a part of these well before our birth. The stories that await us represent a rich mixture of historical, societal, cultural, and family influences.

Family stories speak about our place and role in the family and the hopes and expectations placed on us. They label, explain, and organize our experiences as we grow. They shape our emerging personalities even before we learn to talk. Our caregivers use storytelling as a way to teach us right from wrong. They may impress upon us how important it is to be honest or hardworking by sharing their own experiences of working on the farm or the consequences when they told a lie as a child. These stories transmit to us the lessons and moral values of previous generations within our culture and family.

Much of our socializing consists of sharing personal experiences through stories: laughing or crying over shared events, bragging about personal accomplishments, marveling at athletic prowess, gossiping about friends. As Neimeyer (2000a) said, "Such telling, which views narration as a social performance rather than a cognitive accomplishment, inevitably positions the author in relation to an intended audience and, at least implicitly, calls for an audience response" (p. 233). Telling these stories connects us with other people; our stories convey to them our perspective, or a part of our view of the world. Hearing another's story helps us imagine being in their shoes, feeling the way they do. Knowing stories of the others allows us to understand them better. Simply put, we relate to people by knowing their stories.

Our search for identity often includes trying on many different stories. We attempt to live other people's stories—that is, narratives offered by our culture—while looking for that perfect fit. That is, we use stories to make meaning out of our experience. Each story we try on affects us in at least some small way as we create our own story or self-narrative (cf. Neimeyer, 2000a; Pennebaker & Seagal, 1999). Various threads of the stories that we engage with become more or less integrated into our own story and our identity.

They leave their traces, important or trivial, in the self-narrative. In this process, different stories tend to merge into each other at the edges. However, although the story threads may be woven together in places, they remain identifiable throughout when examined more closely (McLeod & Balamoutsou, 1996).

As we use the term, a *story* is an account of a specific, concrete series of events that has a beginning, middle, and end. It conveys a sense of an active, agentic protagonist. It also implies a moral, evaluative standpoint (McLeod, 1997). Like Russell and Lucariello (1992), we consider that narratives require "a protagonist inspired with intentionality, undertaking some action, physical or mental, real or imagined, within the story itself" (p. 671). The structure of stories (a chronology of events with a beginning and ending) helps organize our experiences, gives us a sense of effectiveness by being the story's protagonist, and provides evaluative meaning. The characters and objects and events that appear in our stories are linked, that is, systematically related by causing, preceding, following, or being in opposition to other story figures (Neimeyer, 2000a). Their relationship to each other makes them understandable in the context of the story. Some story figures are of special significance; they become important units of meaning, both in our lives and in stories we tell of it. When their relationship to other story figures changes, this may have a large impact on the story, lived or told.

In a sense, the self is a story as well as a storyteller, weaving together the overarching story that organizes our life (Neimeyer, 2000a). The central theme in this story of self has been called a *meta-narrative,* or, equivalently, *macronarrative* (Angus et al., 1999; Gonçalves, Korman, & Angus, 2000), personal myth (McAdams, 1996), story of the good life (McLeod & Lynch, 2000), cultural narrative, or life script. This overarching meta-narrative is never fully and explicitly told but is implied in the specific, individual stories that it encompasses (McLeod, 2000). The self is, then, a collection of narratives or stories in complex interaction to each other and also the process by which new stories are added and the existing ones are modified.

There may be ways, however, in which the narratives we employ do not accurately reflect our experiences of living. Within the larger story of the self, some individual story threads may not be elaborated in detail or linked to other threads; rather, they are present but submerged. Such submerged story threads may not be fully acknowledged or integrated into the meta-narrative and may be at odds with it in one way or another. They may be concealed to various extents, hinted at, disguised, avoided, or even actively denied. The result is to make some stories less tellable than they might otherwise be and to keep some stories from ever being told (McAdams, 1998). Their influence on the meta-narrative may not be immediately evident. Uncovering these hidden, problematic stories may suddenly reveal what affects our life without us being fully aware of this influence; such a discovery may transform our life and the narrative about it.

What Makes a Story Problematic?

Stories can become problematic when they fail to serve their functions, such as sharing experiences, forming connections, or accurately reflecting our lived experience. Stories may also become problematic when they reflect personally troubling or problematic experiences. We will explicate each of these sorts of problems in turn.

Some problems may be understood as inadequacies in culturally provided narratives. Some personal experiences do not fit into easily accessible stories. For example, homosexual experiences of dating, falling in love, or developing intimacy remain largely unexpressed in the dominant cultural narratives. Culturally promoted narrative themes may also be personally unsatisfying or problematic when they cast personal experience in damaging ways. Some examples of culturally endorsed self-destructive figures include the superwoman who is trying to be a perfect mother, worker, wife, and social being, all at once; or the tough macho man who denies any fears and vulnerabilities and refuses help and support even when he needs help and support because accepting them would seem a shameful weakness. Other culturally promoted figures may be ineffectual: for example, a good girl, needing approval from others and hoping to be taken care of, or a mother so centered on her children that she has no interests or commitments of her own, resulting in an empty existence once her children are grown. Similarly, story figures may become stereotyped (e.g., the maiden aunt, the martyr). People who recognize in themselves some resemblance to such figures may find themselves drawn into the mold of inflexible *prototype narratives* (Gonçalves et al., 2000), that is, into a destructive identification with the stereotypes, simply because the culture does not offer flexible alternatives.

Images publicized within the culture sometimes result in big personal costs to individual members of the culture. For example, Wiersma (1988) described uniformly optimistic stories told initially by homemakers who had recently joined the workforce and were asked to talk about this experience to the interviewer. Once a better rapport was established, however, it became clear that these "press release" stories disguised fear, confusion, and a sense of loss—feelings that the participants were unable to express when speaking about this topic. The inflexible, culturally provided optimistic plot of a woman assertively entering the workforce and enjoying newfound independence was inadequate to contain personal experiences of the participants. It functioned as a dead symbol in their personal stories. Instead of helping them understand what the workforce meant to them, the story had an oppressive role. It forced participants to distort their experience to fit it into the procrustean bed of rigid, socially expected narrative. Rigid scenarios and figures may thus exclude, indeed banish, alternative understandings. In such cases, as Russell and Wandrei (1996) suggested, "it is no longer the individual's purely personal constructions but the societal constructions that need alteration in order to facilitate contextually diverse narratives that may affirm and thus partially alleviate an individual's or a community's struggle" (p. 331).

A story may be problematic because it is an account of a personally painful experience. For example, a woman sexually abused by a known and trusted relative may have difficulty understanding how she could be suddenly betrayed by someone she was used to seeing as her protector. The sudden change in the plot of her life may render her personal story disjointed and difficult to make sense of (see Neimeyer, 2000a). The incoherent, inarticulate story is problematic because it does not help to make meaning of the woman's experience; the events and feelings surrounding her experience of abuse are unprocessed, unable to be fully communicated and understood by herself and others. She lacks the symbolic (semiotic) tools to make the problematic experience coherent and link it to the rest of her life story. There is evidence that psychological well-being is intimately related to the relative coherence of an individual's life story (Baerger & McAdams, 1999).

Because they are so painful, traumatic experiences are difficult to process and put into words. There is a motivation to avoid feeling pain, often by denying the experience. Trauma survivors often experience blackouts, and stories about trauma often have gaps. Much is left unsaid or outside of the story. In a story about trauma, the language itself may serve the function of containing or concealing personal experience. These masked experiences are ever more difficult to approach and assimilate. Such stories can be damaging because they lock people into traumatic scripts, making them vulnerable to revictimization. For example, a woman with a history of abuse may come to expect this form of treatment from other people, and this can function as a self-fulfilling prophecy (Briere, 1996; Coffey, Leitenberg, Henning, Turner, & Bennett, 1996; Finkelhor & Browne, 1985; Janoff-Bulman & Frieze, 1983).

Problematic stories lead to pain and conflict, intrapsychic or otherwise (e.g., interpersonal, familial, societal). Who feels the pain determines how the problem gets addressed. For example, a mother found to be abusive by child protective services may be required to attend therapy. In this case, it is society's pain, not the mother's, that dictates the treatment.

From the assimilation perspective, the problematic nature of experience is defined by its context. The problem arises from a conflict between the experience and something else, be it culture, the needs of others, or our own expectations or meta-narrative. We consider this perspective as an alternative to pathologizing: The problem is seen as a lack of mutual assimilation, rather than as the experiences themselves. From this point of view, psychopathology may also be seen as a story, a problematic attempt to integrate something (cf. Hillman, 1975; Kelly, 1955; Leitner & Pfenninger, 1994; Mair, 1989; Szasz, 1960, 1990). For example, a substance-abusing husband may have chosen his addiction as a way to assimilate his stresses and insecurities, and the addiction creates a problem in the marriage. Talking about his stresses would address what he himself feels is a problem and encourage him to look for ways of dealing with these problems without drug use. This strategy would address both his own and his wife's concerns. Assimilation provides a framework for understanding problematic experiences and also describes a process by which the problems may be resolved. The process of assimilating problematic experiences seems to follow a similar path, whether in therapy or not. It is a process to which we now turn our attention.

Assimilation as a Lens

When we find ourselves inside a problematic story, we may attempt to ward off the problematic aspects or reject the ill-fitting narratives, denying or refusing to face them. We may remain stuck with a nagging awareness of acting out a script that does not quite fit for us. Or, we may reflect on our stories or explore possible solutions to them.

Organizing and telling one's story—to oneself or to others—often provides a release of tension (Pennebaker, 1997; Rennie, 1994). Some people find relief in rethinking stories by themselves or by talking to a close friend, family member, or spiritual leader. Others seek the help of a professional, such as a psychotherapist, who can listen and offer a unique relationship and understanding. The uniqueness of therapy is that therapists systematically focus on clients' stories and know how to work with them. The therapist attempts to follow the client's untold or hidden problematic stories and encourages their expression through dialogue. This heightened sensitivity to exceptions from dominant themes may be a crucial feature of all narrative therapy approaches (Sluzki, 1992).

The assimilation model (Stiles, 1999, 2002; Stiles et al., 1990) is an account of how problematic experiences become integrated into the client's personality in successful therapy. The model arose out of intensive qualitative analyses of client narratives and describes commonalities in the process of change. The model explains how therapy helps resolve the pain of living problematic stories and how experiences that once were problematic can find their way into a larger dominant narrative, within both the self and the culture.

According to the assimilation model, the self is a community made up of the linked traces of unproblematic experiences. In the voices formulation of the model, these traces of experience are described as internal voices (Honos-Webb & Stiles, 1998; Stiles, 1997, 1999; Stiles, Benjamin, et al., 1997). The metaphor of voice emphasizes that our internal parts actively strive for expression. Voices are traces of experience that involve all of the person's capacities in the moment (i.e., thinking, feeling, motivation, and behavior). When they are addressed, or triggered, voices actively respond; they want to speak and act when called forth by particular situations. The triggering situations somehow resemble experiences that formed these voices, and messages expressed by a voice usually recall aspects of these same experiences. Voices engage in conversations within a person, resulting in the sometimes contradictory nature of an individual's statements or actions.

Contradictions arise from unassimilated voices, experiences that have not been fully linked or integrated and are therefore problematic, as described in the preceding section. Confrontations between unassimilated voices—for example, when a problematic voice emerges and addresses the dominant community—are felt as dysphoric emotion (e.g., fear, anger, shame, disgust). That is, expressions by problematic voices are distressing in some way. A problematic voice might represent a traumatic memory, an unacceptable part of the self, or anything that is threatening or painful to the person. Such voices are opposed by the dominant community of voices and may be kept silent and separate.

The process of assimilation occurs through a dialogue between dominant and problematic voices. The problematic voice is initially weak and vague (although it may occasion intense negative emotion), and it elicits a response (e.g., suppression or avoidance) from a much stronger dominant voice. Through dialogue, problematic voices gradually become integrated into the community. This happens as voices develop shared understandings or meaning bridges. Voices construct meaning bridges through an exchange of signs or stories that convey the experience of one voice to another. A meaning bridge is created when two voices understand a sign in the same way, as when a story successfully represents and encompasses both voices.

The quality of the relationship between the dominant and problematic voices is summarized in the Assimilation of Problematic Experiences Scale (APES; Table 11.1; Stiles et al., 1991), which describes a sequence of stages that characterize the evolution of problematic experiences en route to becoming resources. APES stages describe the problematic voice as warded off or dissociated at first, then feared and actively avoided, then acknowledged and confronted, then dealt with in negotiations, then understood, cooperated with in finding solutions to problems that arise in daily life, and eventually fully integrated and used as a resource. The intrapersonal process of assimilation is similar to the interpersonal process in which a group initially excludes a newcomer, then begins to communicate, and ultimately reconciles their difference, leading to the inclusion of a previously unwanted member into the group. This voice can now interact smoothly with the other voices and engage in coordinated action.

The assimilation model has grown out of qualitative research on psychotherapy. The bulk of this research has been in the form of intensive case studies (e.g., Honos-Webb, Stiles, Greenberg, & Goldman, 1998; Knobloch, Endres, Stiles, & Silberschatz, 2001; Stiles, Meshot, Anderson, & Sloan, 1992; Stiles et al., 1991; Varvin & Stiles,

Table 11.1   Assimilation of Problematic Experiences Scale (APES)

0 **Warded off/dissociated.** Client is unaware of the problem; the problematic voice is silent or dissociated. Affect may be minimal, reflecting successful avoidance. Alternatively, problem may appear as somatic symptoms, acting out, or state switches.

1 **Unwanted thoughts/active avoidance.** Client prefers not to think about the experience. Problematic voices emerge in response to therapist interventions or external circumstances and are suppressed or avoided. Affect is intensely negative but episodic and unfocused; the connection with the content may be unclear.

2 **Vague awareness/emergence.** Client is aware of a problematic experience but cannot formulate the problem clearly. Problematic voice emerges into sustained awareness. Affect includes acute psychological pain or panic associated with the problematic material.

3 **Problem statement/clarification.** Content includes a clear statement of a problem—something that can be worked on. Opposing voices are differentiated and can talk about each other. Affect is negative but manageable, not panicky.

4 **Understanding/insight.** The problematic experience is formulated and understood in some way. Voices reach an understanding with each other (a meaning bridge). Affect may be mixed, with some unpleasant recognition but also some pleasant surprise.

5 **Application/working through.** The understanding is used to work on a problem. Voices work together to address problems of living. Affective tone is positive, optimistic.

6 **Resourcefulness/problem solution.** The formerly problematic experience has become a resource used for solving problems. Voices can be used flexibly. Affect is positive, satisfied.

7 **Integration/mastery.** Client automatically generalizes solutions; voices are fully integrated, serving as resources in new situations. Affect is positive or neutral (i.e., this is no longer something to get excited about).

Source: This table was devised by William B. Stiles and appears in several of his papers. See Stiles, 1999.

Note: Assimilation is considered as a continuum, and intermediate levels are allowed; for example, 2.5 represents a level of assimilation halfway between vague awareness/emergence (2.0) and problem statement/clarification (3.0).

1999). However, there has also been quantitative research on the model (Detert, Llewelyn, Hardy, Barkham, & Stiles, 2002; Field, Barkham, Shapiro, & Stiles, 1994; Reynolds et al., 1996; Stiles, Barkham, Shapiro, & Firth-Cozens, 1992; Stiles, Shankland, Wright, & Field, 1997). These studies collectively show that problematic voices pass through the sequence of stages described in the APES and that more advanced stages of assimilation are related to better psychotherapy outcomes.

Thus, the assimilation model has narrative roots, born out of a search for commonalities in stories and experiences at different phases of therapy. The assimilation model itself can be seen as a narrative, a generic description of the change process in individual cases from the researcher's perspective. It can be considered a meta-narrative—a story about what happens in therapy that is separate from the self-narratives clients bring into therapy.

The Assimilation Process

Therapy can be seen as a process of allowing unwanted voices to emerge in a safe environment, where they do not feel as threatened by other people and other voices. The first step in building a meaning bridge is to allow the problematic voice to emerge fully into the client's awareness. Both the problematic and dominant voices must be present for them to start interacting. Formulating a problematic theme is a starting point for modifying or invalidating it (Hermans, 1999). As summarized in Table 11.1, this emergence transpires across APES Stages 1 (unwanted thoughts/active avoidance), 2 (emergence/vague awareness), and 3 (problem statement/clarification).

Once both voices are fully present and equally acknowledged, they begin listening to each other. As their empathy for each other grows, they are able to co-construct a story that helps explain both of their experiences (Glick, Stiles, & Greenberg, 2002). As both voices contribute to the new story, they reach a shared understanding, and it becomes the meaning bridge that connects them (APES Stage 4: Insight). Once a meaning bridge is in place, it is reinforced and refined as clients apply their understanding to new experiences in the world around them. This is described by APES Stages 5 (working through) and 6 (problem solution). Meaning bridges give voices a common language or way of looking at previous experiences and allow them to act jointly in new situations. Voices retain their separate identity; they do not simply meld into a new voice, but rather the relationship between them changes. Once they are able to talk easily to one another, different voices in the community become resources rather than problems: They can be called on as required by the situation at hand. This allows the person to be open and flexible to a variety of new situations. Voices may eventually become so fully integrated that the problem is no longer salient (APES Stage 7: Mastery).

The Restorying Process As Seen Through the Assimilation Lens

We suggest that the assimilation model can be used as a lens to see how voices that once were problematic, muted, or rejected may become a part of the storied world. Assimilation offers a language in which clinicians and researchers can describe client change.

From the assimilation standpoint, story figures can be viewed as voices, which may be at different levels of integration or mutual acceptance and understanding. The story, then, is a way of putting the figures together, or relating the multiple voices to each other. The story details the relationships between its different characters. Thus, a story can be viewed as a meaning bridge between voices.

In considering story figures as voices and stories as meaning bridges between them, our view extends Polkinghorne's (1996) suggestion that the central protagonist in a self-story is the person's own self, who encounters other characters representing family members and friends. The assimilation model adds that there are many self-characters (voices) interacting with one another as well as with the external figures. We concur that "narrative is the form of meaning that is particularly suited for expressing unity and purpose" with its "capacity to draw together disparate life actions and happenings into a coherent whole" (Polkinghorne, 1996, p. 300).

The assimilation model's understanding also converges with the goals of narrative therapies, which aim to elaborate clients' stories into more coherent, complex, and diverse narratives (e.g., Gonçalves & Machado, 1999). Stronger, more elaborated meaning bridges promote understanding and empathy between voices. More effective communication is facilitated by multiple links between voices; there are multiple ways of putting the same characters or figures together, and these ways may change and evolve.

A client's story may go through a process of evolution that can be examined in terms of its APES stage (see Table 11.1). APES descriptions provide a way of comparing stories to one another, or to themselves across time, by giving a common metric that describes the degree of integration of the voices. This use of the APES responds to Russell and Lucariello's (1992) call for researchers to become more empirical and systematic in supporting their claims that clients' stories change in therapy. Successive versions of a developing story can be placed at different APES levels on the assimilation continuum.

For example, a client comes to therapy because of her compulsive cleaning rituals, which take too much time, disrupt her everyday life, and exasperate her husband. She views these as symptoms of an illness and hopes that an expert professional will do something to make them go away, to restore peace in her family. This is a culturally stereotypical benign story with a clearly defined scenario and an expected happy ending. The protagonists are a sick client needing help; her husband, who suffers as a result of her sickness; and a benevolent authority figure who can fix the problem for everybody's benefit. As therapy progresses and new material emerges, the client notices connections between things that seemed irrelevant before. Her compulsive cleaning rituals began shortly after a miscarriage after her husband threw her down the stairs. This is something he does when he is particularly unhappy with her, usually after another man has paid attention to her, thus making the husband jealous. These facts of the client's life did not fit into the previous story and so they were not articulated but silently stayed in the background of her narrative. Mentioning them in therapy brings them to the forefront of her attention. These facts now have to be accounted for, but there seems to be no place for them in the previous story. The client's story world is shattered (McLeod, 1997); her story becomes fragmented, with mysterious gaps that beg for an explanation, as she struggles to put together images of a loving husband and of being hit, cursed, and thrown down the stairs.

In the benign first version of the story, the relations between some story elements (e.g., the cleaning rituals and the miscarriage) can be rated at APES = 0 (warded off, dissociated; see Table 11.1) or APES = 1 (unwanted thoughts, avoided). The relationship moves to the APES = 2 (vague awareness, emergence) as the woman becomes aware of her own emotional pain. The compulsive rituals lose their ability to make her feel in control; they no longer successfully distract her from her terror of provoking the husband's anger again. This version is a tragedy of being trapped in an abusive relationship that she considers basically loving, albeit marred with occasional miscommunications. Reframing the story of a loving marriage into a story of an abusive one is painful, but it gives voice to the problematic abusive experiences, allowing them to participate in the story. Incorporating these experiences, as story figures, allows the client to define this relationship as a problem and aids her in seeing how she can personally take responsibility for dealing with it. This alters the earlier expectation that her symptoms could be easily or effectively fixed by a benevolent expert-outsider. The story, at APES = 3, is now about an active protagonist examining how she got to this unlikable place in her life and how she can go to a better place. The example could be continued through the remaining APES stages, as the internal meaning bridges grow stronger. At each stage, the voice of the abusive experiences has a different relation to the client's understanding of herself and her symptoms. Increases in her self-understanding are represented in the structure of her narrative, and the APES offers a description of these changes and a way to compare different versions of one client's story or to compare different stories across clients.

Building meaning bridges among internal voices involves processes similar to communication in interpersonal and cultural contexts. As disparate perspectives on the culture become gradually interwoven in the stories of its people, a community encompassing different people's voices emerges. We suggest that the metaphorical community within a person may be understood in much the same way.

Why is dialogue between different voices advantageous, be it within a person or in a larger interpersonal or cultural context? In a society, having a diversified cast makes for a well-rounded community. For example, having a town made up of farmers, police officers, teachers, and artists enables the community to handle a wide array of situations. Having different members with different talents and capabilities is important, and communication among them is equally important. They must be able to talk to one another to decide who might be the best representative to handle a particular task or problem.

The same can be said for internal communities. A rich and diversified cast of voices enables individuals to successfully face a multitude of new experiences as they arise. The internal communities, too, can call forth the representative best suited to meet the demands of a particular situation. The benefit of diversity is that it gives us resources to understand experience in a more nuanced and therefore more accurate way.

Restorying as Assimilation of Voices: A Case Example

The case of Margaret (a pseudonym) will now be presented to illustrate the restorying process as seen through the lens of assimilation. This case has been previously analyzed from a qualitative narrative analysis approach (McLeod & Lynch, 2000). For full assimilation analysis of this case, see Glick (2002; Glick, Stiles, & Greenberg, 2002). In this discussion, we elaborate on linking assimilation and narrative perspectives. Margaret was a 58-year-old Caucasian woman dealing with the departure from home of her adult children and with an ailing marriage. She received 17 sessions of client-centered therapy through her participation in the York Depression Project (Greenberg & Watson, 1998). Like all participants in that project, she met the criteria of the *Diagnostic and Statistical Manual of Mental Disorders* (*DSM-III-R*; American Psychiatric Association, 1987) for mild to moderate major depression. Showing significant improvement on a variety of the outcome measures, she was deemed one of the most successful client-centered therapy cases in the project. As part of a subsequent psychotherapy process study (Greenberg & Angus, 1994) funded by the Social Sciences and Humanities Research Council in Canada, all 17 therapy sessions were transcribed for further intensive process analyses.

Margaret's dominant way of being was an overly responsible caregiver of her family, which we labeled the *Caretaker* community. This dominant community represented both her loving desire and her felt obligation to take care of others, and it guided most of her thoughts, feelings, and actions. This way of interacting with the world had served Margaret well for many years; she was a skilled caretaker and derived a sense of personal worth from this role. However, a conflict arose when a new voice surfaced, which was Margaret's desire to be taken care of. This problematic voice was labeled *Care For Me* and was threatening to the Caretaker community because it conflicted with the selfless manner in which the Caretaker acted. The resulting tension between these two voices led to great frustration over caring for others without receiving any help or support in return. In narrative terms, Margaret had adopted a common cultural narrative for women of her background: Good wives and mothers diligently care for their families, putting others' needs ahead of their own. When Margaret felt the urge to satisfy her own needs, she didn't have access to a story in which getting her needs met was acceptable. As such, she suffered psychological distress in the form of depression.

Over the course of her therapy, Margaret expressed her problematic Care For Me voice in a clearer and stronger manner, moving through APES Stages 2 and 3. Once the two voices were equally represented, they began listening to one another and slowly built a meaning bridge. In the 11th session, the meaning bridge was solidified in a moment of insight (APES Stage 4). Margaret realized that she had been systematically pushing her husband away whenever he offered to help. Consequently, he felt alienated. Not knowing that part of her longed for help, he withdrew his support. The following passage illustrates the joint understanding that was achieved (Care For Me is italicized; Caretaker is bolded).

Margaret ... I never thought about it this way until now but,

maybe, he felt so left out too, maybe! he just felt left out.

Therapist when ... [you] were consumed with what was going on with your family ...

maybe he felt, left out and maybe helpless.

Margaret yeah, you know I never looked at it that way before.

*I just always ... had this feeling of resentment
that my, my sole support [slight laugh] wasn't there*

Therapist uh-huh, like he should have supported you more.

Margaret *yeah,*

*and maybe he just felt left out you know that,
as I say, I was so consumed with my parents,
that maybe I pushed him out of my life? ...*

Therapist maybe he didn't know how to help or?

Margaret yeah.

Therapist maybe he didn't know what you needed at the time

Margaret *... yeah, you know, I never thought of it that way,*

*isn't that strange,
... I guess maybe I was just so angry
and so let down and, you know*

Therapist and maybe there was a lot of hurt there that wasn't being expressed too

(Session 11: lines 1100-1123)

This revised narrative of Margaret's relationship with her husband represented a new joint understanding between the two voices, and it can be viewed from the perspective of either voice. The Care For Me voice might have said to the Caretaker: "You felt threatened when your husband tried to help and ended up pushing him away with your need to be caring." The Caretaker could have responded: "Yes, and you never spoke up to let him know that you really needed some emotional support and recognition so how can we blame him for not helping."

After this, Margaret started communicating her needs (letting her husband know when she wanted help) while also considering her husband's perspective on their marriage. Their relationship started to improve, and she began generalizing this success to other areas of her life. In the final three sessions, Margaret reported specific success in letting go of her Caretaker role, characteristic of APES Stage 6. Her daughter got married while Margaret was in therapy, and Margaret reported that she did not feel responsible for every detail of the wedding. She allowed others to take care of things and was able to relax and enjoy herself. What was once a problem (asking for and accepting help) became a resource. For this to occur, Margaret had to readjust her meta-narrative of what it meant to be a good wife and mother.

In Margaret's reconstructed meta-narrative, both of her internal voices could communicate their needs. She was no longer living out an ill-fitting or limiting script. Rather, with the aid of the therapeutic relationship, she was able to give voice to both her need to care for others and her need to care for herself. The restorying process afforded Margaret the opportunity to find or create a narrative that better described her own lived experience. As her story evolved, Margaret was able to approach new experiences, such as her daughter's wedding, in a more resourceful and flexible manner.

Story Genres Reflect the Characteristics and Hanging Interrelationships of Voices

Characterizing Voices

The voices in client narratives, such as Margaret's Caretaker and Care for Me voices, actively respond to other voices and external situations, and they can be characterized by their distinctive ways of expressing themselves. Consistent features in the form and content of a voice's expression help distinguish which voice is speaking. More specifically, voices may be characterized and distinguished by the following criteria:

> *Intentionality* is what the client seeks or intends to say or do from the perspective of a particular voice. It is the main underlying message, which can be formulated in a short statement of general intent, a behavior pattern with attached meaning.
>
> A related quality of a voice is its *function*, or what the person specifically accomplishes by the verbalization, such as listing events, providing descriptions, expressing emotions, reflecting upon something, asking questions, voicing disagreement, summarizing, drawing conclusions, and so forth.
>
> *Content* is what is spoken about by the voice, for example, a person, event, or emotion, about which a question is asked or about which a disagreement is expressed.
>
> *Affect* characterizes how the content of the voice is spoken about and what emotions are expressed about this content.
>
> *Contextual triggers* indicate what a given voice responds to—the external or internal object that immediately preceded (and apparently prompted) the expression of this voice.
>
> The *dialogical pattern* has to do with placing expressions of particular voices in the context of the entire text. Dialogical patterns are repeatedly encountered sequences or configurations of voices. They are relationships between voices that can be noticed and understood in depth only when considered within the broad context of the entire text.

Characterizing Relationships Between Voices in Stories

When criteria for describing voices, discussed in the previous section, are applied to story figures, intentionality would refer to the main idea carried by this figure or character, or its raison d'être in the story. The other criteria would translate into a function of the character in the plot, contents, and affect that it carries in the context of the story, other figures that immediately precede its appearance, and structural or dialogical relationships between different figures of the story.

Attending to structural features of stories can be useful for detecting changes in the relationship between different voices as they become more assimilated. Some of these changing characteristics include relative cohesion or consistency of the narrative; its theme or moral; the associated affect; types of characters that are a part of the narrative; richness of the description of characters; rules about time, place, and sequence of events; and a relation between the protagonist and the author as well as between the protagonist and other characters or figures of the narrative. There is evidence that relatively poorer narrative form in client stories is associated with more severe pathology (Hambleton, Russell, & Wandrei, 1996; Russell & Wandrei, 1996).

Just as the voices that populate narratives have consistency in their expression, dialogical patterns within narratives themselves have consistent features and typical elements that make them recognizable (Bakhtin, 1986). These combinations of story elements are called *genres*. While there is controversy and disagreement as to whether it is the structure of language or the structure of consciousness that is the primary factor (Bakhtin, 1984, 1986; Foucault, 1971; Habermas, 1990; Heidegger, 1971; Lacan, 1981; Wittgenstein, 1969, 1980), genres are nonetheless useful indicators of the manner in which clients organize and understand their complex reactions to their experiences. Genres typically follow common, well-established rules. Consider the definition of a tragedy:

> [A] dramatic composition . . . dealing with a serious or somber theme, typically that of a noble person whose character is flawed by a single weakness, as pride, envy, etc., which causes him to break a divine law or a moral precept and which leads inevitably to his downfall or destruction. (*Webster's*, 1989, p. 1502)

In the language of assimilation, genres represent distinct configurations of voices that are recognizable story types within the therapy narratives of clients. These story types reflect recurring patterns in the structure of the client's community of voices.

Genres and APES Levels

Connecting APES levels (see Table 11.1) with genres, we speculate that the following patterns may emerge in psychotherapy clients' narratives. At APES Stage 0, one may expect stereotyped, banal stories reflecting the client's alienation from his or her experience. Within narratives at APES Stage 1, fragmented, ghostlike stories emerge, signaling the emergence of painful warded-off experience, albeit with a limited understanding of what the dreaded thing is. At APES Stage 2, one finds tragic stories, reflecting the distress resultant from the full emergence of previously buried psychic trauma. At APES Stage 3, mysteries appear, stories involving the following of clues en route to making sense of problematic experiences. At APES Stage 4, we see psychological novelizations, with well-developed characters and story lines and with an attempt to understand these characters, rather than focusing exclusively on their actions. At APES Stage 5, comic stories emerge wherein a protagonist, using hard work and intelligence, weathers adversity and successfully overcomes obstacles that block the way to gratifying his or her needs. Finally, at APES Stages 6 and 7, epics—stories of achievement, glory, and success—emerge, reflecting the accomplishment that the client has attained in gaining a sense of perspective and integration with respect to the once problematic experience. This progression is reminiscent of Polkinghorne's (1996) observation that the life plots told by individuals undergoing occupational rehabilitation due to some physical or mental disabling condition moved from being victimic to agentic through a series of stages of transformation.

It may be that features of genres are relatively enduring because they reflect basic features of the human process of meaning-making (Bakhtin, 1984). That is, human ways of constructing stories, crystallized over the course of centuries in established genres, may be fundamentally parallel to the human process of making sense of a diverse array of experiences (Bakhtin, 1970/1979; Patterson, 1985). This latter point is captured in the APES; thus, the APES and genres overlap in their attempt to reflect these general features of human processing of experience.

How Does Therapy Help? An Assimilation Perspective on the Value of Narrative

Intrapersonally, decreasing conflict between internal voices reduces negative emotions and symptoms. Clients feel better in the moment when a voice feels heard and understood, and a sense of optimism and purposefulness then follows. Even if a voice is not fully integrated (i.e., it is not at APES Stage 7), once it has emerged fully into awareness (APES Stage 3) and established meaning bridges to the dominant community (APES Stage 4), clients tend to feel more efficacious and confident about handling future problems. Their confidence is not just due to a relief of symptoms or a momentarily feeling better; being in touch with a larger cast of internal characters makes future problems more manageable. Internal meaning bridges allow a person to use the resource or particular voice that is most appropriate for a given situation or context. If the meaning bridges are strong enough, the person may not even consciously be aware of a particular voice emerging. The integration is manifested by a felt sense of knowing how to successfully navigate the situation. For example, assimilating a painful experience of betrayal may eventually result in a greater ability to discriminate between people who are or are not trustworthy.

Assimilation also occurs at an interpersonal level. Being in a relationship demands some common ground, that is, some level of interpersonal assimilation, mediated by meaning bridges. A common form of an interpersonal meaning bridge is a shared story of the relationship, which is interpersonally created, negotiated, and accepted by the participants. The process of interpersonal assimilation proceeds like the intrapersonal assimilation sequence. Because events and words mean different things to different people, personal stories about the same interpersonal event also differ. This may not be a problem as long as these people never meet. However, when they engage in a relationship, they encounter differences in their personal stories, which may clash and cause conflict. To continue their relationship, both participants have to work through the conflict and create a shared story. They may combine and reconstruct their narrative accounts of what happens or has happened in the relationship. The degree to which they are able to negotiate differences determines how deep or superficial their relationship will be.

This assimilative restorying process occurs at the sociological and cultural level as well. Stories and myths exchanged between people become nearly autonomous the more they are shared, almost taking on a life of their own (Gergen, 1985, 1999). Popular stories within a culture are continually reshaped, with each revision reflecting the unique zeitgeist into which each successive generation of storytellers is born. As individuals assimilate their problematic experiences and produce new, more adaptive narratives, these narratives become passed on through interpersonal discourse. Then, the stories gradually become part of the broader, overarching cultural perspective on things such as social interaction, child rearing, marriage, or family. For example, the prevailing American cultural narrative throughout much of the 20th century suggested that good wives did not abandon their husbands and families, no matter how dire or dangerous the marriage.

As many women stepped out of this restrictive cultural script, a feminist movement emerged and restoried the role of women in America today. The assimilation perspective allows noticing and describing these processes of cultural change, rather than focusing only on individual psychological problems, as more traditional models of psychotherapy do.

CONCLUSIONS

We have presented our view of how narrative theory and the assimilation model of change in psychotherapy interact and inform each other. We have discussed what makes stories problematic, how these stories become reconstructed in therapy, and how the assimilation model helps describe and track the changes. Finally, we have speculated about how these changes are beneficial, both to individuals and to the world in which they live. We suggest that the assimilation model, with its roots in qualitative clinical case analyses, its semiotic view of functions and evolution of stories, and its systematic methods for tracking changes in stories offers a useful understanding of the process of narrative meaning-making of the stories, problematic and benign, that clients bring to and work with in psychotherapy.

REFERENCES

American Psychiatric Association (1987). *Diagnostic and statistical manual of mental disorders* (3rd ed., rev.). Washington, DC: Author.

Angus, L., Levitt, H., & Hardtke, K. (1999). The narrative process coding system: Research applications and implications for psychotherapy practice. *Journal of Clinical Psychology, 55*, 1255-1270.

Baerger, D. R., & McAdams, D. P. (1999). Life story coherence and its relation to psychological well-being. *Narrative Inquiry, 9*, 69-96.

Bakhtin, M. M. (1979). *Estetika Slovesnogo Tvorchestva* [Aesthetics of verbal art]. Moscow: Moscow University Press. (Original work published 1970)

Bakhtin, M. M. (1984). *Problems of Dostoevsky's poetics* (C. Emerson, Trans.). Minneapolis: University of Minnesota Press.

Bakhtin, M. M. (1986). *Speech genres and other late essays.* Austin: University of Texas Press.

Briere, J. (1996). *Therapy for adults molested as children: Beyond survival* (2nd ed.). New York: Springer.

Bruner, J. (1986). *Actual minds, possible worlds.* Cambridge, MA: Harvard University Press.

Bruner, J. (1990). *Acts of meaning.* Cambridge, MA: Harvard University Press.

Coffey, P., Leitenberg, H., Henning, K., Turner, T., & Bennett, R. T. (1996). Mediators of the long-term impact of child sexual abuse: Perceived stigma, betrayal, powerlessness, and self-blame. *Child Abuse and Neglect, 20*, 447-455.

Detert, N., Llewelyn, S., Hardy, G. E., Barkham, M., & Stiles, W. B. (2002). *Assimilation in good- and poor-outcome cases of very brief psychotherapy for mild depression.* Manuscript submitted for publication.

Field, S. D., Barkham, M., Shapiro, D. A., & Stiles, W. B. (1994). Assessment of assimilation in psychotherapy: A quantitative case study of problematic experiences with a significant other. *Journal of Counseling Psychology, 41*, 397-406.

Finkelhor, D., & Browne, A. (1985). The traumatic impact of child sexual abuse: A conceptualization. *American Journal of Orthopsychiatry, 55*, 530-541.

Foucault, M. (1971). *The order of things: An archaeology of the human sciences.* New York: Pantheon.

Gergen, K. J. (1985). The social constructionist movement in modern psychology. *American Psychologist, 40*, 266-275.

Gergen, K. J. (1999). *An invitation to social construction.* London: Sage.

Glick, M. J. (2002). *Assimilation analysis of problematic experiences in two cases of client-centered psychotherapy.* Unpublished master's thesis, Miami University, Oxford, OH.

Glick, M. J., Stiles, W. B., & Greenberg, L. S. Building a meaning bridge: Therapeutic progress from problem formulation to *understanding*. Manuscript submitted for publication.

Gonçalves, O. F., Korman, Y., & Angus, L. (2000). Constructing psychopathology from a cognitive narrative perspective. In R. A. Neimeyer & J. D. Raskin (Eds.), *Constructions of disorder* (pp. 265-284). Washington, DC: American Psychological Association.

Gonçalves, O. F., & Machado, P. P. P. (1999). Cognitive narrative therapy: Research foundations. *Journal of Clinical Psychology, 55,* 1179-1191.

Grafanaki, S., & McLeod, J. (1999). Narrative processes in the construction of helpful and hindering events in experiential psychotherapy. *Psychotherapy Research, 9,* 289-303.

Greenberg, L. S., & Angus, L. (1994). How therapy works. *Social Sciences and Humanities Research Council Standard Research Grant (1994-1998).*

Greenberg, L. S., & Watson, J. (1998). Experiential therapy of depression: Differential effects of client-centered relationship conditions and process experiential interventions. *Psychotherapy Research, 8,* 210-224.

Habermas, J. (1990). *Moral consciousness and communicative action* (C. Lenhardt & S. W. Nicholson, Trans.). Cambridge: MIT Press.

Hambleton, G., Russell, R. L., & Wandrei, M. L. (1996). Narrative performance predicts psycho-pathology: A preliminary demonstration. *Journal of Narrative & Life History, 6,* 87-105.

Heidegger, M. (1971). *Poetry, language, thought* (A. Hofstadter, Trans.). New York: Harper & Row.

Hermans, H. J. M. (1999). Self-narrative as meaning construction: The dynamics of self-investigation. *Journal of Clinical Psychology, 55,* 1193-1211.

Hillman, J. (1975). *Re-visioning psychology*. New York: HarperCollins.

Honos-Webb, L., & Stiles, W. B. (1998). Reformulation of assimilation analysis in terms of voices. *Psychotherapy, 35,* 23-33.

Honos-Webb, L., Stiles, W. B., Greenberg, L. S., & Goldman, R. (1998). Assimilation analysis of process-experiential psychotherapy: A comparison of two cases. *Psychotherapy Research, 8,* 264-286.

Janoff-Bulman, P., & Frieze, I. H. (1983). A theoretical perspective for understanding reactions to victimization. *Journal of Social Issues, 39,* 1-17.

Kelly, G. A. (1955). *The psychology of personal constructs*. New York: Norton.

Knobloch, L. M., Endres, L. M., Stiles, W. B., & Silberschatz, G. (2001). Convergence and divergence of themes in successful psychotherapy: An assimilation analysis. *Psychotherapy, 38,* 31-39.

Lacan, J. (1981). *The language of the self: The function of language in psychoanalysis*. Baltimore, MD: Johns Hopkins University Press.

Leitner, L. M., & Pfenninger, D. T. (1994). Sociality and optimal functioning. *Journal of Constructivist Psychology, 7,* 119-135.

Lowe, R. (1999). Between the "no longer" and the "not yet": Postmodernism as a context for critical therapeutic work. In I. Parker (Ed.), *Deconstructing psychotherapy* (pp. 71-85). London: Sage.

Mair, J. M. M. (1989). *Between psychology and psychotherapy: A poetics of experience*. New York: Routledge, Chapman & Hall.

McAdams, D. P. (1996). Personality, modernity, and the storied self: A contemporary framework for studying persons. *Psychological Inquiry, 7,* 295-321.

McAdams, D. P. (1998). The role of defense in the life story. *Journal of Personality, 66,* 1125-1146.

McLeod, J. (1997). *Narrative and psychotherapy*. London: Sage.

McLeod, J. (2000, May 20). *Narrative processes in experiential therapy: Stories as openings*. Paper presented at the British Association for Counselling Annual Research Conference, University of Manchester.

McLeod, J. (2002, June 23-27). *A qualitative narrative analysis of two intake interviews*. Paper presented at the Society for Psychotherapy Research meeting, Santa Barbara, CA.

McLeod, J., & Balamoutsou, S. (1996). Representing narrative process in therapy: Qualitative analysis of a single case. *Counselling Psychology Quarterly, 9,* 61-76.

McLeod, J., & Lynch, G. (2000). "This is our life": Strong evaluation in psychotherapy narrative. *European Journal of Psychotherapy, Counselling, and Health, 3,* 389-406.

McNamee, S., & Gergen, K. J. (Eds.). (1992). *Therapy as social construction*. London: Sage.

Neimeyer, R. A. (2000a). Narrative disruptions in the construction of the self. In

R. A. Neimeyer & J. D. Raskin (Eds.), *Constructions of disorder* (pp. 207-242). Washington, DC: American Psychological Association.

Neimeyer, R. A. (2000b). Performing psychotherapy: Reflections of postmodern practice. In L. Holzman & J. Morss (Eds.), *Postmodern psychologies, societal practice, and political life* (pp. 190-201). New York: Routledge.

Neimeyer, R. A., & Mahoney, M. J. (Eds.). (1995). *Constructivism in psychotherapy.* Washington, DC: American Psychological Association.

Patterson, D. (1985). Mikhail Bakhtin and the dialogical dimensions of the novel. *Journal of Aesthetics and Art Criticism, 44,* 131-139.

Pennebaker, J. W. (1997). Writing about emotional experiences as a therapeutic process. *Psychological Science, 8,* 162-169.

Pennebaker, J. W., & Seagal, J. D. (1999). Forming a story: The health benefits of narrative. *Journal of Clinical Psychology, 55,* 1244-1253.

Polkinghorne, D. E. (1996). Transformative narratives: From victimic to agentic life plots. *American Journal of Occupational Therapy, 50,* 299-305.

Rennie, D. L. (1994). Storytelling in psychotherapy: The client's subjective experience. *Psychotherapy, 31,* 234-243.

Reynolds, S., Stiles, W. B., Barkham, M., Shapiro, D. A., Hardy, G. E., & Rees, A. (1996). Acceleration of changes in session impact during contrasting time-limited psychotherapies. *Journal of Consulting and Clinical Psychology, 64,* 577-586.

Russell, R. L., & Lucariello, J. (1992). Narrative, yes; Narrative ad infinitum, no! *American Psychologist, 47,* 671-672.

Russell, R. L., & Wandrei, M. L. (1996). Narrative and the process of psychotherapy: Theoretical foundations and empirical support. In H. Rosen & K. T. Kuehlwein (Eds.), *Constructing realities: Meaning-making perspectives for psychotherapists* (pp. 307-335). San Francisco, CA: Jossey-Bass.

Sarbin, T. R. (Ed.). (1986). *Narrative psychology: The storied nature of human conduct.* New York: Praeger.

Sluzki, C. E. (1992). Transformations: A blueprint for narrative changes in therapy. *Family Process, 31,* 217-230.

Stiles, W. B. (1997). Multiple voices in psychotherapy clients. *Journal of Psychotherapy Integration, 7,* 177-180.

Stiles, W. B. (1999). Signs and voices in psychotherapy. *Psychotherapy Research, 9,* 1-21.

Stiles, W. B. (2002). Assimilation of problematic experiences. In J. C. Norcross (Ed.), *Psychotherapy relationships that work: Therapist contributions and responsiveness to patients* (pp. 357-365). New York: Oxford University Press.

Stiles, W. B., & Angus, L. (2001). Qualitative research on clients' assimilation of problematic experiences in psychotherapy. In J. Frommer & D. L. Rennie (Eds.), *Qualitative psychotherapy research: Methods and methodology* (pp. 112-127). Lengerich, Germany: Pabst Science Publishers.

Stiles, W. B., Barkham, M., Shapiro, D. A., & Firth-Cozens, J. (1992). Treatment order and thematic continuity between contrasting psychotherapies: Exploring an implication of the assimilation model. *Psychotherapy Research, 2,* 112-124.

Stiles, W. B., Benjamin, L. S., Elliott, R., Fonagy, P., Greenberg, L. S., Hermans, H. J. M., Bucci, W. S., Karon, B. P., & Leiman, M. (1997). Multiple voices: A virtual discussion. *Journal of Psychotherapy Integration, 7,* 241-262.

Stiles, W. B., Elliott, R., Llewelyn, S. P., Firth-Cozens, J. A., Margison, F. R., Shapiro, D. A., & Hardy, G. (1990). Assimilation of problematic experiences by clients in psychotherapy. *Psychotherapy, 27,* 411-420.

Stiles, W. B., Meshot, C. M., Anderson, T. M., & Sloan, W. W., Jr. (1992). Assimilation of problematic experiences: The case of John Jones. *Psychotherapy Research, 2,* 81-101.

Stiles, W. B., Morrison, L. A., Haw, S. K., Harper, H., Shapiro, D. A., & Firth-Cozens, J. (1991). Longitudinal study of assimilation in exploratory psychotherapy. *Psychotherapy, 28,* 195-206.

Stiles, W. B., Shankland, M. C., Wright, J., & Field, S. D. (1997). Aptitude-treatment interactions based on clients' assimilation of their presenting problems. *Journal of Consulting and Clinical Psychology, 65,* 889-893.

Szasz, T. S. (1960). The myth of mental illness. *American Psychologist, 15,* 113-118.

Szasz, T. S. (1990). The theology of therapy: The breach of the First Amendment through the medicalization of morals. *Changes, 8,* 2-14.

Varvin, S., & Stiles, W. B. (1999). Emergence of severe traumatic experiences: An assimilation analysis of psychoanalytic therapy with a political refugee. *Psychotherapy Research*, 9, 381-404.

Webster's Encyclopedic Unabridged Dictionary of the English Language. (1989). New York: Portland House.

Wiersma, J. (1988). The press release: Symbolic communication in life history interviewing. *Journal of Personality, 56*, 205-238.

Wittgenstein, L. (1969). *On certainty*. Oxford, UK: Blackwell.

Wittgenstein, L. (1980). *Culture and value* (P. Winch, Trans.). Oxford, UK: Blackwell.

CHAPTER 12

Minding Our Therapeutic Tales
Treatments in Perspectivism

ROBERT L. RUSSELL
FRED B. BRYANT
WITH CECELIA CASTILINO, MARYLOUISE JONES,
MARY WANDREI, JEANNE PIETTE, KIRSTEN ELLING, AND ROD DAY

Child therapists of every theoretical orientation inevitably encounter or use narratives in their diagnostic or therapeutic work. In terms of diagnostic procedures, for example, some of the most popular assessment tasks are based on narrative production or comprehension (e.g., the Thematic Apperception Test, Henry, 1973; the Children's Thematic Apperception Test, Bellak, 1986; the Means-Ends Storytelling Test, Platt & Spivack, 1975; and the Wechsler Memory Scale, Wechsler, 1945). Clinical interviews also routinely begin with the solicitation of client stories about the circumstances that have brought them to seek treatment. In terms of therapeutic processes, narratives saturate the dialogue between client and therapist in every phase of treatment. In fact, storytelling was found to be the most frequent type of children's linguistic productions in their therapies (Lebo, 1952).

Appreciation of the critical importance of narrative in treating psychosocial problems is becoming more evident, even if not commensurate with the frequency with which they are encountered. For example, only 32% of child and adolescent clinicians indicated that they thought storytelling was at least occasionally useful as a specific therapy technique, and even fewer, a mere 12%, indicated that it was often useful (Koocher & Pedulla, 1977). From a normative, developmental perspective, a higher level of appreciation of the role of narrative in therapy would seem to be warranted, as storytelling is integral to self-formative and coping processes throughout the life span.

Unfortunate, too, is the parallel lack of research interest in clinical uses of narrative in treatment: There is no substantial empirical literature on narrative processes in child treatment, although it is heartening to witness a recent growth of interest in this area. The historical absence of a concentrated focus on narrative and narration is especially surprising because child therapists are regularly challenged to (a) grasp the meaning of child narratives, developmentally and clinically (Gardner, 1971, 1993; Russell & van den Broek, 1988, 1992; van den Broek & Thurlow, 1991), and (b) develop techniques for changing children's maladaptive patterns of narration (e.g., Stiles, Meshot, Anderson, & Sloan, 1992). Unfortunately, few studies of child treatment focus on any aspect of the language used by therapists or clients in the treatment hour (Shirk & Russell, 1996).

To rectify the neglect of narrative processes in child treatments and to help refocus child therapy process research, a concerted effort must be made to demonstrate that (a) key constituents of narratives are clinically and developmentally relevant and (b) methods exist or can be devised to isolate and study them. Moreover, we need to know if therapists differ from ordinary speakers in the extent or kind of narrative processes they already, or can in the future, employ in their clinical work. In effect, "there is no hope of capturing the special ingredients of a therapeutic process without empirically investigating how a psychotherapeutic process differs from an ordinary attempt to change the behavior of a person" (Siegfried, 1995, p. 4).

In the present chapter, we tackle these issues head on. We first attempt to identify key narrative dimensions crucial to child development and, by extension, to child psychotherapy. We then demonstrate how aspects of the identified dimensions can be operationalized. Second, we review data relevant to answering the question of whether therapists' narrative productions are different from those of lay individuals, when the latter have been inducted into a helping parental versus therapeutic role. We do this by presenting results of a study in which an expert therapist's narrative responses to child client stories were compared to lay participants' narrative responses to the same child stories.

DEVELOPMENTAL AND CLINICAL IMPORTANCE OF NARRATIVE

There are several links between aspects of narrative and psychological health (see Russell & van den Broek, 1988; Russell & Wandrei, 1996). In fact, taken as a symbolic form, narrative is a universal means by which individuals come to represent and organize their knowledge of the world, themselves, and others. The scope of this universalism transcends the boundaries of mythic and everyday consciousness as they are organized in everyday life, for narrative provides even the most exact sciences, however much they might begrudge the intrusion, a formalism of sorts with which to track knowledge and its development within their specialized traditions (Danto, 1985; MacIntyre, 1980). In the end, scientific theories are ways of reading/writing the world, where beginnings (causes), middles (processes, laws), and ends (outcomes/effects) are related in attempts at understanding organic and inorganic processes.

When attempting to understand human beings and their peculiar knack for articulating the subjective meaning of all aspects of their existence, narrative begins to play a double role. In everyday life, narration is the symbolic foundry in and through which identities are forged and circulated within the cultural community. In the social sciences, narrative functions as perhaps *the* overarching formalism that best brings descriptive and explanatory coherence to the historicity of our species and individual consciousness. The double duty of narrative in everyday life and in the social sciences attests to its status as a prime constituent of what it means to be human.

Narrative and narration transport speakers and hearers into historical or imagined landscapes of action. At its most basic level, *action* is the transport of bodies through space in a measurable instant of time. In this minimalist sense, a body moving through space would be considered action. However, everyday and real social scientific interest in this type of mechanistic action is roused only when it is enlivened by two evaluative perspectives. In the first perspective, a body moving through space might, for instance, come to signify an unintended pratfall, as when we say, not just that the body moved and came in contact with the ground, but that *it* accidentally fell or that *it* fell intentionally, in a comical manner to create slapstick humor. Here we seem to situate the physical movement of a body in a perspective or frame that imbues it with constitutive meaning having to do with will or intent. Accidents, after all, do not happen *in* nature. In the second perspective, we seem to confer a special status on the body that has fallen when we frame, even denominate, the fall within an intentionalist perspective. Even though we see the same body falling, we now appraise the fall as an action of an *agent* or *subject* with a personal identity, even if that agent or subject is not human in the strictly biological sense. That these two perspectives are correlative indicates how integral intentionality and identity/personhood/agency are when attempting to understand human or humanlike action.

A simple formula might here be proposed: Movement, when inspired with and/or appraised in terms of the intentionalist perspective, becomes action, which correlatively can be carried out only by agents. In this sense, the statement, "John went from home to downtown," is roughly equivalent to "the body moved from such and such geographical coordinates, a place dubbed home, to such and such geographical coordinates, a place dubbed downtown, in such and such time," in its mechanistic gloss. The loss of meaning, if one does occur, happens because of the residual connotative associations we may have with *home* or *downtown* or *John*, all of which entail historical and not only spatial and temporal familiarity with homes, downtowns, and Johns. But note, if we say, "John went from home to downtown in a hurry," we have added information that simply cannot be reduced to the objectivist translation. The phrase, *in a hurry*, cannot be adequately captured by noting land speed. Instead, it adds an irreducible constitutive element of subjectivity or consciousness, and this addition illuminates or rather defines, co-relatively, something about both the unique status of the movement as action and of the body as an embodiment of an actor or agent.

In this sense the landscape of action is always already the landscape of consciousness, whether the latter is presupposed or made explicit linguistically. Even when we attempt to cleanse narratives of subjective perspectives (as in some literary texts, e.g., the nouveau roman of Robbe-Grillet or some passages in Hemingway's *The Sun Also Rises*) and produce objectivist or phenomenological stories, readers fill in what has been left out, inspiriting the "movements" as they unfold even along landscapes bereft of markers of subjectivity (see Bruner, 1986, 1987). However much we might tend to get swept away by sensational movements across these action-scapes, in the end, our concern focuses on what the action has meant or felt like to those actors or agents involved in it. We are more concerned with our take on events, on those processes that seemingly take place somewhere within our interiority, than on the events themselves.

This concern is neither incidental nor sporadic. On the contrary, our take on things is the social target of inexhaustible interest. Our preoccupation with reading other minds is so ubiquitous that the processes that make it possible must have been of the highest value in our evolution as a species; their absence or disruption must have been, and still would be, of equally high cost. Understanding the grammar of motives and their expression in verbal or nonverbal displays would seem essential for survival in social groups, especially during contests of power or conditions of scarcity and of no less importance when negotiating species reproduction.

Happily, every normal child with good-enough parenting and an intact central nervous system develops early in toddlerhood a cognizance of the importance of human subjective states, such as those made manifest by the propositional attitudes (e.g., I think that, I know that, I pretend that) or by markers of modality (including but not restricted to the modal auxiliary verbs: should, could, would, must, can, etc.) or by moral and other emotions. Achieving awareness and appropriate use of the markers of such internal states has been taken as evidence that children have developed a "theory of mind" (e.g., Astington & Gopnik, 1991; Bretherton & Beeghly, 1982; Johnson & Wellman, 1982). Theories of mind enable us to distinguish between "a world of thoughts, beliefs, intentions, [emotions], and knowledge from the world of mere bodily presence" (Johnson & Wellman, 1982, p. 222). As Moore and Frye (1991) point out, a theory of mind has tremendous utility in describing, explaining, and manipulating one's own and others' behavior and may be instrumental in furthering cognitive development.

Lack of development of a theory of mind has been implicated in child psychopathology as well, most consistently in autism through numerous naturalistic and experimental studies (Baron-Cohen, 1991; Baron-Cohen, Leslie, & Frith, 1986; Eisenmajer & Prior, 1991). Descriptive and some experimental research has also revealed that emotional and cognitive perspective taking, theoretically linked to abilities described under the rubric of theories of mind, is less developed in younger than older children (Selman & Byrne, 1974). Furthermore, such perspective taking is less developed in children with conduct problems than in normal children (Selman, 1980). Problems in explicating internal states in narratives told to a variety of experimental prompts have also been demonstrated to predict significant amounts of depressive, anxious, and cognitive difficulties in young adults (Hambleton, Wandrei, & Russell, 1996). Furthermore, normal development of theories of mind have begun to be charted over the preschool and middle school years (Frye & Moore, 1991), offering the needed comparison norms for assessment. Appropriate acquisition and use of a theory of mind should be recognized as essential to normal development.

What is the connection between narratives and theories of mind? Narratives are important because they are thought to be (a) a primary means by which such theories are developed and enhanced in dialogue (Feldman, 1988) and (b) used to convey one's level of interpersonal understanding of human affairs, that is, of the landscape of consciousness as well as the landscape of action (Bruner, 1986, 1987). Narratives enable individuals to interface their theories of mind in symbolic and literal action, through extended dialogic topic/comment sequences that take story form. Such interfacing is evident even at children's one-word stage of linguistic development (Bretherton, 1991), where context is often read to fill in narrative gaps. Later, the exchange and elaboration of stories cements the budding mutuality required of mature cultural participants. In a sense, storytelling serves as a primary normative strategy by which a culture's theory of subjectivity and intersubjectivity can be conveyed, developed, and practiced. Developmental outcomes for individuals who have not attained sufficient mastery of a culture's theories of mind are, conversely, fraught with psychosocial peril.

NARRATIVE, THEORIES OF MIND, AND PSYCHOTHERAPY

Theory and research in child psychopathology and its psychosocial treatment have often focused on distorted representations of experience, such as distorted aspects of self-schemas or biased attributional processes (Crick & Dodge, 1994; Kendall, 1993). However, Russell and van den Broek (1988, see also Russell, 1991) argue that internal representations of behavioral episodes are organized in narrative form. Consequently, it may enhance treatment efficacy to target this narrative representation for intervention because it provides the holistic context, the symbolic form, in which the more piecemeal attributions and schemas are situated and gain their interpersonal meanings. Change the overarching narrative representation and deeper and more extensive opportunities for engaging in novel behaviors can be achieved.

Methods for achieving such changes can themselves take narrative form. Theorists as diverse as Bettelheim (1977), Gardner (1971, 1993), and McMullin (1986) claim that storytelling can help change or "repair" the structure of a client's representation of interpersonal events. Costantino, Malgady, and Rogler (1986) have also demonstrated that the use of fairy tales in treatment of young children achieved greater positive change in trait anxiety than traditional therapy. In development too, "as contrasted with abstract propositional arguments, stories are far more likely to really engage the reader or listener and, with the aid of other factors, develop a person's moral life" (Vitz, 1990, p. 716). In these accounts, however, there is little focus on what aspects of narrative representation may be most fruitful to target for change or repair.

Ellis's (1962) theoretical work is a significant exception. His focus on the debilitating effect of situating action within a harsh and punishing evaluative frame (Freud's masochistic superego) highlights, albeit unwittingly, the linguistic means by which the frame is conveyed and presumably through which events and reactions are distorted. The linguistic system he pinpoints is the modal auxiliary system in English (all languages have the capability of conveying modal concepts, only some have separate syntactic systems for doing so, as in English). His emphasis on "Mustabatory" framing of action as a cause of maladaptation (e.g., excessive anxiety and guilt) forges the link between pathology and types of narration where theories of mind achieve only a fragmented perspectivism. The impact on consciousness can be gleaned by simply juxtaposing a few statements: "I went from home to downtown," "I must go from home to downtown," "I want to go from home to downtown." Only the statement with the *must* clause conveys psychological pressure, even without tonal information, and it seems to adumbrate a future dysphoric state or consequence if the downtown destination is not achieved (e.g., I must ... or else). If we imagine a person who totalizes this "Mustabatory" frame for narrating his or her experience, fragmenting it off and employing it in isolation from the full horizon of perspectives normally available, we can glean what must be a kind of warp or deviation in that person's subjectivity. In other words, the phenomenal world that presents itself to an individual who totalizes the "Mustabatory" frame must be significantly different from that which presents itself to a less pressured consciousness.

There are many other frames and concepts that can be conveyed through modality and other markers of theories of mind, such as desire, belief, and intention, to name only a few. Several empirical studies have also demonstrated links between therapeutic processes and linguistic markers of modality and theories of mind. Lord, Castelino, and Russell (1990), for example, found that greater depths of client experiencing were associated with their use of more internal state language and mental verbs, classic indicators of theories of mind. Client disclosure of internal states, beliefs, desires, intentions, and emotions is also associated with positive therapeutic outcomes (Stiles, 1979). Not coincidentally, such markers of theories of mind are abundant in therapists' talk as well. Essig and Russell (1990) not only could discriminate between Rogers, Ellis, and Perls's therapeutic talk in theoretically driven ways on the basis of their use of markers of theories of mind but also demonstrated that each disclosed his or her own perspective on events far more frequently than standard theories of self-disclosure would have us believe. Essig and Russell (1989b) also demonstrated that sessions judged highest in good therapy processes could be differentiated from sessions judged lowest in good therapy processes based on the distribution of markers of theories of mind solely in the therapists' talk, solely in the clients' talk, or in their interactive discourse.

When we focus on process research with children, much less work has been done, even though childhood is the developmental period in which the presence of markers of theories of mind steadily grows and in which the foundations of character and relatedness are being formed. We attempted to spark interest in this area with a study that sketched out a broad range of markers of theories of mind and modality. In an experimental study, we compared therapists' and lay speakers' retellings of child narratives sampled from actual child treatment sessions. To do this, we used Essig and Russell's (1990) category scheme, which includes 16 different markers of theories of mind and modality. In addition, we adapted Selman's (1980) scales for assessing different types of perspective taking, one that measured degree of self-awareness and one that measured degree of social perspective taking. Because the language used to convey awareness of theories of mind can be more complicated linguistically than language that does not represent perspectives of any kind, we also included two other variables to assess the elaboration and complexity of the narratives. By including this second dimension, we could assess if the participants in our study were sensitive to children's capacities to comprehend and use the complex narrative language that represents theories of mind (Shirk, 1988).

Armed with these notions of narrative, we compared the extent to which markers of theories of mind and modality occurred in children's narratives and their retellings by lay participants or an expert clinician. The lay participants heard verbatim stories told by school-age children during actual treatment sessions. They were asked to retell the stories with three different prompts: exactly as they heard them, as a helpful parent would, and as a concerned therapist.

The design of the study was undertaken to answer several questions. We reasoned that if the participants' stories in the therapy condition differed significantly in the use of markers of theories of mind from their stories in the parent and verbatim conditions, then they might indeed have access to a therapeutic register of narrative storytelling. On the other hand, if the retellings in the parent and therapist condition are both different from the verbatim recall condition but not different from each other, then it would seem that helpful therapeutic and parent retellings were indistinguishable to the participants. In other words, they could not stretch their helpful language any further than that associated with the more common and familiar parenting role. By comparing the participants' narratives in the therapist condition to the experienced therapists' (i.e., Richard Gardner's, 1971) in vivo retellings, we could begin to pinpoint if and how a therapist's narratives differ from what is ready at hand to lay participants. Documentation that such differences exist would help to pinpoint language areas to assess as potential active ingredients in sparking children's subsequent development of theories of mind.

In our study, each of 18 male subjects heard six stories varying from 77 to 425 words in length. The stories they heard had been told by children in therapy with Richard Gardner (1971). We had a child actor tell the stories again so that we could tape them and present standardized versions to each participant. They were prompted to retell two of the stories exactly as the stories were told, as a helpful parent would, and as a helpful therapist would. Consequently, there were 108 stories, 36 in each retelling condition.

Essig and Russell's (1989a) classification scheme was used to appraise the extent and kind of markers of modality and theories of mind in the retold stories. The classification scheme recognizes 16 different ways in which speakers can linguistically represent their subjective perspectives on the events conveyed through simple and complex sentences (see Appendix A). Essig and Russell defined *specifications* as words or phrases that are located between the logical subject and the logical predicate in a sentence. These words or phrases serve to specify the meaning of the event in terms of the subjectivity of the speaker or protagonist and, consequently, elaborate the subjective relationship between the speaker or character and the event (see Appendix A for definitions of specifications). For instance, in the segment, "And unfortunately, he cut the dog in half," *unfortunately* is a specification: It indicates the psychologically relevant manner in which the actor performed the action. Specifications are identified by particular linguistic markers such as adverbs, auxiliary verbs, or prepositional phrases. For instance, the utterance, "He did his best to try to put the dog back together again," contains two specifications. In this utterance, the basic event is "He put the dog back together again," which is modified by the operator "try to." This is called a specification of intention because the basic event is made contingent on the efforts, or the subjective intention, of the subject. Furthermore, the subject's "trying" is also modified by the verb phrase "did his best"; this is considered a specification of manner because it indicates a subjective evaluation of the way in which the "trying" was performed. The eight different types of specifications are especially suited for elaborating a single subject's subjectivity. The other six subtypes of specifications are: mode, duration, initiation, result, aspect, and degree.

Essig and Russell (1989a) identified eight different markers of modality and theories of mind that are commonly used in complex sentences. They termed these markers *predications*. Formally, a predication is identified when a new event, containing a subject and a verb, is added to the basic event and further elaborates the inner worlds of the speaker or actor(s). A predication of knowledge is illustrated in the utterance, "The master didn't really notice [that the dog was in the way]." The implicit basic event is "the dog was in the way," and the predication operator is "The master noticed." The psychological elaboration of the subject/agent in the new verb phrase concerns the possibility of gaining knowledge of the basic event, which, in this instance, includes a different individual as its subject. Consequently, predications are especially relevant in elaborating the perspective of one agent on another agent's action or in elaborating a perspective on one's own action. Note that the new verb phrase is also modified by *really*, a specification of degree. The other subtypes of predications are called: supposition, subjectivation, description, retelling, entreaty, appearance, and attitude (see Appendix B for definitions and examples of predications).

We also assessed the stories with less linguistically intensive scales, which we adapted from Selman's (1980) work on self-awareness and role taking. Following Selman, five levels of self-awareness were employed:

1. *Physicalistic Concept of the Self*, which defines the earliest conceptions of the self as coterminus with physical being (e.g., in a child's story (see Appendix A): "And then his rear feet were turned around/ and then he was like a normal dog")
2. *Differentiation Between Inner and Outer*, representing a dawning awareness of a psychological self with an inner domain of subjective experience (e.g., "I'll be doing . . . anything you want me to do")
3. *Introspective Self*, noted as the child's capacity to acknowledge a second-person social perspective as distinct from internal experience (e.g., "Once upon a time there was a very thin snake who didn't feel very good about being thin. And one day he came upon a fat snake and decided to boast about how great it was to be thin")
4. *Conceptions of the Self as Observer and Observed*, as the articulation of a capacity for third-party perspective taking (e.g., "he felt bad that he couldn't do other things and therefore tried to make up with it by bringing attention to that feature")
5. *The Emergence of the Unconscious*, as the self becomes aware of an internal domain that is not necessarily accessible to conscious scrutiny (e.g., "the snake felt a need from deep within to brag—he didn't understand why, but he did it anyway")

Each story received a rating (1 to 5) for the highest level of self-awareness demonstrated.

Following Selman and Byrne (1974), perspective-taking was measured using four developmental levels:

1. *Egocentric Role Taking*, which involves the recognition of the physical separateness of self and other without being able to differentiate their subjective points of view (e.g., "Once upon a time there was a little dog. Of course, he has . . .")
2. *Subjective Role Taking*, which involves the acknowledgment of the existence of alternative perspectives, but without their synthesis into one's own personal viewpoint (e.g., "The dog awoke and was aware of this unusual condition")
3. *Self-Reflective Role Taking*, which involves a more sophisticated capacity to take a second-person social perspective on the self's actions and intentions (e.g., "The little mouse didn't realize that other people who like the mouse's father would feel very bad if he did such a thing")
4. *Mutual Role Taking*, which involves the adoption of a third-person perspective or rule by the child (e.g., "If you have a complicated disease or medical problem, you have to expect to take a long time and work very hard to help it")

Each story was analyzed as a whole and rated (1 to 4) for the highest level of perspective taking explicitly demonstrated.

Two simple measures of the complexity of the participants' narrative retellings were included: words per segment/clause and the type-token ratio. Words per segment was defined as the number of words per segment of text. Segments generally conformed to the pattern of an independent clause and any of its dependent clauses (Wiener & Mehrabian, 1968). Consequently, words per segment gives an estimate of the degree of lexical elaboration and complexity of text segments. The type-token ratio was computed by dividing the number of new words by the total number of words in the narrative, resulting in an estimate of the degree of lexical novelty or redundancy in the narrative. As the ratio approaches 1.0, more lexical novelty is present in the narrative.

All of the measures were coded with adequate reliabilities. When we analyzed the participants' narratives, participant stories in the parent and in the therapist condition were found to differ from the recall condition by containing more specifications (i.e., markers of theories of mind and/or modality) and more segments evidencing higher perspective-taking levels. These differences, however, were attributable to their induction into a helping role per se, parent or therapist, versus the memorial condition, as there were no significant differences between the participants' stories on any of the six measures when told in the therapist *versus* the parent role.

These findings suggest that when retelling children's stories to be of help to them, adults tend to increase perspectivism by placing the events talked about in the perspectival context of theories of mind and modal frames, on the one hand, and in terms of multiple viewpoints, on the other. The participants' stories pack aspects of mind and motive into their retelling of the children's stories as they increase the developmental level of the characters' role taking. Such packing is presumably helpful because it underscores and marks linguistically those perspectives that enliven movements with interpersonal motives and meaning and, as a consequence, constitute and reveal an agent's character.

It is also interesting to note that the participants' helpful stories did not differ from their memorial stories on the linguistically more complex predications and on the reflexive awareness of self. The perspectivism facilitated by predications and reflexive awareness of self seems to require greater cognitive/linguistic and emotional development, and its facilitation may pose a more difficult narrative challenge. Implicitly, the participants' stories seemed to restrict their helpful retellings to those aspects of theories of mind and modality that explicitly concern enlivening physical movement and the bodies of others in more than one viewpoint. Developmentally, this may make good sense. Others must become agents or selves, and physical movements must become actions, before one's sense of self as an agent capable of intentional action, and reflection on that action and agency, is possible.

When we compare the children's stories to those of the participants' in the therapist condition and to those of the actual therapist, more pronounced differences come to light. The differences between the narrative variables of the experienced therapist and participants were compared relative to the children's scores. To do this, we calculated effect sizes: for example, the difference between the children's and therapists' mean score on a variable divided by the standard deviation of the children's score on that variable. These effect sizes indicated the magnitude of differences between the narrative measures, standardized by the children's standard deviations.

The experienced therapist's scores were .4 and 1.62 standard deviations larger than the children's mean score on specifications and perspective taking. On the same variables, the participants' were 2.4 and .7 standard deviations larger than the children's mean scores. What this means is that the participants' stories placed the events the children narrated in the unfolding perspectives of personal time (four of the eight specifications are concerned with this aspect of action) and of intention, actuality, possibility/necessity, veridicality, and style or manner far more than did the therapist's stories. In contrast, the therapist stories created perspectivism by placing the events within grasp of multiple viewpoints, the actors and the tellers, to a greater degree than the participants' stories.

In effect, the lay participants' implicit and predominant helping strategy was to specify the style by which an event unfolds in temporal, epistemic, and deontic perspectives, thereby underscoring the evaluative frames in and through which activity and movement achieve the status of actions. Only secondarily and derivatively does the actor emerge as the agent responsible for these actions. In contrast, the implicit and predominant helping strategy of the therapist was to explicitly stress the perspectivism of agency itself, thereby stressing the primacy of viewpoint or voice in valuations of action.

The therapist's scores were 1.98 and 1.14 standard deviations larger on self-awareness and predications than the children's mean scores. The participants' scores were 0 and .14 standard deviations *smaller* than the children's mean score on self-awareness and predications. Recall that predications, involving two grammatical subjects, one in the superordinate and one in the subordinate clause, can syntactically counterpoise the perspectives of different agents or of the same agent on him- or herself. It is here that the therapist seems to underscore the primary oppositions of sociality (self/other) and subjectivity (I/me) within which perspectivism finds its foundation and ineradicable evaluative core. Simultaneously, the therapist rounds out the characters in the stories by stressing their reflexive awareness of themselves as actors. Consequently, one's viewpoint itself is made relative and can assume a less privileged place among other valued viewpoints.

On the dimension of elaboration and complexity, there were striking differences between the experienced therapist's stories and the children's and participants' stories. The actual therapist's mean words per segment is .60 standard deviations larger than the children's mean score. The participants in the therapist instruction condition, however, obtained a mean words-per-segment score 5.6 standard deviations larger than the original children's score. This indicates that the complexity of participants' stories as measured by words per segment is over nine times more deviant from the complexity of the children's stories than were the actual therapist's stories. In addition, the original therapist's mean type-token ratio is 2.43 standard deviations less than the children's. The participants' mean type-token ratio is only .28 standard deviations less than the children's. Thus, the degree of conceptual novelty in the expert therapist's retellings was about eight times less than in participants' stories.

Together, these scores on the elaboration and complexity dimension indicated that the expert therapist stayed relatively close to the children's level of linguistic complexity, while introducing a large amount of conceptual redundancy in his narratives. In contrast, the participants in the therapist condition used far more linguistic complexity than the children but increased the conceptual redundancy very little. In comparison to the participants, it seems the therapist was working very hard to introduce and reiterate the role of theories of mind and modality in understanding action while staying very close to the children's linguistic and/or cognitive/emotional capacities (an example of the children's original story and a participant's and therapist's retellings can be found in Appendix B).

CONCLUSIONS

In this chapter, we tried to present some justification for focusing research and clinical attention on narratives and narration in child therapy. We underscored the role narrative and narration play in the development and expression of theories of mind and modality and how the latter seem to be intricately involved in adaptation and adjustment. We attempted to show how aspects of theories of mind and modality could be operationalized and studied, and we demonstrated some ways in which lay participants' helpful stories differ from those of expert therapists. Throughout we tried to emphasize the role theories of mind, modality, and narratives play in developing perspectivism, an essential ingredient in attaining self and other awareness.

We presented evidence to the effect that lay participants do in fact increase markers of theories of mind and modality when trying to retell children's narratives in a helpful way. They seemed to understand that repairing, deepening, or augmenting theories of mind can be of help in furthering the development of the children. This, we propose, is a common tenet of folk wisdom and is regularly used by adults in the process of enculturating their children (Moore & Frye, 1991). The expert therapist, however, appeared to use narration in a more methodical and pervasive way than the lay participants. His narratives seemed to focus far more predominantly on the type of perspectivism that requires the implicit or explicit juxtaposition and even opposition of viewpoints, as in perspective taking, reflexive self-awareness, and predications, each of which involves both a prioritizing and a relativizing of agenthood. The expert therapist was able to do this while constraining the linguistic complexity of the narratives, presumably for ease of child comprehension. This emphasis on intersubjectivity comports with the notion that development of selves and their subjectivity takes place through interpersonal experience, through conversational and narrative exchange, and not the other way around (Shotter, 1995; Vygotsky, 1936/1978).

The therapeutic maxim to be derived from the study's findings might be worded as follows: Embody in your narrative and discourse the richest theory of mind possible, through the prioritization of multiple agentive viewpoints on self and other, but use simplified and conceptually redundant narrative discourse while doing so. Therapeutic narratives model a specific credo, namely, that what one thinks, believes, feels, hopes, imagines, wills, knows, and attests, and how one qualifies and elaborates events through the use of multiple viewpoints, is key in reconstructing or enhancing a sense of identity and social relatedness. Ultimately, the panoply of perspectives from which we are able to articulate self and other determines the form and content of the phenomenological world that seems to show and exert itself as our very own. As much as, or even in spite of, whatever physical description one can give of the circumstances in which we find ourselves, the determination of who we are and how we engage and represent our compeers is fundamentally ideational in character.

Narrative, in other words, provides the means to tell who we and our compeers are and to articulate the interpersonal meaning of what we and they have or have not done. In therapy, even the achievement of the simple temporal coherence of a series of movements is not obtained by establishing a simple chronology of events described in an objectivist manner, for the meanings of events do not transpire in objective time. There is no objective metronome of personal experience. Thus, we saw how even the lay participants attempted to elaborate the children's basic events by the use of specifications marking subjective time. They situated the events in a time denominated with reference to wills and passions and intentions, as the specifications of initiations, continuings, and endings imply. Such demarcations cannot be reduced to or derived from an objective time. In this sense, narrative time provides the form in which human action potentials take shape and can be described, altered, and projected in all of their historicity.

The therapists did this as well. But in addition, their narratives underscored that the way events and agents are instantiated in subjective time—with its constitutive will, desire, hope, sense of obligation, and truth and falsity—always already depends on the agenthood of the being in terms of whose viewpoint the events are articulated. In a sense, we now have the plurality of subjective times nested within the interpersonal space of multiple agents. Narrative and narration used in this way are uniquely suited to expose the plurality of beings and times that constitute the human condition. The perspectivism that such exposure can help to facilitate is essential to child development and, even more so, for children who have had psychosocial problems.

We hope that further refinements of our notions of narrative, theories of mind, and modality will allow more empirically supported use of narratives in child therapy.

APPENDIX A: SAMPLE STORIES

In the following stories, italicized words indicate specifications, bold words indicate predications, underlined words or segments indicate evidence of perspective taking, and uppercase words indicate evidence of self-awareness.

Child's Story (Stimulus Story)

1. *Once upon a time* there was a little dog./ 2. *Of course*, he has a master / 3. and once when his master was chopping wood/ 4. the little dog got in his way./ 5. *By accident* he chopped the dog in half/ 6. so he sewed the dog back together again./ 7. But he sewed the dog back together again *wrong*./ 8. He had the back feet pointing up in the air and the front feet pointing down,/ 9. and that little dog was the most unusual sight in the world./ 10. *Of course*, the dog **said to the master, "Hey, give me a bone**./ 11. *I'[wi]ll* stand on my rear feet/ 12. and *I'[wi]ll* do amazing tricks./ 13. *I'[wi]ll be doing* somersaults for you/ 14. anything you WANT me to do./ 15. Please give me a bone."/16. The dog's name was Snoopy./ 17. So his master fed him a bone/ 18. and then his rear feet were turned around/ 19. and then he was like a normal dog./ (words per segment = 8.0; type/token ratio = 0.51; perspective taking = 1; self-awareness = 2; specifications per segment = 0.53; predications per segment = 0.05)

Therapist Story

1. *Once upon a time* there was a little dog/ 2. and this little dog was standing near his master who was chopping wood./ 3. And *by mistake* or *accident* his master chopped him in half./ 4. Well, his master, although he was a goodhearted person,/ 5. *used* to make a lot of errors,/ 6. and, *by mistake*, the master sewed the dog back in such a way/ 7. that his feet stuck up in the air in the back/ 8. and his other feet were on the ground./ 9. It *really* looked funny./ 10. And <u>this dog **got** the idea</u>/ 11. <u>that he *could* be cured</u> of this/ 12. if only his master *would* give him a bone./ 13. <u>He didn't know</u>/ 14. **<u>that this was foolish idea,</u>**/15. <u>**that cures for such problems do not come** *so easily*.</u>/ 16. <u>You *just* don't get cured by eating a bone.</u>/ 17. So he begged the master for a bone,/ 18. and his master *finally* **said**, "Okay,/ 19. *I'[wi]ll* give you a bone."/ 20. Then he ate the bone/ 21. and <u>was VERY DISAPPOINTED</u> /22. when he **found out**/ 23. **that this did not cure him.**/ 24. And then he <u>wondered what he *could* do.</u>/ 25. So <u>he decided to go to a doctor in town.</u>/ 26. The doctor examined him and **said, "What you need is a special operation followed by exercises on your part and hard work."**/ 27. So he went in for the operation/ 28. and they straightened him out./ 29. They put his feet where they *should* be and/ 30. turned his body around,/ 31. and they prescribed a long series of exercises/ 32. which required a lot of work on his part and/ 33. cooperation with

doctors and therapists./ 34. And *after a long time,*/ 35. he *finally* got back into shape, /36. moved his legs *right,*/ 37. and became a HAPPY, healthy dog./ 38. The moral of the story is that there are no quick cures to complicated diseases—/ 39. if you have a complicated disease or medical problem/ 40. you have to expect to take a long time/ 41. and work *very hard* to help it,/ 42. and your own cooperation is *often* required. (words per segment = 7.8; type/token ratio = 0.42; perspective taking = 4; self-awareness = 2; specifications per segment = 0.50; predications per segment = 0.24)

Subject Story: Verbatim Recall Condition

1. *Once* there was a dog./ 2. And the dog *of course* had a master./ 3. And one day the master was chopping wood/ 4. and he *accidentally* chopped his dog in half./ 5. So, the master sewed the dog together *wrong.*/ 6. He sewed together the dog/ 7. so that the back feet were facing up/ 8. and the front ones were facing down./ 9. The dog's name was Snoopy./ 10. Snoopy, ah, *of course* wanted a bone,/ 11. so one day he asked his master for a bone/ 12. and he **said he *would* do tricks for the bone.**/ 13. He *would* do somersaults/ 14. and he *would* stand on his hind legs./ 15. And the master gave him a bone/ 16. and after that he was back to normal. (words per segment = 7.25; type/token ratio = 0.47; perspective taking = 1; self-awareness = 1; specifications per segment = 0.50; predications per segment = .06.)

Subject Story: Parent Condition

1. *Once upon a time* there was a dog who was close to its master, as a companion./ 2. And on one occasion the man was chopping wood,/ 3. And *unfortunately* he cut the dog in half./ 4. The master then *was able* to reattach the two portions of the dog together./ 5. However, he did it *the wrong way,*/ 6. with the front teeth going one way and the rear teeth going the other way./ 7. The dog awoke/ 8. and **was aware of this unusual condition**/ 9. and *said to his master, "Look, I am going* to more or less forgive you,/ 10. because **I think we *can* make something of it by earning some money.**/ 11. *Just* give me a bone/ 12. and I'*ll be able to* make certain tricks for you/ 13. and we *can* attract a crowd."/ 14. However, the dog, after consuming the bone—/ 15. *By some miracle*, the dog *was able* to reverse itself into its proper condition./ 16. So, **I think the moral of this story** *would* be that when we think things *are looking* the worst,/ 17. that there *is a tendency* that they *will get* better. (words per segment = 10.5; type/token ratio = 0.61; perspective taking = 2; self-awareness = 1; specifications per segment = .95; predications per segment = 0.29)

Subject Story: Therapist Condition

1. *Once upon a time* there was a dog who had a master./ 2. And this dog loved and trusted his master/ 3. And one day when his master was chopping wood,/ 4. the dog was playing/ 5. and got in the way/

6. and the master *didn't really* **NOTICE**/ 7. because he was concentrating on sawing this wood/ 8. and cut the dog in half./

9. Well, the master *did his best* to *try* to put the dog together/

10. and he sewed the dog back together./ 11. Except that he made a mistake/ 12. and he put the front feet on *right*/ 13. but the back feet were pointing up in the air./ 14. So the dog **said to his master, "I want a bone.**/ 15. Give me a bone./ 16. I'[wi]ll do tricks for you./ 17. I'[wi]ll jump on my hind feet and [I will] do somersaults. 18. And so the master gave him a bone./ 19. And *all of a sudden* the dog's back feet were forward again/ 20. and the dog, whose name was Snoopy, was HAPPY/ 21. and they were HAPPY master

and dog again. (words/segment = 8.0; type/token ratio = 0.82; perspective taking = 2; self-awareness = 2; specifications per segment = 0.42; predications per segment = 0.10.)

APPENDIX B: SPECIFICATION AND PREDICATION SUBTYPES

Specification Subtypes

1. Specification of Intention: The basic event is present as an object or goal of the subject's intention or desire, or is the object of a plan: "He wanted to leave home." "She tried to make it work."

2. Specification of Mode: The event is made contingent on some notion of necessity or possibility (includes concepts such as permission, obligation, verification, etc.): "He can't leave home." "She had to make it work."

3. Specification of Manner: The subject's evaluation of or perspective toward an event is represented as being included within the subject's performance of an event: "He gladly left home." "She enthusiastically made it work."

4. Specification of Result: The event is represented as having been completed from the perspective of the subject's evaluation: "He finished leaving home." "She no longer makes it work."

5. Specification of Initiation: The event is represented as beginning from the perspective of the subject's participation within it: "He started to leave home." "She began to make it work."

6. Specification of Aspect: The subject's participation within the event is presented as ongoing with respect to the internal temporal organization of the event: "He is leaving home." "She continues to make it work."

7. Specification of Duration: A temporal perspective toward the event is included and it is nonobjective (i.e., not measured by clocks, calendars, etc.): "He never left home." "She occasionally makes it work."

8. Specification of Degree: The truthfulness or actuality of the subject's participation in the event is either attenuated or accentuated: "He kind of left the ministry." "She really is working."

Predication Subtypes

1. Predication of Appearance: The subject of one event is making it seem as though another event took place or is taking place: "Donna pretended that she loved him." "The kids played at being pilots."

2. Predication of Knowledge: The subject of one event performs some cognitive work to acquire knowledge or awareness of some other event: "Bill learned that she didn't love him." "She remembered when she was with child."

3. Predication of Description: The subject of one event performs an act of public description or behavioral display to transmit knowledge of an event to another subject: "The candidate told his supporters that they had helped during the election." "His grimace showed her how upset he was."

4. Predication of Retelling: The subject of one event performs what is typically an act of public description or behavioral display that is in the form of a direct quotation to transmit knowledge of an event to another subject: "The candidate told his supporters, 'We made a good run at it.'" "She said to herself, 'I didn't work hard enough.'"

5. Predication of Supposition: The subject has an awareness of, knowledge of, or perspective toward an event located in the future: "She thinks he will win." "He expects Mary to leave the party."

6. Predication of Subjectivation: A point of view or perspective is formulated toward an event not located in the future: "He thinks that he won." "John believes that he is Superman."

7. Predication of Attitude: A subject adopts a perspective toward an event and the content of that perspective seems the result of that event: "Cheryl enjoyed it when she went to the gym for the afternoon." "He was confused when she left him."

8. Predication of Entreaty: A subject expresses an intention, wish, or desire that is linked to the action of some other subject: "My first doctor wanted me to discipline my child." "I want you to go to the store."

REFERENCES

Astington, J. W., & Gopnik, A. (1991). Theoretical explanations of children's understanding of the mind. *British Journal of Developmental Psychology, 9*, 7-31.

Baron-Cohen, S. (1991). The theory of mind deficit in autism: How specific is it? *British Journal of Developmental Psychology, 9*, 301-314.

Baron-Cohen, S., Leslie, A. M., & Frith, U. (1986). Mechanical, behavioral, and intentional understanding of picture stories in autistic children. *British Journal of Developmental Psychology, 4*, 113-125.

Bellak, L. (1986). *The TAT, CAT, and SAT in clinical use* (4th ed., rev.). Philadelphia: Grune & Stratton.

Bettelheim, B. (1977). *The uses of enchantment: The meaning and importance of fairy tales.* New York: Vintage.

Bretherton, I. (1991). Intentional communication and the development of an understanding of mind. In D. Frye & C. Moore (Eds.), *Children's theories of mind* (pp. 49-75). New York: Lawrence Erlbaum.

Bretherton, I., & Beeghly, M. (1982). Talking about internal states: The acquisition of an explicit theory of mind. *Developmental Psychology, 18*, 906-921.

Bruner, J. (1986). *Actual minds, possible worlds.* Cambridge, MA: Harvard University Press.

Bruner, J. (1987). Life as narrative. *Social Research, 54*, 11-32.

Costantino, G., Malgady, R. G., & Rogler, L. H. (1986). Cuento therapy: A cultural sensitive modality for Puerto Rican children. *Journal of Consulting and Clinical Psychology, 54*, 639-645.

Crick, N. R., & Dodge, K. A. (1994). A review and reformulation of social formation-processing mechanisms in children's social adjustment. *Psychological Bulletin, 115*, 74-101.

Danto, A. C. (1985). *Narration and knowledge.* New York: Columbia University Press.

Ellis, A. (1962). *Reason and emotion in psychotherapy.* New York: Lyle Stewart.

Eisenmajer, R., & Prior, M. (1991). Cognitive linguistic correlates of "theory of mind" ability in autistic children. *British Journal of Developmental Psychology, 9*, 351-364.

Essig, T. S., & Russell, R. L. (1989a). *Categories for classifying psychological relations between subjects and events in discourse: A scoring manual.* Available from authors.

Essig, T. S., & Russell, R. L. (1989b). *The Vanderbilt Psychotherapy Process Scales and self-disclosing discourse: Good process and subjectivity during inpatient psychotherapy sessions.* Paper presented at the meeting of the Society for Psychotherapy Research, Toronto.

Essig, T. S., & Russell, R. L. (1990). Analyzing subjectivity in therapeutic discourse: Rogers, Perls, Ellis, & Gloria revisited. *Psychotherapy: Theory, research, practice, training, 27*, 271-281.

Feldman, C. F. (1988). Early forms of thought about thoughts: Some simple linguistic expressions of mental state. In J. Astington, P. Harris, & D. Olson (Eds.), *Developing theories of mind* (pp. 126-137). Cambridge, UK: Cambridge University Press.

Frye, D., & Moore, C. (1991). *Children's theories of mind.* New York: Lawrence Erlbaum.

Gardner, R. A. (1971). *Therapeutic communication with children: The mutual storytelling technique.* New York: Jason Aronson.

Gardner, R. A. (1993). *Storytelling in psychotherapy with children.* New York: Jason Aronson.

Hambleton, G., Wandrei, M. L., & Russell, R. L. (1996). Narrative performance predicts psychopathology: A preliminary demonstration. *Journal of Narrative and Life History, 6*, 87-105.

Henry, W. E. (1973). *The analysis of fantasy.* Malabar, FL: Krieger.

Johnson, C. N., & Wellman, H. M. (1982). Children's developing concepts of the mind and brain. *Child Development, 53*, 222-234.

Kendall, P. C. (1993). Cognitive-behavioral therapists with youth: Guiding theory, current status, and emerging developments. *Journal of Consulting and Clinical Psychology, 61,* 235-247.

Koocher, G. P., & Pedulla, B. M. (1977). Current practices in child psychotherapy. *Professional Psychology, 8,* 275-287.

Lebo, D. (1952). The relationship of response categories in play therapy to chronological age. *Journal of Child Psychiatry, 2,* 330-336.

Lord, J. J., Castelino, C. T., & Russell, R. L. (1990, June). *Linguistic aspects of client discourse: Affect, subjectivity, and client experiencing levels.* Paper presented at the meeting of the Society for Psychotherapy Research, Wintergreen, VA.

MacIntyre, A. (1980). Epistemological crises, dramatic narrative, and the philosophy of science. In G. Gutting (Ed.), *Paradigms and revolutions* (pp. 54-73). Notre Dame, IN: University of Notre Dame Press.

McMullin, R. E. (1986). *Handbook of cognitive therapy techniques.* New York: Norton.

Moore, C., & Frye, D. (1991). The acquisition and utility of theories of mind. In D. Frye & C. Moore (Eds.), *Children's theories of mind* (pp. 1-14). New York: Lawrence Erlbaum.

Platt, J. J., & Spivack, G. (1975). *Manual for the Means-Ends Problem-Solving Procedures (MEPS): A measure of interpersonal cognitive problem-solving skills.* Camden: University of Medicine and Dentistry of New Jersey.

Russell, R. L. (1991). Narrative in view of humanity, science, and action: Lessons for cognitive therapy. *Journal of Cognitive Psychotherapy, 5,* 241-256.

Russell, R. L., & van den Broek, P. (1988). A cognitive developmental account of storytelling in child psychotherapy. In S. R. Shirk (Ed.), *Cognitive development and child psychotherapy* (pp. 19-52). New York: Plenum.

Russell, R. L., & van den Broek, P. (1992). Changing narrative schemas in psychotherapy. *Psychotherapy: Theory, Research, Practice, and Training, 29,* 344-354.

Russell, R. L., & Wandrei, M. (1996). Narrative and the process of psychotherapy. In H. Rosen & K. T. Kuehlwein (Eds.), *Constructing realities: Meaning-making perspectives for psychotherapists* (pp. 307-335). San Francisco, CA: Jossey-Bass.

Selman, R. L. (1980). *The growth of interpersonal understanding.* New York: Academic Press.

Selman, R. L., & Byrne, D. F. (1974). A structural-developmental analysis of levels of role-taking in middle childhood. *Child Development, 45,* 803-806.

Shirk, S. (1988). *Cognitive development and child psychotherapy.* New York: Plenum.

Shirk, S., & Russell, R. L. (1996). *Change processes in child psychotherapy: Revitalizing treatment and research.* New York: Guildford.

Siegfried, J. (1995). *Therapeutic and everyday discourse as behavior change: Towards micros-analysis in psychotherapy process research.* New York: Ablex.

Shotter, J. (1995). In conversation: Joint action, shared intentionality, and ethics. *Theory and Psychology, 5,* 49-73.

Stiles, W. B. (1979). Verbal response modes and psychotherapeutic technique. *Psychiatry, 42,* 49-62.

Stiles, W. B., Meshot, T. M., Anderson, W. W., & Sloan, W. W. (1992). Assimilation of problematic experiences: The case of John Jones. *Psychotherapy Research, 2,* 81-101.

van den Broek, P., & Thurlow, R. (1991). The role and structure of personal narratives. *Journal of Cognitive Psychotherapy, 5,* 257-274.

Vitz, P. C. (1990). The use of stories in moral development. *American Psychologist, 45,* 709-720.

Vygotsky, L. (1978). *Mind in society.* Cambridge: MIT Press. (Original work published 1936)

Wechsler, D. (1945). A standardized memory scale for clinical use. *Journal of Psychology, 19,* 87-95.

Wiener, M., & Mehrabian, A. (1968). *Language within language: Immediacy, a channel in verbal communication.* New York: Appleton-Century-Crofts.

Part IV

Narrative Assessment Strategies in Psychotherapy

CHAPTER 13

Self-Defining Memories, Narrative Identity, and Psychotherapy
A Conceptual Model, Empirical Investigation, and Case Report

JEFFERSON A. SINGER

PAVEL S. BLAGOV

OVERVIEW

In previous work, we have provided examples of narrative memories generated by clients in the course of psychotherapy that have become organizing touchstones in the therapeutic dialogue and the client's own self-understanding (Singer, 2001, in press; Singer & Blagov, in press; Singer & Salovey, 1993, 1996; Singer & Singer, 1992, 1994). The goal of this chapter is to describe more recent theoretical and empirical advances that locate these "self-defining" memory narratives in an integrative model of identity and autobiographical memory. After reviewing the recent convergence between cognitive perspectives on the self and memory (Conway & Pleydell-Pearce, 2000) and narrative approaches to identity (Habermas & Bluck, 2000; McAdams, 1999, 2001), this chapter provides empirical support for our model by demonstrating the linkage between self-defining memories and personality adjustment. Finally, we examine this model of memory and personality in psychotherapy by its application to a case example.

THE SELF-MEMORY SYSTEM MODEL

In the early 1980s, a burgeoning new movement in cognitive psychology focused on

AUTHORS' NOTE: Correspondence regarding this chapter should be sent to Jefferson A. Singer, Ph.D., Department of Psychology, Connecticut College, New London, CT 06320, or to jasin@conncoll.edu.

autobiographical memory (as documented in several influential books, Neisser, 1982; Neisser & Fivush, 1994; Neisser & Winograd, 1988; Rubin, 1986, 1996). Although this work made significant progress in a cognitive understanding of memory processes, these advances were relatively independent of developments in personality theory and research. However, among these cognitive studies of memory, Martin Conway's model of autobiographical memory (Conway, 1996; Conway & Rubin, 1993) offered the most promise of integration with contemporary personality research. In a comprehensive review article, Conway and Pleydell-Pearce (2000) laid out a cognitive model that located autobiographical memory in a *self-memory system* that integrated personal goals and other components of personality and identity.

The self-memory system enables the individual to retrieve memories of personal significance by reconstructing specific memories from a base of autobiographical knowledge. When a memory cue occurs, it activates goals relevant to the personality, which are organized hierarchically in a "working self." These goals are linked to a three-level hierarchy of autobiographical knowledge. To retrieve a specific memory relevant to the goals activated by the retrieval cue, the individual instantiates a hierarchical search through the autobiographical knowledge base.

At the first level, and the most abstract, individuals generate "lifetime periods" or large units of time from their lives that reflect particular overarching goals and activities, for example, early years of marriage, graduate school, or a period of financial hardship. Once a lifetime period is defined, individuals search through "general events." General events are categories of events linked across relatively brief time periods (a week, a day, a few hours) or organized by a shared theme (e.g., first-time experiences or academic successes). Finally, these two types of semantic information allow individuals to generate *event-specific knowledge*. Event-specific knowledge encompasses imagery and sensory detail tied to unique and specific episodes in an individual's life. The cumulative search process yields the recollection of a specific and sensory-rich autobiographical memory. The activated goals within the working self both guide and limit the search, ensuring that it is relevant to the exigent cue but does not overwhelm attentional resources. Thus, the self-memory system both encourages and limits the search process.

The working self clearly, then, has a central role in autobiographical memory construction (Brewer, 1986; Conway & Pleydell-Pearce, 2000). It is conceived of as part of working memory, consisting of a temporarily active set of available self-schemas. It has a hierarchy of goals that constrain cognition and behavior and serve as retrieval control processes. There is empirical evidence that self-relevance mobilizes long-term memory resources and results in the preferential episodic encoding of self-relevant material (e.g., Conway & Dewhurst, 1995). Active goals influence autobiographical retrieval (Moffitt & Singer, 1994), as evidenced by a relationship between memory content and personal strivings. Conway and Pleydell-Pearce (2000) review studies that present neuroimaging evidence for the model, based on PET scans and slow cortical potential recordings during experiments with autobiographical recall. (Also see Conway, Pleydell-Pearce, & Whitecross, 2001; Conway et al., 1999; Craik et al., 1998.)

THE LIFE STORY APPROACH TO PERSONALITY

If indeed the autobiographical memory system is guided, in part, by a self that consists of a hierarchy of desired goals, and these goals can be activated by internal processes (e.g., thoughts, fantasies, etc.) or external cues (e.g., interpersonal or situational stimuli), how then do these goal hierarchies emerge, and what goals are likely to take precedence for individuals at a given period of their lives? We have explored this question in detail elsewhere (Singer & Blagov, in press), but briefly, we can suggest that the psychosocial stages of identity construction may play a critical role in how goals are aligned within the self hierarchy at various junctures of individuals' lives. As Erikson (1959) first proposed, individuals face a series of developmental crises, and their ongoing sense of identity emerges from the crucible of their various responses to these challenges of autonomy, intimacy, generativity, and integrity. More recently, McAdams (1988, 1993, 1996) has argued that this identity development takes the form of a life story, actively constructed by individuals in response to the contemporary world's lack of preconceived meaning systems. This life story organizes autobiographical memories (Brewer, 1996) and the goals and fantasies of the self (McAdams, 2001), situating individuals within a sociocultural milieu and integrating their various roles and relationships into an ongoing narrative (see also Bruner, 1997, for a similar position). According to McAdams (1995), a full scientific inquiry into personality requires analysis of the unique identity that is expressed in one's life story.

Aspects of the self match similar features of "good stories" because personality develops through a socialization process that is heavily based in the stories told to, about, and around children (Miller, 1994). In a sense, both our stories and our selves should have a plot structure organized around a desired ending or outcome; they should have a coherence that relates events to each other in an intelligible way; they should have identifiable protagonists, as well as obvious obstacles and nemeses; they should be credible in the sense that they contain elements that do not wildly contradict our understanding of what is plausible for a particular story or person (McAdams, 1996).

The comprehension and remembering of stories coincide with the development of children's ability to tell about their own past (Habermas & Bluck, 2000; McAdams, 2001). Stories become models for autobiographical remembering (Miller, 1994). A coherent life story begins to emerge in adolescence, when modern society expects individuals to make important life choices and to be able to justify them with a consistent and socially acceptable account of who they are, where they come from, and what they want to accomplish (Habermas & Bluck, 2000; McAdams, 1996). In mid-adolescence, young people first become able to have a complex understanding of the biopsychosocial reasons behind the ordering of life events (Bluck & Habermas, 2000, 2001; Habermas & Bluck, 2000). Coincidentally, memory studies have yielded a robust finding that vivid memories from early adulthood (about 20 years of age) are overrepresented in the reports of mature adults (Conway & Pleydell-Pearce, 2000; Holmes & Conway, 1999; Pillemer, 1998a, 1998b; Rubin, Rahhal, & Poon, 1998; Rubin, Wetzler, & Nebes, 1986). One explanation for this "reminiscence bump" is that it reflects the consolidation of identity (Habermas & Bluck, 2000; McAdams, 2001; Thorne, 2000).

McAdams (1996) believes that the organization of the life story can be predictive of mental health. The good adult life story is internally coherent; makes sense to others; has a richness of themes, characters, and events; and has increasing differentiation, generative integration, and a meaningful end. A mature adult identity with these characteristics enables the person to take on successfully different roles in work and relationships in order to be useful to the self and others while preserving integrity.

INTEGRATION OF THE SELF-MEMORY SYSTEM AND THE LIFE STORY NARRATIVE WITH THE LIFE STORY SCHEMA

If the self in Conway and Pleydell-Pearce's autobiographical memory model is linked to a developmentally sensitive life story of identity, which highlights what goals will be most prominent in its hierarchy at any given time, how do specific memories connect to the goals and information contained within narrative identity? Bluck and Habermas (2000, 2001) offer a theoretical connection through their concept of the *life story schema*, which bridges cognitive, affective, and motivational dimensions of personality. Life story schema theory proposes that individuals possess an understanding of how the normative life story is constructed within our culture. This normative structure draws on social cognitive conventions with regard to temporal order, dominant themes, causal attributions, and evaluative stances toward experiences. In a sense, the life story schema is our semantic knowledge structure and contains our abstracted understanding of what our or anyone else's life story should contain. The raw experiences of autobiographical memories are filtered through the life story schema, which in turn helps individuals to assign meaning and value, both to their memories and the goals associated with them. Thus, Bluck and Habermas (2000, 2001) see the life story schema as an interface between the highest-order autobiographical knowledge in Conway and Pleydell-Pearce's (2000) model and the life story narrative identity. It provides the rules and grammar that link the two.

Self-Defining Memories in the Self-Memory System and the Life Story

If we assume that individuals have an overarching life story schema that sets parameters on how goals and memories might be linked in the personality, this schema will also lead individuals to see certain memories as more developmentally critical and thematically central to their immediate life story and its exigencies. These memories are likely to be more highly relevant to current important goals within the self and to generate a consequent greater level of affective intensity. Since they are expressive of salient concerns or conflicts in individuals' overarching narrative identity (i.e., the life story), they have been described as *self-defining memories* (Singer & Salovey, 1993). A self-defining memory is a reminiscence that is "vivid, affectively charged, repetitive, linked to other similar memories, and related to an important unresolved theme or enduring concern in an individual's life" (Singer & Salovey, 1993, p. 13).

Repetitiveness indicates that the memories are related to the recurrent goals in the working self. Singer and Salovey (1993) wrote about the motivational aspect of repetitive memories that serve deliberately or inadvertently as reminders for established goals or important decisions. Although the instance of reminiscence is transient, the relative stability of the basic story lines of repetitive memories has been demonstrated empirically (e.g., Christianson & Safer, 1996; Demorest & Alexander, 1992; Thorne, Cutting, & Skaw, 1998). The affective intensity and vividness of self-defining memories are indirect indicators of the role these memories play in cognition and personality (Singer & Salovey, 1993).

A self-defining memory is likely to show linkage to similar memories based on shared emotions, types of events, participants, goals, outcomes, or lessons. From a cognitive perspective, this would mean complex cross-indexing of knowledge that pertains to different self-defining memories at the higher levels of the self-memory system hierarchy. A similar notion exists in the precursor of narrative theories of personality, Tomkins's (1987) script theory, according to which a process called psychological magnification links memories of similar events, increases their significance to the self, and weaves schemas and scripts out of the memories that later become self-fulfilling aspects of the self.

The self-defining memory construct is similar to Pillemer's (1998a) concept of personal event memories in that self-defining memories are experienced subjectively as truthful representations of past events, may have the quality of reexperiencing the event, and yield a detailed narrative. However, self-defining memories are not restricted to happenings that took place at a specific date and time. In fact, the degree of specificity is one of their measurable properties. The self-defining memory construct is more demanding than the concept of personal event memories in relation to the vividness of the remembered events and, especially, their importance to the person's identity.

The ability to recognize the importance of the memories, to abstract meaning from them, and to integrate that meaning into a life story schema is a developmental achievement (Bluck & Habermas, 2001). The degree to which the self-defining memories of individuals clearly and explicitly reveal their connection to the self is another quantifiable property of the narrative process. As an additional refinement of the life story schema elaboration (Bluck & Habermas, 2001) of the self-memory system model (Conway & Pleydell-Pearce, 2000), it is proposed that self-defining memories constitute the kind of self-memory system output that is integrated by the life story schema. The implication is that processing self-defining memories in working memory can result in changes in the indices of the life story schema and thus reorganize its temporal, thematic, or causal lines.

Measurable Aspects of Self-Defining Memories Including Integrative Meaning

Singer and Blagov (in press) proposed that the relationship of self-defining memories to personality could be examined reliably along dimensions of structure, meaning, and affect. Structure is operationalized as the degree of temporal specificity and the amount of imagistic detail of the memory (Singer & Moffitt, 1991-1992). The dimension of meaning captures memory categorization and integration, that is, the degree to which the narrative contains an elaboration on a theme or issue in the individual's life that goes beyond the particulars of the remembered event. Such elaborations can be considered lessons learned or evidence for psychological wisdom (see Pillemer, 1998a; Staudinger, 2001). The affective tone is measured by means of participants' ratings of how a memory makes them feel at the time of recall, and it has been previously linked to the nature of personal strivings (approach and avoidance) and their attainment and nonattainment (Moffitt & Singer, 1994).

Thorne and McLean (2001) have recently operationalized a fourth dimension of content through a narrative coding system. Their system includes categories such as personal threat and injury, relationship, achievement, and guilt and shame, among others. Due to space limitations, we will only discuss the first dimension of meaning; interested readers can learn about results related to the other three dimensions in Blagov and Singer (in press).

The dimension of meaning The cognitive process by which a tellable and conscious narrative about the past is created has been called narrative processing (Singer & Bluck, 2001) or reminiscence (Conway & Pleydell-Pearce, 2000; Staudinger, 2001). It is to be distinguished from autobiographical reasoning (Singer & Bluck, 2001) or life reflection (Staudinger, 2001), which is the derivation of meaning (interpretations, evaluations, insights, explanations, and lessons) from memory and life narratives. Theorists (e.g., Robinson, 1986) have suggested that the creation of meaning in autobiographical memory functions in affect regulation and relationship maintenance and repair. Making meaning of past struggles and sharing it has been found to predict positive self-regard in college students (Debats, Drost, & Hansen, 1995), less grief over time in bereaved spouses (Bauer & Bonanno, 2001), and well-being, a sense of growth, and enhanced ego development in parents of disabled children (King, Scollon, Ramsey, & May, 2000).

In an attempt to operationalize this dimension, Pillemer (1998a) suggested that personal event memories could be classified into categories based on their implied meaning, for example, originating events, turning points, symbolic messages, and memorable messages. Drawing on Pillemer's reasoning, but unable to validate his typology empirically, Singer and Blagov (2000) offered the more general construct of *integrative memories*: narratives in which the individual ascribes meaning to the memories by relating them to lessons about the self, important relationships, or life in general. A pilot study suggested good reliability of an early version of an integration coding system and a relationship between young people's social-emotional adjustment and the degree to which they sought meaning in self-defining memories (Blagov & Singer, 2000). Based on these observations, Singer and Blagov (in press) suggested that the meaning-making process in the construction of self-defining memories enables autobiographical memory to affect the self. Not only do goals active in the self-memory system influence the construction of memories (Conway & Pleydell-Pearce, 2000), but linking self-defining memories to abstract self-knowledge through the integrative process creates a positive feedback loop that gives additional cognitive, affective, and motivational value to the memory and powerfully reinforces relevant goals in the self-memory system (Singer & Blagov, in press).

Summary of the Overall Conceptual Framework

The working self of healthy conscious adults has the ability to search autobiographical knowledge to inform and assist its efforts toward attainment of current goals active in working memory (Conway, 1996). The autobiographical knowledge base is searched first at the most general and abstract level and, as thematic categories relevant to the current goals are found, the search proceeds toward the specific levels, and details about specific experiences from the past may be activated. The phenomenal conscious experience of a memory is tightly linked to the narrative processing of the activated knowledge, which children have learned to engage in from their earliest years (Habermas & Bluck, 2000; Miller, 1994). In adolescence, more sophisticated autobiographical reasoning becomes possible as memories are elaborated upon and deliberately used as sources of abstract knowledge and lessons (Bluck & Habermas, 2001; Staudinger, 2001; Thorne, 2000). Repetitive, vivid, and emotionally intense memories that are tied to the enduring concerns of the working self become likely candidates for autobiographical reasoning. The abstract knowledge from these self-defining memories becomes integrated with other semantic memories about the self and gives rise to the life story schema, which is a permanent but evolving index of lifetime periods and important themes and concerns (Bluck & Habermas, 2000). With age, the life story schema gains increasing importance with respect to its ability to influence the working

Figure 13.1 A model of the role of the life story schema and self-defining memories in the adult Self Memory System. Episodic memories subject to autobiographical processing become self-defining. They can yield abstracted information that may be integrated into the life story schema. For simplicity, all pathways through which the working self can access the autobiographical knowledge base and the feed-forward pathway from the life story schema to the working self have been omitted.

self as a source of motivation and wisdom (Staudinger, 1999). Figure 13.1 presents the framework visually.

The structure of self-defining memory narratives is their temporal organization and detail specificity (Singer & Moffitt, 1991-1992), and it depends on the extent to which the search through the autobiographical knowledge base has progressed to the most specific level. Overgeneral memories may indicate a working memory deficit due to emotional distress or depression (Williams, 1996). They may also be due to a motivated inhibitory process similar to repression (Singer & Salovey, 1993) or to an inability to put unusual and traumatic experiences into conventional story lines (Barclay, 1996).

The meaning of self-defining memories is their integrative quality, or the extent to which the narrative contains evidence for abstracted knowledge or lessons about the self or the world beyond the remembered events. Integrative self-defining memories indicate that individuals have engaged in autobiographical reasoning about the memory and are explicitly using their past experience to inform their sense of identity and depth of self-understanding.

The content of self-defining memories is their subject matter. It may indicate what kinds of events, interactions, and outcomes the individual is most motivated to attain or to avoid (Moffitt & Singer, 1994; Singer & Salovey, 1993). It may also indicate what kinds of actual events from the past were most important in determining the current personality status. Studying the intrapersonal trends and interpersonal differences in the proposed dimensions of self-defining memories bridges together the study of cognitive processes in autobiographical memory and the study of identity from a narrative perspective. It may also lead to insights about what constitutes a well-developed life story that promotes growth, maturity, adjustment, and wisdom.

In sum, the vivid narrative memories that clients generate in psychotherapy are located in a cognitive framework of personality that encompasses both a self-system and network of autobiographical memory. The glue that holds this framework together is the tendency of individuals to construct ongoing narratives or life stories of their identity, with memories and goals as their vital building blocks. The most important goal-relevant autobiographical memories may be operationalized as self-defining memories in the laboratory and subjected to systematic scrutiny for their relationship to other measures of personality and adjustment. The following section provides an example of this research.

VALIDATION OF THE SELF-DEFINING MEMORY FRAMEWORK: PERSONALITY ADJUSTMENT AND DEFENSES

To demonstrate the utility of this model of autobiographical memory and personality, it would be helpful to show that self-defining memories that contain integrative statements are indeed related to indices of ego development and social-emotional maturity. To test this question, we formulated the following proposition: Individuals with higher numbers of integrative statements in their self-defining memories should show evidence of higher levels of personality adjustment and more sophisticated defensive strategies in coping with stress or emotion.

To measure personality adjustment, we employed the Short Form of the Weinberger Adjustment Inventory (WAI-SF) (Weinberger, 1997, 1998). For this chapter, we focus on the specific relationship of the dimension of meaning, as operationalized by integrative statements in the self-defining memories, to Weinberger's measure. The WAI-SF consists of 37 items that yield scores on two dimensions, self-restraint and subjective experience of distress. Self-restraint covers intrapersonal (impulse control), interpersonal (suppression of aggression and consideration of others), and communal (responsibility) aspects of socialization. Low levels of self-restraint are characteristic of young children or individuals who do not regulate their impulses and affects successfully. High levels reflect strong socialization and attention to social convention; however, individuals who are best socially-emotionally adapted should have moderate self-restraint as they manage affect skillfully and do not resort to overcontrol (Asendorpf & van Aken, 1999; Hart, Hofmann, Edelstein, & Keller, 1997; Weinberger & Schwartz, 1990). Distress has the subdimensions of trait anxiety, depression, low well-being, and low self-esteem. Subjective distress on the WAI-SF correlates with personality measures of depression, anxiety, and self-esteem (Weinberger, 1998).

We hypothesized a curvilinear relationship between integrative statements in self-defining memories and individuals' levels of self-restraint, such that individuals with moderate levels of self-restraint would show the highest level of integration in the self-defining memories, followed by high self-restraint and then low self-restraint. To test the proposed relationship between integrative self-defining memories and self-restraint, 106 student participants received the Self-Defining Memory Task (Singer & Moffitt,

1991-1992) and generated 10 self-defining memories. The Self-Defining Memory Task requests that participants write down memories that are vivid, emotionally intense, repetitive, familiar to the self, and linked to other similar memories. Participants rate memories collected with this method as more important, and they are judged by raters to be more concerned with themes of self-discovery than memories that are collected with more general autobiographical memory requests (Moffitt & Singer, 1994; Singer & Moffitt, 1991-1992). The current version contained a request for the memory to be relevant to an enduring theme, issue, or conflict in the person's life.

The Classification System and Scoring Manual for Self-Defining Autobiographical Memories by Singer and Blagov (2000) is an original protocol that allows raters to be trained to score self-defining memories for structure and meaning. This system has been validated over a series of studies (Blagov & Singer, 2000, in press; Blagov, Singer, & Vergnani, 2002; Moffitt & Singer, 1994; Singer & Blagov, 2000; Singer & Moffitt, 1991-1992; Singer & Salovey, 1993). The scoring system (Singer & Blagov, 2000) discriminates between integrative and nonintegrative self-defining memories, based on a coding of statements made in the written memories. Integrative statements include the following kinds of phrases, "I learned that . . . ," "This experience taught me that . . . ," "Since then, I understood that . . . ," and so on.

We conducted a one-way analysis of variance (ANOVA) statistic with three levels of self-restraint (low, moderate, and high) as the predictor and the number of integrative memories (out of 10 memories for each individual) as the dependent variable. The statistic was significant, $F(2, 96) = 6.14$, $p < .01$, and an inspection of the means plotted in Figure 13.2 reveals the predicted curvilinear relationship. The effect of self-restraint was explored further with Tukey's HSD post-hoc tests. They revealed a significant difference in integrative memories between the low ($M = 1.91$) and the moderate ($M = 4.18$) self-restraint groups ($p < .05$) and between the high ($M = 2.74$) and the moderate groups ($p < .10$). These results suggest that moderately restrained individuals wrote down the highest numbers of integrative self-defining memories.

In Weinberger's (1998) framework, self-restraint is a developmental achievement and a sign of emotional maturity. From a narrative perspective, maturity is synonymous with the ability to engage in autobiographical reasoning to construct a coherent and generative life story (Habermas & Bluck, 2000; McAdams, 2001; Staudinger, 1999, 2001; Thorne, 2000). Individuals with moderate self-restraint scores did indeed write down more integrative self-defining memories than did the low and the high self-restraint groups.

Although the causal relationships remain unclear, we favor the following interpretation. Meaning-making and the construction of integrative self-defining memories are strategies that help people cope with negative emotions. Being more impulsive and less socialized into cultural narrative norms, low-restraint individuals rarely step back to think about the meaning of their actions and memories. Moderate self-restraint suggests an ability to acknowledge and regulate emotions, making it possible for these individuals to engage in high-order processing of their emotional memories. High self-restraint is associated with a desire to conform to cultural norms and narrative constraints, as well as a rigid and overcontrolled coping style. However, high-restraint individuals did show more integrative memories than low-restraint individuals. This finding makes sense if we assume that at least some portion of high self-restraint individuals rely on intellectualization as a defensive strategy. Future research would want to differentiate types of integrative

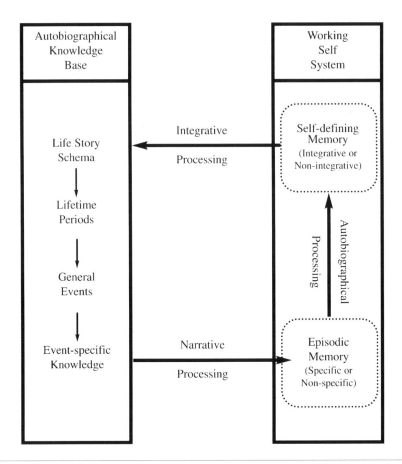

Figure 13.2   Moderate self-restraint on the Weinberger Adjustment Inventory (an indication of emotional maturity) predicts higher numbers of integrative self-defining memories in young adults.

statements in memories; perhaps some types of integrative statements are more linked to other positive aspects of memory recall, such as specificity or affective intensity.

Overall, the findings of this study do indeed suggest that our framework of self-defining memories may be meaningfully related to personality adjustment. Having demonstrated the validity of this linkage of memory and personality in the laboratory, the last section of this chapter returns to the realm of therapy and illustrates how we might apply this same conceptual framework to the narrative memories our clients share in psychotherapy.

APPLICATION OF SELF-DEFINING MEMORY RESEARCH TO CLINICAL PRACTICE: A CASE STUDY

As part of a standard evaluation process, the first author of this chapter routinely asks clients in their initial meetings to share a specific memory or two from their lives that they consider particularly important and self-revealing. At later junctures in the course of therapy, clients invariably share other memories that capture a theme or conflict that has emerged as significant in the therapeutic work. Whether the clients provide memories initially or they surface later on, the amount of emotion and meaning attached to them makes them stand out as prominent episodes in their life stories. Once these memories emerge in the therapy, it is not uncommon that links between them and other memories similar in both plot and sequence of emotions are likely to become apparent (see Tomkins, 1979). Clients also tend to return to these memories at moments when they seek to explain past motives and relationships. To determine how central and self-defining a given memory might be, one can gauge how many self-defining memory attributes are present: that is, vividness, affective intensity, repetitiveness, linkage to other memories, and focus on an enduring concern or unresolved conflict.

If indeed a memory seems to be serving in a self-defining capacity, the therapist can also actively introduce exploration of these particular memories into the therapy process. By examining the meanings and patterns that emerge from the memory, clients may gain insight into certain recurring themes from their lives that appear to dominate interpersonal interactions, including the therapeutic relationship. In fact, the ability of clients to see a connection between a self-defining memory and the manner in which they are interacting with the therapist vivifies their intellectual understanding that past concerns can resurface and affect current relationships.

Once therapist and client have identified and explored a set of related self-defining memories, the images from these memories serve as metaphoric touchstones in the therapeutic dialogue. The use of the self-defining memory as a metaphor in both the therapeutic relationship and ongoing relationships outside the therapy encourages the client to draw lessons or inferences from these linked experiences. As the client articulates and applies these integrative messages, greater self-restraint and better personality adjustment would be expected to emerge. In the following case example, we elaborate these ideas about the value of self-defining memories in psychotherapy and show in more detail how one makes use of these memories in treatment.

Art is a skilled tradesman in his mid-40s who is married with three children. He entered therapy because his wife was threatening to dissolve their 18-year marriage due to their emotional distance and conflicts over sexual intimacy. Through her own therapy, she had gained the confidence to confront his controlling and passive-aggressive behavior toward her. In particular, she claimed that whenever they would draw close and become physically intimate with each other, he would withdraw the next day, pick fights with her, or become thoroughly preoccupied with his work. At other times, he would literally become physically sick the day after they had been intimate. In their actual love making, she felt that he would purposely climax before her to deprive her of physical pleasure. Their relationship had reached such an impasse that they had not made love in the previous 5 months. One of the major sources of contention was his sleep apnea, which led him to snore and twitch at night. The severity of this condition caused them to sleep in separate beds. His wife felt that he had not made a sincere effort to remedy this problem and in fact used it as a way to distance himself from her.

In addition to describing his current difficulties in this first meeting, Art provided some basic background about his family life. He was the middle child of a large family and neither parent displayed much warmth or affection to the children. His father was often away on business and drank a great deal when he was home. He tended to be opinionated and highly critical of his wife and children. Due to this negative atmosphere, Art would often withdraw into silence or just disappear for hikes in the woods. When asked for an important memory, he provided the following one:

As [far back] as I can remember, I had worked to save money for college. I wanted to go to forestry school. I worked as a paperboy, a bus boy, and pumped gas. Every spare moment when I wasn't in school or studying, I was working. I did the papers in the morning and the other jobs at night after school. And I never spent a penny. I just put it into the bank and saved and saved. Well, the summer before my senior year of high school I got a chance to go with a school group to Europe for a few weeks. When I came back from the trip, I went to check my account. The money was gone. I went to my parents and asked them, "What was going on? Where was my money?" My father said he had taken the money to buy a car and when I graduated high school I could have the car. All the money for tuition was gone. I never went to college, even though I was accepted to a forestry school. And you know what, every child after me went to college and my parents paid for their full ride.

When asked what this memory meant to him, Art talked about how he felt that even people who were supposed to love or protect him could easily betray him. He said that he put up a powerful wall around his feelings and when he felt threatened, he retreated behind it by becoming silent and aloof. In subsequent sessions, Art continued to look at multiple examples of this pattern of withdrawal and his heightened sensitivity to possible betrayal by loved ones.

During our fifth meeting, he described a recent incident that linked to his earlier memory. He had recently finished a wall at a construction site when one of his coworkers heard the sound of kittens' meowing. Despite the knowledge that he would have to destroy the wall he had just built, he smashed it down to save the kittens. As he broke the wall, the irony entered his mind that he was able to do this for these animals, but that he was somehow unwilling to break through his protective front to save his marriage.

In the ninth meeting, he described how therapy had brought his wife and him closer and that they had made love, but how he grew distant the next day and became physically sick. He talked about how uncomfortable he was with praise and how he never received positive feedback growing up. He then suddenly returned to the self-defining memory that he had recalled in the first session. He said that the only thing his father had ever praised him for was saving money, but in the end he took all his money away. He realized too that he associated needing someone's approval or love with a loss of control. This loss of control terrified him and also enraged him. He connected his giving up any plan to go to college, and a subsequent period of heavy drinking and drug use after high school, with a desire to lash out at his parents. He recalled an earlier episode of running away from home when he was 14 and needing to spend time with a Youth Services officer. He linked all of these experiences to a general feeling of being betrayed and rejected by his parents. His withdrawal from his wife after increased intimacy was not just a gesture of fear, but also an attack by someone who felt wounded and cornered.

In a meeting several weeks later, Art recalled a self-defining memory about the weekend of his first sexual experience. He was still a teenager and was dating an older woman in her 20s. She was much more experienced than him and took him to a vacation house to lose his virginity. On the car ride home, she revealed to him that she had "deflowered" him in order to take out her anger for being raped as a teenager. He described himself as devastated by this revelation and noted that, true to his subsequent pattern, he became physically sick.

In a session a few months later, he revealed yet another self-defining memory that connected to the same pattern of trust and humiliation. He recalled a time in elementary school when his teacher noticed his dirty fingernails from the playground and forced him to stand in front of the class and show his hands to his classmates. When asked about the connection to his other memories, he explained that yet another figure of supposed trust and protection (in this case, a teacher) had betrayed him.

Connected to this series of memories was Art's revelation that he often became aroused when his wife was most upset and vulnerable. He later linked this admission to the fact that he felt attracted to pornography after periods of conflict and anger with his wife. He saw these responses as ways in which he could express a sense of anger and control after periods in which he himself had been made to feel vulnerable and emotionally open.

As these disclosures and insights accumulated over this first year of therapy, Art made significant progress with his wife. They were making love more regularly, but the pattern of connection and then distance was still quite apparent. This "push-me-pull-you" dynamic had also clearly become a part of the transference relationship. Art expressed a great deal of good feeling toward the therapy and attended faithfully, but he could be counted on to follow a positive session with the news that things had gone backward or were "up and down." Similarly, he might report that he forgot to try a recommendation from the therapy or that it had not worked or only worked for a while.

We were able to identify this pattern of transference behavior and connect it to his sequence of intimacy and withdrawal, as exemplified in his series of self-defining memories. We talked about how it was more effective for him to express his hurt or anger to me directly and then work through these feelings in our dialogue. With his pattern enacted in the therapeutic relationship, it could be felt and not just discussed abstractly. Interpretation of this dynamic and its clear linkage to his memories made a tremendous difference for Art. He was able to take a step forward in his commitment to his treatment and, simultaneously, his marriage. For the first time in therapy, he was able to say how grateful he was for our meetings and how much it mattered to him to come to his sessions.

As this experience of empathy and connection deepened in the therapy, he was able to recall more painful memories of his upbringing and his relationship to his father. He recalled one of the only times that his father had shown affection to him and embraced him. He was in his bed one morning and his father came into his room to wake him. Seeing the room in disarray, his father flung a dresser drawer across the room at the exact moment that Art sat up in bed. The drawer hit Art in the head and almost knocked him cold. As Art cried in pain, his father crossed the room and held him to try to soothe him. In telling this story, Art's mixture of anger and sorrow was palpable, but he still blocked himself from allowing any tears to fall. Although he struggled for control, he was able to recognize his urge to distance himself from me and to diminish the therapy. With the insight he had gained from understanding the patterns in his memories and seeing it enacted in the transference, he stopped himself from withdrawing, despite the strong impulse to do so.

These periods of strong emotional revelation and accompanying insight allowed Art to make continued connections between his self-defining memories and the messages that they offered to him about his pattern of behavior in relationships. He increasingly made reference to "the paper route" memory, linking it to his "first sexual experience" memory and other memories that spoke to his fear of betrayal in intimacy and defenses against it. With his self-understanding growing and his determination to express rather than act out his fear, his marital relations improved to a point where we could cut back on his weekly therapy with the confidence that he could work through the rough passages in his marriage on his own.

To end this case history and its account of how clients can learn about and make use of the thematic meanings of their self-defining memories, we can give one final example of Art's growing self-understanding. In one of his last meetings, he started the therapy by saying he had another "paper route" example that recently happened with his 3-year-old daughter. As they were leaving a store, she announced that she had her own quarters to put in the bubble gum machine. When he inspected the quarters, he realized that they were vintage silver quarters from his boyhood coin collection that he had given to his children as a present. As he felt himself becoming angry, he suddenly recalled an episode from his childhood when his brother had done the exact same thing with his penny collection, using a 1909 penny to purchase gum.

Art came to therapy that day able to make a connection between his memories and to offer his interpretation of how they were linked. His capacity for integration of his remembered experiences (seeing these memories as special cases of his "paper route" self-defining memory) indicated a deepening self-understanding and an emerging sense of freedom from the rigid patterns of his past. Rather than lashing out at his daughter, he was able to see what had provoked his initial feeling and then put this reaction in perspective. His present experience no longer automatically replicated his past.

Art's use of his self-defining memories in his psychotherapy can be expressed more formally in the conceptual model of autobiographical memory and personality that we have advanced in this chapter (see Figure 13.1). Art began with a particular abstraction or life story schema: "My life is a story of how intimacy can't be trusted and is likely to lead to betrayal. My only protection is to withdraw or control others."

From this schema, we can trace the linkage of overarching goals ("to avoid emotional pain" and "to control others who might hurt you") in the working self to autobiographical knowledge in the self-memory system. A developmental crisis precipitated by his wife's demand for intimacy then causes his search through the autobiographical knowledge system to give particular salience and affective intensity to certain lifetime periods ("childhood years raising money"), to general events ("times my parents betrayed me"), and to specific events ("the paper route" memory and other linked specific events). These specific events are organized through narrative processing into episodic memories, which in turn, due to their relevance to the pressing active goals of his working self, take on the special features of self-defining memories.

These memories appear as vivid, affectively intense, repetitive, dense in their connections to other memories, and expressive of an unresolved and ongoing conflict about intimacy. As he recalls them, they provide information both about the emotion associated with similar experiences and the relative possibility of attaining his goals (e.g., in this case, only by withdrawing from intimacy might he minimize his pain).

Finally, the process of psychotherapy allows him to step back from these self-defining memories and apply integrative processing to his understanding of them. Through analysis and interpretation of the memories, he is able to link the memories to a new goal ("Overcoming my fear of intimacy in order to save my marriage"), and this reconfiguration of the self-memory system requires the application of new understanding or reframing of the self-defining memories. As he attaches this new integrative message to his self-defining memories ("My withdrawal may have worked then, but does not work now"), reverberations occur throughout the self-system all the way up to a shift in the life story schema ("My life story is one in which I cautiously and slowly learn to accept love, despite my earlier history of distrust and betrayal"). This modification of the life story schema completes the complex loop and suggests a satisfactory response to the developmental challenge that had been raised at this juncture in his life story, that is, he succeeded in building greater intimacy in his marriage.

CONCLUSIONS

In this chapter, we outlined a conceptual model for understanding the role of self-defining memories in personality, as well as their potential application in psychotherapy. We provided a theoretical bridge between Conway and Pleydell-Pearce's cognitive model of autobiographical memory and McAdams's life story of identity. We suggested that Bluck and Habermas's concept of a life story schema offers an overarching organization for linking memory and personality and that self-defining memories are concrete expressions of how this linkage manifests itself in consciousness. Furthermore, we have introduced the idea of integrative statements associated with self-defining memories as a means of measuring the personality adjustment or socioemotional maturity of individuals. To support this proposal, we provided data from our laboratory and also a case study from psychotherapy practice.

In future work, it would be important to develop more formal assessment procedures for identifying clients' salient goals, related self-defining memories, and progress in expression of integrative statements. One possibility would be to incorporate the following instruments into the initial evaluation of clients: Emmons's (1986) Personal Striving measure, the Self-Defining Memory Task (Singer & Moffitt, 1991-1992), and our scoring system for measuring integrative statements in self-defining memories (Singer & Blagov, 2000). Linkage of these measures taken at the beginning, middle, and end of therapy to indices of therapeutic outcome would provide validation of this model's treatment efficacy.

REFERENCES

Asendorpf, J. B., & van Aken, M. A. (1999). Resilient, overcontrolled, and undercontrolled personality prototypes in childhood: Replicability, predictive power, and the trait-type issue. *Journal of Personality & Social Psychology, 77,* 815-832.

Barclay, C. R. (1996). Autobiographical remembering: Narrative constraints on objectified selves. In D. C. Rubin (Ed.), *Remembering our past: Studies in autobiographical memory* (pp. 94-125). Cambridge, UK: Cambridge University Press.

Bauer, J. J., & Bonanno, G. A. (2001). I can, I do, I am: The narrative differentiation of self-efficacy and other self-evaluations while adapting to bereavement. *Journal of Research in Personality, 35,* 424-448.

Blagov, P. S., & Singer, J. A. (2000, October). *Relationships between identity and social-emotional maturity: Self-defining memories, self-concept clarity, and self-restraint.* Paper presented at the meeting of the New England Psychological Association, Lewiston, ME.

Blagov, P. S., & Singer, J. A. (in press). Four dimensions of self-defining memories (specificity, meaning, content, and affect) and their relationships to self-restraint, distress, and repressive defensiveness. *Journal of Personality.*

Blagov, P. S., Singer, J. A., & Vergnani, M. (2002, March). *Structure and meaning in autobiographical memories: A reliable scoring system.* Poster presented at the meeting of the Eastern Psychological Association, Boston, MA.

Bluck, S., & Habermas, T. (2000). The life story schema. *Motivation and Emotion, 24,* 121-147.

Bluck, S., & Habermas, T. (2001). Extending the study of autobiographical memory: Thinking back about life across the life span. *Review of General Psychology, 5,* 135-147.

Brewer, W. F. (1986). What is autobiographical memory? In D. C. Rubin (Ed.),

Autobiographical memory (pp. 25-49). Cambridge, UK: Cambridge University Press.

Brewer, W. F. (1996). What is recollective memory? In D. C. Rubin (Ed.), *Remembering our past: Studies in autobiographical memory* (pp. 19-65). New York: Cambridge University Press.

Bruner, J. (1997). A narrative model of self-construction. In J. G. Snodgrass & R. L. Thompson (Eds.), *The self across psychology: Self-recognition, self-awareness, and the self-concept*. In *Annals of the New York Academy of Sciences, 818* (pp. 145-161). New York: New York Academy of Sciences.

Christianson, S.-A., & Safer, M. A. (1996). Emotions in autobiographical memories. In D. C. Rubin (Ed.), *Remembering our past: Studies in autobiographical memory* (pp. 218-243). New York: Cambridge University Press.

Conway, M. A. (1996). Autobiographical knowledge and autobiographical memories. In D. C. Rubin (Ed.), *Remembering our past: Studies in autobiographical memory* (pp. 67-93). New York: Cambridge University Press.

Conway, M. A., & Dewhurst, S. A. (1995). The self and recollective experience. *Applied Cognitive Psychology, 9*, 1-19.

Conway, M. A., & Pleydell-Pearce, C. W. (2000). The construction of autobiographical memories in the self-memory system. *Psychological Review, 107*, 261-288.

Conway, M. A., Pleydell-Pearce, C. W., & Whitecross, S. E. (2001). The neuroanatomy of autobiographical memory: A slow cortical potential study of autobiographical memory retrieval. *Journal of Memory & Language, 45*, 493-524.

Conway, M. A., & Rubin, D. C. (1993). The structure of autobiographical memory. In A. F. Collins & S. E. Gathercole (Eds.), *Theories of memory* (pp. 103-137). Hillsdale, NJ: Lawrence Erlbaum.

Conway, M. A., Turk, D. J., Shannon, L. M., Logan, J., Nebes, R. D., Meltzer, C. C., & Becker, J. T. (1999). A Positron Emission Tomography (PET) study of autobiographical memory retrieval. *Memory, 7*(5/6), 679-702.

Craik, F. I. M., Moroz, T. M., Moscovitch, M., Stuss, D. T., Winocur, G., Tulving, E., & Kapur, S. (1998). In search of self: A PET investigation of self-referential information. *Psychological Science, 10*(1), 26-34.

Debats, D. L., Drost, J., & Hansen, P. (1995). Experiences of meaning in life: A combined qualitative and quantitative approach. *British Journal of Psychology, 86*, 359-375.

Demorest, A. P., & Alexander, I. E. (1992). Affective scripts as organizers of personal experience. *Journal of Personality, 60*, 645-663.

Emmons, R. A. (1986). Personal strivings: An approach to personality and subjective well-being. *Journal of Personality and Social Psychology, 51*, 1058-1068.

Erikson, E. H. (1959). Identity and the life cycle: Selected papers. *Psychological Issues, 1*, 5-165.

Habermas, T., & Bluck, S. (2000). Getting a life: The emergence of the life story in adolescence. *Psychological Bulletin, 126*, 748-769.

Hart, D., Hofmann, V., Edelstein, W., & Keller, M. (1997). The relation of childhood personality types to adolescent behavior and development: A longitudinal study of Icelandic children. *Developmental Psychology, 33*, 195-205.

Holmes, A., & Conway, M. A. (1999). Generation identity and the reminiscence bump: Memory for public and private events. *Journal of Adult Development, 6*, 21-34.

King, L. A., Scollon, C. K., Ramsey, C., & May, T. (2000). Stories of life transition: Subjective well-being and ego development in parents of children with Down Syndrome. *Journal of Research in Personality, 34*, 509-536.

McAdams, D. P. (1988). *Power, intimacy, and the life story: Personological inquiries into identity*. New York: Guilford.

McAdams, D. P. (1993). *The stories we live by: Personal myths and the making of the self*. New York: William Morrow.

McAdams, D. P. (1995). What do we know when we know a person? *Journal of Personality, 63*, 365-396.

McAdams, D. P. (1996). Personality, modernity, and the storied self: A contemporary framework for studying persons. *Psychological Inquiry, 7*, 295-321.

McAdams, D. P. (1999). Personal narratives and the life story. In L. A. Pervin & O. P. John (Eds.), *Handbook of personality: Theory and research* (2nd ed., pp. 478-500). New York: Guilford.

McAdams, D. P. (2001). The psychology of life stories. *Review of General Psychology, 5*(2), 100-122.

Miller, P. J. (1994). Narrative practices: Their role in socialization and self-construction. In U. Neisser & R. Fivush (Eds.), *The remembering self: Construction and accuracy in the self-narrative* (pp. 159-179). Cambridge, UK: Cambridge University Press.

Moffitt, K. H., & Singer, J. A. (1994). Continuity in the life story: Self-defining memories, affect, and approach/avoidance personal strivings. *Journal of Personality, 62*, 21-43.

Neisser, U. (Ed.). (1982). *Memory observed: Remembering in natural contexts.* San Francisco: Freeman.

Neisser, U., & Fivush, R. (Eds.). (1994). *The remembering self: Construction and accuracy in the self-narrative.* Cambridge, UK: Cambridge University Press.

Neisser, U., & Winograd, E. (Eds.). (1988). *Remembering reconsidered: Ecological and traditional approaches to the study of memory.* Cambridge, UK: Cambridge University Press.

Pillemer, D. B. (1998a). *Momentous events, vivid memories.* Cambridge, MA: Harvard University Press.

Pillemer, D. B. (1998b). What is remembered about early childhood events. *Clinical Psychology Review, 18*, 895-913.

Robinson, J. A. (1986). Autobiographical memory: A historical prologue. In D. C. Rubin (Ed.), *Autobiographical memory* (pp. 19-23). Cambridge, UK: Cambridge University Press.

Rubin, D. C. (Ed.). (1986). *Autobiographical memory.* Cambridge, UK: Cambridge University Press.

Rubin, D. C. (Ed.) (1996). *Remembering our past: Studies in autobiographical memory.* Cambridge, UK: Cambridge University Press.

Rubin, D. C., Rahhal, T. A., & Poon, L. W. (1998). Things learned in early childhood are remembered best. *Memory and Cognition, 26*, 3-19.

Rubin, D. C., Wetzler, S. E., & Nebes, R. D. (1986). Autobiographical memory across the adult lifespan. In D. C. Rubin (Ed.), *Autobiographical memory* (pp. 202-221). Cambridge, UK: Cambridge University Press.

Singer, J. A. (2001). Living in the amber cloud: A life story analysis of a heroin addict. In D. P. McAdams, R. Josselson, & A. Lieblich (Eds.), *Turns in the road: Narrative studies of lives in transition* (pp. 253-277). Washington, DC: American Psychological Association.

Singer, J. A. (in press). A love story: Using self-defining memories in couples therapy. In D. P. McAdams, R. Josselson, & A. Lieblich (Eds.), *Narrative and psychotherapy.* Washington DC: American Psychological Association.

Singer, J. A., & Blagov, P. S. (2000, June). *Classification system and scoring manual for self-defining autobiographical memories.* Paper presented at the meeting of the Society for Applied Research on Memory and Cognition, Miami Beach, FL.

Singer, J. A., & Blagov, P. S. (in press). The integrative function of narrative processing: Autobiographical memory, self-defining memories, and the life story of identity. In D. R. Beike, J. M. Lampinen, & D. A. Behrend (Eds.), *The self and memory.* New York: The Psychology Press.

Singer, J. A., & Bluck, S. (2001). New perspectives on autobiographical memory: The integration of narrative processing and autobiographical reasoning. *Review of General Psychology, 5*, 91-99.

Singer, J. A., & Moffitt, K. H. (1991-1992). An experimental investigation of specificity and generality in memory narratives. *Imagination, Cognition & Personality, 11*, 233-257.

Singer, J. A., & Salovey, P. (1993). *The remembered self: Emotion and memory in personality.* New York: Free Press.

Singer, J. A., & Salovey, P. (1996). Motivated memory: Self-defining memories, goals, and affect regulation. In L. L. Martin & A. Tesser (Eds.), *Striving and feeling: Interactions among goals, affect, and self-regulation* (pp. 229-250). Hillsdale, NJ: Lawrence Erlbaum.

Singer, J. A., & Singer, J. L. (1992). Transference in psychotherapy and daily life: Implications of current memory and social cognition research. In J. W. Barron & M. N. Eagle (Eds.), *Interface of psychoanalysis and psychology* (pp. 516-538). Washington, DC: American Psychological Association.

Singer, J. A., & Singer, J. L. (1994). Social-cognitive and narrative perspectives on transference. In J. M. Masling & R. F. Bornstein (Eds.), *Empirical perspectives on object relations theory: Empirical studies of psychoanalytic theories* (Vol. 5, pp. 157-193). Washington, DC: American Psychological Association.

Staudinger, U. M. (1999). Older and wiser? Integrating results on the relationship between age and wisdom-related performance. *International Journal of Behavioral Development, 23,* 641-664.

Staudinger, U. M. (2001). Life reflection: A social-cognitive analysis of life review. *Review of General Psychology, 5,* 148-160.

Thorne, A. (2000). Personal memory telling and personality development. *Personality and Social Psychology Review, 4,* 45-56.

Thorne, A., Cutting, L., & Skaw, D. (1998). Young adults' relationship memories and the life story: Examples or essential landmarks. *Narrative Inquiry, 8*(2), 237-268.

Thorne, A., & McLean, K. (2001). *Manual for coding events in self-defining memories.* Unpublished manuscript.

Tomkins, S. S. (1979). Script theory: Differential magnification of affects. In H. E. Howe, Jr., & R. A. Dienstbier (Eds.), *Nebraska Symposium on Motivation 1978* (Vol. 26, pp. 201–236). Lincoln: University of Nebraska Press.

Tomkins, S. S. (1987). Script theory. In J. Aranoff, A. I. Rabin, & R. A. Zucker (Eds.), *The emergence of personality* (pp. 147-216). New York: Springer.

Weinberger, D. A. (1997). Distress and self-restraint as measures of adjustment across the life span: Confirmatory factor analyses in clinical and non-clinical samples. *Psychological Assessment, 9,* 132-135.

Weinberger, D. A. (1998). Defenses, personality structure, and development: Integrating psychodynamic theory into a typological approach to personality. *Journal of Personality, 66,* 1061-1080.

Weinberger, D. A., & Schwartz, G. E. (1990). Distress and restraint as superordinate dimensions of self-reported adjustment: A typological perspective. *Journal of Personality, 58,* 381-417.

Williams, J. M. G. (1996). Depression and the specificity of autobiographical memory. In D. C. Rubin (Ed.), *Remembering our past: Studies in autobiographical memory* (pp. 244-267). Cambridge, UK: Cambridge University Press.

CHAPTER 14

The Narrative Assessment Interview
Assessing Self-Change in Psychotherapy

KAREN K. HARDTKE

LYNNE E. ANGUS

The concept of narrative has captured the attention of many investigators in the psychotherapy research field, as well as practicing clinicians representing a broad spectrum of therapy approaches. The individual as storyteller, the act of storytelling, and the stories individuals tell in therapy are currently considered useful metaphors in our quest to build comprehensive theories of human meaning-making, and they offer a framework to further our understanding of the nature of self-identity and subsequently self-change in psychotherapy.

For the past several years, the narrative processes research team at the York Psychotherapy Research Centre and Clinic at York University in Toronto, Canada, has focused on investigating narrative processing strategies that facilitate the reconstruction and co-construction of clients' life stories in psychotherapy. To this end, we constructed the Narrative Processes Model (Angus, Levitt, & Hardtke, 1999) and Coding System (Angus, Hardtke, & Levitt, 1996)—a transtheoretical heuristic developed for empirical exploration of the narrative processing strategies engaged in by both the client and the therapist in the facilitation of client self-change in the therapy hour.

Working primarily within the context of experiential/humanistic therapy for depression, one of the unique insights generated by the Narrative Processes Coding System (NPCS) has been the discovery that clients, irrespective of therapy outcome, tend to prioritize shifts to personal storytelling, while

AUTHORS' NOTE: Correspondence regarding this chapter should be sent to the authors at York University, 4700 Keele Street, Toronto, Ontario, Canada M3J 1P3, or to hardtke@yorku.ca.

therapists specialize in inviting clients to shift to emotion-focused and meaning-making modes of experiential engagement (Angus et al., 1999; Hardtke, 1996a, 1996b; Lewin, 2001). Telling stories and grounding new understandings of self-in-action and life events seemed to be a particularly important client task in the psychotherapy process of the brief experiential therapy dyads that we have investigated intensively at the York Psychotherapy Research Center (Hardtke, 1996a, 1996b; Lewin, 2001; Lewin & Hardtke, 2000). In light of these findings, we have become increasingly convinced that the stories clients tell about themselves are important threads in the fabric of their self-identities (see McAdams, 1993). Furthermore, in the context of our interest in how stories change in therapy, we became intrigued with the question of whether or not clients see themselves differently after they have experienced significant gains in therapy and, correspondingly, with the degree to which that change is mirrored in the stories they generate to describe themselves posttherapy.

To address this question empirically, we directed our attention to the clients themselves. We asked our clients to turn the focus of their attention to their views of self and to provide us with personal memory narratives that illustrate these self-perceptions in the context of their interpersonal relationships. To this end, the present chapter introduces the Narrative Assessment Interview (NAI) (Hardtke & Angus, 1998), a brief semistructured interview protocol designed to be given at pre- and posttherapy, and/or at various other posttreatment periods, to explore and potentially assess client self-story change in psychotherapy. To provide a context of understanding regarding the development of the NAI, we will first present an overview of the various influences that have impacted thinking regarding the scope and functions of narrative expression in therapy. Next, we will briefly summarize the Narrative Processes Model and NPCS, which have guided our inquiries into narrative processes in experiential therapies and identify the key findings that guided the development of the NAI protocol. Finally, we will present the full protocol for the administration of the NAI and clinical examples illustrating its application in the context of brief experiential/humanistic therapies for depression (Greenberg & Angus, 1998).

BACKGROUND CONTEXT

A review of the psychology and psychotherapy research literature reveals that the narrative metaphor has amassed many suitors. For example, the concept of narrative has been offered as a perspective in or fundamental approach to the study of human nature. Bruner's (1986) seminal work espousing narrative as a "distinct way of knowing," augmented by the growing recognition of the contextual impact and role of intentionality on action (Rennie & Toukmanian, 1992), as well as the co-constructed nature of experience (Angus & Hardtke, 1994; Angus & Rennie, 1989), has presented the research community with a powerful alternative to positivist, paradigmatic approaches to human inquiry.

To date, most psychotherapy researchers have elected to define *narrative* as the description of personal events or stories that occur within the context of the therapy hour (Luborsky, Barber, & Diguer, 1992; Luborsky, Popp, Luborsky, & Mark, 1995; Rennie, 1994). Using this definition, narratives or personal stories are identified as discrete units of text that can be decontextualized from therapy sessions for further intensive analyses. For example, Luborsky and his colleagues have developed the Core Conflictual Relationship Theme (CCRT) (Luborsky & Crits-Cristoph, 1990), a method to identify clients' relationship narratives and to identify recurring action patterns and relational themes in the context of brief psychodynamic psychotherapy. Building on these insights, Howard Book (see Book, 2003, this volume) has identified key therapeutic strategies for working effectively with client relationship narratives and core relational themes in brief dynamic therapy.

Rennie (1994) used the Interpersonal Process Recall procedure (IPR) (Kagan, 1975) to access first-person accounts of client storytelling in person-centered psychotherapy. Using a grounded theory analysis of these client accounts, both facilitating and impeding functions of client narrative expression were identified, and the role of these factors for the development of client and the therapeutic alliance were addressed. More recently, Rennie (see Levitt & Rennie, 2003, this volume) has addressed the critical role of client reflexivity in the inception of narrative expression and knowing in psychotherapy.

Clients' personal stories can also be viewed as points along a continuum of their overall life stories. Accordingly, the narrative metaphor has been used by personality researchers and clinicians to refer to the individual's development of an overall perspective, or view of self(selves) and personal identity, in which discrete events are placed in a temporal sequence and are meaningfully organized along a set of intrapersonal and interpersonal themes (Angus et al., 1999; Baumeister & Newman, 1994; Bruner, 1986; Gergen & Gergen, 1983; Howard, 1991; McAdams, 1993; McAdams, Diamond, de St. Aubin, & Mansfield, 1997; McLeod & Balamoutsou, 1996; Polkinghorne, 1988; Sarbin, 1986; Singer & Blagov, in press; Spence, 1982; White & Epston, 1990). Drawing on the work of Baumeister and Newman (1994) who coined the terms, Angus (Angus & Hardtke, 1994) proposed that the term *micronarrative* may be used to identify the prose-type stories told in the therapy hour, while the term *macronarrative* may be used to refer to the client's life story, which he or she implicitly and explicitly describes and reconstructs over the entire course of the therapy relationship (Spence, 1982). Furthermore, the thematic ordering of the client's micronarratives may be viewed as a key factor in the structure of the overall macronarrative.

THERAPEUTIC CHANGE VIEWED FROM A NARRATIVE PERSPECTIVE

According to White (2001), people begin to experience problems for which they frequently seek therapy when the dominant narratives in which they, or others, are storying their experiences in the world are delimited or truncated. In these circumstances, significant aspects of the person's lived experiences contradict his or her dominant narrative. In other words, although a sense of meaning and continuity is achieved through the storying of experience, it is gained at a price because our lived experience is richer than discourse. As noted by Bruner (1986), narrative structure organizes and gives meaning to experiences, but there are always feelings and lived experiences not fully represented by the dominant story.

Given the gaps between narrative structure and experience, therapy offers clients an opportunity to reauthor their life narratives by identifying individual personal events, feelings, intentions, and thoughts that currently fall outside the dominant narrative. The therapeutic process then becomes a vehicle for the generation of alternative stories and views of self that incorporate vital and previously neglected aspects of the individual's lived experience (Angus & Bowes-Bouffard, 2002; White, 2001). "When persons seek therapy, an acceptable outcome would be the identification or generation of alternative stories that enable them to perform new meanings, bringing them desired possibilities—new meanings that persons will experience as more helpful, satisfying and open-ended" (White & Epston, 1990, p. 15). The identification of unique-outcome personal stories that challenge and destabilize problem-saturated macronarrative plots is viewed as a key strategy to offer new ways of seeing and valuing the self-in-relation to others and to establish alternative narrative plots that facilitate desired outcomes in life.

A similar approach to understanding macronarrative or life story change in therapy, which focuses on the importance of narrative expression, emotional meaning-making and the emergence of new views of self and others in psychotherapy, is the Narrative Processes Model (Angus & Boufffard, 2002; Angus et al., 1999). In contrast to the work of White (2001), which is based in a poststructuralist, social constructionist perspective, the Narrative Processes Model is based on assumptions drawn from a dialectical constructivist (Greenberg & Pascual-Leone, 1995) or contexutualist (Neimeyer & Mahoney, 1995) conceptualization of psychotherapy discourse. Accordingly, the following play lead roles in the consideration of client change on both the micronarrative (i.e., individual story) and macronarrative (i.e., life-story) level: client reflexivity, storytelling, narrative themes in the construction of self-identity, emotion schemes and emotion processing for the facilitation of self-identity change, the co-constructive nature of the client-therapist dialogue, and the conceptualization of productive therapeutic change as a dynamic, dialectical process of processing shifts.

According to the Narrative Processes Model of therapy (Angus et al., 1999), the detailed description of emotionally salient personal narratives, the differentiation of emotions, and the reflexive construction of new perspectives on self and others (i.e., the generation of new personal meaning) facilitate the construction of a more differentiated, coherent, and meaningful understanding of the self and the self-in-relation to others. Grounded in these core assumptions, the Narrative Processes Model operationally defines three basic processing strategies or modes that are proposed to be involved in client macronarrative change in psychotherapy:

1. An external or storytelling mode, which includes autobiographical memories (i.e., micronarratives)

2. An internal or emotion-focused mode, which includes the expression and articulation of affect

3. A reflexive or conceptual meaning-making mode, which draws on both micronarrative and emotion processes in the articulation of new life themes and self-understandings

The articulation of new core themes and shifts in the view of self are expressed in the form of macronarrative or identity change. Not surprisingly, given the theoretical interest in the concept of narrative as foundational to the construction of personal identity and life stories, interest has turned to the possibility of assessing narrative change in psychotherapy.

ADDRESSING THE GAP: ASSESSING NARRATIVE CHANGE IN PSYCHOTHERAPY

Attempts to conduct empirical investigations capturing the dynamic conceptualization of narrative reconstruction and self-change have proven an interesting challenge for researchers. Neimeyer (1994) identifies the difficulty in analyzing narratives within the therapy discourse as follows: "Attempting to specify the particular value of client-generated narratives in therapy is difficult not only because of the generality of the concept of narrative, but also because of the uniqueness of each client's narrative production" (pp. 239-239). Despite these obstacles, several creative and interesting interview protocols designed to capture people's sense of their life stories are emerging in the literature (the Identity Interview, Gonçalves & Machado, 1999; the Life-Story Interview, McAdams, 1993; Autobiographical Writing Tasks, Balamoutsou, 2003). The question not yet addressed is what this narrative change might look like, or sound like, at posttreatment.

Drawing on the Narrative Processes Model (Angus & Hardtke, 1994; Angus et al., 1999), the NPCS (Angus et al., 1996) offers psychotherapy researchers an empirical measure of micronarrative and macronarrative change processes appropriate for the assessment of therapeutic discourse (Hardtke, Levitt, & Angus, in press). The NPCS is a two-step process that enables the researcher:

1. To reliably subdivide and characterize therapy session transcripts into topic segments according to content shifts in verbal dialogue
2. To further subdivide and characterize each topic segment according to shifts in one of the three narrative process sequences, which correspond to the three narrative process modes: external, internal, or reflexive

Working primarily within the context of process experiential and client centered brief treatments (Greenberg, Watson, & Goldman, 1998; Goldman, Greenberg, & Angus, 2003) for depression, one of the unique insights emerging from our narrative processes research program to date has been the discovery that in the context of the therapeutic discourse, clients tend to prioritize shifts to external or storytelling modes (Angus et al., 1999; Hardtke, 1996a, 1996b), while experiential therapists specialize in inviting clients to shift to reflexive and internal processing modes (Gonçalves, Korman, & Angus, 2000; Gonçalves, Machado, Korman, & Angus, 2002; Lewin, 2001). The following clinical example illustrates this cyclical shifting of narrative process modes:

Therapist *[therapist and client currently engaging in reflexive process mode]* So somehow you experienced your husband as becoming more distant during the time you were caring for your mother and having to shoulder the responsibility for her.

Client and, but, you know, to give my husband credit, and I guess, I have blamed him for not being there for me, but actually, I guess I, in a way, to give him credit, he has never brought that up with me. He has never referred to it *[client shifts from a reflexive process mode to an external process mode]* because you know, he always said, like well, he wouldn't say anything. He used to get mad at my sisters. One time, when we had to move my mother into a different nursing home, he got furious that my sisters didn't help and then I would say to him "don't you dare talk to my sisters like that." So it got to the point where he said nothing and then to the point that I withdrew. He spent his days in the basement and I found myself busy in the kitchen, or with friends. We didn't talk.

Therapist *[therapist offers a reflexive summary of the client's story)* So somehow you wanted support, and when he said something and it was against your family *[and then invites a shift to an internal process mode of inquiry]* it kind of hurt you so you kind of pushed him away a bit . . . ?

Client Right, mm-hm. *[client shifts to a reflexive mode of inquiry]* It's my fault too. I was so consumed with my mother but then when I look back on it I think, well, did I have much of a choice?

Research findings emerging from the application of the NPCS to brief experiential therapies for depression (Angus et al., 1999; Hardtke et al., in press; Lewin, 2001) provide promising empirical support for the notion that the disclosure of emotionally salient personal narratives, woven with reflexive meaning-making processes, is a significant factor in the achievement of productive therapeutic outcomes.

This cyclical process of narrative processes shifting appears to serve several key therapeutic functions. First, clients tell personal stories to share their problems with the therapists and in so doing are developing the fundamentals of the therapeutic alliance. In the retelling of emotionally salient memory narratives, clients also gain a heightened experiential access to those events, which facilitates the exploration and differentiation of problematic emotion schemes and sets the ground for reflexive meaning-making and the emergence of new views of self and others in the therapy hour. Finally, the identification of personal narratives in the "real" world of personal relationships, narratives that capture new actions, emotions, and emerging views of self, provides an essential concretization of the "actuality" of perceived self-change. This restorying process is an important vehicle for the integration of new views of self in clients' ongoing self-identity. In essence, these narratives of change are akin to White's (2001) "unique outcome stories" in that they instantiate new ways of acting and being with others that enable preferred outcomes, and they provide the ground for the construction of new ways of understanding and viewing the self as they challenge prior views of self and self-identities.

Moreover, exciting connections have emerged linking the empirical findings of our narrative processes research program with current theoretical thinking about the significance of the storytelling process and its role in human meaning making. Baumeister and Newman (1994) addressed the interplay between the description of events (i.e., focusing on the articulation of specific, context-bound information) and the interpretation of those events (i.e., a focus on the identification of general rules or laws) in human meaning-making in the context of personality psychology. These authors submit that both propositional (or paradigmatic) thought and narrative modes of thought contribute to the process of making sense of one's experience on an ongoing basis. The narrative mode of thought, as conceptualized by Baumeister and Newman (1994), involves stories about particular personal experiences. These stories are temporally structured and context sensitive.

The narrative mode of thought, as defined by Baumeister and Newman (1994), appears to be very similar to the processes characterized by the NPCS's external narrative processes mode, wherein the dialogue primarily reflects the articulation and detailed description of personal events and autobiographical memory narratives that address the question of "what happened" in a person's life. According to Baumeister and Newman (1994), the narrative mode of thought provides the basic grounding for the identification of general themes, or patterns of self, which are subsequently built on by means of reflective and abstractive processes, characteristic of paradigmatic thought. In turn, the concept of paradigmatic thinking (i.e., reflection and abstraction) resembles the processes characterized by the reflexive narrative sequence mode of the NPCS. Furthermore, these authors submit that "each event must be understood in narrative form, in order to grasp what is actually happening, before abstract inferences or generalizations can be made from it" (p. 679).

Hence, the theoretical conceptualization of human meaning making as proposed by Baumeister and Newman (1994) appears to converge with the empirical findings of our narrative processes research program in that it suggests that clients make meaning of their experiences in the world by shifting between personal storytelling (external) and meaning-making (reflexive) narrative modes. Thus, the theoretical descriptions of "narrative modes of thought" and our empirical investigations of "narrative processes" have partnered to create a strong voice heralding the potential significance of narrative meaning-making in psychotherapy.

THE NARRATIVE ASSESSMENT INTERVIEW PROTOCOL

The NAI (Hardtke & Angus, 1998) was developed to provide a heuristic method for the exploration of self-story (macronarrative) change in psychotherapy. Rather than focusing on symptom reduction as an indicator of therapeutic success (in, for example, clients suffering from depression), we turned our attention to developing an instrument that might tap the way treatment affected the unique stories our clients brought to the therapy hour—to capture how, and to what degree, these stories, as illustrations of self-perception, changed after the experience of psychotherapy.

The NAI is a brief, semistructured interview protocol designed to be completed after the initial therapy session, at posttherapy and subsequently during periods of follow-up. The data collection procedure consists of a three-stage process, which entails the completion and audiotaping of a semistructured interview in Stage 1, the generation of a written summary sheet of the pretherapy interview in Stage 2, and the completion of a posttherapy interview including client reflection on the pretreatment NAI sheet in Stage 3. The open-ended format of the interview is intended to promote the exploration of the client's view of aspects of self in narrative form, without imposing the constraints of, for example, adjective checklists.

The NAI was developed for implementation in the York II Clinical Treatment trial for depression (Greenberg & Angus, 1998) conducted at the York Psychotherapy Clinic and Research Center at York University in Toronto, Ontario, Canada. In this study, supported by the Ontario Mental Health Foundation, participants were interviewed at pretreatment, posttreatment, and again 6 months after treatment termination to investigate the impact of brief client-centered and process experiential therapy on clients' sense of self, their stories, and the aspects of self they indicated they wanted to change before entering therapy.

The following section presents the procedural steps entailed in the completion of the NAI. Woven into this presentation are two case summaries taken from an ongoing treatment trial for depression. The first case example, Alan, illustrates the data generated during the various stages of the NAI, as well as the avenues of inquiry regarding narrative change that might be traveled via the application of the interview. The second case example, Marion, illustrates the potential for clients to self-reflect, make meaning, and potentially reauthor their sense of self within the context of the interview itself.

Stage 1: The Narrative Assessment Interview

In Stage 1, the clinician or researcher introduces the NAI to clients or participants immediately after the first session of therapy with the following statement:

> Now I am going to ask you some questions about you. People are complex and although the questions I will ask may at first appear to be quite simple, some people find them difficult to answer. The difficulty may be in part because you have never been asked these types of questions before. I encourage you to take as much time as you feel necessary to think about what I ask you before you respond. The questions are about how you see yourself and how you feel others see you. This shouldn't take more than 10 minutes of your time.

It is important during this first stage of the interview to facilitate a safe, collaborative, nonjudgmental atmosphere within which clients/participants may feel free to explore and describe their stories about themselves and the views they hold about others' perceptions of them. After the completion of the introductory statement, the therapist then asks clients or participants the following questions. (Note: the following presentation of the NAI protocol interchanges the dyads of therapist and client with participant and researcher to emphasize the suitability of the interview in both clinical and research contexts.)

Question 1: How would you describe yourself? If the participant describes herself according to a role (e.g., I am a mother), the interviewer would then ask "What kind of mother are you?" The participant might respond with a description such as, "I am a loving mother." The participant is then asked to provide a recent example from her lived experience that would illustrate this description of herself. If the participant describes himself using adjectives (e.g., "I am very caring"), he is subsequently asked to provide the interviewer with a recent example to illustrate this description in terms of his lived experience. Participants are encouraged to take their time and generate as many descriptions as they can. Following each description, the interviewer prompts the participant to provide a recent example from her or his life to illustrate the description provided.

The purpose of Question 1 is to explore how clients see themselves prior to treatment: positively or negatively, externally or internally oriented in terms of singular or multiple perspectives. Examples, or stories of clients' lived experience that illustrate views of self, are elicited to explore the degree to which these experiences are congruent with the client's view of self or dominant narrative.

The Narrative Assessment Interview: Clinical Case Example—Alan

On entering a brief experiential treatment for depression, Alan was a middle-aged, married father of three children who, for the previous 3 years, had not been able to secure employment in his professional field: "I fell off a cliff 3 years ago; my career, my job, my life went crashing into a wall." The qualities Alan attributed to himself were generally positive: "I'm intelligent and well-educated with a very good sense of awareness of self"; "I am the father of three—a good, caring and conscientious father"; "married"; "a professional"; "I am supportive, a giver, a contributor, a problem solver." When asked by the interviewer what kind of father he was, Alan noted "I wish I knew." Asked to describe his role as a husband, Alan reported "I'm a terrible husband; I can't meet my spouse's needs at this point."

When prompted to provide stories that would illustrate the self-descriptors he generated, Alan either authored sparsely detailed generic autobiographical memory narratives, or else he could not generate a related story at all. For example, when asked to provide a recent story that might illustrate how he viewed himself as intelligent, well educated, and self-aware, Alan described "recently working through a bit of a business deal . . . small stuff but taxing me nonetheless." Asked to generate a story that might illustrate himself as a contributor, Alan stated, "I like to give back good things," but he could not, at this point, generate a current story to illustrate this aspect of himself.

Although the self-descriptors Alan generated in his pretreatment NAI were generally positive, his descriptions of self in the context of the roles he plays in his life stood out as negative. For example, he noted that he cannot meet his wife's needs at the moment and is unsure of his role as a father. The pretreatment NAI appeared to offer Alan insight into his experience of depression in that what seemed to be important to his sense of self-worth was tied to the extent to which he was able to fulfill the roles or threads of the fabric of his self-identity. Alan's current lived experience appeared to fall outside of his dominant narrative or view of self as efficacious and successful. His inability to fulfill his roles or to find success in his profession had a negative effect on his appraisal of himself and his sense of self-worth. This working hypothesis of the potential factors affecting Alan's depression is further evidenced in his response to the second question of the NAI, which encourages the participant to reflect on how they feel others see them.

Question 2: How would someone who knows you really well describe you? The purpose of this question is to tap into the way clients perceive that others view them to assess further their view of self. This concept draws on the notion of the "looking glass effect" (Popper & Eccles, 1997), "just as we learn to see ourselves in a mirror, so the child becomes conscious of herself by seeing her reflection in the mirror of other people's consciousness of herself" (p. 110). This question illustrates our interest in exploring the possible implications of discrepancies between clients' view of themselves and how they feel others view them. In other words, "Do I see myself as I feel others see me or do I feel others see me differently than I see myself?"

When asked to describe how he felt significant others in his life viewed him, Alan said, "I have no idea—this is part of my journey. I don't know who knows me very well anymore." He reported that although he feels his wife generally viewed him as intelligent and hard working, he did not know how his children would describe him beyond "as their dad." Alan was unable at this juncture to generate stories that might illustrate how his wife or his children viewed him, indicating a disconnection between his view of self and his current lived experience.

Toward the end of the interview, Alan said that he felt the most valuable part of the interview was having the opportunity to describe how others saw him. He remarked, "and this ties into the roles of how any human being is seen." He said that some might see him "as a professional who could go out and be the knight of the 21st century, or they used to see me that way. So how people saw me reflects on how I see myself." Alan observed, "People describe themselves differently at different times in their lives. If one would take me 10 years ago, senior executive, corner office, phone ringing off the hook, people standing in line to speak with me." As an unemployed professional, Alan said that he found himself retreating from others, socializing less for fear that someone might ask what he does for a living.

Alan's responses to Question 2 of the protocol suggest that how he felt he might be perceived by others is incongruent with his sense of self; this disparity may be considered a key precipitant to his deteriorated mood and view of himself. Alan seemed to have a stable view of self, but because of his changing life circumstances, he began to question his self-efficacy. Alan indicated that how others view him determines how he views himself. Ten years ago, when he could claim success in his profession, he could socialize. Finding himself unemployed, he had retreated for fear of being criticized; his decreased sense of self-worth and self-efficacy were potentially cornerstones to his depression.

The final question of the NAI focuses clients on what might be their goals in therapy, providing information about the client's personal sense of what might emerge in treatment.

Question 3: If you could change something about who you are, what would you change? The purpose of this question is to gain an understanding, early in treatment, about what if anything clients hope to change about themselves. The responses to this question also provide a concrete pretreatment reference point to reflect on and from which to compare each participant's own conceptualization of change at therapy outcome.

In his pretreatment NAI, Alan reported that if he could change something externally, he would change his life circumstances: "I would like to be back in a situation where I belong and can contribute." Internally, he noted that he would like to be old enough and wise enough to understand what he was going through. He also said that he would like to laugh more.

Stage 2: The NAI Summary Sheet

In the second stage of the NAI procedure, the audiotaped pretreatment NAI is summarized and the key descriptors, generated by clients in relation to the three questions, are recorded. The purpose of the Narrative Interview Summary Sheet is to provide a brief yet comprehensive written record of the outcomes of the pretreatment NAI for the client to reflect on critically during the posttreatment open-ended inquiry interview. Figure 14.1 is the Narrative Interview Summary Sheet generated from Alan's pretreatment interview. Current variations regarding the application of the NAI protocol include exploring the potential benefits of allowing the client to hear the audiotaped pretreatment interview versus presenting the client with a written summary of the interview.

Stage 3: Posttherapy Narrative Assessment Inquiry

To facilitate a critical inquiry into the experiences of change, the final stage of the NAI protocol involves having clients read and judiciously reflect on their own Narrative Interview Summary Sheets within the context of a posttherapy interview. By encouraging clients early in the therapeutic process to reflect on what changes they may hope to address in therapy, a reference point will be established from which to compare clients' experience of change at posttherapy and again during follow-up interviews.

Multiple administrations of the NAI protocol can be conducted over time. For example, in the York II Depression Project (Greenberg & Angus, 1998), participants were called back for an interview 6 months after completing their treatment. In preparation for this interview, the participant's posttherapy therapy NAI was summarized on a Narrative Interview Summary Sheet. During the follow-up interview, the participant was presented both the pretreatment and posttreatment Narrative Interview Summary Sheets to stimulate a critical reflection on responses offering a further opportunity to evaluate potential changes in their views of self and self-in-relation to others, as well as potential changes in the

> **Client Code: Alan**
>
> *If you could change something about who you are, what would you change?*
>
> - externally: I would like to change my life circumstances
> - internally: I would like to be wise enough and old enough to understand what I'm going through
> - I would like to be back in a situation where I belong and can contribute
> - I have to learn to laugh more. I don't know how to have fun
>
> *How would you describe yourself?*
>
> - a very intelligent, well-educated individual with a very good sense of awareness of myself, in many aspects anyway
> - I am the father of three—a good, caring, and conscientious father
> - married, professional; I see myself as a terrible husband
> - I am a problem solver, a giver, a person who contributes to the welfare and benefit of others
>
> *How would someone who knows you very well describe you?*
>
> - I have no idea. That is part of my journey. I don't know who knows me well anymore
> - My wife would describe me as an intelligent, hard-working individual
> - My kids would describe me as their dad

Figure 14.1   A Sample of the Narrative Interview Summary Sheet

stories they generate to illustrate these views of self over time.

Alan's posttreatment responses to a traditional battery of quantitative outcome measures, conducted within the York II Depression Project and a diagnostic interview, indicated that he no longer met the criteria of Major Depressive Disorder according to the *Diagnostic and Statistical Manual of Mental Disorders* (*DSM-IV*; American Psychiatric Association, 1994). During his posttherapy interview, Alan reported that he had experienced a "profound change" and was experiencing a sense of "wholeness and self-identity." "Not that I didn't have identity before but it was a voyage of discovery, a good voyage of self-actualization. Am I changed? Yes, fundamentally." Alan pointed out that "the real crisis was having a loss of identity," and his therapy experience "was a journey of healing and self-awareness."

When reflecting with the interviewer on what he identified at pretreatment regarding areas he hoped would change, Alan said that he was in the process of changing his life circumstances:

> The real world is still the real world and I'm still facing a lot of career things that I faced 3 years ago when I fell off my cliff. The real world doesn't move just because you want to. But there is within myself a new confidence—a confidence in what I have to offer. That was what job hunting was all about. I was getting ostracism. The elimination processes that society has around us are very profound. That can destroy who you are as a person.

Reflecting on his responses to his pretreatment NAI descriptions of self on the Narrative Interview Summary Sheet (i.e., Stage 2 of the NAI), Alan commented, "They do not mean the same thing—I'm richer. I have shifted." Unlike the sparse and generic narratives he provided in the initial NAI (i.e., Stage 1 of the NAI), he proceeded to illustrate his self-descriptions with concrete, specific examples from his current lived experience. For example, Alan said that he felt that he had gained intelligence: "I have parts of myself that I subordinated and I am much more self-aware, to the point where I look back and say 'well gee, how could I have been so cut off from that part of myself?'" Alan went on to describe in detail how he reconnected with his alma mater and began working on a new project.

Alan said that at that juncture he could describe himself as a "better father," and he was able to provide a recent, detailed story involving his son that illustrated this change. He stated that he felt distressed about having called himself a "terrible husband" during his pretreatment NAI. He said, "I'm distressed that I said that. I saw myself as a failure. I remember that was terrible. I was unable to contribute to my other half." He said, "I don't think that I was ever a terrible husband."

Finally, responding to the interviewer's probe about how he feels others see him, Alan said:

> They're just beginning to know me because I'm now open. I had come to a point where I couldn't go out for dinner with anybody; don't dare let people know what I am doing or not doing—I was defined by my work. Now I can't think of too many people that I'm afraid of talking to—there's a richer side that I have to show.

Alan's responses during his posttreatment NAI and his ability to generate current stories appeared to illustrate a new congruence between his lived experience and his sense of self. This, in turn, seemed to contribute to a growing sense of his own self-worth. The threads of his identity, as represented by the stories he generated to describe himself, were now strongly woven, thus giving potential insight into the lessening of his depressive symptoms.

The Narrative Assessment Interview as an Opportunity for Meaning Making: The Case of Marion

Our application of the NAI has also suggested that the interview may provide the opportunity for clients to self-reflect, make meaning, and potentially reauthor their sense of self within the context of the interview itself. The following clinical case example illustrates the potential of the interview to provide clients with this opportunity.

Like Alan's case, Marion's case was deemed a good outcome example because she had achieved clinically significant change in terms of her level of depression at treatment termination. During her posttherapy NAI, Marion's first reaction to the presentation of her pretreatment Narrative Interview Summary Sheet suggested little change with regard to how she saw herself and how she felt others saw her. She said, "Yeah, that's me . . . I think that is what people see of me most of the time." An interesting shift happened when the interviewer probed Marion for stories illustrating others' view of her as "warm, loving, and caring." Marion commented, "I guess I have been bitchier lately. Nastier. Maybe it's all a part of me and my reflections and realizing that I shouldn't share that much of myself." At that point, the interviewer reminded Marion that at first she had indicated no change. The interviewer queried the differences in Marion's responses. Marion replied, "but that's what I am really like. You know, the thing is, this is what I'm really like. It's just that I am putting the brakes on all the time." It was evident that putting the brakes on referred to her spending money on gifts for her close friends and family, as she had generated a number of stories illustrating her generosity in her pretreatment NAI to illustrate herself as "very warm, loving, and caring."

During Marion's posttreatment NAI, she began to generate stories illustrating her continued practice of giving gifts, as well as her attempts to spend less on people. She said that her spending would have to be curtailed if she were to realize her dream to become a homeowner, and she said, "From now on this is me. I'm not buying anybody's love anymore." Marion said, "I think more of myself. My self-esteem will always fluctuate. I'm not going to pretend I am better now."

During this posttherapy inquiry interview, Marion and the interviewer began to further explore the meaning of her gift giving and its impact on her sense of self and self-esteem. It appeared almost as if embedded in her posttherapy NAI was the potential for relapse as she continued to struggle with "buying things," a behavior she considered "unhealthy" and one that negatively affected her self-respect, yet a behavior intimately connected to her sense of self as "loving and warm."

Unlike Alan's case, Marion's posttreatment NAI seemed to suggest a continuing struggle with her sense of self in relation to others. Like Alan, Marion seemed to continue to embrace her pretherapy self-descriptions, but somehow, she appeared to struggle with what these descriptions meant to her and how others saw her. The stories she generated to illustrate herself as "warm and caring" began to take on a different tone—one that somehow fueled the idea that she was buying people's love. Marion reiterated this struggle during her 6-month follow-up NAI. At that time, she was presented with her pretreatment Narrative Interview Summary Sheet, as well as a summary of her responses at posttreatment. During the 6-month follow-up interview, Marion said,

> I have ceased treating people incessantly with gifts, little things, chocolate, you know, except when there is an occasion, like my coming back from Europe . . . the old me would have bought them each a box each . . . I buy less and seem that I respect myself more for it. It is a bit of a struggle still, it's not um, second nature yet. I just love buying things.

Our analyses of the NAI material collected from Alan and Marion suggests that cases in which clients achieve equally significant levels of clinical change, in terms of their scores on standardized measures, may represent contrasting patterns of narrative change. For Alan, a fragmented and largely negative self-narrative woven with stories of failure had shifted into coherent and vivid autobiographical narratives to support a narrative of self as potent and in control. For Marion, it appeared as though much useful therapeutic work had been done to allow her to reflect on the self-limiting stories she told about herself and to identify an alternative, reauthored way of accounting for relationships. However, Marion's new macronarrative was not firmly embedded in her lived experience, indicating a sense of fragility and signaling the potential benefit of further therapeutic work. For example, preliminary analyses of the NAI protocols conducted as part of an ongoing treatment trial for depression appear to indicate that those clients who were able to generate stories from their current lived experience to illustrate their shifting views of self seemed less likely to indicate a relapse at follow-up—perhaps suggesting they have consolidated these shifts and have grounded them in their personal narrative, regaining a congruency between their sense of self and their current lived experience.

FUTURE DIRECTIONS FOR PSYCHOTHERAPY RESEARCH AND PRACTICE

Just as we have proposed the significance of clients grounding their experience in their personal self or selves, so, too, do we emphasize the benefits of exploring our understanding of human meaningmaking/construction and therapeutic change by shifting from the theoretical propositions of change to a grounding of these propositions in the data we gather. The NAI was developed according to this strategy and is presented as an instrument stemming from a narrative perspective to augment our understanding of client change in psychotherapy.

In a presentation at the Society of Psychotherapy Research, John McLeod (2000) reminded his audience that when we are conducting psychotherapy outcome studies, we are essentially asking the question: What "came out" of the process of therapy for the client? Widely used outcome measures, for example, the Beck Depression Inventory (Beck, 1972) and the Symptom Check List-90 (Derogitis, Rickels, & Roch, 1976), are convenient numerical indices of change regarding distressing symptomology. These quantitative measures provide researchers with valuable information, allowing us to ask: Did the therapy help the client to feel less depressed? What quantitative outcome measures do not provide, however, is a rich picture of how the therapy process might have affected the client's unique world of interpersonal relationships and view of self as mediated through, and by, significant others. The investigation and exploration of the potential impact of therapy on the client's own personal world, on his or her day-to-day functioning, is as important as the development and administration of nomothetic indices of change.

The NAI protocol is a practical assessment tool for psychotherapists, clinicians, and researchers. For example, the protocol has recently been used in an industrial/organizational setting to assess the impact of a leadership training program on employees' sense of self and self-in-relation to their coworkers. According to McCollum (personal communication, November 2002), preliminary analyses of the NAI protocols suggest that participants in a leadership training program reported a shift in how they thought other employees perceived them in the organization. The leadership trainees felt that they were more likely to be seen as emerging leaders in the organization. A similar shift was noted in the trainees' own views of themselves, such that they were also more likely to see themselves as assuming future leadership roles in their organization. It appears that the NAI holds some promise as an effective strategy for the assessment of organizational identity and change in organizations.

The NAI protocol is straightforward in its application and provides clinicians and researchers with a quick baseline evaluation of client-generated therapeutic goals, which can be used later in therapy for the evaluation of therapeutic progress. Most important, by creating a context for focused self-reflection on experiences of difference and change, the NAI protocol functions as an effective therapeutic intervention. By stimulating clients to provide meaningful accounts of experiences of shifts or changes in their perspectives on self and others—and to ground those new views of self in storied representations of lived experiences—the NAI contributes to the identification of what Michael White terms "unique outcome stories" and the inception of new plot lines for clients' life narratives. In addition, as Bruner (1986) suggests, it is the fundamental integration of narrative action (actions and events in the world) with the landscape of consciousness (personal meanings, emotions, and views of self and others) that is the axis of personal identity formation and, we would argue in therapy, the fundamental ground from which experiences of personal change and new identity construction emerges.

REFERENCES

American Psychiatric Association. (1994). *Diagnostic and statistical manual of mental disorders* (4th ed.). Washington, DC: Author.

Angus, L., & Bowes-Bouffard, B. (2002). "No lo entiendo": La busqueda de sentido emocional y coherencia personalante una perdida traumatica durante la infancia. *Revista Psicoterapia, 12*(49), 25-46.

Angus, L., & Hardtke, K. K. (1994). Narrative processes in psychotherapy. *Canadian Psychology, 35*(2), 190-203.

Angus, L., Hardtke, K. K., & Levitt, H. (1996). *An expanded rating manual for the narrative processes coding manual.* Unpublished manuscript, Department of Psychology, York University, Toronto, Canada, M3J 1P3.

Angus, L., Levitt, H., & Hardtke, K. K. (1999). The narrative processes coding system: Research applications and implications for psychotherapy practice. *Journal of Clinical Psychology, 55*(10), 1255-1270.

Angus, L., & Rennie, D. (1989). Envisioning the representational world: Metaphoric expression in psychotherapy relationships. *Psychotherapy, 26,* 372-379.

Balamoutsou, S. (2003). *Writing task assignment.* Unpublished manuscript, University of Keele, UK.

Baumeister, R. F., & Newman, L. S. (1994). How stories make sense of personal experiences: Motives that shape autobiographical narratives. *Personality and Social Psychology Bulletin, 20*(6), 676-690.

Beck, A. (1972). Measuring depression: The depression inventory. In T. A. Williams, M. M. Katz, & J. A. Shield (Eds.), *Recent advances in the psychobiology of the depressive illness.* Washington, DC: U.S. Government Printing Office.

Book, H. (2003). The CCRT approach to working with patient narratives in psychodynamic psychotherapy. In L. Angus & J. McLeod (Eds.), *The handbook of narrative and psychotherapy* (pp. 71-85). Thousand Oaks, CA: Sage.

Bruner, J. S. (1986). *Actual minds, possible worlds.* Cambridge, MA: Harvard University Press.

Derogitis, L. R., Rickels, K., & Roch, A. F. (1976). The SCL-90 and the MMPI: A step in the validation of a new self-report scale. *British Journal of Psychiatry, 128,* 280-289.

Gergen, K. J., & Gergen, M. M. (1983). Narratives of self. In K. J. Gergen & M. M. Gergen (Eds.), *Historical social psychology.* Hillsdale, NJ: Lawrence Erlbaum.

Goldman, R., Greenberg, L., & Angus, L. (2003). Experiential therapy for depression: Comparing the effectiveness of process-experiential and client-centered therapy approaches. Manuscript under review.

Gonçalves, O. F., Korman, Y., & Angus, L. (2000). Constructing psychopathology from a cognitive narrative perspective. In R. A. Neimeyer & J. D. Raskin (Eds.), *Constructions of disorder: Meaning-making frameworks for psychotherapy* (pp. 265-284). Washington, DC: American Psychological Association.

Gonçalves, O. F., & Machado, P. P (1999). Cognitive narrative psychotherapy: Research foundations. *Journal of Clinical Psychology, 55*(10), 1179-1191.

Gonçalves, O. F., Machado, P. P., Korman, Y., & Angus, L. (2002). Assessing psychopathology: A narrative approach. In L. E. Beutler & M. L. Malik (Eds.), *Rethinking the DSM: A psychological perspective* (pp. 149-176). Washington, DC: American Psychological Association.

Greenberg, L. S., & Angus, L. (1998). *Examining the relationship between specific treatment factors and sustained change in psychotherapeutic treatment of depression.* Ontario Mental Health Foundation Major Research Grant.

Greenberg, L. S., & Pascual-Leone, J. (1995). A dialectical constructivist approach to experiential change. In R. A. Neimeyer & M. J. Mahoney (Eds.), *Constructivism in psychotherapy* (pp. 168-192). Washington, DC: American Psychological Association.

Greenberg, L. S., Watson, J. C, & Goldman, R. (1998). Process-experiential therapy of depression. In L. S. Greenberg & J. C. Watson (Eds.), *Handbook of experiential psychotherapy* (pp. 227-248). New York: Guilford.

Hardtke, K. K. (1996a). *Characterizing therapy focus and exploring client process: Investigating therapeutic modalities from a narrative approach.* Unpublished master's thesis, York University, Toronto, Canada.

Hardtke, K. K. (1996b, June). *Narrative processes in successful psychotherapy.* Paper presented at the meeting of the Society for Psychotherapy Research International Conference, Como, Italy.

Hardtke, K. K., & Angus, L. (1998). *The Narrative Assessment Interview.* Unpublished manuscript, Department of Psychology, York University, Toronto, Canada, M3J 1P3.

Hardtke, K. K., Levitt, H., & Angus, L. (in press). Investigating narrative processes in psychotherapy discourse: The Narrative Processes Coding System. *Zeitschrift fuer Qualitative Bildungs-, Beratungs- und Sozialforschung.*

Howard, G. S. (1991). Culture tales: A narrative approach to thinking, cross-cultural psychology, and psychotherapy. *American Psychologist, 46,* 187-197.

Kagan, N. (1975). Influencing human interaction: Eleven years with IPR. *Canadian Counsellor, 9*(2), 74-97.

Levitt, H., & Rennie, D. L. (2003). Narrative activity: Clients' and therapists' intentions in the process of narration in psychotherapy. In L. Angus & J. McLeod (Eds.), *The handbook of narrative and psychotherapy* (pp. 299-313). Thousand Oaks, CA: Sage.

Lewin, J. (2001). *Both sides of the coin.* Unpublished master's thesis, York University, Toronto, Canada.

Lewin, J., & Hardtke K. K. (2000, June). *The other outcome: An investigation of narrative processes in poor outcome brief experiential psychotherapy.* Paper presented at the meeting for the Society of Psychotherapy Research, Chicago.

Luborsky, L., Barber, J. P., & Diguer, L. (1992). The meanings of narrative told during psychotherapy: The fruits of a new observational unit. *Psychotherapy Research, 2*(4), 277-290.

Luborsky, L., & Crits-Cristoph, P. (1990). *Understanding transference: The CCRT method.* New York: Basic Books.

Luborsky, L., Popp, C., Luborsky, E., & Mark, D. (1995). The core conflictual relationship theme. *Psychotherapy Research, 4* (3&4), 172-183.

McAdams, D. P. (1993). *The stories we live by: Personal myths and the making of the self.* New York: William Morrow.

McAdams, D. P., Diamond, A., de St. Aubin, E., & Mansfield, E. (1997). Stories of commitment: The psychosocial construction of generative lives. *Journal of Personality and Social Psychology, 72*(3), 678-694.

McLeod, J. (2000, June). *Qualitative outcome research in psychotherapy: Issues and methods.* Paper presented at the meeting for the Society of Psychotherapy Research, Chicago.

McLeod, J., & Balamoutsou, S. (1996). Representing narrative process in therapy: Qualitative analysis of a single case. *Counselling Psychology Quarterly, 9*(1), 61-76.

Neimeyer, R. A. (1994). The role of client-generated narratives in psychotherapy. *Journal of Constructivist Psychology, 7,* 229-242.

Neimeyer. R. A., & Mahoney, M. J. (Eds.). (1995). *Constructivism in psychotherapy.* Washington, DC: American Psychological Association.

Polkinghorne, D. (1988). *Narrative knowing and the human sciences.* Albany: State University of New York Press.

Popper, K. R., & Eccles, J. C. (1997). *The self and its brain.* New York: Springer.

Rennie, D. L. (1994). Storytelling in psychotherapy: The client's subjective experience. *Psychotherapy, 31*(2), 234-243.

Rennie, D. L., & Toukmanian, S. G. (1992). *Psychotherapy process research: Paradigmatic and narrative approaches.* Newbury Park, CA: Sage.

Sarbin, T. (1986). *Narrative psychology: The storied nature of human conduct.* New York: Praeger.

Singer, J. A., & Blagov, P. S. (in press). The integrative function of narrative processing: Autobiographical memory, self-defining memories, and the life-story of identity. In D. R. Beike, J. M. Lampinen, & D. A. Behrend (Eds.), *The self and memory.* New York: The Psychology Press.

Spence, D. (1982). *Narrative truth and historical truth: Meaning and interpretation in psychoanalysis.* New York: Norton.

White, M. (2001). Folk psychology and narrative practice. *Dulwich Centre Journal, 2.* Adelaide, South Australia.

White, M., & Epston, D. (1990). *Narrative means to therapeutic ends.* New York: Norton.

CHAPTER 15

Disorganized Narratives
The Psychological Condition and Its Treatment

GIANCARLO DIMAGGIO

ANTONIO SEMERARI

OVERVIEW

Within the Training School for Cognitive Psychotherapy (*Italian Associazione di Psicologia Cognitiva* or APC), the *Terzo Centro di Psicoterapia Cognitiva* in Rome has been concentrating on the study of the therapeutic process with seriously ill patients, in particular those suffering from personality disorders.

Over the course of 10 years of working together, our clinical practice and empirical research has been aimed in three directions:

1. We analyze patients' narratives and the dialogical component in them (Bruner, 1990; Dimaggio, Salvatore, Azzara, & Catania, 2003; Dimaggio & Semerari, 2001; Gonçalves, 1995; Hermans, 1996; Hermans & Kempen, 1993; Neimeyer, 2000; Salvatore, Dimaggio, & Semerari, 2003).

2. We analyze alterations in metacognitive and metarepresentative skills. We became interested in this area of interest when we observed that patients suffering from personality disorders systematically fail to identify their own mental states correctly, find the right psychological motive for their actions, or formulate suitable hypotheses on the mental functioning of others. They are not therefore good *folk psychologists*.

As a result, clinicians who assume that patients are able, with the simple stimulus of their therapist's questions, to identify their own mental states and to discuss them fail

---

AUTHORS' NOTE: Correspondence regarding this chapter should be sent to Giancarlo Dimaggio, Terzo Centro di Psicoterapia Cognitiva, Via Ravenna 9/c, 00161Rome, Italy. The writing of this chapter has been supported by the University of Nijmegen, The Netherlands, Faculty of Social Sciences.

systematically with patients with personality disorders, as the latter's ability to do this is hampered.

There is an abundance of empirical data and a great deal of theoretical speculation—both in the area called theory of mind (Baron-Cohen, Leslie, & Frith, 1985; Leslie, 1987) and in the analysis of autistic and schizophrenic patients (Baron-Cohen, 1995; Frith, 1992)—supporting the hypothesis that there are modules for the processing of data regarding intentional states and that in some disorders these modules are dysfunctional. Starting out from this basis, we noted that the psychological skills of patients suffering from personality disorders are hampered in various ways, with serious consequences for their relationships and for the outcome of any therapy.

As an example, if patients are not aware of feeling fragile, they cannot tackle this, ask for help, or involve others in overcoming it. Their therapists, in not being able to perceive the feeling because it is not being expressed, do not respond in an empathetic manner. Such problems are likely to make a therapeutic relationship difficult. We have, therefore, found ourselves in an area of study involving authors of various schools, all of them interested in the way in which patients manage (or not) to represent to themselves their own mental states and those of others and to organize coherent and comprehensible narratives from this information (Fonagy & Target, 1996; Liotti & Intrecciagli, 1998; Stiles, Meshot, Anderson, & Sloan, 1992).

We have, therefore, developed a model that (a) describes the deficits in metacognitive skills that we have been able to observe in our clinic; (b) permits the testing of the hypothesis that the various personality disorders are characterized by different failures in these skills—with this in mind, we have created the Metacognition Assessment Scale (Semerari et al., in press); and (c) permits patients with these disorders to be treated successfully (Semerari, 1999).

3. We create psychopathology and psychotherapy models for the personality disorders occurring most frequently in our clinic, showing how the contents and form of the patients' narratives, the profile of their metacognitive dysfunctions, and their interpersonal cycles interact with one another to cause vicious circles that keep their disorders alive.

What is specifically "narrative" about our approach is that we have paid particular attention to structural alterations in patients' narratives, noting that patients can suffer not only on account of the subject matter of their discourse but also because of the way in which it is organized and put together. Stories act as a map of the world. If this map is inadequate, poor, unstable, or chaotic, patients feel paralyzed and do not manage to tell others about their problems; in fact, their narrative and relational style makes their life and their symptoms worse and hampers their ability to ask for help. To sum up, some patients' narratives are poor in content while those of others are disorganized.

In this chapter, we shall concentrate on disorganized narratives, describing their phenomenology, the various forms that they take, the criteria to be used for identifying them in a text, the questions involved in treating them, the way that patient/therapist dialogue gets influenced if they are present, and the strategy to be adopted for tackling them.

THE FUNCTIONS OF NARRATIVE ORGANIZATION

To find their way among the various forms that the future can take, individuals require tools to provide a reliable guide to their actions in the world of relationships. They need to be quick at calculating which scenario to inhabit, among the many different ones available, carried along on a wave of reasonable hope that it is the best choice. Johnson-Laird (1983) maintains that to be effective at making decisions when pressed for time, we use not only the tools of logic but also mental models, three-dimensional portraits of scenes in which we foresee the consequences of our actions. In the opinion of Bruner (1986, 1990), narrative is a form of reasoning that combines significant quantities of information and puts it into structures, that is, stories, that we can quickly lay our hands on to solve identity problems and to use as a guide through the ups and downs of life.

We also supply a narrative structure to phenomena that are not inherently "storied" by attributing cause and effect sequences and intentional actions to constructions of personal experiences (Gonçalves, Korman, & Angus, 2000; Hermans, 1996; Michotte, 1946). This allows us to make order out of the sensorial, inner chaos in which we find ourselves enveloped, to remember experiences, and to communicate them to others (Kelly, 1955; Mandler, 1984; Neimeyer, 2000).

Narrative is not precise like a syllogism; it provides explanations that appear plausible although not true, and in the complex world of social interactions, it performs a mapping function well. Damasio (1994) has noted how mental images marked by pleasant or unpleasant emotions are the main decision-making engine in human beings. Scenes that feature emotionally pleasant images indicate preferred choices, whereas unpleasant images indicate evolutions of the future to be avoided. Conjuring up a clear blue sea with the sun caressing her skin can make a young woman book a holiday by the Sicilian sea, while the memory of his mother telling him off can stimulate a student to study for an exam. Damasio has shown that subjects with neurological damage—those who have lost the ability to emotionally mark images because the circuits connecting the emotional valence to visual images and the propositional reasoning zones are broken—become social idiots. Without an emotionally marked image to put an end to the cost/benefit evaluation, such people may spend days on end calculating whether it is better to go the supermarket on Tuesday or Thursday.

Humans live in a complex world. If they are to adapt to their environment, achieve their desires, and avoid unhappiness, they need a wide range of self-in-the-world representations to guide them in their relationships with others—whether in a sentimental, friendly, or work-related context—and to teach them how to trust a colleague, court a young lady, or calm down a child. Having a wide number of self-in-the-world representations is an indispensable quality requiring organization, so that a subject can set up action hierarchies, giving priority to the activation of one mental model as opposed to another.

In important relationships, in particular, this wide range of self-in-the-world representations is emotionally charged. Are the partners we have before us ready to listen to us, or are their intentions to subjugate us as if we were slaves? Are they asking for help or aiming to deceive or to take advantage of us? Starting with the research contributions of Bowlby (1969/1982; Stern, 1985), it has been observed that we build multiple narratives representing our interactions with caregivers, and these narratives are filed using different representational codes. For example, a young girl may describe her relationship with her mother as one in which her mother is kind and only leaves her child alone because she deserves punishment, while, at the same time, feeling a profound rage toward an unfair mother who is experienced as being cruel and emotionally unavailable.

To be able to adapt, an individual needs to have a wide range of models or narrative scenarios representing interactions of self in relation to others. The absence of these relationship narratives prevents an individual from adeptly moving about, exploring, and interacting with others (Dimaggio et al., in press). But to be adaptive, this multiplicity of relationship scenarios—what we call narrative complexity—needs to be internally organized. A set of self-narratives needs to meet a set of criteria (see below) to have an adaptive function. Some of these criteria come from work done by Grice (1975), who established the principles (quality, quantity, manner, and relevance) required for a conversation to be effective.

With this starting point, we then considered the question in a functional sense: What are the features of the type of narrative individuals need to move around in the world and make their discourses comprehensible for a clinician and others who want to help or cooperate with them? On this question, our thinking was guided by the work by Taylor, Bagby, and Parker (1997) on alexithymia, by Stiles (Stiles et al., 1992) on the assimilation of problematical experience, by Kernberg (1975) on splitting, by Neimeyer (2000) on narrative disruptions, and by studies performed on theory of mind and the ability of human beings to understand others' mental states (Baron-Cohen et al., 1985; Leslie, 1987; Sperber, 2000; Stich & Nichols, 1998).

Other sources for the list of criteria were the transcripts of sessions with patients suffering from personality disorders and excerpts from their diaries. Each time we found ourselves having difficulty in understanding a text, we would systematically ask ourselves what the obstacle was. We then drew up the following list of criteria. A conscious representation needs to:

1. fit the context
2. describe accurately a subject's inner state
3. describe the interaction that is under way in an articulated and "realistic" manner, and therefore provide a report, one that is reliable or at least open to potential confutations from experience, of another's intentions and of the interaction that is being created
4. be kept separate from other narratives; there is a limit to the number of brackets, parentheses, and digressions that we can insert into a story without getting confused and confusing the person to whom we are speaking
5. be placed in the right mental sphere as a dream, an imagined fantasy, or an actual occurrence
6. describe the inner dialogue between the characters entering on stage in such a way that the relationship between them is comprehensible (Hermans, 1996; Hermans & Kempen, 1993) and that each aspect of the self taking the floor has a distinct voice and finds someone willing to listen.

When these criteria are not achieved, we are in the land of disorganized narratives (Dimaggio & Semerari, 2001).

It is possible to use these criteria as a guide in research into the psychotherapy process as well. With our colleagues at the Terzo Centro[1] we have, for example, developed a tool for the testing of Horowitz's (1987) theory about distinct and identifiable states of mind in patients' narratives: the Grid of Problematic States (Semerari et al., 2003). With this tool, it is possible to evaluate whether the elements in a discourse (thought themes and emotions) tend to join together in stable clusters or to move in a chaotic, unstable, and fragmented manner.

Furthermore, the Metacognition Assessment Scale includes an item termed *integration* that concerns a patient's ability to put together a discourse integrating the various elements in a coherent and comprehensible manner. In the first cases we analyzed of patients with personality disorders, we were able to observe how a narcissistic patient demonstrated good integrative skills whereas a borderline patient did not (Semerari et al., in press).

We have also set up a procedure whereby patients undergoing psychotherapy are given the task of keeping a diary with different topics. The instructions require patients, first, to select the topics they want to write about and then to put together a text. In this way, the reviewers are able to assess how much the topic written about corresponds with the intended chosen topic. If there is no topic correspondence (the assessment operation requires a minimal degree of inference), we are again in the area of disorganization. The texts are also assessed for other aspects of consistency: for example, the presence of clear time-space links (Salvatore, Dimaggio, Azzara, Catania, & Hermans, 2000; Dimaggio et al., 2003).

A number of the features of disorganized narratives have been extensively studied in other fields. For example, there is substantial documentation about the deficit in distinguishing between fantasy and reality in obsessive-compulsive patients (the thought/action fusion phenomenon; Salkovskis, 1989). Similarly, research on attachment using the Adult Attachment Interview (which, in a way similar to our work, originates from an evaluation of how much a text complies with Grice's criteria), a pattern defined as disorganized, in which developmental memories are recalled in a chaotic, confused, fragmentary, and contradictory manner (Main, 1991), is well documented.

DISORGANIZED NARRATIVES

The patients we have in psychotherapy often do not adhere to these criteria, relating stories that are confused, disordered, and incomprehensible, characterized by thought themes and emotions that get mixed together without any apparent sense. Patients may provide descriptions of the same character that are intense and at the same time opposite and mutually incompatible, or they may open an infinite number of parentheses without ever closing them, while hundreds of characters come onto the stage competing with each other for the floor (Dimaggio & Semerari, 2001; Salvatore et al., 2003). A therapist in such cases may end up feeling stunned, confused, frightened, or impotent.

A number of clinicians have described disorganized narratives. For instance, Rasmussen and Angus (1997) noted that, when comparing the within-session stories of three borderline patients with those of three patients who did not meet the criteria for borderline personality disorder, the narratives told by borderline clients were experienced as significantly more disorganized by their therapists than those of the non-borderline clients.

In general, however, psychotherapists and clinicians have focused on certain aspects of patient narrative disorganization while neglecting other aspects that, in our opinion, ought to be identified and tackled to make any treatment more effective. The main aspect of narrative deficit highlighted in the clinical practice and research literature is the so-called integration deficit, in which, even if patients have a wide range of representations of the self-other relationship at their disposal, they are unable to account for the rapid and difficult-to-understand transitions that occur when passing from one mental scenario to another. An author who has highlighted this deficit is Kernberg (1975). In his opinion, borderline patients' self-narratives are organized in accordance with self-representations that are dichotomous, contrary to each other, incompatible, and loaded with extreme judgments—all good or all bad—toward the self and significant others. Such patients swing between one type of self-representation and the other and never manage to integrate them.

Liotti (1995) maintains that there are three typical protagonist roles in the narratives of borderline or dissociative subjects: victim, all-powerful savior, and persecutor. In a personal narrative, the self and/or the other can assume, almost at the same time, each one of these roles. Accordingly, when borderline patients enter into affective relationships with others, they can feel they are victims of potential abuse; invert the roles by persecuting another, who then acts as the victim; or else feel that the participants in the relationship are threatened by some hidden persecutor. Sadly, they do not realize that they are feeling threatened by the same person to whom they were just looking to for protection.

Ryle (1997; Golynkina & Ryle, 1999) provides a comprehensive portrait of dissociation in borderline patients and identifies a number of typical self states: *ideal*, in which self and others have relationships of the type, "I trust others" "others admire me"; *abuser rage*, involving schemas of the type, "I want to hurt others," "I am overwhelmed with feelings"; *powerless victim*, which is complementary to the previous state; *angry victim*, in which subjects rebel against abuses of their condition as powerless victim; and *coping state* or *zombie state*, which have the same quality: subjects are trying to master their suffering and frequently cut themselves off from their feelings. Ryle, like Liotti, stresses the dissociation between the various self states.

In fact, by adopting a perspective in which the self is multifaceted (Horowitz, 1987; Markus & Nurius, 1986) and in which a series of characters or voices embody different aspects of a personality (Hermans, 1997, 2001a, 2001b; McAdams, 1995; Stiles, 1999; Stiles, Osatuke, Glick, & Mackay, 2002), we are able to see how the problem in such patients is not only the presence of particular characters but also the crowding together of a multiplicity of voices, struggling to get heard, drowning each other out, competing with each other (Lysaker, Lysaker, & Lysaker, 2001), and subjecting a listener to an unintelligible whir. However, among these, the ones described respectively by Kernberg and Liotti—that is to say, the extreme representations (good/bad) and those of victims, persecutors, and all-powerful saviors—are particularly important clinically.

Fonagy and Target (1996), following Winnicott (1965) and picking up the distinction made by Leslie (1987) between primary (based on reality) and disconnected (based on fantasy) representations, note a deficit in distinguishing between fantasy and reality in borderline patients. The latter tend to draw up imaginary versions of interactions (e.g., "my partner *seems* like a witch to me") and then use them as if they were primary representations ("my partner *is* a witch, and I will deal with her accordingly"). This deficit is not specific to borderline patients; on the contrary, it is very widespread among those with mental disorders. Similarly, phobic subjects consider their fantasies about catastrophes to be real (Gardner, Mancini, & Semerari, 1987), and obsessive patients exhibit a thought/action fusion phenomenon (Salkovskis, 1989).

In addition to these two deficits, Dimaggio and Semerari (2001) point out two other forms of disorganization in narratives: (a) basic integration deficit and (b) overproduction of narratives with hierarchy deficit. A basic integration deficit is present when there is an inconsistency between the meaning of the text being communicated, the type of physical arousal experienced, facial expressions, and posture. Patients might describe having been raped with a smile, with an incongruously relaxed body and an eerie gleam in their eyes. With the overproduction of narratives with organizational deficit, hundreds of stories and characters, all interlinked with each other, crowd onto the stage and drown each other out, with the narrator unable to decide which is the main theme, where the story ends, and in what scenario a patient really wants to get a listener involved. There has been an identical description of this crowding together of voices without any hierarchy in schizophrenic patients (Lysaker & Lysaker, 2002; Lysaker, Wickett, Wilke, & Lysaker, in press).

The Effects of Narrative Disorganization

As we have seen, clinicians have described various ways in which the phenomena linked to disorganized narratives manifest themselves in the therapeutic discourse, ranging from conflicting representations of nonintegrated self-other interactions, to narrative descriptions that are disconnected from the affective state of the patient, to an overwhelming multiplicity of characters and emotionally charged scenarios that coexist without any sense of priority or order of importance.

What is common to these various forms of narrative disorganization? The authors' answer is of a functionalist type. We believe that the impact of all of these different types of narrative disorganization is an inability to prioritize present actions on the basis of past narrative scenarios. Thanks to the integrative and organizational qualities of narratives, mentally complex individuals, possessing a multiplicity of goals and emotions, are able to maintain a certain level of consistency in their behavior. We may, at certain moments, feel furious with the person whom we usually love, but if there is not a memory that is common to the two states and an integrative point of view, our behavior will swing back and forth in opposite directions, each canceling the other out. If, moreover, the representation that we make to ourselves is of multiple and contradictory roles in relationships with others, without a superordinate point of view determining which of these is to predominate, the resulting behavior will be just as chaotic and disorganized.

To succeed in organizing narratives with a view to behaving consistently, we also need suitable metacognitive skills, that is, those that let us reason in terms of intentionality, identify the mental states of ourselves and other individuals, and achieve an adequate mastery of any problematical mental states (Flavell, Miller, & Miller, 1993; Semerari, 1999; Semerari et al., in press; Wells & Purdon, 1999). Being able to represent both our own mental state in a particular narrative scenario, the effects that the course of events will have on this state, and the impact on others provides crucial information for deciding what action to take and for maintaining a particular course, notwithstanding fluctuations in desires and fears.

The classic example of this link between organization of narratives, metacognitive skills, and an effective choice of action is the episode of Ulysses with the Sirens. The hero is aware that he has two potentially incompatible desires: to listen to their song and to return to his home country. He portrays to himself the scene in which he is under the effect of the singing, describing to himself the consequences of the events on his mental states diachronically. Under the effect of the singing, Ulysses' desire for his home country will disappear, and he will be overcome by the impetuous need to get to the divine creatures, thus putting his life at risk. However, the self-narrative continues, and Ulysses foresees a variation in mental state. Away from the influence of the singing, he can see his desire to return home coming back to him, and his usual "I" is again master of his action choices. The action emerges from the integration of these scenes. He has himself tied to the mast and gives appropriate instructions to his comrades; he thus manages to hear the singing while at the same time not deflecting his ship from the way home.

Drawing from the myth of Ulysses, we are suggesting that successfully treating narrative disorganization involves helping patients to maintain courses of action that are consistent with their long-term goals and to set their lives in a stable direction. The focus of this chapter will now turn to the treatment of narrative disorganization in psychotherapy.

IMPLICATIONS FOR PSYCHOTHERAPY

Patients suffering from disorganized narratives present unique challenges for clinicians undertaking treatment interventions. A clinician needs to be attentive not only to dialogue contents and forms but also to the structure of patients' discourse. Patients with an overproduction of narratives will suffer not only because they feel intense and painful emotions, in the context of life themes in which they break down, get abandoned, or are spiritless and purposeless, but also because they are prevented by their narrative style from planning actions, selecting what to give priority and what desires to let go of. They are unable to make use of any past narratives that fit the current relational context and thus have no previous scenarios to guide them. Listeners find themselves in the midst of chaos, and this results in therapists not being able to provide a focus to treatment, program a strategy, or attune themselves empathically to their patients.

The overproduction of narratives also means that treatment should be undertaken in two stages. First, therapists will need to attend to master their own sensations of inner chaos evoked by the interactions with such patients. Next, the treatment should be directed at patients with a view to stimulating the building of a metacognitive point of view (Semerari, 1999; Semerari et al., in press) or an Observing-I position (Cooper, 2003; Dimaggio et al., 2003; Hermans, 2001a, 2003; Leiman & Stiles, 2001), by which part of the self gains the ability to construct a narrative that is self-reflective, provides the relationships between the other characters in a subject's inner dialogue with meaning, and integrates any contrasting, incompatible, or dissociated aspects in a story (Angus, Levitt, & Hardtke 1999; Angus, Lewin, & Hardtke, 2001; Fonagy & Target, 1997; Ryle, 1997).

Interpersonal Cycle in Disorganized Narratives

A problematic relational style is not merely a reflection of past experiences. It is also a part of the present, in that it is continuously creating the conditions for self-perpetuating. The way in which negative relational expectations play the role of self-fulfilling prophecies has been defined as a *cognitive interpersonal cycle* (Safran, 1984; Safran & Segal, 1990; Safran & Muran, 2000): a process in which negative expectations encourage the type of behavior that induces the other into acting in a way that confirms such expectations. When such cycles get activated during therapy, therapists will note that they feel inclined to act in an antitherapeutic manner. It is not simply specific relational beliefs—"he is hostile to me" or "she will despise me"—that activate these cycles. Forms of mental functioning, like disorganized storytelling, can also push another into mental states or behavior that aggravates the problem through an interpersonal process.

Given that the first guiding principle of any therapy should be not to cause further harm, therapists need, in treating disorganized storytelling, to start by controlling those inevitable moments in which they feel drawn toward increasing the chaos existing in the relationship. The best way to do this is to identify those inner phenomena that signal that they have entered a chaotic interpersonal cycle. In less extreme forms, therapists find themselves feeling confused about what to focus treatment on. There may be many different and emotionally significant themes, but therapists are unable to identify an order of importance or a reason for probing first into this one or that one. In this condition, they may catch themselves no longer listening and asking questions merely with a view to using up the time. A conversation thus becomes of a casual nature, and this keeps the patient's narratives fragmented. Therapists may also allow themselves to be drawn along by a patient's discourse and follow along with the patient, noting each change of voice, and this also stokes the mutual confusion. In the end, to stop their own confusion, therapists may try to impose some order forcibly by constantly turning the patient back to a single topic. In this case, the patient's participation in the conversation is restricted to the sole topic permitted by the therapist but at the same time, the patient's mind is full of all the other scenes that are just as pressing emotionally but are not expressed in the relationship. The result is a dissociated therapy where the content of the conversation and a patient's inner states follow different paths.

When a patient's emotional suffering is at its most intense, this chaotic cycle can lead to a sense of frightening urgency: Patients experience intense distress, feel the need for something that will soothe it, and try in a disorderly manner to act in ways that are often harmful to both themselves and the therapy. In such instances, therapists may feel themselves participating in both the sense of urgency and the chaotic scenarios. They portray the patient, and with some reason, as being out of control and imagine catastrophic scenarios for the latter and for themselves. Therapists may feel frightened and wish they had never started that therapy, think about "holding" measures, such as drugs, hospitalization, or strict calls to keep to the therapeutic contract, in a manner that is impulsive and not based on an accurate analysis of the case or the situation. Therapists may behave as if dominated one moment by a tyrannical personality and the next by a frightened one. If acted out, such a trend stimulates the patient's fright and feeling of being out of control.

In the opinion of Safran and Segal (1990), escaping from these problematic cycles requires inner discipline. This well-chosen expression stresses how the goal of such operations is to modify how therapists would naturally be inclined to act. Inner discipline involves two stages of action. Initially, therapists need to focus on their inner state and try to identify the various components distinguishing their own experiences and the characters that populate them vis-à-vis the characters embodied by the patient.

At the second stage, therapists should focus on the patient's experience and try to perceive where there are features complementary or similar to their own experience. In the case of the interpersonal cycles, when they have carried out their "inner discipline" operations, therapists become aware that they are sharing in the patient's basic problem: that of not being able to put the many different representations of self-with-other in order. From an interpersonal point of view, with this knowledge, it becomes possible to overcome the inclination to act in a countertherapeutic way and instead to establish a therapeutic alliance that is cooperative and effective for sorting out common problems. From a technical point of view, the next section will show how these strategies can be applied to advantage during therapy.

Sharing, Metacognition, and Mastery

Knowing that they have a problem that is shared in part with the patient, therapists are

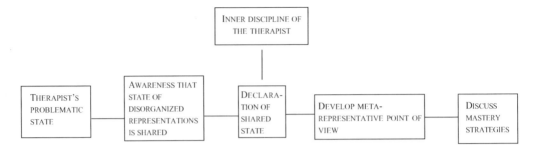

Figure 15.1 Schema of Therapist's Intervention

in a favorable position for two reasons. First, declaring this makes it easier to develop a meta-reflective dialogue on the mutual problem—in this case, the disregulation of narrative scenarios. Second, when a patient has reached an Observing-I position and achieved a superordinate point of view about the problem by mastering his or her own mental state, therapists can demonstrate the way they have achieved a sense of calm and can discuss these strategies with the patient. Figure 15.1 illustrates the general schema (Semerari, 2000) of the kind of conversational interaction that we are proposing is helpful for patients.

We would like to draw the reader's attention to a number of aspects of this strategy. First of all, declaring that the problem is shared helps a patient with confused, disparate, or contradictory relational scenarios to achieve a clearer and more stable representation of his or her relationship with the therapist. Therapists can declare their disorganized narratives in two ways: making a self-disclosure or, in a method similar to that suggested by Safran and Muran (2000), using the "universal we." In the first case, therapists make those aspects of their own mental state that they consider to be shared by the patient plain to the latter, by saying for example, "While listening to you speaking, I too felt a sense of urgency, a need to take action, come what may here and now. But now we need to think about it and decide what's the best thing to do." With the "universal we," therapists intimate that the patient's experience is or could be shared in that it is common to all humanity. For example: "Are you going through one of those times in which we feel overwhelmed by a thousand different problems and all we'd like to do is not see or hear?"

Declaring that the problem is a shared one encourages patients to develop the ability to perceive and describe their own mental states, that is, to obtain a higher level of metacognitive skills, for three reasons:

1. It validates their experience and allows them to contemplate it in a safe interpersonal environment.

2. It focuses not on single scenarios but on the chaotic way in which those scenarios are represented and makes the latter the object of treatment. In this way none of the self's many facets is excluded.

3. The fact that the therapist partially shares the problem creates, in a relationship between equals, the premise for thinking about alternative ways of coping, thus strongly emphasizing that the problem is comprehensible and can be mastered.

For this reason we consider it important that the conversation, as suggested by Linehan (1993), is dialectical and in two phases, with the validation and sharing of experience being followed by a discussion of mastery strategies.

Let's look at an example taken from a course of therapy with Linda, a 25-year-old woman. She alternates between living in fear of being humiliated and terrorized by others and experiencing a profound sense of personal unworthiness and ineffectiveness with, in rare moments, an angry rebelliousness. More frequently, however, she desperately looks for help, which, in turn, can tragically turn out to be a source of vulnerability and danger for her in her relationships with others. From a diagnostic point of view, using criteria from the *Diagnostic and Statistical Manual of Mental Disorders* (DSM-IV; American Psychiatric Association, 1994), Linda suffers from a set of different disorders: Major Depressive Disorder and Dissociative Disorder N.O.S [not otherwise specified], delusional episodes, and Borderline and Paranoid personality disorders (Axis II).

Linda: Well, today I seem to not have any reason for living. Yesterday I seemed... [starts crying]... I cannot say if I was annoyed, angry or anything else because of my family, because I can't stand them! There are things I can't stand and if it depended on me I'd have cancelled them out but I can't do that, and this makes me feel powerless. And then I am powerless in my life and in all that I'm able to do, because I was trying to work hard for my future.

Therapist: What happened?

Linda: I was thinking of my father, because I realized he's a person with some weaknesses. He's timid. He's afraid of everything. He always wants to be understood. He almost wants someone to take care of him. I hate him for this reason because it should be him taking care of me.

Therapist: I see what you mean, but what's this got to do with your feeling powerless in your life?

Linda: This is one of the things why, hum... I was going back over my usual thoughts and then suddenly they became so many! Very real, and quite suddenly I didn't feel well any more.

Therapist: Can you tell me about them?

Linda: Well, I thought of my mother and grandmother, whom I cannot stand. *[angry tone]* She is always poking her nose into other people's business, to criticize them, and I would like her to be on her own but I can't achieve it. My mother is unable to be a role model for me. I think she does it on purpose, that she somehow enjoys denying me her help. I couldn't get this continual need for being helped out of my mind *[starts crying desperately]* because I thought that, if I could get it out of my mind, everything would be all right. But I wasn't able to do it.

Therapist: So yesterday you were in need of help.

Linda: Yes.

Therapist: Why?

Linda: Because I thought of death, I thought that life keeps running on and on and on and my life is running away and I'm not able to do anything of what I would like to do. There's nothing I'm able to do! And I can't manage the concrete things that happen to me. I imagined them piling up, piling up over time and I wouldn't be able to manage them. I seem to not have any kind of power over my life.

The self is made up of a polyphony of different voices (Hermans & Kempen, 1993), but this extract narrated by Linda sounds cacophonous, with critical, weak, abandoned, angry, desperate, or impotent characters crowding together, stealing the scene from each other, and making it impossible for the therapist to identify which character is most important to relate to in the session. We need to focus, therefore, on the chaotic character of the patient's self-narrative representations. Each of the problems she talks about—the meaning of life for her, her control over choices, her need for help, and her relationships with her relatives—has a considerable emotional importance and needs to be treated with care and concern. However, while the problems keep on crowding together in her mind, they cannot be analyzed in depth or adequately addressed, leaving her with a sense of absolute powerlessness. In this case, the therapist decides to focus his attention on the chaotic nature of the patient's mental state rather than on the specific problems that emerge in her discourse. Under the pressure of the patient's numerous problems, all of them urgent, the therapist has been experiencing a feeling of inner chaos, too. He therefore grasps that there is a problem common to both of them and indicates this to the patient, by references to his own mental state and use of the universal "we."

Therapist Well, Linda, while I was listening to you, I felt a little confused. I can see the importance of each single problem but I don't know exactly which one we should concentrate on. You know those moments when we feel attacked by lots of urgent problems all together and our mind seems like it will burst.

Linda Actually there was a moment when I felt so bad that I thought I was going to split in two.

Let's consider the metacognitive shift. Now the patient is thinking not about the single elements making up her mental state but about the nature of her overall state, which she links to her dissociative experience.

Therapist Actually it's too much. Each of the problems you talked about is very important: what life really means for you, your need for help, the difficulties your relatives find in helping you, the possibilities of carrying out your intentions and the suddenness of death, which can prevent us from fulfilling our goals. However, now it is not the content of each single thing. The fact is that we feel confused and powerless if certain problems keep on piling up in our minds all together. The question then is how to get out of this chaotic mental state?

[This speech describes the two phases in the session, with the moment of sharing followed by a discussion on mastery strategies.]

Linda Yes, when my thoughts accelerate I haven't got any positive ones. I don't know how I'll cope.

The patient is now keeping up her new ability to reflect on her own mental states, has got to a higher level of metacognitive skills, and tries to participate in the discussion about mastery strategies, which takes up the rest of the session. In the end, patient and therapist agree that the patient will try to observe her chaotic mental state "from the outside" by writing it down. The next excerpt shows that the metacognitive level she achieved was maintained in the next therapy session.

Linda   I've been feeling a little more self-confident. I've tried to put your advice into practice and since I started to write I've been feeling better and I haven't needed to write more than a line.

Therapist   Could you stop your problems from crowding in?

Linda   Yes, I could. I slowly grasped that I was thinking of too many problems and then I started writing before they became too many.

Therapist   And how many times did you have the feeling you were entering a chaotic state of mind?

Linda   Two or three times, but it wasn't as chaotic as the one I talked about last time.

For self-narratives to act as a guide to action in the world, not only do a hierarchy of importance and a consistency of action need to be established but also a self-correcting mechanism needs to be actively engaged. Narrative scenarios and roles must adapt to changes in the environment and flexibly take into account the complexity of relationships that exist between self and the world. For this to happen, self-narratives need to have the "as if" quality (Vaihinger, 1935) and be approached as possible hypotheses and not a perfect mirror image of reality. Borderline patients can lose this ability to distinguish between what is represented and the real world[2] (Fonagy & Target, 1996). This phenomenon is also included in *DSM-IV*, with transitory delusional states being among the criteria for Borderline Personality Disorder.

In this case, too, the therapeutic relationship can lead to some characteristic interpersonal cycles, of which we shall now describe one of the most frequent, the one involving mutual distrust (Nicolò, Dimaggio, Semarari, & Carcione, 2001). A feature of the therapist's inner state in this case is the feeling of "treading on egg shells," with the impression that patients might interpret every sentence and gesture as being a confirmation of their persecutory anxieties and the fear of maybe saying or doing something that could cause a catastrophic breakdown in the relationship. The natural tendency is to become ever more cautious and to speak ever less, keeping questions to a strict minimum. However, by speaking, the therapist's mind—intentions, caring, and concern—becomes more comprehensible to the patient. If therapists are incomprehensible to a delusional patient, they will almost certainly get included in the delusion, while if they make their evaluations and intentions explicit, this preserves at least the possibility that dialogue can keep going.

We shall see in the next example how a dialogue can evolve between patient and therapist, with a victim character embodied by the patient, feeling threatened by an abusing persecutor, embodied by the therapist. This relationship ought to belong to the "as if" world, in which representation is "disconnected" to use Leslie's term, but the patient approaches it as if it was real. The therapist intervenes and shifts the relationship to the world of fantasy, which both of them can joke about. The objective at this point is not to rewrite the narrative, but to put it in the right mental context, that is, pretend play.

From a technical point of view, too, in this case, inner discipline operations revolve around the question, What is there in my problematic mental state that is shared by the patient? What is shared in this case is the need to know the other's evaluations and intentions in order to be able to regulate the relationship.

Therapists can encourage this process by performing acts of sincere self-disclosure. In the following extract, Linda, in an angry and agitated state, declares that she sees the therapist as part of a conspiracy with the goal being to control her. After an initial stage of cautious exploration, with Linda going so far as to include him in her delusional narrative in a persecutory position, the therapist undertakes an act of self-disclosure. His purpose is to clearly define the primary representation, "the real one," of the therapeutic relationship, as one between equals in a mutually agreed therapy contract.

Linda   And now I'm also annoyed with, well for example with you, with Dr. F, with Dr. P, my father, my mother, my grandmother, their friends (...) "these people are like you; they're on your side" just to be able to imprison me in predefined schemas.

Therapist   And, sorry, in what schema would I be wanting to imprison you?

Linda   But, well, you, you know, you're precisely a component of the overall system.

Therapist   Let's say then [smiles] as a member of the overall system, what schema would I be wanting to imprison you in?

Linda   One in which you convince me that I have to change according to your wishes.

Therapist   Yes, in a certain sense.

Linda   I mean I'm horrified by the idea of being a pup—. I feel I'm a bit of a puppet sometimes.

Therapist   And in what way, how would I be wanting you to change?

Linda   That's it! Because I don't know what to say. . . .

Therapist   No, not that! No, no! You can't tell me you don't know. I've told you that in every way I could!

Linda   No, hang on then. You'd like me to change in the sense of going and picking up again some of those things about my family, wouldn't you?

Therapist   No, quite honestly I couldn't care less about them at this present time. I'd like you to be more critical with regard to your feelings of persecution.

Linda   I can assure you that it's very difficult for me to grasp what you're really trying to say.

The therapist has made clear his intentions: stimulating a change. Therefore, in a certain sense, he enters Linda's scenario with a desire to change her, but in a completely different way from what she fears: to get her to see her ideas of persecution from a new perspective. The fact that the therapist is putting his cards on the table, as it were, causes a break in Linda's delusional state, and she begins to establish a dialogical relationship with the therapist by disclosing, for the first time during the session, a hint of doubt that she is unable to comprehend his mental state. As a result, the therapist continues to pursue this line of action.

Therapist   I'll explain to you, don't get angry, I'll explain to you.

Linda   No, I'm angry because . . .

Therapist   There's no reason. I've nothing to hide on this point. I think your vision of the world is that it's bad and wants to persecute you and this rigid and unquestionable

	vision of the world is at the bottom of many of your problems and prevents you from having a normal life. The intention of my therapy is this: for you to stand back from this impression you have of the world (. . .) and after that, in my opinion, you'll be capable of making your own choices. Do you want me to put this down in writing? That's what my intention is! Now don't tell me that you don't know it because I reckon I've been perfectly clear!
Linda	But since, no, because . . . since I'm unable to realize what you mean in the same way as perhaps when I'm going down the street like I did recently and I was trying to grasp what it meant.
Therapist	Did you have the impression that people had it in for you?
Linda	Yes, very much so.
Therapist	That's what I mean.

Room has been found for talking about the story in which the patient feels threatened without the therapist finding himself in the persecutor position. Linda talks in a very critical tone of her ideas and recognizes that they are symptoms.

Linda	But that's the way I live and think; that's exactly the way I've been made up for a long time now!
Therapist	I think you're capable of being aware of it.
Linda	No, the last few days I've seemed to see prisons wherever I've turned.

Therapist	I agree when you say to me that I want to change something in you: it's this. We can talk about it but I tell you honestly that I think you're unwell. It's this that's making you really unwell.

In the following extract, Linda manages to describe her distress, the feeling of being torn apart inside. The therapeutic dialogue has made it possible for her to disclose a basic inner state, which is probably generating her ideas about being persecuted; as she feels fragile, the patient is convinced that the world is threatening her.

Linda	I feel like I've been torn up into little bits, knocked down from every point of view. I'd just like to stay at home on my own and not let anyone see me any more. However, when I'm there on my own I realize that I'm imagining people nevertheless passing judgment on what I'm doing while I'm on my own and. . . .
Therapist	and you realize it's in your imagination?
Linda	Yes, that's right.

A distinction between fantasy and reality has now been established. There has been no change in the contents of Linda's narrative; in the dialogues between characters, she is still in a weak, criticized, yielding position; but, thanks to the action taken by the therapist, the scene is now unfolding in the world of inner fantasies. The therapeutic relationship can now go ahead without the therapist being seen as part of a world that wants to persecute her. With the atmosphere more relaxed, Linda discloses what was really behind her fantasies: feeling herself obliged to have sexual intercourse.

Linda	I feel obliged to think again about certain things in the sexual sphere too and then gradually I have to transfer them absolutely from my father to guys and then I have to absolutely have contacts with guys and, for example, I can't avoid life.
Therapist	You're convinced that I, your family and the psychiatrists' association are intent on making you have sex.
Linda	*[laughs]* It's not the psychiatrists; it's Italy that won't accept that a girl . . .
Therapist	. . . doesn't have sex. I can assure you that as far as I'm concerned I'm not under any orders *[laughs]* from the Italian government aimed at ensuring that all Italian girls have sex.
Linda	OK, I'm glad to hear it.
Therapist	And in fact I'll be clearer still: At least for the next few months it would be better if you didn't have any sentimental relationships because to get involved emotionally or sexually now could unbalance you. If you like, I'll put it in writing: *[laughs]* you mustn't have sex; abstain from sex.
Linda	OK, *[laughs]* no thanks because I feel reassured by this.

The therapist, using a self-disclosure operation as a starting point, frees himself from the position of being seen as persecuting and sexually threatening, on the one hand; on the other hand, by jokingly ordering her not to have sexual intercourse, he validates the patient's desire to isolate herself. At this point, interpersonal contact is too emotionally charged for Linda; her goal is to achieve a protective distance from a threatening world. As has already emerged, even when on her own, the patient continues to imagine she is being persecuted, but then she experiences this in the form of her own mental images and not as hard fact.

The extracts above were taken from the first 6 months of therapy. Treatment is still under way: Three years have passed, and Linda has stopped having delusional episodes and has started a sentimental relationship with a partner in which she is able to feel an ego-syntonic sexual attraction, without feeling forced into it by anyone.

CONCLUSIONS

With patients suffering from disorganized narratives, therapists find themselves faced with a difficult task: entering a chaotic scenario, in which hundreds of voices are all crowding together and hundreds of fragments of different stories are intertwined. The emotions in these cases are almost always intense and difficult to modulate. Therapists get easily caught up in a relationship that is intense, sometimes irritating, sometimes threatening, and always confusing. The therapeutic strategy that we propose involves certain actions aimed at treating the structural narrative dysfunction in a way that enhances the context for working, observing, and modifying the life themes, the quality of the relationships, and the dialogue between the characters inhabiting a patient's mental world.

The first type of action is aimed at acquiring a higher degree of metacognitive skills and at encouraging an Observing-I position that can endow patients' inner chaos with meaning and acknowledge the breathless multiplicity of their narrative. With this action, patients are able to experience their chaos in a less threatening way and communicate in a more comprehensible fashion with their therapists. By starting with a sharing of the problems caused by the chaos in the narrative, patients and therapists are facilitated in identifying the dominant life themes, the characters that represent these themes, and the way to build more adaptive life narratives.

The second type of action is aimed at recovering the ability to distinguish between fantasy and reality where this has been lost. The goal is not to immediately change the contents of the narratives but to allow the patient to acknowledge that an imaginary narrative is taking the place of the world, with pernicious results. Self-disclosure by therapists can be a valuable tool in this context. As we have shown in the extracts reproduced from therapy sessions, the effect of these actions is, in any case, a change in the quality of the therapeutic relationship. When patients acquire a better level of metarepresentative skills, their position vis-à-vis the therapist changes. Emotions shift flexibly in the context of new narrative scenarios. A therapist and a patient, working together collaboratively, in a position of equals, to implement treatment, see the person of the patient as the object of threats, seductions, and abuses by others. Distinguishing between imagined and actual narrative scenarios makes it possible later to modify the ones in which problematical contents and interpersonal relationships appear.

NOTES

1. Namely: Antonino Carcione, Maurizio Falcone, Giuseppe Nicolò, Michele Procacci, Laura Conti, and Donatella Fiore.

2. Freud (1913) termed this way of thinking "psychic equivalence."

REFERENCES

American Psychiatric Association. (1994). *Diagnostic and Statistical Manual of Mental Disorders* (4th ed.). Washington, DC: American Psychiatric Association.

Angus, L., Levitt, H., & Hardtke, K. (1999). The narrative processing coding system: Research applications and implications for psychotherapy practice. *Journal of Clinical Psychology, 55,* 1255-1270.

Angus, L., Lewin, J., & Hardtke, K. (2001, March 7-10). *Narrative processing modes and therapeutic change in brief experiential therapy for depression: An empirical analysis.* Paper presented at the Society for Psychotherapy Research meeting. Leiden, The Netherlands.

Baron-Cohen, S. (1995). *Mindblindness.* Cambridge: MIT Press.

Baron-Cohen, S., Leslie, A., & Frith, U. (1985). Does the autistic child have a "theory of mind"? *Cognition, 21,* 37-46.

Bowlby, J. (1982). *Attachment and loss* (Vol. 1, 2nd ed.). London: Hogarth. (Original work published 1969)

Bruner, J. (1986). *Actual minds, possible worlds.* Cambridge, MA: Harvard University Press.

Bruner, J. (1990). *Acts of meaning.* Cambridge, MA: Harvard University Press.

Cooper, M. (2003). "I-I" and "I-Me": Transposing Buber's interpersonal attitudes to the intrapersonal plane. *Journal of Constructivist Psychology, 16*(2), 131-153.

Damasio, A. R. (1994). *Descartes's error: Emotion, reason, and the human brain.* New York: Grosset/Putnam.

Dimaggio, G., Salvatore, G., Azzara, C., & Catania, D. (2003). Rewriting self-narratives: The therapeutic process. *Journal of Constructivistic Psychology, 16*(2), 155-181.

Dimaggio, G., Salvatore, G., Azzara, C., Catania, D., Semerari, A., & Hermans, H. J. M. (in press). Dialogical relationships in impoverished narratives: From theory to clinical practice. *Psychology and Psychotherapy.*

Dimaggio, G., & Semerari, A. (2001). Psychopathological narrative forms. *Journal of Constructivist Psychology, 14,* 1-23.

Flavell, J. H., Miller, P. H., & Miller, S. A. (1993). *Cognitive development.* Hemel Hempstead, UK: Prentice Hall.

Fonagy, P., & Target, M. (1996). Playing with reality I: Theory of mind and the normal development of psychic reality. *International Journal of Psychoanalysis, 77,* 217-233.

Fonagy, P., & Target, M. (1997). Attachment and reflective function: Their role in self-organization. *Development and Psychopathology, 9,* 679-700

Freud, S. (1913). Totem and taboo. In J. Strachey (Ed.), *The standard edition of the complete psychological works of Sigmund Freud.* London: Hogarth.

Frith, C. D. (1992). *The cognitive neuropsychology of schizophrenia.* Hove, UK: Lawrence Erlbaum.

Gardner, G., Mancini, F., & Semerari, A. (1987). The construction of psychological disorder as invalidation of self-knowledge. In F. Fransella & L. Thomas (Eds.), *Experimenting with personal construct psychology* (pp. 259-272). London: Routledge & Kegan Paul.

Golynkina, K., & Ryle, A. (1999). The identification and characteristics of the partially dissociated states of patients with borderline personality disorder. *British Journal of Medical Psychology, 72,* 429-445.

Gonçalves, O. F. (1995). Cognitive narrative psychotherapy. In M. J. Mahoney (Ed.), *Cognitive and constructive psychotherapies* (pp. 139-162). New York: Pergamon.

Gonçalves, O. F., Korman, Y., & Angus, L. (2000). Constructing psychopathology from a cognitive narrative perspective. In R. A. Neimeyer & J. D. Raskin (Eds.), *Constructions of disorder* (pp. 265-284). Washington, DC: American Psychological Association.

Grice, H. P. (1975). Logic and conversation. In P. Cole & J. L. Moran (Eds.), *Syntax and semantics* (Vol. 3, pp. 129-178). New York: Academic Press.

Hermans, H. J. M. (1996). Voicing the self: From information processing to dialogical interchange. *Psychological Bulletin, 119,* 31-50.

Hermans, H. J. M. (1997). Dissociation as disorganized self-narrative: Tension between splitting and integration. *Journal of Psychotherapy Integration, 7*(3), 213-223.

Hermans, H. J. M. (2001a). The construction of a personal position repertoire: Method and practice. *Culture & Psychology, 7*(3), 324-366.

Hermans, H. J. M. (2001b). The dialogical self: Toward a theory of personal and cultural positioning. *Culture & Psychology, 7*(3), 243-281.

Hermans, H. J. M. (2003). The construction and reconstruction of a dialogical self. *Journal of Constructivist Psychology, 16*(2), 89-130.

Hermans, H. J. M., & Kempen, H. J. K. (1993). *The dialogical self: Meaning as movement.* San Diego: Academic Press.

Horowitz, M. J. (1987). *States of mind: Configurational analysis of individual psychology* (2nd ed.). New York: Plenum.

Johnson-Laird, P. N. (1983). *Mental models: Towards a cognitive science of language, inference, and consciousness.* Cambridge, UK: Cambridge University Press.

Kelly, G. (1955). *The psychology of personal constructs.* New York: Norton.

Kernberg, O. F. (1975). *Borderline conditions and pathological narcissism.* New York: Aaronson.

Leiman, M., & Stiles, W. B. (2001). Dialogical sequence analysis and the Zone of Proximal Development as conceptual enhancements to the assimilation model: The case of Jan revisited. *Psychotherapy Research, 11,* 311-330.

Leslie, A. M. (1987). Pretense and representation: The origin of "theory of mind." *Psychological Review, 94,* 412-426.

Linehan, M. M. (1993). *Cognitive behavioral treatment of borderline personality disorder.* New York: Guilford.

Liotti, G. (1995). Disorganized-disoriented attachment in the psychotherapy of the dissociative disorders. In S. Goldberg, R. Muir, & J. Kerr (Eds.), *Attachment theory: Social, developmental, and clinical perspectives* (pp. 343-363). Hillsdale, NJ: Analytic Press.

Liotti, G., & Intreccialagli, B. (1998). Metacognition and motivational systems in psychotherapy: A cognitive evolutionary approach to the treatment of difficult patients. In C. Perris & P. D. McGorry (Eds.), *Cognitive psychotherapy of psychotic and personality disorders: Handbook of theory and practice.* New York: John Wiley.

Lysaker, P. H., & Lysaker, J. T. (2002). Narrative structure in psychosis: Schizophrenia and disruptions in the dialogical self. *Theory and Psychology, 12,* 207-220.

Lysaker, P. H., & Lysaker, J. T. (2001). Schizophrenia and the collapse of the dialogical self:

Recovery, narrative, and psychotherapy. *Psychotherapy, 38,* 252-261.

Lysaker, P. H., Wickett, A. M., Wilke, N., & Lysaker, J. T. (in press). Narrative incoherence in schizophrenia: The absent agent-protagonist and the collapse of internal dialogue. *American Journal of Psychotherapy.*

Main, M. (1991). Metacognitive knowledge, metacognitive monitoring, and singular (coherent) vs. multiple (incoherent) models of attachment: Findings and directions for future researches. In C. M. Parkes, J. Stevenson-Hinde, & P. Marris (Eds.), *Attachment across the life cycle* (pp. 126-159). New York: Routledge.

Mandler, J. (1984). *Scripts, stories, and scenes: Aspects of schema theory.* Hillsdale, NJ: Lawrence Erlbaum.

Markus, H., & Nurius, P. (1986). Possible selves. *American Psychologist, 41,* 954-969.

McAdams, D. (1995). What do we know when we know a person? *Journal of Personality, 63,* 365-395.

Michotte, A. (1946). *The perception of causality.* London: Methuen.

Neimeyer, R. A. (2000). Narrative disruptions in the construction of the self. In R. A. Neimeyer & J. D. Raskin (Eds.), *Constructions of disorder* (pp. 207-241). Washington DC: American Psychological Association.

Nicolò, G., Dimaggio, G., Semerari, A., & Carcione A. (2001). Metacognicion y trastorno paranoide de personalidad. *Revista de Psicoterapia, 45,* 117-136.

Rasmussen, B., & Angus, L. (1997). Models of interaction in psychotherapy with borderline and nonborderline clients: A qualitative analysis. *Journal of Analytic Social Work, 4,* 53-73.

Ryle, A. (1997). *Cognitive analytic therapy and borderline personality disorder: The model and the method.* Chichester, UK: Wiley.

Safran, J. D. (1984). Assessing the cognitive-interpersonal cycle. *Cognitive Therapy and Research, 8,* 333-348.

Safran, J. D., & Muran, J. C. (2000). *Negotiating the therapeutic alliance: A relational treatment guide.* New York: Guilford.

Safran, J. D., & Segal, Z. V. (1990). *Interpersonal process in cognitive therapy.* New York: Basic Books.

Salkovskis, P. M. (1989). Cognitive-behavioral factors and the persistence of intrusive thoughts in obsessional problems. *Behavior Therapy and Research, 27,* 677-82.

Salvatore, G., Dimaggio, G., Azzara, C., Catania D., & Hermans, H. J. M. (2000). *Manuale per la siglatura della coerenza e complessità delle narrazioni.* Unpublished manuscript.

Salvatore, G., Dimaggio, G., & Semerari, A. (2003). *A model of narrative development: Implications for understanding psychopathology and guiding therapy.* Manuscript in preparation.

Semerari, A. (Ed.). (1999). *Psicoterapia cognitiva del paziente grave: Metacognizione and relazione terapeutica.* Milan, Italy: Raffaello Cortina Editore.

Semerari, A. (2000, September 19-23). *Metacognition and therapeutic relationship in the treatment of personality disorders: Guidelines for a manual of constructivist therapy.* Paper presented at the 7th International Congress on Constructivism in Psychotherapy, Geneva, Switzerland.

Semerari, A., Carcione, A., Dimaggio, G., Falcone, M., Nicolò, G., Procacci, M., & Alleva, G. (in press). How to assess metacognitive functioning in psychotherapy? The Metacognition Assessment Scale and its applications. *Clinical Psychology and Psychotherapy, 10.*

Semerari, A., Carcione, A., Dimaggio, G., Falcone, M., Nicolò, G., Procacci, M., Alleva, G., & Mergenthaler, E. (2003). Assessing problematic states in patients' narrative: The grid of problematic states. *Psychotherapy Research, 13*(3), 337-353.

Sperber, D. (Ed.). (2000). *Metarepresentation.* Oxford, UK: Oxford University Press.

Stern, D. N. (1985). *The interpersonal world of the infant: A view from psychoanalysis and developmental psychology.* New York: Basic Books.

Stich, S., & Nichols, S. (1998). Theory theory to the max. *Mind & Language, 13,* 421-449.

Stiles, W. B. (1999). Signs and voices in psychotherapy. *Psychotherapy Research, 9,* 1-21.

Stiles, W. B., Meshot, C. M., Anderson, T. M., & Sloan, W. W. J. (1992). Assimilation of problematic experiences: The case of John Jones. *Psychotherapy Research, 2,* 81-101.

Stiles, W. B., Osatuke, K., Glick, M. J., & Mackay, H. (2002, October 20-22). *Encounters between voices generate emotion: An elaboration of the assimilation model.*

Paper presented at the Second International conference on The Dialogical Self, Ghent, Belgium.

Taylor, G. J., Bagby, R. M., & Parker, J. D. A. (1997). *Disorders of affect regulation: Alexithymia in medical and psychiatric illness*. Cambridge, UK: Cambridge University Press.

Vaihinger, H. (1935). *The philosophy of "as if."* London: Kegan Paul, Trench & Trubner.

Wells, A., & Purdon, C. (1999). Metacognition and cognitive-behavior therapy: a special issue. *Clinical Psychology and Psychotherapy*, 6, 1-2.

Winnicott, D. W. (1965). *The maturational processes and the facilitating environment*. London: Hogarth.

CHAPTER 16

Story Dramaturgy and Personal Conflict
JAKOB—A Tool for Narrative Understanding and Psychotherapeutic Practice

BRIGITTE BOOTHE

AGNES VON WYL

Storytelling is one of the important elements of primary socialization. Parents shape the individuality of their children, beginning in the first year of a child's life, by telling and sharing stories. Narrative communication, primarily initiated by the parental interaction partner, develops in the course of children's early lives to a broad and rich spectrum of cotelling and then to children's adopting initiative storytelling (Fivush, Gray, & Fromhoff, 1987; Nelson, 1993; Papousek, 1995; Welch-Ross, 1995). Listener and narrator are empathic partners in a narrative alliance; narrative communication is basic for the emergence of personal acceptance in the parent-child relationship. Narrative communication is important, also, for the emergence of confidence in the surrounding world because parental narrators are ambassadors and mediators of life and world, in the bad and the good sense; the belief in a good-enough environment (Hartmann, 1939, 1950) is mediated by parental narratives on people, creatures, and things as good or bad, inviting or dangerous, aversive or attractive. A child's secure attachment to a sensible and attentive mother figure (Bowlby, 1969) is always partly the product of a narrative mother-child union that enables and internalizes

AUTHORS' NOTE: Correspondence regarding this chapter should be sent to Brigitte Boothe at the Psychological Institute, University of Zürich, Schmelzbergstrasse 40, CH 8044 Zürich, or to boothe@klipsy.unizh.ch.

models of shared experiences, so that the child feels encouraged to explore, to ask for help, and to engage in narrative encounters on troubles, joys, misfortunes, and successes. The emerging self and the self-concept are fruits of narrative interaction (Eder, 1990; Lewis & Brooks-Gunn, 1979; Miller, Potts, Fung, Hoogstra, & Mintz, 1990), and the child's sense of self-continuity, autobiographical remembering, self-presentation, and self-knowledge have some of their roots in a narrative context (Neisser, 1998).

By telling stories, personal experience is expressed and shared with others (Boothe, 1994, 1999; Boothe, von Wyl, & Wepfer, 1999; Gülich & Hausendorf, 2000). Patients and clients also tell stories in the psychotherapeutic situation. In evoking actions, occurrences, events, and incidents, they express what makes them suffer (Eisenmann, 1995; Luborsky, 1977; Schafer, 1979, 1980; von Wyl, 2000a, 2000b). In telling stories, they invite their professional interlocutor, the psychotherapist, to be involved with their feelings (Spence, 1982a, 1982b, 1983). Patients and clients use the power of storytelling to evoke their present state of mind. In telling their story, they invite the psychotherapist to make him- or herself at home in their world and to share what goes on there at an emotional level.

Storytelling is the social articulation of subjectivity (Gergen, 1994; Wiedemann, 1986). The storyteller communicates to the interlocutor: "I am the person who has experienced this and that. As a person with this particular history, I demand acknowledgment, resonance, and acceptance by the important others." The storyteller uses narrative patterns and strategies to attain the ultimate goal of this acknowledgement, namely social integration (Gergen & Gergen, 1988).

Evoking the present and social integration are communicative achievements of storytelling, but storytelling also performs regulative functions in the narrator's mental organization, namely those of wish fulfilment and dealing with anxiety.

The wish-fulfilling or restoring function of storytelling explains why, as tellers of our own stories, we are in a state of positive psychological tension (Boothe, 1998), why storytelling has an "enjoyment potential" for us, as von Matt (1995, p. 36) puts it. In storytelling, we model our experience in the light of our subjective conditions of wish fulfilment (Boothe, 2002a). Storytelling is persuasive and asks for affirmation. Believing what one tells has a latent wish-fulfilling function.

The fear-coping and stabilizing function of the narrative—also qualified here as the reorganization function—allows agitating or thrilling experiences to be subsequently brought under control (Flader & Giesecke, 1980; Freud, 1920/1955). Whatever had excited, irritated, surprised, frightened, afflicted, or threatened us continues to occupy our thoughts. The events remain in our mind's eye irrespective of our wishes. The subsequent storytelling—the continued retelling of the story—relieves the tension and has a stabilizing effect.

Storytelling as an articulation of subjectivity combines functions of psychophysical regulation (restoration and reorganization) with communicative functions of episodic self-construction and the procedural making of personal history and personal continuity (event-evoking or actualization and social integration).

Moving from the narrator to the listener, we find that listeners, too, experience "the narrative suspense as enjoyable" (von Matt, 1995, p. 36). But they experience it quite differently from the narrator, namely as an emotionally committed expectation as to how the narrative sequence continues. Narrative understanding is a sort of practiced plot-intelligence. When the story is new for the listener, he or she is confronted with the setting or start conditions of the story: A scene opens with figures, environment, and wishes that are organized as the starting point and often as the nucleus of an episodic sequence, and this results in a sort of solution or final point. Listeners put themselves—or transfer themselves—into the setting, the initial organization of the scene, the starting point of the story (Bühler, 1976, 1978), which sets up a combination of events that opens up a horizon of expectation (Brooks, 1984; Gülich & Quasthoff, 1986; Labov & Fanshel, 1977; Liedtke, 1990; Werling, 1989). What listeners fear and hope for by intuitively sharing in the dramatic narrative, what they are excited about and how they emotionally evaluate the outcome of the story depends on the specific dramatic technique of the narrative (Brémond, 1964; Fischer, 1996). In this way, listeners experience vicariously and yet in a spirit of assimilation the wish-fulfilling or restoring factors that are placed in the story by the storyteller and the type of fear-coping or reorganization with which the latter is struggling.

FROM NARRATION TO CONFLICT

Everyday verbal narratives by patients have a conflictive and dynamic character. The narrative is of value for the psychotherapist's understanding in terms of his or her psychodiagnostic and treatment technique, thanks to its capacity to actualize and model social integration, restoration, and reorganization. The psychotherapist can use a verbal narrative in four ways. He or she understands the actualization aspect of the narrative as the presence of the past in the here and now and in this way sees how experiences are articulated and expressed verbally in the present situation. In the sense of socially integrative modeling, the psychotherapist takes care to note the strategic impact that is expressed in the client's presentation. The psychotherapist may become involved as a coplayer in the narrative drama and discover both its restoring and reorganizing impact. The unfolding of the narrative organization opens a potential for assessing patients' conflict dynamics. Findings from narrative analysis can be rendered fruitful for the systematic exploration of the narrator's wishes and defense mechanisms, psychosocial compromise, and relationship organization along the path to a reconstructive analysis of the narrative data.

THE DRAMATIC OR ENACTMENT IMPACT OF THE NARRATIVE

In daily psychotherapeutic practice, patients tell narratives in which they reenact and newly enact their experiences in such a way that their declarative view of themselves and the world, as well as their procedural conflict dynamics, are expressed (Boothe, 1994; Boothe, von Wyl, & Wepfer, 1998; Luborsky & Kächele, 1986). The dramatic or enactive impact of the narrative, as well as its dynamics and plot, are extensively treated outside of psychoanalysis, namely in social psychology, sociology, and linguistics (e.g., Brooks, 1984; Bruner, 1987, 1990; Bühler, 1976, 1978; Goffman, 1959; Gülich & Hausendorf, 2000; Gülich & Quasthoff, 1986; Lucius-Hoene, 2000; Propp, 1968; Quasthoff, 1980; Ricoeur, 1996; Spence, 1983; Stanzel, 1988; Von Cranach, Kalbermatten, Indermühle, & Gugler, 1980; White, 1986; Wolfson, 1978). These issues are also of programmatic importance for psychotherapeutic practice and research.

In the narrative-analysis work group at the University of Zurich, we use a systematic disclosure procedure for transcribed verbal narratives that is available in manual form. We call it the *JAKOB narrative analysis system* (Boothe & the JAKOB Group, 2002). Our special interest focuses on narrative plot organization and its dramaturgical and psychodynamic potential (an interest that we also have in relation to dreams, literature, and drama, for example: Boothe, 2001b, 2001c, 2002a, 2002b).

WHAT IS JAKOB AND HOW DOES IT WORK?

The JAKOB analysis is a multistep disclosure procedure that encompasses both descriptive and hypotheses-generating aspects. A short summary and overview of the method is offered here. The approach makes use of the communicative form of storytelling in which narrators articulate their wishes, fears, and relationships, presenting themselves as creators of their own inner drama. For purposes of analysis, specific narrative episodes are selected from transcripts of psychotherapy sessions.

The JAKOB procedure involves the following tasks: (a) extracting narrative episodes from the communicative flow of the interview, (b) documenting these narratives, (c) describing the dramaturgical repertoire of the narrator, (d) explicating the narrative self-presentation of the narrator, (e) formulating the hypothetical happy end and the hypothetical disaster that can be constructed out of the horizon of expectations determined by the story's start conditions, (f) modeling conflict and defense movements, (g) inspecting the narrative enactment of relationships to generate hypotheses about therapeutic collaboration and transference-countertransference patterns.

Our work of reconstruction, reformulation, and interpretation goes on concretely in the following steps. In the redescriptive-reconstructive part, we identify the oral narrative in the patient-therapist dialogue (on the basis of video or audio recordings) and transcribe it using the rules of the Ulm text bank (Mergenthaler, 1992). We divide the transcribed text into segments as a numbered sequence of subject-predicate links. We then code personal details, props, scene, and stage events by using a coding system for lexical units. On this basis, we access the narrative material in a hypothetical-interpretative way (Boothe et al., 1999).

Accordingly, the analysis centers on the interpretative disclosure of the narrative material on the basis of the segmented reformulation of a narrative whose layout is determined and whose lexical elements are reconstructed. Lacking the space required to explain the procedure employed by the JAKOB narrative analysis, we refer interested readers to the *Manual of the JAKOB Narrative Analysis* (Boothe and the JAKOB group, 2002). Computer-aided presentation and coding of narratives has been developed by Luder (1999a, 1999b).

The Initial Narrative of Therese in the First Psychotherapeutic Interview

We will now illustrate the main elements of narrative analysis using JAKOB in the context of some case material. To recapitulate, JAKOB is designed to perform the following tasks: (a) to extract narrative episodes in the communicative flow of the interviews; (b) to document the narrative; (c) to describe the repertoire of figures, props, and actions; (d) to explain the narrative self-presentation of the speaker; (e) to analyze the plot; (f) to model conflict and defence regulation; and (g) to inspect the narrative enactment of relationships and to reflect aspects of therapeutic collaboration and hypotheses of transference/counter-transference.

Rather than discussing all of the findings in great detail, we will focus on the following topics: self-presentation by the narrator, narrative dynamics, narration and conflict dynamics, conflict and defense regulation, enactment, conflict, and confrontation with life challenges. We use one initial narrative followed by a summary.

The young female patient in question will be called Therese. The initial interview was available as transcript from the research project of the Magdeburg work group on qualitative psychotherapy research, run by Jörg Frommer (using the transcription system of the Ulm text bank, Mergenthaler, 1992). In Table 16.1, we present the first narrative in the transcript of the interview, converted from continuous text to a segmented version and structured as a numerical sequence of subject-predicate links.

In general, narrative entries tend to declare an episodic fixing of the past in terms of time and space. In contrast, Therese expresses herself in terms of a thematic orientation: self-originated *spoiling*. Time-space information follows this thematic orientation, but only a small amount. The construction of the time-space context becomes the imaginative task of the listener, who comes to understand in the following speech that the drama relates to a recent students' exhibition at the art academy.

Therese also structures her narrative exit in a different way. She uses a familiar means of rounding off a narrative: the generalized "moral of the story" in the concluding sentence: "Everything falls into my lap and I always spoil everything." To this extent, this initial narrative is also an example of a generalizing self-reproach.

Self-Representation by the Narrator

Narrators present their stories to gain their interlocutors' acknowledgment. Narrators want to and can experience recognition or rejection for very diverse statements. In the JAKOB narrative analysis, interest focuses on how narrators place their ego-figure, the narrating ego, in the scene so as to create the image they hope to project to listeners.

Therese-1 (Therese's first narrative) enacts the rhetoric of remorse: An expected benefit fails to materialize because the ego-figure blocks the potential resource holders by means of aversive interventions. The missed opportunity is brought out in the narrative (Segment 20: "then I would have had a lot of money and no need to go on working"), as is the self-sabotaging action (Segment 21: "but I was so rude") and finally the self-reproaching assessment (Segments 38 and 39: "everything falls into my lap and I always spoil everything"). Highlighting the narrator in terms of her reproach rhetoric brings out the (missed) opportunity, which was offered but not taken up, as particularly valuable and her own status as a self-sabotaging agent as particularly destructive:

> With no effort on my part, one of my artworks met with such great interest that the customer would have been only too happy to have bought it for a great deal of money, had I not scotched the whole thing myself because of my foul mood at the time.

In this narrative structure of a self-handicapping action with the masochistic bonus of suffering self-enactment, Therese invites her interlocutor to affirm the motto that provides her narcissistic gratification: talented, desired, and self-ruining.

Narrative Dynamics and the Initial Narrative of Therese

Why does Therese need to be acknowledged as being gifted, desired, and self-destructive? These questions address the subjective involvement of narrators, the desire that drives them. Some help is provided by looking at the narrative dynamics: What would be a happy end to each of a narrator's stories, that is, what would be the optimum outcome?

What, on the other hand, would be a tragic outcome, a catastrophe or disaster? In addition to the intended self-presentation, we will now examine a key feature of the narrative form of speech: the creation of tension in the narrative, its dynamic construction.

Table 16.1 Therese-1 (English): *People Wanted to Buy My Paintings*

Segment Number	Narrative Sequence
1	I mean
2	I have just spoiled something for myself
3	people wanted to buy my paintings
4	and I just came up
5	I had applied for a scholarship in Paris
6	you know
7	I thought
8III7	it would be good
9III7	half a year in Paris would do you good
10	you know
11III7	you would get out of here
12	because I have the feeling
13III12	I know all the people here or at least many people so superficially
14III12	and they know me
15III12	and I am so caught up here
16III12	because I can't get out of my role
17	and yes and then I came up and saw the lists
18	and that I didn't get the scholarship
19	and then these people pounced on me and wanted to buy my painting
20	then I would have had a lot of money and no need to go on working
21	but I was so rude
22	because I was so angry
23aIII22	that this yes
24	this as well is so typical
25III24	that I can't switch myself to a new situation but that I am totally upset
23bIII22	because I didn't get the scholarship
26	so sad
27	this was now during the exhibition um on the 6th of February or so
28	and then I spoil something for myself like that
29	and then I was so angry afterward
30	it went
31	then I was so angry with myself for so long
32	that I have spoiled even this
33	others of course had got in touch too
34	but they would have really bought the painting
35	you know
36	so that I think
37	I always spoil everything for myself
38	everything falls into my lap
39	and I always spoil everything

Note: A Roman III characterizes a grammatical object appearing as a dependent clause.

How does a narrative generate tension? It sets starting conditions and on that basis gets us to ask: How will the story unfold? What is the outcome? Narrators thus establish a transfer strategy for themselves and their audience on an everyday basis, which obliges both to comply with a series of initial conditions that create a specific narrative dynamic. In other words: A narrative has certain rules of play.

Narrators and listeners agree on the rules of play for the narrative's tension span, rules that are intuitive and implicit in an everyday context. The JAKOB narrative analysis formulates these rules in a systematic way. If we reveal them by analyzing the initial phase of the narrative, we show the initial dynamics and characterize the wish implied by constructing the hypothetically optimal (optimum) and the hypothetically catastrophic (disaster) ends of the expectation horizon. Here is how it is done in more detail.

To determine the initial dynamics, we seek out those segments that define the expectation horizon of the narrative. These segments provide orientation about the who, the what, and the how—all the relevant components of the setting or scene. Now we are able to add the hypothetical fulfillment peak (optimum) and its catastrophic abyss (disaster).

The initial dynamics for Therese-1 were established in Segments 3 to 5 and 7 to 9. Inspecting the material, we find these components: Strangers wish to purchase paintings produced by the ego-figure, the ego-figure meets these strangers. The contact with the strangers was preceded by the ego-figure's search for information about the success of an application for a scholarship as a means of extending her own artistic competence in a particularly stimulating environment. An *expectation horizon* is thus opened up, which involves the mobilization and development of a potential negotiation in which the ego-figure might obtain a benefit and gratify her desire for her own creative development. In brief, it concerns a dynamic of enrichment.

We add to this dynamic initial model its optimum and disaster hypotheses.

Hypothetical optimum: The susscessful sale of the painting yields a handsome profit; the offer of a scholarship opens up the prospect of great gains in artistic wealth and a great career: Therese's work sells at a profit; the path to mastery is open before her.

Hypothetical disaster: Potential wealthy customers turn away from lack of interest; rather than winning a scholarship, she becomes socially marginalized: Therese becomes impoverished and marginalized.

Narration and Conflict Dynamics

The narrative analysis distinguishes between ego and ego-figure. The episodic narrative sequence presents the "I" as the ego-figure or narrated ego. In the transition from the narrative dynamics to psychodynamics, we change the reference point with regard to the personal pronoun "I." At the level of psychodynamics, we no longer refer to the narrated ego or the ego-figure but to the narrator. Matters no longer revolve around the figure as presented but around the psychological situation of the narrator.

Following the rules of play, the development and conclusion of the narrative can be analyzed in the light of its optimum and disaster outcomes. After these outcomes have been formulated on the basis of the initial dynamics, the actual outcome of the narrated events is examined from the perspective of psychodynamics. This actual outcome can be characterized as the effective result in obvious contrast to the optimum and the disaster. This step makes it possible to determine how the narrator moves between the optimum and disaster. On the basis of the initially revealed expectation horizon, the narrator develops a context of action in which she aims to integrate those impulses that were apparent in the initial dynamics. The point here is to develop the specific narrative dynamics, that is, how the narrator actually performs this task as the story unfolds and how she actually concludes it, an outcome designated here as effective result. We do this by focusing on the narrative core and the narrative framework; we examine the development dynamics and the formulated results and assess the course of the narrative in the tension between the optimum and the disaster.

How does Therese as a narrator act in the movement between optimum (my work makes a profit, the path to mastery is open to me) and disaster (I become impoverished and marginalized)?

Rage and hostility because of the scholarship rejection lead her to attribute the failure to sell the painting to herself. She overemphasizes her responsibility for the outcome and her own inability to turn from her rage at the rejected scholarship to the needs of the current situation. She also stresses the strength of the desire shown by the potential customers to buy her paintings. *I am becoming impoverished and marginalized.* These narrative focuses mediate between the optimum and the disaster.

Effective result: I could be rich in terms of financial resources and development potential if only I didn't get in my own way.

This narrative of missed opportunity now enters into the result in the form of a declarative concluding tendency. It is presented as a compromise in view of two failures and holds open a dual fantasized solution: of being great in suffering instead of richly rewarded and yet of being able to hold on to the image of someone who is indeed richly rewarded.

Wish-Defense Movement

Narration has a restorative function. In other words, narrators try to remodel past events to provide wish fulfilment. In doing so, they are confronted not only with psychological impulses that are opposed to the wish fulfilment but also with an audience that is expected to accept the narrative in a positive way. Narrators must, therefore, employ techniques to make their wish fulfilment acceptable to their interlocutors: The wish fulfilment is consequently woven into the narrative and presented in an acceptable light. It attempts to make a restorative impact on the narrative process but can do so only if both narrators and listeners are induced to adopt an affirmative rather than an interrogative stance.

The narration is used in the service of subsequent wish-oriented fulfilment. The idea of wish fulfilment plays a central role in psychoanalysis. What is important here is not the perception of a discrepancy between wish and reality but a kind of mental fading-in technique: The mental evocation of a wish fulfilment temporarily brightens the narrator's mood and thus reduces the negative tension in the short term.

What direction does the correction of past events take toward the desired outcome (discernable in the narrative)? In the course of our narrative analytical studies, we have assembled a provisional series of exemplary wish dynamics (Boothe, 2001a). In Therese's initial narrative, we determine the following restoring and reorganizing factors:

Restoring element: In view of the central importance of the dynamics of gratification and being furnished with resources, the aim is to be in the position of a thriving, loved, and supported child at the center of parental life, to gain acknowledgment, to be nourished and cared for.

Reorganizing element: Fear of being ignored and marginalized, fear of the withdrawal of valuable resources. We are concerned here with the conflict perspective of being cared for versus autonomy.

We examine the organization of the narrative sequence to determine to what extent and by what means the narrative enacts a defense movement. The scrutiny of this sequence in connection with the lexical finding reveals, at the level of the sequential-lexical organization, the defense movement of turning against the self. This defensive movement can be represented here as follows: The experienced quasi-parental failure is processed by means of a self-reproaching enactment: "If the gratifications are not produced, then you alone are to blame. Be a good girl, behave in a friendly and socially adapted way, and the reward is sure to come."

The turning against the self is experienced in addition to the self-reproaches as a rage directed against the self.

Enactment, Conflict, and Challenge

Therese's initial narrative offers a compact and resolute modeling of her experienced conflict and her compromising defensive and compensatory strategies. The inspection of Therese's second (and only other) narrative in the first interview and the communication management in the patient-therapist dialogue reveals a continuous coherent relationship that dramatically enacts a specific conflict dynamics and sounds out its potential. Therese seeks contacts that give her gratification, furnish her with resources, encourage her potential; she replies to rejection of her demands with helpless rage. In the perspective of subjectively important wish-motives, we are dealing with the fantasized position of a child who stands at the center of parental attention and enjoys loving care, resources, and gratifications. In her narrative enactment, Therese shows how she protects her supporting fantasies for the sake of hedonistic regulation. In Therese's initial narrative, rage at her disappointment is regulated by the narcissistically magnificent enactment of a self-reproach. The withdrawal of care, resources, or gratification leads to dysphoria, regressive retreat, and helpless rage.

In psychotherapy, Therese might well initially idealize her therapist as a permissive parental bestower of resources with no selfish claims. She would wish to be nourished and grow through the therapist's agency, while—in the sense of this transference offer—consequently blocking out the particularities and limitations of the object as well as the contact conditions. Learning to cope productively with disappointment crises by seeing them as a challenge to mobilize her own resources, her own potential for work and love, appears to be a key therapeutic task for Therese. It could offer a particular opportunity in relationship (i.e., disappointment) crises between therapist and patient if she feels that the object is withdrawing, rejects her, and refuses to gratify her desires.

The preceding analysis is limited to the initial narratives and has the nature of an excerpt in terms of an analytical penetration. However, we may apply the results to the personality of the narrator. We assume that Therese's wish-motives are reflected in her communicative enactment because the narrative sequence, which unfolds as goal directed, offers a view of the vitality of her mental life in all its conflictive nature.

What patients tell their psychotherapists is not the factual content of their lives. Rather, they suggest this content in their central emotional engagement with its specific complications and consequences. As narrative seducers and persuaders, storytellers enjoy the privilege of placing their personal suffering intensely before listeners who are involved primarily in an affirmatively corealizing and coshaping way and of evoking a resonance. This resonance is an essential element in the formation of trust between therapist and patient. Certainly, the therapeutic process also involves the dissolution of those experiential dramas that have proven to be unsatisfactory crutches in dealing with the adversities and challenges of everyday life, with its mix of pleasure and pain.

CONCLUSION: NARRATIVE ANALYSIS AND PSYCHOTHERAPEUTIC PRACTICE

We will take stock of the complex of storytelling in the psychoanalytical context. Narration can be viewed as a specific way to regulate the contributions of at least two participants in a conversation by giving one of them the right to narrate. To claim this right, narrators need to make introductory, maintaining, and concluding statements. These statements have to be ratified by listeners. To claim and give the right to narrate, the participants use more or less standardized communication techniques; however, these techniques are not used ritually, unlike the techniques used in professional storytelling situations. In everyday storytelling, the narration is not initiated by an assignment but by personal motives, and it is shaped accordingly. A speech sequence only qualifies as a narrative if it describes a process that is confined by space and time and is driven by emotions. This emotional drive should not only be active in the past but also in the present. Narrations are very evocative; in other words, the narrative suggests things to listeners as well as to narrators. The narrative speech sequence is dynamically organized and is characterized by the tension between a desired situation and an actual situation. The narrative can only have its place in the conversation if this tension affects narrators and listeners as well. This happens when they both become involved in the concern that stands behind the narrative, without mentioning it explicitly because mentioning it would distance the participants from each other and counteract the motivation of the narrative.

By telling stories, we take possession of the world. Everybody can narrate. We use this ability every day. To narrate enables us to express our experiences in a personal way and to involve other people in our own personal drama. It furnishes our experiences with an individual and unmistakable physiognomy. Narrators are moved and touched by what has happened to them, and they bring these feelings to life by telling their story.

Patients tell stories during psychotherapy sessions. This is their personal way of telling what the problem is and what makes them suffer. The narrative expression of tragedy and hope demands an emotional engagement of listeners. Furthermore, listeners should be able to discern and establish connections between sequences and to judge them. This allows the psychoanalyst to detect psychological conflicts and to document the psychotherapeutic process in a way that does justice to the individual patient.

What Can Be Gained by Applying Systematic Narrative Analysis?

We suggest that these are some of the practical benefits of using this method of narrative analysis:

- The narrative expert gains insight into the rules of the narrative process in psychotherapy.
- The narrative expert understands the way the listener gets involved in the narration.
- The focus of attention is on the way experiences are evoked and structured by narrative speech.
- The narrative expert gains experience with establishing relationships in a narrative process.
- The experiences become explicit and can be expressed.
- The narrative expert is able to detect the logic of social relations in the narrative models: Narrations contain social intelligence.

From Psychoanalysis to Narrative Dynamics

From the beginning of the 20th century to this day, practice and theory of psychoanalysis have developed in many different directions, with the foundation of a multitude of schools and camps (see Erwin, 2002; Mertens, 1981, 1992, 1997; and Krause, 1997, for a historical and systematic presentation). Dream, scene, enactment, and narration were always concepts of fundamental importance for the understanding of the relationship between patient and psychoanalyst, the psychodynamic case conceptions, and the research questions. Thinking in dynamic configurations, orienting oneself in and by relationships, and pointing out and participating in enactments (Boothe, 1992; Lorenzer, 1974, 1983; Straub, 1999,

p. 280f). characterize psychotherapeutic practice, particularly if psychoses, traumas, and psychosomatic and personality disorders are to be treated. Psychoanalytic therapy has been subjected to controlled empirical research for a long time and quite successfully (Wallerstein, 1997). Grawe, Donati, and Bernauer (1994) and Roth and Fonagy (1996) have reviewed the outcomes of empirical studies on the efficacy of several psychodynamic therapeutic methods. Furthermore the Stockholm Outcome of Psychotherapy Project (STOP) (Sandell, 1997; Sandell, Blomberg, & Lazar, 1999), a large-scale study directed by Leuzinger-Bohleber and Stuhr (1997), and a study on psychoanalytic practice directed by Rudolf (Grande, Rudolf, & Oberbracht, 1997) have produced promising results.

Most important, there is a new interdisciplinary interest in the subjectivity of the patient and in systematic case studies. This interest focuses on narrative communication. At present, self-articulation and self-modification are becoming subjects of practice-oriented research. For the study of these subjects, the methodology of qualitative research plays a key role (Flick, 1995; Frommer & Rennie, 2001).

Psychoanalytic therapy is based on a theory of motivated ignorance that describes a dynamic of a conflictive offense against the self. A conflictive offense against the self leads to interference in and disarrangement of psychological and psychosocial regulations and communication, social and physical resources in case of crisis. Patients and psychoanalysts cooperate to enable patients to regain the capability to perceive, to judge, and to make decision by sensitizing them to psychological defensiveness and its motives. Furthermore, the relationship provides the patients with an environment that helps them to confront their selves.

To communicate and to understand narrative self-presentation not only is a valuable way to detect the patient's subjective entanglements but also provides a verbal representation of the individual relationships between patients and therapists. Narrative competence and the competence to analyze narrations allow patients and psychoanalysts, working together, to gain access to different kinds of relationships and memories by the process of enactment and reenactment, clarification and interpretation. Patients are then able to experience their vital concerns (wishes), which are wrapped in narrations and yearning to be expressed. Those concerns can characterize the lives of patients if they become elements of pleasure and happiness.

REFERENCES

Boothe, B. (1992). The unavailable relationship, the capacity to be alone, and the female oedipal development. *International Forum of Psychoanalysis, 1*, 104-109.

Boothe, B. (1994). *Der Patient als Erzähler in der Psychotherapie* [The patient as narrator in psychotherapy]. Göttingen, Germany: Vandenhoeck und Ruprecht.

Boothe, B. (1998). Einige Bemerkungen zum Konzept des Wünschens in der Psychoanalyse [Remarks on the concept of wishing in psychoanalysis]. In B. Boothe, R. Wepfer, & A. von Wyl (Eds.), *Über das Wünschen* (pp. 203-249). Göttingen, Germany: Vandenhoeck & Ruprecht.

Boothe, B. (1999). Narrative episodes and the dynamics of psychic conflict. *Journal for Gestalt Theory and its Applications (GTA), 21*, 6-24.

Boothe, B. (2001a). Erzähldynamik und psychischer Verarbeitungsprozess. Eine narrative Einzelfallanalyse [Narrative dynamics and psychological processing. A narrative case study]. *Psychotherapie und Sozialwissenschaft, 3*, 28-51.

Boothe, B. (2001b). Non-individuation and wedding with death in the works of Friedrich Dürrenmat. *PSYART: A Hyperlink Journal for the Psychological Study of the Arts*, article 010424. Retrieved January 23, 2003, from http://www.clas.ufl.edu/ipsa/journal/articles/psyart2001/boothe01.htm

Boothe, B. (2001c). The rhetorical organisation of dream-telling. *Counselling and Psychotherapy Research, 1*, 101-113.

Boothe, B. (2002a). Looking a hundred years back: Remarks on the concept of "wishing" in psychoanalysis. *International Forum of Psychoanalysis, 11*, 188-197.

Boothe, B. (2002b). Oedipus complex. In E. Erwin (Ed.), *The Freud encyclopedia. Theory, therapy, and culture.* (pp. 397-404). New York: Routledge.

Boothe, B., & the JAKOB Group. (2002). *Manual der Erzählanalyse JAKOB.* [Manual of the JAKOB narrative analysis]. Zürich. Switzerland: Psychologisches Institut.

Boothe, B., von Wyl, A., & Wepfer, R. (1998). *Psychisches Leben im Spiegel der Erzählung. Eine narrative Psychotherapiestudie* [Psychological life as it manifests itself in narration. A narrative study of psychotherapy]. Heidelberg, Germany: Asanger.

Boothe, B., von Wyl, A., & Wepfer, R. (1999). Narrative dynamics and psychodynamics. *Psychotherapy Research, 9*, 258-273.

Bowlby, J. (1969). *Attachment and loss: Vol. 1. Attachment.* New York: Basic Books.

Brémond, C. (1964). *Logique du récit* [Logics of narrative]. Paris: Seuil.

Brooks, P. (1984). *Reading for the plot: Design and intention in narrative.* New York: Knopf.

Bruner, J. (1987). Life as narrative. *Social Research, 54*, 11-32.

Bruner, J. (1990). *Acts of meaning.* London: Harvard University Press.

Bühler, K. (1976). *Die Axiomatik der Sprachwissenschaften* [The axiomatic theory of language sciences]. Frankfurt, Germany: Klostermann.

Bühler, K. (1978). *Die Darstellungsfunktion der Sprache* [The descriptive function of language]. Frankfurt, Germany: Suhrkamp.

Eder, R. (1990). Uncovering young children's psychological selves: Individual and developmental differences. *Child Development, 61*, 849-863.

Eisenmann, B. (1995). *Erzählen in der Therapie. Eine Untersuchung aus handlungstheoretischer und psychoanalytischer Perspektive* [Narration in therapy. A social action approach and a psychoanalytical approach]. Opladen, Germany: Westdeutscher Verlag.

Erwin, E. (Ed.). (2002). *The Freud encyclopedia: Theory, therapy, and culture.* London: Routledge.

Fischer, P. (1996). *Die Spielregel—Ein Konzept der erzählanalytischen Methode JAKOB, angewendet und erprobt an autobiographischen Traumaufzeichnungen Franz Kafkas* [The rules—a concept of the narrative analysis JAKOB tested on and applied to the autobiographical dream recordings Franz Kafka's]. Unpublished master's thesis, University of Zürich, Switzerland.

Fivush, R., Gray, J., & Fromhoff, F. (1987). Two-year-olds talk about the past. *Cognitive Development, 2*, 393-409.

Flader, D., & Giesecke, M. (1980). Erzählen im psychoanalytischen Erstinterview: Eine Fallstudie [Narrations in the first psychoanalytical interview: A case study]. In K. Ehlich (Ed.), *Erzählen im Alltag* (pp. 209-262). Frankfurt, Germany: Suhrkamp.

Flick, U. (1995). *Qualitative Forschung. Theorie, Methoden, Anwendung in Psychologie und Sozialwissenschaften* [Qualitative research. Theory, methods, applications to psychology and social sciences]. Reinbek, Germany: Rowohlt.

Freud, S. (1955). Jenseits des Lustprinzips [Beyond the pleasure principle]. In *Gesammelte Werke* (Vol. 13, pp.1-69). London: Imago Publishing Co. (Original work published 1920)

Frommer, J., & Rennie, D. L. (Eds.). (2001). *Qualitative psychotherapy research: Methods and methodology.* Lengerich, Germany: Pabst Science.

Gergen, K. (1994). Mind, text, and society: Self-memory in social context. In U. Neisser & R. Fivush (Eds.), *The remembering self: Construction and accury in the self-narrative* (pp. 78-104). New York: Cambridge University Press.

Gergen, K. J., & Gergen, M. M. (1988). Narrative and the self as relationship. In L. Berkowitz (Ed.), *Advances in experimental social psychology* (Vol. 21, pp. 17-56). New York: Academic Press.

Goffman, E. (1959). *The presentation of self in everyday life.* New York: Doubleday.

Grande, T., Rudolf G., & Oberbracht, C. (1997). Die Praxisstudie Psychoanalytische Langzeittherapie: Ein Projekt zur prospektiven Untersuchung struktureller Veränderungen in Psychoanalysen [The empirical study of a psychoanalytical long-term therapy: A prospective study of structural changes in psychoanalyses]. In M. Leuzinger-Bohleber & U. Stuhr (Eds.), *Psychoanalysen im Rückblick* (pp. 415-431). Giessen, Germany: Psychosozial-Verlag.

Grawe, K., Donati, R., & Bernauer, F. (1994). *Psychotherapie im Wandel: Von der Konfession zur Profession* [Changing psychotherapy: From confession to profession]. Göttingen, Germany: Hogrefe.

Gülich, E., & Hausendorf, H. (2000). Vertextungsmuster Narration [Narrative text pattern]. In K. Brinker, G. Antos, W. Heinemann, & S. F. Sager (Eds.), *Text- und Gesprächslinguistik: Ein internationales Handbuch zeitgenössischer Forschung* (pp. 369-385). Berlin, Germany: De Gruyter.

Gülich, E., & Quasthoff, U. M. (1986). Storytelling in conversation: Cognitive and interactive aspects. *Poetics, 15,* 217-241.

Hartmann, H. (1939). Ich-Psychologie und Anpassungsproblem [Ego psychology and problem adaptation]. *Internationale Zietschrift für Psychoanalyse, 24,* 62-135.

Hartmann, H. (1950). Psychoanalysis and developmental psychology. *Psychoanalytic Study of the Child, 5,* 7-17.

Krause, R. (1997). *Allgemeine Psychoanalytische Krankheitslehre* [General psychoanalytical pathology]. Stuttgart, Germany: Kohlhammer.

Labov, W., & Fanshel, D. (1977). *Therapeutic discourse: Psychotherapy as conversation.* New York: Academic Press.

Leuzinger-Bohleber, M., & Stuhr, U. (Eds.). (1997). *Psychoanalysen im Rückblick: Methoden, Ergebnisse und Perspektiven der neueren Katamneseforschung* [Retrospective psychanalyses: Methods, results and perspectives of the latest catamnestic research]. Giessen, Germany: Psychosozial-Verlag.

Lewis, M., & Brooks-Gunn, J. (1979). *Social cognition and the acquisition of the self.* New York: Plenum.

Liedtke, J. (1990). *Narrationsdynamik: Analyse und Schematisierung der dynamischen Momente im Erzählprodukt* [Narrative dynamics: Analysis and schematizing of the dynamic moments in narrations]. Tübingen, Germany: Niemeyer.

Lorenzer, A. (1974). Wittgensteins Sprachspiel: Konzept in der Psychoanalyse [Wittgenstein's language game: The concept of the psychoanalysis]. *Psyche, 28,* 833-852.

Lorenzer, A. (1983). Sprache, Lebenspraxis und szenisches Verstehen in der Psychoanalyse [Language, experience of life and scenic comprehension in psychoanalysis]. *Psyche, 37,* 97-115.

Luborsky, L. (1977). Measuring a pervasive structure in psychotherapy: The core conflictual relationship theme. In N. Freesman & S. Grand (Eds.), *Communicative structures and psychic structures* (pp. 347-395). New York: Plenum.

Luborsky, L., & Kächele, H. (1986). *Der zentrale Beziehungskonflikt. Ein Arbeitsbuch* [The crucial relational conflict]. Ulm, Germany: PSZ-Verlag.

Lucius-Hoene, G. (2000, November). *Narrative Bewältigung von Krankheit: Versuch einer konzeptuellen Fassung im Vergleich mit der Coping-Forschung* [Narrative coping with illness: Attempt to compare a conceptual version with the coping-research]. Paper presented at the Symposium "Qualitative linguistische Verfahren und klinische Forschung," am Zentrum für Interdisziplinäre Forschung in Bielefeld, Germany.

Luder, M. (1999a). *Die computerunterstützte Erzählanalyse JAKOB: Handbuch* [The computer assisted narrative analysis JAKOB: A manual]. Zürich: Psychologisches Institut.

Luder, M. (1999b). *Kategorien und Codes: Auf dem Weg zu einer computerunterstützten Fassung der Erzählanalyse JAKOB* [Categories and codes: Toward a computer assisted analysis JAKOB]. Unpublished master's thesis, University of Zürich, Switzerland.

Mergenthaler, E. E. (1992). *Die Transkription von Gesprächen* [The transcription of conversations] (3rd ed.). Ulm, Germany: Ulmer Textbank.

Mertens, W. (1981). Krise der psychoanalytischen Theorie? [Crisis of psychoanalytical theory]. In W. Mertens (Ed.), *Neue Perspektiven der Psychoanalyse* (pp.13-82). Stuttgart, Germany: Kohlhammer.

Mertens, W. (1992). *Einführung in die psychoanalytische Therapie* [Introduction into psychoanalytical therapy] (Vols.1-3) (2nd ed.). Stuttgart, Germany: Kohlhammer.

Mertens, W. (1997). *Psychoanalyse: Geschichte und Methoden* [Psychoanalysis: History and methods]. München, Germany: Beck.

Miller, P., Potts, R., Fung, H., Hoogstra, L., & Mintz, J. (1990). Narrative practices and the social construction of self in childhood. *American Ethologist, 17,* 292-311.

Neisser, U. (1998). Stories, selves, and schemata: A review of ecological findings. In M. Conway, S. Gathercole, & C. Cornoldi (Eds.), *Theories of memory* (Vol. 2, pp. 171-186). Cambridge, UK: Polity Press.

Nelson, K. (1993). Explaining the emergence of autobiographical memory in early childhood.

In A. Collins, S. Gathercole, M. Conway, & P. Morris (Eds.), *Theories of memory* (Vol. 1, pp. 355-385). Hove, UK: Lawrence Erlbaum.

Papousek, M. (1995). Origins of reciprocity and mutuality in prelinguistic parent-infant dialogues. In I. Marková, C. F. Graumann, & K. Foppa (Eds.), *Mutualities in dialogue* (pp. 28-81). Cambridge, UK: Cambridge University Press.

Propp, V. (1968). *Morphologie des Märchens* [Morphology of fairy-tales]. Frankfurt, Germany: Suhrkamp.

Quasthoff, V. M. (1980). *Erzählen in Gesprächen* [Narrations in conversations]. Tübingen, Germany: Niemeyer.

Ricoeur, P. (1996). *Das Selbst als ein Anderer* [The self as other]. Munich, Germany: Fink.

Roth, A., & Fonagy, P. (1996). *What works for whom? A critical review of psychotherapy research*. New York: Guilford.

Sandell, R. (1997). Langzeitwirkung von Psychotherapie und Psychoanalyse [Long-term impact of psychotherapy and psychoanalysis]. In M. Leuzinger-Bohleber & U. Stuhr (Eds.), *Psychoanalysen im Rückblick* (pp. 348-365). Giessen, Germany: Psychosozial-Verlag.

Sandell, R., Blomberg, J., & Lazar, A. (1999). Wiederholte Langzeitkatamnesen von Langzeit-Psychotherapien und Psychoanalysen [Repeated long-term catamnesis of long-term psychotherapies and psychoanalyses]. *Zeitschrift für Psychosomatische Medizin und Psychoanalyse, 45,* 43-56.

Schafer, R. (1979). The appreciative analytic attitude and the construction of multiple histories. *Psychoanalysis and Contemporary Thought, 2,* 3-24.

Schafer, R. (1980). Action and narration in psychoanalysis. *New Literary History, 12,* 61-85.

Spence, D. P. (1982a). *Narrative truth and historical truth: Meaning and interpretation in psychoanalysis*. New York: Norton.

Spence, D. P. (1982b). Narrative truth and theoretical truth. *The Psychoanalytic Quarterly, 1,* 43-69.

Spence, D. P. (1983). Narrative persuasion. *Psychoanalytical Contemporary Thought, 6,* 457-481.

Stanzel, F. K. (1988). *Theorie des Erzählens* [Narrative theory] (2nd ed.). Göttingen, Germany: Vandenhoeck und Ruprecht.

Straub, J. (1999). *Handlung, Interpretation, Kritik: Grundzüge einer textwissenschaftlichen Handlungs- und Kulturpsychologie* [Action, interpretation, critique: Outlines of a linguistic action and culture psychology]. Berlin, Germany: Walter de Gruyter.

Von Cranach, M., Kalbermatten, U., Indermühle, K., & Gugler, B. (1980). *Zielgerichtetes Handeln* [Purposive action]. Bern, Switzerland: Huber.

Von Matt, P. (1995). *Verkommene Söhne, missratene Töchter: Familiendesaster in der Literatur* [Debased sons, ill-bred daughters. Family disasters in literature]. Munich, Germany: Hanser.

Von Wyl, A. (2000a). *Magersüchtige und bulimische Patientinnen erzählen: Eine narrative Studie der Psychodynamik bei Essstörungen* [What anorexic and bulimic patients have to tell: A narrative study of anorexic patients' psychodynamic situation]. In B. Boothe & R. Volkart (Eds.), *Psychoanalyse im Dialog* (Vol. 9). Bern, Switzerland: Peter Lang.

Von Wyl, A. (2000b). What anorexic and bulimic patients have to tell: The analysis of patterns of unconscious conflict expressed in stories about everyday events. *European Journal of Psychotherapy, Counselling and Health, 3,* 375-388.

Wallerstein, R. S. (1997). Katamnesen in der Psychoanalyse: Zu ihrem klinischen und empirischen Wert [Catamnesis in psychoanalysis: The clinical and empirical value]. In M. Leuzinger-Bohleber & U. Stuhr (Eds.), *Psychoanalysen im Rückblick* (pp. 46-60). Giessen, Germany: Psychosozial-Verlag.

Welch-Ross, M. (1995). An integrative model of the development of autobiographical memory. *Developmental Review, 15,* 338-365.

Werling, S. (1989). *Handlung im Drama* [Action in drama]. Bern, Switzerland: Lang.

White, H. (1986). *Auch Klio dichtet oder Die Fiktion des Faktischen* [Klio also writes poetry or the fiction of the actual]. Stuttgart, Germany: Klett-Cotta.

Wiedemann, P. M. (1986). *Erzählte Wirklichkeit* [Narrated reality]. Weinheim, Germany: Psychologie Verlags Union.

Wolfson, N. (1978). A feature of performed narrative: The conversational historical present. *Language in Society, 7,* 215-237.

Part V

Emerging Trends and Future Directions

CHAPTER 17

Narrative Activity
Clients' and Therapists' Intentions in the Process of Narration

HEIDI M. LEVITT

DAVID L. RENNIE

Narrative is a hot topic these days. Linguistically, narrative has been understood as a major discursive form involving a beginning, protagonist, plot, and end (e.g., Aristotle, 1954; Frye, 1957; Ricoeur, 1983/1990). Epistemically, it has been related to narrative knowing, or knowing in terms of particular persons or experiences, in contrast with paradigmatic knowing, or knowing in terms of general considerations or even laws (Bruner, 1986; Polkinghorne, 1988; Sarbin, 1986; Spence, 1986). In light of these understandings, psychotherapy has been construed as a situation where clients are helped to retell their lives in ways that reduce their emotional pain and help them move forward (McLeod, 1997; Neimeyer, 1994; Schafer, 1976; White & Epston, 1990).

Most of the research on narrative in psychotherapy has been directed to the spoken discourse between the client and the therapist, with a focus on the client's contribution to it. This focus on conversation has taken a variety of forms. In some approaches, the interest has been in organizing the client's discourse into typological structures (Angus, Levitt, & Hardtke, 1999; Levitt & Angus, 2000), which in turn may be examined in terms of their coherence over time

AUTHORS' NOTE: The authors wish to thank the clients and therapists who volunteered to participate in the studies leading to this chapter as well as the Social Sciences and Humanities Research Council of Canada for its support of this research. Correspondence regarding this chapter should be sent to Heidi M. Levitt, University of Memphis, Psychology Department, Psychology Building, Room 202, Memphis, TN 38152, or to hlevitt@memphis.edu.

(Gonçalves, Korman, & Angus, 2000). In others, narrative has been examined inductively in terms of major themes evident during the course of therapy (McLeod & Balamoutsou, 1996, 2001). In still others, the themes of interest have been framed by theories of various sorts (e.g., Luborsky & Crits-Cristoph, 1990; Stiles et al., 1990; Stiles, Meshot, Anderson, & Sloan, 1992). A feature of these discursive approaches to narrative research is that, by limiting analyses to the researchers' perspective, they are free to interpret features of clients' stories about which the clients themselves may not have been aware.

A disadvantage of these varied approaches to narrative psychotherapy research, however, has been the absence of the clients' and therapists' self-reflections on their experiences of narrative communication (unless they happen to talk about them in the session). A branch of research has been developed, however, in which investigators examine the intentions in and experience of constructing the psychotherapy narrative. These studies can investigate this experience when narrative is construed as instances in session when clients relate stories characterized by a plot and having a beginning-middle-ending structure. They can also study narrative when it is construed as a discursive process that engulfs *all* of the clients' in-session communication. The rationale for the latter approach is that all thought ultimately leads to the restructuring of clients' own autobiographical narratives (see Labov, 1997; Polkinghorne, 1995; or Vogel, 1994; for further discussion of the meanings attributed to this term). Indeed, in this chapter, research is presented that uses both traditional and inclusive definitions of narrative.

Both authors have used the technique of Interpersonal Process Recall (IPR) (Elliott, 1986; Kagan, 1975) to access the client's inner experience of engaging in discourse with the therapist (Rennie) or both the client's and the therapist's experience (Levitt). As will be seen, when clients are given the opportunity to describe what they were doing at particular moments in therapy, they reveal intentions, purposes, and motives that often are not mentioned to the therapist. Uncovering the inner activities directing therapeutic discourse increases the density and richness of our understanding of the discourse and of the relationship between the partners in the therapy exchange. These returns are made even greater when therapists are consulted about their experiences of the same moments.

Our joint interest in the inner intentions, purposes, and motives guiding the production of narrative from moment to moment thus differs from much of the research that has been conducted on narrative. While most of this previous work focuses on the narrative speech as separate from the internal experience during narration, when IPR is used, the participants' reports of their recollections of what they were experiencing in the moment under attention is what is of interest. In these reports, participants explain what they were doing in their discourse. Their explanations are limited to what they were aware of; they cannot, of course, comment on whatever unconscious determinants may also have been involved unless those determinants entailed processes that occurred automatically at the time but can be identified once attention is directed to them retrospectively. Those who are skeptical of any person's ability to explain what he or she was doing in therapy or any other form of discourse will, of course, dismiss the returns from such research as uninteresting. We counter that it is equally appropriate to be skeptical of any explanation of discourse that does not take into account conscious intentions. In this vein, then, our research helps to fill in the one side of this two-sided way of looking at discourse.

In focusing on the functions of narrative in therapy, accordingly, we begin with a summary of such functions of narratives in the light of clients' reports given in the study by Rennie (1994b). We proceed to integrate into this picture the understandings coming from the IPR studies of narrative processes as they contribute to the telling of clients' life stories. Here, in the interest of exploring the more general processes in depth, we will draw on Levitt's work. In that fashion, we present a case study of a narrative therapy entailing IPR interviews with both a client and her therapist describing their experiences of the client's narration and storytelling where, interestingly, part of it was about the client's interest in her family's story. This analysis illustrates the functions that the narrative had not only for the client but also for the therapist.

Activities in Narrating a Specific Story

Rennie's (1994b) study was derived from a larger one in which 14 clients were presented with replays of either audio- or videotapes of most of an entire session of psychotherapy that they had just finished. In IPR inquiries, they were invited to stop the tape replay at any point where they recalled having experienced something interesting or significant and to describe what they remembered. Two of these clients were interviewed about two separate therapy sessions each, so that a total of 16 therapy sessions were studied (all 16 sessions are addressed in Rennie, 1992). Of these, 11 entailed recollections of experiences of storytelling. A grounded theory (Glaser & Strauss, 1967; Rennie, Phillips, & Quartaro, 1988) analysis of the transcripts of the reports on these experiences provided glimpses into why these clients had engaged in storytelling and how they went about doing it. Some of these reasons had to do with a desire to penetrate authentically into inner experience, others with a desire to alter it nonauthentically.

To a considerable extent, this authentic versus inauthentic use of storytelling distinguished clients who had entered the therapy session in either of two different frames of mind. Some clients had intended to get to the bottom of burdening troubles, if possible. Noteworthy in this regard was a client who had had, prior to the therapy session studied, a bad week at work. She was a master's-level counselor who was underemployed as a waitress to help her husband get through graduate school. Earlier that week, her employer had required her to polish furniture in the restaurant, which meant she had to get on her knees, which had been humiliating. This humiliation had catalyzed questions and concerns about her life and what she should be doing with it, at this particular juncture and in the future. These questions and concerns, it seemed, had to some extent been not only difficult to entertain but inchoate as well.

In the IPR inquiry, the client indicated that, in dealing with these concerns in the therapy session, she had begun by telling the story of the humiliating experience at work, knowing that there was more beneath the story. She had not wanted to launch directly into a frank discussion of her deeper concerns, however. Instead, she hovered, as it were, above the concerns, keeping emotionally in touch with them but at a comfortable distance through the telling of the story. In the same token, the therapist's responses to her story had given her a sense of the extent to which he had understood and accepted her, which she had needed to step below the story into its deeper significance. Later in the session, she left the story to engage in a more direct discussion of her deeper concerns.

Thus, it became apparent that clients in this frame of mind used stories in therapy as a means of delaying direct entry into an inner disturbance. Moreover, this delaying activity was useful in its own right in several ways. It provided a way of keeping the inner disturbance in sight, if at a distance for a while. It evoked images, memories, and feelings that were all connected with the inner disturbance. It provided a meaning space where helpful realizations came to her, realizations that she kept to herself because she was not yet ready, as indicated, to broach them directly with her therapist. The storytelling also enabled her to get rid of some of the disturbing feeling around the humiliating event. Overall, in the analysis of this kind of authentic engagement with disturbing experience, it became apparent that storytelling was used to allow time to develop the comfort needed to engage in an eventual direct exploration of the disturbance.

Alternatively, clients who were in a different frame of mind used stories nonauthentically. Here, something had occurred in their lives that was too disturbing to accept. It was also vivid in memory, poignant, even searing. These clients entered the session with an inchoate desire to deal with the disturbance without getting to the bottom of it. Thus, among these clients, one told his therapist a story about his girlfriend having spent the night with his best male friend. In an intense outpouring of this story, he worked hard at believing that his girlfriend had simply slept on his friend's couch. He told the story in this way with great passion. Yet, in the IPR session, he indicated that he had been trying vigorously to convince both himself and his therapist that the given version of events was the true one. Throughout, however, he had thoughts, feelings, and images that told him otherwise, which he had not revealed to his therapist. Thus, it became apparent that stories may be used by some clients to manage, even at the expense of distortion, their beliefs about something that is extremely important to them. It also came to be understood that, parallel with this activity, these clients had realizations of their true beliefs of the story stirred up by the act of telling it defensively, as it were. In this sense, then, it was apparent that storytelling can lead to insight even when the intent behind the storytelling was to prevent this outcome.

Activities in Narrating a Life Story

In her work on silences, Levitt (2001a, 2001b, 2002) conducted IPR interviews in which she asked clients to describe what was happening for them as they reviewed moments of silence within their psychotherapy sessions. She has described (Levitt, 2002) how, in these silent moments, they had been intensely in touch with their internal experience to the point that they needed to break away from the therapy discourse to focus inwardly. It was often within these moments that they came into contact with novel elements that acted to refine the narrative expression that followed. This research was conducted within the perspective, described previously, that views all psychotherapy discourse as an effort to reshape the clients' autobiographical narrative.

Accordingly, three types of productive pauses were identified. The first was what Levitt has referred to as *emotional* pauses, where clients attended to both incipient and strong feeling. The second was *expressive* pauses, where they sought labels or symbols to represent their experiences within the therapy dialogue. The third was *reflective* pauses, or moments when connections and interpretations were made. Clients described experiencing these pauses as therapeutic in that the silences helped them to identify, analyze, and communicate their internal experiences and to recognize new dimensions of their experience that they would use to transform the session discourse. At the same time, clients also reported that they had felt pressured to carry on with the conversation when what they wanted was more time to focus on their selves. As lengthy pauses were felt to be awkward, clients reported prematurely reengaging in narrative activity at the potential cost of realizing new insights or emotions. Thus, these processes, carried out silently, appeared to be the moments in which new awareness was developed. Therefore, these introspective moments can be positioned as the goal of psychotherapy because they lead to a narrative that reflects a deepened awareness of self. The narrative then becomes the supporting framework that guides clients to greater comfort with self-examination, enabling them to reach new depths of awareness and, in turn, a more comprehensive narrative. This formulation appears circular, but it is not because of the person's capacity to shift an experience through an attempt to articulate it while all the while staying within that same experience (Gendlin, 1996; Taylor, 1989). By subverting the primacy of the spoken word, the intentions, purposes, or motives that generate psychotherapeutic narrative discourse emerged as vital activities.

Levitt (2001a) also has described other types of pauses, termed *obstructive*, in which cognitive/affective activities prevent a deepening of awareness. Thus, disengaged silences occurred when the threat of a painful or anxiety-provoking emotion caused clients to avoid exploration. These moments were described as being consciously willed at times, when clients felt that a topic was dangerous (cf. Rennie, 1994b). At other times, the avoidance was reported to have occurred without deliberation, automatically, as it were. Second, *interactional* pauses occurred when clients switched from exploring their own issues to think about those of their therapists. Most often, these silences had happened when clients were confused about their therapists' instructions or comments, worried about their therapists' experiences in session, or protecting the alliance from concerns they had about the treatment. Some of these pauses resulted in clients being deferential to their therapist. This connection of pauses with deference thus amplifies what has been brought to light about deference in other IPR studies (e.g., Grafanaki & McLeod, 1999, 2002; Rennie, 1994a; Rhodes, Hill, Thompson, & Elliott, 1994; Timulak & Lietaer, 2001; Watson & Rennie, 1994). Unless the concerns motivating them were addressed in the session, these silences interfered with the clients' inner exploration because they had altered their narrative discourse for these reasons and limited or distorted the information available for exploration. Thus, one client entered a series of interactional pauses when her cognitive therapist asked her to imagine what a friend might tell her to help her raise her self-esteem. The client sat silently, thinking about her friends who in fact had abandoned her in her depression but knowing that a disgruntled reply would not meet the task demands set before her. She replied, after the resulting silence, "I don't know." Trying another approach, the therapist then asked her to consider what she might tell a friend. But being placed in the position of supporting the friends who had hurt her was even more difficult. In an attempt to provide the therapist with the expected answer, the client gave a disingenuous response, while doubting the purpose of the entire exercise. This study points to clients' agency not only in generating meaningful narratives but in avoiding them when narration might prove too threatening either to themselves or to the therapeutic alliance.

Two Principal Narrative Intentions

Thus, the various IPR studies converge in indicating two fundamental sets of intentions underlying storytelling and narrative discourse. The first has to do with emotional exploration and expressive symbolization prompted by a desire to understand oneself more fully. The second pertains to the management of anxiety arising in intrapersonal exploration and interpersonal interaction and is manifested in defensive activities such as belief management, disengagement, interactional contemplation, and deference. These activities, usually carried out covertly, are purposeful. As such, they are either carried out deliberately and are conscious or they are automatic in the moment but accessible to awareness when reflected on. Thus, whether telling stories in the traditional sense of the term or engaged in narrative in the inclusive sense, clients may conduct either authentic or inauthentic self-exploration, or both, depending on the exigency of the moment and their characteristic way of addressing inner experience.

An Example of Narrative Activities and Intentions

To illustrate an inquiry into the intentions behind discourse, we present below segments of the transcripts of a therapy session and of IPR interviews with both the client and the therapist about these moments in the session. This material comes from a larger study by Levitt and Adams (2003) on therapists' and clients' reports on significant events occurring in one of their therapeutic sessions. Therapists and clients were interviewed separately within a day of a session, and both were asked to review the taped session, pausing it at moments that they deemed to be significant. At these points, they were asked to describe what was important about that moment.

Segment of session transcript. The following dialogue took place between a therapist and client of the same ethnic background. The 22-year-old client had been discussing family issues with her therapist in the context of a university counseling clinic; the therapist had shared with her in a previous session some of his own writing on family dynamics within their shared Hispanic culture, referring to his own family of origin to exemplify points. It is noteworthy that the therapist practices a humanistic approach influenced by narrative therapy, thereby lending a second layer of relevance to this case study. At this particular moment in the session, the client finished a lengthy story, describing the dynamics she had seen within her boyfriend's family. The therapist responded by identifying the common theme within her and her boyfriend's family histories.

Therapist So, you both [client and her boyfriend] share that, that you have these, this, these vivid traumas in your life and you both tried to overcome them, and

Client Yeah.

Therapist you both are put in situations where you, as the kid, had to try to get the family together.... You could say that his parents literally don't talk to each other, and yours talk to each other, but not really.

Client Right. *[laughs]*

Therapist So it's the same thing, it's like "I can't believe these adults can't get along."

Client Yeah. After so many years *[pause]*

Therapist So, you really found someone [your boyfriend] who can understand you? And you can understand him.

Client Mm hm. Yeah. Er, I try to make him understand me *[both laugh]*, because a lot of the times he doesn't. *[laughing]* But, um.

Therapist He doesn't?

Client A lot of the times he, like I told you

Therapist	Yeah.
Client	like he doesn't see things, like, how things can *[pause]* can *[pause]* like from your past
Therapist	Yes
Client	like he doesn't understand why I come to counseling.
Therapist	Yes.
Client	He's like, "That's weird."
Therapist	Hmm
Client	I'm like "I don't care if it's weird, I need to go," and whatever. And he just he's like "What do you guys talk about?" *[laughing]*
Therapist	Right.
Client	"Do you talk about me?" *[still laughing]* And, what, what do you say? *[laughing]* He just, he doesn't understand the whole
Therapist	Right
Client	concept, concept and *[pause]* I don't know *[longer pause]*
Therapist	So, that's the difference. You really are trying to deal with your past and he's not?
Client	Oh, he's not.
Therapist	Yeah.
Client	He's not, he's, he's very much like, very closed, and very and I think *[pause]* that's bad for him. *[A description of his withdrawal from his family members follows.]* He's always been the type to, like, hold things inside and never really talk about his feelings. *[The therapist asks how she has changed since they got together. She tells him that her boyfriend motivated her scholastically.]*
Client	So I think that we both have done things like for each other. That is completely different. Like I can't imagine my parents ever being like this. I wonder how their *[pause]* my parents' relationship was when they first started going out or
Therapist	Mm hm
Client	*[pause]* I know they only knew each other for like 3 months before they got married *[pause]*. Which is I think is crazy. . . . I just I wonder, I'm there, my parents are not very big on storytelling, and I'm like *[softly]*
Therapist	Mm hm
Client	they really haven't told us much. Never *[pause]*
Therapist	Mhm. That's funny because you, you are a storyteller
Client	Yeah
Therapist	and . . .
Client	and, so is my brother, and my brother and I always talk about, you know, "Mom and dad never say any stories to us. They never." *[pause]* My uncle actually, my brother went to go visit my uncle in Kentucky, my uncle owns a restaurant there, my mom's brother, and he is a big story tell, teller.
Therapist	Mm hm
Client	and he is just like, you know, "me and your Mom," he was telling all this to my brother, and my brother started telling me some of the stories he told him. I

was like *[pause]* really, I was like, "Wow! I never knew that" and *[pause]* it was just, and I want to go visit my Uncle just so that he can tell me stories. *[laughing]*

Therapist Sure!

Client just so he can, you know, talk to me, cause my parents are just *[pause]* you know, just so concerned with everyday life. They just never stop and, you know, enjoy *[softly]* or whatever. Talk about, you know the good times that they have had, or the struggles they've been through, or anything.

Therapist Mm hm. So they have really not shared that part with you.

Client Mm hm. Yeah.

Therapist *[pause]* You had to get it somewhere else, or not get it.

Client Right, right.

Therapist Makes you wonder about your parents, what were they like and what did they go through

Client Mm hm

Therapist and did they ever like love each other or?

[Client switches topic and continues talking about parents' problematic present-day dynamics.]

The conversation seems smooth and both participants appear to have been fruitfully exploring the client's relationship and her desire to gather stories about her parents as a means toward her own growth.

The therapist's perspective. In an IPR interview, the therapist recalled his engagement in this portion of the therapy session. He understood the client's open exploration as a response to his disclosure of his family dynamics in the previous session. As he said, "What seemed to really be important to her is being able to tell me her story. And that could be because she just read mine... So she kind of needs to reciprocate." This understanding **was** in keeping with his general co-construction of the narrative. Both he and the client had Hispanic backgrounds, and his mention of what the client had read in the quotation above refers to a writing that drew on his own life story, to that effect, which he had given to her to read earlier. He remarked on how their cultural connection added depth to the relationship and put him in sync with her stories.

He also understood the storytelling about the boyfriend's trauma as a vicarious way of talking about her own trauma and felt that doing so had allowed her to deepen her experience of her trauma. He commented,

> It's gotten much easier to do [talking about her own trauma], but sometimes she can kind of vicariously talk about her boyfriend's trauma easier than she can talk about hers..... [I] let her go to a certain extent and then to bring it back. "So what is it about you? How are your feelings toward your parents the same or different?" ... I think that, um, it [my guidance] lets her explore a little farther the way that what she might otherwise... It's a little deeper, um, I think.... She was telling it very, very differently [than before, so]... that's exciting [to me]....

As a narrative therapist, he also was aware of his activity in assisting and reinforcing her agency in the creation of stories.

> I think it's a need to, just this need to—to have what her parents don't have. It's like she doesn't have this story [of theirs].... And that there *is* a story ... [which is] a sign of intimacy.... Intimacy with whoever

you share it with. But really the basic intimacy is [with] the person you're telling the story about.... It's intimacy with him because it's a story building about their relationship.... What's therapeutic about it is the particular part of how this relationship is mutual. And, her part in that rather than [being passive] I'm just listening for signs of her, her, her agency.... And, uh, not really having to work too hard to do that. And then there's also, a lot of feelings of like getting pride that she's worked so hard that she could get to where she could say some things that are very insightful.

The purposes behind his conarrating for the therapist thus had been to increase the client's comfort, to stimulate her self-awareness, and to assist her in building a history of narratives about her relationship with her boyfriend. As it turned out, the therapist's sense of what was going on in her discourse in the therapy session about this last aspect, especially—the relationship with the boyfriend—had been both similar in some ways and quite different in others from the client's sense of it.

The client's perspective. Before describing the client's commentary, it is important to note that, throughout the IPR interview, she indicated how much she liked and admired her therapist and enjoyed the therapy experience. It is, thus, not surprising that the fewest differences pertained to their respective senses of their relationship with each other. She too felt that his self-disclosure was important. She put less emphasis on it than he did, however. For her, it was one of the many ways in which he had managed to convey to her that he was a real person, and one with whom she could feel comfortable. In other respects, their views were different, some subtly so, others more widely divided. A subtle difference pertained to the matter of trauma. When describing the client's experience as vicarious in this regard, the therapist implied that the client reexperienced her own trauma through her focus on her boyfriend's experience. In part, this seems to have been her sense as well, but the dialogue about her boyfriend's trauma held other significant meanings for her. She indicated that when she talked about how her boyfriend was confiding in her, she wanted to get across that her life had been tougher than his had been. In the IPR, she proclaimed that the abandonment her boyfriend experienced did not come close to what she had been through. She felt that everyday life for him was OK, unlike her everyday life. This sense also was present in her tacit comparison of the lack of stories in her own family as compared to the stories told in his family:

Client	I'm saying how my parents are not storytellers how they really never told us stories every day. They just really never told us anything. I know I [don't] want to be like that with my kids.... It's not normal and it's important for your kids to hear what your mom was like when she was 9 years old or what your dad was like at 16.... 'Cause you get to know your parents and, I don't know, [it] helps you relate to your kids and make them feel umm like, "I was a human being like you." I think that's important for parents to say that.... And I don't think my parents ever gave me that
Interviewer	a sense of relating to them?
Client	Yeah. I just always felt abused. I thought that they were like superior. "Oh, she's just a kid."... I kinda felt sad. It's kind of like an emptiness.... Or it kind of

feels unfair because other people had this. And I guess that's what I was kind of talking [thinking] about here, because before I was talking about my boyfriend's parents.

But a wider difference pertained to another sense of what she had also been doing when talking about her relationship with her boyfriend. She revealed that she had been trying to convey pride in the fact that her boyfriend was confiding in her and that she could help him, in spite of having endured greater suffering. Moreover, she had wanted to help her therapist assist her in the role of helper. This sense had not been on the therapist's radar screen at all. To complicate matters further, it is clear from her report that she withheld communicating her pride at her relative success in her own healing to manage the therapist's impression of her. She had done this out of fear that he would think she was being conceited about the hurdles she had overcome. As she said, "I just doubt myself. I'm like, 'No, I'm going to be selfish' or 'That's not right to say' . . . . I think 'What would the therapist think of me if I said something like that?' . . . Is that wrong for me to say? . . . It's not right to be competitive about your pain."

Thus, the discrepancies between what is revealed in the three transcripts are striking in some respects. The therapy transcript reads as though the conversation between the client and the therapist was about the client's quest to recover from a traumatic history similar to her boyfriend's and about the hunger for family stories to make her parents seem more human. In contrast, the transcript of the IPR with the therapist reveals that his intention in encouraging the client's storytelling about the family stories was to foster new narrative formulations. Beneath this intention was a supporting one that involved the belief that their shared cultural histories

and his encouragement to go deeper would strengthen not only their therapeutic alliance but also her intimacy with her boyfriend. To complicate matters further, what the client had been doing as far as she was concerned was to convey subtly—so as not to violate feared judgments by her therapist—her own strength at having faced greater obstacles and suffered greater deprivation than her boyfriend.

This case illustrates the unpredictability that can exist in judging the internal experience of either the therapist or the client on the basis of the discourse alone. Three stories may be occurring at once: the story in the dialogue between the client and the therapist, the client's inner story, and the therapist's inner story. Moreover, doubtless beneath such conscious, alternative intentions are often unconscious determinants as well. Whenever this happens, the process of narrative unfolding is even more complex.

This message is especially compelling in this case because it entailed a strong working alliance. Even here, the therapist had been disconnected in some ways from the client and had guided the exploration only in a faltering way, in the client's reported experience. That this kind of disjunction can occur even in a good working alliance has profound implications for the practice of and research on psychotherapy.

THERAPEUTIC AND RESEARCH STRATEGIES TO EXPLORE NARRATIVE INTENTIONALITY

Integrating Conversational and Intentional Approaches in Research

There are several advantages to studying narrative therapy through the analysis of conversation as an approach to discourse analysis. This approach is less threatening to clients and therapists than are studies entailing interviews with them about the experience of therapy, and especially IPR interviews. Correspondingly, the plan to study therapy conversation makes it easier to get research participants. Furthermore, the contributions of both the client and the therapist are available for study. As indicated above, the external perspective entailed in this approach enables the analyst to interpret therapy discourse in ways that may be beyond the ken of the therapy participants.

The disadvantage of this approach is that, although it provides one way of interpreting the meaning of discourse, it precludes another equally important one, which is the meaning it holds for those producing it. The handicap imposed on the attempt to make sense of the surface of text is brought home by Spence (1986) and Steele (1986). They describe the problems encountered in the attempt to understand the meaning of narrative text on the basis of its content alone. They point out that problems such as omission and the deliberate "smoothing" of narratives can rob the interpreter of important detail and context that could guide accurate interpretation. This state of affairs does not mean that interpretations are not possible, of course. But it does mean that any interpretation has to be made within a theoretical framework, whether psychoanalytic, social constructionist, feminist, and so on. Such frameworks may be very different from those used by the originators of the discourse themselves. This consideration opens up the question about the way to truth: Does the best account of the meaning of discourse have to do with what its originators intended by it or with interpretations of it from an external perspective that are presumed to reach beyond where the originators' awareness can go? This question divides even philosophical (e.g., Gadamer, 1960/1992) and methodical (e.g., Dilthey, 1961) hermeneuts, let alone poststructuralists (e.g., Rose, 1990) and phenomenologists (e.g., Giorgi, 1970) as they wrestle with questions of interpretation.

Our view is that despite the persuasiveness of the arguments, coming from many sides, that much of what goes on in thinking and discourse is beyond awareness, it is a mistake to ignore the intentions that thinkers and conversationalists attribute to their thinking and talking. The case study above and its supporting empirical research illustrate the point. As it happens, and also as illustrated, the development of intention-accessing techniques such as IPR, combined with the development of sophisticated methods of textual analysis such as the grounded theory method, provides ways to reveal and study systematically such covert activities.

It is distinctly possible and perhaps even to be recommended that the qualitative approach to understanding such activity goes hand in hand with more conventional research strategies. In fact, one of us (Levitt) has been doing just that in her development of the Pausing Inventory Categorization System (Levitt, 1998). The instrument provides a way of interpreting, from the surface of therapy text, the kinds of thoughts and feelings likely carried out and experienced by clients during pauses in their discourse with their therapists. The categories used in the inventory are derived from her qualitative research, have strong indices of interrater and client-rater reliability (see Levitt, 2001b), and can be applied to any therapy transcript or tape.

Recommendations for the Practice of Psychotherapy

Some qualities of the psychotherapy relationship may widen the gulf between experience and its expression. The power imbalance inherent in a therapist-client relationship certainly plays a role (e.g., Brown, 1994; Grafanaki & McLeod, 1999, 2002;

Rennie, 1994a; Rhodes et al., 1994; Timulak & Lietaer, 2001; Watson & Rennie, 1994). Thus, it is important for therapists to emphasize to their clients that their feedback is appreciated and to assure them that the alliance can withstand their corrections and perhaps even be strengthened by them. Otherwise, clients usually remain apprehensive about conveying their hesitations about suggestions or interpretations—even when a strong alliance is present.

As for narrative therapy, Newman and Holzman (1999) suggest that it is an activity that challenges modernist conceptions of human activity and emotion. In their view, the act of telling a story allows clients to delineate their individuated selves and establish social relations. These theorists eschew the view that narrative has merely explanatory utility for the therapist, noting instead, as we do, that the act of narration is therapeutic in and of itself. Along this line, it is important that therapists ask clients directly about their experiences in therapy and especially when subtle clues signifying ripples in the flow of therapy seem to call for it (Levitt, 2001a, 2001b, 2002; Rennie, 1998, 2002). By such metacommunicating (cf. Kiesler, 1996), or entering into dialogue about the dialogue, therapists can help clients become more aware of the processes that are either facilitating or impeding their progress. In particular, they can help clients to identify when their expression is misshapen deliberately, either to preserve the therapeutic relationship or to avoid emotional distress. Through this exploration, clients can become attuned to their styles of interacting interpersonally as well as the ways in which they defensively protect themselves. They can decide how they wish to manage the anxieties of discovery and interaction and can learn to intentionally guide their narrating processes to enhance and maintain states of therapeutic introspection.

Thus, for example, in the above case study, had the therapist been more attuned to possible disparities between what clients say and think, supported by subtle nonverbal clues (such as pauses, for example), he might have been able to detect moments when the spoken narrative and his client's inward experience were at cross-purposes. Had he also invited her to share what was behind the signs that all was not smooth for the client, she likely would have felt safe in revealing what she had been thinking. This being so, she might have been able to disclose her concerns about displeasing her therapist, potentially leading to greater assertion and honesty in therapy, and perhaps beyond it.

CONCLUSION

The work outlined and illustrated in this chapter brings into somewhat greater relief the extent to which both clients and therapists are self-aware agents with purposes behind their conversations in therapy (see also Bohart & Tallman, 1996, 1999; Rennie, 2000, 2001; for more on clients' agency). These purposes often are not expressed in the actual discourse of the therapy for many reasons. Perhaps the work's greatest value is in its illustration of the importance of the conscious nature of these intentions, the role of unconscious factors notwithstanding. It highlights the value of obtaining reports on experiences of therapy, and especially reports stimulated by the technique of IPR. The work supports the notion that for clients, storytelling is therapeutic in its own right, and it calls on therapists to be patient with storytelling and actively to help clients with it. It illustrates the utility of qualitative research methods as ways of making sense of such reports. It points out how clients and therapists can easily be in conflict without knowing it. Last but not least, the work sanctions an active role for therapists in the defusing of the power differential preventing clients from revealing what they are thinking in sticky moments, including moments entailed in narrative activity. It goes without saying that therapists need to appraise such activity sensitively so as not to interfere unduly with the flow of the clients' experience. But it is our strong view that, properly managed, this kind of bid for transparency cannot but enhance the almost infinitely complex activity of psychotherapeutic engagement, including the fathoming of the meaning of clients' stories and narrative activity in the broader sense.

REFERENCES

Angus, L., Levitt, H., & Hardtke, K. (1999). Narrative processes and psychotherapeutic change: An integrative approach to psychotherapy research and practice. *Journal of Clinical Psychology, 55* (10), 1255-1270.

Aristotle. (1954). *Rhetoric and poetics* (W. Rhys Roberts & I. Bywater, Trans.). New York: Random House.

Bohart, A., & Tallman, K. (1996). The active client: Therapy as self-help. *Journal of Humanistic Psychology, 36,* 7-30.

Bohart, A. C., & Tallman, K. (1999). *How clients make therapy work: The process of active self-healing.* Washington, DC: American Psychological Association.

Brown, L. S. (1994). Boundaries in feminist therapy: A conceptual formulation. *Women & Therapy, 15,* 29-38.

Bruner, J. (1986). *Actual minds, possible worlds.* Cambridge, MA: Harvard University Press.

Dilthey, W. (1961). *Meaning in history: Wilhelm Dilthey's thoughts on history and society* (H. P. Rickman, Ed., Trans., and Introduction). The Hague, Netherlands: Nijhoff.

Elliott, R. (1986). Interpersonal Process Recall (IPR) as a process research method. In L. Greenberg & W. Pinsoff (Eds.), *The psychotherapeutic process: A research handbook* (pp. 503-528). New York: Guilford.

Frye, N. (1957). *Anatomy of criticism: Four essays.* Princeton, NJ: Princeton University Press.

Gadamer, H.-G. (1992). *Truth and method* (2nd rev. ed.) (J. Weisheimer & D. G. Marshal, Trans.). New York: Crossroad. (Original work published 1960)

Gendlin, E. T. (1996). *Focusing-oriented psychotherapy: A manual of the experiential method.* New York: Guilford.

Giorgi, A. (1970). *Psychology as a human science: A phenomenologically based approach.* New York: Harper Row.

Glaser, B. G., & Strauss, A. (1967). *The discovery of grounded theory: Strategies for qualitative research.* Chicago: Aldine.

Gonçalves, O. F., Korman, Y., & Angus, L. (2000). Constructing psychopathology from a cognitive narrative perspective. In R. A. Neimeyer & J. D. Raskin (Eds.), *Constructions of disorder: Meaning-making frameworks for psychotherapy* (pp. 265-284). Washington, DC: American Psychological Association.

Grafanaki, S., & McLeod, J. (1999). Narrative processes in the construction of helpful and hindering events in experiential psychotherapy. *Psychotherapy Research, 9,* 289-303.

Grafanaki, S., & McLeod, J. (2002). Experiential congruence: Qualitative analysis of client and counselor narrative accounts of significant events in time-limited person-centered therapy. *Counselling and Psychotherapy Research, 2,* 20-32.

Kagan, N. (1975). *Interpersonal process recall: A method of influencing human interaction.* Unpublished manuscript, University of Houston, Houston, TX.

Kiesler, D. J. (1996). *Contemporary interpersonal theory and research: Personality, psychopathology, and psychotherapy.* New York: John Wiley.

Labov, W. (1997). Some further steps in narrative analysis. *Journal of Narrative & Life History, 7,* (1-4), 395-415.

Levitt, H. (1998). *Pausing inventory categorization system: Classifying clients' experiences of silences in psychotherapy.* Unpublished manuscript, University of Memphis, Memphis, TN.

Levitt, H. M. (2001a). Clients' experiences of obstructive silence: Integrating conscious reports and analytic theories. *Journal of Contemporary Psychotherapy, 31*(4), 221-244.

Levitt, H. M. (2001b). The sounds of silence in psychotherapy: Clients' experiences of pausing. *Psychotherapy Research, 11*(3), 295-309.

Levitt, H. (2002). Voicing the unvoiced: Narrative formulation and silences. *Journal of Counseling Psychology Quarterly, 15,* 333-350.

Levitt, H., & Adams, K. (2003). *A comparison of clients' and therapists' experiences of one therapy session*. Manuscript in preparation.

Levitt, H., & Angus, L. (2000). Psychotherapy process measure research and the evaluation of psychotherapy orientation: A narrative analysis. *Journal of Psychotherapy Integration, 9*(3), 279-300.

Luborsky, L., & Crits-Christoph, P. (1990). *Understanding transference: The Core Conflictual Relationship Theme method*. New York: Basic Books.

McLeod, J. (1997). *Narrative and psychotherapy*. Thousand Oaks, CA: Sage.

McLeod, J., & Balamoutsou, S. (1996). Representing narrative process in therapy: Qualitative analysis of a single case. *Counselling Psychology Quarterly, 9*, 61-76.

McLeod, J., & Balamoutsou, S. (2001). A method for qualitative narrative analysis of psychotherapy transcripts. In J. Frommer & D. Rennie (Eds.), *Qualitative psychotherapy research: Methods and methodology* (pp. 128-152). Lengerich, Germany: Pabst.

Neimeyer, R. A. (1994). The role of client-generated narratives in psychotherapy. *Journal of Constructivist Psychology, 7*, 229-242.

Newman, F., & Holzman, L. (1999). Beyond narrative to performed conversation ("In the beginning" comes much later). *Journal of Constructivist Psychology, 12*, 23-49.

Polkinghorne, D. E. (1988). *Narrative knowing and the human sciences*. Albany: SUNY Press.

Polkinghorne, D. E. (1995). Narrative configuration in qualitative analysis. *Qualitative Studies in Education, 8*, 5-23.

Rennie, D. L. (1992). Qualitative analysis of the client's experience of psychotherapy: The unfolding of reflexivity. In S. G. Toukmanian & D. L. Rennie (Eds.), *Psychotherapy process research: Paradigmatic and narrative approaches* (pp. 211-233). Thousand Oaks, CA: Sage.

Rennie, D. L. (1994a). Clients' deference in psychotherapy. *Journal of Counseling Psychology, 41*, 427-437.

Rennie, D. L. (1994b). Storytelling psychotherapy: The client's subjective experience. *Psychotherapy, 31*, 234-243.

Rennie, D. L. (1998). *Person-centred counselling: An experiential approach*. Thousand Oaks, CA: Sage.

Rennie, D. L. (2000). Aspects of the client's control of the psychotherapeutic process. *Journal of Psychotherapy Integration, 10*, 151-167.

Rennie, D. L. (2001). The client as a self-aware agent in counseling and psychotherapy. *Counselling and Psychotherapy Research, 1*, 82-89.

Rennie, D. L. (2002). Experiencing psychotherapy: Grounded theory studies. In. D. J. Cain & J. Seeman (Eds.), *Humanistic psychotherapies: Handbook of research and practice* (pp. 117-144). Washington, DC: American Psychological Association.

Rennie, D. L., Phillips, J. R., & Quartaro, G. K. (1988). Grounded theory: A promising approach to conceptualization in psychology? *Canadian Psychology, 29*, 139-150.

Rhodes, R. H., Hill, C. E., Thompson, B. J., & Elliott, R. (1994). Client retrospective recall of resolved and unresolved misunderstanding events. *Journal of Counseling Psychology, 41*, 473-483.

Ricoeur, P. (1990). *Time and narrative* (Vol. 1). Chicago: University of Chicago Press. (Original work published 1983)

Rose, N. (1990). *Governing the soul: The shaping of the private self*. London: Routledge.

Sarbin, T. R. (1986). *Narrative psychology: The storied nature of human conduct*. New York: Praeger.

Schafer, R. (1976). *A new language for psychoanalysis*. New Haven, CT: Yale University Press.

Spence, D. P. (1986). Narrative smoothing and clinical wisdom. In T. Sarbin (Ed.), *Narrative psychology: The storied nature of human conduct* (pp. 211-232). New York: Praeger.

Steele, R. S. (1986). Deconstructing histories: Toward a systematic criticism of psychological narratives. In T. Sarbin (Ed.), *Narrative psychology: The storied nature of human conduct* (pp. 256-275). New York: Praeger.

Stiles, W. B., Elliott, R., Llewelyn, S. P., Firth-Cozens, J. A., Margison, F. R., Shapiro, D. A., & Hardy, G. (1990). Assimilation of problematic experiences by clients in psychotherapy. *Psychotherapy, 27*, 411-420.

Stiles, W. B., Meshot, C. M., Anderson, T. M., & Sloan, W. W., Jr. (1992). Assimilation of problematic experiences: The case of John Jones. *Psychotherapy Research, 2*, 81-101.

Taylor, C. (1989). *Sources of the self: The making of modern identity*. Cambridge, MA: Harvard University Press.

Timulak, L., & Lietaer, G. (2001). Moments of empowerment: A qualitative analysis of positively experienced episodes in brief person-centered counseling. *Counselling and Psychotherapy Research, 1*, 62-73.

Vogel, D. (1994). Narrative perspectives in theory and therapy. *Journal of Constructivist Psychology, 7*, 243-261.

Watson, J. C., & Rennie, D. L. (1994). A qualitative analysis or clients' subjective experience of significant moments in therapy during the exploration of problematic reactions. *Journal of Counseling Psychology, 41*, 500-509.

White, M., & Epston, D. (1990). *Narrative means to therapeutic ends*. New York: Norton.

CHAPTER 18

"To Tell My Story"
Configuring Interpersonal Relations Within Narrative Process

TIMOTHY ANDERSON

My father-in-law likes to tell a story about my wife when she was 11 years old. She was determined to cut the lawn but couldn't keep the lawn mower running. He watched as she became increasingly flabbergasted, but he remained on the sidelines because she didn't want his help. She wanted independence and mastery of the machine and the yard. When her frustration had peaked, she finally signaled for his assistance. At that time, her father walked over to the lawn mower, simply flipped a belt back into position, and presto, the lawnmower started with little effort. She sensed that he had known this all along as she stewed in her own juices and tried to make the lawn mower work. The 11-year-old responded with even more frustration, now directed at her father. At this point, my father-in-law, a master storyteller, tightens up his face and dramatically changes his voice to capture the young girl's resentment—and this is the punch line, "I'm sorry my mom and me ever married you!"

The above story communicates meanings that are mostly to the storyteller's liking, preserving himself and his daughter in an interpersonal field in which his helping hand will always remain indispensable—even if it's the last thing that she wants. Many of the same principles associated with interpersonal relations are also found within narrative structure. The storyteller places characters in various relationship configurations, and the

---

AUTHOR'S NOTE: Correspondence regarding this chapter should be sent to the author at Ohio University, Department of Psychology, Athens, OH, 45701, or to andersot@ohiou.edu.

interactions unfold through the course of the narrative, usually concluding with the most meaningful moments. But that's not the end of the story. The listener coparticipates in the story's telling and may validate the narrator's construction or even provide alternative versions—all of which shape the perceived interpersonal *movements* of the characters. For example, the above story might be shaped by my wife's need for independence and mastery and by the way she perceived her father's initial restraint as cold mastery over her attempts to learn how to fix the lawn mower, as if he were waiting for her to fail. Each narration of the story takes on a different voice and allows for a resituation, a reinterpretation. As long as the story is told, it remains alive and dynamic, with the interactions among the multiple-voiced characters always up for negotiation and new meanings. That is, the characters in the story live independent lives that are not limited to the personal identity, or life story, of the narrator. For example, the above story could be used for several purposes and told in many voices: (a) as part of a personal autobiography, (b) as a response to my wife when she asserts her independence, (c) as a story told to the lawn mower repair person, or even (d) as part of an argument between my father-in-law and mother-in-law as an illustration of how mother and daughter were solidly allied against him.

Narrative exists in a wide variety of contexts and formats. The storyteller may speak from different temporal vantage points, from ancient history or deep within the vault of personal memory, or alternatively a narrator may provide a nearly real-time report as events occur. The storyteller's intent may range from providing an accurate rendering of events to creating a fantasy that seemingly cannot be linked to anything real. The context of the storytelling and the audience may also vary dramatically. The perspective on interpersonal narrative process outlined here will be limited mostly to spoken dialogue of personal stories such as those found within the intimate disclosures of psychotherapy sessions.

TOWARD A DEFINITION OF NARRATIVE

Most specific definitions of narrative have focused on narrative as a cognitive activity and constructive process that involves meaning making (Neimeyer & Stewart, 2000). Polkinghorne (1988) defines narrative as a cognitive and meaning-making process in which "human beings give meaning to their experience of temporal and personal actions" (p. 11). Narratives can also be understood in regard to the project of defining the self through a lifelong biography, which serves the more encompassing function of forming personal identity (e.g., McAdams, 2001). Habermas and Bluck (2000) describe stories in the context of the more advanced goal of the life narrative project. The cognitive and meaning-making aspects of narrative are directed to the specific purpose of understanding the self. This meaning-making activity is referred to as *autobiographical reasoning,* which "involves forming links between elements in one's life and the self in an attempt to relate one's personal past and present" (p. 749). Thus, autobiographical reasoning is the process of selecting and finding meaning among events so that events coherently fit within the ongoing process of constructing the larger life narrative. Autobiographical reasoning is a metaphorical device similar to what Stiles (1999) refers to as the process of building *meaning bridges,* which are also built for the purpose of self-definition.

The above definitions of narrative do not include a simpler observation. Almost all stories, especially those told in very personal settings such as psychotherapy or the family hearth, involve interactions between or among characters. Characters are usually people in relationship to each other or the narrator (or "elements" in the George Kelly sense). Interpersonal narratives also involve a cognitive process that gives meaning to temporal actions and involves building bridges that can be coherently articulated and reasoned. However, the nature of narrative can be understood differently when seen primarily as an *inter*personal process. Stories are a unique human tool that allows for the construction of interpersonal portraits in motion. Each story serves as a new stage in which the narrator repositions the characters in his or her life within a constantly moving interpersonal field. Hence, a narrative can be defined as the organization of the transactions among characters (i.e., events), experience, and time. The narrator imposes meaning and identity on these events by fixing a cast of characters who are continuously moving toward and away from each other. Interactions among characters in the opening of the story initiate a chain reaction among them and a movement toward a conclusion. I expand on related issues below.

Characters and Conflict

Characters roam the interpersonal field within the frame of the story, their jurisdiction partially defined by the narrator. Characters' movements toward and away from other characters will almost certainly alter the construed balance of interpersonal affairs. This *conflict* is the plot that the narrator attempts to resolve. Characters exhibit various controls over or away from each other as the narrator experiments with various interpersonal configurations. The conflict is concluded when the narrator imposes a new interpersonal configuration, one that is more in line with some facet of the narrator's construal of the interpersonal field. This is not to say that the interpersonal goals of the narrator are met in the outcome, but within the story, there will be some indication of the narrator's interpersonal *goals* or *the wish*.

Interpersonal Complementarity

One of the more central propositions of interpersonal theory is *complementarity*, which predicts how characters within the interpersonal field will respond to each other. Dominant interpersonal behaviors evoke submissive responses; submissive acts impel others to respond by taking charge. Warm and affiliative actions evoke similar warmth and affiliation, and likewise, hostile initiatives evoke hostile responses. Until recently, interpersonal complementarity was best understood as defining predictable behavioral reactions, which may not necessarily convey how people think and feel about relationships and, more important, how people choose their stories or how they might change these stories and make sense of their relationships. Benjamin (1993) has expanded these behavioral acts to include the intended focus of communication, which may affect how the interpersonal communication is received, and this has implications for how speakers may complement these intended communications. Horowitz, Dryer, and Krasnoperova (1997) have suggested that interpersonal complementarity cannot be understood without knowing one's interpersonal *goals*. The theoretical developments of Benjamin and Horowitz (among others) make it possible to understand narrative as a fundamentally interpersonal phenomenon.

The storyteller may experiment with various arrangements of the interpersonal field by constructing multiple stories or even multiple versions of the same story. From an interpersonal perspective, the events and conflict within a story represent the unfolding of interpersonal complementarity in the relationships between characters. Stories provide an opportunity to address critical incidents in the construction of the interpersonal field. For example, in the story that opens this chapter, the daughter challenges a submissive position by attempting to master the task of mowing the lawn, returns to a submissive position by needing father's help, and then, in a burst of protest, she re-asserts herself in a coup on paternal dominance. Each interpersonal movement in the story is a search for renegotiation of the energies that hold the characters in their relative positions within the interpersonal field. The meaning of the story can be interpreted from a variety of perspectives because the story itself only serves to situate the characters within the interpersonal field (see below). For example, the father may perceive the story as reinforcing paternal power, whereas the daughter may find meaning in having challenged the dominance over her.

Each narrative movement offers the possibility for construing alternatives in the interpersonal configuration of the characters. Interpersonal complementarity becomes useful as a tool for understanding a constructed landscape (including interpersonal goal states) and not behavioral reactions. It might even be said that narratives provide people with imaginary landscapes for exploring how shifts in interpersonal relationships may (or may not) lead to a chain reaction throughout the interpersonal field.

Interpersonal Power and Character Impermeability

Narrative conflict, then, is necessarily linked to interpersonal transactions between characters, which then dynamically ripple through the interpersonal field, reshaping interpersonal alliances and conflicts. An altered alliance adjusts the interpersonal space between characters, altering the interpersonal *gravity* among all characters within the interpersonal field. If the intensity of the narrative conflict is too great for the community of characters, there will be repercussions for those characters that have disrupted the balance. The interpersonal movements of the offending characters have led to a destabilization of relational balance among other characters. The community of characters must have sufficient resources to absorb the change in balance that occurs after any character's movement within the interpersonal field. Instead of reshaping the community of characters and already defined interpersonal alliances, it is often more parsimonious for the community of characters to recoil from allowing any shift and to pressure the offending characters back into place.

It might be argued that stories in which the interpersonal field is not significantly altered are more typical of everyday life. The interpersonal equilibrium is reestablished without a larger revolution of the interpersonal field, even while using a host of defensive strategies to deny the real limits of interpersonal freedom. In their actions, most people may accept a very limited number of degrees of interpersonal freedom and rarely if ever challenge the interpersonal status quo, living lives, to paraphrase Thoreau, in quiet, not fully realized desperation. In their stories, people may be quiet revolutionaries of the interpersonal field, experimenting and challenging the interpersonal status quo in ways often not realized in everyday encounters.

The point here is not so much that stories reflect some form of hegemonic oppression of social forces or expression of some repressed intrapsychic wishes. The real point is that narratives provide a unique level of representation, a step removed from overt interactions, in which interpretations of interpersonal configurations may be represented, hypothesized, and proposed by the narrator. Narratives are meaning bridges between the island of wishes and the direct interpersonal declarations of others. In psychologically healthy people, such declarations cannot exist for long without being incorporated into a narrative.

Stories as Change Opportunities

Narratives are especially important to psychotherapy because they inherently involve the potential for change events, even when concluding with a return to the status quo. Reworking one's life story is ultimately a change event itself, which is why most psychotherapy is almost completely filled with stories. For example, a client in psychotherapy who had been married for 35 years to a highly controlling man often told stories filled with personal encounters of vulnerability, loss, and intrusion. He would take things from her without informing her or give specific instructions on her activities. As therapy progressed, she began telling stories such as the following:

> I met him after we talked. I don't know what came over me but I just looked him in the eye and stared him down and told him to return my stuff. And he looked away and it was clear that he didn't want to listen to *me*. And I didn't back down this time. I just kept looking at him until he finally said that he would do it. It was really surprising! And I was surprised at how firm I was able to be but I'm sure I'll be back to where I was the next time around.

This transformation of this client's narratives was a beginning sign of change occurring with therapy, quite heartening to both client and therapist. In this sense, insight-oriented psychotherapists and their clients are revolutionaries, plotting with the client for the larger transformation of the self within the narrated interpersonal field, often working to reshape old alliances for the overthrow of a hegemonic interpersonal field and replaced with a more harmonious expression and sequencing of narrative voices.

Further implications of an interpersonal view of narrative are explored below, including some of the uses and functions of narrative when viewed through an interpersonal lens, as well as the interpersonal and experiential processes of narrative construction.

Multiple Voices

The view of interpersonal narrative presented thus far is that stories are performed activities that allow for reexperiencing and constructing various interpersonal constellations. As an experimental apparatus (as in George Kelly's analogy of how the personal construing process is analogous to experimental hypothesis testing), narratives allow for experiencing or reexperiencing other voices in a way that allows for meaningful understanding without somehow being incorporated into the self project. Some have argued that the narrative voice is largely singular and that the goal of storytelling optimally should be in the service of forming identity and thematic integration (e.g., Tantam, 2002). McAdams (2001) argues that a narrator uses stories to meaningfully integrate disparate aspects of self through time. As noted, Habermas and Bluck (2000) also argue that the self is active in creating a single life narrative in which events are integrated into the larger fabric of one's identity.

From an interpersonal view, it might be argued that narrators speak in multiple voices, in narrative forms that are not their own but defined by culture. It might be said that we do not fully "own" ourselves and that we choose to "give voice" to some of the many voices that surround us. For example, in observing French culture, Abigail Adams, wife of the second U.S. president, noted that life itself had become theater to the extent that it could be said, "Every man of the nation an actor, and every woman an actress" (McCullough, 2001, p. 308). If Shakespeare was correct in that all the world is a stage, then the stories we tell each other are the scripts to the plays, always in revision and negotiation with the actors. Gergen (1991) argues that it is thus impossible to "possess" one's own story, to construct an identity that is independent and outside of the influence of relationships. According to Gergen,

> The genres of story offered by a culture at any given time are also likely to be limited.... We are generally prepared to accept as "true" only those life stories that conform to existing conventions. Yet one's personal history is not a cultural possession only in the sense of story forms. Indeed, the very content of such stories also depends on social relationships. (pp. 161, 163)

That is, interpersonal relationships and the larger social context determine the narratives and not the self or the formation and integration of identity. In fact, it could be argued that having a self-narrative and integrated identity is the conventional narrative form of contemporary culture and that narratives that fall outside of this motif are less likely to be seen as plausible.

The self-narrative view is overdetermined, even though some narrative activity may focus on understanding self actions. Shafer (1992), for example, states that narration is a process, an action: "Nothing here supports the common illusion that there is a single self-entity that each persona has and experiences, a self-entity that is, so to speak, out there in Nature where it can be objectively observed" (p. 26). Spence (1982), who also operates from a psychodynamic perspective, states the case for multiple-voiced narratives more strongly:

> Only rarely do we find a patient speaking to the analyst in a two-person dialogue; rather the patient is speaking with multiple voices to a variety of loosely defined "others," and the conditions of the conversation—who is speaking to whom and for what reason—become critical determinants of what is being said. (p. 124)

The interpersonal perspective of narrative recognizes that the narrator speaks in multiple voices. Narratives involve understanding self in relation to the entire social context in which one is embedded. Hermans (1996) eloquently described these dialogues among characters as if they are playing to "private audiences" (p. 39) in which characters respond to the narrator with feelings and evaluations. Meaning making is achieved through understanding others; or for that matter, it may be achieved through the multiplicity of voices spoken through the narrator. Much of this activity is indeed an attempt to resolve conflicts of these voices, but it is a significant point that these relational transactions may not always be focused on constructing a self-narrative.

Some self-narrative theorists suggest, however, that there is compelling developmental evidence that advanced narrative skills coincide with psychologically equivalent landmarks (Habermas & Bluck, 2000). For example, relatively early in life, a child develops the capacity to describe scripts, or event-sequences. Between the ages of 9 and 10, children attain the capacity to tell stories, which include a plot or "complicating event." Habermas and Bluck note that it is not until adolescence that skills are attained to begin to link themes of events back to an ongoing life narrative. These observations might suggest to some that since the life narrative project appears to be a developmentally advanced activity, it also correlates with optimal psychological and emotional functioning. However, the developmental abilities that emerge in adolescence and are necessary for forming a life narrative are also abilities that are equally suited for other tasks, such as comprehending the larger social world and communicating the complexity of conflicts among characters within it. That is, nothing inherent in these abilities specifically suits them to a self-narrative or to a reflexive process that is explicit (can understanding be tacit?) or makes these skills best suited to integrative and comprehensive understandings.

It remains unclear if the absence of the complete, integrated life narrative is related to problems in living. While the absence of the most basic narrative skills appears to be related to developmental disabilities such as autism (Baron-Cohen, 1996), it remains unclear if the absence of significantly more advanced skills in forming a life narrative is linked to emotional and psychological suffering. Since the ability to organize and synthesize relatively disparate events to a single identity requires relatively advanced cognitive abilities, such as those found in the attainment of formal operations (see Damon & Hart, 1988), their use in narration may be like other formal operational characteristics, which may or may not be involved in the tasks necessary within psychotherapy and the attainment of well-being. For example, to what extent does the search for meaning require the complex, integrative reflexive processes found in life stories? People who do not resolve the conflict inherent in life stories may appear less psychologically minded and less reflective, but to what extent are such individuals less capable of making meaning of their lives, even if they might remain blind to inconsistencies, and of living happy, meaning-filled lives? Perhaps future research may provide more definitive answers.

Who Owns Our Stories?

After all had been lost, Hamlet's dying words to Horatio were a plea for remembrance:

> *If thou didst ever hold me in thy heart,*
> *Absent thee from felicity for a while,*
> *And in this harsh world draw thy breath in pain*
> *To tell my story.*
>
> Hamlet, Act V, ii

Hamlet's plea was for Horatio to change, to alter his consciousness, in order to tell "his" story. It is through our interpersonal alliances that we embrace others' stories, and as suggested above, their voices creep into our own stories as well. The voices that we accept, then, are our experiences of our encounters in the relational space between us or among characters.

The faithful remembrance of these voices is unavoidable, even when the consequences appear negative and unwanted. For example, from an interpersonal perspective, people develop psychopathology out of a desire to be faithful to parental wishes. For example, children might inhibit themselves in response to a parent who does not want to be bothered by children. As adults, such people may develop problems in being assertive and engage in self-effacing behaviors, still maintaining the pattern of behaviors that was originally designed to please the parent. As Benjamin (2001) has frequently noted, "psychopathology is a gift of love"; children would sacrifice their own desires, and ultimately their psychological health, to meet the wishes of the parent. Internalizing other voices or self-other relational schemes (Hermans, 1996) is similar to narrative-based relational descriptions in psychotherapy like the Core Conflict Relational Theme (CCRT) (Luborsky & Crits-Christoph, 1990) and the Cyclical Maladaptive Pattern (CMP) (Strupp & Binder, 1984). When these private audiences become dispossessed and fixed from their more public expressions, there is the potential for loss of experiencing and expression. The narration becomes a "canned act" in which the voices become subjugated to the self and not able to interact directly with their real relational sources.

It is not surprising that there is great potential for possessive mischief in the expression of multiple voices in narrative since the act of narration of past events is usually an attempt to recapture experience.

Stories about moments with our most cherished loved ones may yield the most "true" version of past interaction, the story. Yet, the story itself is a step removed from the experienced interpersonal interaction, as words fail to capture what it was like at the time. It might be said that the most that can be hoped for is new relational moments with others in the retelling of the story. The new moments are different stories and allow for reinterpretation. Like Horatio, we may be compelled to take on voices of others, voices that are likewise multiply determined. Similarly, history might be seen as multiplied voices, filtered by each generation and reinterpreted through contemporary culture. The voices of history attempt to remember the story as it was "in reality" even as the story is transformed through the multiple voices (culture), all attempting to remain true to each other. Even so, the power of culture cannot help but transform the story, just as ideals such as "freedom" change meaning as they are filtered through culture and time (Foner, 2002). Like history, our stories are culturally determined as they are sifted through retellings, relationships, and time. Can we tell our own story? Perhaps we can, in the sense that we own our experience in the moment of telling the story, but the events themselves become distanced from us as soon as they occur. Of course, we can keep telling the story, but as I will argue, each telling is a separate experience with new listeners and/or at different times.

Situating Experience: Building Meaning Bridges

Stories are ultimately told somewhere between the unified and cohesive life narrative and the multiple-voiced narrative. As Stiles (1999) notes, "Multiple voices within people can represent depth of resources and flexibility, or they can represent fragmentation and dissociation. The difference is the strength of the meaning bridges—the sign-mediated links between voices" (p. 3). In identifying optimal narrative process, the ability to build meaning bridges may be a more critical factor than identifying which characters and events are meaningfully linked. Self-narrative theorists ultimately require that the meaning bridges link back to the self, which might be thought of as the "tyranny of the self" (Weibel, 2002).

Perhaps equally important to building meaning bridges (Stiles, 1999) is the ability to craftily construct meaning bridges in strategic locations. For example, Angus, Levitt, and Hardtke (1999) note that the location of meaning bridges (reflexive sequences) in the story may be critical to the optimal use of the story. When a story's meaning bridges are built prematurely or excessively (e.g., before the story structure and emotion have had time to develop), the overall story may appear shallow. No doubt, constant bridge building has its benefits, and yet identifying the critical events and voices to link to could also save considerable psychological resources. Ultimately, the narrator decides which events to narrate, where to place the characters, and which emotions and expressions to emphasize within the story. When an event is chosen or constructed for narration, critical decisions about how or why a particular configuration of characters might have the potential for meaning must be made before the story is told. From a constructivist perspective, Newman and Holzman (1999) suggest, "Stories appear to be more fundamental than meaning or even than our experience; they 'situate our experience' and enable us to 'perform meaning'" (p. 37). For Newman and Holzman, meaning making ultimately occurs after the critical decisions about story construction have been made, and the storytelling is critical because "situating our experience" through storytelling affords the opportunity to locate experience.

A growing number of research findings support the theoretical position that meaning-making activities occur after the basic structure of the story has been constructed. Research on emotional disclosure of stressful and traumatic events that take place over several days has even found that at the beginning of storytelling, there is greater emotional expression. Then in later days, the narrator shifts to more meaning-making processes (Keefe, Lumley, Anderson, Lynch, & Carson, 2001). To some extent, narrators have to relinquish an interpretive stance to allow themselves to flow into the story before beginning to understand where they are situated and where the characters will lead. Applied to an interpersonal perspective, to "situate our experience" is always done in relation to other characters, which is critical to the task of identifying the most meaningful relationship events before they happen. In other words, if an experiment could be performed where two disparate characters are brought together whom the narrator knows to be especially observant of the interaction, it could make for a "good story" later on.

Critical Balance of Narrative Processes

The observation that there may be an optimal ordering of narrative processes raises other questions about how stories are constructed. A useful schematic is Angus et al.'s (1999) narrative process theory, which proposes three basic narrative processes as being part of narrative formation: (a) external processes are basic, descriptive details, which include the setting and actions of characters; (b) internal processes are the subjective and especially emotional reactions that the narrator expresses within the story; and (c) reflexive processes are the interpretive, meaning-making statements made by the narrator (the meaning bridges; see above). Angus et al.'s work considers the sequences within any narrative to be predominantly one of the three activities and has demonstrated that these basic processes can be reliably identified with psychotherapy sessions.

As a thought experiment, consider what a story would be like if it were exclusively constructed of any of these single narrative processes. If the story were entirely external, without any emotional and interpretive processes infusing the basic descriptions, the story would make no assumptions about what the listener knows or does not know. There would be no emotional identification or emphasis of critical developments. In fact, it is questionable whether critical developments would be identifiable since the descriptions might be so bland and external that it would be impossible to infer the agency or intentionality of the characters. Such a story would likely look very similar to the stories of autistic people. People with autism tend to be very precise in describing objects and characters but fail to include agency and emotion within their characters. In fact, such descriptions would not be recognized as stories by most people (Baron-Cohen, 1996). In contrast, most people will add intentionality and goal seeking to completely inanimate objects, and this might be considered an essential narrative device (Baron-Cohen, 1996; Bruner, 1986; Hermans, 1996).

Continuing the thought experiment, would it be possible to construct a story that is completely filled with internal narrative process? Such a story would be all emotion and no external or reflexive process. To assist with answering the question, it is also useful to consider what happens when stories are predominantly internal. Rasmussen and Angus (1996) found that borderline clients have more rapid topic shifts, which occur in the context of core client issues. One explanation proposed for this interesting finding was that the topic shifts were initiated in these borderline clients at points when they were feeling emotionally overwhelmed within the therapy sessions. It is as though intense emotion disrupts the developing story before it can be fully formed. Also, consider a basic clinical observation of clients who are emotionally overwhelmed with posttraumatic stress. Often, these patients are unable to escape from the intensity of their emotion, have difficulty recounting their trauma, and become stuck when approaching the emotion-laden points in the story. Consider the common clinical observation of nightmares and stories of some of these patients: It is as if a second or two of highly charged emotion replays itself in a seemingly endless loop. Indeed, the story disintegrates and cannot be told when all experience is internal.

It might also be interesting to consider what might happen to a story if there were an absence of emotional processes. Depressed people have difficulty identifying specific external elements of stories when asked to narrate positive experiences (Moffitt, Singer, Nelligan, Carlson, & Vyse, 1994). One explanation for this is that the depressed person cannot readily draw on the emotion needed to construct the story, and therefore, the story is poorly constructed. Finally, the problems with a narrative that is filled with reflexive processes have been considered above when discussing the building of meaning bridges.

Unfortunately, if the thought experiment were a research project on narrative, it would have been an utter failure since there would be no narratives produced by the subjects, and hence, there would be no data to analyze. Perhaps, the experimenter should consider performing some manipulation checks before conducting another experiment. While speculative, the thought experiment may point the way for some actual experiments. First, if people tend to experience constricted and guarded affect, then narratives in which emotional disclosure is encouraged might serve to facilitate the generation of narratives and well-being. Pennebaker (1991) has suggested that one reason emotional disclosure of negative emotional events has had positive effects is possibly because of a current cultural climate in which affect is overregulated. Second, if intense emotion leads to the disruption of narration, then it might stand to reason that clients who have problems around emotional expression, such as those who are traditionally given borderline, antisocial, and histrionic labels, would not respond well to narratives in which emotion is activated. There is some support for this since clients who attempt emotion- and experience-based therapies tend to have a more guarded outlook (e.g., Greenberg, Rice, & Elliott, 1993).

In addition to matching treatments by interpersonal characteristics, it might be worth considering how conarration may be enhanced through the matching of storyteller and listener. For example, is it possible that people who fail to employ any one of the three narrative process modes might improve their narrative abilities if they were matched to a listener who is especially strong in that quality? Is it possible that the depressed storytellers in Moffitt et al.'s (1994) study might have told more complete and specific stories about positive experiences if only they co-constructed their stories with someone who experiences more positive emotions?

Fitting Experience Into the Story Structure

Are there some events, such as certain traumas or nonverbal experiences, that can be experienced without the building of meaning bridges? In other words, if narratives serve to situate our experience and not necessarily to define it, then the narrative framework might serve to hold inferred experiences that are communicated only because the gestalt of the narrative allows for the expression—the signs alone (verbal labels) do not allow for an effective communication of the experience. Ultimately, narratives cannot "describe things as they are, or . . . capture their essences" (Gergen, 1991, p. 108) because the signs of language ultimately gain their power from textual maneuvers and cultural conventions. As Spence (1982) warns, "language is the persistent seduction" since the narrator is constantly forced to relinquish the true image or sensory experience "and use whatever words are available to come up with an approximation" (p. 123). For example, in the story about my wife that opened this chapter, simply describing her level of frustration when the lawn mower was fixed not only decontextualizes the experience from the event but also makes the sign ineffective. Even more ineffective is the simple label, "frustration." The sequence of events situates and grounds the experience in relation to the characters, and hence it is the totality of the narrative sequences that gives power to the signs.

Maintaining Meaning Bridges

It follows that narratives allow for situating experiences where meaning bridges do not exist, providing a stage for the expression of those experiences that cannot be labeled or more parsimoniously identified. If meaning is made by connecting signs and voices (Stiles, 1999), is it possible that narratives are just as likely to situate one's experience toward the developing chasms between signs and voices as they are to locate where meaning has been made? This use of narrative has not been fully explored. If Newman and Holzman (1999) are correct in their argument that stories serve to situate experience and meaning making occurs later, then it would stand to reason that storytelling could lead to some surprises in the meaning-making process. The very act of storytelling, then, allows us to identify areas where meaning bridges may be in need of repair or to anticipate where new meanings may be needed in the future. Stories may allow for anticipating meaning-making tasks that are on the horizon, while the identification of emotional states ("frustrated") or behavioral acts in isolation only signify that which exists (or its negation). It is as if the constellation of characters unwinds and somewhere along the way, the narrator might observe the landscape and privately exclaim, "Here I am! And the bridge is now out and the water is high. I can't make sense enough here right now!" Of course, it might correctly be noted that this self-observation itself is a paradoxical meaning.

New voices in the wilderness, new canyons, new dissociations may develop from these interpersonal movements. Narratives express the interpersonal positioning of these voices, but by no means can the unfolding of orderly relationships and meaning be predicted. Some meaning bridges are more easily built than others. Some voices are hopelessly separated in time and space, and no bridge can be built regardless of the amount of brick and mortar (the signs) available. Some narrators may undertake construction of impossible meaning bridges; others may be happy using the bridges that have been built before. The difference is that more adventurous meaning makers recognize the waterways that have not been crossed and attempt to construct novel meaning bridges. Most may fail, but the attempt itself is a partial construction of a meaning bridge. At least the voices are brought into juxtaposition through the narrative, even if there is no language to link them.

Stories as Co-Constructions

It is apparent that stories are interpersonal by the simple fact that the telling is a communication from one person (the narrator) to another (the listener). Some stories are truly co-constructions as this (mostly) hypothetical example of a conversation between two college students illustrates:

Student A Do you remember the time when we wore all those goofy clothes and went out in the wee hours of the morning? Remember, how we chose the most outrageous things that we could possibly find to wear?

Student B And we just barely caught this bus, just because we said, "Hey, a bus. Let's just get on it."

Student A Yeah, and we had no idea where it was going to go. We were really crazy.

Student B And then we got worried about being on this bus and not being able to get back.

Student A And you asked the driver, "How late is this bus going to run?"

Student B Remember, how he said in such a choppy voice, "two-fifteen. Seven-days-a-week."

Student A And we just laughed our head off about that. Why?

Student B Yeah, that was really crazy. That was so much fun.

Who is the narrator? Of course both voices are narrating.

Other stories are co-constructions in that the person narrating may alter the story for the sake of the listener. It seems plausible to suggest that the construction of stories may be quite similar to other activities that involve the use of language. Clark and Wilkes-Gibbs (1986) have demonstrated that in paired activities, even when there is an assigned speaker who is assigned responsibility for problems, problem solving takes place through the active moment-by-moment collaboration with the assigned partner. Even more convincing are the findings of Bavelas, Coates, and Johnson (2000) in which the nature of the communication was experimentally controlled. Some listeners were instructed to give either general or specific responses as they listened to stories told by participants, whereas another group was distracted while they listened to the storyteller. Storytellers in the group with distracted listeners were less skilled in telling their stories. Bavelas et al. suggest that listeners are conarrators, even when the listeners give very limited, general responses, such as nodding their head and saying "Mm-hm." The collaboration of the narrator and the listener also was found in research by Anderson, Carson, Keefe, and Darchuk (in press), in which there was greater emotional expression by the narrator when *both* the narrator and listener had high social skills than in all other listener pairings.

Recent developmental research has suggested that narrative might be a collaborative process continuously practiced between child and parent throughout childhood. Continued collaborative storytelling would seem to be inconsistent with the notion of "scaffolding," the view that parents teach the basic skills of narration and then retreat as children master these skills. Instead, Haden, Haine, and Fivush (1997) found that as children develop more advanced narrative skills, parents also develop more sophisticated narrative strategies. This has led Haden et al. to propose that the more appropriate model for narrative acquisition is a "collaborative 'spiral' rather than a scaffold" (p. 304). They also note that the storytelling process may take place less for the specific purpose of telling stories and more to promote the "social goals of establishing and reestablishing interpersonal bonds through collaboratively co-constructing shared stories of the past" (p. 304).

Even when there is a clearly defined narrator, stories are arguably an interpersonal event because the narrator must translate experience into a format that can be comprehended by the listener. The experience is altered and translated into words, and the narrator must have some empathy for how the story will be heard by the listener. Experiences that are socially unacceptable cannot readily be translated into words (i.e., made understandable to the audience), and large parts of that experience can never be shared with others. Even more, as narratives are told, the listener co-constructs the narrative, which ultimately alters the story. Describing this phenomenon within the psychoanalytic communication of narrative, Spence (1982) notes that misunderstandings expressed by the analyst can alter the experience of the story and "can easily be substituted for the target image, part of the past is now placed forever out of reach" (p. 63). Part of the reason that a client may come to therapy is because experience cannot find narrative expression. The original experience may never have been communicated and remains locked inside, without the signs available for expression. The experience may also have been effectively quashed and replaced with a hand-me-down narrative in which experience is bartered away for social acceptance, the supreme currency within any culture. Such a narrative would create further distance from the narrator's experience, which is abandoned with the promise that a culturally approved narrative will allow for experiencing with the listener. It is as if one's experience becomes boiled down into an easily communicated and easily understood form that others can easily identify with, which might be thought of as more of a "press release" (Wiersma, 1988) than an opportunity for sharing experience. The socially acceptable press release is like a role in that it may ease the difficulties of shared experience, but both roles and socially approved press-release narratives cannot substitute for more intimate and difficult interpersonal relating (Leitner & Thomas, in press).

However, most storytelling may be much more open to co-constructive processes. With each retelling, the story is slightly revised, often based on the reactions of those who heard the story on previous narrations and the co-construction of the story by listeners. Some of the same events may have various versions, sometimes with different audiences, sometimes with the same audience at different times—all retellings being similar in the way that a musician's unique recordings of the same song or Monet's many water lilies are similar. Our stories offer the opportunity for a uniquely creative human activity or a "flow" of concentration and experiencing (Csikszentmihalyi, 1993). In such moments, stories transcend the simple concatenation of events, and the participants attempt to reexperience the event by becoming totally engrossed in the retelling of those interpersonal interactions, experiencing the events as if they were happening anew. A picture may paint a thousand words, but a good narrator can breathe life into the same portrait a thousand times and even tell a different story each time, a new experience with each listener.

REFERENCES

Anderson, T., Carson, K. L., Keefe, F., & Darchuk, A. C. (in press). The influence of social skills on private and interpersonal emotional disclosure of negative events. *Journal of Social and Clinical Psychology*.

Angus, L., Levitt, H., & Hardtke, K. (1999). The narrative process coding system: Research applications and implications in psychotherapy practice. *Journal of Clinical Psychology, 55*, 1255-1270.

Baron-Cohen, S. (1996). *Mindblindness: An essay on autism and theory of mind*. Cambridge: MIT Press.

Bavelas, J. B., Coates, L., & Johnson, T. (2000). Listeners as co-narrators. *Journal of Personality and Social Psychology, 79,* 941-952.

Benjamin, L. S. (1993). *Interpersonal diagnosis and treatment of personality disorders.* New York: Guilford.

Benjamin, L. S. (2001). A developmental history of a believer in history. In M. R. Goldfried (Ed.), *How therapists change.* Washington, DC: American Psychological Association.

Bruner, J. S. (1986). *Actual minds, possible worlds.* Cambridge, MA: Harvard University Press.

Clark, H. H., & Wilkes-Gibbs, D. (1986). Referring as a collaborative process. *Cognition, 22,* 1-39.

Csikszentmihalyi, M. (1993). *The evolving self: A psychology for the third millennium.* New York: Harper Collins.

Damon, W., & Hart, D. (1988). *Self-understanding in childhood and adolescence.* Cambridge, UK: Cambridge University Press.

Foner, E. (2002). *Who owns history? Rethinking the past in a changing world.* New York: Hill & Wang.

Gergen, K. J. (1991). *The saturated self: Dilemmas of identity in contemporary life.* New York: Basic Books.

Greenberg, L. S., Rice, L. N., & Elliott, R. (1993). *Facilitating emotional change: The moment-by-moment process.* New York: Guilford.

Habermas, T., & Bluck, S. (2000). Getting a life: The emergence of the life story in adolescence. *Psychological Bulletin, 126,* 748-769.

Haden, C. A., Haine, R. A., & Fivush, R. (1997). Developing narrative structure in parent-child reminiscing across the preschool years. *Developmental Psychology, 33,* 295-307.

Hermans, H. J. M. (1996). Voicing the self: From information processing to dialogical interchange. *Psychological Bulletin, 119,* 31-50.

Horowitz, L. M., Dryer, D. C., Krasnoperova, E. N. (1997). The circumplex structure of interpersonal problems. In R. Plutchik & H. R. Conte (Eds.), *Circumplex models of personality and emotions.* Washington, DC: American Psychological Association.

Keefe, F. J., Lumley, M., Anderson, T., Lynch, T., & Carson, K. L. (2001). Pain and emotion: New research directions. *Journal of Clinical Psychology, 57,* 587-607.

Leitner, L. M., & Thomas, J. (in press). Experiential personal construct psychotherapy. In F. Fracella (Ed.), *Personal construct psychology handbook.* Chichester, UK: Wiley.

Luborsky, L., & Crits-Christoph, P. (1990). *Understanding transference: The CCRT method.* New York: Basic Books.

McAdams, D. P. (2001). The psychology of life stories. *Review of General Psychology, 5,* 100-122.

McCullough, D. (2001). *John Adams.* New York: Simon & Schuster.

Moffitt, K. H., Singer, J. A., Nelligan, D. W., Carlson, M. A., & Vyse, S. A. (1994). Depression and memory narrative type. *Journal of Abnormal Psychology, 103,* 581-538.

Neimeyer, R. A., & Stewart, A. E. (2000). Constructivist and narrative psychotherapies. In C. R. Snyder & R. E. Ingram (Eds.), *Handbook of psychological change: Psychotherapy process and practices for the 21st century.* New York: John Wiley.

Newman, F., & Holzman, L. (1999). Beyond narrative to performed conversation ("In the beginning" comes much later). *Journal of Constructivist Psychology, 12,* 23-64.

Pennebaker, J. W. (1991). *Opening up: The healing power of confiding in others.* New York: William Morrow.

Polkinghorne, D. (1988). *Narrative knowing and the human sciences.* Albany: State University of New York Press.

Rasmussen, B., & Angus, L. (1996). Metaphor in psychodynamic psychotherapy with borderline and non-borderline clients: A qualitative analysis. *Psychotherapy, 33,* 521-530.

Shafer, R. (1992). *Retelling a life: Narration and dialogue in psychoanalysis.* New York: Basic Books.

Spence, D. P. (1982). *Narrative truth and historical truth: Meaning and interpretation in psychoanalysis.* New York: Norton.

Stiles, W. B. (1999). Signs and voices in psychotherapy. *Psychotherapy Research, 9,* 1-20.

Strupp, H. H., & Binder, J. L. (1984). *Psychotherapy in a new key: A guide to time-limited dynamic psychotherapy.* New York: Basic Books.

Tantam, D. (2002). *Psychotherapy and counseling in practice: A narrative framework.* Cambridge, UK: Cambridge University Press.

Weibel, D. (2002). *Tyranny of the self.* Unpublished manuscript. Ohio University.

Wiersma, J. (1988). The press release: Symbolic communication in life history interviewing. *Journal of Personality, 56,* 205-237.

CHAPTER 19

The Contributions of Emotion Processes to Narrative Change in Psychotherapy
A Dialectical Constructivist Approach

LESLIE S. GREENBERG

LYNNE E. ANGUS

OVERVIEW

According to Damasio (1999), the first impetus to story an experience is the awareness of an inner bodily feeling. He argues that at the most fundamental level of consciousness, "knowing" springs to life when changes in the status of the body-self are connected to environmental impacts. Sarbin (1995) suggests that at a higher level of consciousness, all emotions are storied and that personal stories are shaped by—emplotted within—the trajectory of emergent emotion themes. It is often the rise and fall of emotional themes—and the conflicting desires, intentions, goals, and purposes they represent—that provide the connective thread that weaves together disparate experiences and events to create a meaningful and coherent whole: a storied experience.

Take, for example, the experience of grief. After the shock of the death of a loved one, we often move into anger and then sadness before reaching an acceptance of the loss and an appreciation of the other. In classic stories of love's difficulties, in which events and circumstances conspire to thwart the course of love, we find stories of enchantment and ecstasy coupled with jealousy and betrayal,

AUTHORS' NOTE: Correspondence regarding this chapter should be sent to the authors at York University, 4700 Keele Street, Toronto, Ontario, Canada M3J 1P3, or to lgrnberg@yorku.ca.

attachment coupled with loss, all coupled with conflict, anger, and despair.

In contrast, when circumstances unfold in such a way as to enable the course of true love, a different story emerges, one that moves from enchantment and desire through difference and struggle to secure attachment, comfort, and familiarity. In either love story, the shifting emotional landscapes function as key markers for our assessment of what is "really going on" in the hearts and minds of the lovers, their inner world of intentions, purposes, goals, hopes, and desires. It is important to note that the narrative organization of emotional experience—in which intentions, purposes, expectations, hopes, and desires are articulated—is what allows us to reflexively understand what an experience means to us and says about us.

While client narrative expression (Angus & Bouffard, 2002, in press; Angus, Levitt, & Hardtke, 1999; Baumeister & Newman, 1994; Book, 1998; Botella & Herrero, 2000; Bruner, 2002; Dimaggio & Semerari, 2001; Gonçalves, Machado, Korman, & Angus, 2002; McLeod, 1997; Neimeyer, 1995; White, 2001) and emotion processes (Greenberg, 2002; Greenberg & Paivio, 1997; Greenberg & Pascual-Leone, 2001) have each received increasing attention in the psychotherapy change literature, the interrelationship between narrative and emotion processes has rarely been addressed. The purpose of this chapter is to address this question in the context of a dialectical-constructivist model of therapeutic change (Angus & Korman, 2002; Arciero & Guidano, 2000; Greenberg & Pascual-Leone, 1995, 1997, 2001; Greenberg, Rice, & Elliott, 1993; Guidano, 1991, 1995; Mahoney, 1991; Neimeyer, 1995; Pascual-Leone, 1987, 1990a, 1990b, 1991; Watson & Greenberg, 1996; Watson & Rennie, 1994). In this chapter, the contributions of tacit-schematic, attentional, and reflexive information processing systems to the construction of emotional experience and narrative knowing are explored, and the implications of this heuristic model for future psychotherapy research and practice will be addressed.

In particular, the contributions of emotion and narrative processes for the construction of new personal meanings will be addressed in terms of the articulation of individual stories and in the construction of an overall life story or self-identity. In the dialectical constructivist model, the organization of internal experience into a coherent narrative (Whelton & Greenberg, 2000) is the basis of a sense of self. The self is viewed as a multiprocess, multilevel organization emerging from the dialectical interaction between ongoing, moment-by-moment experience and higher-level reflexive processes that attempt to interpret, order, and explain elementary experiential processes. In this view, affectively toned, preverbal, preconscious processing is seen as the major source of self experience. Articulating, organizing, and ordering this experience into a coherent narrative is the other major element. Individuals, thus, constantly create the self they are about to become by synthesizing biologically based information and culturally acquired learning. While biology and culture may occasionally conflict, they are not inherently antagonistic to one another. Rather they are both necessary streams of a dialectical synthesis. People live most viably by managing to integrate inner and outer, biological and social, emotional and rational.

In a series of ongoing process-outcome research studies (Goldman & Greenberg, in press; Greenberg & Angus, 1995; Greenberg & Toukmanian, 1999; Hardtke, Levitt, & Angus, in press; Levitt & Angus, 2000) at the York Psychotherapy Research Center, we have begun to explore empirically the interrelationship between storytelling and emotion processes in client-centered and experiential psychotherapy. Early returns from the intensive analyses of a number of single cases suggest that clients' disclosures of emotionally charged personal narratives is foundational to the process of change in therapy (see Angus, Lewin, Bouffard, & Rotondi-Trevisan, 2003, this volume). At the level of individual stories or micronarratives (Angus et al., 1999; Baumeister & Newman, 1994), it is our view that emotional expression is a key marker of the personal significance of autobiographical memory narratives. In turn, the meaning of an emotion is fully understood when organized within a sequential narrative framework that identifies what is felt, about whom, and in relation to what need or issue. Thus, it appears that in psychotherapy as in life, all significant emotions are embedded in important stories, and all significant stories revolve around important emotional themes.

At the macronarrative level of the overall self-story, we view personal identity as an organized network of emotionally significant, autobiographical memory narratives that represent core beliefs and key values about self and others. The salient emotional tone of the autobiographical memory narrative—anger, sadness, joy, or fear—appears to be one of the primary associative connections that links one individual memory with another. Accordingly, implicit emotion themes and the narratives they contain become one of the lenses through which we classify, story, and make meaning of our new interpersonal experiences with others in the world.

THE DIALECTICS OF MEANING MAKING: INTEGRATING NARRATIVE AND EMOTION PROCESSES

From a dialectical-constructivist perspective (Greenberg & Pascual-Leone, 1995; Greenberg et al., 1993; Pascual-Leone, 1987, 1990a, 1990b, 1991), the reflexive construction of new personal meanings involves the self-organization and articulation of felt emotional experiences. The following core assumptions have been identified as crucial for the emergence of new personal meanings in psychotherapy: (a) client agency, (b) human reflexivity and meaning-making processes, (c) the importance of emotion schemes and emotion processing for the facilitation of second-order or identity change, and (d) the co-constructive nature of the client-therapist dialogue (Greenberg, 2002; Greenberg et al., 1993).

Within this framework, we will suggest that the narrative framing of emotional processes, at both tacit and conscious levels of awareness, is important in promoting personal change experiences in psychotherapy. For instance, drawing on recent developments in the study of human consciousness, Antonio Damasio (1999) argues that human beings essentially live and breathe in a world that is ordered and experienced as an unfolding story in time. He states:

> The entire construction of knowledge, from simple to complex, from non-verbal imagetic to verbal literacy, depends on the ability to map what happens over time, inside our organism, around our organism, to and with our organism, one thing followed by another, causing another endlessly. Telling stories, in the sense of what happens in the form of brain maps, is probably a brain obsession and precedes language, since it is, in fact, a condition for language. (p. 188)

In essence, knowing springs to life in the unfolding story of changes to the body's state.

For Damasio (1999), human consciousness comes into being with the creation of this tacit narrative account, and it is manifested in the feeling of knowing. As such, both narrative and emotion processes, operating at tacit levels of consciousness, are fundamental to the generation of an emotional felt-sense or experience. In turn, the awareness of a bodily felt-referent, so central to experiential therapy (Gendlin, 1962), is symbolized within the context of an unfolding external (environmental) or internal (memory-based) narrative scene. It is the interaction of this bodily felt-sense within the narrated scene that leads to meaning being carried forward, the organization of new self-experiences, and the construction of new views of self and others. To better understand themselves, people continually symbolize, story, and explain themselves to themselves—and in so doing construct an ongoing, emergent self-narrative that organizes their personal stories and provides a sense of self-coherence. In this manner, their stable identity emerges. The result is an integration of reason and emotion, a combining of head and heart.

A dialectical-constructivist approach to self-awareness and human meaning-making identifies four key stages in which narrative and emotion processes are at play. The first stage involves the rapid synthesis of affective responses, from sensations and tacit narrative scenes, to create inner bodily feelings or an inner felt-sense. The second stage entails the allocation of attentional resources to the bodily felt-sense to symbolize, reflexively differentiate, and name the feeling state to create a known subjective reality. The reflexive symbolization occurs in the context of the tacit narrative scene and results from naming the tacitly synthesized bodily felt-sense and narrative context.

The third stage entails the conscious articulation of new meaning. New personal meanings are articulated in relation to the experiences of both self and others. At this stage, a conscious, causal explanation of experienced emotions is provided in the form of a narrative account. Stages 1 through 3 address the interrelationship of emotion and narrative processes in the context of processing individual life events or micronarratives. In these stages, not only are emotions put into narrative form, but narratives are given significance by fusing them with emotion.

The fourth and final stage entails the consolidation of an identity narrative. This occurs by either (a) the integration of the new narrative and personal meanings into preexisting views of self or others or (b) the inception of a radical reorganization of the self-narrative and the articulation of new emotionally significant ways of viewing and understanding the self. This provides a new identity narrative. This final stage addresses the role of emotion and narrative processes at the level of self-identity construction or macronarrative change. The combination of these four stages—synthesis, symbolization, meaning making, and identity consolidation—is key to significant client shifts and self-change events in psychotherapy. Each of these stages, in turn, offers different opportunities for therapeutic intervention.

Consider how this process occurs when a client is telling the following story about a surprise encounter at a movie theater the night before. He states that while standing in line for a movie, he turned around to look at some movie posters and suddenly realized that standing behind him was someone whom he either wished desperately to avoid or whom he was amorously longing to meet. Depending on which set of emotions, desires, and feelings prevailed in the moment, he would be able to narrate two entirely different senses of internal complexity that were generated in the context of the unfolding story of the chance meeting at the movie theater. In relation to each story, he could talk about how he felt in and about the unfolding narrative scene and explicate complex felt meanings such as the intentions, beliefs, purposes, and goals of self and other.

Many of these tacit meanings, and the "story" of the event, were not processed consciously in the moment before he opened his mouth to greet the other person at the movie theater. What was actually said would either be coolly dismissing or charmingly disarming, depending on, in part, the past history of the relationship of the client and the other person, as well as current goals, intentions, expectations, and appraisals. If no clear experience had emerged at the moment of the surprise encounter at the movie theater, this person's performance might have appeared to be clumsily awkward, in response to feeling overwhelmed by a complex tangle of mixed emotions and feelings. Thus, beyond the specific performance generated—what is actually said or done—there lies at the periphery of awareness a host of tacitly synthesized bodily felt-meanings that, with attentional allocation, can be brought to focal awareness and symbolized, their meaning articulated (James, 1890/1950; Perls, Hefferline, & Goodman, 1951). If further reflected on, they could influence the person's identity narrative.

The bodily felt-referent (Gendlin, 1962), which becomes the focus of attention and reflection, is the experiential ground from which situated meanings are differentiated and articulated. Thus, in the case of our client, seeing a person with whom he desired contact, he becomes filled with feelings, wishes, hopes, dreams, and evaluations of self-worth, including appraisals of his looks, body, intelligence, and social abilities as well as many other idiosyncratic feelings and meanings. This complex set of personal meanings, contained within the bodily felt-sense, is differentiated within the context of the unfolding narrative scene. The particularities of the narrative scene influence the expression of desired actions and the nature of the self-evaluations undertaken in the moment. For instance, if the client happens to meet a person to whom he is strongly attracted but he is holding hands with a current partner, he may feel constrained in his expression of inner desires for contact with the other. Moreover, with current partner in hand, acknowledging and/or articulating the longing for contact with the other may be accompanied by pangs of guilt and shame.

In the case of a surprise encounter with someone with whom he dreaded having contact, his fears and concerns, evaluations of self-worth, competence, rights, and abilities to deal with conflict are all differentiated within the specific local context of the unfolding narrative scene. For instance, if the dreaded other is holding hands with his best friend, he is likely to feel constrained in his desire to run away and avoid contact. The evocation of the bodily felt-sense—longing and desire or fear and dread—as well as specific features of the narrative scene interact to enable or constrain the expression of action tendencies in the unfolding event. The first step in therapy is to focally attend to the client's bodily felt-sense of experience. From this experiential ground, personal meanings are differentiated and symbolized, articulated in the context of an unfolding narrative scene, and meaningfully understood.

Syntheses of Bodily Feelings

As noted earlier, Damasio (1999) identifies the linking of simple narrative maps with emotional reactions as the root of human consciousness and the emergence of emotional awareness. This first narrative, experienced at a tacit level of processing, entails the linking of a nonverbal representation of the self, in the process of modification, with the cause or stimulus of that modification (Dimaggio & Semerari, 2003, this volume). Damasio explains,

> What happens when an organism interacts with an object is a simple narrative without words ... it has characters, it unfolds in time and has a beginning, a middle and an end. The end is made up of reactions that result in a modified state of the organism. (p. 188)

According to Damasio, the endpoint of the wordless narrative is an emotional reaction, which in turn provides a complex array of experiential information about the status of the body in the context of the unfolding narrative scene. Affective reactions function as key markers of the significance of an event for personal well-being and are responsible for the allocation of further attentional resources in the organism (Forgas, 1995; Le Doux, 1996) and, presumably, further emotion schematic processing.

In agreement with Damasio's (1999) emphasis on the constructive nature of emotion, Russel (2003) argues that the conscious awareness of emotion is the outcome of a complex constructive process, one that is not simply the result of the activation of a biologically based, psycho-motor-affective program. He proposes that many emotions are complex constructions that are the outcome of the progressive synthesis of basic elements of core affect. He proposes the degree of pleasantness and the degree of arousal as the core affective processes. These generate the automatic perception of the affective quality of pleasantness/unpleasantness experienced in relation to a specific object and/or event (narrative scene). Changes in core affect, in terms of pleasantness/unpleasantness, are then rapidly linked to a perceived stimulus or cause to provide an explanation for the experienced affect shift. It is only after this causal attribution that people start to experience something like a discrete emotion, such as being angry at a friend who has let them down or sadness in response to the loss of a loved one. Emotion is, thus, simultaneously discovered and constructed.

Damasio (1994) suggests that the automatic formation of systematic connections between categories of objects and narrative scenes, on the one hand, and primitive, pre-organized emotions, on the other, leads the maturing human to be capable of a second, higher-order type of emotion experience. In the context of Damasio's account of the origins of affective reactions, feelings do not arise as singular discrete emotions, such as anger or sadness, divorced from past history or the current narrative context. Instead, emotions generate complex feelings based in part on a person's emotional learning history. Much adult emotional experience is of this higher order, generated by learned, idiosyncratic schemes that serve to help the individual to anticipate future outcomes. This higher-level synthesis of a variety of levels of processing has been referred to as an emotion scheme (Oatley, 1992; Pascual-Leone, 1991) and has been identified as a principal target of intervention and therapeutic change (Greenberg & Paivio, 1997; Greenberg et al., 1993). When activated, emotion schemes serve as the basis for human experience and self-organization (Greenberg, 2002; Greenberg & Paivio, 1997; Greenberg et al., 1993).

Emotion schemes are complex feeling states that are based on a person's past emotional experiences, contextualized within narrative scenes, and are often represented as salient autobiographical memories. These high-level, complex feelings provide people with an overall sense of things or a "gut feeling" and become available as a bodily felt-referent to which people can attend to create meaning. Once formed, emotion schemes produce more complex bodily felt-feelings. These feelings are generally no longer a result of purely innate responses to specific situational cues experienced in the context of a particular narrative scene. Rather they emerge from the repeated occurrence of specific emotional outcomes, linked to explicit or implicit interpersonal interactions or narratives that compose the history of a person's lived emotional experience. An example of this second higher-level type emotion would be the nostalgia that a person might experience on returning to a cherished childhood scene. Regardless of whether or not the experience can subsequently be fully articulated (i.e., exactly what and why one feels the way one does), the experience nonetheless is tacitly generated. Perhaps most important, these emotion-based organizations serve as memory-based schemes associated with emotional experiences that guide appraisals and serve as blueprints for physiological arousal and action.

Depending on the nature of past intimate relationships, emotion schemes can either be adaptive or maladaptive in current interpersonal relationships. An example of the development of a maladaptive emotion scheme is seen in a child whose initiatives for closeness are met with unpredictable responses of either love or abusive rejection from parents. As a consequence, the child is likely to develop schemes in which intimacy and fear are associated with beliefs or expectations that others will either reject them or cause them harm. Later in life, when the individual becomes close to others, these schemes may become activated, and patterns of physiological arousal associated with the original abuse, plus associated negative beliefs or expectations formed by their past experiences, will be evoked. The person may at any time be organized to be afraid, to physically shrink away from closeness, and to tacitly appraise intimacy as threatening, even though the individual knows consciously that this reaction may be unfounded in the context of the current interpersonal interaction or narrative scene. The following therapy session excerpt, drawn from the York I Depression study (Greenberg & Watson, 1998), illustrates the activation of just such an emotion scheme in a client's life.

Client   What happens with Mark is when I see him enter the room I feel emotion toward him... *[shift to emotional differentiation]* just like different emotions but up until about a week ago, like friendship.

Therapist   Is that kind of like.... a feeling of warmth? *[empathic conjecture, differentiating emotional experience and symbolizing]*

Client   Exactly! I was about to say a trust, a warmth...just this complete contentment. *[symbolizing the synthesized bodily felt-sense]*

Therapist   That feels really good inside.

Client   Exactly and um it's followed by this gut-wrenching, sick feeling of dread *[symbolizing and then shifts to reflexive mode and explains experience]* because the only other person in the last 4 years that has made me feel that way was Raoul and it turned out to be exactly opposite to everything that was really going on... like when I thought he most liked me, and most accepted me for who I was, it was a huge act.

The quest for knowing and naming what is felt, and for knowing what it means or says about me in the context of a specific situation or relationship, heralds the shift to the next level of experiential processing.

In Emotion-Focused Therapy (EFT), the therapist would follow a two-stage approach of arriving at and then leaving emotional experience (Greenberg, 2002). In the first stage, the therapist listens and lets the story and its emotional significance emerge. In this stage, the therapist above works with the emotion schemes of dread and distrust, ensuring that the client had fully arrived at the experience by focusing back on the activated maladaptive emotional experience of dread. To further attend to, welcome, symbolize, and explore it, the therapist might say, "Let's stay with this feeling of sickness and dread that just hits you in the gut when you are reminded of Raoul. Can you stay with it and breathe?" This draws the client's attention to the trauma-based emotion memory schemes and the responses associated with them. Articulating a belief that helps narrate the experience, the client might now say, "It's like I can't open up, I'll just be hurt again."

Having arrived at a core maladaptive feeling and an articulated sense of its personal meaning, the goal in therapy will then shift to having the client access a more adaptive emotional resource as an antidote to the maladaptive feeling. This shift heralds the movement to the second stage of the EFT approach. Focusing on the alternate feeling already present in the room, the feeling of "trust, a warmth . . . just this complete contentment," might do this. If this were not present as the source of an alternate voice, the therapist could access a more adaptive emotional response by helping the client articulate a need, asking, "What do you need in this deep feeling of hurt and distrust?" The client might respond, "I just need to be held and to be comforted. I do so want some of the warmth." The therapist would then put this more adaptive voice in a dialectical interaction with the voice of dread by saying, "So what are you saying to the dread and to the voice that says, 'I can't open up?'" The client might say, "I know I need to go slow to protect myself, but I also need to recognize what is different in this relationship."

Symbolizing

Tacit or implicit meaning and the accompanying bodily felt-sense, when attended to, articulated, and differentiated in awareness, is referred to by therapists as experiencing (Bohart & Wugalter, 1991; Gendlin, 1962, 1996; Greenberg et al., 1993). This experiential (holistic) processing of patterns of emotional relevance is different from conceptual processing (Epstein, 1994; Greenberg et al., 1993). In experiential processing, the bodily felt-sense acts as a constraint on the possible conscious conceptual constructions that can satisfy it, eliminating many other possible meanings. Preconceptual, tacit felt-meanings carry implications that act to constrain but not fully determine the construction of personal meanings. Rather, felt-meanings are synthesized with conceptual, explicit meanings to form narrative descriptions of personal events (Greenberg & Pascual-Leone, 1995, 2001).

A crucial part of this meaning-making process is the production of linguistic distinctions to express this implicit bodily felt-sense of meaning. A bodily felt-sense or feeling arises by means of a dynamic synthesis of an internal set of emotionally based schemes that are evoked in the context of a specific narrative scene or situation. The reflexive decentering from the direct experience of the emotional responses, in combination with other self-reflexive processes such as appraisals and attributions in the context of a specific narrative scene, facilitates the articulation of what was felt, in relation to whom, and about what issue.

For instance, we might symbolize a given internal sense as feeling tired or overwhelmed in the context of a particular narrative scene or set of circumstances. Both of these synthesized meanings of internal felt-senses, feeling tired and feeling overwhelmed, convey aspects of the experienced situation in a way that saying that we are feeling "exhausted" or "afraid" would not. The symbols "tired" or "overwhelmed" are each adequate but capture different aspects of the total experience. Conscious experience, thus, is not simply "in" us and fully formed. Instead, it emerges from a dialectical dance in which there is movement between (a) attention to an internal bodily felt-sense (I am tired) and (b) reflexive differentiation and naming of that felt-sense (and I feel exhausted with meeting the endless stream of demands at work these days) contextualized within the particular circumstances of a narrative context. The outcome is the articulation of the inner felt-sense in which the "right words" have been found to capture and represent an inner felt-sense and provide a platform for the differentiation of new personal meanings and understandings. How we articulate our feelings, most often in language and embedded within unfolding narrative frames, is thus crucial for the creation of new conscious experiential meaning.

As Greenberg et al. (1993) point out, it is crucial that therapists remain sensitively attuned to the nuances of their clients' inner felt-sense and not oversimplify the idea of reflecting feelings. They argue that therapist phrases such as, "you feel really angry," are not sufficiently differentiated and may well be marginally helpful for clients. Rogers (1959) suggested that experiencing a feeling "denotes an emotionally tinged *experience*, together with its personal meaning. Thus it includes the emotion but also the cognitive content or the meaning of the emotion in its *experiential context*" (p. 198). For Rogers, an inner felt-sense was understood to stand in relation to, and to be embedded within, a specific context or scene. Accordingly, it is very important that therapists accurately capture both the internal feeling and the external context—in essence what the feeling is about—in their empathic reflections. This may be as simple as saying to a client, "after she said that *[external narrative context of an unfolding conversation]*, you felt kind of undermined *[client inner felt feeling]*."

Greenberg, Rice, and Watson (1996) concur with Rogers when they suggest that therapists need to help clients to open up their experience and to explore the impact of people and events on them. The following example provides a demonstration of how a therapist's empathic response can succinctly capture and integrate the salient aspects of an unfolding narrative scene with the client's evoked emotional response.

Client I had a lot of difficulties with my parents . . . like when I was little, my parents would make me eat every last piece of food on my plate, they stood watching over me, and I hated it! And I felt so helpless. . . .

Therapist Just this sense of standing over you . . . watching . . . forcing you to eat. . . . was almost more than you could bear.

In her response, the therapist captures the particularity of salient aspects of the unfolding narrative scene (standing over and watching you), the reflexive meaning of those actions from the client's perspective (forcing you to eat) along with the idiosyncratic quality of the inner felt-meaning (was almost more than you could bear) evoked for the client in the context of the childhood memory. By capturing both sides of the client's experience, external scene and internal subjective feelings and meanings, the therapist helps the client to engage in further reflexive processing and differentiation of the evoked feeling response in the context of the external scene.

One of the unique insights generated by the narrative processes research program (Angus et al., 1999; Lewin, 2001) at York University has been the discovery that good-outcome cases could be distinguished from poor-outcome cases by a particular pattern of narrative processing. In these good cases, therapists focused clients inward when they were engaged in reflexive processing, and clients, once focused internally, then reflected on their emotional experiences to create new meaning. Therapists shifted the clients' focus from reflexive to emotion processes, and then clients shifted from internal emotional differentiation back to reflexive processing.

In her intensive case analysis of three good-outcome and three poor-outcome process experiential therapy dyads from the York I Depression study (Greenberg, Watson, & Goldman, 1998), Lewin (2001) found that in good-outcome cases, almost a third (30%) of the therapists' shifts in mode of processing were from reflexive modes to internal emotional differentiation. It appeared that the therapist's specific focus on the differentiation of emotional meanings, in the context of the client's own self-reflections, helps the client to enter more fully into a sustained elaboration of his or her own internal world of felt emotions, as experienced in the therapy session.

In the context of process experiential psychotherapy in particular, two-chair and empty-chair role-play scenarios, in which clients engage in an imaginative dialogue with self and others, seem to play a particularly important role in the facilitation of client self-reflexive processing in relation to core emotional responses. The following excerpt, drawn from a good-outcome process experiential therapy dyad (Greenberg & Angus, 1995), illustrates the dialectical dance between reflexive and emotion-focused processing modes unfolding within the context of a chair dialogue. In this empty-chair intervention, the client is playing the role of her husband and describing how he pushes her away and makes her feel unimportant.

Therapist   Like be him [husband] how do you make her feel bad, how do you make her feel like a child?

Client   By laughing—just straight—not taking her seriously.

Therapist   Ah. Tell her how you feel. You feel more powerful that way, right, like—sort of brush her off, how do you do that—how do you make her feel?

Client   Um, you don't need that, or, you know, you can do without her, you've got to stay home, and

Therapist   What's this, like pushing her back? [client gesturing]

Client   Um, forget it, you don't need this, and—move out of my way so I can try to get dressed and go out. [client elaboration of narrative action in the context of imagined scenario] [laugh]

Therapist   Mm-hm

Client   You're not important, [client self-reflexive shift to husband's assessment of her overall importance to him] and you're just there for, because the kids are there, not because— [sigh] [crying] [client active expression of bodily felt-sadness and hurt in response to feeling unwanted as wife]

At this point, the client indicates to the therapist that she is now experiencing her own emotional responses and no longer able to role-play her husband.

Client   I'm myself again.

Therapist   OK, come here. [client changes chairs] What are you feeling? [therapist shifts focus to differentiation of bodily felt-sense/emotional response]

Client   [crying] As I was saying, that—that he just doesn't love me. [client shift to reflexive meaning of feeling unloved in her marriage]

Therapist   So he sweeps you aside, and you feel unloved. [therapist evocative reflection of client experience in which both feeling and narrative action is integrated]

Client   [sniff] Yeah.

Therapist Tell him about that feeling. *[therapist encourages reflexive differentiation of the feeling of being unloved in the context of a dialogue with her husband]*

Client Um—it's like, I try so hard but you continue stepping on me, um, I feel like I'm there just for his slave, just, but not as your wife. *[in the context of reflecting on her own emotional responses to her husband's action, the client articulates a relational metaphor that captures a differentiated sense of being treated unfairly in the relationship and feelings of humiliation and denigration; of being stepped on]*

Therapist Uh-huh, what's it like to feel like a slave? *[therapist encourages a further differentiation of complex feelings connected to the symbolized experience of being treated like a slave]*

Client Just, to do everything for, for you and the kids or everybody that, you know; but not to do anything together. *[client shift to reflexive meaning of husband's actions and identifies feeling unwanted as his wife]* It's like not having me there, you don't want me there.

Therapist Tell him what it's like to feel unwanted and unloved.

Client It's—it's very resentful, I resent you when *[client shift to articulation of emotions and feelings experienced in response to being treated as a slave and unwanted as a wife]*

Therapist Uh-huh

Client When you push away, I resent you, I resent you...

Therapist I resent you, tell him. *[therapist encourages client to differentiate her feelings of resentment in the context of the imagined audience of her husband, in the empty chair]*

Client Yeah, why don't you want me to be there? *[client shift to reflexive questioning of the intentions and motives for her husband's hurtful actions and her need to know why he neglects her as a partner in life, as a wife]* For us to go out and have time to ourselves? Is there something about me, that you don't like me being there with you?

Therapist So you start to question yourself, right?

Client Yeah...

In this example, both client and therapist focus on the differentiation of the client's emotional responses and their symbolized meanings in the context of an imagined empty-chair dialogue with her husband. In addition, it is clear that the therapist helps the client shift from reflection on the meanings of actions and statements by her husband—"You're not important (to me)"—to the active expression of emotional reactions, crying and tears, in response to hearing these statements in the context of the imagined dialogue. The therapist stays with the client's leading edge, focusing on and symbolizing emergent feelings of resentment. Meanwhile, the client reflects on her experience: "I'm there just for his slave... but not as your wife" and "Is there something about me...?"

In contrast, it was found that in the York I Depression study, poor-outcome process experiential therapists initiated significantly fewer reflexive to internal processing shifts (16.75%) than did their good-outcome counterparts. Poor-outcome therapists and clients were much more likely to shift from external narrative storytelling to emotional differentiation, without a reflexive interval, than their good-outcome counterparts. The following therapy session excerpt, drawn from a poor-outcome process experiential dyad (Greenberg & Angus, 1995), illustrates how difficult it is for a therapist to shift a client toward emotional differentiation and meaning making when the client is not actively engaged in a self-reflexive processing stance. The client also appeared to play a more passive role when exploring her feelings, which were more likely to be described as discrete bodily sensations rather than experienced and symbolized as feelings or emotions.

Client   Yeah, yeah. I find that I'm, I'm ah I feel short of breath a lot. *[client description of bodily felt sensations]*

Therapist   Short of breath a lot? *[therapist focuses on client bodily felt-sense with implicit invitation for client elaboration]*

Client   Mm-hm. And just panting and huffing and puffing you know I *[lets out breath]* breathing and yawning and like I can't get enough air. *[client describes further aspects of bodily sensations]*

Therapist   So it's almost as if you're suffocating. *[therapist evocative-metaphoric reflection and shift to a reflexive symbolization of bodily felt-sense]*

Client   Yeah. *[client passive agreement]*

Therapist   So, what's that sense of suffocating? *[therapist invites client to reflexively articulate and differentiate the symbolized-metaphoric experience of feeling suffocated]*

Client   Well, I'll pick up the phone, I can be sitting... *[client shift away from focus on bodily felt-sense and reflexive meaning-making to description of external event]*

It is interesting to note that, in this example, the client initiated movement away from focusing on her internal experience and shifted into storytelling rather than self-reflection and differentiation of experience. This example illustrates that the activation of bodily felt-experiences and emotional responses is not the only crucial element for therapeutic change in therapy; emotional responses need to be accompanied by client reflexivity, an elaboration and transformation of the personal meaning surrounding an emotionally charged event. This excerpt reveals the importance of both emotional processing and reflexivity for successful outcomes in process experiential therapy.

A primary goal of process experiential task interventions, such as two-chair and empty-chair tasks, is the heightening of client emotional arousal to facilitate shifts in client emotional processes. Emotion shifts can mean moving from maladaptive secondary emotions to more primary adaptive emotional responses or accessing new adaptive emotional responses in the context of personal memory narratives. Experiencing new and sometimes contradictory emotional responses in the context of past life events can lead to significant shifts in the intentions, hopes, beliefs, wishes, and feelings that we attribute to the actions of self and others. At these moments, people see themselves and others in a new light and are impelled to construct a new, emotionally coherent narrative that accounts for what happened, why it occurred, what was felt, in relation to whom, and about what need or issue. It is our contention that emotions are "understood" and have personal meaning when organized within a narrative framework that identifies what is felt, about whom, and in relation to what need or issue.

Experience does, however, have its own implicit structure, based on inborn emotional/motivational/narrational tendencies; it does not always follow the order imposed on it by language and culture. No socially derived symbol can accurately reflect a given experience. Meaning does not come simply from social construction. An inaccurate, externally imposed symbol cannot create new lived experience, and it might ultimately cause greater disturbance and confusion if mistakenly accepted. People must be guided by their own emotionally based bodily felt-feelings, which arise from an interaction with the particularities of the unfolding narrative scene or situation. This internal complexity induces a "bodily felt sense" of meaning (Gendlin, 1962, 1996), which must be attended to and articulated for conscious experience to unfold. Once clients have expressed and clearly articulated their feelings, they are in a position to reflect on and evaluate their experiences and actions in the light of current goals, needs, and values. These activities are essential for the emergence of an explicit personal narrative that coherently organizes emotional experiences, goals, intentions, and beliefs within the context of the events of the unfolding narrative scene.

ARTICULATING NEW MEANINGS: EXPLAINING

The reflexive symbolization of identified emotions and their inclusion in the unfolding narrative enable the experience to be fully understood and accepted as part of the life story. Narratives serve to sequence events temporally, to coordinate actions, objects, and people in our lives; they provide perspectives and meaning to our experiences. Narratives guide future actions, communication, and relationships and help us fit into our culture. Satisfaction with our lives often depends on how events conform to our narrative expectations. When our story breaks down, our sense of continuity, coherence, and control breaks down. Narratives are also offered as models through the life stories of other people, fairy tales, folklore, film literature, and fiction. We use these as standards to guide our own narratives and against which to evaluate them.

The reflexive system is a conscious, controlled level of emotional processing that generates "cooler" emotional representations with lower arousal levels. The activation of the reflexive schematic system facilitates the organization and narrative representation of emotional experiences, and this enables the construction of an emotionally salient and meaning-filled narrative account of our interpersonal experiences with others in the world. Pennebaker and Seagal (1999) have shown that talking and writing about emotionally traumatic experiences immediately causes a drop in skin conductance and blood pressure and improves long-term health and immune function. Analyzing research participants' essays, Pennebaker and Seagal observed that the writing appears to force people to stand back and reorganize their thoughts and feelings in terms of a coherent story in which emotions, thoughts, and actions are organized into a narrative framework with a clear beginning, middle, and end. Subjects commented that the process of writing made them think things out and look at themselves from outside, from a self-reflexive position. This report suggests that reflective elaboration, narrative structuring, and meaning creation are all important therapeutic consequences of emotional expression.

In a similar vein, Angus et al. (1999) argue that accessing and articulating the client's world of emotions, beliefs, expectations, intentions, and goals—what Bruner (1990) has termed the landscape of consciousness—is crucial for the emergence of new ways of seeing and experiencing longstanding relationship problems and coming to terms with significant personal loss. The reflexive decentering from and then reengagement with distressing life experiences, from different relational vantage points, facilitates the articulation of new understandings about the self in relation to others. The reflexive processing of emotions, beliefs, hopes, needs, motives, intentions, and goals (landscape of consciousness) and their inclusion in the events of the problem stories or narratives (landscape of action) enables the experience to be fully understood and accepted as part of the life story. In essence, the integration of the landscape of action (a description of the sequential, linear unfolding of an event, which answers the question of what happened) with the landscape of consciousness (the internal responses of self and others, which addresses the question of what was felt and what does it mean) enables the construction of a coherent and meaning-filled narrative account of our interpersonal experiences with others in the world (see Angus et al., 2003).

For instance, the full personal significance of an interpersonal interaction or event often emerges in the context of a narrative inquiry that addresses three important questions: What did I feel? In relation to whom? About what personal need, value, goal, or issue? The reflexive differentiation of one's own and others' feelings, wishes, intentions, goals, and purposes, which emerge from the articulation and differentiation of felt emotions, are now connected with the unfolding sequences of narrative action to create a fully articulated and coherent narrative account. A key marker of narrative coherence is the presence of causal inferences or connectors that link the internal worlds—intentions, emotions, wishes, hopes, and purposes—of self and others with the actions undertaken in the scenario. Longer-term autobiographical memory storage and later retrieval are also enhanced by the narrative integration of the landscapes of action and consciousness, of events and emotions. The capacity to return to emotionally salient, autobiographical memories (Singer & Salovey, 1993) increases the likelihood that new views of self, self-experiences, and ways of relating to others will be remembered and transferred to a range of interpersonal contexts and domains in the future. Roger Schank (2000) goes as far as to say that narrative storytelling is autobiographical memory: "We need to tell someone else a story that describes our experiences because the process of creating the story also creates the memory structure that will contain the gist of the story for the rest of our lives" (p. 115). For Schank, telling a story is not a rehearsal, it is an act of creation, which in turn is a memorable experience itself.

Finally, the narrative organization of emotional experience enables people to coherently articulate and share their personal experiences with others and increases the likelihood of receiving support from others in times of need. In psychotherapy, it is our contention that effective therapists tacitly recognize the importance of both systems and actively facilitate client shifts to the processing of emotion schematic experiences and to fuller reflexive narrative making, in a bid to help them make conscious sense of their own emotional experiences.

In healthy meaning making, people's self-reflections are based predominantly on their bodily felt-sense, generated bottom-up by emotional and sensorimotor processing. Explaining, however, can also be based on more socially acquired cognitive schemes, which were obtained from others or inferred from past experience. Although often useful, these may also be sources of psychological difficulty. Those explanations that favor image maintenance over experience and interfere with here–and-now perception have been viewed as guided by "learned conditions of worth" (Rogers, 1959) or "introjects" (Perls et al., 1951) or "faulty assumptions" (Beck, 1976). Whenever identity is overly controlled by these determinants, people are not grounded in their own primary experience, and dysfunction may result.

Narrative Identity Construction and the Embodied Self

A level of organization of self even higher than that of stable self-organizations can be referred to as a narrative identity (Whelton & Greenberg, 2000). This identity involves the integration of accumulated experience and of various self-representations into some sort of coherent story or narrative. Identity cannot be understood outside of these narratives. To assume coherence and meaning, human lives must be "emplotted." In this process, events are organized by narrative discourse such that disparate actions and experiences of a human life are formed into a coherent story. These stories are influenced in that every culture has complex rules about the form meaningful narratives can take. These stories are not merely descriptive; they are creative and interpretive. Rationality, imagination, myth, and metaphor all come into play in trying to organize into a story the temporal sequence of events that make up the flow of life. Narratives, however, are not constructed arbitrarily, nor do they come only from culture but rather they are grounded in experience. The stories that tell us who we are emerge in a dialectical interaction between the experiencing and the narrative-making selves. At core, the self is embodied, but a body needs a story to act meaningfully, to relate past and future, to situate dreams, goals, regrets, plans, lost opportunities, hopes, and all the stuff of a truly human life (Whelton & Greenberg, 2000). Life is inherently a story the structure of which we make explicit when we reflect on our past and our possible future.

These stories of what happened constitute a discursive account of identity as it emerges over time (Angus & Bouffard, 2002, in press; Angus & Hardtke, 1994; Angus et al., 1999). The self-story or narrative is part of a constructivist dialectic. It establishes a sense of the coherence and stability of the self by symbolizing patterns in experience across situations. It also provides discursive explanations for the sometimes inconsistent meanings and aspects of self that predominate in different situations and relationships. All of these efforts contribute to the ongoing life project of achieving a sense of self-understanding and identity in which the questions of "who am I?" and "what do I stand for?" are addressed. Narrative identity is as complex as every other aspect of self, consisting of a dialogical array of often contradictory self-representations whose underlying coherence is as intricate as the point-counterpoint arrangements of layered musical scores. Given that the self experientially is a set of complex self-organizations in constant flux, the creation of the self-narrative is crucial to the establishment of a stable identity (Hermans & Hermans-Jansen, 1995).

What this view suggests is that the many voices that compose the self are given coherence, not just in the stories that people tell to account for themselves, but in the body, which irreducibly situates the self in the environment (Damasio, 1999; Gendlin, 1996; Mahoney, 1991). Narrative is one pole of the dialectic. The other pole, the intricate network of bodily, sensorimotor, and affective subsystems whose information is organized and synthesized into experientially available self-states is fundamental to embodied human experience.

CONCLUSIONS

It is our contention that in psychotherapy, effective therapists actively facilitate client shifts to the processing of emotion schematic experiences and to fuller reflexive narrative making in a bid to help them make conscious sense of their own emotional experiences. Converging evidence in experimental and social psychology and in neurophysiology suggests that much of the processing involved in the generation of emotional experience occurs independently of and prior to conscious, deliberate, cognitive operations and influences conscious thought. Therefore, working at the purely conceptual or linguistic level to effect emotional change may not produce enduring change. Instead, therapeutic interventions are more likely to succeed if they target the schematic processes that automatically generate the emotional experience that underlies clients' felt-senses of themselves as well as the way people construct meaning from their experience. We are suggesting that these schemes are complex affective structures and are themselves based on an integration of biology, experience, and culture.

Next, the experience is consciously reflected on, and the tacit representation of the unfolding "wordless" narrative scene (Damasio, 1999) associated with the evoked affective reaction is made explicit. In essence, a synthesis occurs between the tacit representation of felt emotional experiences and the imagined representation of the wordless narrative scene (Damasio, 1999). The narrative scaffolding of emotional experiences provides an effective framework for the organization and integration of felt emotions with unfolding action sequences. It is important to understand that this integration of emotion processes and narrative structure facilitates the construction of a storied explanation of what happened, an explanation that can then be told to others and reflected on for further understanding and personal meaning construction. Therapy, then, is a process of coming to know one's own stories, understanding them, and in so doing changing them. In the process of articulating and reflecting on life experiences in psychotherapy, personal narratives become deeper—fused with emotional meaning and significance—as well as larger—taking more information into account. In essence, personal stories become both meaningful and "meaning filled." In therapy, stories thus emerge from the body if there is a facilitative listener there to receive them, and they are brought into the world through the help of language.

In an emotion-focused narrative view, the self is seen as being constructed continually in an ongoing, self-organizing process. The self is best understood as an emergent organization of more basic elements. In this synthesis, embodied emotional experience and language-based narrative views are fundamental components of a higher-order synthesis process, both conscious and agentic, that determines who we create ourselves to be. Constructing the self involves an ongoing process both of identifying with and symbolizing experience as our own and constructing an embodied narrative that offers temporal stability and coherence. This process acts to identify our experience as our own and allows certain experiences to be seen as continuous within ourselves. The constantly evolving self operates as a synthesizing process, creating and being created anew in each moment and situation (Greenberg & Paivio, 1997; Greenberg et al., 1993; Greenberg & van Balen, 1998; Perls et al., 1951; Rogers, 1959).

REFERENCES

Angus, L., & Bouffard B. (2002). "No lo entiendo": La busqueda de sentido emocional y coherencia personalante una perdida traumatica durante la infancia. *Revista Psicoterapia, 12*(49), 25-46.

Angus, L., & Bouffard, B. (in press). The search for emotional meaning and self coherence in the face of traumatic loss in childhood: A narrative process perspective. In J. Raskin & S. Bridges (Eds.), *Studies in meaning* (Vol. 2). New York: Pace University Press.

Angus, L., & Hardtke, H. (1994). Narrative processes in psychotherapy. *Canadian Psychology, 35*, 190-203.

Angus, L., & Korman, Y. (2002). Coherence, conflict, and change in brief therapy: A metaphor theme analysis. In S. Fussell (Ed.), *The verbal communication of emotions: Interdisciplinary perspectives* (pp. 151-165). Hillsdale, NJ: Lawrence Erlbaum.

Angus, L., Levitt, H., & Hardtke, K. (1999). The Narrative Processing Coding System: Research applications and implications for psychotherapy practice. *Journal of Clinical Psychology, 55*, 1255-1270.

Angus, L., Lewin, J., Bouffard, B., & Rotondi-Trevisan, D. (2003). The CCRT approach to working with patient narratives in psychodynamic psychotherapy. In L. Angus & J. McLeod (Eds.), *The handbook of narrative and psychotherapy* (pp. 87-101). Thousand Oaks, CA: Sage.

Arciero, G., & Guidano, V. (2000). Experience, explanation, and the quest for coherence. In R. Neimeyer & J. Raskin (Eds.), *Constructions of disorder: Meaning-making frameworks for psychotherapy* (pp. 91-118). Washington DC: American Psychological Association.

Baumeister, R. F., & Newman, L. S. (1994). How stories make sense of personal experiences: Motives that shape autobiographical narratives. *Personality and Social Psychology Bulletin, 20*(6), 676-690.

Beck, A. (1976). *Cognitive therapies and the emotional disorders*. New York: International Universities Press.

Bohart, A., & Wugalter, S. (1991). Changes in experiential knowing as a common dimension in psychotherapy. *Journal of Integrative and Eclectic Psychotherapy, 10*, 14-37.

Book, H. (1998). *How to practice brief psychodynamic psychotherapy: The Core Conflictual Relationship Theme approach*. Washington, DC: American Psychological Association.

Botella, L., & Herrero, O. (2000). A relational constructivist approach to narrative therapy. *European Journal of Psychotherapy, Counselling, and Health, 3*, 1-12.

Bruner, J. (1990). *Acts of meaning*. Cambridge, MA: Harvard University Press.

Bruner, J. (2002). *Making stories: Law, literature, life*. New York: Farrar, Strauss & Giroux.

Damasio, A. (1994). *Descartes' error: Emotion, reason, and the human brain*. New York: Putnam's.

Damasio, A. (1999). *The feeling of what happens*. New York: Harcourt Brace.

Dimaggio, G., & Semerari, A. (2001). Psychopathological narrative forms. *Journal of Constructivist Psychology, 14*, 1-23.

Dimaggio, G., & Semerari, A. (2003). Disorganized narratives: The psychological condition and its treatment. In L. Angus & J. McLeod (Eds.), *The handbook of narrative and psychotherapy: Practice, theory and research* (pp. 263-282). Thousand Oaks, CA: Sage.

Epstein, S. (1994). Integration of the cognitive and psychodynamic unconscious. *American Psychologist, 49*(8), 709-724.

Forgas, J. (1995). Mood and judgments: The Affect Infusion Model (AIM). *Psychological Bulletin, 117*(1), 39-66.

Gendlin, E. (1962). *Experiencing and the creation of meaning: A philosophical and psychological approach to the subjective*. Glencoe, IL: Free Press.

Gendlin, E. T. (1996). *Focusing-oriented psychotherapy: A manual of the experiential method*. New York: Guilford.

Goldman, R., & Greenberg, L. (in press). Depth of emotional experience and outcome. *Psychotherapy Research*.

Gonçalves, O. F., Machado, P. P., Korman, Y., & Angus, L. (2002). Assessing psychopathology: A narrative approach. In L. E. Beutler & M. L. Malik (Eds.). *Rethinking the DSM: A psychological perspective* (pp. 149-176). Washington, DC: American Psychological Association.

Greenberg, L. S. (2002). *Emotion-focused therapy: Coaching clients to work through their feelings*. Washington, DC: American Psychological Association.

Greenberg, L. S., & Angus, L. (1995). How does therapy work? *Social Sciences and Humanities Research Council Standard Research Grant (1995-1998)*.

Greenberg, L., & Paivio, S. (1997). Varieties of shame experience in psychotherapy. *Gestalt Review 1(3), 205-220.*

Greenberg, L. S., & Pascual-Leone, J. (1995). A dialectical constructivist approach to experiential change. In R. A. Neimeyer & M. J. Mahoney (Eds.), *Constructivism in psychotherapy* (pp. 169-194). Washington, DC: American Psychological Association.

Greenberg, L. S., & Pascual-Leone, J. (1997). Emotion in the creation of personal meaning. In M. J. Power & C. R. Brewin (Eds.), *Transformation of meaning in psychological therapies: Integrating theory and practice* (pp. 157-173). New York: John Wiley.

Greenberg, L. S., & Pascual-Leone, J. (2001). A dialectical constructivist view of the creation of personal meaning. *Journal of Constructivist Psychology, 14,* 165-186.

Greenberg, L. S., Rice, L. N., & Elliott, R. (1993). *Facilitating emotional change: The moment-by-moment process.* New York: Guilford.

Greenberg, L., Rice, L., & Watson, J. (1996). *Manual for client-centered therapy.* Unpublished manual, York University, Toronto, Ontario, Canada.

Greenberg, L., & Toukmanian, S. (1999). Emotional change processes. *Social Sciences and Humanities Research Council Standard Research Grant (1999-2002).*

Greenberg, L., & van Balen, R. (1998). Theory of experience-centered therapy. In L. Greenberg, J. Watson, & G. Lietaer (Eds.), *Handbook of experiential psychotherapy: Foundations and differential treatment* (pp. 28-57). New York: Guilford.

Greenberg, L., & Watson, J. (1998). The treatment of depression in experiential therapies. In R. Fuhr, M. Sreckowic, & M. Gremmler-Fuhr (Eds.), *Das handboek der gestalt therapie.* Gottingen, Germany: Edition Humanitische Psicologie.

Greenberg, L. S., Watson, J. C., & Goldman, R. (1998). Process-experiential therapy of depression. In L. S. Greenberg & J. C. Watson (Eds.), *Handbook of experiential psychotherapy* (pp. 227-248). New York: Guilford.

Guidano, V. F. (1991). *The self in process.* New York: Guilford.

Guidano, V. F. (1995). Self-observation in constructivist therapy. In R. A. Neimeyer & M. J. Mahoney (Eds.), *Constructivism in psychotherapy* (pp. 155-168). Washington, DC: American Psychological Association.

Hardtke, K., Levitt, H., & Angus, L. (in press). Investigating narrative processes in psychotherapy discourse: The Narrative Processes Coding System. *Zeitschrift fuer qualitative Bildungs-,Beratungs- und Sozialforschung.*

Hermans, H. J. M., & Hermans-Jansen, E. (1995). *Self-narratives: The construction of meaning in psychotherapy.* New York: Guilford.

James, W. (1950). *The principles of psychology.* New York: Dover. (Original work published 1890)

Le Doux, J. E. (1996). *The emotional brain: The mysterious underpinnings of emotional life.* New York: Simon & Schuster.

Levitt, H., & Angus, L. (2000). Psychotherapy process measure research and the evaluation of psychotherapy orientation: A narrative analysis. *Psychotherapy Integration, 9(3),* 279-300.

Lewin, J. K. (2001). *Both sides of the coin: Comparative analyses of narrative process patterns in poor and good outcome dyads engaged in brief experiential psychotherapy for depression.* Unpublished master's thesis, York University, Toronto, Ontario, Canada.

Mahoney, M. (1991). *Human change processes.* New York. Basic Books.

McLeod, J. (1997). *Narrative and psychotherapy.* London: Sage.

Neimeyer, R. (1995). Client-generated narratives in psychotherapy. In R. Neimeyer & M. Mahoney (Eds.), *Constructivism in psychotherapy* (pp. 231-246). Washington, DC: American Psychological Association.

Oatley, K. (1992). *Best laid schemes: The psychology of emotions.* New York: Cambridge University Press.

Pascual-Leone, J. (1987). Organismic processes for neo-Piagetian theories: A dialectical causal account of cognitive development. *International Journal of Psychology, 22,* 531-570.

Pascual-Leone, J. (1990a). An essay on wisdom: Toward organismic processes that make it possible. In R. J. Sternberg (Ed.), *Wisdom: Its nature, origins, and development* (pp. 244-278). New York: Cambridge University Press.

Pascual-Leone, J. (1990b). Reflections on life-span intelligence, consciousness, and ego development. In C. Alexander & E. Langer (Eds.), *Higher stages of human development:*

Perspectives on adult growth (pp. 258-285). New York: Oxford University Press.

Pascual-Leone, J. (1991). Emotions, development, and psychotherapy: A dialectical-constructivist perspective. In J. Safran & L. Greenberg (Eds.), *Emotion, psychotherapy, and change* (pp. 302-335). New York: Guilford.

Pennebaker, J., & Seagal, J. (1999). Forming a story: The health benefits of narrative. *Journal of Clinical Psychology, 55*, 1243-1254.

Perls, F., Hefferline, R. F., & Goodman, P. (1951). *Gestalt therapy*. New York: Dell.

Rogers, C. R. (1959). A theory of therapy, personality, and interpersonal relationships, as developed in the client-centered framework. In S. Koch (Ed.), *Psychology: A study of a science* (Vol. 3, pp. 184-256). New York: McGraw-Hill.

Russel, J. A. (2003). Core affect and the psychological construction of emotions. *Psychological Review, 110*(1), 145-172.

Sarbin, T. (1995). *Narrative psychology: The storied nature of human conduct*. New York: Praeger.

Schank, R. (2000). *Tell me a story: Narrative and intelligence*. Evanston, IL: Northwestern University Press.

Singer, J., & Salovey, P. (1993). *The remembered self: Emotion and memory in personality*. New York: Free Press.

Watson, J., & Greenberg, L. (1996). Emotion and cognition in experiential therapy: A dialectical-constructivist position. In H. Rosen & K. Kuelwein (Eds.), *Constructing realities: Meaning making perspectives for psychotherapists* (pp. 253-276). San Francisco: Jossey-Bass.

Watson, J., & Rennie, D. (1994). Qualitative analysis of clients' subjective experience of significant moments during the exploration of problematic reactions. *Journal of Counselling Psychology, 41*, 500-509.

Whelton, W., & Greenberg, L. (2000). The self as a singular multiplicity: A process experiential perspective. In J. Muran (Ed.), *Self-relations in the psychotherapy process* (pp. 87-106). Washington, DC: American Psychological Association.

White, M. (2001). Folk psychology and narrative practice. *Dulwich Centre Journal*, No. 2. 1-37.

CHAPTER 20

Social Construction, Narrative, and Psychotherapy

JOHN MCLEOD

Social constructionism is the term used to describe a set of philosophical ideas that have become influential within the social sciences during the latter half of the 20th century. Probably the most important writers within this approach have been Peter Berger and Thomas Luckmann (1966) and Kenneth Gergen (1985, 1994a, 1994b). The work of these authors reveals that social constructionism represents an integration of several diverse strands of thought, for example, the social phenomenology of Alfred Schutz (1932/1972), the hermeneutics of Hans-Georg Gadamer (1975), and the poststructuralist ideas of Mikhail Bakhtin (1929/1973) and Michel Foucault (1980). There has been considerable debate around what some commentators regard as tensions within the social constructionist position, for example, in two Special Issues of *Theory and Psychology* (Stam, 2001, 2002) and elsewhere (Danziger, 1997; Nightingale & Cromby, 1999). Despite these debates, it is possible to identify a set of key ideas that characterize a social constructionist framework for understanding social life. My purpose in this chapter is to offer a brief outline of social constructionist thinking and then to consider some of the ways in which this philosophical perspective can be used to inform an appreciation of the role of narrative within psychotherapeutic practice.

Social constructionism can be viewed as a critical stance that provides a set of questions that can be applied to any aspect of culture and society. The primary question a social constructionist approach brings to bear on any social/cultural practice is: How do people act together? Any piece of action can be regarded as a joint "accomplishment" on the part of those who perform or construct it. How do people act or work together to

AUTHOR'S NOTE: Correspondence regarding this chapter should be sent to the author at University of Abertay Dundee, Tayside Institute for Health Studies, Dunhope Castle, Dundee DD3 6HF Scotland, or to j.mcleod@tay.ac.uk.

accomplish, for example, a moment of insight in a therapy session, "these feelings of being depressed all the time," a therapeutic relationship, a series of therapy sessions that "changed my life," a response to an item on an outcome questionnaire, or other aspects of the experience of psychotherapy?

The central question of "how do people act together?" leads to further questions that open up different aspects of the ways that action is accomplished:

> In acting together, does one person or persons have power and control over others? What are the sources of this power and control?
>
> How is this power manifested and used?
>
> When people are acting together, how do they use language to organize what they are doing? Is there a structure of turn-taking, interrupting, and silence, and what could this signify? What words are used? What are the layers of cultural meanings that are implied by these words? Is there evidence of the use, or contested use, of generalized and organized ways of talking (discourses)?
>
> What are the cultural resources (stories, myths, practices, rituals, technologies, rules, virtues, and values) that are drawn on in the making of meaning?
>
> What are the wider cultural horizons within which this piece of action can be understood?
>
> What part does physical embodiment and material culture play in the construction of action?

From a social constructionist perspective, counseling and psychotherapy can be viewed as a cultural arena that people who are experiencing difficulties or tensions in their lives can use to construct or reconstruct a sense of agency, personal identity, and belonging. Psychotherapy exists alongside many other cultural arenas in which identity can be reshaped, for example, the workplace, religious institutions, political organizations, and sport (Giddens, 1991). Why is it that psychotherapy has become a major site for "identity work" as the 21st century begins? In what ways has the meaning of psychotherapy shifted as a result of its incorporation into bureaucratic health care systems? A social constructionist interpretation of psychotherapy is inevitably reflexive, inviting researchers and other interested people to explore and define the cultural assumptions and projects that inform the questions they ask.

PSYCHOTHERAPY AS A RESPONSE TO MODERNITY

At the heart of social constructionism is the idea that our possibilities as human beings arise from the culture, society, and "tradition" within which we live. We construct—socially, together, through history—what we define as "real" and "true." Social constructionist ideas and practices are particularly well suited to the forms of life that are typical of postmodern societies, as people strive to reflect on, and create alternatives to, the structures, institutions, and beliefs that characterize modernity. The quality of being in modern society has been described by the social constructionist sociologist Peter Berger (1965) in these terms:

> The individual in modern society is typically acting and being acted upon in situations the motor forces of which are incomprehensible to him. The lack of intelligibility of the decisive economic processes is paradigmatic in this connection. Society confronts the individual as mysterious power, or in other words, the individual is unconscious of the fundamental forces that shape his life. One's own and the others' motives, meanings and identities, insofar as they are comprehensible, appear as a narrow foreground of translucency, the background of which is provided by the massive structures of a social world that is opaque, immensely powerful and potentially sinister. (pp. 40-41)

How can any of us deal with such a world? The complexity and existentially terrifying nature of the 21st-century world can be seen as driving individuals to seek enclaves of personal safety. Cushman (1990, 1995) has suggested that, in such a world, each person is under pressure to construct an autonomous and bounded self as a buttress against the "mysterious powers" of the social. But, as Cushman (1990) has argued, this self is necessarily empty, detached from sources of meaning generated by a commitment to a common good. For many people within Western societies, Cushman (1990) has observed, the empty self came to be filled through the accumulation of possessions and travel (consumerism) or through engaging in a journey of self-discovery (therapy).

Within the professional communities of counseling and psychotherapy today, there is a growing appreciation that an overindividualized approach to therapy has the effect of reinforcing tendencies toward bounded autonomy and separateness and away from connectedness and that this represents a cultural direction of travel that is potentially destructive. The discourse of therapy, as an enterprise concerned with the structure of an individual self, has gradually been supplanted by a discourse of relatedness. A pivotal move within this refocusing of psychotherapy has been the shift from a relatedness that refers to abstract structures in people's heads (interpersonal schemas, object relations, and the like) to a relatedness that is about what happens between actual people on an everyday basis (Sullivan, 1953). There has been a realization that resistance to the mysterious powers of global capitalism is best accomplished at a local level. While the therapist may be a valuable ally, a wider network of people—adversaries, supporters, audiences, guides, consultants—can usefully be involved in the work of therapy. Beyond this, there is a locality that is constituted not in flesh and blood but in physical and material terms: places, rituals, literature, networks. Viewed in this light, therapy can be a means of enabling people to build personally meaningful communities, to become better able to work together for a common good.

The shift from an individualized, psychologized image of the person to a sociocultural or *postpsychological* (McLeod, 1999) perspective required the adoption and development of a new language, one that would allow discussion of a different type of therapeutic process. The key concept, for those therapists involved in this transition, has been the idea of *narrative*. The concept of narrative has turned out to be enormously useful in relation to an understanding of how localities are constructed and maintained and what they mean to people.

NARRATIVE, THE CULTURAL TRADITION, AND SUBJECTIVITY

A locality is a place that is densely "storied" for a person. It is a place that is associated with many overlapping and interconnected stories about the people (alive and dead) who inhabit that place and what they did. Places and objects that have meaning for people also have voices. In any such place, it is possible, if one stops and listens, to hear these voices (Basso, 1984). Places that have meaning for people are also places where they themselves have some kind of voice, where they may speak, and where there is someone to hear them. Narrative and voice are important constructs for those who engage in localizing therapeutics because they provide a means of identifying the threads of meaning that link the individual person with the other people in his or her life, the physical environment in which he or she lives, and the set of virtues or sense of the "good life" that guides his or her actions.

A social constructionist approach to narrative does not share the individual-centered perspective around which modern psychology and psychotherapy have been built:

> ... the story of my life is always embedded in the story of those communities from which I derive my identity. I am born with a past; and to try to cut myself off from the past, in the individualist mode, is to deform my present relationships. The possession of an historical identity and the possession of a social identity coincide. Notice that rebellion against my identity is always one possible way of expressing it.... What I am, therefore, is in key part what I inherit, a specific part that is present to some degree in my present. I find myself part of a history and that is generally to say, whether I like it or not, one of the bearers of a tradition. (MacIntyre, 1981, p. 221)

For a social constructionist perspective, it makes little sense to attempt to understand a person, or understand ourselves, in isolation from the tradition within which the person lives. This is not to assume that personal behavior is "determined" or controlled by social forces; individual and collective agency and processes of co-construction are always at work. The tendency of most theories of psychology and psychotherapy to ignore social experience can be interpreted as constituting a form of social control that involves isolating people from collective sources of support and resistance.

The value of concepts of narrative and voice as tools for opening up an appreciation of the experience of being a person embedded within a locality or tradition can be found in analysis of published fiction. Novels are complex stories that encompass—usually—the voices of multiple characters and an overarching voice of the narrator. The majority of published novels are conventional thrillers and romances that reinforce dominant cultural narratives, for example, around gender, consumerism, militarism, and imperialism. Typically, readers do not find their own individual lives and localities portrayed in such novels. Some novels, however, seek to tell the stories and capture the voices of particular localities. Nations and smaller cultural groupings are constructed as "imagined communities" through a published fictional literature that provides a set of cultural narrative reference points. In my own community in Scotland, the work of modern novelists has played an important role in the struggle to maintain a sense of cultural (and personal) identity in the face of incorporation, globalization, and social change (Craig, 1999). Authors such as Lewis Grassic Gibbon, Robin Jenkins, and Alasdair Gray have documented and allowed readers to reflect on the landscapes of action and consciousness of 20th-century Scotland.

The vast body of narrative, including both an oral tradition and a written literature (and other media, such as cinema and television), represents a resource that people in a locality can use in constructing lives. The resource comprises an interlocking, layered set of stories about identity (what kind of a person can I be?) and relationships (what do people do together?). Within a culture or social group, language is used in many complex ways to convey the meanings carried by these stories. For example, the story of the birth of Jesus, the Nativity, is written in the Bible and, on some occasions, may be read aloud word for word at a church service. The same story may be performed as a play by young children at school. The structure of the story may operate as a template for stories told by people about many different topics. There may be moments when the use in a conversation of the word *Jesus* invokes the story of the Nativity. For any individual, each retelling or hearing of the story evokes memories of previous telling and hearings and connects that person with the thread of his or her life history. There will be many other ways in which this story operates as part of the sense-making apparatus of people in

Christian societies. It is a story that permeates the culture (Gaarder, 1996). It is a resource that is part of the tradition within which we make our lives.

As Foucault (1980) pointed out, the narrative resources available to members of a culture are bound up with issues of power and control. Stories are not equally valued within a culture. The idea of discourse can be used to refer to sets of story templates and ways of narrating that are found within a culture. To keep a cultural tradition alive requires multiple discourses (MacIntyre, 1981), contrasting voices in dialogue. Everyday life—being a person, being in relationships—therefore involves a process of positioning ourselves within these discourses or being positioned by others. By focusing on the ways in which a sense of self is maintained through talk, a social constructionist approach to individual identity and subjectivity highlights the theme of *multiplicity*: We exist in a fragmented, divided world (Van den Berg, 1974).

Some discourses and stories gain authority and become dominant within a culture while other discourses and stories become silenced or shamed. Everyone is aware of the dominant narratives and discourses associated with being a man and being a woman, and the wide range of means that exist for controlling and disciplining those who tell different stories. Everyone is aware, at some level, of the narrative and discourse of the "lunatic" and the penalties, in terms of degradation and disaffirmation, that accrue to anyone who becomes positioned within that discursive domain (Laing, 1960, 1961).

The dominant narratives and discourses that prevail within a culture are generally linked to structures and institutions of power and control. For example, Western culture is highly militarized, with regular wars and a significant proportion of national product spent on weapons and armies. It is perhaps not surprising that narratives and metaphors of war (fight, attack, defend, defeat) are commonplace (Lakoff & Johnson). Over the past 200 years, a narrative industry has also developed, which has taken the production of stories away from the everyday life practice of oral storytelling and constructed a new tradition of passive consumption of narratives and "spectacles" (Gergen, 2000). The growth of pornography as a large-scale commercial activity represents a striking example of a 21st-century narrative industry that has generated new and deeply destructive narratives in the shared cultural resource for making sense of embodiment, sexuality, and relationship.

From a social constructionist perspective, the idea of narrative operates as a means of bridging the multiple realities of contemporary life. A narrative can be a brief joke or story told by one person to another. It can be a structure for organizing individual experience. It can be a myth or an autobiography. Narrative is a form of language use and meaning making that is embedded in place and forms of life. The concept of narrative is, therefore, central to therapy—any kind of therapy—because it conveys a sense of the interwoven quality of subjectivity and social context. It is impossible to imagine a form of psychotherapy that did not involve the telling and retelling of stories.

CONSTRUCTIONIST PERSPECTIVES ON PSYCHOTHERAPY

There are many ways in which a social constructionist approach can be used to develop an appreciation of the role of narrative in psychotherapy. As a method of inquiry, social constructionism pays particular attention to the language through which realities are created and maintained within everyday life. It is a critical approach that is sensitive to the operation of ever-present processes of power and domination. It is a form of inquiry that aims to generate practical possibilities in relation to documenting and disseminating tools and strategies for promoting mutuality. Some examples of a constructionist perspective on narrative and psychotherapy are briefly outlined next.

The Story of the "Good Life"

My own research has centered on seeking to understand issues such as how the stories told by clients in therapy change, what seems to make such change possible, and how the complexity of co-constructed narrative action in therapy can be investigated in a respectful way. This research has involved the development of a set of strategies for carrying out qualitative, hermeneutic, narrative analyses of single cases (McLeod & Balamoutsou, 2001) and building a framework for understanding narrative processes in therapy through carrying out a series of case studies (Grafanaki & McLeod, 1999; McLeod, 1997; McLeod & Balamoutsou, 1996, 2000; McLeod & Lynch, 2000). The findings and implications of this research are discussed in McLeod (2002).

One of the most striking discoveries to emerge from these investigations is the extent to which the work of therapy centers around exploration and reflection on deeply implicit assumptions that both client and therapist hold about what makes life worth living. Gordon Lynch and I have described these assumptions as the "story of the good life" (McLeod & Lynch, 2000). The "good life" story clients tell is always their own personal story, but it also reflects their personal interpretation of a broader cultural narrative (Taylor, 1989).

In one case, Margaret, a Canadian woman in her 50s, received 16 sessions of client-centered psychotherapy,[1] which were highly effective in helping her to overcome depression (McLeod & Lynch, 2000). In the first session, Margaret described a series of stressful events that she believed had contributed to her difficulties. She then talked about the importance for her of her relationship with her husband and how this relationship had recently been marked by tension and conflict. In the middle of this problem-focused narrative, she commented:

... I always sort of felt that
when your children grew up
and we based our whole life on our children
you know
we have to
and you know
we had
it was always family holidays
and that type of thing
like we never left our children
and this was an agreement that
this is our life
you know
and we were very happy with it
but I always had sort of
the feeling
that
when the children grew up
and were independent
we would become a couple again
and of course the timing of all of this just
just
that's just not what happened
and I think I just felt so let down
that um I couldn't cope with it very well
you know
(can I?
I have some in my purse
but to rummage through would be...)
it wasn't what was happening
and
and I think I became very frustrated
and very angry
and I'm just having a hard time
getting over all of this anger
you know

In this passage, Margaret stands aside from providing the therapist with a chronicle of her troubles and instead places these troubles in the context of an overarching metanarrative: her story of what her life was about ("we based our whole life on our children... but... when the children grew up and were independent we would become a couple again"). The personal significance of this metanarrative is underscored by tears, and its relevance to the task of therapy lies in the fact that it is, for Margaret, a shattered narrative ("that's just not what happened and I think I just felt so let down").

From a social constructionist point of view, the process of co-constructing meaning is of particular importance. In the case of Margaret, it was possible to examine the cultural metanarrative within which the therapist positioned herself, by analyzing the therapist's statements within therapy sessions. Clearly, the therapist did not disclose a story of troubles. Nevertheless, her responses to Margaret revealed a consistent implicit story of what goes wrong in people's lives and what can help. A selection of the therapist's statements during the first session included:

> *inside you're just feeling really angry about this*
> *and it's coming out in anger?*
> *and yet inside you said it's really something the fear is there*
> *what's really going on for you is hard for you to express*
> *so it's kind of affected how you can sort of negotiate and sort of communicate*
> *a lot of feeling that never really got expressed to him.*

These statements reflect the cultural narrative of the good life associated with humanistic psychology: the notion of a deep personal interior or inner self that requires exploration as a prerequisite for fulfillment.

These stories of the good life, within which therapist and client position themselves during their time together, represent the meaning context within which therapy takes place. The process of therapy can be understood, at least in part, as circling around two types of activity. In Margaret's case, the client began to apply the therapist's metanarrative to the events of her own life, which opened up a wider narrative repertoire for her. The client also engaged in a search for ways to repair her own good-life story by trying to find out how and why it went wrong and what would be required to restore/restory it. In this case and other cases we have studied (particularly McLeod, 1997, Chapter 7), the task of metanarrative repair, or the construction of an alternative metanarrative, appears to be central to the work of therapy, even if the therapist and client do not appear to be consciously aware that they are engaged in such a quest.

The Personal Niche

The social constructionist image of the person is that of a being who is continually engaged in constructing identity and making meaning, knowing and being known, in interaction and conversation with others in the context of a complex and fragmented social world. A useful approach to making sense of how personal identity is constructed under the conditions of modern life is through the idea of the personal *niche*: the physical, occupational, interpersonal, and narrative space within which a life is lived out (Willi, 1999). The social and cultural world can be viewed as similar to an ecology. Just as organisms evolve their own niche within an ecological system, people are faced with the task of constructing niches within the social ecology that confronts them. Cultural and personal narratives are some of the elements of a personal niche, for example, the fiction a person reads, the family stories that are told at Christmas, the individual's life narrative and autobiographical memories. But the niche also consists of institutions and organizations (the workplace, a sports club), friendship networks and places (the park, the shopping center). In a city, many thousands of people may occupy the same neighborhood, but they exist within quite different personal niches within that social environment. When some aspect of this niche or personal world is disrupted, problems in living arise, and help may be sought. The niche may be disturbed by changes associated with stages in a life course, for example, having a baby or retiring from work. It may be affected by actions of others, such as abuse and hostility, bereavement, exile, or illness. In all of these scenarios, the person is faced by a need to stand back, reflect, and arrive at some decisions about how to reconstruct or repair what has been or construct a new niche.

It is perhaps worth noting that the idea that personal troubles can be understood in terms of the construction of a meaningful personal niche is quite different from the idea that personal troubles are due to personal "deficits" such as mental illness (Gergen, 1990). Research into the personal worlds of individuals who have had lengthy histories of severe "mental health" problems found that people who might be considered highly disabled and psychotic in the context of dominant cultural narratives of health and sanity in fact lead lives that are satisfying to them if they can construct a meaningful niche for themselves, perhaps from activities such as spending time in a coffee bar, listening to music, and being a member of a church. Corin (1998; Corin & Lauzon, 1992) has described a strategy of "positive withdrawal" through which a meaningful life can be constructed by those who experience close personal relationships as overwhelmingly stressful.

The concept of the personal niche captures several key aspects of a social constructionist approach to engaging with problems in living. A personal niche is always co-constructed. It requires action on the part of the individual, but in collaboration (whether overt or tacit) with others. It is personal and unique but, at the same time, a fragment of a cultural mosaic. It leads to an appreciation that narratives are not merely communication structures that exist in a purely linguistic or cognitive space but are situated ways of talking that make reference to a shared world.

Positioning: The Construction of Subjectivity and Identity in Conversational Interaction

The concept of subject positioning within conversational interaction has been developed by Rom Harre and his colleagues (Davies & Harre, 1990; Harre & Van Langenhove, 1991; Van Langenhove & Harre, 1994) and has been used by many social constructionist theorists. If we live, as people, within a culture comprising multiple discourses, then our identity or subjectivity can be understood in terms of how we position ourselves, or are positioned by others, in relation to these discourses or dominant narratives. The idea of subject positioning makes it possible to explore the ways in which a sense of self may be experienced in some situations as unitary and stable (when we settle in to one form of discursive practice) and in other situations as fluid and multiple (when we shift positions). It also provides a means of appreciating the moment-by-moment construction of identity within talk because every statement made in a conversation implicitly positions speaker and listener(s) in relation to social roles and discourses. This idea is a valuable tool for psychotherapists because it helps to explain how the individual subjectivity of clients is constructed on a moment-by-moment basis through interaction with the therapist. The concept of subject positioning draws therapists' attention to the ways in which the language they use brings into being certain emotions and capabilities in the client.

An example of an exchange between a therapist and client which illustrates the operation of subject positioning in therapy is provided by the narrative therapist John Winslade:

> When I spoke about my daughter who had died some 10 years earlier and was slightly overcome by the emotions that returned with her memory, I was once asked by a counselor, "Are you still grieving for her?" In this moment, I experienced being called into a position as a patient with some pathological condition. The word *still* implied some normal length of time for which it would be appropriate to grieve and, by inference, that I should think about myself as needing treatment if I was abnormally prolonging my grieving. The invitation was into a particular relation with the counselor's authority to assess and prescribe treatment (e.g., the corrective expression of "repressed" emotion). . . . What made the position call particularly potent was the impossibility of answering the question without taking up this pathological view of myself. If I had said *yes*, I would have entered into the position I was being offered. If I had said *no*, I would clearly have denied the evidence of my emotional response within the counselor's discursive framework, thereby proving her repression hypothesis. (Drewery, Winslade, & Monk, 2000, p. 253)

This therapist-client conversational interaction can be understood in terms of the dominant therapeutic discourse that Gergen (1990) has characterized as a "language of deficit." The person seeking help communicates a feeling of sadness, which is reified as a pathological state (grieving). Through this conversational strategy, the client is positioned as abnormal, and the therapist is positioned as someone who possesses the "authority to assess and prescribe treatment." The therapist is in control of the situation, and it is difficult for the client to resist the call to enter a subjective position and go on to further elaborate a set of symptoms.

The narrative therapy procedure of externalizing the problem represents a contrasting form of subject positioning (Epston & White, 1995; White & Epston, 1990). In narrative therapy, rather than reify a concern or problem expressed by the client as a deficit "in" the person, the problem is treated as an entity outside the person, which he or she is able to resist and control. For example, a person may visit a therapist as a result of experiences of losing his or her temper and becoming violent with family members. A narrative therapist working with such a client might make use of responses such as "I understand you are here because you've been visited by anger more often than you would like" and "How much of the time would you say that anger is in charge of your life these days?" (Parry & Doan, 1994, p. 89). These conversational strategies invite the client into a position of being a subject who is separate from the anger, who has the capability of controlling the anger, who is an expert on the role of anger in his or her life, and who is not always, or only, an angry person. The person is also positioned as an active agent and coinquirer, someone who will work together with the therapist to resolve this issue. The therapist positions himself or herself as an individual who is curious and cares about the person enough to want to know more and to help. The therapist is further positioned as someone who is outside of an expected professional "psych" role, insofar as he or she is making some rather unusual statements (e.g., anger in charge of your life). The spatial metaphor implied by the concepts of positioning and externalizing can be extended to an appreciation of the proximity of person, therapist, and problem in the room. At the beginning of the session, the problem is in the client or *is* the client, and the client addresses the therapist face to face as a powerful "other." As soon as the therapist engages in the discursive practices of narrative therapy, it is as though the client and the therapist become equals, sitting side by side to inspect and observe the problem, which can be imagined as occupying a separate chair.

The kind of positioning that is enabled by externalizing questions has implications for the manner in which the conversation "goes on." A form or genre of discourse is established that is like an investigation made by a journalist or researcher. The statements that the client makes about the problem do not refer to the "I" who is talking. It therefore becomes possible for the "I" to be indexed by attributes that are not deficiencies, such as "Yesterday I stopped anger in its tracks by. . . ." Externalizing questions also provide scaffolding for meaning making. The interrogative form invites the client to reflect by assembling and classifying examples of the problem. The proposition that the problem can be talked about as some kind of agentic entity that can "visit," "be in charge," or be "sneaky" supplies the beginnings of a framework for constructing a narrative or story around anger, which serves to integrate the investigative data that the person is collecting.

The use of externalizing questions represents an example of sensitivity-to-subject positioning in therapy. In practice, in the narrative therapy developed by White and Epston (1990), this conversational strategy is embedded within a number of other strategies that also align therapist and client with a constructionist worldview that emphasizes connectedness and collaboration. For example, narrative therapists position clients not as bounded, autonomous individuals but as members of networks and communities, and the therapists are curious about the role of other people in a person's struggle with a problem such as anger. Clients are positioned as consultants who can teach their therapists about how certain problems can be overcome, rather than as clients expected to adopt a supplicant role. Narrative therapists draw on a wide repertoire of linguistic strategies to accomplish this type of positioning (Kogan & Gale, 1997). These strategies are not techniques that can be applied independently but are part of a coherent *discourse technology* (Fairclough, 1992) that draws clients into a way of talking about life that reflects the principles and values of social constructionism. A discourse technology is a way of talking—words, phrases, metaphors, forms of questioning—that reflects a dominant cultural narrative or discourse. All approaches to therapy can be viewed as employing discourse technology, and all competent therapists are highly consistent in the way they talk with clients.

Cultural Tools

A "common factors" perspective on counseling and psychotherapy suggests that a number of shared elements underpin all effective therapies: the creation of a safe space in which to disclose troubles and express emotion, a relationship with a "healer," and the instillation of hope or positive expectations (Frank, 1973; Hubble, Duncan, & Miller, 1999). Within the therapeutic space or arena created through the enactment of these common factors, therapists deploy specific interventions that reflect the therapeutic tradition within which they work. These "healing rituals" need to be credible to the client and to operate as rituals or routines that generate personal learning and change. Peavy (1999) has suggested that, from a social constructionist perspective, interventions or rituals can be viewed as cultural tools. In therapy, actions that are part of everyday cultural experience—engaging in eye contact, shaking hands, asking a question—are used in a strategic, intentional manner by therapists. There are also more complex sequences of activity that can be viewed as therapeutic cultural tools. Examples of therapeutic use of cultural tools include: keeping a diary, writing letters, reading novels, reading myths, watching movies, making pictures, sculpting, dancing, participating in theater (Anderson, 1977). Each of these tools represents a format or structure for the narration of life stories.

Within therapies that are informed by social constructionism, particular emphasis is placed on cultural tools that promote collaboration, co-construction, and membership (in contrast to more individual-oriented tools such as keeping a diary or reading a self-help book). A widely known example of the use of cultural tools in narrative therapy is the sending of letters and certificates to clients in which therapists document the person's narrative and perhaps celebrate how it is changing (White & Epston, 1990). Another example can be found in the use of map making in therapy:

> A map is a cultural tool for showing *how to navigate* (social life); *how to find one's way* (to a preferred future); *how to explain the lay of the land* to another (common understanding); and *how to talk about complex configurations* in a simplified manner (decomplexifying), and *how to articulate the unseen* (making invisible parts of life visible). Very young children, almost all children in school, and many adults are natural mappers. The maps may take the form of doodling, charting, drawings, artwork, or scribbles. It is not much of a stretch to call people *homo cartigraphicus* for in our mapping, doodling, charting, drawing, and scribbling, we are usually "mapping" aspects of our personal experience. . . . It is certainly a common, everyday experience to ask another for directions about how to get to a destination and have the other say: "Here, I'll draw you a map." In [social constructionist] counseling, mapping is taken to be a primary method for assisting help-seekers to analyze complex situations, construct plans for action, construct decisions, invent strategies for problem-solving, and build futures. A map is a visual method for building answers to such dilemmas as "Where (in the world am I)?" "What futures do I have?" "What pathways in social life are open to me and how do I get on them?" "How can this mess I am in become articulated in a sensible way?" "What are my stepping stones for getting where I want to be?" (Peavy, 1999, p. 11)

A letter or a map is a document that remains with the person, and they can continue to use it either as a reminder of their connectedness and working relationship with the therapist or to show and explain things to other people in their life. In some cases, the cultural tool can be employed as a means of deliberately involving a wider audience in the task of generating new understandings. For example, Madigan (1999) describes his work with a man who wrote to a large number of people he knew, asking for their observations around his "depression."

Another cultural tool that has been adapted by constructionist therapists is the idea of the *campaign* or *league*. In their work with people who have experienced difficulties around eating, David Epston and his colleagues have found it valuable to establish anti-anorexia leagues (Epston, Morris, & Maisel, 1995). These leagues operate as campaigns against the images of women and body size that prevail in modern society and against the diet industry. Participating in a league allows people to be members of a community in which language and narrative can be used to construct alternative forms of life and in which they can "re-member" the people they were before compulsive eating behaviors entered their life.

The importance of cultural tools, from a social constructionist perspective on therapy, lies in the fact that they represent an enormous, preexisting resource for the creation of narratives. In addition, these everyday cultural resources—maps, letters, political campaigns—are familiar to people. They can never be seen by users of therapy as mystifying "techniques" that can only be used by those who have undergone special professional training. They are not a vehicle through which people are subjected to the controlling "gaze" of the professional.

SOCIAL CONSTRUCTION AND THERAPY: FUTURE CHALLENGES

The concepts of subjective positioning, the personal niche, cultural tools, and the story of the good life provide examples of some of the ways in which aspects of the process of psychotherapy can be understood from a social constructionist perspective. Narrative activity runs through all of these activities. Many other examples might be given; social constructionism represents a fertile resource for therapists. In conclusion, it is perhaps useful to consider some of the challenges facing those who might seek to follow this path.

The first challenge to constructionist therapists can be characterized as resisting the reification of the narrative metaphor. Some narrative-informed approaches to therapy, such as the CCRT model of Lester Luborsky, have developed specific definitions and measurement strategies to pin down what they mean by a narrative. Constructionist narrative therapy is not like this. Within constructionism, the idea of narrative is intended as a way of referring to a necessary aspect or quality of human beings, in the sense described by Ricoeur (1980). For example, the concept of narrative can be used to talk about silence, the space *between* words (Cornforth, 2001; Lynch, 1997). The pressure within constructionist therapy may be that, as the approach becomes more explicitly codified in textbooks, its rich oral and communal tradition, which has sustained the ambiguity of being built around a metaphor, may give way to a more rational stance. Textbooks, case studies, and conference presentations are, to a large extent, context-stripping forms of communication that do not readily allow audiences to appreciate the local, embodied nature of therapist-client contact.

A second challenge facing constructionist therapies can be described as that of actively engaging in the debate over legitimacy. In most industrialized societies, there has been increasing pressure on psychotherapy to demonstrate its effectiveness through controlled outcome studies. So far, constructionist therapy has not entered this arena. There are substantial barriers. At present, research into psychotherapy outcomes is conducted in a monological style and uses change in psychiatric/psychological symptoms as the main index of "improvement." None of this fits a social constructionist worldview. From a constructionist perspective, useful knowledge is co-constructed, for example, through collaboration between therapists and client consultants. What changes in therapy is not symptoms but the stories told by the person and the ways in which these stories can be used by the person to enable membership, inclusion, and engagement in meaningful action. There is a huge research agenda here, in terms of developing a narrative constructionist approach to psychotherapy outcome. It is necessary to develop a systematic critique of the social construction of existing knowledge of outcome (McLeod, 2001a) and to create strategies for documenting and analyzing outcome in different ways (McLeod, 2001b). The Narrative Assessment Interview (Hardtke & Angus, 2003, this volume) provides a glimpse of what is possible.

A final challenge is to find ways of addressing the hostility to constructionism that seems to exist in some sections of the academic and professional community.

Social constructionism has been characterized by its critics as irredeemably relativistic and as denying the reality of personal agency and subjectivity. Some elements of the response of social constructionist writers to these criticisms have been, perhaps inevitably, somewhat defensive. It is time to move beyond this polarization. Social constructionism is a means of giving close attention to the flexibility and inventiveness of language. It is a reminder of the importance of history, of the fact that everything we say and do is constructed from layer upon layer of what Gadamer called "historical consciousness." Constructionism affirms the power that people have to do things together and to resist and reinvent in the face of oppression.

NOTE

1. I would to thank Dr. Leslie Greenberg and Dr. Lynne Angus of the Psychotherapy Research Group, York University, Toronto, for permission to use this case material for research purposes.

REFERENCES

Anderson, W. (Ed.). (1977). *Therapy and the arts: Tools of consciousness*. New York: Harper & Row.

Bakhtin, M. (1973). *Problems of Dostoevsky's poetics*. Ann Arbor, MI: Ardis. (Original work published 1929)

Basso, K. H. (1984). "Stalking with stories": Names, places, and moral narratives among the Western Apache. In E. M. Bruner (Ed.), *Text, play, and story: The construction and reconstruction of self and society* (pp. 19-55). Washington, DC: American Ethnological Society.

Berger, P. L. (1965). Toward a sociological understanding of psychoanalysis. *Social Research, 32*, 26-41.

Berger, P., & Luckmann, T. (1966). *The social construction of reality*. New York: Penguin.

Corin, E. (1998). The thickness of being: Intentional worlds, strategies of identity, and experience among schizophrenics. *Psychiatry, 61*, 133-146.

Corin, E., & Lauzon, G. (1992). Positive withdrawal and the quest for meaning: The reconstruction of experience among schizophrenics. *Psychiatry, 55*, 266-278.

Cornforth, S. (2001). Culture: The song without words. *Counselling and Psychotherapy Research, 1*, 194-199.

Craig, C. (1999). *The modern Scottish novel: Narrative and the national imagination*. Edinburgh, Scotland: Edinburgh University Press.

Cushman, P. (1990). Why the self is empty: Toward a historically situated psychology. *American Psychologist, 45*, 599-611.

Cushman, P. (1995). *Constructing the self, constructing America: A cultural history of psychotherapy*. Reading, MA: Addison-Wesley.

Danziger, K. (1997). The varieties of social construction. *Theory and Psychology, 7*, 399-416.

Davies, B., & Harre, R. (1990). Positioning: The discursive production of selves. *Journal for the Theory of Social Behaviour, 20*, 43-63.

Drewery, W., Winslade, J., & Monk, G. (2000). Resisting the dominant story: Toward a deeper understanding of narrative therapy. In R. A. Neimeyer & J. D. Raskin (Eds.), *Constructions of disorder: Meaning-making frameworks for psychotherapy* (pp. 243-364). Washington, DC: American Psychological Association.

Epston, D., Morris, F., & Maisel, R. (1995). A narrative approach to so-called anorexia/bulimia. In K. Weingarten (Ed.), *Cultural resistance: Challenging beliefs about men, women and therapy* (pp. 69-96). New York: Harrington Park Press.

Epston, D., & White, M. (1995). Termination as a rite of passage: Questioning strategies for a therapy of inclusion. In R. A. Neimeyer & M. J. Mahoney (Eds.), *Constructivism in psychotherapy* (pp. 339-354). Washington, DC: American Psychological Association.

Fairclough, N. (1992). *Discourse and social change*. Cambridge, UK: Polity Press.

Foucault, M. (1980). *Power/knowledge: Selected interviews and other writings, 1972-1977* (C. Gordon, Ed.). New York: Pantheon.

Frank, J. D. (1973). *Persuasion and healing: A comparative study of psychotherapy*. Baltimore, MD: Johns Hopkins University Press.

Gaarder, J. (1996). *The Christmas mystery*. (E. Rokkan, Trans.). New York: Farrar, Straus & Giroux.

Gadamer, H. (1975). *Truth and method* (2nd ed.). New York: Continuum.

Gergen, K. J. (1985). The social constructionist movement in modern psychology. *American Psychologist, 40,* 266-275.

Gergen, K. J. (1990). Therapeutic professions and the diffusion of deficit. *The Journal of Mind and Behavior, 11,* 353-368.

Gergen, K. J. (1994a). *Realities and relationships: Soundings in social construction*. Cambridge, MA: Harvard University Press.

Gergen, K. J. (1994b). *Toward transformation in social knowledge* (2nd ed.). London: Sage.

Gergen, K. J. (2000). The self: Transformation by technology. In D. Fee (Ed.), *Pathology and the postmodern: Mental illness as discourse and experience* (pp. 100-115). Thousand Oaks, CA: Sage.

Giddens, A. (1991). *Modernity and self-identity: Self and society in the late modern age*. Cambridge, UK: Polity Press.

Grafanaki, S., & McLeod, J. (1999). Narrative processes in the construction of helpful and hindering events in experiential psychotherapy. *Psychotherapy Research, 9,* 289-303

Hardtke, K. K., & Angus, L. (2003). The Narrative Assessment Interview: Assessing self-change in psychotherapy. In L. Angus & J. McLeod (Eds.), *The handbook of narrative and psychotherapy: Practice, theory, and research* (pp. 247–262). Thousand Oaks, CA: Sage.

Harre, R., & Van Langenhove, L. (1991). Varieties of positioning. *Journal for the Theory of Social Behaviour, 21,* 393-407.

Hubble, M. A., Duncan, B. C., & Miller, S. D. (Eds.). (1999). *The heart and soul of change: What works in therapy*. Washington, DC: American Psychological Association.

Kogan, S. M., & Gale, J. E. (1997). Decentering therapy: Textual analysis of a narrative therapy session. *Family Process, 36,* 101-126.

Laing, R. D. (1960). *The divided self: An existential study in sanity and madness*. Harmondsworth, UK: Penguin.

Laing, R. D. (1961). *Self and others*. Harmondsworth, UK: Penguin.

Lakoff, G., & Johnson, M. (1980). *Metaphors we live by*. Chicago: University of Chicago Press.

Lynch, G. A. (1997). Words and silence: Counselling and psychotherapy after Wittgenstein. *Counselling, 8,* 126-128.

MacIntyre, A. (1981). *After virtue: A study in moral theory*. London: Duckworth.

McLeod, J. (1997). *Narrative and psychotherapy*. London: Sage.

Madigan, S. (1999). Inscription, description, and deciphering chronic identities. In I. Parker (Ed.), *Deconstructing psychotherapy* (pp. 150-163). London: Sage.

McLeod, J. (1999). Counselling as a social process. *Counselling, 10,* 217-226.

McLeod, J. (2001a). An administratively created reality: Some problems with the use of self-report questionnaire measures of adjustment in counselling/psychotherapy outcome research. *Counselling and Psychotherapy Research, 1,* 215-226.

McLeod, J. (2001b). *Qualitative research in counselling and psychotherapy*. London: Sage.

McLeod, J. (2002). Lists, stories, and dreams: Strategic invitation to relationship in psychotherapy narrative. In W. Patterson (Ed.), *Strategic narrative: New perspectives on the power of personal and cultural stories* (pp. 89-106). Lanham, MD: Lexington.

McLeod, J., & Balamoutsou, S. (1996). Representing narrative process in therapy: Qualitative analysis of a single case. *Counselling Psychology Quarterly, 9,* 61-76.

McLeod, J., & Balamoutsou, S. (2000). Narrative process in the assimilation of a problematic experience: Qualitative analysis of a single case. *Zeitschrift fur qualitative Bildungs- , Beratungs- , und Sozialforshung, 2,* 283-302.

McLeod, J., & Balamoutsou, S. (2001). A method for qualitative narrative analysis of psychotherapy transcripts. In J. Frommer & D. Rennie (Eds.), *Qualitative psychotherapy research: Methods and methodology* (pp. 128-152). Lengerich, Germany: Pabst.

McLeod, J., & Lynch, G. (2000). "This is our life": Strong evaluation in psychotherapy narrative. *European Journal of Psychotherapy, Counselling and Health, 3,* 389-406.

Nightingale, D. J., & Cromby, J. (Eds.). (1999). *Social constructionist psychology: A critical analysis of theory and practice*. Buckingham, UK: Open University Press.

Parry, A., & Doan, R. E. (1994). *Story revisions. Narrative therapy in the postmodern world*. New York: Guilford.

Peavy, R. V. (1996). Counselling as a culture of healing. *British Journal of Guidance and Counselling, 24,* 141-150.

Peavy, R. V. (1997). A constructive framework for career counseling. In T. L. Sexton & B. L. Griffin (Eds.), *Constructivist thinking in counseling practice, research, and training* (pp. 122-140). New York: Teachers College Press.

Peavy, R. V. (1999). *An essay on cultural tools and the sociodynamic perspective for counselling.* Unpublished manuscript.

Ricoeur, P. (1980). Narrative time. *Critical Inquiry, 7,* 169-193.

Schutz, A. (1972). *The phenomenology of the social world.* London: Heinemann. (Original work published 1932)

Stam, H. J. (2001). Introduction: Social constructionism and its critics. *Theory and Psychology, 11,* 291-296.

Stam, H. J. (2002). Introduction: Varieties of social constructionism. *Theory and Psychology, 12,* 571-576.

Sullivan, H. S. (1953). *The interpersonal theory of psychiatry.* New York: Norton.

Taylor, C. (1989). *Sources of the self: The making of modern identity.* Cambridge, UK: Cambridge University Press.

Van den Berg, J. H. (1974). *Divided existence and complex society.* Pittsburgh, PA: Duquesne University Press.

Van Langenhove, L., & Harre, R. (1994). Positioning and autobiography: Telling your life. In N. Coupland & J. F. Nussbaum (Eds.), *Discourse and lifespan identity* (pp. 81-100). London: Sage.

White, M., & Epston, D. (1990). *Narrative means to therapeutic ends.* New York: Norton.

Willi, J. (1999). *Ecological psychotherapy: Developing by shaping the personal niche.* Seattle, WA: Hogrefe & Huber.

CHAPTER 21

Toward an Integrative Framework for Understanding the Role of Narrative in the Psychotherapy Process

LYNNE E. ANGUS

JOHN MCLEOD

OVERVIEW

The concept of narrative and psychotherapy has proved to offer fertile ground for innovation in psychotherapy theory and practice. The authors of this *Handbook* represent a rich array of cultural backgrounds—European, North American, Australian—and reflect a variety of distinct therapeutic approaches (including narrative therapy, brief dynamic, client-centered, experiential, relational, and cognitive-constructivist). They draw on a range of epistemologies (social constructionist, poststructuralist, dialectical constructivist), employ different assessment strategies and research methods, and work with a spectrum of client groups. All of these writers have identified client narrative expression as the common ground of social discourse in psychotherapy and an essential constituent of client reflexivity and human agency. Behind the writings of these authors lies the work of other important narrative-oriented therapists and researchers, whose ideas could not be directly included in the *Handbook* because of space limitations. Massive contributions to

AUTHORS' NOTE: Correspondence regarding this chapter may be sent to Lynne Angus at York University, 4700 Keele Street, Toronto, Ontario, Canada M3J 1P3, or to langus@yorku.ca.

the appreciation of the role of narrative in psychotherapy have been made by James Pennebaker (1990), in his research into the health benefits of storytelling, and by Jeremy Holmes and other psychodynamic psychotherapists, in painstaking research into the effects on adult narrative competence of insecure patterns of attachment in childhood (Holmes, 2001). Much of the constructivist tradition in using narrative in therapy has grown out of the writings of Miller Mair (1988, 1990), Haim Omer (Omer & Alon, 1997), and Theodore Sarbin (1986). It is essential to celebrate cultural diversity in story making: Dwivedi (1997) and Alida Gersie (1997) have highlighted the therapeutic use of narratives and storytelling practices from cultures outside of the dominant European/North American worldview. Powerful examples of how narrative ideas can be applied in practice can be found in the life story and reminiscence therapy tradition in work with older people (Birren, Kenyon, Ruth, Schroots, & Svensson, 1995; Butler, 1963) and in the therapeutic creative writing workshops developed by Bolton (1998) and Hunt (2000). There are many other fine examples of narrative-informed therapeutic theory and practice that might be added to this list.

In this final chapter, we offer a succinct distillation of the most significant practical implications emerging from both the writing presented in this *Handbook*, and from the wider narrative and psychotherapy literature. Our aim is to stimulate reflection on the future impact and importance of the narrative turn for psychotherapy theory, practice, and research by formulating some fairly brief statements that, we believe, capture the key points of convergence and divergence within current theory, research, and practice around narrative and psychotherapy. We hope that these formulations will resonate with readers who have immersed themselves in the book.

PRACTICAL IMPLICATIONS FOR RESEARCH AND PRACTICE

Narrative Expression Is a Fundamental Self-Making Practice

Jerome Bruner (Chapter 1) beautifully articulates the assertion that narrative and self are inextricably interlinked. For Bruner, the sense of self originates in the embodied act of storying our experiences in the world to share those experiences with others as well as to facilitate self-understanding. In terms of self-understanding, telling ourselves about ourselves is like making up a story about who and what we are, what has happened, and why we are doing what we are doing. The construction of personal identity, or selfhood, cannot proceed without a capacity to narrate. Once we are equipped with that capacity, we can produce a selfhood that joins us with others and permits us to hark back selectively to our past while shaping ourselves for the possibilities of an imagined future.

In addition, narrative is a form of discourse that links events together across time; thus, it can display the temporal dimension of human existence and represent the subjective experience of time. Narrative form captures the notion that human lives are "becomings" or journeys in which actions and happenings occur before, after, and at the same time as other actions and happenings. The role of narrative in contextualizing human actions as expressions of underlying intentions, purposes, goals, and wishes—referred to as theory of mind—in childhood development was highlighted by several authors in the *Handbook*. The capacity to narrate personal experiences in terms of human intentions, purposes, and goals was viewed by these authors as foundational to the development of the capacity to adopt the perspective of another, in relation to the self, and to articulate new personal meanings from this vantage point.

Through the very act of articulating a specific point of view, including intentions, purposes, and goals, in relation to a set of actions and unfolding events, narrative storytelling gives expression to human agency.

The Concept of Narrative Encompasses a Number of Different Storytelling Structures

When people construct narratives about their experience in therapy, it is useful to identify different story subtypes that have contrasting functions in terms of both identity work (understanding self) and relationship work (the development of the alliance with the therapist). *Habitual narratives* are accounts of what usually happened. *Chronicles* or *reports* are like empty stories; they give information about what happened, but with no sense of drama, purpose, or meaning. Such stories provide a background, contextual understanding of the client's world but convey relatively little information about intentionality or emotional meaning. By contrast, *personal stories* (micronarratives, autobiographical memories, relationship episodes) are vivid, concrete accounts of specific events, and they provide the therapist with an entry into the lived experience of the client. While psychodynamic and experiential therapists focus on client narrative accounts of conflict and distress in their therapy sessions, narrative therapists help clients identify and make stories of life experiences that represent unique or preferred outcomes for the client. The *macronarrative* (life story, life script, self-concept) is a term used to refer to the overall integration of salient personal stories into an organized narrative framework that tells the story of a life. It is an implicit narrative structure that reflects the overall autobiographical account that the person can give of his or her life as a whole.

It is also possible to identify *cultural narratives* (discourses, dominant narratives), which represent a culturally normative story of the "good life"; these may be implicit in habitual and personal narratives. They act as a kind of organizing principle for both everyday stories and the life narrative by providing a narrative framework (the story of how things *should* be or ideally *can* be) for evaluating action. Numerous authors in this *Handbook* have reinforced the view of Michel Foucault and other poststructuralist theorists that narrators speak through narrative forms that are not their own but defined by culture. Bruner (Chapter 1) argues that we gain the self-told narratives that make and remake ourselves from the culture in which we live. However much we may rely on a functioning brain to achieve our selfhood, we are virtually from the start expressions of the culture that nurtures us. Culture itself is dialectic, replete with alternative narratives about what self is or might be. The stories we tell to create ourselves reflect that dialectic. As Polkinghorne (Chapter 3) suggests, the plots that people employ as templates for interpreting the events in their lives often are provided by their cultural discourse. Life stories are intelligible within a particular cultural frame, and yet they also differentiate one person from the next. The repertoire of cultural plots is thought to reflect plots in which the person's performance matches the functional needs of the society. The socially authorized plots are adapted by people to make sense of their particular lives. The plots provide meaning and value to their past actions; that is, these actions have served to forward the plot (good actions) or have impeded the plot development (bad actions). Plots also serve in the planning of future actions in that people choose those actions that are consistent with the needs of the plot's completion (to live a good life).

Different approaches to therapy appear to focus on different storytelling structures, or different levels of storytelling (concrete and specific vs. abstract and generalized). It seems clear that the narrative therapy of White (Chapter 2) and Combs and Freedman (Chapter 8) seeks to enable clients to explore the relationship between dominant cultural narratives and their personally constructed life stories or macronarratives, while psychodynamic therapy concentrates more on working with clients to gain insight into the linkages between personal stories (relationship episodes) and the life story. Constructivist therapies, found in the work of Botella, Gonçalves, and Greenberg (Chapters 7, 6, and 19, respectively), seem open to all three types of narrative construction. However, it is also true that clients in narrative therapy tell vivid personal stories, and clients in psychodynamic therapy identify cultural narratives that operate in their lives. The difference in narrative emphasis across approaches to therapy may reflect the therapist's theory more than it does their actual practice with clients.

Narration Is in Itself a Basic Therapeutic Process

The therapy setting makes it possible for clients to articulate their life narratives (or parts of them) with support and without interruption or competition. This gives clients a chance to reflect on their stories and to consider whether there are any parts of the stories that they might want to update, reconstruct, or repair. Many contributors to the *Handbook* suggest that the act of storying experience is an essential self-organizing process that provides a platform for subsequent reflection and personal meaning making in psychotherapy. The term *autobiographical reasoning* has been used to refer to this narrative meaning-making activity. A narrative schema or structure organizes the ever-unfolding cacophony of lived experience into bounded episodes that by definition have a beginning, middle, and an end and enable perspective taking and reflection. Client narrative meaning making in psychotherapy is also viewed as evidence of client agency, which is the source of new meanings in psychotherapy, for example, as the client actively engages in reflexive processing. In summary, there is a basic therapeutic value in allowing troubled people to tell their stories.

The Therapeutic Alliance Emerges From the Storytelling Activity of the Client

The therapeutic relationship arises from a recognition that people find it helpful to have an opportunity to tell their stories in a setting in which what they have to say is accepted and valued by others. Therapy is an interpersonal activity rather than one in which a subject knower seeks to comprehend a client as an at-a-distance object. The basic experience of another person becoming a witness to our account of troubles is meaningful and worthwhile. The role of the counselor or psychotherapist includes being both witness to and coeditor of the stories told by the person seeking help. The quality of the therapeutic relationship is largely determined by how effective the therapist is in carrying out these tasks.

Narrative communication is basic for the emergence of personal acceptance in the therapy relationship. In storytelling, the listener and narrator are empathic partners, and they join in a narrative alliance. Autobiographical memory storytelling facilitates the development of a strong, trusting therapeutic bond in which both client and therapist cocreate a sense of shared experiencing, knowing, and interpersonal understanding. Narrative understanding in psychotherapy is regarded by Brigitte Boothe and Agnes von Wyl (Chapter 16) as a sort of practiced plot intelligence. Therapists put or transfer themselves into the setting, the initial organization of the scene, the starting point of the story, which sets up a combination of events that open up a horizon of expectation. The therapist's capacity to attend empathically to a client's key concerns, as conveyed in personal stories, contributes to an early development of a strong, secure therapeutic alliance by instilling a sense of basic trust in the client toward the therapist.

Effective Therapeutic Work Involves Sensitivity to Narrative Multiplicity

When people narrate the important events and experiences of their lives, the text that emerges can be viewed as similar to a polyphonic novel, containing within it a multitude of internalized voices that "speak" to each other in dialogue. These voices can be understood in different ways: as the discursive expressions of different subject positions constituted in internalized conversations, as reflections of dominant cultural narratives or discourses, or as unheard or warded-off problematic experiences. All life stories are formulated with both external and internalized audiences in mind. As McAdams (Chapter 9) suggests, someone is always listening or watching—be it friends and acquaintances, parents and children, therapists, or Freud's superego, Mead's generalized other, Perls's Top Dog, internalized attachment objects, or God. Given the dialogical nature of subject positions and discursively expressed narrative voices, there is always more than one way to tell our life story, more than one voice to be heard, and more than one plot to be voiced. It is precisely this reconstructive potential that is the essence of human change in general and psychotherapy in particular. Various therapeutic strategies can be employed to facilitate dialogue between multiple voices: externalizing conversations, role-play, two-chair work, position repertoires, and letter writing.

Effective Therapeutic Work Involves Sensitivity to Shifts Between Different Forms of Narrating

There is a rhythm to storytelling with a therapy session. A typical pattern is that clients talk about what "generally" happens (habitual narratives), then shift into an actual story that exemplifies, dramatizes, and makes concrete/specific what is being talked about. In doing so, clients draw the listener (therapist) into their subjective, emotional, and moral world. The story is often followed by a period of reflection, evaluation, and interpretation, where the meaning of the story is explored. This process of sense making helps to develop a perspective on the "problem." There is also a rhythm within the telling of a story, expressed through repetition, contrast, reported speech dialogue, pace, and voice quality. Effective therapists are aware of the possible narrative trajectories that may occur during a therapy session and have expertise in facilitating client movement from one mode of narrating to another.

Emotion as a Marker of Subjective Significance in Stories

Therapists pay particular attention to emotional stories for further articulation and elaboration in psychotherapy. Emotions are "understood"—and have personal meaning for clients—when organized within a narrative framework that identifies what is felt, about whom, and in relation to what need or issue. In addition, the differentiation of client emotional experiences, in the context of salient personal stories, may be an effective intervention strategy for facilitating client narrative change in psychotherapy. When clients experience new and sometimes contradictory emotional responses in the context of reflection on personal stories, significant shifts in the intentions, hopes, beliefs, wishes, and feelings attributed to the actions of self and others can occur. At these moments, clients see themselves and others in a new light and are impelled to construct a new, emotionally coherent narrative, which accounts for what happened, why it occurred, what was felt, in relation to whom, and about what need or issue. Alternatively, unstoried affect may exert a disorganizing influence on personal meaning making and result in negative impacts on psychological (Dimaggio & Semerari, Chapter 15) and physiological (Pennebaker & Seagal, 1999) states.

Narrative Coherence as an Indicator of Client Well-Being

The work of Dan McAdams (Chapter 9) suggests that the narrator uses stories to meaningfully integrate disparate aspects of self through time. Identity takes the form of an inner story, complete with setting, scenes, character, plot, and themes. Internalized life stories are based on biographical facts but go considerably beyond the facts as people selectively appropriate aspects of their experience and imaginatively construe both past and future to construct stories that make sense to them and to their audiences. These stories vivify and integrate life and make it more or less meaningful. People appear to find it important to create a single life narrative in which different events and aspects of self are integrated into the larger fabric of their identity. By constructing a single life story that integrates a wide range of self-characterizations, the adult can resolve what William James first identified as the "one-in-many-selves paradox." Singer and Blagov (Chapter 13) have identified the importance of integrative processes and autobiographical memory narratives for the creation of self-coherence and understanding.

Numerous authors in this *Handbook* view the coherent organization of narrative diversity or complexity as a marker of positive therapeutic outcomes in psychotherapy. For instance, Dimaggio and Semerari (Chapter 15) suggest that to be able to adapt, an individual needs to have a wide range of models or narrative scenarios representing interactions of self in relation to others. The absence of these relationship narratives prevents an individual from adeptly moving about, exploring, and interacting with others. But, they add, to be adaptive, this multiplicity of relationship scenarios—this narrative complexity—needs to be internally organized. A key goal of therapy is the coherent integration of multiple views of self and self-identities.

When clients identify unique outcome personal stories, White (Chapter 2) and Combs and Freedman (Chapter 8) use narrative-focused questioning to help clients challenge and destabilize unitary problem-saturated identities or dominant plots. The emergence of preferred identity subplots that coherently organize the detailed description of unique outcome stories, and the meanings they hold for the client, is a major goal of the narrative therapy approach. These authors argue that the deconstruction of dominant narrative plots leads to a more diverse and complex self-narrative, and this in turn leads to preferred outcomes, identity, and a different future.

Several authors identified narrative incoherence as a marker of psychological distress in psychotherapy and identified narrative assessment strategies for the assessment of incoherence in client storytelling. Dimaggio and Semerari (Chapter 15), for example, pay particular attention to structural alterations in patients' narratives, noting that patients can suffer not only on account of the subject matter of their discourse but also because of the way in which it is put together. In this view, stories act as a map of the world. If this map is inadequate, poor, unstable, or chaotic, clients feel paralyzed and do not manage to tell others about their problems.

One of the major challenges for psychotherapy researchers over the next few years will be to further develop methods for describing, exploring, and measuring narrative coherence and incoherence, as well as narrative change in psychotherapy. While contributors to the *Handbook* have demonstrated the application of a variety of innovative research strategies for the intensive case analysis of client narrative expression in therapy, a comprehensive analysis of client and therapist contributions to narrative change in psychotherapy has yet to be completed. Virtually all of the writers in this *Handbook* assert, implicitly or explicitly, that the stories told by clients change as a result of effective therapy in the direction of being more coherent, accessible, differentiated, and evocative. However, there is still very little research evidence that bears directly on this assumption. Michael White and David Epston have argued that therapy can help people to "reauthor" their life stories. What does a reauthored life story look like? How does a therapist know when reauthoring has taken place?

CONCLUSIONS

These propositions represent a tentative first step in the direction of an integrative approach to narrative-informed therapy. In compiling these statements, we have been aware that there also exist some stark polarizations within the set of ideas and practices associated with the narrative turn in psychotherapy. For example, on the face of it, there would appear to be a major contrast between the emphasis placed on "unique outcome" or "solution" stories in narrative therapy and the focus on repetitive problem stories found in brief psychodynamic psychotherapy using Core Conflictual Relationship Theme (CCRT) analysis (described in Chapter 4). There is also a distinct difference between the socially oriented nature of narrative therapy and the largely individual, "inner self" orientation of most other forms of therapy described in this *Handbook*. Other points of tension are also apparent. However, we suggest that an integrative framework may allow many of these tensions to be resolved. For example, clients in narrative therapy do talk about problems, even though their therapists may be more interested in unique outcomes. Conversely, clients in dynamic therapy do talk about their successes, even if their therapists are concentrating on collecting information they need to identify the client's CCRT pattern of wishes and responses. In both cases, what is happening can be viewed as the narrativization of experience, a process of being known to an audience (the therapist) and an opening out of the multiplicity of voices or selves within the individual's life narrative.

We find ourselves surprised that we have not been drawn to categorize the themes emerging from our reading of these chapters in terms of competing theoretical, ontological, and epistemological traditions. No poststructuralist approach to narrative is irreconcilable with a psychodynamic or experiential approach, at least as we see it. We believe that this is an interesting and significant conclusion because the surface rhetoric of these approaches is so different. It seems as though the concept of narrative is so fundamental to human psychological and social life, and carries with it such a rich set of meanings, that it provides a genuine meeting point between theoretical schools of therapy that have previously stood apart from each other.

We feel that the discovery of narrative as a nontrivial point of convergence for the therapy field is to be greatly welcomed for two reasons. First, it is important for those of us in the therapy business to be able and willing to listen to each other and learn from each other. We expect our clients to be able to do this. Second, the organization of therapy training, practice, and research around allegedly competing and alternative models has been gradually dissolving. The majority of practitioners define themselves as eclectic or integrationist. The research shows that the specific therapy model used by a therapist is not a particularly powerful factor in predicting outcome. At the same time, however, there has not been so far an integrative conceptualization of therapy that has captured the imagination of therapists and clients. While the common factors theory as an integrative model may be true, it seems to lack a generative spark. It has not inspired groundbreaking research or innovative practice. It does not have a creative edge. The concept of narrative, on the other hand, breaks plenty of new ground in opening up therapy to insights from anthropology, linguistics, philosophy, neuroscience, cultural studies, developmental psychology, and many other disciplines. It is certainly creative and innovative, as reflected in the many new therapeutic strategies developed by contributors to this *Handbook*. It may be the spark.

REFERENCES

Birren, J. E., Kenyon, G., Ruth, J.-E., Schroots, J. J. F., & Svensson, T. (Eds.). (1995). *Aging and autobiography: Explorations in adult development*. New York: Springer.

Bolton, G. (1998). *The therapeutic potential of creative writing*. London: Jessica Kingsley.

Butler, R. N. (1963). The life review: An interpretation of reminiscence in the aged. *Psychiatry, 26,* 65-76.

Dwivedi, K. (Ed.). (1997). *The therapeutic use of stories*. London: Routledge.

Gersie, A. (1997). *Reflections on therapeutic storymaking: The use of stories in groups*. London: Jessica Kingsley.

Holmes, J. (2001). *The search for the secure base: Attachment, psychoanalysis, and narrative*. London: Routledge.

Hunt, C. (2000). *Therapeutic dimensions of autobiography in creative writing*. London: Jessica Kingsley.

Mair, M. (1988). Psychology as storytelling. *International Journal of Personal Construct Psychology, 1,* 125-137.

Mair, M. (1990). Telling psychological tales. *International Journal of Personal Construct Psychology, 3,* 121-135.

Omer, H., & Alon, N. (1997). *Constructing therapeutic narratives*. New York: Jason Aronson.

Pennebaker, J. W. (1990). *Opening up: The healing power of confiding in others*. New York: William Morrow.

Pennebaker, J., & Seagal, J. (1999). Forming a story: The health benefits of narrative. *Journal of Clinical Psychology, 55,* 1243-1254.

Sarbin, T. (Ed.). (1986). *Narrative psychology: The storied nature of human conduct*. New York: Praeger.

Name Index

Adams, A., 319
Adams, J. F., 131
Adams, K., 304
Adams-Westcott, J., 145
Affleck, G., 166
Alexander, I. E., 232
Alexander, K., 82
Alleva, G., 264, 266, 267, 269, 270
Alon, N., 104, 368
Alves, A., 104, 114
American Psychiatric Association, 202, 257, 273
Andersen, T., 147
Anderson, H., 57, 58, 188
Anderson, T., 56, 323, 326
Anderson, T. M., 198, 264, 266, 300
Anderson, W. W., 212
Angus, L. E., 88, 89, 90, 91, 92, 103, 104, 126, 128, 183, 193, 195, 196, 202, 247, 248, 249, 250, 251, 252, 253, 256, 265, 267, 270, 299, 300, 322, 323, 332, 333, 339, 340, 342, 344, 345, 361, 362
Arciero, G., 332
Aristotle, 299
Arnett, J. J., 161
Arnold, M., 6
Asendorpf, J. B., 236
Astington, J. W., 214
Augustine, 8, 9
Azzara, C., 186, 263, 266, 267, 270

Baerger, D. R., 104, 160, 196
Bagby, R. M., 266
Bakan, D., 183
Bakhtin, M. M., 121, 176, 177, 205, 206, 351
Balamoutsou, S., 193, 195, 249, 251, 300, 356
Bamasio, A., 331, 333, 335, 336, 345, 346
Barber, J. P., 72, 74, 248
Barclay, C. R., 235

Barkham, M., 132, 199
Barlow, D. H., 134
Baron-Cohen, S., 214, 264, 266, 321, 323
Bartlett, F. C., 120
Basso, K. H., 353
Bateson, G., 41, 42, 54, 58
Bateson, M. C., 127
Bauer, J. J., 234
Baumeister, R. F., 249, 252, 253, 332, 333
Bavelas, J. B., 326
Beck, A., 260, 345
Becker, J. T., 230
Beckett, S., 8-9
Beeghly, M., 214
Beels, C., 21, 49
Bellak, L., 211
Benjamin, L. S., 188, 198, 316, 321
Bennett, R. T., 197
Berger, P. L., 351, 352
Bernauer, F., 293
Best, S., 59, 64
Bettelheim, B., 215
Beutler, L. E., 114, 115
Bhatia, S., 178
Binder, J. L., 72, 321
Birren, J. E., 368
Blagov, P. S., 229, 231, 233, 234, 237, 243, 249
Blomberg, J., 293
Bluck, S., 162, 163, 166, 168, 229, 231, 232, 233, 234, 237, 316, 319, 320
Bohart, A., 87, 310, 338
Bolton, G., 368
Bonanno, G. A., 234
Bonarius, H., 184
Book, H., 71, 72, 79, 249, 332
Boothe, B., 284, 285, 286, 290, 292
Botella, L., 103, 120, 125, 126, 127, 130, 131, 133, 332

Boucault, M., 205
Bouffard, B., 91, 332, 333, 344, 345
Bowers-Bouffard, B., 249, 250, 333, 344
Bowlby, J., 265, 283
Bowman, P. T., 160, 166
Boxer, A., 159
Breger, L., 160, 162
Brémond, C., 285
Bretherton, I., 214
Brewer, W. F., 230, 231
Briere, J., 197
Brooks, P., 285
Brooks-Gunn, J., 284
Brown, L. S., 309
Browne, A., 197
Bruner, E. M., 25, 62
Bruner, J. S., ix, 3, 6, 19, 20, 21, 22, 34, 48, 49, 50, 89, 90, 96, 119, 137, 139, 145, 194, 213, 214, 231, 248, 249, 260, 263, 265, 285, 299, 323, 332, 344
Bucci, W. S., 198
Bühler, K., 285
Butler, R. N., 368
Byrne, D. F., 214, 218

Calvin, J., 5
Capps, L., 104
Carcione, A., 264, 266, 267, 269, 270, 275
Carlson, M. A., 324
Carson, K. L., 323, 326
Casey, K., 159
Castelino, C. T., 216
Catania, D., 186, 263, 266, 267, 270
Cather, W., 12
Childress, A., 82
Christianson, S.-A., 232
Clark, H. H., 326
Clifford, J., 25
Coates, L., 326
Coffey, P., 197
Cohen, K., 82
Cohen, S. M., 147
Cohler, B. J., 159
Combs, G., 59, 65, 145, 146, 147, 148
Connell, J., 132
Conway, M. A., 159, 229, 230, 231, 232, 233, 234
Cooper, M., 180, 270
Corbella, S., 126, 127, 130, 131, 133
Corin, E., 358
Cornforth, S., 362
Costantino, G., 215
Cozolino, L., 103
Craig, C., 354

Craik, F. I. M., 230
Crick, N. R., 215
Crits-Christoph, P., 72, 82, 83, 248, 300, 321
Cromby, J., 351
Crossley, M., 167
Csikszentmihalyi, M., 327
Curtin, T. D., 113
Curtis, J., 72
Cushman, P., 352
Cutting, L., 232

Dabats, D. L., 234
Dafforn, T., 145
Dahl, H., 72
Damasio, A. R., 265
Damon, W., 177, 321
Danto, A. C., 212
Danziger, K., 57, 65, 351
Darchuk, A. C., 326
Davies, B., 358
Day, R., 183
Deacon, T., 115
de Beauvoir, S., 12
DeLaurenti, B., 147
DeLaurenti, P., 147
Demorest, A. P., 232
Denzin, N., 159
Derogatis, L. R., 132, 260
Derrida, J., 41, 42, 61
Descartes, R., 63
de Shazer, S., 54, 55, 61, 126
de St. Aubin, E., 164, 165, 166, 249
Detert, N., 199
Dewey, J., 6
Dewhurst, S. A., 230
Dews, P., 58
Diamond, A., 165, 166, 249
Diguer, L., 71, 72, 74, 248
Dilthey, W., 309
Dimaggio, G., 103, 186, 263, 264, 266, 267, 268, 269, 270, 275, 332, 335
Doan, R. E., 60, 359
Dodge, K. A., 215
Donati, R., 293
Dostoyevsky, F., 176
Drewery, W., 359
Drost, J., 234
Dryer, D. C., 316
Duarte, Z., 104
Duncan, B., 133, 360
Dwivedi, K., 368

Eakin, P. J., 10, 13
Eccles, J. C., 255

Ecker, B., 132
Edelstein, W., 236
Eder, R., 284
Eells, T. D., 71
Efran, J. S., 121
Eisenmajer, R., 214
Eisenmann, B., 284
Elder, G. H., Jr., 164
Elkind, D., 162, 163, 168
Elliott, R., 88, 91, 193, 197, 198, 300, 303, 310, 324, 332, 333, 336, 338, 339, 346
Ellis, A., 215, 216
Emmons, R. A., 243
Endres, L. M., 198
Epstein, S., 338
Epston, D., 34, 39, 50, 54, 58, 59, 61, 62, 63, 104, 137, 139, 140, 142, 145, 146, 147, 159, 167, 168, 169, 170, 249, 250, 299, 359, 360, 361
Erikson, E. H., 12, 23, 162, 164, 231
Eron, J. B., 55
Erwin, E., 292
Essig, T. S., 216, 217
Evans, C., 132

Fairclough, N., 360
Falcone, M., 264, 266, 267, 269, 270
Fanshel, D., 285
Faude, J., 72
Feldman, C. F., 214
Field, S. D., 199
Figueras, S., 125
Finkelhor, D., 197
Firth-Cozens, J. A., 193, 197, 198, 199, 300
Fisch, R., 55
Fischer, P., 285
Fish, V., 61
Fivush, R., 159, 163, 230, 283, 326
Flader, D., 284
Flavell, J. H., 269
Flick, U., 293
Fonagy, P., 198, 264, 268, 270, 275, 293
Fonda, J., 12
Foner, E., 322
Forgas, J., 336
Foucault, M., ix, 20, 33, 39, 49, 59, 61, 64, 65, 137, 138, 139, 141, 351, 355
Frank, J. D., 360
Franz, C., 167
Freedman, J., 59, 65, 145, 146, 147, 148
Freud, S., 3, 4, 12, 82, 166, 215, 275, 279, 284, 371
Fried, D., 82
Frieze, I. H., 197

Frith, C. D., 264
Frith, U., 214, 264, 266
Fromhoff, F., 283
Frommer, J., 287, 293
Frye, D., 214, 221
Frye, N., 299
Fung, H., 284

Gaarder, J., 355
Gadamer, H.-G., 309, 351, 363
Gale, J. E., 360
Gallagher-Thompson, D., 114
Gardner, G., 268
Gardner, R. A., 212, 214, 217
Gazzaniga, M., 115
Geertz, C., 24, 25, 39, 61, 62, 63, 138, 139
Gendlin, E. T., 303, 334, 335, 338, 343, 345
Georgaca, E., 186
Gergen, K. J., 25, 57, 61, 110, 121, 128, 134, 161, 167, 170, 193, 206, 249, 284, 320, 325, 351, 355, 358, 359
Gergen, M. M., 25, 167, 249, 284
Gersekovich, I., 160
Gersie, A., 368
Giddens, A., 352
Giesecke, M., 284
Giorgi, A., 309
Glaser, B. G., 126, 133, 301
Glick, M. J., 200, 202, 268
Goffman, E., 62, 285
Goldman, R., 91, 198, 251, 332, 340
Golynkina, K., 268
Gomez, A. M., 133
Gonçalves, O. F., 90, 103, 104, 105, 112, 114, 115, 193, 194, 195, 196, 200, 251, 263, 265, 300, 332
Goodman, P., 335, 345, 346
Goolishian, H., 57, 58, 188
Gopnik, A., 214
Grafanaki, S., 193, 303, 309, 356
Grande, T., 293
Grawe, K., 293
Gray, J., 283
Greenberg, L. S., 87, 88, 91, 92, 178, 179, 185, 198, 200, 202, 248, 250, 251, 253, 256, 324, 332, 333, 336, 337, 338, 339, 340, 342, 345, 346
Greer, G., 12
Gregg, G., 159, 160, 167, 178
Grice, H. P., 266
Gugler, B., 285
Guidano, V. F., 332
Gülich, E., 284, 285
Gutmann, D., 164

Habermas, J., 205
Habermas, T., 162, 163, 166, 168, 229, 231, 232, 233, 234, 237, 316, 319, 320
Haden, C. A., 326
Haine, R. A., 326
Hambleton, G., 205, 214
Hansen, P., 234
Harber, K. D., 89
Hardtke, H., 88, 90
Hardtke, K., 88, 89, 90, 91, 103, 104, 126, 128, 183, 193, 195, 247, 248, 249, 250, 251, 252, 253, 270, 299, 322, 323, 332, 333, 339, 344, 345, 362
Hardy, G., 193, 197, 199, 300
Hare-Mustin, R., 141
Harper, H., 198
Harré, R., 177, 358
Hart, D., 177, 236, 321
Hartmann, H., 283
Harwood, M., 115
Harwood, T. M., 114
Hausendorf, H., 284, 285
Haw, S. K., 198
Hefferline, R. F., 335, 345, 346
Hegel, G. W. F., 6
Heidegger, M., 205
Heilbrun, C. G., 167
Hemingway, E., 213
Henning, K., 197
Henriques, M. R., 104, 114
Henry, W. E., 211
Hermans, H. J. M., 103, 159, 166, 167, 176, 178, 179, 180, 181, 182, 183, 184, 186, 193, 198, 200, 263, 265, 266, 267, 268, 270, 274, 320, 321, 323, 345
Hermans-Jansen, E., 103, 167, 181, 182, 183, 186, 345
Herrero, O., 103, 120, 125, 126, 133, 332
Hill, C. E., 303, 310
Hillman, J., 197
Hoffman, B. J., 183
Hofmann, V., 236
Hole, A., 82
Holmes, A., 231
Holmes, J., 368
Holmes, J. G., 159
Holzman, L., 310, 322, 325
Honos-Webb, L., 178, 179, 185, 198
Hoogstra, L., 284
Horowitz, L. M., 72, 316
Horowitz, M., 72, 266, 268
Hostetler, A. J., 159
Howard, G. S., 113, 249
Hoyt, M. F., 57

Hubble, M. A., 360
Hulley, L., 132
Hunt, C., 368

Indermühle, K., 285
Intreccialagli, B., 264
Iser, W., 34, 50

JAKOB Group, 285, 286
James, W., 21, 164, 176, 177, 335, 372
Janoff-Bulman, P., 197
Jimenez, B., 133
Johnson, C. N., 214
Johnson, M., 110, 355
Johnson, S., 72
Johnson, T., 326
Johnson-Laird, P. N., 265
Josephson, B. R., 166
Josselson, R., 160, 167

Kächele, H., 285
Kagan, N., 249, 300
Kalbermatten, U., 285
Kapur, S., 230
Karon, B. P., 198
Kaye, J., 110
Keefe, F. J., 323, 326
Keller, M., 236
Kellner, D., 59, 64
Kelly, G. A., 57, 124, 125, 126, 184, 197, 265
Kempen, H. J. G., 159, 166, 176, 178, 263, 266, 274
Kempis, T. à, 9
Kendall, P. C., 215
Kenyon, G., 368
Kerby, A. P., 61
Kermode, F., 165
Kernberg, O. F., 266, 267, 268
Kerouac, J., 9
Kets de Vries, M. F. R., 84
Kevitt, H., 332
Kierkegaard, S., 127
Kiesler, D. J., 310
Kim Berg, I., 126
King, L. A., 234
Klohnen, E. C., 164
Knobloch, L. M., 198
Knowles, E. S., 164
Kogan, S. M., 360
Koocher, G. P., 211
Korman, Y., 90, 195, 196, 251, 265, 300, 332
Kotre, J., 165
Krasnoperova, E. N., 316

Krause, R., 292
Kuebli, J., 159, 163

Labov, W., 285, 300
Lacan, J., 205
Laing, R. D., 355
Lakoff, G., 110, 355
Larimer, D., 147
Lauzon, G., 358
Lazar, A., 293
Lebo, D., 211
Le Doux, J. E., 336
Leiman, M., 179, 198, 270
Leitenberg, H., 197
Leitner, L. M., 197, 327
Lejeune, P., 5
Leslie, A. M., 214, 264, 266, 268
Leuzinger-Bohleber, M., 293
Levant, R. F., 54
Levine, F., 82
Levinson, D. J., 164
Levitt, H., 88, 89, 90, 91, 103, 104, 126, 128, 183, 193, 195, 247, 248, 249, 250, 251, 252, 270, 299, 301, 302, 303, 304, 309, 310, 322, 323, 332, 333, 339, 344, 345
Lewin, J. K., 95, 98, 99, 248, 251, 252, 270, 333, 339, 340, 344
Lewis, M. L., 160, 166, 284
Lieblich, A., 160, 167
Liedtke, J., 285
Lietaer, G., 303, 310
Lincoln, Y., 159
Linehan, M. M., 272
Linell, P., 178
Linn, R., 167
Liotti, G., 264, 268
Llewelyn, S. P., 193, 197, 199, 300
Lloyd, G., 5
Logan, J., 230
Logan, R., 165
Lord, J. J., 216
Lorenzer, A., 292
Lowe, T., 193
Luborsky, L., 71, 72, 74, 82, 83, 248, 284, 285, 300, 321, 362
Lucariello, J., 195, 201
Lucius-Hoene, G., 285
Luckmann, T., 351
Luder, M., 286
Lukens, M. D., 121
Lukens, R. J., 121
Lumley, M., 323
Lund, T. W., 55
Lynch, G., 195, 202, 356, 362

Lynch, T., 323
Lyotard, J.-F., 61, 120
Lysaker, J. T., 179, 189, 268, 269
Lysaker, P. H., 179, 189, 268, 269

Machado, P. P., 90, 112, 114, 193, 194, 200, 251, 332
MacIntyre, A., ix, 169, 212, 354, 355
Mackay, H., 268
Madigan, S., 361
Maerlender, A. C., 113
Mahoney, M. J., 57, 193, 250, 332, 345
Maia, A., 104
Main, M., 267
Mair, J. M. M., 197
Mair, M., ix, 368
Maisel, R., 139, 361
Malgady, R. G., 215
Malik, M., 114
Mancini, F., 268
Mandler, J., 265
Mann, S., 142
Mansfield, E., 165, 166, 183, 249
Mansfield, K., 12
Marcia, J. E., 160
Margison, F. R., 193, 197, 300
Mark, D., 248
Markus, H., 111, 164, 268
Maruna, S., 160, 166
Mascolo, M. F., 56
May, T., 234
McAdams, D. P., 104, 159, 160, 161, 162, 163, 164, 165, 166, 167, 168, 169, 171, 183, 193, 195, 196, 229, 231, 237, 248, 249, 251, 268, 316, 319
McCandless, C., 10, 11, 12
McCullough, D., 319
McLean, K., 233
McLeod, J., 103, 159, 167, 193, 195, 201, 202, 249, 260, 299, 300, 303, 309, 332, 353, 356, 357, 362
McMullin, R. E., 215
McNamee, S., 57, 193
Mead, M., 166, 371
Meares, R., 21
Mehrabian, A., 218
Mellon, J., 82
Mellor-Clark, J., 132
Meltzer, C. C., 230
Mergenthaler, E., 266, 286, 287
Mertens, W., 292
Meshot, C. M., 198, 264, 266, 300
Meshot, T. M., 212
Meyerhoff, B., 137, 145

Michotte, A., 265
Miller, P., 284
Miller, P. H., 269
Miller, P. J., 231, 234
Miller, S., 133
Miller, S. A., 269
Miller, S. D., 360
Ming, S., 82
Mintz, J., 284
Modell, J., 167
Moffitt, K. H., 92, 230, 233, 235, 236, 237, 243, 324
Moleiro, C., 114
Monk, G., 359
Moore, C., 214, 221
Moreira, P., 115
Morgan, A., 144
Moroz, T. M., 230
Morris, F., 139, 361
Morris, M., 72
Morrison, L. A., 198
Moscovitch, M., 230
Muran, J. C., 270, 272
Murray, S. L., 159
Myerhoff, B., 34, 50
Myers, P. R., 113

Nebes, R. D., 230, 231
Neimeyer, G. J., 57, 120
Neimeyer, R. A., 57, 103, 120, 124, 125, 193, 194, 195, 196, 250, 263, 265, 266, 299, 316
Neimeyer, T., 332
Neisser, U., 6, 10, 230, 284
Nelligan, D. W., 324
Nelson, K., 283
Newman, F., 310, 322, 325
Newman, L. S., 249, 252, 253, 332, 333
Nichols, S., 266
Nicolò, G., 264, 266, 267, 269, 270, 275
Nightingale, D. J., 351
Nurius, P., 111, 164, 268

Oatley, K., 336
Oberbracht, C., 293
Ochs, E., 104
O'Hanlon, W. H., 55
Olney, J., 8, 9
Omer, H., 103, 368
Osatuke, K., 268
Oxenhandler, N., 5

Pacheco, M., 125, 126, 127, 130, 131, 133
Paivio, S., 332, 336, 346

Papousek, M., 283
Parker, J. D. A., 266
Parry, A., 60, 359
Pascual-Leone, J., 88, 250, 332, 333, 336, 338
Patten, A., 160, 166
Patterson, D., 206
Peavy, R. V., 360, 361
Pedulla, B. M., 211
Pennebaker, J. W., 89, 104, 194, 197, 324, 343, 368, 372
Perls, F. S., 91, 216, 335, 345, 346, 371
Perry, J. C., 72
Perry, W. C., 164
Peterson, B. E., 164
Pfenninger, D. T., 197
Phillips, J. R., 301
Piaget, J., 23, 57
Pillemer, D. B., 231, 233, 234
Pinker, S., 115
Piorkowski, R., 160
Platt, J. J., 211
Pleydell-Pearce, C. W., 159, 229, 230, 231, 232, 233, 234
Poch, G., 133
Polkinghorne, D. E., ix, 200, 205, 249, 299, 300, 316
Pollack, R. D., 56
Polo, M., 160
Poon, L. W., 231
Popp, C., 72, 248
Popper, K. R., 255
Potts, R., 284
Prior, M., 214
Procacci, M., 264, 266, 267, 269, 270
Propp, V., 10, 285
Purdon, C., 269

Quartaro, G. K., 301
Quasthoff, V. M., 285

Rahhal, T. A., 231
Ram, A., 178
Ramsey, C., 234
Rasmussen, B., 267, 323
Rees, A., 199
Reichelt, S., 188
Rennie, D. L., 87, 197, 248, 249, 293, 301, 303, 310, 332
Reynolds, J., 160, 166
Reynolds, S., 199
Rhodes, R. H., 303, 310
Rice, L. N., 88, 91, 324, 332, 333, 336, 338, 339, 346
Rickels, K., 260

Ricoeur, P., ix, 285, 299, 362
Robinson, J. A., 234
Roch, A. F., 260
Rogers, C. R., 91, 216, 339, 345, 346
Rogler, L. H., 215
Romanelli, R., 114
Rosaldo, M., 25
Rosas, M., 114
Rose, N., 309
Rosenberg, M., 176, 177
Rosenwald, G. C., 166, 169, 170
Roth, A., 293
Rotondi-Trevisan, D., 92, 333, 344
Rousseau, J.-J., 5, 9
Rowan, J., 180
Rubin, D. C., 166, 230, 231
Rudolf, G., 293
Russel, J. A., 336
Russell, R. L., 104, 195, 196, 201, 205, 212, 214, 215, 216, 217
Russell, S., 142
Ruth, J.E., 368
Ryle, A., 268, 270
Ryle, G., 138

Sacks, O., 13
Safer, M. A., 232
Safran, J. D., 270, 272
Safran, J. S., 270, 271
Salkovskis, P. M., 267, 268
Salovey, P., 159, 166, 229, 232, 235, 237, 344
Salvatore, G., 186, 263, 266, 267, 270
Sandell, R., 293
Sarbin, T., ix, 159, 193, 249, 299, 331, 368
Saver, J., 13
Schafer, R., 53, 284, 299
Schaffer, N., 72
Schaffler, P., 72
Schank, R., 344
Schmidt, K., 72
Schroots, J. J. F., 368
Schutz, T., 351
Schwartz, G. E., 236
Scollon, C. K., 234
Seagal, J., 89, 194, 343, 372
Segal, Z. V., 270, 271
Selman, R. L., 214, 216, 218
Semerari, A., 103, 263, 264, 266, 267, 268, 269, 270, 272, 275, 332, 335
Senner, R., 64
Shafer, R., 320
Shakespeare, W., 319
Shankland, M. C., 199

Shannon, L. M., 230
Shapiro, D. A., 134, 193, 197, 198, 199, 300
Shirk, S., 212, 216
Shotter, J., 221
Shulman, D., 147
Shweder, R., 6
Sibicky, M. E., 164
Siegel, D. J., 115
Siegfried, J., 212
Silberschatz, G., 198
Singer, J., 344
Singer, J. A., 92, 122, 159, 160, 166, 167, 229, 230, 231, 232, 233, 234, 235, 236, 237, 243, 249, 324
Singer, J. L., 229
Skaw, D., 232
Sloan, W. W., Jr., 198, 212, 264, 266, 300
Slobin, D., 7
Sluzki, C. E., 197
Soares, L., 104, 114
Spence, D. P., 4, 25, 53, 249, 284, 285, 299, 309, 320, 325, 327
Spencer, S., 176
Sperber, D., 266
Spivack, G., 211
Stam, H. J., 351
Stanzel, F. K., 285
Staudinger, U. M., 233, 234, 235, 237
Steele, R. S., 309
Stern, D. N., 265
Sterne, P., 145
Stewart, A. E., 316
Stewart, A. J., 167
Stich, S., 266
Stiles, W. B., 178, 179, 185, 193, 197, 198, 199, 200, 202, 212, 216, 264, 266, 268, 270, 300, 316, 322, 325
Straub, J., 292
Strauss, A., 126, 133, 301
Strupp, H. H., 321
Stuhr, U., 293
Stuss, D. T., 230
Sullivan, H. S., 352
Surko, M., 178, 179, 185
Sveaass, N., 188
Svensson, T., 368
Szasz, T. S., 197

Tallman, K., 310
Tantam, D., 319
Target, M., 264, 268, 270, 275
Taylor, C., 169, 178, 303, 356
Taylor, G. J., 266
Tennen, H., 166

Thomas, J., 327
Thomas, M. B., 54
Thompson, B. J., 303, 310
Thompson, L., 114
Thoreau, H. D., 10, 318
Thorne, A., 160, 166, 231, 232, 233, 234, 237
Thurber, J., 6
Thurlow, R., 212
Timulak, L., 303, 310
Tomkins, S. S., 159, 233, 239
Toukmanian, S. G., 248, 332
Tulving, E., 105, 230
Turk, D. J., 230
Turner, T., 197
Turner, V., 25, 137

Vaihinger, H., 275
van Aken, M. A., 236
van Balen, R., 346
Van den Berg, J. H., 355
van den Broek, P., 212, 215
Van Geel, A. L. M., 186
Van Langenhove, L., 177, 358
Van Loon, R. J. P., 178
van Ravenswaay, P., 82
Varvin, S., 198
Velásquez, P., 133
Vergnani, M., 237
Vico, G., 8-9
Vitz, P. C., 215
Vogel, D., 300
Von Cranach, M., 285
Von Matt, P., 284
von Wyl, A., 284, 285, 286
Vygotsky, L., 221
Vyse, S. A., 324

Walkover, B. C., 167
Wallerstein, R. S., 293
Wandrei, M. L., 104, 196, 205, 212, 214
Wang, Q., 6
Watson, J. C., 91, 202, 251, 303, 310, 332 337, 339, 340
Watzlawick, P., 55

Weakland, J., 55
Webster's Encyclopedia Unabridged Dictionary, 205
Welch-Ross, M., 283
Wechsler, D., 211
Weibel, D., 322
Weinberger, D. A., 236, 237
Weiner-Davis, M., 55
Wellman, H. M., 214
Wells, A., 269
Wepfer, R., 284, 285, 286
Werling, S., 285
Werner-Wildner, L. A., 125
Wetzler, S. E., 231
Whelton, W., 332, 345
White, H., 285
White, M., 33, 34, 39, 42, 49, 50, 54, 58, 59, 60, 61, 62, 63, 65, 104, 137, 139, 141, 142, 145, 146, 147, 159, 167, 168, 169, 170, 249, 250, 252, 260, 299, 332, 359, 360, 361
Whitecross, S. E., 230
Wickett, A. M., 269
Wiedemann, P. M., 284
Wiener, M., 218
Wiersma, J., 196, 327
Wilke, N., 269
Wilkes-Gibbs, D., 326
Willi, J., 357
Williams, J. M. G., 235
Winnicott, D. W., 268
Winocur, G., 230
Winograd, E., 230
Winslade, J., 359
Wittgenstein, L., 61, 121, 125, 205
Woike, B. A., 160
Wolfson, N., 285
Woolf, V., 9
Wright, J., 199
Wugalter, S., 338
Wylie, M. S., 65

Young, K., 13

Subject Index

Action, 213
Adjectifying process, 107-108
Adult Attachment Interview, 267
Agency, 128, 131, 133. *See also* Client agency; Personal agency; Self-agency
Agentive self, 145
Alexithymia, 266
Alliance, working, 133. *See also* Therapeutic alliance, client storytelling and
Alternate narrative:
    construction, 111
    historical grounding, 111
    projection, 111
Alternatives, openness to. 128
Alternative narratives/stories, 32, 33, 34, 43, 148, 369
    versus dominant stories, 33-34
Alzheimer's disease, 13
American cultural narrative, 20-thcentury, 206-207
Anti-anorexia leagues, 361
Assimilation, interpersonal, 206
Assimilation perspective, 197-204
    restorying process seen through, 200-202
Assimilation model, 193-197, 207
    narrative roots, 199
    narrative therapies and, 200
    qualitative research and, 198, 207
    quantitative research and, 199
    self in, 198
    value of narrative, 206-207
    See also Assimilation lens; Assimilation process; Meaning bridges; Voices
Assimilation of Problematic Experiences Scale (APES), 185, 198, 200-201
    stages, 199, 200-201, 203, 204, 205-206
Assimilation process, 199-200
Associative availability, construction of, 106
Authenticity, 34

Authentic story, 33, 34
Autism:
    lack of theory of mind in, 214
    narrative processes and, 323
    patients with, 264
Autobiographical knowledge, hierarchy of:
    event-specific, 230, 234, 242
    general events, 230, 234, 242
    lifetime periods, 230, 234, 242
Autobiographical memories, 336, 369. *See also* Autobiographical memory; Autobiographical memory narratives; Autobiographical memory storytelling
Autobiographical memory, 88, 92, 229, 230, 232, 242, 243
    cognitive processes, 236
    narrative context and, 284
    narrative structure, 166
    retrieval, 344
    socially constructed, 166
    storage, 344
    See also Autobiographical memories; Autobiographical memory narratives; Autobiographical memory storytelling
Autobiographical memory narratives, 333
    self-coherence creation and, 372
    See also Autobiographical memories; Autobiographical memory; Autobiographical memory storytelling
Autobiographical memory storytelling, 92, 95, 370
    See also Autobiographical memories; Autobiographical memory; Autobiographical memory narratives
Autobiographical reasoning, 233-234, 316, 370
Autobiographical Writing Tasks, 251
Autobiography, 8, 11-12
    literary, 8
    written, 4, 12
Autonomous self, 32-33

Beck Depression Inventory, 260
Behaviorism, radical, 21, 22
Biography:
    cultural concepts, 166-167
    Western culture, 167
Blanquerna Psychotherapy Unit (Barcelona), 120
Borderline patients:
    all-powerful savior role narrative, 268
    narrative processes and, 323-324
    persecutor role narrative, 268
    self-narratives, 267, 275
    self states, 268
    victim role narrative, 268
Brief dynamic therapy, 367

Campaign, 361
Catharsis injunction, 23
Cellularization of life, 33
Center for Cognitive Psychotherapy, University of Minho (Portugal), 112
Character construction, 128
Child psychopathology, lack of theory of mind in, 214
Child psychotherapy, narrative processes in, 211-212, 215-222
    fairy tales, 215
    predication subtypes, 224-225
    sample stories, 222-224
    specification subtypes, 224
    See also Narrative
Children's Thematic Apperception Test, 211
Chronicles, 369
Classification System and Scoring Manual for Self-Defining Autobiographical Memories, 237
Client agency, 88, 333, 352, 367, 370. *See also* Agency; Personal agency; Self-agency
Client-centered therapy, 91, 202, 251, 367
    storytelling and emotion processes in, 332
Client reflexivity, 249, 250, 367
Client self-reflections on narrative communication, 300, 301
Client-therapist dialogue, 250, 333
    constructive nature, 88
Client well-being, narrative coherence and, 372-373
Clinical Outcomes in Routine Evaluation (CORE) system, 132
Cognitive behavior therapy, 22
Cognitive-constructivist therapy, 367
Cognitive interpersonal cycle, 270
Cognitive narrative psychotherapy, 104-112
    adjectifying (phase 2), 107-110

main objective, 105
projection (phase 3), 110-112
recollection stage (phase 1), 105-107
researching, 112-115
Cognitive psychology, 22, 122, 229
Cognitive scientists, 159
Coherence, 128, 345, 346
    biographical, 162-163
    causal, 162-163
    key marker, 344, 372-373
    loss of narrative, 125
    temporal, 162
    thematic, 163
    See also Coherent narrative
Coherent narrative:
    client well-being and, 372-373
    emotions and, 372
    See also Coherence
Commitment story, 166. *See also* Contamination sequences; Redemption sequences
Conceptual meaning-making mode, 250
Conflict dynamics, narration and, 289-290
Constructionism, psychotherapy and, 355-362
    co-constructing meaning, 357
    cultural tools, 360-362
    personal niche, 357-358, 362
    story of "good life," 195, 356-357, 362, 369
    subjective positioning, 358-360, 362
    See also Social constructionism
Constructivism, 56-58
    narrative therapy and, 368
Constructivism and Discourse Processes Research Group, Ramon Llull University, 120
Constructivist psychotherapy, 57, 170, 367, 368, 370. *See also* Constructivism; Social constructionism
Constructivists, 120
    radical, 170
Contamination sequences, 166
Conversations, subject positions and, 121
Core Conflictual Relationship Theme (CCRT), beginning phase of, 78-80
    Response from the Self (RS), 79
    Response of the Other (RO), 79
    therapist confrontation technique, 79
    Wish (W), 79, 80
Core Conflictual Relationship Theme (CCRT), second phase of, 80-81
    interpretive focus, 81
    Response from the Self (RS), 81
    Response of the Other (RO), 80
    Wish (W), 81

Core Conflictual Relationship Theme (CCRT), third phase of, 81-83
   enactments, 82
   Relationship Episodes (REs), 82, 83
   Response from the Self (RS), 82
   Response of the Other (RO), 82
   termination issues, 81
   transference, 82
   Wish (W), 82
Core Conflictual Relationship Theme (CCRT) psychotherapy approach, 71-72, 78-84, 248-249, 321, 362, 373
   appearance, 72-77
   benefits, 83
   during assessment phase, 72, 74, 77
   effectiveness, 83-84
   future, 84
   goals, 77-78, 83
   history, 71-72
   presenting, 72
   validity, 72
   See also specific phases of CCRT; Relationship Episodes (REs)
Creative writing workshops, therapeutic, 368
Critical self, 91
Cross-cultural psychology, 21
Cultural anthropology, new, 24, 49
Cultural narratives, 195, 369, 370. *See also* Cultural plots
Cultural plots, 369
   as constricting, 59-60
   future actions and, 60
   meaning-generated, 63
   repertoire, 59
   socially acceptable, 59
   socially authorized, 369
   See also Cultural narratives; Plots
Culture, 38-48
   as didactic, 369
   as historically constructed, 38
   as socially constructed, 38
   life stories and, 53
   narrative as vehicle of, 39, 42-43
   narrative study of lives and, 166-167
Cyclical Maladaptive Pattern (CMP), 321

Daily alternate narratives, identification of, 111
Daily episodic narratives recall, 106
Daily narratives, 106
   metaphorizing, 110
   objectification, 107
Decellularization of life, 33
Deconstructive questions, 142

Depressed patients, narrative processes and, 324
Determinacy, indeterminacy within, 39, 40-42
Developmental psychologists, 159, 166
Developmental psychology, 23
Dialectical constructivism, 367
Dialogical approach, narrative-informed psychotherapy, 175-176
   acknowledgment of client's specific expertise, 176
   affective components of storytelling, 183-184
   as reconstruction of position repertoire, 178-184
   evaluation of success, 185-186
   future, 189-190
   goal, 178-179, 189-190
   gradual transition between assessment and change, 176
   self-listening, 176
   therapeutic process, 184-189
   therapeutic relationship, 186-189
   treatment contraindications, 189
   treatment indicators, 189
   See also Dialogical self
Dialogical dominance, 178
Dialogical interchange, 178
Dialogical self, 176-178
Dialogical space, 175, 189
Disciplines of the self, 39
Discourses, 369
Discourse technology, 360
Discursive expressions, 371
Disorganized narratives, 264, 267-270, 278, 372
   effects, 269-270
   integration deficit, 267, 268
   interpersonal cycle in, 270-271
   main aspect, 267
   overproduction of narratives with hierarchy deficit, 268-269, 270
   See also Narrative disorganization, implications of for psychotherapy
Dominance, 178
Dominant stories/narratives, 33, 60, 61, 249, 355, 369, 370
   extracting, 60
   reflections, 371
   versus alternative stories, 33-34
   See also Dominant stories/narratives, deconstructing
Dominant stories/narratives, deconstructing, 60-61, 64, 372
   externalizing the problem, 60
   unique outcomes, 60, 62, 144-146, 252, 373

Double description, 41
Dysnarrativia, 13
  selfhood and, 13

Ego:
  versus ego-figure, 289
Egocentric role-taking, 218
Ego identity, 160, 166
Emerging adulthood, 161, 164
Emerging self, narrative interaction and, 284
Emotion:
  marker of subjective significance, 371-372
Emotional differentiation, 95, 96, 100
Emotional pauses, 302
Emotion-focused mode, 250
Emotion-Focused Therapy (EFT), 337
Emotion processes, integrating narrative processes and, 333-334
Emotion processing, 88
Emotion schemes, 88, 250, 333, 336, 346
  adaptive, 337
  bodily felt-feelings, 336
  maladaptive, 337
Emotion shifts, 98, 342
Emphatic attunement, 87, 96
Emphatic response, 339
Empowerment, 54
Empty-chair work, 91, 97, 340, 342
  goal, 98
Episodic memory, 105, 106
Episodic recall, 106
Essential self, 23
Existentialism, narrative therapy and, 62-63. *See also* Personal agency; Responsibility
Expectation horizon, 289
Experience, organizing through narrative, 115
Experiencing self, 91
Experiential psychology, 87-88. *See also* Process experiential psychotherapy, narrative processes and
Experiential therapists, 369. *See also* Experiential psychology; Experiential therapy
Experiential therapy, 251, 334, 367, 373
  NPCS and, 252
  storytelling and emotion processes in, 332
Expressive pauses, 302
Externalization, 142
Externalizing conversations, 32, 33, 371
External narrative sequences, 88-89, 90, 92, 93, 95, 97, 98
External voices, 178

Family:
  as communication system, 54, 55

Family counseling, narrative therapy in, 62, 168. *See also* Family therapy
Family therapy, 22
  history, 54-55
  meaning-based, 55
  See also Family counseling, narrative therapy in; Family therapy theory; Marriage and family counseling
Family therapy theory, 54
  biological approach, 55
  ecological approach, 55
  structural approach, 54
Faulty assumptions, 345
Feedback listening, 175
Feminist movement, 207
Feminists, 167, 309
Flow, 327
Folk psychologists, 263. *See also* Folk psychology
Folk psychology, 15, 19-20, 31, 32, 42, 48-49
  criticisms, 20-21
  everyday life uses, 19
  features, 20
  mindedness, 25, 30
  reinstatement, 23-25
  theory of mind, 20
Free association, 105
Functionalism, new, 22

Generalized other, 166, 371
Generativity:
  narrative identity and, 164-165
  various ways of addressing, 165
Gestalt therapy, 91, 97
  unfinished business, 91
God, 166, 371
Grid of Problematic States, 266
Grief, experience of, 331-332
Guided imagery exercise, 106

Habitual narratives, 369, 371
Healing rituals:
  as cultural tools, 360
Hermeneutics, 351
Historical consciousness, 363
History, 38-48
Houston Galveston Institute, 57
Human agency, 22, 23, 24
Humanistic psychology, 357
Human reflexivity, 333
Hypothetical disaster, 289
Hypothetical optimum, 289

Identity:
  as problem, 161

defining, 160-163
   Erikson's concept, 161
   hypothetico-deductive thinking and, 162
   inner story and, 372
   narrative perspective, 236
   self-narrative construction and, 122
   self-understandings and, 161
   sexual development and, 161
   social relationships and, 162
Identity claims:
   alternative, 43
   preferred, 34
Identity conclusions, 32, 33
   alternative, 32
Identity construction, psychosocial stages of, 231
Identity Interview, 251
Identity work, 352
Images, culturally publicized, 196
Imagined communities, 354
Imagoes, personal, 164
Information theory, 22
Inhabited lives, 31, 49
   production, 35
"Inner reality," 122
Inner self:
   versus outer self, 218
Inner story, 160
Integrative memories, 234, 372
Integrative self-defining memories, construction of, 237, 243
Intentional state notions, 33
Intentional states, 21, 22, 23, 24, 30-38, 48, 49
   rich description, 25
   See also Folk psychology
Internalized attachment objects, 166, 371
Internal narrative sequences, 88, 89, 90, 93, 97, 98
Internal state categories, 33
Internal state psychologies, 21, 22, 23, 31
   challenges to, 21
   Eastern philosophy and, 23
   new consumer culture and, 23
   personal liberation philosophies and, 23
   revival, 22-23, 24
   See also Developmental psychology; Structuralism
Internal states, 21, 25, 32, 33, 214, 271.
   See also Internal state psychologies
Internal voices, 178
Interpersonal goal states, 318
Interpersonal narratives, 316-317
Interpersonal Process Recall procedure (IPR), 249, 300, 301, 310-311

activities in narrating life story, 302-303
activities in narrating specific story, 301-302
advantage, 308-309
client delaying activity, 301-302
client inner story, 308
client managing own beliefs of disturbances, 302
client/therapist dialogue, 308
disadvantage, 309
increased richness/density of discourse understanding, 300
recommendations for psychotherapy practice, 310
therapist inner story, 308
See also Narrative activities/intentions, example of; Narrative intentionality, therapeutic/research strategies to explore; Narrative intentions, principal
Interpersonal Process Recall (IPR) studies of narrative processes, 301
Interpersonal relations, narrative structure and, 315-316
   characters' interpersonal movements, 316, 317
   conflict, 317, 318
   interpersonal complementarity, 317-318
   interpersonal gravity, 318
   interpersonal power/character impermeability, 318-319
Intimate memories, 166
Introjects, 345
Introspective self, 218
I-position, 176-177

JAKOB narrative analysis system, 285-291
   initial narrative/first psychotherapeutic interview, 286-287
   narrative dynamics/initial narrative, 287-289
   narrator self-representation, 287
   rules, 289
   tasks, 286
   wish-defense movement, 290-291
Joined lives, 31, 33, 49
   production, 32-33

Knowledge, power and, 39, 40
Korsakov's syndrome, 13

Landscape of action, 90, 93, 96, 99, 145, 146, 344
   historical, 213
   imagined, 213
Landscape of consciousness, 90, 93, 95, 96, 99, 145, 213, 344

Landscape of identity, 146
Language games, 125, 126, 131
Language of deficit, 359
League, 361
"Learned conditions of worth," 345
Life course, life story and, 163-166
Life narrative:
   absence of integrated, 321
   adolescents and, 320
   research methods, 159
   research theories, 159
Life reflection, 234
Life scripts, 195, 369
Life span narratives:
   episodic recall, 106
Life stages model, Erikson's, 12, 164
Life stories, 58-59, 369
   as cultural texts with moral perspectives, 169
   as meaning-making constructions, 169
   as psychosocial constructions, 169
   culture and, 369
   integrative, 162
   internalized, 372
   mental health and organization of, 231
   personal, 370
   reauthoring, ix, 373
   revised, 65
   successful psychotherapy and articulation of, 88
   successful psychotherapy and elaboration of, 88
   See also Life narrative; Life story; Life story, life course and; Life story schema, integration of self-memory system and life story narrative with; Plots;
Life story:
   change, 250
   successful psychotherapy and transformation of, 88
Life story, life course and, 163-166
   adolescence, 163-164
   early to middle adulthood, 164
   emerging adulthood, 164
   mid-life, 164
Life-story Interview, 251
Life story personality theory, 230-231, 232
Life story schema, integration of self-memory system and life story narrative with, 232-236. *See also* Self-defining memories
Life story therapy, 368
Linguistic strategies, narrative therapists', 360
Listeners, 316
Love, experience of, 332

Macronarratives, 89, 105, 195, 249, 250, 333, 369, 370
   change in psychotherapy, 250, 251, 253
Map, 361, 372
Map making, 361
Marriage and family counseling, 54. *See also* Family therapy
Meaning:
   as interpretive achievement, 120-121
   as linguistic achievement, 120-121
   construing, 120
Meaning bridges, 198, 316, 322
   building, 199-200, 202, 317, 322-323
   maintaining, 325
   narratives as, 318-319
   stories as, 194, 200
   See also Voices
Meaning making, 42, 49, 100, 237, 320, 325, 334, 370
   dialectics, 333-334
   narrative, 207
   Narrative Assessment Interview (NAI) as opportunity for, 258-259
   narrative processes and emotional, 87, 92, 95-99, 100
   processes, 333, 338
   reflexive, 88, 89-91, 252
   relationally sustained, 121
   social inquiry and, 24
   See also Meaning bridges
Meaning making activity, 38
Meaning questions, 146
Meanings:
   articulating new, 343-346
   as maps, 58
   See also Narrative identity construction, embodied self and
Means-Ends Storytelling Test, 211
Me-position, 176-177
Metacognition Assessment Scale, 264, 266
   integration, 266
Metacognitive dysfunctions, 264
Metacognitive shift, 274
Metacognitive skills, 263, 269, 278
Metacommunication, 310
Metanarrative repair, 357
Metanarratives, 120, 195, 197, 199, 357
   constructing alternative, 357
Metaphorizing, 110
Metaphors:
   mirrored room, 141
   narrative, 137-138
   war, 355
Metarepresentative skills, 263

Micronarratives, 105, 249, 250, 333, 369
   change in psychotherapy, 251
"Moral of the story," generalized, 287
Multi-intentioned lives, 31, 49
   production, 31-32
Multiple authenticities, 31, 34, 49
   production, 33-34
Multiple discourses, cultural traditions and, 355
Multiple voices, 319-321, 322, 373
Multiplicity, 355
Multivoiced self, 178
Multivoiced society, 178
Mustabatory framing of action, 215
Mutual role taking, 218

Narcissistic patients, 267
Narrating, shifts between different forms of, 371. *See also* Storytelling
Narration:
   as therapeutic, 310, 370
   conflict dynamics and, 289-290
   restorative function, 290
   See also Storytelling
Narrative, 265, 353, 354
   alliance, 370
   as metaphor for psychological functioning, 120
   as primary mode of knowing, 38
   assimilation perspective on value of, 206-207
   as vehicle of culture, 39, 42-43
   competence, 293
   complexity, 266
   consciousness level, 128
   cultural tradition and, 353-355
   definitions, 58, 248, 300
   disruptions, 266
   dramatic/enactment impact, 285-286
   endpoint, 128
   form, 128
   importance, 214, 220
   incoherence, 372
   in everyday life, 212
   in social sciences, 212, 213
   mapping function, 265
   metaphor, 248, 249
   modes of thought, 253
   organization, 264-267
   psychological health and, 212-215, 220
   reflexivity, 126
   self and, 368
   subjectivity and, 353-355
   temporal dimension of human existence and, 368
   transformation, 133
   worldview, 140
   See also Narrative activities/intentions, example of; Narrative analysis; Narrative assessment strategies; Narrative communication; Narrative expression; Narrative identities; Narrative identity; Narrative practices; Narrative processes; Narratives
Narrative activities/intentions, example of, 304-308
   client's perspective, 307-308
   session transcript segment, 304-306, 308
   therapist's perspective, 306-307, 308
Narrative analysis, 104
   narrative dynamics, 293
   practical benefits, 292
   psychoanalysis, 292-293
   psychotherapeutic practice and, 291-293
Narrative Assessment Interview (NAI) protocol, 247-248, 253-259, 362
   background context, 248-249
   future for psychotherapy research/practice, 259-260
   narrative assessment interview (stage 1), 253, 254-256, 258
   posttherapy narrative assessment inquiry (stage 3), 253, 256-259
   stage 1 clinical case example, 254-256
   stage 3 case, 258-259
   summary sheet (stage 2), 253, 256, 257, 259
Narrative assessment strategies, 250-253, 372. *See also* Narrative Assessment Interview (NAI) protocol
Narrative beings, human beings as, 103
Narrative brain, 103
Narrative change in psychotherapy, emotion processes and, 331-333, 346
   dialectical-constructivist model, 332, 333, 334, 345
   good outcome cases versus bad outcome cases, 339-340
   identity consolidation stage, 334
   meaning-making stage, 334, 343-346
   symbolization stage, 334, 338-343
   synthesis stage, 334, 335-338
   See also Narrative processes, integrating emotion processes and
Narrative coding system, 233
   dimension of meaning, 233-234
Narrative communication:
   emergence of confidence and, 283
   personal acceptance and, 283

Narrative disorganization, implications for psychotherapy, 270-278
  interpersonal cycle in disorganized narratives, 270-271
  sharing/metacognition/mastery, 271-278
  therapist self-disclosure, 272, 274, 276, 279
  therapist use of "universal we," 272, 274
Narrative expression:
  as self-making practice, 368-369
  therapeutic alliance and, 92-95
Narrative genres, 320. *See also* Story genres
Narrative identities, 160, 169-170. *See also* Identity; Narrative identity; Narrative model of identity, McAdams; Narrative therapy
Narrative identity, 345
  embodied self and construction of, 345
  psychotherapy and reconstruction of, 132
Narrative industry, 21st-century, 355
Narrative intentionality, therapeutic/research strategies to explore, 308-310
  integrating conversational/intentional research approaches, 308-309
Narrative intentions, principal, 303-308
  emotional exploration/expressive symbolization, 303
  management of anxiety, 303-304
Narrative metaphor, 137-138
Narrative model of identity, McAdams, 160, 164, 168, 169, 171, 243
Narrative multiplicity, therapist sensitivity to, 371
Narrative practices, 19-20, 140-148
  asking questions about problems, 141-142
  developing history of present and extending story into future, 146
  developing stories from unique outcomes, 144-146
  documenting/circulating new stories, 147-148
  externalizing conversations, 142
  mapping statement of position, 142-143
  naming problem/project, 143-144
  reflecting, 146-147
  unique outcomes, 60, 62, 144-146, 252, 373
Narrative processes:
  critical balance, 323-324
  emotional meaning making, 87, 92, 95-99
  external, 323
  integrating emotion processes with, 333-334
  internal, 323
  reflexive, 323
Narrative Processes Coding System (NPCS), 90-91, 95, 126, 247, 248, 251
  brief experiential therapies and, 252
  external narrative processes mode, 252
  internal narrative sequence mode, 90
  reflexive narrative sequence mode, 253
Narrative processing, 233
Narrative Process Model (NPM), 88-91, 92, 247, 250, 251
  basic processing strategies, 250
  external narrative sequences, 88-89, 90, 92, 93, 95, 97, 98
  internal narrative sequences, 88, 89, 90, 93, 95, 97, 98
  personal identity in, 88
  reflexive narrative sequences, 87, 88, 89-91, 90, 95, 96, 97, 100
  therapeutic change in, 88
  underlying core assumptions, 88
  See also Autobiographical memory; Emotional differentiation; Emphatic attunement
Narrative process theory, 323
Narrative researchers:
  versus narrative therapists, 170-171
Narrative resources, culture and, 355
Narratives, 159, 343
  as interpersonal process, 317, 320
  as meaning bridges, 318-319
  collective, 122
  conflictive character of verbal, 285
  definitions, 316-317
  dialogical component, 263
  dynamic character of verbal, 285
  individual, 122
  social context and, 320
  therapist use of verbal, 285
  voices as, 121-122
  See also Stories
Narrative scenarios, disregulation of, 272
Narrative schema, 370
Narrative skills, advanced, 320
Narratives of identity, 127
  psychological problems and construing, 122
Narrative structures, 42, 43, 49
  reflexive engagements and, 35, 38
Narrative study of lives, culture and, 166-167, 168
  adoptive parents, 167
  expectant parents, 167
  HIV patients, 167
  Israeli soldiers, 167
  young Moroccans, 167
Narrative therapies:
  assimilation model and, 200
  of personality, 159

See also specific narrative therapies;
 Narrative therapy
Narrative therapists, 369
 as narrative change agents, 169
 See also specific types of narrative therapists
Narrative therapy, ix, 19, 25, 32, 34, 43, 49,
 53-54, 55, 63-65, 137, 167-171, 310,
 367, 370
 culture and life stories, 168-169
 development, 53
 effects on identity/personality
  development, 168
 emancipation metaphor, 167-168
 example, 148-154
 existential themes, 54, 62-63
 family counseling and, 168
 future convergence of diverse perspectives,
  373-374
 importance of life stories' developmental
  dimensions, 168
 intelligibility as goal, 121
 polarizations among diverse
  perspectives, 373
 postmodern influences, 54, 61-62
 primary focus, 55, 63
 purpose, 59
 story types as psychological ideals, 169
 theoretical foundation, 59
 transformation as goal, 121
 versus postmodern therapy, 63
 See also specific types of narrative therapy;
  Narrative therapy, themes in
Narrative therapy, themes in, 55-61
 adaptation of constructionist approach
  to meaning, 55, 56-58
 emphasis on client strengths, 55-56, 58
 emphasis on narrative/story form of
  meaning, 55, 58-61
 view of clients and therapists as partners, 55,
  56, 58
 See also Constructivism; Reflecting teams;
  Solution-focused therapy
Narrativization of experience, 373
Neural plasticity, 115
New functionalism, 22, 23
New psychologies, 20-22, 48
Novels, 354. *See also* Polyphonic novel

Objectifying, 107-108
Objectivist assumption, 122
Obstructive pauses, 303
One-in-many-selves paradox, 164, 372
Ontario Mental Health Foundation, 253
Open-ended questions, 181

Origin, 128, 131
Other as alter ego, 177
Outsider witness groups, 147, 154

Paradigmatic thinking, 253
Pausing Inventory Categorization System, 309
 interactional pauses, 303
 productive pauses, 302
Pedagogy, 5-6
Penn Psychotherapy Project, 74
Personal agency, 20, 25, 30-38, 48, 49, 64
 deemphasis, 21
 See also Agency; Client agency; Self-agency
Personal event memories, 233
 memorable messages, 234
 originating events, 234
 symbolic messages, 234
 turning points, 234
Personal identity, 333, 352
 narrative and construction of, 368
Personality:
 adjustment/defenses, 236-238
 life story approach, 230-231, 242
Personality disorders, 263, 264, 266-267
Personal meanings, new:
 core assumptions, 333
Personal memory, 166
Personal memory narratives, 248
Personal myth, 195
Personal stories/narratives, 346, 369, 370, 371
 disclosure, 252
Personal Striving measure, 243
Person-centered psychotherapy, 249. *See also*
 Client-centered therapy
Perspective-taking, 219, 221-222
 levels, 218
 predications and, 219
 reflexive self-awareness and, 219
Phenomenologists, 309
Plot intelligence, practiced, 370
Plots, 63, 64, 104, 128, 159, 205, 317, 369
 life stories and, 58
 planning and, 369
 reauthoring one's, 59, 65
 revisioning one's, 60
 See also Cultural plots; Life stories;
  Narratives; Stories
Polyphonic novel, 176, 177, 189, 371
 self as, 166
Pornography, 355
Position repertoire, 371
 examples, 180-183, 184, 188-189
 See also Position repertoire,
  reconstruction of

Position repertoire, reconstruction of, 178-184, 186
   psychotherapy innovations, 178-179
   valuation of significant story parts, 181-183
Positive withdrawal, 358
Possible selves, 164
Postmodern anthropology, 61-62
Postmodernist philosophers, 61-62, 64
Postmodern philosophy, 61, 62, 63-64
Postmodern therapy, 54
   narrative therapy versus, 63
Postpsychological perspective, 353
Poststructuralism, 351, 367, 373
Poststructuralists, 137, 309, 369
Posttraumatic stress disordered patients, narrative processes and, 324
Power, 138-139
   knowledge and, 39, 40
   modern, 138-139, 141
   traditional, 138
Predications, 217
   subtypes, 218, 224-225
   types, 217
Preferred claims, 34
Preferred identity subplots, 372
Primary attribution error, 5
Problematical experience, assimilation of, 266
Problem-focused narrative, 356
Process experiential psychotherapy, narrative processes and, 87, 88, 91-100
   central task, 91-92
   objective, 91
   See also Client-centered therapy; Empty-chair work; Gestalt therapy; Narrative expression, therapeutic alliance and; Narrative processes, emotional meaning-making and; Two-chair work
Process experiential therapists, 92-93, 95, 96-97
   good-outcome, 96-97
   poor-outcome, 98-99
Projecting processes, 112
Projection:
   introduction, 111
   modeling, 111
Prototype narratives, 196
   construction, 106
   metaphorizing, 110
Psychoanalysis, 3-4, 309
   narrative therapy and, 53
Psychodynamic therapists, 368, 369
Psychodynamic therapy, 370, 373
Psychological dysfunction, 108. *See also* Psychological problems
Psychological health, narrative and, 212-215

Psychological magnification, 233
Psychological problems:
   construing narratives of identity and, 122
   loss of personal agency and, 122
   unintelligibility and, 122
Psychological tension, positive, 284
Psychopathology:
   as signifying process, 104
   as social production, 104
   narrative construction and, 103-104
Psychotherapeutic practice, narrative analysis and, 291-293
Psychotherapy, 122, 134
   as liberation, 133
   as reconstruction of position repertoire, 178-184
   as response to modernity, 352-353
   as specialized human conversation, 122
   constructionist perpectives, 355-362
   goal, 179, 372
   narrative change assessment in, 250-253
   purpose, 104
   value of self-defining memories in, 239
   See also specific types of psychotherapy
Psychotherapy practice, Interpersonal Process Recall (IPR) and, 310

Reauthoring conversations, 43
Reauthoring plots, 59, 65
Recalling process, 105
Recollection process, 106-107
Redemption sequences, 165, 166
Reflecting teams, 56, 147, 154
Reflexive construction, 333, 344, 346
Reflexive engagements, narrative structures and, 35
Reflexive meaning-making, 88, 89-91, 252
Reflexive narrative sequences, 88, 89-91, 322
Reflective pauses, 302
Reflexive processing, 370
Reflexive system, 343
Reflexivity, 133
Reframing, 55
Relational constructivism, 120
   constitutive assumption, 123
   historical context, 120
   main assumptions, 120-122, 124
   See also Relational constructivism, therapeutic practice guidelines for
Relational constructivism, therapeutic practice guidelines for, 123-134
   dialogue/relationships/subject positions, 125-127

experience/meaning/interpretation/language, 123-125
   narrative and identity, 127-131
   reconstruction of narrative identity, 132
Relational therapy, 367
Relationship Episodes (REs), 74, 75-76, 78, 82, 83, 369, 370
   Regressive Wish, 78
   Response from the Self (RS), 72, 74, 75, 76, 77, 78, 83
   Response of the Other (RO), 72-73, 74, 75, 76, 77, 83
   RO-actual, 73
   RO-affect, 73
   RO-behavior, 73
   RO-expected, 73, 75
   Wish (W), 72, 73, 74, 75, 76, 77, 78, 83
   See also specific phases of CCRT
Relationships as conversational, 121
Relaxation induction exercise, 106
Relevance, 128
Reminiscence, 233
Reminiscence bump, 231
Reminiscence therapy, 368
Reorganizing element, 290
Repetitive memories, 234
   motivational aspect, 232
Repetitive problem stories, 373
Reports, 369
Research psychologists, 159
Responsibility, 54, 64
Restoring element, 290
Restorying process, 252
   assimilation of voices example, 202-204
   cultural level, 216
   seen through assimilation lens, 200-202
   sociological level, 216
Retelling, 154
"Retreat of the omniscient narrator," 176
Revisioning plots, 60
Rhetoric, Classical, 5
Rites of passage, 12
Role-play, 371

Scaffolding, 326, 346
Scaling questions, 126
Schizophrenic patients, 264, 269
Scripts, 159
Script theory, 233
Self, 23
   as knower, 177
   as known, 177
   as object, 177
   as observed, 218

as observer, 218
as other, 5, 13
as polyphonic novel, 166
as story, 195
as storyteller, 195
defining, 3
descriptions, 6-9
multiple views of, 372
narrative and, 368
patterns of, 252-253
physicalistic concept of, 218
soul and, 5
techniques, 64
Self-agency, 54. *See also* Agency; Client agency; Personal agency
Self-awareness, 221, 334
   levels, 218
Self-concept, 369
   narrative interaction and, 284
Self-confrontation method, 181
   spatial position, 181
Self-constituting subject, 64-65
Self-continuity, narrative context and, 284
Self-defining memories, 229, 242, 243
   affective intensity, 239
   as metaphors, 239
   content, 235-236
   definition, 232
   focus on enduring concern/unresolved conflict, 239
   in self-memory system and life story, 232-234
   integrative, 235
   linkage to other memories, 239
   meaning, 235
   measurable aspects, 233
   repetitiveness, 239
   structure, 235
   value in psychotherapy, 239
   vividness, 239
Self-defining memory research, application of to clinical practice, 238-243
Self-Defining Memory Task, 236-237, 243
Self-destructive figures, culturally endorsed, 196
Self-exploration:
   authentic, 304
   inauthentic, 304
Self-fulfilling prophecy, 197, 270
Selfhood:
   as public issue, 5-6
   as relational, 13
   as verbalized event, 7
   creating, 13
   recreating, 13

Self-identities, integration of multiple, 372
Self-identity
   change, 250
   narrative themes in construction of, 250
Self-in-the-world representations, 265
Self-knowledge, narrative context and, 284
Self-making, 6
   as narrative act, 4
   narrative, 10-13
   through self-narrating, 12
Self-memory system model, 229-230, 243
   personality adjustment and, 238
   summary, 234-236
   validation, 236-238
   See also Life story schema, integration of self-memory system and life story narrative with; Self-defining memories; Self-defining memory research, application of to clinical practice
Self-narrative construction, identity and, 122
Self-narratives, 4, 58, 105, 175, 176, 184
   dimensions of, 128
   See also Narratives; Stories
Self-presentation, narrative context and, 284
"Self psychologies," 23
Self-reflective role taking, 218
Self-reproach, generalizing, 287
Self revival, era of, 23
Self-story, 200, 345. *See also* Narrative; Self-narratives; Stories; Story
Self-telling, 6, 8-9
   appropriate, 5
   function, 3-5
   See also Storytelling
Semantic memory, 105
Sense making process, 371
Silences, 302-303. *See also specific types of pauses*
Social constructionism, 57, 170, 309, 351-352, 367
   narrative therapy versus, 63
   See also Social constructionism, narrative therapy and
Social constructionism, narrative therapy and, 351, 353-355
   criticisms, 362-363
   future challenges, 362-363
Social constructionists, 120, 309
Social phenomenology, 351
Social power, 178
Social psychologists, 159
Social sciences, interpretive turn in, 15, 24, 25, 49, 139
Social Sciences and Humanities Research Council (Canada), 202
Society of Psychotherapy Research, 260
Solution-focused therapy, 55-56
Specifications:
   definition, 217
   subtypes, 224
   types for elaborating subject's subjectivity, 217
Splitting, 266
Spoiling, self-originated, 287
"Statement of Position Map," 142
Stereotyped story figures, 196
Stockholm Outcome of Psychotherapy Project (STOP), 293
Stories, 140, 160, 193, 194-195, 316-317, 325
   as change opportunities, 319
   as co-constructions, 325-327
   as models for autobiographical remembering, 231
   changes due to therapy, 193
   constructivist perspective, 322
   culturally determined, 322
   family, 194
   good, 231
   meaning making through, 194
   socializing through, 194
   tips for telling/writing, 7
   unpacking, 42, 43
   See also specific types of stories; Macronarratives; Metanarratives; Micronarratives; Narratives; Self-narratives; Story
Story:
   as meaning bridge between voices, 200
   definition, 195
   problematic, 195-197, 207
   self as, 195
   See also Narrative; Narratives; Self-narratives; Stories
Story figures:
   as voices, 200
   self-destructive, 196
   stereotyped, 196
Story genres, 205
   APES levels and, 205-206
   characterizing relationships between voices, 204-205
   characterizing voices, 204
   See also Narrative genres
Story making, cultural diversity in, 368
Story structure, fitting experience into, 324-325
Storytellers, 284, 315, 316, 317-318
   as narrative persuaders, 291

as narrative seducers, 291
evoking resonance, 291
intent, 316
self, 195
See also Storytelling
Storytelling, ix, 89, 95, 99, 250, 252, 291-292, 301, 310, 322-323, 325
as self-organizing, 370
assessment strategies, 372
as social articulation of subjectivity, 284
as therapeutic, 310
audience, 316
authentic use, 301, 302
collaborative, 325-326
concrete versus abstract levels, 369
context, 316
enjoyment potential, 284
fear-coping function, 284
human agency and, 369
inauthentic use, 301, 302
mode, 250
restoring function, 284
rhythm, 371
shifts between different forms of, 371
social integration as ultimate goal, 284
socialization and, 283
stabilization function, 284
structures, 369-370
therapeutic alliance and, 370-371
wish-fulfilling function, 284
See also Storytelling, affective components of
Storytelling, affective components of, 183-184
contact/union with others (O-affect), 183, 184
general negative (N) affect, 183, 184
general positive (P) affect, 183, 184
self-affirmation (S-affect), 183, 184
Structuralism, 23
Sub-cellularization, 33
Subjectifying, 108-109
daily narratives, 109
introduction, 109
modeling, 109
process, 109-110
prototype narratives, 109
Subjective role taking, 218
Subjective significance, emotion as marker of, 371-372
Subjectivist assumption, 122
Subject positions:
conversations and, 121
voices and, 121

Superego, 166, 371
masochistic, 215
Supplementation process, words/actions and, 121
Symbolic interactionism, 122
Symptom Check List, 132, 260
Systems theory, 22

Technologies of the self, 39
Temporal regression exercise, 106
Tension, narrative, 287-289
Terzo Centro, 263, 266
Thematic Apperception Test, 211
Theme, 128
Theories of mind, 220-221
markers, 216, 217
narratives and, 214
See also Predications; Specifications; Theory of mind
Theory of mind, 214, 264, 266, 368
appropriate acquisition, 214
appropriate use, 214
folk psychology, 20, 21
See also Theories of mind
Therapeutic alliance, client storytelling and, 87, 92-95, 252, 370-371
personal acceptance, 370
quality of relationship, 370
trust, 371
Therapeutic change, narrative perspective of, 249-250
Therapeutic conversations, 33, 34, 35, 43
Therapists:
as coeditors, 370
as witnesses, 370
self-reflections on experiences of narrative communication, 300, 301
sensitivity to narrative multiplicity, 371
See also specific types of therapists; Therapeutic alliance, client storytelling and
Thick descriptions, 138, 141
Top Dog, 371
Training School for Cognitive Psychotherapy, 263
Turning points, 12
Two-chair work, 91, 97, 340, 342, 371
goal, 98

Unconscious mind, 21
emergence of, 218
Unique outcome stories, 60, 62, 144-146, 252, 373
University of California, Santa Barbara, 114
University of Zurich, 285

Validation/invalidation process, 184-185
    anchoring, 185
    attending, 185
    creating, 185
    Investigation-Validation-Investigation (IVI), 185
Valuations, 183-184, 185-186
    types, 186-187
Verbalized events, 7
Virtual leagues, 147
Virtual teams, 147
Voices, 200, 321, 325, 353, 354
    as narratives, 121-122
    characterizing relationships between, 204-205
    characterizing, 204
    dominant, 198
    external, 178
    in assimilationist model, 198
    internal, 178, 198, 202, 206
    internalizing other, 321
    metaphor, 198
    multiple, 319-321, 322, 373
    problematic, 198, 200
    stories as meaning bridge between, 200
    subject positions and, 121
    unassimilated, 198

Wechsler Memory Scale, 211
Weinberger Adjustment Inventory:
    moderate self-restraint on, 238
    Short Form (WAI-SF), 236
Working self, 230, 232, 234, 242

York I Depression study, 126, 202, 337, 340, 342
York Psychotherapy Research Centre and Clinic, York University (Toronto), 93, 247, 248, 253, 332, 339
York II Clinical Treatment Depression Project, 253, 256, 257

About the Editors

Lynne E. Angus, C.Psych, is Associate Professor of Clinical Psychology at York University and is president-elect of the North American Chapter, Society for Psychotherapy Research. She has published more than 30 research articles and chapters relating to the contributions of narrative expression and metaphor to psychotherapy outcomes. She is the originator of the Narrative Processes Coding System (NPCS), which was developed with Heidi Levitt and Karen K. Hardtke and has been translated into Portuguese, Spanish, Finnish, and German. Her therapeutic practice and ongoing research program are centrally concerned with understanding the role of client narrative expression and emotion processes in experiences of significant self-change in psychotherapy.

John McLeod, PhD, is Professor of Counselling at the University of Abertay Dundee. He is author of *Narrative and Psychotherapy* (Sage, 1997), *Qualitative Research in Counselling and Psychotherapy* (Sage, 2001), and other books and articles on a range of therapy topics. He is interested in the development of socially and culturally informed approaches to counseling and psychotherapy, and in the promotion of research that can make a difference to practice.

About the Contributors

Timothy Anderson, PhD, is Associate Professor of Psychology at Ohio University. He has published extensively on psychotherapy processes and the integration of research into clinical practice. He is particularly interested in the nature of the interpersonal processes in psychotherapy that lead to effective interventions. Recently, he has extended his work toward health populations in order to address the interpersonal contributions to the treatment of chronic pain.

Pavel S. Blagov is a student affiliated with the Laboratory for Personality and Psychopathology at Emory University. After studying literary analysis, human biology, and painting, he learned English and developed an interest in psychology at the American College in Bulgaria. At Connecticut College, he explored links between self-defining memories and personality with Jefferson Singer. At York University in Toronto, Canada, he studied emotional memories in relation to psychotherapy outcome with Lynne Angus.

Howard Book, MD, DPsych, FRCPC, FAPA, is Associate Professor in the Department of Psychiatry at the University of Toronto and coordinator of brief psychotherapy training there and at the Centre for Addiction and Mental Health in Toronto, Canada. He is founding Executive Director of the brief psychotherapy center for women at the Women's College Hospital. He has published more than 20 papers on psychotherapy and is the author of a manual on the Core Conflictual Relationship Theme Method.

Brigitte Boothe is Professor of Clinical Psychology, Psychotherapy and Psychoanalysis at the University of Zürich, where she has been a faculty member since 1990. Born in Germany, she completed studies in philosophy, literature, and psychology. Her main research topics are narrative and dream analysis in the clinical context; narration and qualitative research methodology; psychoanalysis, conflict, and communication; narration, text analysis, and literature.

Luis Botella, PhD, is Professor of Psychotherapy in the Department of Psychology, Ramon Llull University, Barcelona, Spain, where he also directs the master's course in clinical psychology and psychotherapy and is the main researcher of the Constructivism and Discourse Processes Research Group. His publications and research interests include postmodern thought, constructivism and social constructionism, psychotherapy, personal construct theory, and narrative psychotherapy. He coordinates the Psychotherapy Service at his university.

Beverley Bouffard is a doctoral student in the clinical psychology program at York University, Toronto, Canada. Her master's thesis investigated trauma-related autobiographical memories in process experiential therapy for unfinished business. She has recently coauthored several chapters and papers on resolving distress and on emotional meaning making in response to traumatic loss. Her academic interests involve traumatic loss and its manifestations in therapy.

Jerome Bruner, PhD, is Adjunct Professor at the New York University School of Law. He has written many seminal works on education and cognitive studies, including *The Culture of Education* (1996), *Acts of Meaning* (1990), *On Knowing: Essays For the Left Hand* (1962), and *The Process of Education* (1961). Through his distinguished career, first as Professor of Psychology at Harvard and then as Watts Professor at Oxford University, he has been at the forefront of what became, in the 1960s, the much-heralded cognitive revolution. During the Kennedy and Johnson administrations, he served on the President's Science and Advisory Committee and helped to found Head Start.

Fred B. Bryant is Professor of Psychology and Director of the graduate program in applied social psychology at Loyola University Chicago, where he teaches courses on social psychology, research methods, and statistics. He is the author of more than 90 professional publications on a variety of topics in personality and social psychology, including psychological well-being, hindsight bias, and the measurement of cognition and emotion. He also conducts research on discourse processes in psychotherapy.

Gene Combs, MD, and **Jill Freedman, MSW,** are codirectors of the Evanston Family Therapy Center in Evanston, Illinois. They have been invited presenters at many national and international conferences and have led workshops on narrative therapy all over the world. They have written many pieces on narrative approaches to therapy. Their first two books, *Symbol, Story, and Ceremony: Using Metaphor in Individual and Family Therapy*, and *Narrative Therapy: The Social Construction of Preferred Realities*, were chosen as main selections by the Behavioral Science Book Service. Their most recent book is *Narrative Therapy With Couples . . . and a Whole Lot More!*

Sergi Corbella, PhD, is Professor of Research Methods in the Department of Psychology, Ramon Llull University, Barcelona, Spain, where he is a psychotherapist in the Psychotherapy Service. He is a member of the Constructivism and Discourse Processes Research Group. His publications and research interests include psychotherapy integration, psychotherapy (process and outcome research), compatibility between therapist and patient, psychopathology, and constructivism.

Giancarlo Dimaggio, MD, is a psychiatrist, psychotherapist, and founding member of *Terzo centro di Psicoterapia Cognitiva*. He trains students at the *Società Italiana di Psicoterapia Cognitiva e Comportamentale* (SITCC) and at the *Associazione di Psicologia Cognitiva*. He is editing a book, *The Dialogical Self in Psychotherapy* (with Hubert J. M. Hermans), and supervises research on dialogical processes and narrative dysfunctions in psychotherapy funded by Nijmegen University.

Meredith J. Glick is a graduate student in clinical psychology at Miami University in Oxford, Ohio. Her research centers on the assimilation model of client change, using a qualitative method of linking process to outcome in psychotherapy.

Óscar F. Gonçalves, PhD, is Professor and Director of Clinical Psychology at the University of Minho, Portugal. His main area of research interest is experimental and clinical psychopathology, mainly the study of language and narrative processes combining behavioral, cognitive, and neurobiological methodologies. He has authored more than 150 papers and chapters and 13 books. He currently teaches several graduate and undergraduate courses in psychopathology and psychopharmacology.

Michael A. Gray is a graduate student in clinical psychology at Miami University in Oxford, Ohio. His interests include the assimilation model and psychotherapy process research, narrative approaches to the study of psychotherapy, archetypal psychology, and phobia and anxiety disorders. He is also an avid reader of poetry.

Leslie S. Greenberg, PhD, is Professor of Psychology at York University in Toronto, Ontario, and Director of the York University Psychotherapy Research Clinic. He has coauthored major texts on emotion-focused approaches to treatment of individuals and couples. His most recent book is *Emotion-Focused Therapy* (2001). He coedited *Empathy Reconsidered* and the *Handbook of Experiential Psychotherapy*. He is a founding member of the Society of the Exploration of Psychotherapy Integration (SEPI) and a past President of the Society for Psychotherapy Research (SPR). He is on the editorial board of a number of psychotherapy journals, including the *Journal of Psychotherapy Integration* and the *Journal of Marital and Family Therapy*.

Karen K. Hardtke, MA, is a doctoral candidate in clinical psychology at York University, Toronto, Canada, and is counselor and counseling supervisor at York University's Counselling and Development Centre. Her dissertation assesses the impact of psychotherapy from a narrative perspective. She codeveloped the Narrative Processes Coding System (NPCS) and the Narrative Assessment Interview (NAI), tools used to investigate clients' reconstruction and co-construction of their life stories.

Margarida R. Henriques, PhD, is Professor of Psychology at the University of Oporto, Portugal. She works in clinical psychology with children, adolescents, and adults, using a cognitive-narrative model and systemic therapies. Her main research interest is the narrative as a system of constructing means in the contexts of psychopathology and psychotherapy. Besides teaching courses in her field, she has published a number of journal articles on the use of narrative in psychotherapy.

Hubert J. M. Hermans, DPsych, is Professor of Psychology at the University of Nijmegen, The Netherlands. He developed a valuation theory and self-confrontation method, an idiographic procedure for assessing a person's meaning system. He has published several books; his most recent work is on the multivoiced and dialogical qualities of the self. He is First International Associate of the Society for Personology and President of the International Society for Dialogical Science.

Olga Herrero is a doctoral fellow at Ramon Llull University, Barcelona, Spain. She codirects the master's course in clinical psychology and psychotherapy. She is a psychotherapist in the Psychotherapy Service at her university and a member of the Constructivism and Discourse Processes Research Group. Her publications and interests include psychotherapy, constructivism, constructionism, PCP, narrative, postmodern thought, grief, and terminal illness.

Carol L. Humphreys is a graduate student at Miami University in Oxford, Ohio. She received her master's degree in clinical psychology from California State University, Dominguez Hills. She is most interested in the experience of dissociation, internal multiplicity, and how change occurs in psychotherapy.

Lisa Janis is a doctoral student in clinical/personality psychology at Northwestern University. Her research interests are in wisdom and integrity in old age and the clinical dimensions of adult development and aging.

Heidi M. Levitt, Ph.D., is Assistant Professor of Clinical Psychology at the University of Memphis. Her research concentrates on processes of personal change. Within this broad rubric, she studies those processes that span psychotherapeutic orientation, such as narrative, significant moments, metaphor, and silences within psychotherapy. She is interested in gender issues and conducts research on eating disorders, domestic violence, and lesbian gender. She is an experiential psychotherapist, and her approach to therapy and research is rooted within humanistic and constructivist traditions.

Jennifer Lewin is a doctoral candidate in clinical psychology at York University, Toronto, Canada. She holds degrees in both molecular biology and clinical psychology. She is involved in psychotherapy research on depression; specifically, she is interested in examining client and therapist interactions that encourage productive therapeutic moments from within a narrative framework.

Paulo P. P. Machado, PhD, is Associate Professor of Clinical Psychology at the University of Minho, Portugal. He has also held faculty positions or visiting appointments in Canada, Spain, and Brazil. His main area of research interest is psychotherapy process and outcome research, primarily the study of emotions and the process of change, and monitoring of mental health service provision. He has authored several papers, chapters, and articles in international journals.

Dan P. McAdams is Professor of Human Development and Social Policy and Professor of Psychology at Northwestern University in Evanston, Illinois. He is also the Director of the Foley Center for the Study of Lives, a small research enterprise dedicated to the study of prosocial aspects of adult personality development. His research has focused on generativity in adult development and the construction of self-defining life stories. His most recent book is *The Redemptive Self: A Narrative Psychology of American Identity*.

Katerine Otasuke is a doctoral candidate in clinical psychology at Miami University in Oxford, Ohio. Her clinical interests center on severe trauma and personality disorders, especially borderline personality. Her dissertation is on methods of tracking clients' multiple parts through therapy using the sounds of their voice, in which she is drawing on her formal education in linguistics and her work experience as a simultaneous translator in Russia, as well as her clinical and research education in psychology in the United States. Her other research interests include psychotherapy process and theories of internal multiplicity.

Meritxell Pacheco is a doctoral fellow at Ramon Llull University, Barcelona, Spain, where she is a member of the Constructivism and Discourse Processes Research Group and works as a psychotherapist and supervisor. She is a member of the Society for Constructivism in the Human Sciences, the European Personal Construct Association, the Society for Psychotherapy Research, and the Spanish Association of Cognitive Psychotherapies.

Her main research focus is the narrative process of identity construction in psychotherapy.

Donald E. Polkinghorne, PhD, holds the Attallah Chair in Humanistic Psychology at the University of Southern California, where he is a professor in the counseling psychology program. Before coming to USC, he served as president of the Saybrook Institute in San Francisco from 1975 to 1987. His scholarly writing has generally focused on the relation between research developed knowledge and psychotherapy practice, and he has advocated that qualitative and narrative approaches to knowledge are more useful to therapeutic practice than traditional measurement-based approaches. He has written articles and chapters on these topics, and is the author of *An Existential-Phenomenological Approach to Education, Methodology for the Human Sciences, Narrative Knowing and the Human Sciences,* and *the Case for Judgment-Based Practice in a Technological World* (in press).

David L. Rennie is Professor of Psychology at York University, Toronto, Canada. His research interests are in qualitative research methodology and its application to the client's experience of psychotherapy. A Fellow of the Canadian and American Psychological Associations, he is author of *Person-Centered Counseling: An Experiential Approach* (Sage, 1998) and coeditor of *Psychotherapy Process Research: Paradigmatic and Narrative Approaches* (Sage, 1992) and *Qualitative Psychotherapy Research: Methods and Methodology* (2001).

D'Arcy J. Reynolds, Jr. is a doctoral student in clinical psychology at Miami University (Ohio). He was a research assistant to Dr. Robert Gifford for five years, during which he authored two journal article publications. His main research interest Internet therapy, and he is currently is preparing a study of the comparison between participant's evaluations in e-mail therapy and face-to-face therapy.

Debra Rotondi-Trevisan, MA, is doctoral candidate in clinical psychology at York University, Toronto, Canada. Her dissertation will investigate the psychosocial risk factors for cardiovascular disease and the coping styles of post-myocardial infarction patients participating in a cardiac rehabilitation and risk reduction program. Her master's thesis explored the narrative coherence of single-event autobiographical memories in experiential psychotherapy for depression.

Robert L. Russell is Professor of Psychology in the Department of Pediatrics and the Director of Research at the Child Development Center, Medical College of Wisconsin. He has authored or edited three books on aspects of treatment research and child psychotherapy. His research focuses on processes of communication as they are encountered in normal and abnormal development, with particular interest in narrative, discourse, and theory of mind.

Lisa M. Salvi is a graduate student in clinical psychology at Miami University in Oxford, Ohio. She earned a master's degree in social work from Hunter College in 1992. Her research interests include using the assimilation model of change in psychotherapy to explore how traumatic experiences affect parenting skills.

Antonio Semerari, MD, is a psychiatrist and psychotherapist who also teaches at the Specialist School, *Associazione di Psicologia Cognitiva,* of Rome. Since 1995, he has directed the research group of *Terzo Centro di Psicoterapia Cognitiva,* in Rome, which specializes in the treatment of personality disorders. The research group's main interests involve the analysis of metarepresentative functions, variations of mental states, and the analysis of narrative forms in the psychotherapeutic process. He is author or editor of several books.

Jefferson A. Singer, PhD, is Professor of Psychology at Connecticut College in New London, CT. He is the author or coeditor of three books and has published more than 50 articles and chapters. He is a Fellow of the American Psychological Association and a recent recipient of a Fulbright Distinguished Scholar Award to conduct memory research at the University of Durham in England. In addition to his teaching and research, he maintains a private practice in clinical psychology in Waterford, Connecticut.

William B. Stiles, PhD, is Professor of Clinical Psychology at Miami University in Oxford, Ohio, and is a psychotherapy researcher and a psychotherapist. He taught previously at the University of North Carolina at Chapel Hill, and he has held visiting positions at the Universities of Sheffield and Leeds in England, at Massey University in New Zealand, and at the University of Joensuu in Finland. He is the author of *Describing Talk: A Taxonomy of Verbal Response Modes*. He is a past president of the Society for Psychotherapy Research, and he is currently North American editor of *Psychotherapy Research*.

Agnes von Wyl, PhD, is a research scientist and clinical psychologist in the Department of Child and Adolescent Psychiatry at the University of Basel and a lecturer in psychoanalytic psychotherapy at the University of Zurich. Her fields of interest are in the area of psychotherapy research, particularly narrative analyses. She is author, coauthor, and coeditor of several articles and books about this topic. The focus of her current research is narrative development.

Michael White is codirector of the Dulwich Centre in Adelaide, South Australia, which is a center for therapy and for community action. He originally trained in social work and family therapy, developing new and original ideas and practices out of dissatisfaction with many of the ways of thinking and working traditionally found in those fields. He is the most prolific and influential figure in the development of narrative therapy. He is the subject of many articles in the professional press and draws large audiences on his overseas teaching tours.

Printed in the United States
By Bookmasters